the process of

special education

administration

the process of
special

CHARLES H. MEISGEIER

Coordinator
Center for Human Resources Development
and Educational Renewal
Houston Independent School System

INTERNATIONAL TEXTBOOK COMPANY

education

administration

JOHN D. KING

Assistant Professor
Department of Special Education
Department of Educational Administration
The University of Texas at Austin

an **Intext** *publisher*   *Scranton, Pennsylvania 18515*

ISBN   0-7002-2271-5

Library of Congress Catalog Card Number: 77-117425

foreword

"Special education" has become part of the national jargon of education in recent years as programs for exceptional children and youth have expanded rapidly. There are those who wish that education of the most able and the least able — the exceptional — had never been called "special education." It has caused confusion as well as occasional resentment. It is not likely, now, however, that the association will be altered. The utilization is too widespread, too consistent.

Thus, when one refers to the organization or administration, or supervision, or financing or other aspects of "special education" one is referring to *either* education of the gifted and handicapped or education of *some* of the gifted and handicapped and in many cases to education of the handicapped only. The latter occurs where school systems label as special education only those programs for specified types of educationally disabled pupils and keep programs for the bright and gifted, if they exist, under "regular" rather than "special" education's jurisdiction.

Practices vary greatly. State laws and regulations govern for the most part. The size of populations subject to single school system administration; the definitions of mental retardation; the authorization for special education programs; certification requirements of "special" teachers; and just about every aspect of special education varies from state to state, often in most significant ways. As an example, the responsibility for the special education of the trainable mentally retarded is removed from the school districts of the state by state law in one state. As a further example, the "ceiling" IQ for educable mentally retarded is 70 in one state and 85 for adolescents in another state. Thus, with a minimum IQ for classification as educable mentally retarded of 50 in each state, there is a higher proportion of the population between the two ceilings, 70 and 85, than between the minimum of 50 and the ceiling in the lower ceiling state.

The Council for Exceptional Children in 1965 took an important standardizing step when it endorsed and published a policy of professional standards for personnel in special education.[1]

The volume in which this Foreword appears is a second major step toward a reduction of confusion and inconsistency in the nation's programs for exceptional children and youth. At least it is a hoped for outcome.

Except for the scattered bits and pieces, much of it reported in the bibliography enclosed, there is no body of literature recognized as authoritative in the organization and administration of special education. Thus, a job, very much in need of being done, has now been done by Dr.'s Meisgeier and King. The need for it is evident in the courses in colleges and universities of corresponding titles. It is evident in the emergency of special programs in tertiary education for the preparation of administrators of special education, one of which is the primary business of the authors. The need is evident in conferences held, legislation sought and passed at state and federal levels, and plans drawn for organizing and administering special education effectively.

It is, therefore, a unique privilege for me to recommend the contents of this volume as a valuable beginning of formal compilation of relevant contributions in this emerging field of specialization in educational administration.

These two most able young scholars have brought together some of the more insightful observations and advocacies of recent years which, while not all in harmony one with the other, are unfailingly provocative — the stimulating kind of stuff from which progress is fabricated.

JOHN W. KIDD, Ed.D.
Assistant Superintendent, M.R.

Special School District of St. Louis County
St. Louis, Missouri 63119
February 20, 1970

[1] Available from CEC, Suite 900, 1499 Jefferson Davis Highway, Arlington, Virginia 22202.

introduction

The field of special education has passed through several critical phases in its development. It has survived the critics, and the advocates have been honored. Programs in all areas of exceptionality have expanded, some with more structure than others. None has had clear cut guidelines or precedents. Chance has often been the rule rather than the exception in the classroom and in the administrative realm. The process of extrapolation from many fields of inquiry has filtered in bits and pieces of information to the worker in special education. But the expanding fields of organization and administration of special education can no longer afford this oblique approach in dealing with the problems and issues of providing special services for exceptional children, youth, and adults.

The process and function of special education administration have only recently begun to emerge into a formalized structure and discipline. To describe this emerging discipline and trace its implications for current practice the authors made an exhaustive search of the literature that included not only sources of information germane to special education but also to general education, psychology, business, management, personnel and guidance, architecture, and computer science, among others. From these sources more than 1,500 articles, books, unpublished dissertations, and other related materials were carefully analyzed for their potential contribution to this representative collection of readings that would form a baseline of knowledge for the special education administrator, the general school administrator, and others concerned about and involved with the administrative process from both a theoretical and pragmatic point of view.

The selection of those articles for final inclusion was a long and deliberate task. The authors attempted first to build parameters by structuring nine separate sections that would lead the reader from basic concepts to more specific and central considerations in the process of special education administration.

In several areas of interest to the authors, few articles could be located and were of questionable value. As a result, several sections are limited in scope and content; namely, those dealing with supervision of special education, facilities and technology, coordination, international perspectives, and programming for rural and sparsely populated areas.

Apparently, there is a need for articles relating system strategies and organizational theory to the processes of special education administration. However, few such articles were found in the extensive survey conducted. There is a paucity of published material relating to the processes of special education organization, supervision, and administration, in the journals and publications dealing with general administration and supervision. The lack of such articles is somewhat compensated for by the availability of many good texts and other specific publications relating to system strategies, organizational administrative theory, and the conceptual processes in general education. Therefore the authors reluctantly decided not to include these kinds of articles in this publication.

The amount and quality of material that was reviewed but not utilized seemed too significant simply to discard and was subsequently developed into an annotated bibliography which appears in the ninth section of the book.

Prior to the comprehensive process of reviewing and selecting articles, a survey was made of sixteen educational journals with national circulation to administrators, supervisors, and teachers to determine the number of special education articles appearing in these journals. Of the journals surveyed, four were directed primarily to teachers, eight to administrators, and four were of general educational interest. These journals were surveyed for the years 1951, 1959, and 1967. In the years surveyed, there were fifty-nine articles published in the sixteen journals concerned with the general area of special education, or an average of 1.4 articles per journal per year. The articles appear with decreasing frequency over the years surveyed, the averages being 1.8 in 1951, 1.6 in 1959, and 0.8 in 1967. Very few of the articles were written by school administrators, and of the total articles reviewed, only nine were written for school administrators. Of these nine several had nothing to do with the process of administration, organization, or supervision of special education. It appears that as the number of special education programs in the public schools increases, there is a decreasing number of articles written about them in the sixteen journals that were part of the survey. There are fewer articles in the journals for administrators than for teachers, and the number appears to be decreasing every year. Most of the reviewed data, particularly in recent years, are to be found only in highly specialized journals. It appears that there is a trend away from the presentation of special education articles in general educational journals which is partly a result of the addition and expansion of more specialized journals, such as *Exceptional Children*, *The Journal of Mental Deficiency*, *Mental Retardation-CEC*, and *Teaching Exceptional Children*, etc.

As more leaders from both the public and private sectors become sensitive to the educational needs of the exceptional individual, so in turn will they be asking more critical and basic questions about frameworks, strategies and models, supervision, coordination, issues, state and federal programming and legislation, perspectives and trends, and facilities and technology of special education. These individuals will also be concerned with personnel considerations and basic research designs for evaluating programs.

The philosophy of this compilation is to give the reader basic insights and understandings into the area mentioned above with little emphasis upon "categories" of exceptionality as such but rather upon the administrative process as it relates to all areas of special education. Those who are familiar with the tremendous growth of special education in the past decade know that the complexity of structuring for the exceptional individual is going to continue to be a major challenge. Educational developments in the 70's will require that special education carefully evaluate existing programs and develop strategies that will make more effective use of learning theory and developing technology.

Special education, functioning for the most part in the past as a separate or sub-system, will increasingly find the need to become an integrated and essential part of the main system. For a child who could not fit into the general educational pattern, alternatives have been limited.

The main alternative to a regular class has been placement in a special self-contained class. However, new sequential arrangements of instructional alternatives suggest that only a small number of exceptional children will require self-contained settings. The greatest number may be able to remain in and profit from the main system if resource help is available and if that system makes use of concepts such as differentiated staffing and provides viable mechanisms for the individualization of instruction. It is our hope that this collection of readings will be a starting point for those facing this challenge.

This publishing project has involved the cooperation and efforts of a great many persons. We were fortunate to receive publication permission from the authors of the articles selected or from their representatives. The encouraging notes that accompanied many of the permission letters were received with gratitude. Special acknowledgment for assistance in abstracting articles is made to students of the editors at the University of Texas and Fort Hays Kansas State College. We have greatly appreciated the help and encouragement of our wives, Connie and Jane.

CHARLES H. MEISGEIER
JOHN D. KING

Austin, Texas
June, 1970

contents

part i

conceptual frameworks for special education

Special education programs for exceptional children are increasing at a staggering rate. Enrollments in special education programs have increased approximately 500% between 1948 and 1966, or almost seven times faster than the 70% increase in the nation's school-age population during the same period. The 1966 estimated enrollment of over two million exceptional pupils, however, only accounts for between 35-40% of pupils who might benefit from special educational services. Partly, this increase has been a result of the interest and financial help available from the federal government. Increased understanding, acceptance and readiness of people everywhere to establish and maintain special education is a result of the efforts of active professional and parent organizations.

In the lead article, the late Ray Graham, one of the great leaders of special education, reviews the growth of this movement, defines the essential aspects of administration, and identifies trends which are still of interest today. Graham outlines the challenges for education in finding the administrative structures, and developing the philosophy and facilities for exceptional children — a significant segment of the school population with major and complex problems. In a more recent article, Lloyd Dunn reviews and challenges present practices and patterns for the mentally retarded and other exceptional children. He forcefully outlines his impression that special education has sacrificed quality programs for quantity and concludes with Graham's statement that "we have a long way to go."

Both Graham and Dunn have focused attention on the issue of

the efficacy of self-contained classrooms for the handicapped and the need for more viable administrative and organizational strategies in special education. Evidence is accumulating that new administrative and organizational mechanisms are being designed to provide for a shift of emphasis from the categorical segregated classroom to a behavioral approach emphasizing the needs of the child in a highly integrated instructional program.

Maynard Reynolds develops a schematic framework for considering certain issues in special education and utilizes this framework to discuss current issues. Samuel Levine proposes a theoretical framework relating to physical and mental disability from which hypothetical propositions are deduced and offers direction for future research in his article.

In the final article of this section, Thomas E. Jordan focuses on a basic problem that has received little attention until quite recently and discusses conceptual issues in the development of a taxonomy for special education.

responsibility of public education for exceptional children*

RAY GRAHAM†

Lincoln Steffens in his autobiography tells the story of a man and the devil walking together down the street of a busy city. They saw a man reach out and grasp a fine and worthy idea — right out of the air. The man said to the devil, "Did you see that? And aren't you afraid of it? A worthy idea can grow and grow until it becomes so powerful it will destroy you." The devil replied, "No, I am not afraid of it. First they will give it a name. Then they will organize and promote it — and then there will be so many ideas of how to handle it that they will become confused and controversial among themselves and the worthy idea will weaken and destroy itself. No, I am not afraid of it."

The history of education is replete with many fine ideas. In spite of the devil many have grown and endured — the steadfast belief in public education in a democracy; the growth of colleges and universities; a dedicated faith in children and youth; worthy objectives of education; and high professional standards. In the development of every one of these ideas, it has been necessary to whip the several devil's advocates: (1) misconception as to purpose and plan, (2) conformity to past patterns and established beliefs, and (3) lethargy of action. One of the more recent (in terms of the long

*Reprinted from *Exceptional Children*, Vol. 28 (January 1962), pp. 255-259, by permission of the author's widow and the Council for Exceptional Children.

†Ray Graham, before his death, was Illinois State Director of Special Education.

history of public education) is what is commonly referred to as special education for exceptional children.

It is not easy to determine just when this worthy idea was "plucked out of the air." Possibly it was when special institutions for handicapped were developed, first in Europe and later in this country. Possibly the idea began with the adoption of our state constitutions guaranteeing an educational opportunity to all the children. (I have never been able to find any interpretation that said these state constitutions meant to say "all the children but those who were mentally retarded, or severely crippled, or totally blind, or brain-damaged, or deaf, or bed-fast, or delinquent and incorrigible." The interpretation is that *all* means *every* child.)

The idea may have been born again as various states passed compulsory attendance legislation. Or it may have developed naturally through the processes of conception of an idea, pregnancy, birth, and growth from the emergent democratic philosophies that have been the seeds of all progress in government and politics, in culture, in economics, in science and in education. For instance, the children's charter which said in Article XIII: "For every child who is blind, deaf, crippled, or otherwise physically handicapped, and for the child who is mentally handicapped, such measures as will early discover and diagnose his handicap, provide care and treatment, and so train him that he may become an asset to society rather than a liability. Expenses of these services should be borne publicly where they cannot be privately met."

Suffice it to say that in the middle of the twentieth century it has become an accepted responsibility, with special legislation enacted in every one of the states, to set up a plan whereby all the children including the handicapped may secure a school opportunity. It is not an opportunity for the mentally retarded child if he is expected to do the same work with the same achievement that is required of children with average ability. It is not an opportunity for the physically handicapped child who is limited in physical perform- ance to have to adjust to the same curricula in every detail as does the non-handicapped. It is not acceptable opportunity to deprive the superior child by limiting him to an average program. It is not an opportunity for a child to learn to adjust to all the complexities of the society in which he must live if we isolate and segregate him by placing him only with the handicapped of his own type.

Education today has a major challenge to find the ways and means, and to develop the philosophy and the facilities, to provide for this rather new adventure in education — a group that is by no measure insignificant in numbers or in the kinds and degrees of their complex problems.

DEFINING THE
RESPONSIBILITY

In the United States responsibility for education is a state function. Under our system of government local school districts derive their authority from their state legislature. Local districts may do what they are given legislative permission to do. For many years — and especially in the 19th century — the only specific legislation for the education of the handicapped provided for state institutions or residential schools. In a vague way the legislative provisions for common schools may have been interpreted as providing for the handicapped along with all other children.

But realistically they could not fit into the regular classes and make progress. As a result most of them made no attempt to attend school. It is true that in larger centers of population local boards of education provided some special classes and facilities long before legislation began to develop specific provisions. For instance, the first day school classes for blind children were opened in Chicago in the year 1900.

Today all states have some legislation that defines the responsibilities of local districts for exceptional children. Most of the states have specialists in the state department of education giving leadership at that level. A majority of the states appropriate funds for assisting local districts in meeting the increased costs of such programs.

The federal government has taken cognizance of the problem and some financial help is available from that source. Generally this has been emphasized in the area of mental retardation and is providing money for research, and fellowships designed to develop leadership in these newer developments of education.

As a rule, the authority for establishing and maintaining special education is left to the local district. The progress that has been made is generally proportionate to the understanding, acceptance and readiness of the local community and district. Of course there are problems of financing the programs, of finding suitable building facilities in these times of expanding school populations, and of recruiting, selecting, training and placing adequately trained personnel. Too often it is urged that the development of special services is retarded because of these problems of finance, building, and personnel. But I am proposing that in my opinion the basic road blocks are in the lack of understanding, acceptance and readiness.

I am amazed to note that when the local community opinion becomes strong enough, or the parents apply the pressures of their organized group, the ways and means are found. The community of the concerned generally finds ways of setting the objectives of education and the policies of a board of education. Where understanding of the children, their problems, and the advantages to both the children and society are clearly set forth we find progress. Where the community accepts these children and its responsibility to them we find results. Where the professional staff understands and accepts we always find readiness to do the job.

ESSENTIAL ASPECTS OF ADMINISTRATION

In evaluating any educational program I am interested in four aspects:

Philosophy

A person, or a community, functions no better than the philosophy that motivates. If a school administrator, teacher, or community believes in children and education, and if their concepts of service are triggered by attitudes that include acceptance of handicapped children they will generally provide most acceptably for them. But if they go no further than to question whether this is a problem of education or welfare; or if they ask "we must first take care of the regular children;" or "we will do the job if the state pays for it," then they will generally do nothing, or do it inadequately. If the philosophy is one of getting out of accepting responsibility, the individual or community can generally find a way to realize the objective.

Leadership

A team may have great players, but their winnings are pretty much determined by the caliber of coaching and quarterbacking. A business generally pays dividends in proportion to the quality of its directing executives. A school board turns to its professional leadership. A mediocre teacher with a good principal may be more effective than an excellent teacher with a poor building leader. Leadership sets the pace, coordinates the programs, interprets within and without the school. Leadership inspires. It supports the discouraged as well as the ambitious. Leadership is creative and creativity is contagious. Leadership gives status and balance. Leadership gets results.

Organization

In special education organization starts with objectives. It includes lines of authority and methods of communication. It is much more than providing facilities and assigning personnel. In special education it includes such intricate details as identification of pupils, determination of their eligibility through careful study, diagnosis, and proper placement. In identifying one handicapped child a whole chain of reactions is set in motion of telephone calls, visitations to home and to clinics, conferences with doctors, psychologists, community agencies, principals, nurses, teachers, and others. Organization of special education is concerned with pupil-teacher ratios, or class size, that in turn are related to age range, grade levels and types and degrees of handicaps. Organization is concerned with equipment, materials of instruction, curriculum, teacher selection and supervision, and school-home relationships. In special education this means making special education as definite, as accepted, as permanent, and as respected as is the third grade, reading, or geometry.

The Look Ahead

No special education program can succeed if it is designed to meet only an immediate condition. The handicapped child that is six today will be 16 in 10 years. The exceptional children in special classes today will be reaching forks in the road ahead. Some will still be handicapped when they are adults. Some will improve, some will regress. Some will go through high school, some to college, and some will find work. Even in school the roads will fork. Some will be in a special class all day. Some will be integrated gradually into some regular classes, and finally into all.

Planning for the future is two fold. It includes the future of each child. It includes the expansion of programs within the school. Each type of handicapped child has special needs. As the school develops services for one type it creates awareness of the needs of others. A small program managed by the superintendent or principal may grow into one where specially qualified directors and supervisors will be needed. The look ahead means planning for the future — planning for buildings, rooms, surveys, financing, personnel selection. Future planning is evidence of growth. Lack of growth is evidence of decay.

CURRENT TRENDS

Three noteworthy considerations stand out among others in developing a good special education program.

1. Legislation

In most states the existing legislation for special education has been enacted within the last decade. In all states it has developed piecemeal. In some instances it is quite limited in that it may apply to only certain types of exceptional children. The patterns of authority for administration and the patterns of reimbursement vary greatly. In some states legislation requires rather high standards and in some they are very weak and would be difficult to defend professionally. The provisions for special education vary in order to coincide with legislative patterns for regular education in the same state. Since special education in most states has developed within the last decade or two this has been beneficial in some respects. It has enabled the state and local districts to study their situations and develop slowly but more soundly.

However, children are children the world over. Education and special education represent a rather definite philosophy whether in one state or another, and medical, social, educational and rehabilitation needs are similar because the kinds and degrees of handicaps are much the same wherever they are found.

Special education has reached a stage of national development where it seems reasonable to assume that it would be most profitable to make a study of legislation in all states so that the best points of each could be evaluated and considered. Such a study should include a comparative study of total legislation. What are essential patterns in all special education legislation? How does legislation relate special education to all education? What are the administrative responsibilities at state and local levels? What administrative rules, regulations and standards are necessary to supplement the legislation? Which features should be permissive and which ones mandatory? What patterns of state financial aid are most appropriate? How does the legislation for day school programs integrate with those for public residential schools? How do they integrate with programs for private schools, and also with other public and private services such as medical and social agencies.

2. Status of Special Education

The rapid growth of special education programs has often resulted in a growing apart instead of together with the total education framework. Special education developed because regular educators were concerned about children with problems. And they asked for those special facilities to be furnished to supplement the regular facilities. Too often we find them operating entirely unrelated to each other. This leads to misunderstandings and poor functioning. We should probably return frequently in our thinking to the original premise that "special education has no justification for existence except as special facilities not available in the regular school are needed."

Special education needs status. Status comes only from understanding and acceptance. It is easy to set up special services that are so separate in administration, in housing, and in program that it soon becomes a school within a school. No child should be in a special class if he can be fairly and adequately served in a regular class. He should be returned to that regular class for any part of the program where he can adjust to it. Special education should never become possessive of these children, nor should regular education ever totally release them.

Status of special education will be attained when it is considered a definite part of the regular school faculty in the building where he teaches. Special education should have no better — and no worse — rooms or equipment than other classes. Exceptional children should not be pampered in school anymore than they should at home. They should be given work they can do and then be expected to do it. Special teachers should be on the same salary schedule as any other teacher with similar amounts of training and experience. If differentials of salary are given for extra work or responsibilities they should be defined and made available to all who qualify — whether special or regular teachers.

Most fundamental to this problem of status is the acceptance of the exceptional child and the special education program by the school in which the class is located, by the Board of Education, and by the local community. Too often the statement comes from the local community that "this is a state function," or "the state should pay most or all of the costs." This is rejection — not acceptance. Status will be attained only when the local community recognizes the handicapped child as one of its precious possessions — a child. And when they have a desire to meet his needs they will tackle the job whether the state has a little Marshall Plan or not to bail them out as to extra costs. The community that accepts the child and the job of serving him gives status to the program.

Only when special education earns status will it have status.

3. A Balanced Program

Balance in program means many things. It means not just programs for one or a few types of handicapped, but for any and all children who need special services. Balance means an adequate and appropriate program at all levels — primary, intermediate, and high school. Balance means a total program, not just one in academic training.

Handicapped children need attention to their growth and development in physical fitness, social adjustment, emotional security, spiritual welfare, and mental growth. Handicapped children need extra curricular activities, vocational or prevocational training, counseling and all other resources of the school. A balanced program relates the school program with the child's program in the home and community. A balanced program coordinates the special with the regular classes. It coordinates the educational services with those given by the nurse, the guidance staff, the psychologist, the school social worker, and the total staff. A program — like a person — that loses its balance will fall.

A CREDO OF FAITH

This I do believe:

That every child is important.

That every child is basically a normal child and that even the so-called handicapped child is rather a normal child with a handicap.

That public education can and should render a service to all children including those with handicaps.

That the basic consideration is not the lowness of the child but rather the highness of our ability to help him.

That special education is *a part of* and not *apart from* regular education.

That every child is entitled to a program of education wherein he can experience success.

That in education it is not as important what we do for a child as it is what we do to him.

That laws do not so much give schools the authority to serve children as it does give opportunity.

That our success in special education should be measured not in the numbers we have served, but in the degree of our success with the most difficult ones.

That no reward in life surpasses that spiritual reward of helping the child to overcome his handicap by adjusting to it.

Yes, special education is a worthy idea. Those of us who work in the field can become confused and controversial, and thus destroy it. Or we can be so clear and so united that together we can make it grow in stature and favor with God and man.

special education for the mildly retarded — is much of it justifiable?*

LLOYD M. DUNN†

In lieu of an abstract to this article, I would like to preface it by saying this is my swan song for now — as I leave special education and this country for probably the next two years. I have been honored to be a past president of The Council for Exceptional Children. I have loyally supported and promoted special classes for the educable mentally retarded for most of the last 20 years, but with growing disaffection. In my view, much of our past and present practices are morally and educationally wrong. We have been living at the mercy of general educators who have referred their problem children to us. And we have been generally ill prepared and ineffective in educating these children. Let us stop being pressured into continuing and expanding a special education program that we know now to be undesirable for many of the children we are dedicated to serve.

A better education than special class placement is needed for socioculturally deprived children with mild learning problems who have been labeled educable mentally retarded. Over the years, the status of these pupils who come from poverty,

*Reprinted from *Exceptional Children*, Vol. 35 (September 1968), by permission of the author and the Council for Exceptional Children. Copyright 1968 by the Council for Exceptional Children.

†Lloyd M. Dunn has been Director, Institute on Mental Retardation and Intellectual Development, George Peabody College for Teachers, Nashville, Tennessee.

broken and inadequate homes, and low status ethnic groups has been a checkered one. In the early days, these children were simply excluded from school. Then, as Hollingworth (1923) pointed out, with the advent of compulsory attendance laws, the schools and these children "were forced into a reluctant mutual recognition of each other." This resulted in the establishment of self contained special schools and classes as a method of transferring these "misfits" out of the regular grades. This practice continues to this day and, unless counterforces are set in motion now, it will probably become even more prevalent in the immediate future due in large measure to increased racial integration and militant teacher organizations. For example, a local affiliate of the National Education Association demanded of a local school board recently that more special classes be provided for disruptive and slow learning children (Nashville *Tennessean*, December 18, 1967).

The number of special day classes for the retarded has been increasing by leaps and bounds. The most recent 1967-1968 statistics compiled by the U. S. Office of Education now indicate that there are approximately 32,000 teachers of the retarded employed by local school systems — over one-third of all special educators in the nation. In my best judgment, about 60 to 80 percent of the pupils taught by these teachers are children from low status backgrounds — including Afro-Americans, American Indians, Mexicans, and Puerto Rican Americans; those from nonstandard English speaking, broken, disorganized, and inadequate homes; and children from other nonmiddle class environments. This expensive proliferation of self contained special schools and classes raises serious educational and civil rights issues which must be squarely faced. It is my thesis that we must stop labeling these deprived children as mentally retarded. Furthermore we must stop segregating them by placing them into our allegedly special programs.

The purpose of this article is twofold: first, to provide reasons for taking the position that a large proportion of this so called special education in its present form is obsolete and unjustifiable from the point of view of the pupils so placed; and second, to outline a blueprint for changing this major segment of education for exceptional children to make it more acceptable. We are not arguing that we do away with our special education programs for the moderately and severely retarded, for other types of more handicapped children, or for the multiply handicapped. The emphasis is on doing something better for slow learning children who live in slum conditions, although much of what is said should also have relevance for those children we are labeling emotionally disturbed, perceptually impaired, brain injured, and learning disordered. Furthermore, the emphasis of the article is on children, in that no attempt is made to suggest an adequate high school environment for adolescents still functioning as slow learners.

REASONS FOR CHANGE

Regular teachers and administrators have sincerely felt they were doing these pupils a favor by removing them from the pressures of an unrealistic and inappropriate program of studies. Special educators have also fully believed that the children involved would make greater progress in special schools and classes. However, the overwhelming evidence is that our present and past practices have their major justification in removing pressures on regular teachers and pupils, at the expense of the socioculturally deprived slow learning pupils themselves. Some major arguments for this position are outlined below.

Homogeneous Grouping

Homogeneous groupings tend to work to the disadvantage of the slow learners and underprivileged. Apparently such pupils learn much from being in the same class with children from white middle class homes. Also, teachers seem to concentrate on the slower children to bring them up to standard. This principle was dramatically applied in the Judge J. Skelly Wright decision in the District of Columbia concerning the track system. Judge Wright ordered that tracks be abolished, contending they discriminated against the racially and/or economically disadvantaged and therefore were in violation of the Fifth Amendment of the Constitution of the United States. One may object to the Judge's making educational decisions based on legal considerations. However, Passow (1967), upon the completion of a study of the same school system, reached the same conclusion concerning tracking. The recent national study by Coleman, et al. (1966), provides supporting evidence in finding that academically disadvantaged Negro children in racially segregated schools made less progress than those of comparable ability in integrated schools. Furthermore, racial integration appeared to deter school progress very little for Caucasian and more academically able students.

What are the implications of Judge Wright's rulings for special education? Clearly special schools and classes are a form of homogeneous grouping and tracking. This fact was demonstrated in September, 1967, when the District of Columbia (as a result of the Wright decision) abolished Track 5, into which had been routed the slowest learning pupils in the District of Columbia schools. These pupils and their teachers were returned to the regular classrooms. Complaints followed from the regular teachers that these children were taking an inordinate amount of their time. A few parents observed that their slow learning children were frustrated by the more academic program and were rejected by the other students. Thus, there are efforts afoot to develop a special education program in D.C. which cannot be labeled a track. Self contained special classes will probably not be tolerated under the present court ruling but perhaps itinerant and resource room programs would be. What if the Supreme Court ruled against tracks, and all self contained special classes across the nation which serve primarily ethnically and/or economically disadvantaged children were forced to close down? Make no mistake — this could happen! If I were a Negro from the slums or a disadvantaged parent who had heard of the Judge Wright decision and knew what I know now about special classes for the educable mentally retarded, other things being equal, I would then go to court before allowing the schools to label my child as "mentally retarded" and place him in a "self contained special school or class." Thus there is the real possibility that additional court actions will be forthcoming.[1]

Efficacy
Studies
The findings of studies on the efficacy of special classes for the educable mentally retarded constitute another argument for change. These results are well known (Kirk, 1964) and suggest consistently that retarded pupils make as much or more progress in the regular grades as they do in special education. Recent

[1] Litigation has now occurred. According to an item in a June 8, 1968, issue of the *Los Angeles Times* received after this article was sent to the printer, the attorneys in the national office for the rights of the indigent filed a suit in behalf of the Mexican-American parents of the Santa Ana Unified School District asking for an injunction against the District's classes for the educable mentally retarded because the psychological examinations required prior to placement are unconstitutional since they have failed to use adequate evaluation techniques for children from different language and cultural backgrounds, and because parents have been denied the right of hearing to refute evidence for placement. Furthermore, the suit seeks to force the district to grant hearings on all children currently in such special classes to allow for the chance to remove the stigma of the label "mentally retarded" from school records of such pupils.

studies such as those by Hoelke (1966) and Smith and Kennedy (1967) continue to provide similar evidence. Johnson (1962) has summarized the situation well:

> It is indeed paradoxical that mentally handicapped children having teachers especially trained, having more money (per capita) spent on their education, and being designed to provide for their unique needs, should be accomplishing the objectives of their education at the same or at a lower level than similar mentally handicapped children who have not had these advantages and have been forced to remain in the regular grades [p. 66].

Efficacy studies on special day classes for other mildly handicapped children, including the emotionally handicapped, reveal the same results. For example, Rubin, Senison, and Betwee (1966) found that disturbed children did as well in the regular grades as in special classes, concluding that there is little or no evidence that special class programing is generally beneficial to emotionally disturbed children as a specific method of intervention and correction. Evidence such as this is another reason to find better ways of serving children with mild learning disorders than placing them in self contained special schools and classes.

Labeling
Processes

Our past and present diagnostic procedures comprise another reason for change. These procedures have probably been doing more harm than good in that they have resulted in disability labels and in that they have grouped children homogeneously in school on the basis of these labels. Generally, these diagnostic practices have been conducted by one of two procedures. In rare cases, the workup has been provided by a multidisciplinary team, usually consisting of physicians, social workers, psychologists, speech and hearing specialists, and occasionally educators. The avowed goal of this approach has been to look at the complete child, but the outcome has been merely to label him mentally retarded, perceptually impaired, emotionally disturbed, minimally brain injured, or some other such term depending on the predispositions, idiosyncracies, and backgrounds of the team members. Too, the team usually has looked for causation, and diagnosis tends to stop when something has been found wrong with the child, when the why has either been found or conjectured, and when some justification has been found for recommending placement in a special education class.

In the second and more common case, the assessment of educational potential has been left to the school psychologist who generally administers — in an hour or so — a psychometric battery, at best consisting of individual tests of intelligence, achievement, and social and personal adjustment. Again the purpose has been to find out what is wrong with the child in order to label him and thus make him eligible for special education services. In large measure this has resulted in digging the educational graves of many racially and/or economically disadvantaged children by using a WISC or Binet IQ score to justify the label "mentally retarded." This term then becomes a destructive, self fulfilling prophecy.

What is the evidence against the continued use of these diagnostic practices and disability labels?

First, we must examine the effects of these disability labels on the attitudes and expectancies of teachers. Here we can extrapolate from studies by Rosenthal and Jacobson (1966) who set out to determine whether or not the expectancies of teachers influenced pupil progress. Working with elementary school teachers across the first six grades, they obtained pretest measures on pupils by using intelligence and achievement tests. A sample of pupils was randomly drawn and labeled "rapid learners" with hidden potential. Teachers were told that these children would show unusual intellectual gains and school progress during the year. All pupils were retested late in the school year. Not all differences were statistically significant, but the gains of the children who had been arbitrarily labeled rapid learners were generally significantly greater than those of the other pupils, with especially dramatic changes in the first and second grades. To extrapolate from this study, we must expect that labeling a child "handicapped" reduces the teacher's expectancy for him to succeed.

Second, we must examine the effects of these disability labels on the pupils themselves. Certainly none of these labels are badges of distinction. Separating a child from other children in his neighborhood — or removing him from the regular classroom for therapy or special class placement — probably has a serious debilitating effect upon his self image. Here again our research is limited but supportive of this contention. Goffman (1961) has described the stripping and mortification process that takes place when an individual is placed in a residential facility. Meyerowitz (1965) demonstrated that a group of educable mentally retarded pupils increased in feelings of self derogation after one year in special classes. More recent results indicate that special class placement, instead of helping such a pupil adjust to his neighborhood peers, actually hinders him (Meyerowitz, 1967). While much more research is needed, we cannot ignore the evidence that removing a handicapped child from the regular grades for special education probably contributes significantly to his feelings of inferiority and problems of acceptance.

Improvements in
General Education

Another reason self contained special classes are less justifiable today than in the past is that regular school programs are now better able to deal with individual differences in pupils. No longer is the choice just between a self contained special class and a self contained regular elementary classroom. Although the impact of the American Revolution in Education is just beginning to be felt and is still more an ideal than a reality, special education should begin moving now to fit into a changing general education program and to assist in achieving the program's goals. Because of increased support at the local, state, and federal levels, four powerful forces are at work:

Changes in School Organization.   In place of self contained regular classrooms, there is increasingly more team teaching, ungraded primary departments, and flexible groupings. Radical departures in school organization are projected — educational parks in place of neighborhood schools, metropolitan school districts cutting across our inner cities and wealthy suburbs, and, perhaps most revolutionary of all, competing public school systems. Furthermore, and of great significance to those of us who have focused our careers on slow learning children, public kindergartens and nurseries are becoming more available for children of the poor.

Curricular Changes.   Instead of the standard diet of Look and Say readers, many new and exciting options for teaching reading are evolving. Contemporary mathematics programs teach in the primary grades concepts formerly reserved for high school. More programed textbooks and other materials are finding their way into the classroom. Ingenious procedures, such as those by Bereiter and Engelmann (1966), are being developed to teach oral language and reasoning to preschool disadvantaged children.

Changes in Professional Public School Personnel.   More ancillary personnel are now employed by the schools — i.e., psychologists, guidance workers; physical educators, remedial educators, teacher aides, and technicians. Furthermore, some teachers are functioning in different ways, serving as teacher coordinators, or cluster teachers who provide released time for other teachers to prepare lessons, etc. Too, regular classroom teachers are increasingly better trained to deal with individual differences — although much still remains to be done.

Hardware Changes. Computerized teaching, teaching machines, feedback typewriters, ETV, videotapes, and other materials are making autoinstruction possible, as never before.

We must ask what the implications of this American Revolution in Education are for special educators. Mackie (1967), formerly of the U. S. Office of Education, addressed herself to the question: "Is the modern school changing sufficiently to provide [adequate services in general education] for large numbers of pupils who have functional mental retardation due to environmental factors [p. 5]?" In her view, hundreds — perhaps even thousands — of so called retarded pupils may make satisfactory progress in schools with diversified programs of instruction and thus will never need placement in self contained special classes. With earlier, better, and more flexible regular school programs many of the children should not need to be relegated to the type of special education we have so often provided.

In my view, the above four reasons for change are cogent ones. Much of special education for the mildly retarded is becoming obsolete. Never in our history has there been a greater urgency to take stock and to search out new roles for a large number of today's special educators.

A BLUEPRINT FOR CHANGE

Two major suggestions which constitute my attempt at a blueprint for change are developed below. First, a fairly radical departure from conventional methods will be proposed in procedures for diagnosing, placing, and teaching children with mild learning difficulties. Second, a proposal for curriculum revision will be sketched out. These are intended as proposals which should be examined, studied, and tested. What is needed are programs based on scientific evidence of worth and not more of those founded on philosophy, tradition, and expediency.

A
THOUGHT

There is an important difference between regular educators talking us into trying to remediate or live with the learning difficulties of pupils with which they haven't been able to deal; versus *striving to evolve a special education program that is either developmental in nature, wherein we assume responsibility for the total education of more severely handicapped children from an early age, or is supportive in nature, wherein general education would continue to have central responsibility for the vast majority of the children with mild learning disabilities — with us serving as resource teachers in devising effective prescriptions and in tutoring such pupils.*

A Clinical
Approach

Existing diagnostic procedures should be replaced by expecting special educators, in large measure, to be responsible for their own diagnostic teaching and their clinical teaching. In this regard, it is suggested that we do away with many existing disability labels and the present practice of grouping children homogeneously by these labels into special classes. Instead, we should try keeping slow learning children more in the mainstream of education, with special educators serving as diagnostic, clinical, remedial, resource room, itinerant and/or team teachers, consultants, and developers of instructional materials and prescriptions for effective teaching.

The accomplishment of the above *modus operandi* will require a revolution in much of special education. A moratorium needs to be placed on the proliferation (if not continuance) of self contained special classes which enroll primarily the ethnically and/or economically disadvantaged children we have been labeling educable mentally retarded. Such pupils should be left in (or returned to) the regular elementary grades until we are "tooled up" to do something better for them.

Prescriptive Teaching. In diagnosis one needs to know how much a child can learn, under what circumstances, and with what materials. To accomplish this, there are three administrative procedures possible. One would be for each large school system — or two or more small districts — to establish a "Special Education Diagnostic and Prescription Generating Center." Pupils with school learning problems would be enrolled in this center

on a day and/or boarding school basis for a period of time —
probably up to a month and hopefully until a successful prescription
for effective teaching had been evolved. The core of the staff would
be a variety of master teachers with different specialties — such as in
motor development, perceptual training, language development,
social and personality development, remedial education, and so
forth. Noneducators such as physicians, psychologists, and social
workers would be retained in a consultative role, or pupils would be
referred out to such paraeducational professionals, as needed. A
second procedure, in lieu of such centers with their cadres of
educational specialists, would be for one generalist in diagnostic
teaching to perform the diagnostic and prescription devising functions on her own. A third and even less desirable procedure would be
for one person to combine the roles of prescriptive and clinical
teacher which will be presented next. It is suggested that 15 to 20
percent of the most insightful special educators be prepared for
and/or assigned to prescriptive teaching. One clear virtue of the
center is that a skilled director could coordinate an inservice training
program and the staff could learn through, and be stimulated by, one
another. In fact, many special educators could rotate through this
program.

Under any of these procedures, educators would be responsible
for the administration and interpretation of individual and group
psychoeducational tests on cognitive development (such as the WISC
and Binet), on language development (such as the ITPA), and on
social maturity (such as the Vineland Social Maturity Scale).
However, these instruments — with the exception of the ITPA which
yields a profile of abilities and disabilities — will be of little use
except in providing baseline data on the level at which a child is
functioning. In place of these psychometric tests which usually yield
only global scores, diagnostic educators would need to rely heavily
on a combination of the various tools of behavior shapers and clinical
teachers. The first step would be to make a study of the child to find
what behaviors he has acquired along the dimension being considered. Next, samples of a sequential program would be designed to
move him forward from that point. In presenting the program, the
utility of different reinforcers, administered under various conditions, would be investigated. Also, the method by which he can best
be taught the material should be determined. Different modalities for
reaching the child would also be tried. Thus, since the instructional
program itself becomes the diagnostic device, this procedure can be
called diagnostic teaching. Failures are program and instructor
failures, not pupil failures. In large measure, we would be guided by

Bruner's dictum (1967) that almost any child can be taught almost anything if it is programed correctly.[2]

This diagnostic procedure is viewed as the best available since it enables us to assess continuously the problem points of the instructional program against the assets of the child. After a successful and appropriate prescription has been devised, it would be communicated to the teachers in the pupil's home school and they would continue the procedure as long as it is necessary and brings results. From time to time, the child may need to return to the center for reappraisal and redirection.

Clearly the above approach to special education diagnosis and treatment is highly clinical and intuitive. In fact, it is analogous to the rural doctor of the past who depended on his insights and a few diagnostic and treatment devices carried in his small, black bag. It may remain with us for some time to come. However, it will be improved upon by more standardized procedures. Perhaps the two most outstanding, pioneering efforts in this regard are now being made by Feuerstein (1968) in Israel, and by Kirk (1966) in the United States. Feuerstein has devised a *Learning Potential Assessment Device* for determining the degree of modifiability of the behavior of an individual pupil, the level at which he is functioning, the strategies by which he can best learn, and the areas in which he needs to be taught. Also, he is developing a variety of exercises for teaching children with specific learning difficulties. Kirk and his associates have not only given us the ITPA which yields a profile of abilities and disabilities in the psycholinguistic area, but they have also devised exercises for remediating specific psycholinguistic disabilities reflected by particular types of profiles (Kirk, 1966). Both of these scientists are structuring the assessment and remediation procedures to reduce clinical judgment, although it would be undesirable to formalize to too great a degree. Like the country doctor versus modern medicine, special education in the next fifty years will move from clinical intuition to a more precise science of clinical instruction based on diagnostic instruments which yield a

[2] By ignoring genetic influences on the behavioral characteristics of children with learning difficulties, we place responsibility on an inadequate society, inadequate parents, unmotivated pupils, and/or in this case inadequate teachers. Taking this extreme environmental approach could result in placing too much blame for failure on the teacher and too much pressure on the child. While we could set our level of aspiration too high, this has hardly been the direction of our error to date in special education of the handicapped. Perhaps the sustained push proposed in this paper may not succeed, but we will not know until we try it. Insightful teachers should be able to determine when the pressures on the pupil and system are too great.

profile of abilities and disabilities about a specific facet of behavior and which have incorporated within them measures of a child's ability to learn samples or units of materials at each of the points on the profile. If psychoeducational tests had these two characteristics, they would accomplish essentially the same thing as does the diagnostic approach described above — only under more standardized conditions.

Itinerant and Resource Room Teaching. It is proposed that a second echelon of special educators be itinerant or resource teachers. One or more resource teachers might be available to each sizable school, while an itinerant teacher would serve two or more smaller schools. General educators would refer their children with learning difficulties to these teachers. If possible, the clinical teacher would evolve an effective prescription for remediating the problem. If this is not possible, she would refer the child to the Special Education Diagnostic and Prescription Generating Center or to the more specialized, prescriptive teacher who would study the child and work out an appropriate regimen of instruction for him. In either event, the key role of the resource room and itinerant clinical educators would be to develop instructional materials and lessons for implementing the prescription found effective for the child, and to consult and work with the other educators who serve the child. Thus, the job of special educators would be to work as members of the schools' instructional teams and to focus on children with mild to moderate school learning problems. Special educators would be available to all children in trouble (except the severely handicapped) regardless of whether they had, in the past, been labeled educable mentally retarded, minimally brain injured, educationally handicapped, or emotionally disturbed. Children would be regrouped continually throughout the school day. For specific help these children who had a learning problem might need to work with the itinerant or resource room special educator. But, for the remainder of the day, the special educator would probably be more effective in developing specific exercises which could be taught by others in consultation with her. Thus, the special educator would begin to function as a part of, and not apart from, general education. Clearly this proposed approach recognizes that all children have assets and deficits, not all of which are permanent. When a child was having trouble in one or more areas of learning, special educators would be available to devise a successful teaching approach for him and to tutor him when necessary. Perhaps as many as 20 to 35 percent of our present special educators are or could be prepared for this vital role.

Two Other Observations. First, it is recognized that some of today's special educators — especially of the educable mentally retarded — are not prepared to serve the functions discussed. These teachers would need to either withdraw from special education or develop the needed competencies. Assuming an open door policy and playing the role of the expert diagnostician and the prescriptive and clinical educator would place us in the limelight. Only the best will succeed. But surely this is a responsibility we will not shirk. Our avowed *raison d'etre* has been to provide special education for children unable to make adequate progress in the regular grades. More would be lost than gained by assigning less than master teachers from self contained classes to the diagnostic and clinical educator roles. Ainsworth (1959) has already compared the relative effectiveness of the special class versus itinerant special educators of the retarded and found that neither group accomplished much in pupil progress. A virtue of these new roles for special education is that they are high status positions which should appeal to the best and therefore enhance the recruitment of master regular teachers who should be outstanding in these positions after having obtained specialized graduate training in behavior shaping, psycho-educational diagnostics, remedial education, and so forth.

Second, if one accepts these procedures for special education, the need for disability labels is reduced. In their stead we may need to substitute labels which describe the educational intervention needed. We would thus talk of pupils who need special instruction in language or cognitive development, in sensory training, in personality development, in vocational training, and other areas. However, some labels may be needed for administrative reasons. If so, we need to find broad generic terms such as "school learning disorders."

New Curricular
Approaches

Master teachers are at the heart of an effective school program for children with mild to moderate learning difficulties — master teachers skilled at educational diagnosis and creative in designing and carrying out interventions to remediate the problems that exist. But what should they teach? In my view, there has been too great an emphasis in special classes on practical arts and practical academics, to the exclusion of other ingredients. Let us be honest with ourselves. Our courses of study have tended to be watered down regular curriculum. If we are to move from the clinical stage to a science of instruction, we will need a rich array of validated prescriptive programs of instruction at our disposal. To assemble these programs will take time, talent, and money; teams of specialists including creative teachers, curriculum specialists, programers, and theoreticians will be needed to do the job.

What is proposed is a chain of Special Education Curriculum Development Centers across the nation. Perhaps these could best be affiliated with colleges and universities, but could also be attached to state and local school systems. For these centers to be successful, creative educators must be found. Only a few teachers are remarkably able to develop new materials. An analogy is that some people can play music adequately, if not brilliantly, but only a few people can compose it. Therefore, to move special education forward, some 15 to 20 percent of our most creative special educators need to be identified, freed from routine classroom instruction, and placed in a stimulating setting where they can be maximally productive in curriculum development. These creative teachers and their associates would concentrate on developing, field testing, and modifying programs of systematic sequences of exercises for developing specific facets of human endeavor. As never before, funds are now available from the US Office of Education under Titles III and VI of PL 89-10 to embark upon at least one such venture in each state. In fact, Title III was designed to support innovations in education and 15 percent of the funds were earmarked for special education. Furthermore, most of the money is now to be administered through state departments of education which could build these curriculum centers into their state plans.

The first step in establishing specialized programs of study would be to evolve conceptual models upon which to build our treatments. In this regard the creative teachers would need to join with the theoreticians, curriculum specialists, and other behavioral scientists. Even the identification of the broad areas will take time, effort, and thought. Each would require many subdivisions and extensive internal model building. A beginning taxonomy might include the following eight broad areas: (a) environmental modifications, (b) motor development, (c) sensory and perceptual training, (d) cognitive and language development including academic instruction, (e) speech and communication training, (f) connative (or personality) development, (g) social interaction training, and (h) vocational training. (Of course, under cognitive development alone we might evolve a model of intellect with some ninety plus facets such as that of Guilford [1967], and as many training programs.)

In the area of motor development we might, for example, involve creative special and physical educators, occupational and physical therapists, and experts in recreation and physical medicine, while in the area of language development a team of speech and hearing specialists, special educators, psychologists, linguists, and others would need to come together to evolve a conceptual model, to identify the parameters, and to develop the specialized programs of exercises. No attempt is made in this article to do more than provide an overview of the problem and the approach. Conceptualizing the specific working models would be the responsibility of cadres of experts in the various specialties.

Environmental Modifications. It would seem futile and rather unrealistic to believe we will be able to remediate the learning difficulties of children from ethnically and/or economically disadvantaged backgrounds when the schools are operating in a vacuum even though top flight special education instructional programs are used. Perhaps, if intensive around the clock and full calendar year instruction were provided beginning at the nursery school level, we might be able to counter appreciably the physiological weaknesses and inadequate home and community conditions of the child. However, the field of education would be enhanced in its chances of success if it became a part of a total ecological approach to improve the environments of these children. Thus special educators need to collaborate with others — social workers, public health officials, and other community specialists. Interventions in this category might include (a) foster home placement, (b) improved community conditions and out of school activities, (c) parent education, (d) public education, and (e) improved cultural exposures. For optimal pupil development, we should see that children are placed in a setting that is both supportive and stimulating. Therefore, we must participate in environmental manipulations and test their efficacy. We have made a slight beginning in measuring the effects of foster home placement and there is evidence that working with parents of the disadvantaged has paid off. The model cities programs would also seem to have promise. But much more human and financial effort must be invested in this area.

Motor Development. Initial work has been done with psychomotor training programs by a number of persons including Delacato (1966), Oliver (1958), Cratty (1967), Lillie (1967), and others. But we still need sets of sequential daily activities built around an inclusive model. Under this category, we need to move from the early stages of psychomotor development to the development of fine and large movements required as vocational skills. Programs to develop improved motor skills are important for a variety of children with learning problems. In fact, one could argue that adequate psychomotor skills constitute the first link in the chain of learning.

Sensory and Perceptual Training. Much of our early efforts in special education consisted of sensory and perceptual training applied to severe handicapping conditions such as blindness, deafness, and mental deficiency. Consequently, we have made a good beginning in outlining programs of instruction in the areas of auditory, visual, and tactual training. Now we must apply our emerging technology to work out the step by step sequence of activities needed for children with mild to moderate learning difficulties. In this regard, visual perceptual training has received growing emphasis, pioneered by Frostig (1964), but auditory perceptual training has been neglected. The latter is more important for school instruction than the visual channel. Much attention needs to be given to this second link in the chain of learning. Children with learning problems need to be systematically taught the perceptual processes: they need to be able to organize and convert bits of input from the various sense modalities into units of awareness which have meaning.

Cognitive and Language Development Including Academic Instruction. This is the heart of special education for slow learning children. Our business is to facilitate their thinking processes. We should help them not only to acquire and store knowledge, but also to generate and evaluate it. Language development could largely be included under this caption — especially the integrative components — since there is much overlap between the development of oral language and verbal intelligence. However, much of receptive language training might be considered under sensory and perceptual training, while expressive language will be considered in the next topic.

A major fault of our present courses of study is failure to focus on the third link in the chain of learning — that of teaching our children systematically in the areas of cognitive development and concept formation. A major goal of our school program should be to increase the intellectual functioning of children we are now classifying as socioculturally retarded. For such children, perhaps as much as 25 percent of the school day in the early years should be devoted to this topic. Yet the author has not seen one curriculum guide for these children with a major emphasis on cognitive development — which is a sad state of affairs indeed!

Basic psychological research by Guilford (1959) has provided us with a useful model of intellect. However, little is yet known about the trainability of the various cognitive processes. Actually, Thurstone (1948) has contributed the one established set of materials for training primary mental abilities. Thus, much work lies ahead in developing programs of instruction for the training of intellect.

We are seeing more and more sets of programed materials in the academic areas, most of which have been designed for average children. The most exciting examples today are in the computer assisted instruction studies. Our major problem is to determine how these programed exercises need to be modified to be maximally effective for children with specific learning problems. Work will be especially needed in the classical areas of instruction including written language and mathematics. Hopefully, however, regular teachers will handle much of the instruction in science and social studies, while specialists would instruct in such areas as music and the fine arts. This will free special educators to focus on better ways of teaching the basic 3 R's, especially written language.

Speech and Communication Training. This area has received much attention, particularly from speech correctionists and teachers of the deaf. Corrective techniques for specific speech problems are probably more advanced than for any other area, yet essentially no carefully controlled research has been done on the efficacy of these programs. Speech correctionists have tended to be clinicians, not applied behavioral scientists. They often create the details of their corrective exercises while working with their clients in a one to one relationship. Thus, the programs have often been intuitive. Furthermore, public school speech therapists have been spread very thin, usually working with 75 to 100 children. Many have been convinced that only *they* could be effective in this work. But remarkable changes have recently occurred in the thinking of speech therapists; they are recognizing that total programs of oral language development go far beyond correcting articulation defects. Furthermore, some speech therapists believe they could be more productive in working with only the more severe speech handicaps and devoting much attention to the development and field testing of systematic exercises to stimulate overall language and to improve articulation, pitch, loudness, quality, duration, and other speech disorders of a mild to moderate nature. These exercises need to be programed to the point at which teachers, technicians, and perhaps teacher aides can use them. Goldman (1968) is now developing such a program of exercises to correct articulation defects. This seems to be a pioneering and heartening first step.

Connative (or Personality) Develop-ment. This emerging area requires careful attention. We must accept the position that much of a person's behavior is shaped by his environment. This applies to all aspects of human thought, including attitudes, beliefs, and mores. Research oriented clinical psychologists are providing useful information on motivation and personality development and before long we will see reports of research in shaping insights into self, the effects of others on self, and one's effects on others. It is not too early for teams of clinical psychologists, psychiatric social workers, creative special educators (especially for the so called emotionally disturbed), and others to begin developing programs of instruction in this complex field.

Social Interaction Training. Again we have an emerging area which overlaps considerably with some of those already presented, particularly connative development. Special educators have long recognized that the ability of a handicapped individual to succeed in society depends, in large measure, on his skill to get along with his fellow man. Yet we have done little to develop his social living skills, a complex area of paramount importance. Training programs should be developed to facilitate development in this area of human behavior.

Vocational Training. Closely tied to social interaction training is vocational training. Success on the job for persons that we have labeled educable mentally retarded has depended on good independent work habits, reliability, and social skills, rather than on academic skills. Consequently, early and continuing emphasis on developing these traits is necessary. In fact, it is likely to be even more important in the years ahead with fewer job opportunities and increasing family disintegration providing less shelter and support for the so called retarded. Therefore sophisticated programs of instruction are especially needed in this area. Even with our best efforts in this regard, it is likely that our pupils, upon reaching adolescence, will continue to need a variety of vocational services, including trade and technical schools, work study programs, and vocational training.

Another Observation. It seems to me to be a red herring to predict that special educators will use these hundreds of specialized instructional programs indiscriminately as cookbooks. Perhaps a few of the poor teachers will. But, the clinical teachers proposed in this article would be too sophisticated and competent to do this. They would use them as points of departure, modifying the lessons so that each child would make optimal progress. Therefore, it seems to me that this library of curriculum materials is necessary to move us from a clinical and intuitive approach to a more scientific basis for special education.

EPILOGUE

The conscience of special educators needs to rub up against morality. In large measure we have been at the mercy of the general education establishment in that we accept problem pupils who have been referred out of the regular grades. In this way, we contribute to the delinquency of the general educations since we remove the pupils that are problems for them and thus reduce their need to deal with individual differences. The *entente* of mutual delusion between general and special education that special class placement will be advantageous to slow learning children of poor parents can no longer be tolerated. We must face the reality — we are asked to take children others cannot teach, and a large percentage of these are from ethnically and/or economically disadvantaged backgrounds. Thus much of special education will continue to be a sham of dreams unless we immerse ourselves into the total environment of our children from inadequate homes and backgrounds and insist on a comprehensive ecological push — with a quality educational program as part of it. This is hardly compatible with our prevalent practice of expediency in which we employ many untrained and less than master teachers to increase the number of special day classes in response to the pressures of waiting lists. Because of these pressures from the school system, we have been guilty of fostering quantity with little regard for quality of special education instruction. Our first responsibility is to have an abiding commitment to the less fortunate children we aim to serve. Our honor, integrity, and honesty should no longer be subverted and rationalized by what we hope and may believe we are doing for these children — hopes and beliefs which have little basis in reality.

Embarking on an American Revolution in Special Education will require strength of purpose. It is recognized that the structure of most, if not all, school programs becomes self perpetuating. Teachers and state and local directors and supervisors of special education have much at stake in terms of their jobs, their security, and their programs which they have built up over the years. But can we keep our self respect and continue to increase the numbers of these self contained special classes for the educable mentally retarded which are of questionable value for many of the children they are intended to serve? As Ray Graham said in his last article in 1960: [p. 4.]

We can look at our accomplishments and be proud of the progress we have made; but satisfaction with the past does not assure progress in the future. New developments, ideas, and facts may show us that our past practices have become out-moded. A growing child cannot remain static — he either grows or dies. We cannot become satisfied with a job one-third done. We have a long way to go before we can rest assured that the desires of the parents and the educational needs of handicapped children are being fulfilled [p.4].

REFERENCES

Ainsworth, S. H. *An exploratory study of educational, social and emotional factors in the education of mentally retarded children in Georgia public schools.* US Office of Education Cooperative Research Project Report No. 171 (6470). Athens, Ga.: University of Georgia, 1959.

Bereiter, C., & Engelmann, S. *Teaching disadvantaged children in the pre-school.* Englewood Cliffs, N.J.: Prentice-Hall, 1966.

Bruner, J. S., Olver, R. R., & Greenfield, P. M. *Studies in cognitive growth.* New York: Wiley, 1967.

Coleman, J. S., et al. *Equality of educational opportunity.* Washington, D. C.: USGPO, 1966.

Cratty, P. J. *Developmental sequences of perceptual motor tasks.* Freeport, Long Island, N.Y.: Educational Activities, 1967.

Delacato, C. H. (Ed.) *Neurological organization and reading problems.* Springfield, Ill.: Charles C. Thomas, 1966.

Feuerstein, R. *The Learning Potential Assessment Device.* Jerusalem, Israel: Haddassa Wizo Canada Child Guidance Clinic and Research Unit, 1968.

Frostig, M., & Horne D. *The Frostig program for the development of visual perception.* Chicago: Follett, 1964.

Graham, R. Special education for the sixties. *Illinois Educational Association Study Unit,* 1960, 23, 1-4.

Goffman, E. *Asylums: Essays on the social situation of mental patients and other inmates.* Garden City, N. Y.: Anchor, 1961.

Goldman, R. *The phonemic-visual-oral association technique for modifying articulation disorders in young children.* Nashville, Tenn.: Bill Wilkerson Hearing and Speech Center, 1968.

Guilford, J. P. *The nature of human intelligence.* New York: McGraw-Hill, 1967.

Hoelke, G. M. *Effectiveness of special class placement for educable mentally retarded children.* Lincoln, Neb.: University of Nebraska, 1966.

Hollingworth, L. S. *The psychology of subnormal children.* New York: MacMillan, 1923.

Johnson, G. O. Special education for mentally handicapped — a paradox. *Exceptional Children*, 1962, 19, 62- 69.

Kirk, S. A. Research in education. In H. A. Stevens & R. Heber (Eds.), *Mental retardation.* Chicago, Ill.: University of Chicago Press, 1964.

Kirk, S. A. *The diagnosis and remediation of psycholinguistic disabilities.* Urbana, Ill.: University of Illinois Press, 1966.

Lillie, D. L. The development of motor proficiency of educable mentally retarded children. *Education and Training of the Mentally Retarded*, 1967, 2, 29- 32.

Mackie, R. P. *Functional handicaps among school children due to cultural or economic deprivation.* Paper presented at the First Congress of the International Association for the Scientific Study of Mental Deficiency, Montpellier, France, September, 1967.

Meyerowitz, J. H. Family background of educable mentally retarded children. In H. Goldstein, J. W. Moss & L. J. Jordan. *The efficacy of special education training on the development of mentally retarded children.* Urbana, Ill.: University of Illinois Institute for Research on Exceptional Children, 1965. Pp. 152- 182.

Meyerowitz, J. H. Peer groups and special classes. *Mental Retardation*, 1967, 5, 23- 26.

Oliver, J. N. The effects of physical conditioning exercises and activities on the mental characteristics of educationally sub-normal boys. *British Journal of Educational Psychology*, 1958, 28, 155- 165.

Passow, A. H. *A summary of findings and recommendations of a study of the Washington, D. C. schools.* New York: Teachers College, Columbia University, 1967.

Rosenthal, R., & Jacobson, L. Teachers' expectancies: Determinants of pupils' IQ gains. *Psychological Reports*, 1966, 19, 115- 118.

Rubin, E. Z., Senison, C. B., & Betwee, M. C. *Emotionally handicapped children in the elementary school.* Detroit: Wayne State University Press, 1966.

Smith, H. W., & Kennedy, W. A. Effects of three educational programs on mentally retarded children. *Perceptual and Motor Skills*, 1967, 24, 174.

Thurstone, T. G. *Learning to think series.* Chicago, Ill.: Science Research Associates, 1948.

Wright, Judge J. S. *Hobson vs Hansen: U. S. Court of Appeals decision on the District of Columbia's track system. Civil Action No. 82-66.* Washington, D. C.: U. S. Court of Appeals, 1967.

a framework for considering some issues in special education*

MAYNARD C. REYNOLDS†

Growing attention is being given to creating a conceptual framework for consideration of special education problems. Outlined below is one way of thinking about the broad range of services provided under special education. The framework is presented schematically, along with a brief discussion of its features, and then utilized to discuss some current issues. Consideration is given only to handicapped children, since programs for the gifted seem not to fit the structure as developed here.

THE HIERARCHY OF SPECIAL EDUCATION PROGRAMS

The variety of programs which comprise special education may be summarized in a chart which takes the form of a triangle (see page 34). At the first level, across the broad base of the chart, is represented the large number of exceptional children, mainly those with minor deviations, who are enrolled in regular classes in the schools. Much of the effort to provide needed services for these children must be directed through regular classroom teachers.

Many exceptional children will not receive all required services

---

*Reprinted from *Exceptional Children*, Vol. 28 (March 1962), pp. 367–370, by permission of the author and the Council for Exceptional Children. Copyright 1962 by the Council for Exceptional Children.

†Maynard C. Reynolds is Director, Special Education, University of Minnesota.

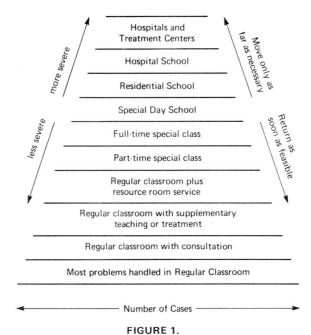

FIGURE 1.

SPECIAL EDUCATION PROGRAMS

in regular classes and thus the chart includes a number of more specialized services, organized in a succession of levels. The gradual narrowing of the chart indicates the smaller numbers of children involved as programs become more specialized.

The second level of service is referred to as "Regular Classroom with Consultation." Some children may be retained in regular classes if consultation is available to teachers and parents to help in understanding children and in making minor modifications in the school program. The schools are rapidly becoming employers of school psychologists, special education consultants, school social workers, and other personnel who provide such consultation.

Children presenting more complex problems will sometimes need specialized services in the form of "Supplementary Teaching or Treatment." This third level of service is illustrated by the work of itinerant speech correctionists who frequently work with individuals or small groups of children for brief periods each day or several times weekly. Similarly, some disturbed children may be given brief periods of counseling help on a regular schedule. Children with hearing or vision problems frequently receive needed supplementary help from specialists while basically enrolled in regular classes.

A next level in the chart is labeled "Regular Classroom plus

Resource Room Service." This type of program has probably been most fully developed for visually handicapped children and in the field of remedial reading, but illustrations may be found in other fields of special education as well. In such programs children are enrolled in regular classes, but special resource rooms are provided in their schools. The children spend a part of each day in the resource room, sometimes on a definite schedule and sometimes on an irregular schedule according to special needs as they arise through the school day. A blind child, for example, may take most instruction in regular classes with normal children but go to the resource room in his building for instruction in braille, mobility, or typing. The resource room includes all necessary special equipment and materials and is in the charge of a specially trained teacher who carefully coordinates her teaching with that of regular classroom teachers.

Succeeding levels, in order, are the "Part-time Special Class," the "Full-time Special Class," and the "Special Day School." Programs of these types are well known and need no description for present purposes. Each represents a further step or extension of program to a more specialized level.

Nearer the top of the chart is the "Residential School." Placement in such schools involves separation from the home environment as well as further specialization in the educational program.

Finally, two programs are listed in which the primary emphasis is on treatment, protection, or care, in contrast to the educational emphasis in programs of lower levels. The first of these is called the "Hospital-School" and the latter, "Hospitals and Treatment Centers." School departments in institutions of these types may have importance, but usually referral of children to such institutions is based upon factors other than educational need. Over-all program control is usually not in the hands of educators.

FEATURES OF THE FRAMEWORK

Several features of the organization of the above chart need to be indicated. In considering the several levels of program, proceeding from the bottom to the top of the chart, a number of changes may be observed:

1. the problems of children placed in programs tend to become more severe or more complex;
2. programs tend to become more expensive;

3. responsibility for administration of programs shifts from
   school authorities to health, welfare, or correction authorities;
4. children are more separated from ordinary school and home
   life;
5. demands for highly specialized personnel increase;
6. parent and general public understanding of programs decreases.

Perhaps the major feature of the scheme is that it presents the
broad range in types of special education programs in an organized
fashion. The descriptions of the various levels have been given with
no thought that they represent the ultimate in types of programs.
Indeed, many other types of programs exist and still others will be
devised. Within this conceptual framework several current issues in
special education may now be considered.

ISSUES IN
SPECIAL EDUCATION

Segregation

One of the continuing issues in special
education is that of segregation — the separation of individuals or
groups of children. It is correctly argued, for example, that removing
a child from his home and neighborhood school for placement in a
residential school is a serious matter. It may be convenient to make
such placements routinely, but conflicting values emerge which in
fact place extraordinary responsibility upon those who make such
placement decisions. Similarly, it can be a disturbing experience for a
child to be placed in a special class or any other type of special
program. But it is also inexcusable to delay or deny special services
when they are needed.

The framework outlined above may be useful in stating a
general attitude or policy toward these continuing problems of
separation or segregation. The prevailing view is that normal home
and school life should be preserved if at all possible. When a special
placement is necessary to provide suitable care or education, it
should be no more "special" than necessary. In terms of the chart,
this is to say that children should be moved upward only as far as
necessary and be returned downward as soon as feasible. By stating
such a principle within the structure of programs as proposed here,
views about the segregation issue can be made quite explicit.

If programs are operated according to the above principle or
attitude, we would find increasing numbers of blind and hearing-

handicapped children returning from residential to day schools after they have achieved special skills through intensive early training. Enrollments in special orthopedic schools at the junior high school level should be lower than at the elementary school level if elementary school programs are effective. Movement among the various levels will perhaps be less possible for the mentally retarded, but in most cases problems of transition would loom large and significant.

The strategy proposed here requires variety and range in programs for all handicapping areas, continuing assessment procedures to assure changes in placement at appropriate times, and coordinated planning and placement services covering all levels.

THE RESPONSIBILITY OF THE SCHOOL TO SEVERELY HANDICAPPED CHILDREN

Between the levels of responsibility well established in the schools, mainly for those with relatively mild handicaps, and programs operated by other public agencies, such as mental hospitals and training schools for delinquent children, there is a zone of indefiniteness in public responsibility. Trainable retarded children and many of the multiply handicapped fall in this "in-between" zone of responsibility. These children have more serious handicaps than the schools are prepared to consider and yet they often do not fit into programs of institutions geared to the very seriously handicapped. In recent years this "in-between" zone has become very active, with many voluntary groups goading public agencies to establish programs. Because programs for children in these categories have never been provided, agencies of all types can "beg off" on precedent.

An interpretation of the problems of these "in-between" groups is suggested by the present conceptual framework. Historically, health, welfare, and correction authorities were given early responsibility in most states for the operation of institutions for the most severely deviant. In recent years, these programs have often been extended into the community in the form of out-patient mental health centers, growing numbers of social casework agencies, improved probationary services for delinquent youth and in other ways. Schools, starting from the level of regular classrooms, have gradually extended their programs to more specialized levels and strengthened relationships with all varieties of community agencies. The separation of schools and other agencies has been lessened; levels of the "chart" have gradually merged.

Problems of the "in-between" children will need to be solved by even closer cooperation among agencies of many types. The trainable retarded, for example, often present life-long dependency problems. It is futile to think about responsibility for these children in terms of "education versus welfare." They need health, welfare, and educational services — not just one or another. The challenge in this field, as in many others, is to establish new and effective interagency community programs. One of the real and current dangers is that programs for such "in-between" children will develop in expedient forms without a clear formulation of public responsibility. Already, too many programs exist with only fragile support and token administrative services by public agencies. Such conditions bode ill for the quality and durability of these programs.

OTHER PROBLEMS
CONSIDERED BRIEFLY

Two additional problems will be examined briefly in the present framework. The first of these concerns the form of special aids as provided mainly by state governments. When the variety of programs is considered, it may be seen that financial aid programs tied to only one or a limited number of types of programs may introduce rigidities in programing. Aids on a per-classroom unit or per-pupil basis are probably less desirable than are aids tied to professional personnel, leaving some variety in the ways they may work with exceptional children.

Implications for terminology and classification may also be mentioned. First, the emphasis on "flow" of children among levels of program implies that categorization of children is always tentative and subject to revision. Second, it is suggested that more attention needs to be given to classification of programs rather than so exclusively to classification of children. The essential problem in educational placement is to allocate children to programs likely to be most valuable for them. Methods of classifying children now used in special education seem to have developed with all too little attention to subtle differentiations necessary to make the most effective placements. As more attention shifts to the program side of the classification and placement problem, it seems likely that approaches to individual child study and classification will be greatly revised. A child's potential is not independent of his situation, or of the methods used in his education, yet we so often proceed as if abstract study of the child himself is sufficient.

SUMMARY

A summary of special education programs has been presented in the form of a hierarchy, ranging from regular classes, through several intermediate levels of special services, to hospitals and treatment centers. The levels of the hierarchy were ordered according to increasing specialization. As children are placed in higher level programs their separation from normal home and school life increases. Responsibility for programs at the highest levels of specialization has generally been placed with health, welfare or corrections authorities. Schools have carried responsibility for programs serving the larger numbers of less severely handicapped children. Within this context, certain current issues in special education were discussed.

It was suggested that having a broad range of services is important and that children should be placed in programs of no more special character than absolutely necessary. There should be continuing assessment of children in special programs with a view toward returning them to more ordinary environments as soon as feasible. Problems of providing services to certain groups of children, such as the trainable retarded, have been interpreted as being partly historical in origin for reason of their "in-between" status in regard to school responsibility and functions of other agencies. To serve these "in-between" children, new patterns of interaction among a variety of agencies will be necessary. Finally, the importance of developing financial aid patterns which stimulate the development of a fuller range of services is stressed and a plea is made for more attention to program differentiation in developing systems of classification and terminology to be applied to handicapped children.

a proposed conceptual framework for special education*

SAMUEL LEVINE†

There has been a paucity of investigations in regard to the personal and social development of the exceptional child,[1] in spite of the growing body of knowledge and increased research activities on non-disabled children. In part this is because special education, to a great degree, has remained at a highly pragmatic level; the major concerns relating to program organization, curriculum development and therapeutic devices and procedures. The need for systematic theoretically oriented research in special education has been stressed recently by Block (1955), Kvaraceus (1958), and Meyerson (1955). This paper proposes a theoretical framework relating to physical and mental disability from which hypothetical propositions are deduced, offering some direction for future research.

*Reprinted from *Exceptional Children*, Vol. 28 (October 1961), pp. 83-90, by permission of the author and the Council for Exceptional Children. Copyright 1961 by the Council for Exceptional Children.

† Samuel Levine is Professor, Psychology and Education, San Francisco State College, California.

[1] Exceptional child refers to all categories of children with mental and physical deviations other than the "gifted." Much of what is proposed here is not applicable to that group and it would appear preferable to exclude them from the present discussion. For the purposes of the article, the exceptional child is defined after Barker, *et al* (1952) as a person having a physical and/or mental handicap and who is generally perceived in his cultural group as deviating sufficiently in these respects to prevent him from participating in important activities on terms of equality with normal individuals of his own age.

The writer is aware that the basis of the differentiations for exceptional children may be a physical, emotional or intellectual deviation or any combination of these. The fact that the group is heterogeneous in regard to disability does not deny the usefulness of the proposed framework. One might modify, amplify or make more specific any particular hypothesis based on one of the exceptionalities. However, as an orienting frame of reference the theoretical propositions and their hypothetical derivations appear heuristic.

This paper will not be concerned with the resolution of the practical implications of the proposed framework. However, it would be profitable to stipulate some of the more salient theoretical questions and their practical counterparts in regard to physical and/or mental deviation. The pervasive concern among special educators has not been with the "a" set of questions, but, rather, with the "b" set of questions. A list of these concerns follows:

1. (a) What is the effect of physical and/or mental deviations on group cohesion?
   (b) How can families who have such children be helped in order to reduce intra-family conflict and increase family integration?
2. (a) What are the effects of a physical and/or mental handicap on personality development?
   (b) What kind of educational and vocational planning is necessary for these children in order to reduce maladjustment?
3. (a) What is the relationship between the learning of stereotypes toward deviants and concept formation?
   (b) How can we reduce stereotyping toward individuals with physical and/or mental handicaps so as to reduce certain restrictive barriers to their adjustment and to improve their social acceptance?
4. (a) How does physical and/or mental deviation affect the socialization of the child, particularly in relation to parent-child interaction?
   (b) How can we reduce parental overprotection of the handicapped child and increase the child's self-direction and psychological independence?
5. (a) In what way does a physical and/or mental handicap affect one's status, position or role expectations in society?
   (b) How can we reduce the marginality or isolation of

individuals with such deviations so as to maximize their contribution to self and society?

CONCEPTUAL FRAMEWORK

Social psychological research regarding the exceptional child has been oriented primarily toward the phenomenon of acceptance-rejection. The major sources of such information have been sociometric and attitude studies. The effect of rejection on personality development has been inferred from these studies, the basis for the rejection being posited in the disability. They have generally sought to confirm or deny the existence of rejection without specifying the conditions under which rejection (or acceptance) may be increased, lessened or modified. In effect, the obtained relationships between disability and acceptance-rejection have been interpreted solely in terms of the deviation as the basis for the findings.

The single variate approach in studies of disability is due, the writer believes, to the assumption that physical and/or mental deviations are sufficient conditions for explaining the observed or measured relationships. The lack of theoretical propositions has minimized other sources of variation as explanatory variables. Berreman (1954, p. 347) states that the problem is to determine how much the psychological and social maladjustment of the disabled child is "an inescapable consequence of physical or other impairment, and how much results from social factors — from the status accorded such individuals in our culture and the position accorded to them by 'normal' people."

The implication of the above is that the concern regarding physical and mental variation must extend beyond solely some objective assessment of the individual's disability. Meyerson (1955, p. 9) points out that the effect of such variations "is strictly relative to the expectations of the culture in which the person lives, the tasks that are required of him and the meaning the person himself and others may assign to the variation." "Disability," Meyerson (1955, p. 12) contends, "is not an objective *thing in a person*, but a social value judgment."

These values relate to society's perception of leadership, contributions toward improving society, being a good citizen, being a family head and other essential aspects for maintaining society. These values are criteria against which behavior is assessed in terms of deviation. All members of society, whether handicapped or not, are evaluated primarily by these values. Where an individual cannot meet these demands, or where there are questions as to the adequacy of the individual in relation to these demands, there will be some devaluation of him on society's part (Barker, *et al*, 1953; Garrett, 1953; MacGregor, 1951; Meyerson, 1948 and 1955; Mussen and Barker, 1944; and Wright, 1960).

Disabled individuals are treated as members of a category which communicates to society some statement of the individual's present and/or potential contribution. These categories, e.g., blind, deaf, mentally retarded, cerebral palsied, orthopedic, or the more general inclusive category, disabled or exceptional, contain the stereotypes, biases and sets toward individuals who are members of these groups. Vinacke (1957, p. 239) suggests that the distinctive element in stereotyping is the social significance of the behavior: "The fact is that traits represented in stereotypes depend solely upon properties which a group of people agree are typical of a class just as is the case in practice for classes of other objects. In this sense the properties of stereotypes have a social reality regardless of whether objective measurement would support them or not. Indeed, it is very likely that such measurement would support, at least to some degree, some traits but would not in the least substantiate others."

CATEGORICAL TERMS

Society "understands" or conceptualizes the disabled individual in categorical terms. Those attributes which society utilizes for categorizing the disabled we term the defining attributes of the category.[2] Each behavior in the category has a degree of defining value in respect to its predictability to the stereotype. Those behaviors that afford maximal prediction to the category have a high defining value and are crucial to the stability of the category. Although these categories may be modified in relation to a particular individual, to a great degree they represent categorization based on biological resemblances. In a sense, these exceptionalities have a common or shared stimulus function. This leads to certain social distinctions and culturally imposed differentiations (Anastasi, 1958; Barker, *et al*, 1953; Heider, 1941).

The disabled individual may not share society's frame of reference in regard to his disability. He will develop for himself a way of understanding and of differentiating those aspects of his disability that present difficulties for him and those that he feels are of no

---

[2] The terms "defining attribute" and "criterial attribute" are borrowed from Bruner, Goodnow and Austin (1956).

consequences to his general functioning. Those aspects of his behavior he defines as most differentiating relative to his deviation we call the criterial attributes of his disability. The criterial attributes are specific to the particular individual's assessment of his abilities, interest and aspirations. Vinacke (1957) makes the point that, in his studies, there is a marked general similarity in the content of self-stereotyping as compared to those stereotypes held by others. Dembo, Ladieu and Wright (1948) found that disabled individuals tend to place themselves in positions on a fortune-misfortune scale similar to non-disabled individuals; whereas nondisabled placed the disabled low on this scale. These findings suggest that a study of the perception of disabled individuals' criterial attributes (self-attributes) as compared to the defining attributes may be fruitful.

The disabled individual will at times come into conflict with the existing structure, whether it be in regard to educational, vocational or social aspirations. Conflict will be evidenced by overt rejection of the individual's aspirations, denial of his competence, and/or a refusal to extend consideration to him equal to that of a non-disabled individual. It is hypothesized that the greater the difference between the individual's criterial attributes and society's defining attributes, the greater will be the conflict. The obvious question arises as to whether conflict is a necessary condition in such situations.

It should be remembered that the defining attributes of a category represent attitudinal or behavioral stereotypes toward particular groups or individuals (i.e., blind, deaf, etc). Insofar as these stereotypes have restrictive or devaluating effects on the individual, the basis for conflict is always present. It could be asked if conflict might be reduced, or perhaps eliminated, by having the disabled accept all of, or most of, society's defining attributes in respect to his disability. Meyerson (1955, p. 56) says, in this respect: "It is easy to contend that the disabled person must 'accept' his disability, but this is only a meaningless and contradictory platitude if the underlying situation of disability is not understood. If 'acceptance' means that the person must be content with an inferior position that requires him to acknowledge his inferiority as a person and permits him to strive only for intrisically less satisfying goals, 'acceptance' is difficult. If there is no assurance that society will 'accept' the disability also and not penalize the person for it, it is unrealistic to endow 'acceptance' with the qualities of a panacea."

Depending upon the frequency with which conflict occurs and the degree of difference between the criterial and defining attributes, there will be a greater or lesser sense of isolation or non-belonging.

To the degree that the individual feels this sense of isolation or non-belonging, there will be psychological and social distance[3] between society and the disabled person (Barker, *et al* 1953; Meyerson, 1948 and 1955; Tenny, 1953).

The individual who seeks participation and acceptance in areas where the stereotypes are firmly established will come into conflict situations. The more crucial the stereotypes are for the definition of that category the greater will be the resistance to the disabled individual's participation. Bruner (1951, p. 208) has pointed out that expectancies mold perceptual organizations in a self-sustaining fashion. That is, " . . . most people come to depend upon a certain constancy in their environment and, save under special conditions, attempt to ward off variations from this state of affairs."

PSYCHOLOGICAL AND SOCIAL DISTANCE

The creation of psychological and social distance is a reciprocal process. The disabled individual may become sensitized to group feelings and non-membership, or if he has had membership, it may have been unrewarding, and he may withdraw from social contact. The individuals in the disabled person's environment may interpret the withdrawing behavior as a confirming instance of the defining attributes. The stereotype is in part confirmed and the group acts in such a way as to reinforce the disabled individual's feelings of difference and isolation. Thus, psychological and social distance is increased. The withdrawal of the disabled person from the environment decreases the communication between him and those around him, lessening the possibility of understanding his interests, aspirations and the ways of his dealing with society's perception of his deviancy. The lessening of communication, of course, will tend to increase the psychological and social distance and more firmly establish the existing stereotypes.

To a great degree this psychological and social distance is

---

[3] The term social distance has had long and considerable usage in sociology. Von Wiese and Becker (1932, p. 241) regard such distance "as a condition resulting from the inhibition of tendencies toward association by tendencies toward dissociation from personal and/or situational factors." Newland (1957, p. 150) speaks of psychological distance and sees this process as both a general, attitudinal reaction as well as a highly situational phenomenon. He states, "attitudes, tempered in forms of certain value systems, may be regarded as indicative of such distance." The term psychological and social distance is used here in order to convey the sense of the interaction of the pervasive, generalized attitudinal system with the personal situational factors.

anticipatory in nature. As the individual's sense of difference and non-belonging is reinforced, the greater will be the anticipation of non-acceptance in future situations. The effect will be for the individual to avoid general social contact, thus increasing psychological and social distance and leading to a personal sense of inadequacy. The anticipation of psychological and social distance is an anticipation of failure. The individual may rationalize his feeling of inadequacy by, in fact, attributing to himself the existing stereotypes and perhaps seek what might be termed a "deviant adjustment." A relatively extreme form of this is removing oneself from general societal contact and seeking companionship solely within the disabled group.

Murphy (1947, p. 767) points out that the deviant has his own world, his own deviant group, in which membership is experienced. One can only speculate about the effect of such deviant groups (such as associations and clubs for the deaf, blind, etc.) on the individual. It is suggested that the greater the individual's dependency on such organizations, the greater the reinforcement of existing stereotypes and the greater the psychological and social distance. The implications of the above statements for the present system of segregated special training schools and institutions appear obvious. To a great degree the educational channels for exceptional children are comprised primarily of children who are themselves disabled.

Meyerson (1948, p. 4) contends that variations in physique lead to a highly negative value and for more extreme deviations, positive restrictions. It is hypothesized that the more obvious or visible the defect and the greater the apparent relevance of the exceptionality for the performance of a task, the greater will be the psychological and social distance. These predictions are given some credence by the findings of Schachter (1951, p. 201) in a study of non-conformity. His data indicate that people who strongly reject the deviate perceive a greater difference between themselves and the deviate than do people who do not reject them. Force (1956, p. 107) concludes, in discussing his findings, "It would seem that a factor of visibility was also operating in which acceptance is more of a task for the child with a disability which is readily discernible or obvious to the viewer."

Kvaraceus (1956, p. 331) measured the degree of acceptability of deviations in children among professional workers. He concludes," . . . apparently this group of professional workers feel most comfortable with the most respectable and perhaps the least offensive of the deviates." Johnson (1950) found that as intellectual ability decreased, acceptance by other children decreased and rejection increased. Lewis (1947, pp. 32-33) found that teachers assign traits that have definite mental health value, as determined by mental hygienists, differentially based on the child's intelligence. The geniuses and high IQ group were assigned the high value traits more frequently than the normative group. Both the retarded and the "problem" groups were assigned these traits less frequently than the normative group.

The hypothesis concerning the obviousness of the defect and the creation of psychological and social distance needs qualification. Wright (1960, pp. 53-54) cautions, "Doubtless there are other factors associated with degree of disability, some favoring and some hindering adjustment, the resultant effect being quite removed from the objective fact of severity." One factor offered here relates to the role of achievement in the modification of the defining attributes and the lessening of psychological and social distance. It is hypothesized that, holding degree of disability constant, there will be an inverse relationship between the child's achievement and the amount of psychological and social distance engendered by the disability. More than likely there will be an interaction between the degree of disability and the child's competence with the amount of psychological and social distance created.

Evidence supporting this proposition is not readily available but some suggested support for our thesis can be found. deGroat and Thompson (1949, p. 74) found that children who show evidence of having acquired more subject matter receive a higher proportion of teacher approval as rated by the pupils. They conclude that "children who experience a high degree of teacher approval have a better opinion of themselves, are more 'outgoing' and have more confidence in their ability to adjust to social situations." As expected, they also found that the more intelligent children receive a significantly greater amount of teacher approval, while the less intelligent pupils experience larger amounts of teacher disapproval. Wright (1960, p. 153) conjectures that attributes such as "perseverence, independence, intelligence, moral stamina, etc. may give genuine support to an ego that may be undermined by the negatively evaluated attributes of the disability itself."

CRITERIA FOR INFERRING PSYCHOLOGICAL AND SOCIAL DISTANCE

Any proposed scheme from which psychological and social distance is to be inferred must assess the strength of existing stereotypes as well as the effect of non-conforming or non-exemplary behavior on the reduction of these stereotypes. The categories within this scheme indicate the strength of the behavioral stereotypes toward the general category of disability or exceptionality or toward any specific category, such as blind or deaf.

We would have a non-exemplar of a specific category where the group's expectations are not borne out in regard to the individual's abilities. For example, each time the statement is made, "I didn't know blind people could do that," there is a tendency to break down that category. For that individual, at least, there is less predictability to the category, "blindness," and therefore less validity to the defining attributes of that category. This suggests some fluidity in regard to the defining attributes.

The following categorical scheme permits the determination of the defining attributes and the criterial attributes from which the inference of psychological and social distance is made.

Category One:

This category contains all of the behavioral stereotypes shared by society, relevant to a particular disability. These stereotypes apply to all individuals having a particular disability. Category One is akin to "biological determinism" in regard to physical disability. That is, the stereotypes are taken as a statement regarding the human nature of the disabled individual.

Category Two:

A particular disabled individual performs in such a way on a defining attribute so as to make his behavior indistinguishable from a nondisabled individual. The disabled individual will be seen as a non-exemplar relative to that particular behavior by all persons who come into contact with him. In this case, the disabled person is seen as the non-exemplar rather than the behavior. There are undoubtedly many disabled individuals who, relative to a specific behavior, are non-exemplars. The particular behavior in question may vary from individual to individual. It is possible to predict for these individuals in respect to all other defining attributes.

Category Three:

A particular behavioral stereotype through non-exemplary confirmation gradually becomes less important or less differentiating in regard to the defining attributes. This may occur through mechanical or other modifications that permit the disabled individual to now meet certain expectations that were not before possible. When a sufficient number of disabled individuals do not confirm the expectation relative to a particular defining attribute, this behavior becomes non-exemplary for all individuals. In this instance the behavior is the non-exemplar rather than the individual. The behavior now becomes non-defining, as it does not contribute to the scheme of attributes that have predictive value.

Category Four:

A particular disabled individual, although evidencing some structural limitation, may not be differentiated from the non-disabled on a functional basis. For this individual, most defining attributes are non-predictive and for all intents and purposes he is a non-exemplar. For example, "It's hard to think of him as a blind person" would be appropriate for such an individual. The defining attributes will, however, be present for other individuals having these same physical limitations. The non-exemplar is, again, the individual, but here he is, in effect, not thought of as disabled; whereas in Category Two the individual is so considered. Category Four is a considerable step or movement toward breaking down the defining attributes. Despite the fact that a few individuals are involved, the inability to predict for these individuals to any or hardly any important defining attributes raises two fundamental questions:

1. What are the conditions in the life situation of these individuals that permitted the development of non-differentiated behavior?
2. Could many, or most, or all such disabled individuals function in this way, given these or similar conditions?

Category Five:

Here the defining attribute breakdown has been virtually accomplished. A sufficient number of meaningful behaviors have become non-differentiating for most (or all) members of a particular disability. The defining attributes have no functional utility, except in those areas dealing with specific structural limitations. Functional questions regarding any disabled individual will be determined at the empirical level. However, no prejudgments will be made, as no stereotypes exist.

SUMMARY

The study in special education of variation in physical and mental development has been concerned primarily with the solution of practical problems rather than with theoretically oriented research.

The author proposed a conceptual framework from which hypothetical propositions were deduced relative to the personal and social development of individuals with physical and/or mental deviations. It has been suggested that these disabilities have both objective and value dimensions associated with them.

The generalized attitudinal set by which society conceptualizes such deviations are referred to as defining attributes. The personal, self-evaluative aspects of the individual's disability are termed criterial attributes. A scheme for assessing the strength of these attributes was presented in terms of categories offering the possibility of determining the relationship between cultural biases and stereotypes and the disabled individual's self-perceptions and personal aspirations.

The concept of psychological and social distance was suggested as a criterion measure of social interaction. Various hypotheses have been set forth specifying the conditions under which psychological and social distance will vary.

REFERENCES

Anastasi, A. *Differential psychology*, (Third Ed.) New York: The McMillan Co., 1958.

Barker, L. S., Schoggen, M., Schoggen, P., and Barker, R. G. The frequency of physical disability in children: a comparison of three sources of information. *Child Devopm.*, 1952, 23, 215–226.

Barker, R. G., Wright, B. A., Meyerson, L., and Gonick, M. R. *Adjustment to physical handicap and illness: a survey of the social psychology of physique and disability.* New York: Social Science Research Council, 1953.

Berreman, J. V. Some implications of research in the social psychology of physical disability. *J. Exceptional children*, 1954, 20, 347–350, 356–357.

Block, W. E. A study of somatopsychological relationships in cerebral palsied children. *J. Exceptional Children*, 1955, 22, 53–59, 77–83.

Bruner, J. S. and Postman, L. On the perception of incongruity: a paradigm. *J. Personality*, 1951, 18, 206–223.

Bruner, J. S., Goodnow, J. J., and Austin, G. A. *A study of thinking.* New York: John Wiley and Sons, Inc., 1956.

deGroat, A. F. and Thompson, G. G. A study of the distribution of teacher approval and disapproval among sixth-grade pupils. *J. Exper. Ed.*, 1949, 18, 57-75.

Dembo, T., Ladieu, G., and Wright, B. A. Adjustment to Misfortune: a study in social-emotional relationships between injured and non-injured people. Final report to the Army Medical Research and Development Board. Office of the Surgeon General, War Department, 1948.

Force, D. G. Social status of physically handicapped children. *J. Exceptional Children*, 1956, 23, 104-107, 132-133.

Garrett, J. F. (Ed.) *Psychological aspects of physical disability.* Washington, D. C.: Office of Voc. Rehab. Dept. of Health, Education and Welfare, Bulletin No. 210, 1953.

Heider, F. and Heider, G. M. Studies in the psychology of the deaf, No. 2: II. The adjustment of the adult deaf. *Psychol. Monogr.*, 1941, 53, 57-158.

Johnson, G. O. A study of social position of mentally-handicapped children in the regular grades. *Amer. J. Ment. Def.*, 1950, 55, 60-89.

Kvaraceus, W. C. Acceptance-rejection and exceptionality. *J. Exceptional Children*, 1956, 22, 328-331.

Kvaraceus, W. C. Research in special education: Its status and function. *J. Exceptional Children*, 1958, 24, 249-254.

Lewis, W. D. Some characteristics of children designated as mentally retarded, as problems, and as geniuses by teachers. *J. Genetic Psychol.*, 1947, 70, 29-51.

Macgregor, F. C. Some psycho-social problems associated with facial deformities. *J. Abn. Soc. Psychol.*, 1951, 16, 629-638.

Meyerson, L. Physical disability as a social psychological problem. *The Journal of Social Issues*, 1948, 4, 2-10.

Meyerson, L. Somatopsychology of physical disability. In Cruickshank, W. M. (Ed.) *Psychology of Exceptional Children and Youth.* New Jersey, Prentice Hall, Inc., 1955, 1-60.

Murphy, G. *Personality.* New York: Harper and Bros., 1947.

Mussen, P. H. and Barker, R. G. Attitudes toward cripples. *Child Devopm.* 1944, 39, 351-355.

National Society for the Study of Education, forty-ninth yearbook, Part II. *The education of exceptional children.* Chicago: Univ. of Chicago Press, 1950.

Newland, T. E. Psycho-social aspects of the adjustment of the brain-injured. *J. Exceptional Children*, 1957, 23, 149-153.

Schachter, S. Deviation, rejection, and communication. *J. Abn. Soc. Psychol.*, 1951, 46, 190-207.

Tenny, J. The minority status of the handicapped. *J. Exceptional Children*, 1953, 19, 260-264.

Vinacke, E. W. Stereotypes as social concepts. *J. Soc. Psychol.*, 1957, 46, 229-243.

von Wiese, L. and Becker, H. *Systematic sociology.* New York: John Wiley and Sons, Inc., 1932.

Wright, B. A. *Physical disability — a psychological approach.* New York: Harper and Bros., 1960.

conceptual issues in the development of a taxonomy for special education*

THOMAS E. JORDAN[†]

One of the trends of the last several years has been an increasing dissatisfaction with the naiveté of work in disciplines concerned with the welfare of children (Siegel, 1956). This dissatisfaction is due to the lack of an adequate rationale for methods of instruction and child study. In all young disciplines there is a period when precedent and simple utilitarianism suffice as explanations. This soon passes as people acquire enough experience to view their work in perspective, and feel sufficiently secure to ask if there is a better way. There generally is a better way, and is found by programmed refinement of existing knowledge rather than by the serendipity which characterized the first defensible procedures.

This general observation applies to all fields of knowledge and is equally applicable to special education. It is no longer adequate to use precedent as a rationale for our practices. It is no longer defensible to ignore advances in disciplines continuous with special education. Programmed research in the behavioral sciences has much to tell us, much to show. Increasingly, experimental evidence demonstrates the relevance of conceptual thinking and research to current practice. For example, Rosenstein's (1960) studies of the deaf clearly dictate some changes in the thinking of educators. Beliefs hoary with age and hallowed by precedent do not always

---

*Reprinted from *Exceptional Children*, Vol. 28 (September 1961), pp. 7-12, by permission of the author and the Council for Exceptional Children. Copyright 1961 by the Council for Exceptional Children.

†Thomas E. Jordan is Professor of Education, University of Missouri, St. Louis.

stand the light of critical thinking, and "the best current thinking" may be firmly grounded in error. What is needed is examination of our beliefs about handicapped children in a systematic fashion, substituting detached scholarship for the clichés. Two examples will illustrate the heart of the matter. The first is from one of the disciplines dealing with children, the other from the history of science.

1. Child study is approached by contemporary home economists in light of some of the most advanced thinking of the 1920's. At a recent meeting with some thirty to forty deans of schools of home economics the writer was cautioned to remember "the whole child" (as if one could forget him) and to "study him" (meaning naive observation with no perception of the methodological problems involved). At the same time a child-development specialist from a major center of study attempted to transmit his ideas and found little basis for communication. It is submitted that home economists influence child care practices very greatly. What a tragedy if their leaders should be incapable of responding to new findings. Their lack of responsiveness may be an inability to think in an idiom now current, and thirty years beyond their own. Their thinking was firmly grounded in the idiom of the 1920's isolating them from contemporary thought.

2. A historical example of refinement of thought by conceptualization may be considered. It is an example of a very serious medical problem yielding to better conceptualization:

Over the centuries scurvy was the sailor's worst enemy. Neither storms nor battles incapacitated as many men as did this vitamin deficiency. The crucial work on this disease was performed by James Lind (1753), the Scottish physician. Consider "the best current thinking" just prior to Lind's publication of *A Treatise of the Scurvy* in 1753. Gideon Harvey, physician to Charles II, considered the disease as follows; "preliminary, liminary, recent, inveterate or terminative." He described "a mouth scurvy, leg scurvy, joint scurvy, an asthmatic scurvy, a rheumatic scurvy, a diarrheous scurvy, an emetic or vomiting scurvy, a flatulent hypochondriac scurvy, a cutaneous scurvy, an ulcerous scurvy..." and so on. Lind proceeded to reduce the number of entities to one, a single disease, and demonstrated the requisite cure, lime-juice.

PROGRESS BASED ON THINKING

Now what have these two examples to offer special education. The first example illustrates the danger of a discipline, indifferent to new ideas, finding itself unable to communicate with the main-stream of thought about child behavior and growth. The second illustrates that "the best current thinking" is never a protection against what is wrong, and what is later shown to be patently so. A third comment is in order. Special educators need to realize that progress is based on thinking. Thinking which leads to progress in a discipline is usually a self-conscious attempt to analyze the form and structure of knowledge. Today we need to impose form and structure on what we know about handicapped children. Merely citing precedent and popular prejudice will not result in progress; it will merely result in a good deal of satisfaction.

Over the years much of the difficulty in educating handicapped children developed because we knew very little about them. We were not sure what was wrong with them, or we did not know how they felt, how they were motivated, or their limitations. Advances in education during the last decades have remedied this situation. In most cases we can find a medical opinion about a child and there are some handicapped students on whom we have rather bulky folders full of medical and psychological information.

It would be interesting to make a blind comparison of children, guessing which youngsters had been studied in detail by scientific personnel, using the manner of instruction and the technique of teaching as the clue. In all probability we could not distinguish between the children with elaborate histories and those without them, at least on the basis of how they were taught. Put another way, we may say that a mass of clinical data about handicapped children does not necessarily mean they will receive better instruction.

There are several ways to explain this. The least useful is to say that special teachers are indifferent to the welfare of their children and ignore much useful information. A more sensible comment is to ask if the information gathered by doctors, psychologists, social workers, and the like has any bearing on the enterprise of teaching. Current practices suggest that information may not say anything to teachers, that there is a breakdown in the communication of information from one discipline to another.

It would be naive to think that communication problems consist of one party in a discussion not knowing all the big words that the other party uses. The matter is more complicated than that. What is at the heart of the difficulty is the lack of conventions about what matters should be raised. This is far more difficult than the matter of big words. We may ask the question, "what needs to be known about a child by any professional person?" What are the categories, if you please, that basically define the functioning child?

THE FUNCTIONING
CHILD

Important aspects of children's functioning may be identified as follows:

Somatic

This term refers to those instructionally significant factors which reflect (e.g.) neuromotor problems, or the problems of accommodating an amputee to the instructional process. A problem which will illustrate an item not in this category would be a metabolic disease such as those receiving attention in the literature of mental retardation, Folling's Disease,[1] Maple Sugar Disease, or Oasthouse disease. This is because such physical considerations are the irrelevant substratum to educational functioning.

Intellectual

The diseases just mentioned probably produce intellectual behavior which is relevant to educational processes. Children with Folling's Disease are commonly mentally retarded. Certainly the intellectual behavior of children is relevant to instruction and should be handled in a taxonomy.

Behavioral

To use the metabolic diseases for a third time, Folling's Disease produces abnormal behavior. It really does not matter what the disease is, but the hyperirritability and motoric excitement which occur in this and other diseases do matter. The disease underlying the behavior is irrelevant, since we do not cope with a medical entity but with its behavioral consequences, and, also, several diseases may produce similar behavior.

Communicative disorders are the disturbed processes of expressive and receptive language. Aphasia is often considered a 'symbolic' disorder, but operationally it is either a disruption of expressive or receptive communication.

These categories do not avoid all problems, but they may facilitate communication. People in various coteries may still consider stuttering a neurotic problem (behavioral), or a phenomenal problem (communicative), or the result of an irritable nervous system (somatic). Whatever their formulation, it would be clear by their choice of terms.

A further advantage is that we can state the functional

---

[1] Sometimes referred to as phenylketonuria.

precedence of handicaps. To speak of a mentally retarded, physically handicapped child is to use syntactic precedence to communicate children's problems. The use of four categories with the convention of functional precedence can eliminate much confusion.

A final observation is conceptual. Two decades ago the theoretician J. R. Kantor (1942) pointed out the need to make sure that there is no hiatus between constructs and the events to which they relate. The four categories described seem to observe that stricture.

It is important to realize that a conceptual issue has just been introduced into the discussion. There are several reasons for this: first, a taxonomy is a conceptual model of a substantive area, of a body of knowledge; second, a taxonomy cannot be developed on the basis of naive realism; third, a taxonomy must permit manipulation of knowledge in such a fashion as to elucidate relationships not immediately apparent in the primary data; and fourth, a taxonomy must act as the formal language of an area, much as mathematics is the formal language of physics and the natural sciences.

To elucidate, a taxonomy is a conceptual model of a substantive area. It reflects in its categories either a broad or a narrow range of concerns. Being a classification system it rejects and accepts items for consideration. It is a model that either has or has not a place to incorporate certain salient factors. If the framework is insufficient it will exclude vital matters.

THE UTILITY OF THE SYSTEM

A taxonomy must be developed with great care. Perhaps the matter that gives the greatest procedural difficulty in the end is the utility of the system. One thing which militates against utility is an endless list of categories. We need to apply Occam's Razor, the principle of Parsimony, to our taxonomy. It is appropriate to recall Lind's (1753) work: " . . . it was found necessary to expunge all such terms as were contrived to give an air of wisdom to the imperfections of knowledge." The easiest way to break that rule is to simply start listing items that should be recorded. This is seen in the studies of parent-child, or teacher-child interaction when interminable lists of such descriptive terms as "hostility," "cooperation," "affection," and the like are compiled. These are then used to record and evaluate behavior. Perhaps the best advice is to set up criteria for judging the inclusiveness, the consistency, the coherence, and the construct validity of the terms employed.

A taxonomy is helpful if it helps us do things that are otherwise impossible. One such value is the need to describe relationships that are not obvious to the simple observer. A taxonomy should be a research tool, a technique for describing and communicating the processes of instruction in special education. It should help us understand how and why learning takes place (Wright, 1959).

If we were to compare growth in the various branches of knowledge it would be clear that the natural sciences have advanced further than most others. In considering why this is so it is well to compare their present form with their historical form. Mathematics, for example, began with the simple proposition that one needs to keep track of the number of one's progeny. It no doubt moved along to keeping track of arrows when man was a hunter, and to the length of building materials when he became an artisan. Today simple mensuration has been replaced by a wholly conceptual mathematics which deals with non-representational matters, and probes relationships in a fashion quite impossible when we deal with the "practical." This is possible because the number two or the quantity X is not restricted to two children, or X paces. Number is used in a theoretical, or to choose a less invidious word, conceptual, sense. Number is used as a formal language, as a set of notations ultimately reducible to reality, but used to escape the limitations of the here and now, used to permit the imagination to deal with things outside of the accident of a particular place and a particular moment.

A taxonomy of special education should have the value of allowing us to leave the problem of what to do about a given child's problems in favor of grasping the heart of similar children's problems. In this way a taxonomy can help us solve our difficulties much as a problem expressed as an algebraic problem can be solved for more than one factor. In this fashion a formal language allows us to grow beyond the stage that accumulated knowledge would indicate. It is no accident that we say it takes four years to train a teacher and five years to make one. What we are really saying is that we can transmit just so much knowledge to a would-be teacher — there are vital matters that simply cannot be communicated to the beginner. Put another way we can say that there are items of knowledge that cannot be codified or transmuted in such a fashion that we can phrase meaningful, communicable statements. In terms of this discussion we may say that we have not been able to handle the accumulated wisdom of a master-teacher's experience. The reason, one might argue, is that there is no formal language available to the teacher and the student, there is no set of terms that are adequate to codify, to express, to manipulate the information. To use Bruner's (1957) expression, taxonomy of special education should permit us to go beyond the information given.

APPLIED CONSIDERATIONS

The assumption on which this presentation rests is that a taxonomy of special education is a practical tool. As an example we may consider the problem of educating emotionally disturbed children. This particular practical problem is chosen because of the attention currently being given to the matter. Also, it is a good example of how not to go about developing an educational schema. At the moment, the education of emotionally disturbed children consists of a series of acts which are justified by either the criterion of precedent, or by the accident of the discipline under whose auspices the problem is placed by an omniscient state legislature. It can be either psychiatrically endorsed babysitting until the play-therapist arrives, or it may be quasi-normal instruction under the care of a motherly, non-neurotic teacher.

Looking to the future, and asking the question, "where do we turn next?," we may see a little light if we try to use a taxonomic approach. One of the functions of a taxonomy is the reduction of data to basic, irreducible terms in data language. In this fashion the path for educating emotionally disturbed children may be laid out by converting psychiatric terms and data into educational terms and data. Since this is a preliminary analysis, and is not intended to be the solution of this problem, let us take the least educationally responsive child, an autistic child. Our task here is to make statements in the same data language about an autistic child as a psychiatric problem, and an instructional problem. For reasons best discussed elsewhere we will use contemporary behavioral theory as the data language.

The psychiatric feature of an autistic child is the "aloneness." The youngster has object rather than person relationships. Educationally, the child simply does not make progress. The hiatus which causes much of our difficulty is the lack of articulation between what the psychiatrist knows and what the teacher does.

Viewed taxonomically, and using a specific data language, we might say that the problem should be formulated as one of interaction. Very briefly, interactions are contingent when one person's behavior produces changes in that of the other. When there is no give and take we say there is asymmetric contingency, or non-contingency. The autistic child's problem is that his chief attribute in either educational or psychiatric settings is a lack of contingent behavior. He does not learn when the teacher teaches, he does not communicate when the therapist attempts to understand him. At the risk of blunting Occam's razor we might say there is no "initiation of structure," in his role behavior.

Now what has this discourse on the autistic child done? It has not given a pedagogy for the autistic child. That would be beyond the scope, though not the implications, of this article. What it has done is to describe a behavior pattern, or a segment of it, in a language which can be applied to two disciplines. It has provided a *lingua franca* for psychiatry and education; it has described a problem in a fashion which is common to two disciplines. Secondly, it has related the emotional disability of a child to the emotional handicap of a learner. It has put in psychiatric data and produced educational data. The fact that it was possible to do this demonstrates the care to be used in choosing a data language. If the idiom worked for some conditions, but not for others, we might have a way of distinguishing those conditions which are disabilities in the organic sense, from those which are handicaps in the functional sense. For example, it is probable that colorblindness, an obvious disability, does not produce any meaningful data in interbehavior. If it did, it would be a problem requiring our sustained attention as educators. Failing that, it would not be a handicapping condition.

Another applied consideration is the value of a simple taxonomy as an aid in communication. A practical problem in instruction is deciding what to do with children who have several handicaps. Which handicap is functionally most important? Where shall we start? A third matter arises when we ponder whether a child should be placed in a special class on the basis of his motor handicap or his sensory handicap, or his intellectual handicap. A taxonomy can help solve these problems.

Recently Willenberg (1961) discussed safety matters affecting handicapped children. His approach was to develop a taxonomic model of factors in the external environment — modifiers — and factors in the internal environment — things to be modified. By plotting these items two-dimensionally he indicated certain conclusions that applied to three sorts of handicaps.

I should like to offer a third area of taxonomic endeavor. This is the understanding of factors affecting vocational success in the period after special instruction. A taxonomy of instruction is not necessarily applicable to post-instructional matters. In some ways there are common elements, but there are some significant differences. It is much like using a checker-board to play chess. The board is the same, by analogy the ecology of home and community, but there are different strategies and some extra ploys.

Figure 1 shows some elements on which post-school life may depend. *Intellect* is the same as in the instructional period, but its relevance decreases. *Concepts* of self, the world, and work, emerge as salient matters. *Motives* vary: *achievement motivation* is probably still important, and new motives, *affiliation, power, money, advancement,* and *level of occupation* emerge. *Skills* refers to motor and perceptual abilities. In the post-school success-and-failure of the cerebral palsied, discrete abilities are important. Of equal importance may be what is referred to as *intermodal* skills, the input through one system and output through another: hand-eye, ear-hand-eye, for example. *Communication* acquires a new significance when we consider that young people may have been taught by people who could grasp the intent of students with poor propositional speech. As barriers are dissolved by communication they are erected by inability to give and receive ideas. The only occupation that is exempt from this consideration is probably that of lighthouse keeper. Were this choice, or a comparable one available it might well represent flight from reality into minority status, a step contrary to the spirit of all previous special education endeavors.

It is unrealistic to relate all abilities to all occupations, and such an attempt would vitiate a taxonomy. For this reason we may consider three terms that apply selectively. *Irrelevant* would describe

INTELLECT	a. verbal b. non-verbal	UNFAVORABLE	IRRELEVANT	FAVORABLE
CONCEPTS	a. work b. world c. self			
SKILLS	a. motor b. perceptual c. intermodal			
MOTIVES	a. occupational level b. money c. affiliation d. advancement e. independence			

COMMUNI-
CATION
	Expressive a. oral
	              b. written
	Receptive a. oral
	              b. written			

FIGURE 1.

the application of colorblindness (see *skills*) to many tasks. On the other hand, serious hearing loss (see *communication*) might be favorable in places where a high background of noise is disruptive, in fact where a disability is no handicap. *Unfavorable* would describe the everyday limitations imposed on the special education graduate choosing an occupation.

SUMMARY

A comprehensive taxonomy is needed. This article has discussed two miniature and overlapping structures and commented on a third, that of Willenberg.

The development of a comprehensive taxonomy will occur when special education has developed a comprehensive data language.

Curriculum can acquire construct validity, as opposed to the face validity of many current procedures when it employs taxonomic refinements.

A taxonomy is a device to solve practical problems; it is also a conceptual model, and so emphasizes the comprehensive needs of special education theory.

A comprehensive taxonomy can restore what has been lost since the demise of Herbart, the unity of theory and practice. It can further lead to a sophisticated pedagogy. This in turn has implications for the increased professionalization of practitioners in special education.

REFERENCES

Bruner, J. "Going beyond the information given." *Contemporary Approaches to Cognition.* Harvard U. Press, 1957.

Kantor, J. R. "A preface to interbehavioral psychology." *Psych. Rec.* . 5, 173 - 193, 1942.

Lind, J. *A treatise on the scurvy.* Edinburgh, 1753.

Rosenstein, J. R. "Cognitive abilities of deaf children." *J. Sp. Hear. Res.* . 3, 108- 119, 1960.

Sigel, I. The need for conceptualization in research on child development. 27, 241-252, 1956.

Willenberg, E. P. "A conceptual structure for safety education of the handicapped." *Excep. Child.* 27, 302- 306, 1961.

Wright, E. M. J. "Development of an instrument for studying verbal behaviors in a secondary mathematics classroom." *J. Exper. Educ.* . 28, 103-122, 1959.

part ii

organizational and administrative strategies and models in special education

Divided into four sections, Part II lays the groundwork for a basic understanding of the organization and administration of special education programs. Consideration is given to the general areas of organization and administration, coordination of services to sparsely populated areas and recurring and emerging issues in special education.

In Section A, Leo E. Connor begins with the preliminaries to a theory of Administration touching upon the evolution of special education as it developed and separated itself from Public School Administration as a whole. There is a survey of the theory and philosophy — the Special Education rationale — behind the very existence of "Special" Education offered by Voelker and Mullen and by John W. Kidd in their articles on Organization, Administration and Supervision. Frank M. Hodgson discusses facts and varied attitudes reflected by State Agency and University personnel and other groups. Ernest P. Willenberg concludes the section with a discussion of Internal Organization. An addendum to Section A presents instructional and organizational alternatives by Willenberg, Deno, and Reynolds.

Specific services and their vital interaction are dealt with extensively in Section B. Robert M. Isenberg's realistic assessment of existing school district structures has been included along with Richard Kothera's creative proposals on the whole question of coordinating services. Practical problems in providing supervisory services are dealt with from both the local and state point of view in Kenneth R. Blessing's discussion of the Modern State Department of Education.

Traditional problems associated with the developing of practical designs and strategies for special education in sparsely populated areas are discussed in Section C by Robert Isenberg. The article resulted from a national research conference co-sponsored by the Western Interstate Commission for Higher Education and the Montana State Department of Public Instruction.

Section D overviews recurring issues in this emerging field. Stressed by Maynard Reynolds is the need for evaluation — not only of the child, but of the program as a whole and the results finally produced by it in the lives of the children it serves. George Brabner examines the meaning of the term "integration" as it applies to special class programs and discusses ways integration can be accomplished most effectively.

Lastly, there is a review by Howard Sparks and Leonard Blackman of the much debated question of whether special teaching skills are needed to educate special children or do similarities outweigh differences when comparing special students with regular students.

The scope of the material covered in this part is very broad. Its content is both theoretical and practical. The problems outlined urgently press upon the educational community demanding answers.

section A

organization
and
administration

preliminaries to a theory of administration for special education*

LEO E. CONNOR†

Educational administration, as the art and science of leadership for all school programs, has been evolving within the past decade toward the formulation of general principles and of a theoretical structure. The Kellogg Foundation-sponsored investigations during the 1950's, and numerous publications since then, have explored successful administrative practices and the contributions of other professions to school leadership (Moore, 1957). More recently, the bases of a theory of education administration have been discussed and research-oriented conclusions have vied with conceptual models to provide better insight into the complexity of administering a regular school program (Griffiths, 1959).

To those involved or interested in the administration of special education programs, the paths and direction blazed by regular school administrators have been both fascinating and disturbing. The new findings and insights offered in the many studies and books emanating from educational administrative sources are spurs for the advances which special education is bound to attain. Yet this decade of investigation of administrative behavior and its resultant theoretical statements seems to be reflected "in absentia" by special education literature, doctoral preparation programs and research efforts.

*Reprinted from *Exceptional Children*, Vol. 29 (May 1963), pp. 431-436 by permission of the author and the Council for Exceptional Children. Copyright 1963 by the Council for Exceptional Children.

†Leo E. Conner is Assistant Superintendent and Educational Director, Lexington School for the Deaf, New York City.

The present article covers some of the points which should be considered if a theory of special education administration is to develop.

THE BASIS OF
SPECIAL EDUCATION

Education is a social science and educators are, or should be, behavioral scientists. Human behavior, the reason for and the end of administrative existence, forms the integrating denominator of the various fields studying and influencing human activity. Instruction as the basic concern of education forms the warp and woof from which emanate all aspects of the schools' activities.

Educators and the traditional social and behavioral scientists have recently increased their cooperation in a cross-fertilization endeavor. In particular, the educator is reacting with the anthropologist, psychologist, linguist, sociologist and economist more often around conference tables and delving into the readings and research of their fields (Thompson, 1959). Progress is slow, however, and the establishment of strong colleges of education in many American university settings may have tended to isolate the practitioners of education from the theorists of most other social sciences.

Educational administration is the art of leadership for school programs. At the same time, an educational administrator is an applier of science similar to a general physician or an engineer who utilizes varied scientific findings to attain desirable objectives. Thus, the psychological laws of learning, the economic and social bases for taxation, the philosophical theories and moral goals undergirding the American way of life — all are factors which educational administrators must weave into a pattern of leadership values.

Special education in all of its areas of exceptionality is an aspect of the instructional function of regular education. Its relationships with the welfare, guidance, clinical or medical professions, and governmental services are necessary, but subordinate to the main purpose of teaching handicapped and gifted children and helping them develop into first class citizens. Special education administrators must be increasingly prepared for and conversant with the body of facts, attitudes and competencies that make up the field of general educational administration. Thus, the commonalities of the educational efforts fundamental to special education and regular education should at least equal the emphasis placed upon the specialized techniques, preparation and pride of various exceptional specialities (Connor, 1960).

Administrators of special education must recognize the foundation stones of their professional endeavor. As administration is common to all human organizations, it is a process of directing and controlling life in some kind of social structure. For special education administration, the field of social science is represented by education. Whatever their prior preparation or professional commitments, the instructional objectives and nature of the educational program for exceptional children take precedence in shaping administrative emphases and decisions by all who head special education programs. Upon the base of instruction must be built the theory of special education administration which is destined to best meet the needs of exceptional children.

CHARACTERISTICS OF A THEORY OF SPECIAL EDUCATION ADMINISTRATION

"A striking feature of our recent past has been the transformation into routine practice of the actions we once treated as exceptional" (Neustadt, 1960).

Special education has no choice but to emulate the history of specialities which have charted the course of step-by-step achievement on the road to higher professional status. Among these main phases are the definition of a body of specialized knowledge and its conceptualization in terms of principles (inner order) and objectives (unique functions). The place of the administration of these enterprises will occupy a larger sphere of attention as special education attempts to answer the oft-repeated question, "Where shall we go next?"

If special education has reached the maturity level of interest in generalizations and principles of administration, then into the literature must pour the insights and conclusions of theorists and practitioners alike to produce a dialogue aimed at researchable topics and eventual theories. Without a broad base of discussion and readiness, the appearance of a theory to explain and predict administrative actions may result in little consideration or acceptance.

Administrators, perhaps more than other special educators, need a firm concept of the nature and goals of their wide ranging activities. They must know the hypotheses and rationale of their programs and possess the creativity and stamina for dealing with growth, experiences, and future events. This complex combination of knowledge, skills and attitudes demanded by administrative responsibilities can be effectively assisted by the organization and delineation of guidelines and predictors and the clarification available through the formulation of a theory of administration.

The following statements are some of the characteristics of a theory of special education administration worthy of consideration. Illustrations are offered that seem to possess the needed guidelines for administrators of special education programs.

A Theory Is
Descriptive

The problems besetting the description of special education programs, at first sight, are overwhelming. Dealing with 12 to 14 exceptionalities and the gamut of 50 state organizational patterns through nursery, elementary, secondary, college and university levels of operation — these name but a few of the divisive elements. Yet a theoretical model which describes the administrative process must remain applicable to the varieties of special education settings. Further, it should be universal enough to include all variety of administrative programs, penetrating enough to satisfy the superspecialist and valuable enough to attain general assent to its propositions.

Litchfield (1956) has proposed a series of statements which are essentially descriptions of the general administrative process to form the bases for a theory.

1. Administration includes decision-making, programming, communicating, controlling and reappraising.
2. Administration functions through policy, resources and execution.
3. Administration must consider the administrator, the ongoing process, its own structure and the community in which it functions.
4. Administration is interaction and achievement within the environment of the institution.
5. Administration is substantially the same in educational, industrial, governmental or military organizations.

Recent attempts have been made to describe the special education field as a whole rather than its specific handicapping and gifted aspects (Jordan, 1961; Reynolds, 1962). As a generalized aspect of this field, the administration of programs will need increased discussion and research. Doctoral studies, conference meetings and continued periodical articles should gradually focus attention on the advantages of dealing with the identifiable elements which make all special education work a common endeavor.

A Theory Is
Explanatory

Special education is in urgent need of an accepted body of insights that will explain the relationships that pertain to the content, techniques and observations relating to exceptional children. A set of statements that will interrelate the data with which special education administrators deal is long overdue. These propositions, to have any effectiveness, must include tenable definitions of special education phenomena and while characterized by reliability, objectivity, comprehensiveness and organization, they must facilitate study and action. A theory must not merely impose another set of symbols between the practitioner or student and the administrative realities of the special education enterprises.

Barnard (1938), for example, has written with great insight concerning the functions of an administrator. The following few excerpts indicate how a theory may explain, with profit, frequently observed and described administrative behavior:

1. All complex organizations grow from and consist of unit organizations whose inherent properties are the determining factors in the character of the complex.
2. The properties of unit organizations are determined by physical, biological and social factors which must be understood for administration.
3. The essential process of adoption in organizations is decision, whereby the physical, biological and social factors of the situation are selected for specific combination by action of the administrator.
4. Informal organizations are found within all formal organizations, the latter being essential to order and consistency, the former to vitality. They are mutually reactive and dependent.
5. The strategic factor in cooperation is leadership, which is the name for relatively high personal capacity for both technological attainments and moral complexity.
6. Some principal errors of administration are (a) an oversimplification of the economy of organizational life; (b) a disregard of the fact and of the necessity of informal organization; (c) an inversion of emphasis upon the objective and the subjective aspects of authority.

The scientific process, in general, should apply to the multitude of facts and attitudes that make up special education programs. The examination of the greatest number of administrative happenings and practices will reveal factors of time, space or causality that permit substantial coordination and summary. Similarities and dissimilarities will emerge and permit formulization for easier comprehension and effective insight. The regulation of administrative conduct is then possible through the understanding of the explanations offered by theories.

A Theory Is
Predictive
A theory must be proven by its success in dealing with new and unknown events. Though created from a study of the past, it should provide direction for the future. Basic to this characteristic is the assumption that administration is a generalized type of behavior that can be productively analyzed for guidelines. As the King said to Alice in Wonderland, "If there is no meaning that saves a world of trouble, you know, we needn't try to find any."

Miller (1955) indicates that one criterion of a real theory is the extent that it guides toward previously unknown knowledge. Thus, astronomy and chemistry provide famous examples of predicted planets and elements that were later discovered. Whether the future history of a social science like education will contain examples of similarly prophesied events in special education is not, at this time, within the realm of our speculative knowledge of administrative theory.

A Theory Is
Economical
The number and complexity of special education administrative activities often tend to confuse the viewpoint held by researchers and practitioners. Thus, the quantity of necessary daily activities in special education, the financial and community factors at the local, state and national levels which affect programs, the research findings and the problems of making effective decisions, among others, tend to keep new and experienced on-the-job administrators glued to the seat of this "bucking bronco." Another way of stating the problem is that of Griffiths (1959), who indicated that "the content of educational administration has in the past been comprised of folklore, testimonials of reputedly successful administrators, and the speculations of college professors."

While it must be admitted that all efforts to discover and organize general principles of administrative behavior rest upon the depth and adequacy with which they reveal the reality of administrative behavior, the need is becoming greater than ever to shortcut the vast areas of knowledge, skills and attitudes which successful administrators must routinely possess. The dangers in the special education field are already evident when specialists in one exceptionality area advance to the head of a broad program serving a variety of exceptional children which involve factors and services beyond the specialist's knowledge and immediate grasp.

A Theory Helps
Decision-Making
Among recent writers, the role of decision-making seems to occupy the key spot in analyses of administrative processes (Gregg, 1957). This essential skill of the executive insures that decisions are made throughout an organization most effectively and that they work to the accomplishment of the stated objectives.

Griffiths (1959) has listed four major propositions concerning decision making which are the bases for an on-going research study of the development of criteria for success in school administration.

1. The structure of an organization is determined by the nature of its decision-making process.
2. If the formal and informal groups in an organization approach congruency, then the total organization will reach maximum achievement.
3. If the administrator confines his behavior to making decisions on the decision-making process, his behavior will be more acceptable to his subordinates.
4. If the administrator perceives himself as the controller of the decision-making process, rather than the maker of the organization's decisions, the decisions will be more effective.

Special education administrators generally are in the first stage of the generalization process with questionnaire studies and descriptive analyses of successful administrative practices. As trends in the executive process can be identified, attempts will be made to group components or functional elements. A theory of special education administration as a set of principles upon which action may be predicted eventually will have to come to grips with the heart of administrative action — the complex and endless decisions of an executive.

A perceptive study of administrative decisions or experience in a top position of a school organization will bear out the usually unnoticed fact that some of the same conditions that promote a school superintendent's leadership in form preclude a guarantee of leadership in fact. Thus, the parents of school children are frequently the same people who act as employers of the school staff or as the group which seeks legislative and organizational improvements for school programs. The understanding and explanation of such seeming paradoxes involve the checks and the balances inherent in the democratic arrangement. Ideally, free people will do their best to lead and to serve at the same time with understanding and maturity. The balancing of the factors of authority, improvement and agreement must be encompassed by a theory of special education administration if it is to assist decision making.

OBSTACLES TO PROGRESS

The terminology and language utilized, the mathematical theorems outlined, and the models or taxonomies drawn up must explain to all members of a profession what they really mean. Jargon, obscura and trivia too often take over in the writings of theorists. Theories that confound and confuse, that do not benefit the practitioners, are better left unborn.

Descriptions and reviews of research and literature which limit the functions of educational administration to transportation, organization, finance, services and plant operation are millstones around the neck of progress in the conceptualization of administration. Special education administrative articles, studies and explanations which ignore the body of recent research findings from the entirety of the social sciences are perpetuating untenable patterns of administration. Views of the administrative field which stress only specific elements, vaguely related activities and "practical" matters, must be replaced by considerations in the context of theories that describe, explain, predict, economize and assist decisions.

To make decisions for and lead in a program with professional integrity is to act consistently within a framework of values shared by the majority of a profession (Hearn, 1958). A profession must be able to define, evaluate, simplify and explain its activities throughout the history of its existence. To fail or to retreat from this demand for improved communication is an act of intellectual delinquency and an admission of eventual disappearance. A theory, however, is always policy and never creed, since dynamic forces and new data and insights may confirm or refute the nature of an explanation (Conant, 1952).

CONCLUSION

The organizational processes of special education, the key skills and competencies that make for effective leadership in programs for atypical children and the values and traditions which mark the history of education of children who are exceptional have been coming of age. The lunge toward expansion that earmarked the late 1940's and the alliances with parent, legislative and research groups that distinguished the 1950's must be consolidated in an active maturity that codifies and earmarks this unique branch of education. Special education must make its administrative patterns professional, in fact and theory, and the knowledge and skills of this endeavor generalized for present growth and future training. The research, analyses and theory building which this article calls for are but one of the major areas of endeavor in the 1960's march of special education.

REFERENCES

Barnard, C. *The function of the executive.* Cambridge, Mass.: Harvard Univer. Press, 1938.

Conant, J. B. *Modern science and modern man.* New York City: Columbia Univer. Press, 1952.

Connor, L. *Administration of special education programs.* New York City: Bureau of Publication, Teachers College, Columbia Univer., 1960.

Gregg, R. In R. Campbell & R. Gregg. *Administrative behavior in education.* New York City: Harper & Brothers, 1957.

Griffiths, D. E. *Administrative theory.* New York City: Appleton-Century-Crofts, 1959.

Hearn, G. *Theory building in social work.* Toronto, Canada: Univer. of Toronto, 1958.

Jordan, T. Development of a taxonomy for special education. *Except. Child.,* 1961, 28, 7-12.

Litchfield, E. Notes on a general theory of administration. *Administr. Sci. Quart.,* 1956, I, No. 1.

Miller, J. Toward a general theory for the behavioral sciences. *Amer. Psychologist,* 1955, 10, No. 9.

Moore, L. *Studies in school administration.* Washington, D. C.: Amer. Assoc. of School Administrators, NEA, 1957.

Neustadt, R. *Presidential power.* New York City: John Wiley & Sons, 1960.

Reynolds, M. A framework for considering some issues in special education. *Except. Child.,* 1962, 28, 367-370.

Thompson, A. *Gateway to the social sciences* (rev. ed.). New York City: Henry Holt & Co., 1959.

organization, administration, and supervision of special education*

PAUL H. VOELKER[†] and
FRANCES A. MULLEN

This chapter is concerned with research directed at the over-all task of providing special education services. As background for the organization of special education, reports on general philosophy and theory of special education, legislation, prevalence studies, and surveys of special education in other countries are reviewed preliminary to discussion of the three areas indicated in the title of the chapter.

At the outset, we must point out the dearth of real research in this area. With the exception of a few specific topics, problems of organization, administration, and supervision have received little attention from researchers. Even factual surveys of present practice that might form the basis for establishing research hypotheses have been scarce.

Bibliographies of the literature on exceptional children give evidence of the paucity of studies on organization, administration, and supervision. The *Elementary School Journal* has continued its series of selected references on special education each year, compiled by Kvaraceus (1960, 1961) and McInnis (1962).

*Reprinted from *Review of Educational Literature*, Vol. 33, No. 1 (February 1963), pp. 5-19, by permission of the author and the American Educational Research Association. Copyright 1963 by the American Educational Research Association.

†Paul H. Voelker is Professor and Chairman, Program in Special Education and Rehabilitation, University of Pittsburgh. Frances A. Mullen is Consultant in Education of the Handicapped and retired Assistant Superintendent of Schools, Chicago.

BACKGROUND

Philosophy and Theory

Jordan (1961) stressed the need for a comprehensive taxonomy of special education. He presented two miniature and overlapping taxonomic structures, arguing that a comprehensive data language would lead to a sophisticated pedagogy, assist in developing a curriculum with construct validity, and provide a basis for special education theory. Levine (1961) postulated a conceptual framework for the social psychology of disability as a basis for derivation of research hypotheses in special education. Wright (1960), in a comprehensive summary of research on the psychology of physical disability, stressed the evidence that the psychological effects of a disability may vary widely for different individuals and in different environments. This theme was further developed in a series of three articles on the social psychology of exceptional children by Hollinshead (1959), Trippe (1959), and Reynolds (1960).

Research Theory

The administrator of special education is becoming increasingly concerned with research, not only as an administrator but also as a consultant and as a consumer of research findings. Goldstein (1959), in a discussion of methodological problems in research in special education, emphasized the need for a comprehensive study of many variables and the difficulty inherent in studying any one of the dynamic factors in isolation.

Hollister and Goldston (1962a, b) undertook to organize data from existing reports into a "beginning taxonomy" of the procedures and considerations involved in conducting classes for emotionally handicapped children.

Wilcox (1961) reported the findings of a special seminar on strategies for behavioral research in mental retardation. He and his colleagues pointed out deficiencies in existing research in the field and called attention to the problems of research design and of formulation of promising research problems.

Legislation

Legislative activity at the federal and state levels increased in tempo during the past several years. Connor (1961b) reviewed the federal legislation of the past five years and stated basic assumptions and unresolved issues facing the Council for Exceptional Children as it formulates policy on legislation for the education of exceptional children. He pointed out the need for increased federal partnership in special education. Green (1961) reported the need for more teachers of exceptional children. She discussed the relative importance and feasibility of omnibus legislation for all types of handicaps as distinguished from piecemeal legislation for each handicap.

Need for and
Extent of Services

Mackie and Robbins (1960), reporting on exceptional children in local public schools, stated that the number of children enrolled in special education programs had more than doubled (from 378,000 to 861,000) in the decade 1948-58. The rate of growth was three times as great as in regular grade enrollments as a consequence of increasing acceptance of education of exceptional children by public school administrators. The authors estimated, however, that only one-fourth of those needing special education were obtaining these services.

That many public school districts plan to expand their services for handicapped pupils in the near future was reported by the National Education Association, Research Division (1961). Data from 875 questionnaires sent to 1,495 urban school districts revealed that (a) a much larger percent of large urban districts than of smaller districts provides separate classes for the handicapped, (b) more separate classes are provided for the mentally retarded than for any other group of handicapped children, and (c) fewest classes are provided for emotionally disturbed children.

Sprague and Dunn (1961) made a survey of special education needs for the Western Interstate Commission for Higher Education. They estimated that .5 million school-age children in the Western states were either handicapped or gifted enough to require special education services but that only approximately one-half of this group was receiving any kind of special service that year. Geer and Wolfe (1960) reported on an investigation of needs for the cerebral palsied in 15 Southern states.

Gardner and Nisonger (1962) stated that data that permit a precise statement of the prevalence of mental retardation are not presently available. They estimated that approximately 3 percent of the school population falls within this classification. Goldstein (1962) estimated that 6-7 percent of the school population in a below-average socioeconomic community would have IQ's below 75 on a *Stanford-Binet Scale* as compared with 3-4 percent in an average-to-superior socioeconomic community.

Connor (1961c) reviewed the various estimates of numbers of individuals with hearing loss and concluded that, because of the diversity of reports, certain improvements in appraisal were required to determine more accurately the prevalence of hearing-impaired children.

Comparative
Special Education

Reports of special education programs around the world have increased in number. United Nations Educational, Scientific, and Cultural Organization (1960), in a statistical survey of 95 countries, reported that 1.58 million children were enrolled in special classes and schools. Those so enrolled represented varied proportions of the school-age population of each country, ranging from less than 1 to more than 20 per 1,000 children. Taylor and Taylor (1960) found, in an extensive study of special education of physically handicapped children in Western Europe, that in almost all countries authority for such programs is centralized in one or more departments of the national government, that problems of overlapping jurisdictions were common, and that voluntary agencies continued to have a large role in the total program.

ORGANIZATION

At the Federal
Level

The U. S. Congress, House of Representatives Committee on Education and Labor, Subcommittee on Special Education (1960), published a comprehensive survey of all federal services to special education and rehabilitation. The U. S. Department of Health, Education, and Welfare, Office of Education (1960), in a handbook describing its operations, showed its organization for special education; the report of the U. S. Department of Health, Education, and Welfare, Office of Education (1961), on its Committee on Mission and Organization recommended a reorganization of the Office's services with respect to exceptional children and higher status within the Office for this work.

Mackie (1962) reviewed the operation of the U. S. Office of Education with respect to special education and indicated that the higher status for special education recommended in the previous reference had been achieved. Data were presented on the operation of the various services of the Office that affect exceptional children.

The U. S. Department of Labor, Labor Standards Bureau (1960), and the President's Panel on Mental Retardation (1962) each issued statements of philosophy and purpose for these special projects of the federal government.

At the State Level

Blessing (1960) discussed the role of the state department charged with responsibility for the education of exceptional children on a statewide basis. He stressed the duality of its functions and pointed out that the administrative duties of regulating and supervising programs sometimes interfered with optimal development of consultative functions. Mackie and Littlefield (1961) published a directory of special education personnel in state departments of education that provided some picture of state organization of services for special education. Connor (1961a), in a brief review of state functions and personnel, suggested that staff at the state level had not increased in proportion to the growth of special education programs to be serviced. Smith (1961) reported surveys of provisions for the gifted at the state level.

Johns and Morphet (1960), in a general text on financing the public schools, devoted a chapter to "Financing Special Services" and reported several plans of state aid. The National Association for Retarded Children (1961) summarized state financing provisions for classes for the trainable; the fourth edition of Hathaway's (1959) standard text on the partially seeing gave a review of state financing for that group.

The American Association on Mental Deficiency completed a five-year project on technical planning in mental retardation with the publication of a manual on program development on state and local levels by Gardner and Nisonger (1962) and a manual on terminology and classification by Heber (1959, 1961).

At the Local Level

The particular problems of organizing special education services, both in large cities and in sparsely settled areas, have received attention. The Los Angeles City School Districts (1960) reported the results of a study of the organization and administration of special education in large cities. Wide divergences of opinion and practice were reported with regard to the role of special education in the school hierarchy, especially with reference to the decentralization of administrative responsibilities into districts within the city. Conant (1961) commended the decentralization of school administration as seen in such cities as Chicago, Detroit, and Philadelphia, but showed awareness of the problem of achieving decentralization of line authority without sacrificing the staff services that the central office can provide. He noted favorably that in St. Louis the central office coordinated a large staff of personnel responsible for the education of many types of exceptional children. Connor (1961a) gave examples of organization of special education in four types of local districts. The differing problems in rural areas were the subject of research by Annas (1960) in Maine and of review by Travelstead (1960) in New Mexico. The Council for Exceptional Children began publication of a series of monographs on administration of special education in small school systems. In the first of these, Streng (1960) provided guidelines for services for children with impaired hearing in small school systems; Erdman (1961) produced a parallel monograph dealing with the educable mentally retarded. Both reports were based on national studies, described a variety of operating programs, and discussed patterns of organization and administration.

The duties of a director in special education were analyzed by the Board of Examiners of the New York City Schools as a basis for establishing an examination for a position. Harold Fields (1961) reported those duties and the examination procedures adopted.

One of the few available large-scale studies of a city program of special education made by an outside agency was reported by Fouracre, Rooke, and Botwin (1961). Finance, physical plant facilities, personnel, transportation, cooperation with community agencies, and public relations were reviewed, and recommendations were made.

Segregated and Integrated Programs of Instruction

Much research has been devoted to the attempt to evaluate special classes, especially for the mentally retarded and the gifted. This material, (1961) found in a survey in Indiana that in many schools speech therapists were given inadequate space and facilities for their work.

Transportation

Featherston (1960) summarized legal provisions in 50 states for transportation to and from school, including provisions for special groups. Bishop (1960) described a bus patrol system utilizing pupil leadership in promoting safe use of buses by crippled children. Wallace (1960) reported that 56 of 98 urban communities surveyed provided transportation for the pupils in programs for the mentally handicapped. Wallace and Starr (1960) found that transportation was provided almost universally for orthopedically handicapped children in special education programs in urban areas and with less uniformity for other types of physically handicapped children.

SUPERVISION

Evaluation of Instruction
In view of the many problems related to instruction of handicapped children, it is remarkable that more well-designed research studies have not been conducted in this important area. Very few reports may be found in the literature for the period covered by this chapter. Zwarensteyn and Zerby (1962) described an experimental program for severely multiple-handicapped blind children in the Michigan School for the Blind. Brill (1960) compared three matched groups of deaf children enrolled in the California School for the Deaf on a five-point rating scale of social adjustment. It was found that the adjustment of deaf children having deaf parents was no better than those with hearing parents.

Groelle (1916) reported on a reading survey of mentally retarded pupils enrolled in special classes in Oakland, California. Data were compared on test findings obtained in October 1956 and October 1959. The author concluded that older pupils read less well than might be expected from their mental age scores.

Interest in evaluation of programs for the trainable mentally retarded continued. Tisdall (1960) in a follow-up study reported little difference between children who had been in trainable mentally handicapped classes and those who had remained at home; Jubenville (1962) described the Ohio program of day care centers under welfare auspices; and Tisdall and Moss (1962) reviewed a number of inconclusive studies on the value of special classes for the trainable and recommended a total program from the cradle to the grave (including the school-age program) to be carried on at the community level by a new agency separate from the school system. Williams and Wallin (1959) suggested that much research remains to be done before complete evaluation of programs for trainable retarded children can be made.

Results from special techniques for teaching emotionally disturbed children were studied by Phillips and Haring (1959). Advantages of a structured-type classroom environment for these children were reported.

Guidance, Placement, and Follow-Up

The importance of providing specialized guidance, placement, and follow-up services for handicapped youth received considerable attention in recent literature. Hunt (1960) observed that the task of providing adequate guidance to exceptional children is too great to be assumed by the teacher alone. He emphasized the need to utilize the specialized guidance services of school and agency personnel. Helen Fields (1961) reported on the responsibilities of the guidance counselor assigned to the Bureau for the Education of Visually Handicapped in the New York City public schools.

Findings of a seven-year pilot study, conducted by the New York Heart Association (1962), of children with heart disease or a history of rheumatic fever revealed that it is not the physical disability alone but the concomitant emotional and social effects that create the handicaps. Early and intensive vocational counseling for these handicapped children is indicated.

Special educators are becoming increasingly concerned with the development of educational programs designed to help handicapped children make a better adjustment in the world of work. Syden (1962) reviewed the literature pertaining to secondary school programs for the mentally retarded for the past 10 years. He found that increasing numbers of school systems had inaugurated programs with special curriculums including both traditional school subjects and vocational training and work experience opportunities. The Detroit Public Schools (1962) issued a pamphlet that related the purposes of a demonstration-research project jointly sponsored with the U. S. Office of Vocational Rehabilitation. This project was designed to study the results of an intensive program of education and vocational rehabilitation services on the employability of mentally retarded boys and girls.

Several follow-up studies were conducted to determine the level of adjustment of handicapped individuals in the community in postschool life. A comprehensive study of social adequacy and social failure of mentally retarded youth was undertaken in Wayne County, Michigan, through Wayne State University (Lee, Hegge, and Voelker, 1959), under grant from the Cooperative Research Branch of the U. S. Office of Education. Four hundred mentally retarded boys and girls previously enrolled in the special classes of the Detroit Public Schools and the Wayne County Training School (200 from each) were selected on a random basis for intensive study. Among other findings, the report showed that many retarded subjects experienced long periods of unemployment, left jobs for poor reasons, or were discharged because of poor behavior. Evidence appeared to support the recommendation for more adequate vocational training, specialized counseling, and job placement and follow-up services.

Dinger (1961) reported on a follow-up study of 100 subjects formerly enrolled in special education in Altoona, Pennsylvania. From the data he drew this conclusion: There is an imperative need for successful occupational training and placement which is primarily the responsibility of the school. Peterson and Smith (1960) compared the findings of a follow-up survey of 45 mentally retarded adults and 45 individuals with normal intelligence formerly enrolled in the schools of Cedar Rapids, Iowa. The characteristics investigated and compared were educational, occupational, home, familial, social, and civic. Lunde and Bigman (1959) reported on a national survey of occupational conditions among the deaf. This survey showed a marked concentration of the deaf in skilled and semiskilled manual occupations with proportionately few in wholesale or retail trade occupations.

Community and
Parent Relationships

The role of parents, parent groups, and community agencies in the education and habilitation of the handicapped continued to receive considerable emphasis. While little research was reported, numerous articles were published on the subject.

Essex (1962) outlined five ways parents and teachers could work effectively together to improve special education programs. Mullen (1960) stressed the need for teamwork between home and school. She stated that this relationship is doubly important when the child is exceptional. Kvaraceus and Ulrich (1959) emphasized the importance of gaining the cooperation of the parent of the delinquent pupil if treatment is to be effective. Wright (1960) summarized research on the role of parents of the handicapped child. Katz (1961) traced the historical development of four representative parent groups of handicapped children. He related their rapid growth in a short period of time and pointed out the impact of these groups in community planning. Hunt (1960) stressed the importance of school personnel working with parent groups. Belinkoff (1960) reported observations on community attitudes toward mental retardation in locating suitable subjects for an experimental class for mentally retarded children. One of the reasons noted in the failure to obtain referrals was the stigma attached to "mental retardation" in the name of the project. When the term was changed to "special education," there was a noticeable increase in the number of parents applying for admission. Fuller (1962) noted the important role of the parents of deaf children in minimizing the handicap of deafness. He discussed the attitudes to be developed by the parents and those to be taught to the deaf children.

NEEDED
RESEARCH

A review of the literature clearly points up the paucity of well-designed research in this area. While some studies provided valid findings, others were inconclusive because of inadequate samples or faulty research techniques. Several lines of investigation should receive priority consideration: (a) determination of the most effective methods of organizing special education programs, (b) evaluation of instruction, (c) more complete inquiry into the incidence and prevalence of the various areas of exceptionality, and (d) well-conceived longitudinal follow-up studies of exceptional youths and adults.

Valid data from such research would assist administrators and supervisors in constructing better programs of special education and in designing more fruitful instructional services.

BIBLIOGRAPHY

Annas, Philip A. *Development of a Program for Mentally Retarded Children in Rural Schools*, 1958-59. U. S. Department of Health, Education, and Welfare, Office of Education, Cooperative Research Project No. 382. Augusta: Maine State Department of Education, 1960. 96 pp.

Barber, Gertrude A. "Teaching the Blind: The Resource Room Approach." *Education* 80:333-36; February 1960.

Belinkoff, Cornelia. "Community Attitudes Toward Mental Retardation." *American Journal of Mental Deficiency* 65: 221-26; September 1960.

Bigman, Stanley Kermit. "The Deaf in American Institutions of Higher Education." *Personnel and Guidance Journal* 39: 743-46; May 1961.

Bishop, Lucy. "Bus Patrol High on Premiums." *Safety Education* 40: 12-13; November 1960.

Blessing, Kenneth R. "A Survey of Public School Administrators' Attitudes Regarding Services for Trainable Retarded Children." *American Journal of*

Mental Deficiency 64: 509-19; November 1959.

Blessing, Kenneth R. "The Function and Role of the Modern State Department in Providing Special Educational Services for Exceptional Youth." *Exceptional Children* 26: 395-400, 408; April 1960.

Bower, Eli M. "The Emotionally Handicapped Child and the School." *Exceptional Children* 26: 6-11; September 1959. 26: 182-88; December 1959.

Brill, Richard G. "A Study in Adjustment of Three Groups of Deaf Children." *Exceptional Children* 26: 464-66, 470; May 1960.

Bruce, Wallace "Social Integration and Effectiveness of Speech" *Volta Review* 62: 368-72; September 1960.

Conant, James Bryant. *Slums and Suburbs.* New York: McGraw-Hill Book Co., 1961. 147 pp.

Connor, Leo E. *Administration of Special Education Programs.* Teachers College Series in Special Education. New York: Bureau of Publications, Teachers College, Columbia University, 1961. 123 pp. (a)

Connor, Leo E. "CEC's Federal Legislative Activity." *Exceptional Children* 28: 135-39; November 1961. (b)

Connor, Leo E. "Determining the Prevalence of Hearing-Impaired Children." *Exceptional Children* 27: 337-43; February 1961. (c)

Detroit Public Schools. *Detroit Special Education — Vocational Rehabilitation Project.* Detroit: Board of Education, 1962. 12 pp. (Mimeo.)

Diedrich, William M.; Allender, Barbara; and Bryne, Margaret C. "The Value of a Preschool Treatment Program for Severely Crippled Children." *Exceptional Children* 27: 187-90, 195; December 1960.

Dinger, Jack C. "Post-School Adjustment of Former Educable Retarded Pupils." *Exceptional Children* 27: 353-60; March 1961.

Dorward, Barbara. *Teaching Aids and Toys for Handicapped Children.* Washington, D. C.: Council for Exceptional Children, a department of the National Education Association, 1960. 64 pp.

Erdman, Robert L. *Educable Retarded Children in Elementary Schools.* Washington, D. C.: Council for Exceptional Children, a department of the National Education Association, 1961. 60 pp.

Essex, Martin. "How Can Parents and Special Educators Best Cooperate for the Education of Exceptional Children?" *Exceptional Children* 28: 478-82; May 1962.

Falconer, George A. "Teaching Machines for the Deaf." *Volta Review* 62: 59-62, 276; February 1960.

Featherston, E. Glenn. *State Provisions for Transporting Pupils.* U. S. Department of Health, Education, and Welfare, Office of Education, Circular No. 453. Revised edition. Washington, D. C.: Government Printing Office, 1960. 15 pp.

Fields, Harold. "Examination for the Post of Director in Special Education." *Clearing House* 35: 533-37; May 1961.

Fields, Helen W. "How New York City Educates Visually Handicapped Children." *New Outlook for the Blind* 55: 337-40; December 1961.

Fouracre, Maurice H.; Rooke, M. Leigh; and Botwin, Perry. *The Report of the Study of the Educational Needs of Physically Handicapped Children in Pittsburgh, Pennsylvania, 1958-1959.* Pittsburgh: School of Education, University of Pittsburgh, 1961. 415 pp.

Fuller, Carl W. "Your Child, Maturity, and You: A Talk with Parents." *American Annals of the Deaf* 107: 320-28; May 1962.

Gallagher, James John. *Analysis of Research on the Education of Gifted Children.* Springfield, Ill.: Office of Superintendent of Public Instruction, 1960. 148 pp.

Gardner, William J., and Nisonger, Herschel W. *A Manual on Program Development in Mental Retardation.* American Journal of Mental Deficiency, Vol. 66, Monograph Supplement. Albany, N. Y.: American Association on Mental Deficiency, January 1962. 192 pp.

Geer, William C., and Wolfe, William G. *Education of the Cerebral Palsied in the South.* Atlanta: Southern Regional Education Board, 1960. 74 pp.

Golden Anniversary White House Conference on Children and Youth. *The States Report on Children and Youth.* Washington, D. C.: the Conference, 1960. 232 pp.

Goldstein, Herbert. "Methodological Problems in Research in the Education Programs for the Treatment of the Mentally Retarded." *American Journal of Mental Deficiency* 64: 341-45; September 1959.

Goldstein, Herbert. *The Educable Mentally Retarded Child in the Elementary School.* What Research Says to the Teacher, No.25. Prepared by the American Educational Research Association in cooperation with the Department of Classroom Teachers. Washington D. C.: National Education Association, May 1962. 33 pp.

Graham, Ray. "Safety Features in School Housing for Handicapped Children." *Exceptional Children* 27: 361-64; March 1961.

Green, Edith. "Quality Education Requires Constructive Legislation." *Exceptional Children* 28: 187-90; December 1961.

Groelle, Marvin C. "Some Results and Implications of Reading Survey Tests Given to Educable Mentally Retarded Children." *Exceptional Children:* 443-48; April 1961.

Hathaway, Winifred. *Education and Health of the Partially Seeing Child.* Fourth edition, (Revised by Franklin M. Foote, Dorothy Bryan, and Helen Gibbons.) New York: Columbia University Press, 1959. 201 pp.

Heber, Rick. *A Manual on Terminology and Classification in Mental Retardation.* American Journal of Mental Deficiency, Vol. 64, Monograph Supplement. Albany, N. Y.: American Association on Mental Deficiency, September 1959. 111 pp.

Heber, Rick. "Modifications in the Manual on Terminology and Classification in Mental Retardation." *American Journal of Mental Deficiency* 65: 499-500; January 1961.

Hollinshead, Merrill T. "The Social Psychology of Exceptional Children: Part I." *Exceptional Children* 26: 137-40; November 1959.

Hollister, William G., and Goldston, Stephen E. *Considerations for Planning Classes for the Emotionally Handicapped.* Washington, D. C.: Council for Exceptional Children, a department of the National Education Association, 1962. 30 pp. (a)

Hollister William G., and Goldston, Stephen E. "Psychoeducational Processes in Classes for Emotionally Handicapped Children." *Exceptional Children* 28: 351-56; March 1962. (b)

Hunt, J. T. "Guidance and Exceptional Children." *Education* 80: 344-48; February 1960.

Johns, Roe Lyell, and Morphet, Edgar L. *Financing the Public Schools.* Englewood Cliffs, N. J.: Prentice-Hall, 1960. 566 pp.

Jordan, Thomas E. "Conceptual Issues in the Development of a Taxonomy for

Special Education." *Exceptional Children* 28: 7-12; September 1961.

Jubenville, Charles P. "A State Program of Day Care Centers for Severely Retarded." *American Journal of Mental Deficiency* 66: 829-37; May 1962.

Katz, Alfred H. *Parents of the Handicapped.* Springfield, Ill.: Charles C. Thomas, 1961. 155 pp.

King, Robert W., and Dunlap, Jerry. "Oklahoma's Optical Aids Clinic." *Exceptional Children* 28: 111-12; October 1961.

Kvaraceus, William C., compiler. "Selected References from the Literature on Exceptional Children." *Elementary School Journal* 60: 343-48; March 1960.

Kvaraceus, William C., compiler. "Selected References from the Literature on Exceptional Children" *Elementary School Journal* 61:338-44; March 1961.

Kvaraceus, William C., and Ulrich, William E. *Delinquent Behavior: Principles and Practices.* Washington, D. C.: National Education Association, 1959. 350 pp.

Lee, John J.; Hegge, Thorleif G.; and Voelker, Paul H., research directors. *Social Adequacy and Social Failure of Mentally Retarded Youth in Wayne County, Michigan.* Detroit: Wayne State University, 1959. 530 pp.

Levine, Samuel. "A Proposed Conceptual Framework for Special Education." *Exceptional Children* 28: 83-90; October 1961.

Los Angeles City School Districts. *Major Report: Special Education Study.* Los Angeles: Office of the Superintendent, the Districts, 1960. 145 pp.

Lunde, Anders S., and Bigman, Stanley K. *Occupational Conditions Among the Deaf.* Washington, D. C.: Gallaudet College, September 1959. 66 pp.

McInnis, Irene M., compiler. "Selected References from the Literature on Exceptional Children." *Elementary School Journal* 62: 334-39; March 1962.

Mackie, Romaine P. "Education of Exceptional Children: Program, Progress, Problems." *School Life* 44: 10-12; July 1962.

Mackie, Romaine P., and Littlefield, Lynell. *Directory of Special Education Personnel in State Departments of Education.* U. S. Department of Health, Education, and Welfare, Office of Education, Publication OE 35003-61. Washington, D. C.: Government Printing Office, 1961. 11 pp.

Mackie, Romaine P., and Robbins, Patricia. "Exceptional Children in Local Public Schools." *School Life* 43: 14-16; November 1960.

Morin, Arline. "Waukegan Finds Advantages in the Itinerant Teacher Plan." *Sight-Saving Review* 30: 33-35; Spring 1960.

Mullen, Frances A. "The Teacher Works with the Parent of the Exceptional Child." *Education* 80: 329-32; February 1960.

National Association for Retarded Children. *Summary of Status of State Level Support of Programs of Special Education in the Public Schools for Children Classed as "Trainable" Mentally Retarded or Equivalent.* New York: the Association (386 Park Avenue, South), 1961. 1 p.

National Education Association, Research Division. "Special Classes for Handicapped Children." *NEA Research Bulletin* 39: 43-46; May 1961.

National Education Association, Research Division, *Special Education Teachers — Salary Schedule Provision, 1961-62.* NEA Research Memo No. 20. Washington, D. C.: the Association, 1962. 20 pp.

Newman, Ruth G.; Redl, Fritz; and Kitchener, Howard L. *Technical Assistance in a Public School System.* Washington, D. C.: School Research Program,

Washington School of Psychiatry (5410 Connecticut Ave., N. W.), 1962. 75 pp.

New York Heart Association. *Vocational Counseling for Children with Heart Disease or a History of Rheumatic Fever: A Pilot Study.* New York: the Association, 1962. 236 pp.

New York State Education Department, Bureau for Handicapped Children. *Challenge of Educating the Blind Child in the Regular Classroom.* Albany: University of the State of New York, 1959. 16 pp.

Nugent, Timothy J. "Design of Buildings To Permit Their Use by the Physically Handicapped." *New Building Research.* Building Research Institute, National Academy of Sciences, National Research Council, Publication No. 910. Washington, D. C.: the Council, 1960. pp. 51-66.

Peterson, Leroy, and Smith, Lloyd L. "A Comparison of Post-School Adjustment of Educable Mentally Retarded Adults with That of Adults of Normal Intelligence." *Exceptional Children* 26: 404-408; April 1960.

Phillips, E. Lakin, and Haring, Norris G. "Results from Special Techniques for Teaching Emotionally Disturbed Children." *Exceptional Children* 26: 64-67; October 1959.

President's Panel on Mental Retardation. *A National Plan To Combat Mental Retardation.* Washington, D. C.: Government Printing Office, 1962. 12 pp.

Reynolds, Maynard C. "The Social Psychology of Exceptional Children: Part III." *Exceptional Children* 26: 243-47; January 1960.

Smith, Carol Cordes. "The '600' Schools." *Education* 80: 215-18; December 1959.

Smith, Eugene H. "State Level Educational Services to Gifted Pupils." *Exceptional Children* 27: 511-13; May 1961.

Sprague, Hall, and Dunn, Lloyd. "Special Education for the West." *Exceptional Children* 27: 415-21; April 1961.

Stolurow, Lawrence M. "Automation in Special Education." *Exceptional Children* 27: 78-83; October 1960.

Streng, Alice. *Children with Impaired Hearing: Administration of Special Education in Small School Systems.* Washington, D. C.: Council for Exceptional Children, a department of the National Education Association, 1960. 72 pp.

Syden, Martin. "Preparation for Work: An Aspect of the Secondary School's Curriculum for Mentally Retarded Youth." *Exceptional Children* 28: 325-32; February 1962.

Taylor, Wallace W., and Taylor, Isabelle Wagner. *Special Education of Physically Handicapped Children in Western Europe.* New York: International Society for the Welfare of Cripples, 1960. 497 pp.

Tisdall, William J. "A Follow-Up Study of Trainable Mentally Handicapped Children in Illinois." *American Journal of Mental Deficiency* 65: 11-16; July 1960.

Tisdall, William J., and Moss, James W. "A Total Program for the Severely Mentally Retarded." *Exceptional Children* 28: 357-62; March 1962.

Travelstead, Chester R. "Problems in the Education of Handicapped Children in Sparsely Settled Areas." *Exceptional Children* 27: 52-55; September 1960.

Trippe, Matthew J. "Social Psychology of Exceptional Children: Part II." *Exceptional Children* 26: 171-75, 188; December 1959.

United Nations Educational, Scientific, and Cultural Organization. *Statistics on Special Education.* New York: the Organization, 1960. 154 pp.

U. S. Congress, House of Representatives Committee on Education and Labor, Subcommittee on Special Education. *Federal Services to Special Education and Rehabilitation: Part I.* Washington, D. C.: Government Printing Office, 1960. 532 pp.

U. S. Department of Health, Education, and Welfare, Office of Education. *Handbook.* Washington, D. C.: Government Printing Office, 1960. 49 pp.

U. S. Department of Health, Education, and Welfare, Office of Education. *A Federal Education Agency for the Future: Report of the Committee on Mission and Organization of the U. S. Office of Education.* Washington, D. C.: Government Printing Office, 1961. 56 pp.

U. S. Department of Labor, Labor Standards Bureau. *This Is the President's Committee on Employment of the Physically Handicapped.* Washington, D. C.: Government Printing Office, 1960. 10 pp.

Wallace, Helen M. "School Services for Mentally Retarded Children in Urban Areas." *American Journal of Mental Deficiency* 64: 679-88; January 1960.

Wallace, Helen M., and Starr, Helen M. "School Services for Handicapped Children in Urban Areas." *American Journal of Public Health* 50: 173-80; February 1960.

Wexler, A. *Experimental Science for the Blind: An Instruction Manual.* New York: Pergamon Press, 1961. 97 pp.

Wilcox, R. W., editor. *Strategies for Behavioral Research in Mental Retardation: A Seminar Report.* Madison: School of Education, University of Wisconsin, 1961. 162 pp.

Willey, Norman R. "An Examination of Public School Speech and Hearing Therapy Facilities." *Exceptional Children* 28: 129-34; November 1961.

Williams, Harold M., and Wallin, J. E. Wallace. *Education of the Severely Retarded Child.* U. S. Department of Health, Education, and Welfare, Office of Education, Bulletin 1959, No. 12. Washington, D. C.: Government Printing Office, 1959. 26 pp.

Wright, Beatrice A. *Physical Disability — A Psychological Approach.* New York: Harper & Brothers, 1960. 408 pp.

Zwarensteyn, Sarah B., and Zerby, Margaret. "A Residential School Program for Multi-Handicapped Blind Children." *New Outlook for the Blind* 56: 191-99; June 1962.

the organization of special education services*

JOHN W. KIDD†

An educator who is committed to the welfare of exceptional children may habitually leave unstated certain philosophical principles in dialogue with colleagues, assuming that such principles have universal acceptance. However, the sometimes harsh realities of the "firing line" serve as a reminder that this assumption is not necessarily a safe one. The appearance in print of such principles as related to a program may symbolize lip service rather than commitment, window dressing rather than substance, or the dedication of a few professionals rather than the profession.

Such principles of special education, therefore, are explicitly stated as a preamble to the paper which follows:

1. All children and youth in this society are entitled to free education to the limit of, commensurate with, and appropriate to their capacities; further, the society, as well as the individual educated, benefits from the presence of an educated citizenry in direct proportion to the completeness of that education, individually and collectively.
2. As a corollary to the first principle, equality of educational opportunity for all the nation's children and youth should prevail such that none is penalized by his place or other circumstances of birth or rearing.

*Reprinted by permission of the author and the Director of Special Education, State of Ohio, 1968.

†John W. Kidd is Assistant Superintendent, Special School District of St. Louis County, St. Louis, Missouri.

3. Clearly implied by both principles 1 and 2 is the proposition that a child who differs from the average to the extent that his educational potential can best be nurtured only by alterations in and/or additions to the curriculum for the average child shall receive such special education services; equality of educational opportunity cannot be symbolized by equal money spent per child but only by the provision of optimal means of enhancing the learning capabilities of each child irrespective of inequalities in cost.

INTRODUCTION — THOSE TO BE SERVED

Special education services are viewed as those services, including instruction, which should be provided by the school to exceptional children and youth — they being those whose disabilities and/or superabilities are such as to warrant elements and types of school services for the development of their educational potentials which are not needed by the average child.

Thus, children and youth to be served by special education are, at this point in educational theory and practice, one-half or less of the school-age population. Definitions, points of view, and estimates range from 10% to as high as 40 or 50% — from the traditional categories of gifted and handicapped — mentally, physically, socially, or emotionally to emerging inclusion of the culturally disadvantaged, the educationally disadvantaged, the experientially deprived, and those with learning disabilities including those with specific maturational lags in academic skill development. Some view these emerging groups, who are of increasing concern, as a threat by special education to engulf all children who fail to lodge in the niche of the statistical average.

It has been said that special education would never have emerged in this society had traditional education sufficiently practiced what it has long preached — the individualization of instruction based upon exhaustive and continuing differential diagnosis of every child. Now some see the return to the nomenclature of a past era, an era when "special education" did not exist, as feasible only through special education itself. As *all* education becomes "special," no longer will *any* education need to be *called* special. Thus the cycle may complete itself but, as many fear, it may not only see the disappearance of the nomenclature, of the categories of children singled out for special education services, but the disappearance of the special services, too. Hence, those of us who are so concerned about the special child are reluctant to surrender his special designation since it seems that without special labels and until they emerged there were few efforts to meet their special needs.

Thus, while emergent knowledge must continue to lead to altered practice, a frame of reference for special educational services, which can survive both new knowledge and altered practice must be based upon a fundamental educational rationale as well as linguistic integrity. Such frame of reference, therefore, must be identified with the educative process and its goals and must relate directly rather than tangentially to learning. To be "brain-injured," for example, is related, as such, only tangentially to learning as is "crippled" and as is "partially sighted." Yet all of these are used today in American education as the bases for *special* education services. A brain-injured child may show no outward manifestations of a minor or non-critical injury and, indeed, may operate as a genius — or he may be epileptic, or cerebral palsied, or mentally retarded, or hyperactive or even a helpless, crib-bound blob. Thus, one may find a special education program including categories of services for the hyperkinetic (brain-injured in some cases), the educable mentally retarded or as exclusively in Ohio "slow-learner" which everywhere else means "between mentally retarded and average," or as in a few states "mentally handicapped" which in those states means "mentally retarded" but everywhere else means "mentally ill or mentally retarded" (a few of whom are brain-injured), and yet none of these is directly an educational consideration. They have to do with etiology, functional deficits, cell impairment, and disease which have varying degrees of implications for educability.

It is, therefore, suggested that education insist upon the establishment of an educational need couched in educational language as the only acceptable basis for program alteration — for special education service.

Such an approach was initiated by Stevens[1] when he taxonomized the educationally significant attributes of children with body disorders.

Kidd's recent proposal[2] strikes at all categories of special education needs and leaves room for limitless alteration in light of emergent knowledge by maintaining that all special education must find its rationale in learning disability or superability.

---

[1] Stevens, Godfrey Daniel, *Taxonomy In Special Education For Children With Body Disorders*, doctoral dissertation, Teachers College, Columbia University, 1962.

[2] Kidd, John W., "President's Message, Time for Change," *Education and Training of the Mentally Retarded*, 1967, 1, 4-5.

Schematically, then, it may be maintained that a special education service may be provided only upon the establishment of the existence of a learning superability or disability 1) of such significance as logically to warrant special help and 2) of such nature as to warrant the application of one or more known special methods or techniques of education. This means, of course, that criterion #1, i.e., the significant learning variant, may exist without criterion #2, i.e., a known and logically warranted technique or method, being available at the point of need (in time and space). This schema may be presented as

General Learning Superability	Specific Learning Superabilities
1	2
3	4
General Learning Disability	Specific Learning Disabilities
Learning Variants	

or it may be viewed as

LEARNING VARIANTS

I.   Learning superability

    A.   General (genius)
    B.   Specific (talent)
        1.   Mental strength
            a.   speed
            b.   agility
            etc.
        2.   Physical strength
            a.   speed
            b.   agility
            c.   size

(1) large
(2) small
     (this can be advantageous as in the
     riveter inside a small space)
     etc.

II. Learning disability (may be totally, partially or not remediable)

    A. General (mental subnormality)
    B. Specific
       1. Language
          a. Auditory
             (1) Cognitive (agnosia)
             (2) Partially hearing
             (3) Deaf
          b. Vision
             (1) Cognitive
                (a) Word blindness (dyslexia or
                     hypolexia)
                (b) Word caller (hyperlexia)
                (c) Reversals (strephosymbolia)
             (2) Partially seeing
             (3) Blind
          c. Speech
             (1) Fluency
                (a) Stuttering
                (b) Apraxia
             (2) Articulatory
             (3) Quality (pitch, tone, etc.)
             (4) Content (linguistic sterility)
          d. Associative (aphasia or aphasoid)
       2. Motor and/or orthopedic
          a. Coordinative
          b. Crippled
          c. Health
       3. Behavioral
          a. Inhibitory (hyperdistractibility, Strauss syn-
             drome)
          b. Emotional (sick psyche, road to psychosis)
             (1) Mild
             (2) Moderate
             (3) Severe

c.   Social
   (1)   Nonconformity
   (2)   Sociopathic (asocial or antisocial)

    II above, "Learning Disability" may be viewed taxonomically as follows illustrating the three educationally significant dimensions of specificity, severity, and remediability. [One university (in Ohio) has restructured its program of preparation of teachers of the exceptional along these lines and based upon this rationale.]

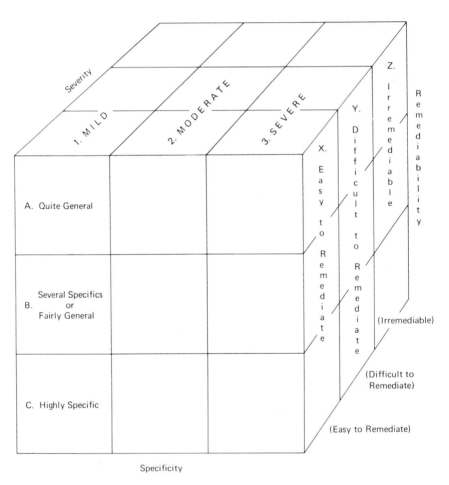

FIGURE 1.

LEARNING DISABILITIES

To recapitulate:

       1. special education services are justifiable only for a significant learning variance of such a nature as logically to warrant the application of a known special method(s) and/or technique(s);

thus 2. conditions warranting special education services must be identifiable as learning disabilities or superabilities;

thus 3. special education service(s) may be provided only when it is logically warranted, i.e., there is convincing evidence of its efficacy.

In general, it is contended here, that organization and administration are means to an end—in education the end is the optimal enhancement of the child's potential for learning – in special education, the principle holds for the child with special needs. Thus, no plan for organization and administration logically precedes the determination of the goals and philosophy. Yet traditional public schooling has proceeded in the opposite manner. Organization and administration have been first by and large, then as new goals emerge, and philosophies develop, the old managerial system is expected to adapt to meeting the emergent needs. In an undertaking of state-wide magnitude, concerned with new goals and concepts if not philosophy, it would be well if the only administrative and organizational assumption made were that the state as a political unit will persevere. However, even at this level, the assumption should not preclude organizational and/or administrative units and patterns of multi-state units of approach if they hold greatest promise for efficiency and economy in achievement of the goals envisioned.

SPECIAL EDUCATION SERVICE
AS A FUNCTION OF NUMBERS

As a society becomes increasingly organized, it allocates the implementation of its wishes to government by and large. Other non-governmental institutionalized entities and processes volunteer to engineer the implementation of selected and often partial wish-fulfillment of the populace. Consideration here of the means of implementing this society's wish for its youth to be educated, and particularly in view of the special needs of many of them, will relate itself to the governmental, i.e., public sector of such wish-fulfillment. It is not to be construed as ruling out the possibility that private, i.e., voluntary efforts may be efficacious.

It has long been held in those states having multiple so-called local school districts that consolidation of such small population units into sizeable demographic (rather than geographic) units is essential to quality programs of education. A simple extrapolation of smallness into unity serves to illustrate the economic nature of this long-held position. Were the school age population to be a single child all would agree that the cost of a teacher, a school, public free transportation including a salaried driver, the materials and equipment of instruction including pre-placement diagnosis by medicine, psychology, education, audiology, speech pathology, etc., would be exhorbitant. Too, all will agree that for the same or slightly more total cost, 10, 20 or 30 children may be provided with that school and teacher and bus and so forth. So it is that cost per child of quality education is reduced as the number of children in one time and place increases, though there may be varying points of diminishing utility as numbers grow larger, as in the number of children per teacher.

Another aspect of numbers has to do with the simplification of the enterprise of educating — simplification as a means of achieving efficiency. A single teacher with a room of ideal size, let 10 serve only as an example, should be the more efficient as the 10 children are reduced in chronological age range from 12 years to 12 months; in mental age range in a similar manner; and in types of learning variance from many to one.

While it may fail in a slight way to meet the rigid criteria of science, from the point of view of radical empiricism, of hard-nosed but compassionate pragmatism, it may be held that certain elements are essential to the most effective implementation of special education services. These in turn may relate to numbers to be served. As an example, a pre-placement and post-placement diagnostic staff is essential. This means the employment, as a minimum, of a psychological examiner, an educational examiner, and a speech-hearing examiner. Additional elements can be justified. Now one does not readily find economic justification for such expenditures of public funds if only a handful of children is to be served. To take another step, it is acknowledged by all that a child with inhibitory disability is most likely to profit from a special education enterprise involving as a minimum a full-time teacher. Yet it is difficult economically to justify the expenditure if the class consists of a single child.

Then there is a *place* for the diagnostic staff to work — not a medical place, not a social agency place, not a psychological place, but an educational place. There is also the *place* for special education services to be rendered. One does not justify to the ever skeptical taxpayer the purchase of land and construction of buildings for special education without a positive knowledge of significant numbers of special children to be served.

So, there are the children to be served and the service. As a minimum the service includes teachers, evaluators and enterprise manipulators — administrators. All need special knowledge and special skills. All need to be engaged essentially full-time in the enterprise in order that this constitute their major commitment, their over-weening concern.

Assuming the principles heretofore enunciated and starting with homogeneity of grouping, it becomes an axiomatic deduction that *the more frequent the occurrence of a learning variant warranting special education, the smaller the general population base necessary to yield the necessary number of subjects for an economically efficient program of high quality.*

The converse, too, is axiomatic: *the more infrequent the occurrence of a learning variant warranting special education, the larger the general population base necessary to yield the necessary number of subjects for an economically efficient program of high quality.*

It then follows that organization may vary in respect to the necessary number in two ways. A special education program for a high incidence exceptionality may be maintained in and for a relatively small general population base, while a special program for a low incidence exceptionality must relate to a relatively larger general population base. These programs may be separately organized and administered as in a small city for the "general learning disability" children since this is a high incidence variant, or in a multi-city region for "hyperlexia", a possible specific neurological precocity and a low incidence exceptionality. *Or* both programs *may* be organized and administered at the regional level.

Thus, other considerations, legal, fiscal and related to administrative integrity must be examined, in addition to the matter of needed general or particular population base, before wise decisions are possible. However, it is reasonably clear at this point that special services for school age children needing full-time special class for high "general learning disability" (now slow-learners in Ohio, and educable mentally retarded or handicapped elsewhere in the nation) may be both economically efficient and of high quality on a general population base of 50,000 since some 12,500 will be of school age, and some 250 to 625 (2% to 5%) will be of this classification, and since both reasonable homogeneity of grouping (if proximity manipulation is unfettered) and economically justifiable evaluating, teaching and enterprise manipulating (administrating) staff may be engaged as well as appropriate space for all be provided at something like less than triple the cost of quality education of the average child. As an example, for 250 children, 20 teachers at $10,000 equals *$200,000*; evaluation staff of 3 full-time plus part-time help from medicine and/or other specialists at $15,000 equals up to *$75,000*; two administrative-supervisory persons at $17,500 equals *$35,000*; space and all overhead for the enterprise may be *$150,000* per year; the annual cost of materials and supplies should be not more than *$15,000* and, thus, the total of $475,000 is only $1,900 per child. (Here we have assumed an average class size of 12½ children, and used typical 1968 monetary standards; salaries included typical perquisites such as employer paid retirement, etc.).

However, it may be quite a different matter to provide the special education services needed for a low incidence exceptionality — for autistic children or PKU children who may occur only once in 10,000. Assuming that special services are needed for autistic children, that they should be provided by the school, that they are significantly different from services needed by other exceptional children — diagnostically, educationally and financially — a general population of this same size of 50,000, 15,000 of whom are of school age, typically will yield one or two autistic children. If the minimum number which can be served efficiently and effectively is 6 or 8 or 10 — or 50 or 100, then a general population base of 300,000 to 5,000,000 will be needed — from a major city to a multi-state region except in more populous states. If one accepts 20 such children as the minimum necessary for service from an organizational unit rendering special education services, and it may well be the magic number as relates to costs, distances, ages, degrees of severity and responsiveness — then a population base of approximately 1,000,000 is necessary with which to work — a city or county or intra-state region, or a state or a multi-state region.

At this point, it becomes clear that if one's concern is this American society — no single present educational or political unit should plan special education services, and organization and administration, therefore, in isolation. In view of problems presented by the presence and absence of transportation facilities, of geographic and time barriers, it may be held that *the more sparsely populated the area the more important that it not plan alone in respect to the development, management and rendering of special education services.*

It is suggested here that a general population base of at least ½ million, 150,000 typically of school age, is necessary to efficient and effective special education service organization and administration *if* such services are to be rendered by a single unit of administration.

INTEGRITY OF THE MINIMUM
UNIT OF ADMINISTRATION

The prospects for development of ideal special educational services vary with density of population, the probable limitations of finance, professional and lay attitudes toward the special needs of special children, and the long-term commitment of a population to meeting these needs. Assuming the ideal in respect to professional and lay concern, and assuming that all-but-instant transportation is just around the corner or that sparsely populated areas are not the immediate concern, and assuming that a state has a population of several million and wishes to plan for meeting the special education needs of its children and youth, those concerned may well look at current practice relative to finance.

What is the state's commitment to education? For example, the three states with which the writer is most familiar are spending $618, $591 and $532 per year per pupil in average daily attendance this year. (These and other such figures are from the National Education Association.) These three states are a southern, a northern and a midwestern one — Louisiana $618, Ohio $591, Missouri $532. They rank among the states 21st (La.), 25th (Ohio), and 35th (Mo.). This, however, is only part of the picture. In percent of income spent for education in 1966-67 Louisiana ranked 7th, Ohio 45th, and Missouri 46th. In their efforts to equalize the tax load and educational opportunity these three states varied greatly in their reliance on local tax resources. Louisiana public schools were supported by 60% of school revenue from the state, Missouri by 34% and Ohio by 32%. Dollars per pupil from state funds were in Louisiana $394, ranked 5th among the states, while in Ohio and Missouri state funds provided per pupil were $187 — exactly the same in the two states — in a tie for 36th, 37th, and 38th rank with Rhode Island. The national average in dollars per pupil from state revenue estimated for this year is $262 — 40% of school funds in the average state coming from the state revenues.

Thus a state planning significant educational program expansion may well need a revolution in financing education to make feasible such expansion if the revenue source or the administrative unit is to be intra-state.

Organization and administration is either facilitated or impeded by law, both statutory, including constitutional, and regulatory. Ideally the special educator might hope for a legal base delegating to the educational profession the responsibility for determining and providing needed special education services. The statutory element might take the form: Each school district or special school district shall maintain such special services, including special classes, as are determined to be needed by the State Department (or Board) of Education for educationally exceptional children. The cost of such special education services and programs shall be borne by the state insofar as their costs exceed those of programs for other children and youth.

It is conceivable that statutory authority may be needed to read: A school district of less than 500,000 total general population shall not render educational services to educationally exceptional children and youth who need full-time special education services. All such school districts in this state shall be parts of larger special school districts as designated by the State Board of Education; each such special school district to have not less than 500,000 general population, nor more than 3,000,000 general population; each such school district to have an elected Board of Education, the rights including tax rights, of other school districts except that it shall not levy local taxes in excess of 25% of that of the regular school district in the state levying the highest local tax.

Regulatory law, rules and regulations promulgated by the state's education authority, amenable to change — professionally desirable change in view of emergent knowledge, should designate types of special services to types of educationally exceptional children and youth.

As to the debate on merits and demerits of separate administrative units for special education, it should focus on the efficacy for service and not upon tradition or vested interest. There are several models of intermediate and overlapping school districts upon which one may draw.

In many of the states the county is the only school district. In others one may find hundreds of local school districts, including some which operate no schools. In the latter the county plays varying roles in education from none in Missouri to the gap-filling role of the county unit in local district states such as Ohio and Pennsylvania.

There is the model of joint agreement districts in Illinois, the model of 20 regional vocational education districts in Iowa and even the metropolitan authority in all aspects of a learning disability, there called mental retardation, in Los Angeles.

The model for a special school district overlapping but independent of several (25) local school districts is the Special School District of St. Louis County, Missouri.

Originally a district to train and educate the handicapped from all 25 local school districts in the county, it recently was given a second mission by the legislature and the voted approval of the county citizenry — that of providing vocational-technical senior high schools for the entire County. Here the general population base is approaching 1,000,000 and a tax base of 25 cents per $100 assessed evaluation is proving to be barely adequate, perhaps in the next year or two depending upon state support, not adequate for quality programming.

If one seriously contemplates moving in this direction it behooves him to re-examine many of his most cherished beliefs about education. As an example, such a special district may find that local districts within its boundaries are not able or willing to provide space for special classes in their schools. The special district may face the necessity of providing its own schools for children who traditionally have been placed in special classes in regular schools. One of the more common and cherished beliefs among parents and educators is that the educable mentally retarded should be in regular school buildings even if in special classes.

A re-examination of this traditional assumption, i.e., that educable mentally retarded children and youth are far better off if placed in a school with normal youngsters, may take this form:

> *Why and how did this notion get started? It is likely that the National Association for Retarded Children, when it organized in 1950, found many of the public school classes for the educable mentally retarded housed in attics and basements, in rooms abandoned by other programs, in annexes and churches, and in rented and donated rooms around the community. It is understandable that these parents insisted that their children have rooms just like other school children. These rooms existed only in "regular schools". Instead of demanding "Place them in nice rooms, or in regular schools", their campaign to get the retardates out of the attics and basements took the form "Integrate them with normal children". Much was made of the possible values of this arrangement, particularly the so-called socialization which would occur.*
>
> *What actually happens when a class of educable retardates is placed in a regular school? Too often (and once is too often), the building administrator learns of the*

arrangement from his superintendent. He may not have been consulted — just told. The building principal, in turn, tells certain members of his faculty and staff that they have to work with the retardates — his physical education teacher, his lunchroom and playground supervisors, and his home economics and shop teachers. They may resent it, or be afraid and uncertain. It is the exception, rather than the rule, for the building administrator and his faculty to ask for the special class and to take a role of leadership in seeing that it is accepted by the school and community. It can be a beneficial experience but it doesn't just happen because the retarded class is placed in a regular building.

What about having the educable retarded in a separate building? If given a modern building, a good and attractive faculty, special teachers of physical education, shop and home economics, what is it that can be done in an integrated class which cannot be done in a segregated one? About the only answer that can be given has to do again with the theoretical advantages of the physical proximity of normal children — the so-called advantages of socialization. Now, if a school system has enough educable retardates (say, two or three hundred) to justify a special building, then it can have special teachers of shop and physical education and home economics working full time with the retarded. Further, it can group the children much more homogeneously than it is likely to be able to do by integrating them. Surely, in such a special school, everything can be done as well or better than by integrating classes except for that one intangible — the possible benefit of the presence of average children.

Two thoughts occur on this theoretical advantage of the so-called socialization with the normal. In the first place, the retarded special class in the regular school is often subject to rejection and derogation both individually and collectively. Secondly, children are in school less than 1,000 hours per year; they sleep about 3,000. This leaves nearly 5,000 hours of before and after school hours, weekends, and vacations during which awareness of and association with the normal world is all but inevitable. It suggests that the advantages of the integrated class are, at least partially, a myth. The advantages are not automatic. The critical factor is not whether the class is in a regular school building — "integrated" — or in a special building.

*The critical factor is the totality of learning experiences
provided for the children — the curriculum, teachers,
supervisors, and administrators of the program.*[3]

Thus, other traditional assumptions and practices may need the
most objective analysis prior to program planning. Among those
which may need such attention are beliefs, assumptions and/or
practices relative to the most able pupils — should they be a
managerial responsibility of special educators? — do they need
differentiated programs? — if so, what programs and for which pupils
among the most able? — and should any really bright child ever be
labeled as in any grade?

And what about the so-called emotionally disturbed? — should
the schools get into residential treatment? — should the schools be
able to separate the child totally from his home, perform what is
sometimes called "parentectomy", cutting the parents out of the
child's life long enough to assess the significance of his habitual
environment in the emotionally sick child's etiology of distress?

And what about social maladjustment? Are we falling into a
trap as we have been accused by an esteemed Negro colleague, to be
unnamed here, of having programs for the emotionally disturbed that
just happen to be all white and one for socially maladjusted that just
happens to be all black?

And the experientially deprived? — and the value-system
deviant? — and the linguistically sterile? — and the pre-delinquent
and delinquent? — and the nearly homeless, living with one part-time
and ineffective if not retarded parent? Are their needs different, the
one from the other as well as from all the others? If we agree that
children from urban black depressed ghettos respond only to a
different educational approach, and that it can be applied only if
they are separated from the common herd for this application,
sometimes called compensatory education, how can we deal with the
accusation which must follow that we are not *separating* for
educational advantage but segregating on the basis of race?

And what about speech therapy? Are we still providing it to
children whose parents complain about their children's imperfect
speech just because they complain and without respect to the child's
capacity to benefit therefrom? — are we aware the vast majority of
children to whom speech therapy is provided from age five or six or

[3] Kidd, John W., "Some Unwarranted Assumptions in the Education and
Habilitation of Handicapped Children," *Education and Training of the Mentally
Retarded*, 1966, 2, 55–56.

seven might, by age 10 or 12, develop speech as well without the therapy as with it?

And what about the child's health? Are we to continue to permit a parent to legally murder his child by refusing to permit physical examination or treatment on religious or some other grounds as is now common among the states?

What have such questions to do with organization and administration of special education? Simply this — until they are answered the rationale for and objectives of special education cannot be stated and no plan of attack can be organized and administered without an awareness of purpose. To do otherwise would be tantamount to saying, "Let's organize special education services so we can administer them when and if we can decide *what* they are and *to whom* they should be provided. "Cart" before "horse"? — more like "end" before "beginning."

SUMMARY

To summarize, it has been contended that:

1. Delineation of philosophy and purpose of a program should precede its organization.
2. Special help for children with special needs emerged in American education only as such children received special designations (categories) (and incidentally emerged by and large through the efforts of parent groups rather than educators, and at state level rather than local); and such special help may dwindle away if and when special designations for special children disappear from the laws and the educational lexicon.
3. A rationale for special education, and subsequent types of services and programs, as well as categories of needs to be met, should derive from *educational* considerations and should be linguistically precise; toward this end it is urged that learning disabilities and superabilities, varying in specificity, in severity and in remediability, provide such frame of reference.
4. Assuming that there are two major criteria of any program — efficiency and effectiveness — and recognizing significant numbers of children to be served as necessary to such special education services; and since exceptionalities meriting special education vary in incidence such that a high incidence exceptionality may occur with sufficient fre-

quency as to make effective and efficient programming for them feasible in a demographic unit of 50,000; while a low incidence exceptionality will call for a demographic unit of ½ million for effective and efficient programming; and since all special education services are more likely to be of high quality in an area if managed by full-time special educators completely responsible for such services in the area; a demographic unit of ½ to 3 million general population is recommended for the Administration of *all* special education services within its area.

special education — facts and attitudes*

FRANK M. HODGSON[†]

For the purpose of acquiring data regarding the (a) definition, (b) function, (c) organization, and (d) administration of a special education program, a study national in scope was conducted in 1960. The investigation was made possible by the Los Angeles Board of Education which allocated the necessary funds to appoint a research coordinator for the project. The post-war growth in pupil population and subsequent rapid expansion of special education services in the Los Angeles Unified City School District had made evident the need to analyze the Los Angeles special education program and to acquire information regarding practices and attitudes from other sections of the nation.

In order to accomplish the selected objectives, one technique used for acquiring information was a questionnaire. The questionnaire study included the following three basic sources for developing data on which to formulate recommendations:

Special Education Specialists

A review of the literature found that there were at the time of the study 26 universities with departments of special education headed by a director or coordinator. The director

*Reprinted from *Exceptional Children*, Vol. 30 (January 1964), pp. 196-201, by permission of the author and the Council for Exceptional Children. Copyright 1964 by the Council for Exceptional Children.

†Frank M. Hodgson is Principal, Fairburn Avenue Elementary School, Los Angeles City School System, California.

or coordinator and staff members, for the most part, were known to devote full time to the field of special education. Accordingly, this group of respondents is referred to as specialists and experts throughout this report.

State Departments
of Education

It was assumed that the state department of education individual responsible for special education would be well informed regarding current research and practice in his state. Since it may also be assumed that state departments of education are responsible for acting in an advisory and leadership position, recommendations indicated by this source would reflect state recommendations and consequently, to a degree, possible trends.

Professors of
School Administration

This group of respondents represents recommendations from generalists as opposed to specialists in the preceding two categories. Selected professors of school administration were obtained from a list of names of individuals who were in attendance at the National Conference of Professors of Educational Administration, August 1959, Buffalo, New York.

The total percentage of usable replies received was as follows: (a) 82 percent from state departments of education, (b) 69 percent from special education experts, and (c) 50 percent from professors of school administration.

Selected findings from one portion of the Los Angeles Study on Special Education are here presented in summary form.

SCOPE OF
SPECIAL EDUCATION

In an attempt to define the scope of special education, a list of physical, mental, and learning classifications was presented. The respondent was requested to indicate approval or rejection of the item as a function of special education. Questionnaire respondents indicated that special education should include the following classifications and educational provisions:

Gifted	Orthopedically handicapped
Mentally retarded	Chronic medical
Mentally deficient	problems

Emotionally and/or   Hospital teaching
   socially disturbed   Home teaching
Blind   Deaf
Partially seeing   Hard of hearing
Cerebral palsied   Speech reading
                                     Speech correction

Questionnaire respondents indicated that special education should not include the following educational provisions:

Remedial reading   Foreign adjustment
                                        classes
Remedial arithmetic   Corrective physical
                                        education

It was interesting to note that there was an apparent reluctancy to include the mentally deficient (children with an IQ range of 0 to 50) in special education. This reluctancy was reflected in a negative response by 33 percent of the professors of school administration, 28 percent of the specialists, and 25 percent of the state department of education respondents.)

The professors of school administration were also less favorably disposed to including the gifted (children who have an intelligence quotient of 125 or 130 and above) as a classification of special education. Approximately 47 percent favored and 43 percent opposed the inclusion of the gifted. Ten percent of the professors of school administration failed to respond to the item. This finding was in contrast to the specialists and state department of education respondents. All specialists recommended that the gifted should be included, and only 12 percent of the state department of education respondents indicated exclusion. This discrepancy may reflect a difference in philosophy, method, and means for meeting the needs of gifted children.

Categories Included in a Public School Department of Special Education

All areas defined as special education were recommended for inclusion in a public school department of special education with the exception of the gifted and the mentally deficient. A majority of professors of school administration indicated a negative response for the inclusion of these two categories. State department of education respondents and specialists, however, were in agreement that the gifted and mentally deficient should be the responsibility of a public school department of special education.

School District Responsibilities for
Handicapped Children

Agreement was found among state department of education respondents, special education experts, and professors of school administration regarding school district responsibilities for making provisions for the following classifications and educational opportunities:

Mentally retarded	Partially seeing
Emotionally and/or socially disturbed	Hard of hearing
Cerebral palsied	Speech reading
Orthopedically handicapped	Speech correction

General agreement was also found among the respondents for accepting school responsibility for the following categories but with less enthusiasm on the part of professors of school administration:

Blind
Deaf
Chronic medical problems

Seventeen percent of the professors of school administration were opposed to including the blind; 17 percent were opposed to including the deaf; and 28 percent were opposed to including those with chronic medical problems.

Agreement was not found among the respondents regarding the school district responsibility for preschool education for the deaf, blind, or cerebral palsied pupil. The specialists were the most enthusiastic in recommending school responsibility for preschool education, followed by state departments of education. By a majority of approximately two to one, professors of school administration indicated that the public school should not be responsible for preschool education of the deaf, blind, or cerebral palsied student.

Only state department of education respondents indicated that the mentally deficient should be the direct responsibility of the school district. Seventy percent of the state departments of education indicated that training of the mentally deficient is the responsibility of public education as opposed to 25 percent of the same group who indicated a negative response. Five percent did not respond to the item. Both the specialists and the professors of school administration indicated a negative answer to school responsibility for training the mentally deficient. Analysis of data received from specialists indicated 33 percent in favor of and 33 percent opposed to accepting public school responsibility for the mentally deficient. Approximately 33 percent of the specialists failed to respond to this item. Analysis of data from professors of school administration found 53 percent opposed to and 31 percent in favor of accepting school responsibility for the mentally deficient.

ORGANIZATION

The degree of segregation or integration of handicapped children is implemented in the form of pupil organization. Philosophically, the minimum goal for all mentally and physically handicapped children is placement in normal or regular classroom situations whenever possible. Although it is assumed that the stated goal would be accepted by most authorities and lay individuals, the problem arises in the inclusion of the words "whenever possible."

Two diametrically opposing viewpoints may be observed. One viewpoint indicates that a considerable number of youngsters within a given category of special education may never be emotionally and socially integrated with success within a regular classroom situation. In addition, doubt is also manifested regarding the meeting of specialized educational needs in an integrated classroom situation.

The opposite viewpoint tends to emphasize the need to accept the handicapped and give them an opportunity to learn to adjust to a normal classroom environment. This goal may demand that placement within a normal environment is the major means of developing social and emotional adjustment. In the sense of emphasis, one school of thought tends to stress the provision of specific educational and physical services; the other school of thought tends to emphasize social and emotional adjustment to a normal environment. Both points of view subscribe to the general philosophical goal of rehabilitation and habilitation.

Pupil
Organization

In order to determine the best means for the education of handicapped children, five descriptive pupil organizational plans were obtained from the literature: the segregated plan, partial segregation, the cooperative plan, the resource room, and the itinerant teacher. The organizational plans were carefully defined in the questionnaire with the recognition that more than one pupil organizational plan may be necessary for a given category of special education. Respondents were requested to indicate one or more of the following types of organization that they would recommend for each category of special education:

> *Segregated Plan.* Special classes or school not on the same site as regular school.
>
> *Partial Segregation.* Section of regular school reserved for special education classes, or special education school on the same site as regular school. No plan to specifically integrate children with regular classroom activities. Partial integration recognized by attendance at school assemblies, events, lunch room, etc., where feasible.
>
> *Cooperative Plan.* Special education class or classes in which pupil may spend some portion of the day in the regular classroom.
>
> *Resource Room.* Pupil registered in regular classroom, does all his work with the regular group, and only goes to the resource room and the special education teacher for materials and special training.
>
> *Itinerant Teacher.* Pupil registered in regular classroom, does all his work with the regular classroom teacher, and receives periodic specialized training, help, and materials from a traveling special education teacher.

State department of education respondents, specialists, and professors of school administration were found to be in agreement relative to giving highest frequency to the following pupil organizational plans in elementary (E) and secondary (S) schools:

Deaf	Partial Segregation (E)
	Cooperative Plan (S)
Mentally Deficient	Segregated Plan (E, S)
Crippled and Delicate	Cooperative Plan (S)
Mentally Retarded	Partial Segregation (E)

State department of education respondents and professors of school administration gave highest frequency to the Cooperative Plan for educating the elementary crippled pupil. Specialists gave highest frequency to a Partial Segregation Plan.

Specialists were strongly in favor of a Cooperative Plan for educating the secondary level mentally retarded student. State department of education respondents gave equal frequency to the

Partial Segregation Plan and the Cooperative Plan. Professors of school administration gave highest frequency to the Partial Segregation Plan.

State department of education respondents and professors of school administration gave highest frequency to the Cooperative Plan for educating elementary hard of hearing pupils. Specialists gave highest frequency to the use of a Resource Room. Specialists and state department respondents gave highest frequency to the use of a Resource Room for educating the secondary level hard of hearing pupil. Professors of school administration gave highest frequency to the Cooperative Plan.

Respondent categories differed in the pupil organizational plan given highest frequency for education of the elementary blind pupil. State department of education respondents gave highest frequency to the Cooperative Plan; specialists gave highest frequency to the Partial Segregation Plan; and professors of school administration gave highest frequency to the Segregated Plan. State department of education respondents and specialists gave highest frequency to the use of a Resource Room for educating the secondary level blind student. Professors of school administration gave equal frequency to the Segregated Plan, Partially Segregated Plan, and Cooperative Plan for educating the secondary level blind student.

State department of education respondents and professors of school administration gave highest frequency to the Cooperative Plan for educating the elementary partially seeing pupil. Specialists gave highest frequency to the use of a Resource Room. State department of education respondents and specialists were in agreement in giving highest frequency to the use of a Resource Room for educating the secondary level partially seeing pupils. Professors of school administration gave highest frequency to the Cooperative Plan.

State department of education respondents and specialists gave highest frequency to the Partial Segregation Plan for educating the elementary emotionally and/or socially disturbed child. Professors of school administration gave highest frequency to the Cooperative Plan. State department of education respondents and professors of school administration gave highest frequency to the Cooperative Plan for educating the emotionally and/or socially disturbed secondary student. Specialists gave highest frequency to the Partial Segregation Plan.

PROFESSIONAL TRAINING FOR SCHOOL PRINCIPALS

An attempt was made to determine the extent of college training in the field of special education recommended for (a) principals of special education schools and (b) principals of regular schools containing special education classes. Respondents were requested to check one of the following three categories to indicate the degree of college training recommended:

1. Basic work in special education (four to six hours)
2. Possession of a special education credential
3. No special requirements or training.

All three categories of respondents were in agreement that the principal of a special education school should possess a special education credential. No state department respondent or specialist indicated that there was no need for requirements or training. Only two percent of the professors of school administration indicated that no special training or requirements should be necessary.

All three categories of respondents were in general agreement that the principal of a regular school containing special education classes should have at least four to six hours of college credit in the field of special education. Specialists were found to be the most concerned regarding training in the field of special education. Twenty-eight percent of the specialists indicated that the principal of a school containing special education classes should possess a special education credential. The majority of specialists, 67 percent, recommended that the principal should have from four to six hours of college credit in the field of special education.

TYPES OF ADMINISTRATIVE FRAMEWORK

An earlier analysis by the author of line and staff charts received from 49 cities with a population of 200,000 or more found three descriptive forms of administrative framework for the special education program.

Fifteen city school districts (31 percent) were found to have an administrative framework that placed the special education leader within the operational division or district. In all instances, the special education leader was vested with advisory or staff relationship with schools and personnel involved in educating the exceptional child. Responsibility for special education schools, as defined by line and staff authority, was found to be assigned to the district superintendent.

Eighteen city school districts (36 percent) were found to have an administrative framework that placed the special education department in a division other than operational. In all instances, the special education leader was vested with advisory or staff relationship with school personnel. Administrative responsibility for special education schools and classes was assigned to the district superintendent. School districts which placed the department of special education in a division other than operational or as a separate entity tended to favor three types of divisions: (a) curriculum branch, (b) pupil personnel services or similar title, and (c) guidance.

Sixteen school districts (33 percent) were found to grant line authority over schools and classes of special education to the special education leader.

It was concluded from the data received that there is no one single form of administrative organization currently in operation for the special education program in large city school districts throughout the United States. It may be inferred that the variety cf special education administrative framework patterns found in large city school systems is a reflection of local district internal needs rather than carefully planned administrative design.

It was of particular interest to determine the type of administrative framework for special education that would be recommended by authorities. Accordingly, four possible administrative organizational plans were developed, defined, and evaluated. The four plans are as follows:

Plan 1 — The special education principal is directly responsible to the district operational superintendent of regular schools in the area in which his school is located.

Plan 2 — The special education principal is directly responsible to the central operational (deputy or associate) superintendent who has responsibility for the various districts and line authority over the district superintendents. The district superintendent has no direct responsibility for special education schools in his district.

Plan 3 — The special education principal is directly responsible to a separate operational director or superintendent responsible only for special education schools. In this instance, the district superintendent has no direct responsibility for special education schools in his district.

Plan 4 — The special education principal has dual responsibility to two superintendents. The principal is responsible to the special education superintendent or director (who is responsible only for special education schools) and the district superintendent in which his school is located.

Respondents were requested to select the plan most suitable for administrative framework for (a) special education schools and (b) regular schools containing special education classes.

FRAMEWORK FOR
SPECIAL EDUCATION SCHOOLS

Data received from state department respondents and specialists found a considerable spread in responses among the four administrative framework plan categories. No single plan received more than a 40 percent positive response.

State department respondents and professors of school administration gave highest frequency to the administrative plan whereby the principal of a special education school was directly responsible to a district superintendent (Plan 1). The same respondents indicated for second choice the plan in which a separate department or division of special education is formed for administrative control of special education schools (Plan 3).

Specialists gave highest frequency to the administrative framework plan whereby the special education principal was directly responsible to a separate department or division of special education (Plan 3). Second choice was evenly divided in frequency count between direct line relationship with the operational district superintendent (Plan 1) and the plan whereby dual line authority stemmed from both the separate department of special education and the operational district superintendent (Plan 4).

FRAMEWORK FOR SCHOOLS
CONTAINING SPECIAL
EDUCATION CLASSES

The respondents gave clear evidence of preference for the recommendation that partial or full administrative control should be vested in the district superintendent relative to regular schools containing special education classes.

The majority of specialists favored the administrative framework (Plan 4) whereby the principal of a school containing special education classes would be under the dual control of two superintendents: the local district superintendent and the head of the department or division of special education.

Professors of school administration were in agreement, as determined by a majority of frequencies, in recommending that the local superintendent be responsible for the schools in his district which include special education classes (Plan 1).

Data received from state department of education respondents found a considerable spread in responses among the four administrative framework plan categories. No single plan received more than a 43 percent positive response. When the frequency responses for Plans 1 and 2 were totalled, however, and compared to the total frequency for Plans 3 and 4, it became evident that the majority of state department respondents favored regular administrative control over schools containing special education classes.

critical issues in
special education:
internal organization*

ERNEST P. WILLENBERG†

     The January, 1964, issue of *Exceptional Children* carried an article by Frank M. Hodgson entitled "Special Education, Facts and Attitudes." This article reported the results of a one year study, including the status of the organization for special education programs and services in local public school systems throughout the nation. Dr. Hodgson failed to find conclusive evidence of major trends or professional agreement relative to the best form or types of internal organization to serve exceptional children. In addition to questions relating to minimum school populations and bases of tax support and structural configurations of effective local public school agencies, there is concern for the echelon of organization which involves service to the exceptional child within the school jurisdiction responsible for his education and training.

     In an earlier issue of this publication (December, 1966) the writer delineated some of the basic criteria for special education leadership at the federal level. Arguments were presented in favor of the establishment of a Bureau for Exceptional Children and Youth in the U. S. Office of Education. It is becoming increasingly evident at state and local levels that effective program planning and development will follow the same general guidelines for centralized

*Reprinted from Exceptional Children, Vol. 33 (March 1967), pp. 1-2, by permission of the author and the Council for Exceptional Children. Copyright 1967 by the Council for Exceptional Children.

†Ernest P. Willenberg is Director of Special Education, Los Angeles City School System, California.

administration as proposed for strengthening the federal leadership potential. While no single pattern suitable for all exceptional children's needs can be outlined for the internal organization of special education in all local school systems, there is ample experience to support the advocacy of various forms of centralized units to provide for the planning, development and coordination of special education. In every instance, the internal organization should support the ebb and flow of pupil placement, instructional resources, and other services as needed.

The unit for educational service is the individual exceptional child. The goal is that child's optimum education and rehabilitation. When the prime consideration focuses attention upon the child and his changing requirements, the organizational scheme within the educational system should facilitate flexible programing and attract the child toward progressive levels of independence and self direction. On the other hand, another child who for various reasons moves in just the opposite direction may require prolonged specialized programs of a more intensive or categorical nature. The concept of flexible internal organization can be scaled from a base where one finds the majority of exceptional pupils requiring minimal modifications. Each successive level above the base represents the need for greater modification in the social milieu of the child and, in many cases, the extent and nature of instruction and other services. With a flexible system of internal organization, the special education program provides such an array of offerings as to match the child's changing requirements throughout the course of his school years.

Level One. Organization for child who needs adjunctive services only, such as special transportation, medication, etc. No modifications in content or procedures of learning opportunities are required. The child is educated in the regular school program.

Level Two. Organization for child who requires some supplementary teaching in the regular classroom. Such a child, given special attention by the regular classroom teacher, may also need some modifications in the materials and methods used in his instruction.

Level Three. Organization for child who requires specialized supplementary teaching such as that provided in integrated programs for the visually handicapped children enrolled in regular grades. Programs include modifications in content and/or materials and techniques.

Level Four. Organization for child who requires special day class instruction. Class is located in a regular school where child may participate part time incidentally and on a planned basis with regular class pupils. Program includes fundamental modifications in content, materials, and methods of instruction.

Level Five. Organization for child who requires full time instruction and ancillary services in a special day school such as that for multi-handicapped or trainable mentally retarded children. Program includes comprehensive and basic modifications in the nature, scope, and sequence of instructional offerings and in supportive services needed.

Level Six. Organization to provide for child who is homebound or hospitalized. Child is unable to attend other organized school programs. Instruction offered may vary in scope and sequence, or in the materials and methods used. This level differs from the others in that the instruction is usually organized to compensate for the circumstances associated with the child's confinement at home or in a hospital.

Level Seven. Organization for child who is placed in an institution. In addition to treatment and care for those who require hospitalization or physical management, also in this category are those children in attendance at residential schools such as those for the blind and deaf. When institutional placement includes education, the instruction may vary in practically every conceivable way to compensate for differences in behavior, learning, and physical ability.

The internal organization is designed to fit the child. The local school system should be structured in such a way as to nurture flexibility in pupil placement practices so that the full resources for special education and rehabilitation can obtain maximum benefits. Such benefits inevitably derive from vigilant and creative leadership with support from outside as well as inside the school system.

administrative structures for special education *

Educational developments in the 70's will require special education to carefully evaluate existing programs and to develop strategies that will make more effective use of learning research and developing technology.

There are significant implications for special education administration in the (a) changing patterns of handicapping conditions, (b) recent technological developments in hardware and software, (c) increasing research and understanding of the processes of human development and learning, (d) advances in the techniques and systems for individualization of instruction, and (e) increasing realization of the benefits and the need for a multidisciplinary approach to solving educational problems.

Special education, functioning for the most part as a separate or sub-system, increasingly will find the need to become an integrated and essential part of the main system. For a child who could not fit into the general educational pattern, alternatives have been limited. The main alternative to a regular calss has been placement in a special self-contained class.

The following sequential arrangements of instructional alternatives by Willenberg, Deno, and Reynolds (Figures 1, 2, and 3) suggest that only a small number of exceptional children will require self-contained settings and that the greatest number can remain in and profit from the main system if resource help is available, and if that system makes use of differentiated staffing and provides viable mechanisms for the individualization of instruction.

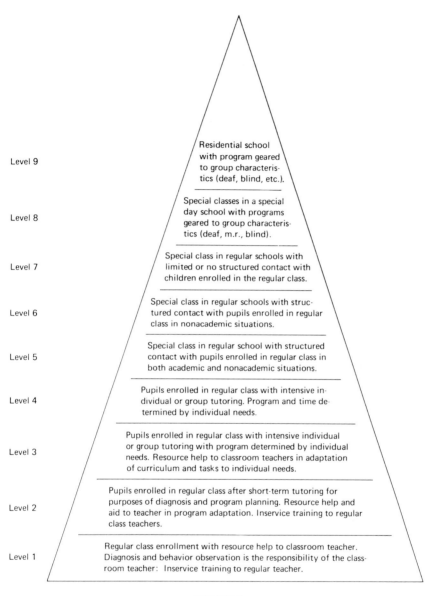

FIGURE 1.

**LEVELS OF INSTRUCTIONAL INTERVENTION WITHIN PUBLIC SCHOOL
SPECIAL EDUCATION PROGRAMS (WILLENBERG, 1968)**

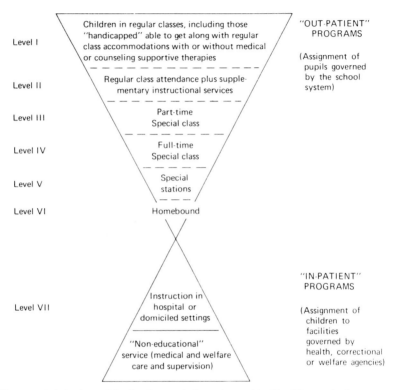

The tapered design is used in the chart to indicate the considerable difference in the numbers involved at the different levels and call attention to the fact that the system serves as a diagnostic filter. The most specialized facilities are likely to be needed by the fewest children on a long-term basis. This organization model can be applied to development of special education services for all types of disability.

FIGURE 2.

THE CASCADE SYSTEM OF SPECIAL EDUCATION SERVICE (EVELYN DENO)

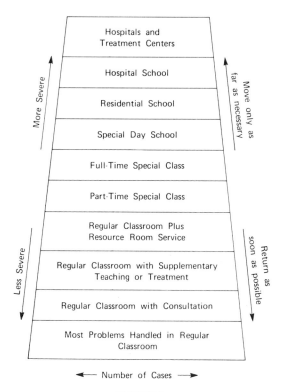

FIGURE 3.

A FRAMEWORK FOR CONSIDERING SOME ISSUES IN SPECIAL EDUCATION.
(SEE MAYNARD REYNOLDS, PART I, PP. 3-36.)

section B

coordination
of
services

various approaches to developing area programs*

ROBERT M. ISENBERG†

There is a long established characteristic of the American people, sometimes called "Yankee ingenuity," which holds that a way can be found to do anything worth doing and then sets about the task of finding it. Our incidence of success is remarkable. It must be admitted, however, that the devices and processes developed range from the efficiency of Henry Ford's production line to many kinds of Rube Goldberg contraptions.

It can be argued that school organization throughout the United States is considerably more than the result of "Yankee ingenuity," but the variations of ability among local school systems to provide appropriate educational opportunities for all children cannot be disputed. A brief review of some of today's realities regarding school districts demonstrates clearly why those who are struggling to implement specialized educational services are trying to discover or create some kind of organizational device for developing programs on a regional or other interschool district basis.

REALITIES OF EXISTING SCHOOL DISTRICT STRUCTURE

There are fewer than 30,000 operating school systems in the United States today, enrolling more than 40

---

*Reprinted from *Cooperative Programs in Special Education* by Robert M. Isenberg and F. E. Lord, 1964 by permission of the Department of Rural Education and the Council for Exceptional Children.

†Robert M. Isenberg is Associate Secretary, American Association of School Administrators, National Education Association.

million children in their elementary and secondary grades. This is the smallest number of separate school administrative units since before westward expansion and the largest enrollment ever. The contributions these educational systems make to our well-being defy estimate. But these school systems of today have not always been what they are nor are they likely to remain so. School organization has been more responsive and adaptive to changing circumstances than any other segment of local government. In the days before hard-surfaced roads and automobiles, it was essential that the school designed to serve each community be located so as to permit the attendance of children coming on foot or on horseback. It was in this setting that our earliest schools were established and school districts were formed. The common school was a one-teacher school — in most instances the only school in the district.

School district structure was not destined to be static, however. As our country grew and better means of doing the things that needed to be done were developed, alternative organization patterns became possible. People combined and consolidated schools and districts in their efforts to form school systems better able to provide for a greatly expanding curriculum and vast increase in demand for educational services. The approximately 30,000 school systems of today were well over 100,000 only a dozen years ago, and because of continuing reorganization efforts, the total number will be further reduced — perhaps to as few as 5,000 districts within the next few years.

There is no longer much doubt that the extensive reorganization of local school districts, vigorously resisted in some areas, has produced administrative units better able to provide for expanding educational programs. This has been sufficiently documented and is generally understood. This success with school district reorganization and the improved educational programs resulting has some tendency to block further progress, however. There is little general understanding that, in spite of all the changes in school district structure, most school systems are still unable to undertake many types of specialized educational service essential to an efficient and comprehensive school operation. More than 80 percent of all of today's school districts, for example, do not employ even as many as 40 teachers. Most of the 20 percent meeting this size criterion are also relatively small; there are only a few large school systems. On January 1, 1963 only 1,054 school systems had enrollments of 6,000 or more pupils — a number well below the population base required for the efficient provision of most specialized service programs.

Those who are serious about implementing programs designed

to serve groups making up a relatively small segment of our school population (for example, blind, orthopedically handicapped, perceptually different, emotionally disturbed, and severely mentally retarded) or to serve specialized functions requiring a large base of operation to achieve efficiency (for example, educational television, data processing, instructional materials, vocational and technical education, and junior college programs) must be realistic about the ability and resources of local school systems. Most are too small to undertake such efforts. Many are so small that even basic programs of guidance, library, and health services are more than can be provided economically and with a high degree of quality. Neither is continued district reorganization, assuming the present rapid rate of progress, likely to create school systems able to provide them.

There are two alternatives — do without these programs or find a way other than through local school systems to provide them. The discussion of various possible approaches to interdistrict programs identified in this article and the descriptions of operating programs which follow will probably have little appeal to those who would be willing to do without.

The greatest barrier to expanding and extending specialized educational service programs in areas where they are not now provided is not really any tendency to discount their value and potential contribution to children and communities. Neither is it the absence of an adequate structure to administer such programs, even though this is a definite lack. The major obstacle seems to be the unwillingness of those working at all levels in our state systems of schools to acknowledge that the traditional local school district by local school district approach cannot do the job. A realistic review of school district organization in any state can lead only to this conclusion.

APPROACHES TO AN ORGANIZATIONAL FRAMEWORK

As pointed out above, the step that seems most difficult to make is recognizing the limitations of local school systems. This is not to suggest that the local school district is not the best device yet conceived to administer the bulk of what makes up an elementary and secondary school program, either now or in the future. It is only to emphasize that what local schools can do must be supplemented. And more and more programs requiring highly specialized personnel and equipment are coming on the scene.

Assuming, then, that the first step has been taken and some way to supplement local school district programs is sought, we recognize that there is a variety of approaches through which the specialized needs and services of school districts can be met. Not all have equal merit in terms of criteria for adequate and appropriate organization. But all are approaches which can be illustrated by one or more operating programs. In each of these instances, regardless of the method developed, the approach has had some degree of success in that services not otherwise available are being provided.

When it has been acknowledged that most local districts are too small to undertake certain services, it is obvious that programs undertaken must include two or more districts. The approaches possible range from two separate districts setting up some mutually satisfactory way of working together to the development of a statewide program. The following sections describe various organizational approaches which fall in this range with comments on their apparent strengths and weaknesses. This is followed by an identification of what are considered general characteristics of desirable structure. An attempt is made to make each of the approaches described as discreet as possible. It is recognized and should be emphasized, however, that two or three of these separately described approaches can be and are used simultaneously by a single operating program without serious confusion.

CONTRACTING FOR SERVICE

Local school districts are established and empowered by state law to administer a public school or a system of public schools. They have quasi corporate powers including making contracts. It is possible for any school district to contract with any other school district, agency, or private individual or business enterprise, unless specifically prohibited by state law or regulation, for any service it wishes either to purchase or furnish. Unless the terms of contracts are unusual or unreasonable, they will be upheld and binding on the parties involved.

A small school district, for example, may have only one or two children who need a "trainable" program. Unable to provide a class, they contract with a neighboring district and arrange to have their children transported to that district for this special program. The neighboring district may be relatively large and have several such classes and may, in fact, contract for this or other services with several other of its smaller neighbors. Often, however, there is no large district with an established program nearby. This contract system has possibilities even for areas where there is no large district with an established program. Several small districts can get together and select one of their number to establish and operate a program, each agreeing by contract to support the undertaking. Together in this way these small districts may well have a sufficient number of children and funds to develop an efficient program.

This contract system is used not only for these severely mentally retarded children but also for blind, partially seeing, deaf, orthopedically handicapped, and many others. It is the common method used by many small elementary school districts for purchasing high school education for their children. It also has other possibilities. Two or more districts can go together to contract for and share the services of a speech therapist, psychologist, dental hygienist, occupational therapist, or some other specialist. Psychiatric service, the services of a child guidance clinic, and many other types of needed service can be arranged through mutually agreed-upon contracts.

One of the chief advantages of contracting for services is that it is relatively easy to do. If a service is needed and some nearby school district, agency, or individual is available and willing to provide it, a contract can be negotiated and service begun. No special legislation or special dispensation is required. In the area of programs for exceptional children, there is additional incentive in that very often state funds are provided to cover all or most of the additional costs.

The contract approach usually requires initiation by the school district needing a service. It assumes recognition that service is needed and that the funds required when not covered by state reimbursement are available. This is more than can often be assumed. The approach also has the disadvantage of being a temporary or terminal relationship. Most contracts are on a year to year basis, although some slight tendency for contracts to cover a longer period of time can be noted. This dependence upon annual renewal gives little assurance to those who work in a contract program or those who attempt to coordinate it that efforts will continue beyond the current year. It discourages long range planning and makes the purchase of expensive specialized equipment a gamble. The approach also imposes a great deal of coordinating responsibility and administrative detail on the school district or agency providing the service.

Other problems of the contract approach arise from attempts to arrive at appropriate pro rata shares of the cost when a number of districts are involved and from the seemingly continuous need to assure a direct relationship between amount of service provided to participating districts and their proportion of support. There is the always present possibility, too, that one or more of the participating districts may discontinue their contractual relationship, either to abandon the particular service or to set up their own separate program. When this occurs, it is sometimes necessary for remaining districts desiring to continue the contract approach to discontinue also.

DEVELOPING A
STATE OPERATION

The extreme from instances where two neighboring school districts negotiate a contractual relationship is having the state education agency undertake direct provision of services which local units cannot provide. This approach is more often used in such operations as film libraries, vocational and technical education programs, and educational television than for services for exceptional children. But there are those who believe the state can and most appropriately should provide all the supplementary services local school districts need. It is certainly true that in some states the only major efforts in behalf of exceptional children outside of what a few local school districts can do are through the services of state employed psychologists and special education consultants.

If there is advantage to a statewide approach to service operations, it is inherent simply in the existence of the agency. A state department of education is a reality and has an interest in and concern about program development. Lacking any other existing agency, it is perhaps natural for the state to try to fill the gap and provide service programs which local districts cannot undertake. Further, specialized educational service programs are often expensive and for some of them (for example, a statewide educational television network) it may be easier to justify and secure the necessary funds by a united statewide approach.

The disadvantages of state operation of services are many. Local schools, teachers, and children are a long way from personnel working out of the capital city. It is extremely difficult to get state administered services on the scene at the place and time they are needed. Real needs for help cannot be scheduled on an annual, monthly, or weekly time chart or work plan. They come as crises, emergencies — major and minor. Help must be "on call" or "within 24 hours" if it is to be of real value. It is sometimes suggested that the way to resolve this handicap is through the creation of a series of regional offices of the state agency closer to schools and school problems. While the suggestion has some merit, the question of why these regional offices should be state operated rather than controlled by the region or area they serve should be considered.

There are a number of other shortcomings to the statewide approach. Programs undertaken are automatically handicapped by the "psychology of state operation," that is, the obligation the state level has to treat all areas of the state equally. Except in experimental or pilot ventures, the state must be prepared to move uniformly statewide when it moves at all. It cannot show preference for one area over another — to a particular area ready to move when others are not. This necessity of moving an entire state at once makes progress slow and difficult and precludes "light-house operations."

Another handicap to developing effective statewide service programs is that their financing is directly tied to legislative action or inaction. The establishment, expansion, and continuation of services are made responsive to the whims of state legislators. Even if it could be assumed that this dependence on state appropriations is not a problem, the funds appropriated to operate services are included as part of the state department of education budget. This by itself creates a new problem. Service programs are costly, and the financing required by a state education department undertaking service functions creates an appearance of serious imbalance in relation to other departments of state government. This is often difficult to understand, may result in interdepartment tension, and sets up a ready target for those eager to reduce state spending. Education and specialized service programs are too important to place in such jeopardy.

In addition, question can be raised regarding the role appropriate for a state education agency. Maintaining an orderly state system of schools through the enforcement of laws and regulations is accepted, sometimes grudgingly, as a necessary function. There is also general agreement that the state is the proper agency to establish standards. But there is little agreement on the state's responsibility for operational functions. Because our history is one in which all operational responsibilities are delegated to local agencies, there is reason to challenge the development of state service programs when equally efficient alternatives closer to the schools and communities to be served are possible.

FORMING A
COOPERATIVE

Cooperation is an old and familiar Yankee characteristic. In earlier years, it found expression in quilting bees, corn huskings, and barn raisings and more recently as a means for distributing electric power and marketing agricultural produce. It has been a way by which people could join together to undertake tasks impossible for individuals. It is a concept directly applicable to the need for developing service programs which school systems individually cannot provide with efficiency and economy.

The formally organized cooperative is made up of members who directly or through their representatives manage and control its operation and who share equally or proportionally in its benefits. In the area of educational services, the members of a cooperative are separate school systems. They are the owners, managers, and receivers of whatever services the cooperative is designed to furnish. They participate in developing the policies which guide service, in selecting the personnel employed, and in financing the operation. The financial contribution each member district supplies may be an equal share with other members or may be based on its average attendance, membership, or some other measure. In this way, school districts voluntarily bind themselves together to form an agency which they collectively control and regulate and from which they receive some share of a larger service.

One of the reasons that more educational cooperatives have not been formed is the extreme difficulty in getting one organized and underway. Initial organization and operation require a dedication of leadership for which no one has responsibility. In education, there are no professional cooperative organizers to spark the approach and guide establishment. On the other hand, many are available to point up problems which may be encountered and to otherwise create suspicion of such a plan. Further, development of an educational cooperative requires a vision of potential and confidence in ultimate success not only on the part of those willing to devote the time required for promotion but by all would-be member districts as well. This is not easy to achieve. It is a path filled with discouragement and frustration.

Where these organizing obstacles are overcome and a cooperative is established, there are additional limitations. Cooperatives tend to be single purpose agencies. They are organized to undertake a specific task. Member school districts align themselves in a particular combination because of their mutual desire to make some specific service available. The cooperative is staffed in relation to this area of functions. Consequently, no matter how well or how efficiently its services are provided, it appears virtually impossible in practice to use the same organization to undertake other types of educational service. The specialized service orientation of the cooperative's leadership and staff, the fact that the collective alignment of member districts for one service may be different for another, and the tendency to fear that expansion of operations may dilute the service already developed are among the reasons that expansion into other service areas is difficult.

Another shortcoming of the educational cooperative is the fact that it tends not to be part of the formal school organization of the state. It is nothing more than a voluntary association of school districts to accomplish in a cooperative way what they cannot do separately. It is not a school district nor a legally recognized agency of school government, even though it may be incorporated. While this does not lessen its effectiveness as a service agency, it does preclude it from receiving direct financial support from the state, from direct access to funds other than through assessments of its members, and from other benefits which may derive from being an integral part of formal school structure.

ORGANIZING A
SPECIAL DISTRICT

The special school district is an alternative to the voluntary special purpose agency illustrated by the educational cooperative. As an integral part of school government, except for such limitations of function as may be specified in its establishment, it operates in much the same way and with the same powers and responsibilities as any school district. It has distinct boundaries, a board of education, tax-levying authority, and is entitled to direct state financial support as may be provided by the state finance plan.

The special district, where permitted by state law, is usually organized by procedures similar to those used in the reorganization of regular school districts. The area to be included is determined and the voters of the area are given opportunity through a referendum to approve or disapprove the proposal. If approved, the special district becomes a fact and regular procedures for the election of its board of education and approval of its budget and tax levy are followed. The only major difference between this type of district and a regular district is that its purpose is specified and limited. It may be a special education district, a vocational education district, a junior college district, or have some other specific area of functions. It is *special* in the sense that it is organized for a special purpose.

Special districts almost always include within their boundaries a number of regular school districts, each responsible for the usual or regular aspects of elementary and secondary school programs. They provide services within this larger multidistrict area as a unified operation responsible directly to the total constituency rather than to individual school districts within the area. Essential articulation between regular school programs and the special service program is thus more dependent upon operating procedures than on direct organizational involvement or participation in policy development. The special district is its own legally constituted unit responsible for its own policies and budget determination and subject only to legal limitations and the responsiveness of its patrons.

Special school districts for various purposes are more common than is generally recognized. While they are not easy to establish and are not provided for by law in a number of states, their creation where permitted is not much more difficult than most school district reorganization efforts. Too, state assistance can usually be called upon to help with organization procedures. In some instances, substantial state leadership is encouraging this type of organization, especially in the establishment of junior college districts.

When carefully planned and organized, the special district will generally have a large enough base of operation to provide a type of service which other school districts cannot appropriately undertake. Its establishment makes it the local agency responsible for such services. This means that the boards of education and administrators of regular school districts can in whole or in part absolve themselves of any further responsibility for such service. An additional advantage with much appeal is that the services they receive from the special district do not show up in their own local budgets. The special district has its own separate sources of funds. Individual local districts in this way are relieved of both financial responsibility and administrative involvement in the area program.

The special district is not without problems, however. Because it has a large constituency to serve, there is often a great divergence of views among its patrons. This becomes somewhat serious when those responsible for local school operations are dissatisfied with either the quality or types of services provided or the philosophy which guides them — in spite of the fact that, by virtue of its establishment, the special district has full and independent responsibility for its program.

The greatest handicap of the special district approach to service results from the limitations of its scope of operation. The special district is established to provide certain specified services and not others. Regardless of how well it does its job, it cannot take on other and different functions which may at a later time be desired.

Inherent in the special district approach is the necessity, when a new type of function emerges and is desired, to create still another special district. This, in fact, is done. The new special district may or may not have identical boundaries and tax base as the first. There are instances, for example, where special education districts, vocational education districts, and junior college districts share in some degree the same general geographic area and tax base as a number of regular school districts. Yet each has a separate legal status, a separate board of education, a separate administration, a separate tax levy, and a separate set of policies. It is not difficult to see that any area utilizing this special district approach for developing specialized educational services can rapidly develop at the same time a cumbersome and confusing system of overlapping districts for which articulation becomes a major problem.

DEVELOPING AN
EFFECTIVE INTERMEDIATE UNIT

The intermediate administrative unit or intermediate school district has received a great deal of attention and discussion in recent years as the type of agency which can provide the specialized services needed to supplement local school district programs. Slowly but increasingly its potential is being recognized and accepted. More rapid progress in developing this approach has been held up both by the general reluctance to acknowledge that local districts cannot do all that needs doing and a fear that strong intermediate units might dominate and usurp local district functions.

Contrary to a rather widely held view, an *intermediate unit* is not a fixed, formalized, clearly-defined organizational pattern ready to be imposed. It is a broad and general concept. Simply defined, it is the middle or intermediate member of a three-level system of organization, that is, a number of basic school administrative units at one level, the state education department at another, and functioning between them, some kind of intermediate agency. As the middle member in an organizational framework for school administration, this agency could have a wide range of specific characteristics and still be an intermediate unit.

Some of the confusion over the intermediate unit approach to developing specialized service programs arises from the fact that the concept is an old one. Most states have or at one time had some type of intermediate unit. In some form, the intermediate unit has existed nearly as long as this country has had public schools. Traditionally, the intermediate agency has been the county school office and the county superintendent of schools. Only recently have substantial alternatives to county school offices been suggested.

The county school office, an agency of the state established to provide administration and general supervision for the multitude of small school districts once existing, served its original purposes reasonably well. Most states developed such an organization during the period from 1829 to 1880, a time when school programs and school needs were vastly different from today. Yet, in a number of states, this agency still functions with a legal framework and assignment of duties which have changed very little. State legislatures and state leadership have not applied themselves to keeping a well-conceived concept up to date.

A charge of complete obsolescence is not entirely valid, however. Recent modifications of intermediate unit structure in some states have been sufficient to demonstrate that when it is properly organized, staffed, and financed, the potential of this type of agency for providing specialized services to both the state and local districts is greater than that offered by other approaches. Appropriate reorganization and a redirection of its functions would necessitate a base of operation in most instances considerably larger than a single county. It would also require professional administration and staff, the elimination of political entanglements, and a level of financial support not now provided. Such a revamping is long overdue.

One of the major advantages to developing the intermediate unit as a regional service agency is that it is automatically in the direct stream of state school organization. Functions which support and supplement those of local school districts can be assigned. If its geographic area is made sufficiently large, its general orientation would permit it to undertake on a regional basis any or all supplementary services needed by local school systems. It could easily adapt to changing circumstances and take on different or additional service functions. Because of this freedom from specific purpose orientation, its potential could be developed simultaneously in such diverse areas as data processing, clinical or diagnostic services, instructional materials, curriculum coordination and development, and inservice staff development. For most school districts, the initiative and resources required by other approaches are likely to prevent their development. Yet all districts in a state could be served by specialized programs if an appropriate number of service-oriented intermediate units were created.

CHARACTERISTICS OF
DESIRABLE STRUCTURE

Each of the several approaches to developing regional or interdistrict service programs included in the foregoing paragraphs is workable. All have potential for supplementing local school district programs. All, in the form described or with some variation, now exist. Such a variety of approaches demonstrates that there is more than one way to develop an area service program.

Since the success of any regional service undertaking depends to a large extent on the organizational framework which permits its development, the following general characteristics considered desirable to assure efficient operation are suggested.

Broad and comprehensive responsibility for both elementary and secondary education and their specialized aspects.

Broad and generally oriented professional administration.

An area of operation large enough to permit the efficient development of most services local school systems cannot provide for themselves.

Adequate and dependable financial support with some degree of flexibility in its use.

The ability to adapt programs and direction as circumstances and needs change.

A sufficient stability to assure the continuation of service in spite of changes and realignments among participating local school systems.

A responsiveness to the needs and desires of local school systems as seen from the local level.

The ability to secure a staff sufficiently competent to have something substantially worthwhile to offer participating districts.

Any regional approach meeting such general characteristics in its organization and operation, assuming appropriate facilities and equipment for whatever it undertakes, is certain to extend educational opportunities far beyond what local school systems will ever be able to do by themselves.

the
cooperative
special education
program*

RICHARD J. KOTHERA†

Because of their highly individual needs, not all school age children are able to realize a maximum benefit from the established regular school curriculum. Physical, mental, and emotional differences are thus provided for by highly specialized and stylized programs referred to as special education. Many school districts throughout this country, because of population and financing, are unable to adequately provide for specialized needs. Through cooperation of a number of school districts, a well rounded program in special education may be offered these children. Cooperation among school districts extends not only to a verbal commitment, but to a legal, financial, and philosophical relationship as well. By combining the populations of a number of school districts as well as by multiple financing, the formation of multidistrict cooperatives in special education is feasible, practical, and of the utmost necessity in providing well rounded programs adequately staffed and populated, and in maintaining an administrative force for securing stability, equity, and educational responsibility in operation.

*Reprinted from *Selected Convention Papers, 46th Annual International CEC Convention, New York City, New York, April 14-20, 1968*, pp. 187-194, by permission of the author and the Council for Exceptional Children. Copyright 1968 by the Council for Exceptional Children.
†Richard J. Kothera is Superintendent of Schools, Roseland School District, Shawnee Mission, Kansas.

NEED FOR MULTIDISTRICT COOPERATIVES

Because of their highly individual needs, not all school age children are able to realize maximum benefit from established regular school curriculum due to physical, mental, or emotional differences. Teachers cognizant of special needs, and of the methodology required to meet them, aid in the realization of human potential through special education services with resulting social adjustment and economic usefulness providing ample return for the investment made by the community in special education. Yet as this philosophy has developed over the years, it becomes apparent that only large school districts have the space, the personnel, and the fiscal stability necessary to establish and maintain well rounded special education programs. While the processes of unification and consolidation have expanded both scope and size of affected school districts, many are still not large enough to adequately maintain a complete program of special education. There exist unified Kindergarten through 12th grade school districts with fewer than 500 children. In some states in the southern portion of the Middle West and Southwest, areas are so sparsely populated it is almost an impossibility to establish and maintain more than a room for housing materials and a sympathetic teacher who attempts to "handle" the problems of those children which cannot be adequately approximated in the regular classroom. If the needs of these children are to be adequately served, specialized programs must be offered them. But at the same time, how is the small school district to care adequately for these needs which, because of lack of enrollment, create a tremendous financial burden for the school district? One means of countering this problem of small school districts, other than consolidation, is the cooperative program, whereby adjoining school districts use the services of special education personnel on the basis of mutual cooperative agreements.

Exemplary in this area are shared speech therapy and psychological services as well as programs for the mentally retarded. Many school districts today, unable to afford the highly specialized personnel utilized in special education programs, have joined together with one district maintaining the paper work and the other school districts reimbursing on a time spent or per pupil cost basis. Yet, if two districts join together in an area such as has been suggested, the type of program resulting still does not adequately meet the needs of all special education children who potentially might enroll in either school district. Another most important question is the direction special education takes. Can two districts afford a director? None have in the past, except to place the responsibility upon a teacher or administrator already functioning full time in another capacity who may lack the sophistication necessary to blend policy, budget, personnel, and facilities to achieve the auspicious results possible in special education. Is there any means avaiable to low enrolled districts that allow the establishment of total special education programs? Perhaps the best answer, unification and consolidation notwithstanding, is the multidistrict cooperative formed to join together enrollments of such size that, regardless of incidence, a total program is possible to meet the exceptionalities of the student population in addition to providing specialized administrative leadership essential to the maintenance and continued growth of the program.

FORMING A
COOPERATIVE

Certain strategies and tactics are necessary to overcome the initial problems of forming a cooperative. Superintendents are known to be concerned about the loss of authority, financial insecurity, state laws, and such, and one must consider these very real problems of district administrators in establishing a cooperative program. First and foremost, the necessity for such a program and its potential benefits need to be presented. What basically is being established in a cooperative is a marriage in which divorce can be so punishing that it is almost an impossibility, if only from the standpoint of public relations. In the formation of our cooperative program in Kansas, we found much hesitancy on the part of superintendents to commit themselves because, at the time, we had little financial stability due to the initiation of a highly questionable foundation finance plan and the lack of permissive legislation directed towards the formation of cooperative programs. It took a certain amount of politicking, convincing, and propagandizing to get eleven superintendents on the same track.

First, we gained a philosophical agreement on the part of each superintendent that the means of meeting the children's needs were not being accomplished with our present form of "I'll send you my mentally retarded; you send me your emotionally disturbed and in June we'll figure out what we owe each other." We requested — in fact demanded — a commitment that the needs of all children must be met. Surveys were taken and the entire program discussed with our state director, Dr. Jim Marshall, who greatly encouraged us. After four years of operation we can only say that the cooperation, encouragement, and understanding of our problems by our State Department made is possible for us to establish and maintain the cooperative.

The cooperative was formed via contract and contains basically four elements:

1. Ground rules used to establish and maintain the program such as: Who will sponsor the program? Who was eligible to participate? In our case, policy is established through a quasi board of education which we refer to as the board of directors.
2. Operations — this concerns the director of special education and establishes duties and reimbursements as well as the hierarchy under which he operates.
3. Facilities — In the cooperative program the facilities are widely scattered and basically consist of free classrooms in elementary schools around the area. It establishes a rental plan for these classrooms which is paid for by the cooperative in terms of credit on a yearly bill.
4. Finance — the contract spells out the financial duties of the sponsoring district in regard to maintaining fiscal responsibility for the cooperative and establishing administrative fees for the administration of the program and operational fees which basically reimburse teachers, teachers' aides, purchase equipment and materials.

All school districts who wish to become a part of the cooperative then enter into a legal contract with all other school districts for the establishment of the cooperative.

Did we have a law on the books which specifically allowed us to form a special education cooperative? The fact is that it was not until two years after the formulation of our cooperative program that a few people questioned the legality of the cooperative, and a bill was sponsored in the Senate which allowed the formulation of special education cooperatives. However, the program was legally established without a specific law for one good reason: the formation of a cooperative is a contractual obligation upon boards of education. The only legal basis necessary is that boards of education be legally endowed with the right to enter into contractual arrangements with other boards of education; or less specifically, that boards of education are allowed to enter into all types of contractual obligations. This law has been in Kansas for a long time and is used every year by boards of education; thus the necessity of establishing a special law perhaps will satisfy the purists, but it is not a legal necessity.

ESTABLISHING THE BOARD OF DIRECTORS

Once the contract was signed, the board of directors was established. There are several ways to establish a board of directors for cooperatives. It may be operated with lay citizens by appointment, with elected members representing boards of education, or with superintendents of cooperating school districts. In our case, the board of directors was made up of the superintendents of cooperating school districts with the idea that within several years this would slowly transfer to a board of directors composed of school board members representing the cooperative districts. At the present time, not one member of a board of education sits on the board of directors; the board is still made up of the superintendents of the cooperating districts. Our director seems to prefer it this way in that he feels his work is less difficult and the amount of sympathy he receives from fellow administrators is much greater than if the board of directors were made up of lay citizens or of members of cooperating school districts' boards of education. This may be true; however, it is important to consider the possibility that more rapid development in the cooperative would be possible with a board of directors who were not superintendents of schools. Because of the problem of vested interest and salary schedule competition, and since the cooperative is maintained as an entity into itself, the board of directors operating as a quasi board of education, perhaps it would be well to do away with that sometime shadow called vested interests by doing away with a board of directors human enough and competitive enough to hold down one area in hopes of developing another. This situation will not always present itself but it is a potential problem in any cooperative, as well as in any special education program. Since special education, as a highly particular field of its own, could very well take a backseat to other programs and not be funded proportionately to support innovation, research, development, and investigation, and perhaps a cooperative program, as it is operated under a board of directors, it could possibly operate more freely with even more adequate financing by operating with a lay board.

FINANCING

Special education is more expensive per pupil than regular education, even if nothing more than enrollment is considered. In the past, special education for students who were orthopedically handicapped, blind, partially seeing, deaf, and hard of hearing required special equipment which was expensive and still is expensive today. However, the difference in cost between special and standard educational equipment is not what it was fifteen or twenty years ago, since regular education has entered into a purchasing era of electronic equipment. The classroom cost of equipment has increased tenfold over what we normally spent in the past, so the mechanical and electronic area of special education expenses have basically decreased in their relationship to the cost of maintaining a regular classroom, since the regular classroom is no longer devoid of its share of mechanical and electronic equipment. However, costs still accrue disproportionately due to special transportation, facilities, and the levy of administrative expenses as well as teachers salaries over a limited number of children. Yet this is offset by increased financing on the part of the state which in many areas provides additional funds for the maintenance of specialized educational programs. In addition to this, there are also incentive plans by various state departments which encourage the formation of a cooperative in special education. In Kansas, a district that takes students from another school district for the purpose of special education is paid $100 per out of district child. In a cooperative such as ours with an enrollment of approximately 260 students of which our district only furnished approximately 25, $23,500 immediately accrues to the cooperative because all students other than the sponsoring district's students are out of district.

Those who are familiar with Kansas and Kansas educators probably have heard a number of disparaging remarks made about its foundation plan and its 104 percent limit. In arriving at the formulation for this foundation plan, Kansas legislators must never have considered special education, and if they did, they deserve praise because they have funded the state very well for a cooperative program.

Money accrues to the cooperative in the state of Kansas in several ways. First, several thousand dollars per program is funded by the department of special education plus reimbursement for a proportionate amount of supplies and equipment. In addition to this, $100 is paid per out of district student in special education. Also, the state foundation program pays a certain sum of dollars per teacher to the school district and that sum of dollars is dependent upon the amount of training the teacher has, with the highest amount paid for the teacher with the most graduate hours. Educationally, teachers in special education are proportionately more highly trained than the average faculty. Also, our cooperative program transports all children and figures transportation from the home to the sponsoring district, and additional money accrues through this.

There are drawbacks to our foundation plan. Since the pupil teacher ratio is a factor, the ratio in a district could fall under the minimum standard mandated by the state, which means a reduction in foundation monies, and an increase in property tax. However, the cooperative maintains that the sponsoring district will only incur normal financial obligations acquired by cooperating districts, so it will not be hurt by a lowering of their pupil teacher ratio. We compile two budgets, one for the school district without the cooperative sponsorship and the other with it included. If the difference is negative, it is paid by the cooperative to the sponsoring school district. If the difference is positive, it is paid by the sponsoring district to the cooperative program. This puts the cooperative on its own financial feet and operates as fiscal financial security for the sponsoring district.

In addition, funds are received from participating districts. At present these funds cover administration and operation. Administration costs are figured by dividing total costs into total school enrollment of the cooperative, which results in a cost of 70 to 80 cents per pupil, paid as a participation fee once a year to maintain the director's office, secretarial salaries, equipment, maintenance, and materials. The second fee paid by districts is the per pupil assessment. After state monies are figured, the remaining costs of the total number of programs is computed and divided by the number of children. The result is per pupil fee of approximately $400. So, if a school district has twenty children in the program and an enrollment of 2,000 children in their school district, their total cost would be $8,000 as the total per pupil assessment plus $1,400 participation fee. That school district thus has any one of a number of programs to place children, in addition to psychological and administrative services for the relatively low cost of $9,400 a year to the participating district.

The cooperative program presently maintains the following classes in special education in Northeast Johnson County:

TABLE 1.

No. of Classes	Area	Students
1	Primary Trainable Mentally Retarded	8
1	Intermediate Trainable Mentally Retarded	8
3	Primary I Educable Mentally Retarded	33
3	Primary II Educable Mentally Retarded	33
3	Intermediate I Educable Mentally Retarded	31
3	Intermediate II Educable Mentally Retarded	33
2	Primary Learning Disabilities	18
3	Intermediate Learning Disabilities	33
1	Primary Emotionally Disturbed	10
1	Intermediate Emotionally Disturbed	5
1	Primary I Hard of Hearing	8
1	Primary II Hard of Hearing	9
1	Intermediate Hard of Hearing	8
1	Primary Orthopedically Handicapped	7
1	Itinerant Program, Visually Impaired	
2	Homebound Fulltime Teachers	} 15
3	Homebound Parttime Teachers	
	Total Number of Children Served	259

Staff

	Total number of Teachers Serving	31
	Total number of Administrators	2
	Total number of Psychologists	2
	Total number of Noncertified Personnel	2
	Total Staff	37

With approximately 260 students enrolled, we have what we consider an excellent beginning program that adequately provides for a large number of students who need specialized programs to meet their needs. In addition to these programs there are hospital and home bound programs with administration by a director and his assistant. Two secretaries serve the administrators and two psychologists. The total cost of this program is just over $300,000 per year including both state monies and participating district fees. The program serves approximately 260 children in classrooms and approximately 425 children per year including money spent for psychological testing for children who do not enter into the program, hospitalized and home bound, as well as itinerant visually impaired children.

The cooperative program in turn cooperates with other area programs. For instance, Kansas City, Kansas, places its primary orthopedically handicapped children in our program. In turn, we place our intermediate children in their program. Both programs are housed in the same facility which happens to be the University of Kansas Medical Center, Children's Rehabilitation Unit.

Additionally, students are taken into the program from districts that have not joined the cooperative. These districts pay a special rate of approximately $900 per year. The tuition is paid by the school district sending the child.

A number of cases have arisen where nonparticipating school districts were unwilling to pay the tuition fee while the parents were extremely willing. However, our rule and our philosophy of special education services, as an obligation of the school district, has been maintained by allowing tuition fees only from districts, not from parents.

The same is true of transportation fees. We contract only with school districts, not with parents. What agreement or arrangement is reached between each school district and parents of exceptional children is up to the school district, not to the cooperative.

Since we have a parochial enrollment in the area, parochial children who need special education facilities transfer back into their public school district and from there are placed in special education.

PROBLEMS

Any cooperative program as well as any program in special education has certain problems relative to the fact that operations in special education are somewhat different than one finds in either elementary or secondary education.

Transportation is perhaps the largest problem in our cooperative program even though our children do not travel relatively large distances. We exist in an area of approximately 80 square miles with the majority of children being bussed to their special education classrooms. It is amazing that a simple thing like bus transportation, which has a minute part to play, can have such tremendous impact upon this program. Many of the children are picked up at their home, delivered to the program, and returned to their front steps. Some are carried up those steps. The overriding philosophy is basically to get the children to class. Since the placement of classes is dependent upon elementary schools where rooms are available, few children are placed within their own local area. In fact one finds children traveling ten miles one direction. Since the bus route of each bus is dependent upon a particular class, the child could easily travel 50 miles before getting to school, he thus could travel for over one and one half hours. We have managed to change the bus company's thinking on this problem to the point that no child travels more than one hour. Probably the majority of problems with transportation relate to the caliber of personnel driving buses, since the special needs of the children must be considered. For instance, some drivers fail to pick up children or the driver has not been informed that the child to be picked up is orthopedically handicapped and therefore the bus driver arrives at the home, sits in the bus and waits, while the mother of the child is inside the door with the child in a wheelchair waiting for the bus driver. Due to lack of communication the child is not taken to class. One bus driver could not make his scheduled run because he was taking his own child to school using the school bus and the child wasn't allowed in the building prior to 8:30 in the morning; therefore, until this problem was solved this bus was running thirty to thirty five minutes late every day.

It would seem that in establishing a transportation program for a cooperative there is the choice between having transportation arranged by the cooperative program or having it handled by the parent, and from what we have seen, the majority of parents are willing to assume this responsibility. In a number of cases, with the children in my own district, when an impasse has been reached between what potentially can take place in bus transportation versus the desires of the parent, the child has been taken out of the bus transportation pool and his transportation handled by his parent.

Another problem is whether or not there should be a fee for transportation. We have a number of arrangements according to the policies of various cooperative districts in Kansas. There is no policy in the cooperative as transportation is left on a fee or free basis with each district. Some districts pay the entire fee which is high compared to the transportation of nonexceptional children. Others mandate the same payment for exceptional children as for the non-exceptional. In my district, parents of both exceptional and nonexceptional children are expected to pay $6.50 per month for transportation with the district paying the remainder. Of course, transportation of the nonexceptional child costs much less than transportation of the exceptional child, but our decision was for equity.

Additional problems are found in the administrative area, and these relate to the director's relationship with the board of directors. They have not clearly defined for our director his responsibility and his relationship to the board. The resultant confusion is being cleared up by an adequate set of policies, rules, and regulations. Also in dealing with a ten member board composed of school administrators, the director must deal with a power structure and, depending upon the item under discussion, the power structure changes.

Other problems relate to the duties and functions of the director of special education for the cooperative. In Kansas, our director has a long distance to travel to reach program after program. Yet basically the director is also a supervisor, and until the program reaches that degree of sophistication at which supervisors become operational in the program, he must operate as a supervisor. Yet at the same time he is held to his office by finance, transportation, and relationship problems, and literally the director has to fight his way out of the office and into the classrooms, because this is what superintendents expect him to do. It seems that superintendents want to get directors of special education into the supervisory role. Yet the director has a special problem. His faculty is spread throughout the cooperative in various buildings under the jurisdiction of principals. If the special education teacher identifies with the faculty and administration of the building, the teacher is prone to program changes that relate his class more towards the accepted practices and principles inherent in the building, which may be detrimental to acceptable practice in special education. If the teacher relates to the special education director, the teacher risks isolation from the building faculty and perhaps illicits unfavorable responses from the building principal. The quandary exists whenever supervisory control is lacking and programs are spread over large geographical distances. But even in a well-balanced program where individualized special education programs are coterminous, nuances that limit the alternatives of choice both for the teacher and the director can exist and result in a limiting of administrative sufficiency and efficiency.

CONCLUSION

Basically the philosophy behind our program has been that special education services can be provided for all children regardless of the size of the school district. Student population and geological area are problems, but are not impossible to overcome. Through a cooperative arrangement, we are well on the road to providing for individual differences regardless of what they may be. This same program is feasible in any state, as long as there are administrators willing to cooperate one with another in a democratic fashion with the ultimate aim of helping all children in the satisfaction of their needs.

providing special educational services for exceptional youth*

When one considers American public education at this present stage of its evolution, one is immediately struck by the influence and impact of democratic personnel administration and supervision on the public schools. Education in the second half of this 20th century is "big business" in a literal sense. Just as industry has concerned itself with democratic personnel policies and practices, so educational administration at the local, intermediate and state levels has undergone a number of distinct changes. Present-day state educational departments, affected as they are by a mobile, industrialized and astronaut-conscious society, have been forced to recognize the need for a reorganization in structure and function to meet these changing demands. It is the purpose of this discussion to consider the functions and role of the modern state department of education, specifically in its provision of special educational services for exceptional children and youth.

CURRENT VIEWPOINT OF STATE DEPARTMENT FUNCTIONS

Local attitudes and understanding of the changing roles of state departments in modern public school

*Reprinted from *Exceptional Children*, Vol. 26 (April, 1960) pp. 395-400, by permission of the author and the Council for Exceptional Children. Copyright 1960 by the Council for Exceptional Children.

†Kenneth R. Blessing is Coordinator, Educational Services, Wisconsin State Department of Public Instruction.

education play an important part in the scope and extent of state supervision. When school districts originally existed in what might be termed educational isolation, state functions were purely statistical, clerical, and regulatory. Current philosophy with respect to state level administration and supervision suggests that the leadership functions of (1) *Planning*, (2) *Research*, (3) *Advising and Consulting*, (4) *Coordinating* and (5) *Public Relations* are infinitely more appropriate to the public school in this satellite age (1). Closely aligned with these leadership functions are those commonly referred to as *operational* and *regulatory*. However, leadership and service functions predominate and these services are being recognized as indispensable in correcting inequities in special education. Since antagonistic elements of local isolation and desire for local autonomy remain to effect the role played by state departments of education, these divisive elements must be made aware of their responsibility in challenging state departments to provide the quality of special education leadership essential in this era of compulsory school attendance. Out of the experience of the past a newer concept has evolved which recognizes that state departments and local units are partners in developing superior special education services for exceptional children and youth.

CONSULTATIVE NATURE OF STATE SUPERVISION

We might consider the modern point of view regarding the consultative function of supervision on the state level in the light of historical development of this function, and illustrate how democratic personnel practices, changing curricular needs, and evolving concepts of state functions are affecting special education. This point of view was reflected in some detail in the Wisconsin Department of Public Instruction's 35th Biennial Report to the Legislature (7). This philosophy should be evaluated by those concerned with state-local cooperation in order that better understanding and improvement in existing special services may result. Where weaknesses and inadequacies exist in terms of actual practices, local agencies should seek to stimulate state department personnel to a greater realization of their leadership and consultative roles.

The 35th Biennial Report (7) states that supervision on the state level seeks to be democratic in nature as it strives to stimulate the growth and development of local administrative and supervisory leadership. Under this kind of *leadership supervision* the finest educational experiences may be made available if stated principles are exercised in practice. Moore and Walters (4) have developed this principle in another framework when indicating that matters of human relationships among school personnel cannot be separated from the organization and the administrative function in either theory or practice.

HISTORICAL DEVELOPMENTS IN STATE SUPERVISORY PRACTICES

Supervision as a function of the state department is as old as the office of the state superintendent. During the century or more of its existence it has evolved through a number of stages including inspectorial, supervisory, and presently consultative. The day is past when state supervision was an accepted annual tyranny to be lived with while the state inspector was visiting the area. Emphasis during this stage was on the more tangible aspects of the school plant such as ventilation, lighting and heating of classrooms. During the supervisory stage strong emphasis on instructional techniques and practices was necessary to provide for inadequacies and gaps in the limited undergraduate training of teachers. Elsbree and Reutter (2) point to the historical role of supervision as being primarily a teacher-training function designed to bolster up programs that otherwise would have tottered because of the inadequate preparation of teachers for the tasks confronting them. Many temporary arrangements were made to meet the need for training prospective and experienced teachers, and such devices as institutes, summer schools and reading circles became popular. This concept of supervision continued throughout the nineteenth century and, until a few decades ago, principals and supervisors were looked upon as a kind of foreman who through close supervision helped to compensate for ignorance and lack of skill in their subordinates.

THE MODERN CONSULTATIVE FUNCTION OF STATE SUPER-VISION

The consultative point of view has evolved as a result of a number of educational developments including such factors as more competently trained instructors, newer concepts of child development and the idea that supervision as properly conceived has many of the same objectives as the modern curriculum program. Elbree and Reutter (2) have noted that many teachers today are commonly as well prepared in their field of specialization as are principals and supervisors in theirs. As the people in the states have recognized the state department's leadership role, they have encouraged, through their legislatures, the strengthening of department services by addition of qualified special supervisors, in such areas as transportation, mental health, driver education, school lunch, surplus property, school buildings and special education. However, the impact of child development theory and the influence of the child-centered curriculum have played a major role in effecting this change in function. Nevertheless, these same authors (2) feel that concepts underlying current supervisory practices in many school systems still have a stifling influence on the growth of teachers. Responsible freedom is essential for the release of a teacher's full creative potentialities. Schools must recognize that in the development of a well-informed, effective citizenry, democratic practices must begin with and pervade the school and the individual classroom, and to be an effective democratic leader a teacher must be free to exercise her talents within the framework of democratic personnel organization and administration. Other authorities have pointed out the urgent need to establish principles and patterns of democratic personnel administration since present personnel policies are as varied as the differences in district and community size.

Wisconsin's state department supervisors have expressed their point of view in the following principles:

1. If special curriculum properly means group study, so special supervision should use consultation and group methods.
2. If special curriculum should focus on the exceptional child, so should supervision.

Therefore, to achieve these ends, state special education supervisors should:

1. Assist local leaders in helping all teachers to gain a better understanding of children and particularly exceptional children.
2. Assist local leaders in helping teachers provide for meeting individual needs, and particularly those of the atypical child.
3. Help local leaders evaluate the total educational program. Are services available for deviate children which help equalize educational opportunities?
4. Focus major attention upon the complex school program rather than upon the work of the individual classroom.
5. Recognize that in general more effective use can be made of a special supervisor's time if he works with *groups* of teachers rather than with individuals. Democratic principles

for teacher participation should be observed in group consultation by the state supervisor if this method is to produce an improvement in instruction.

6. Welcome requests to serve as a special education consultant, recognizing that most effective help can be given in response to call.
7. Help local leaders with their continuous programs of school improvement.

ADMINSTRATIVE AND CONSULTATIVE FUNCTIONS OF STATE SPECIAL EDUCATION PERSONNEL

With this point of view in mind regarding consultative and leadership functions, let us examine the nature of the work performed by state supervisors of special education as well as the competencies required by these individuals to carry out their duties. The duties of most special education supervisors may be divided into two broad general categories: (1) *Administrative* and (2) *Consultative*.

Under *the administrative function* are found such responsibilities as the operation of residential schools for the deaf and blind; the formulation of state policies and standards to assure efficiency in management and safeguards for minimum performance of teaching responsibilities; the preparation of budgets; the development and evaluation of legislation affecting exceptional children and the distribution of state aids for encouragement to communities providing special services. As states have increased their financial participation in local special education services, greater state interest has been expressed in concern for the prudent and economical expenditure of these funds on an equalized basis, thus assuring all exceptional children opportunities for maximal growth and learning.

The consultative functions include such activities as assistance to local communities in establishing new programs; the evaluation of existing special services in local areas; research activities pointed toward educational improvement; formulation of long-term policies and objectives; the provision of leadership in the up-grading of local services beyond the minimal standards set; the pre-service and in-service education of special education teachers throughout the state; the integration and coordination of special services with the total school programs and with the programs of other non-educational agencies serving exceptional children; the determination of pupil eligibility through complete diagnosis and psychological evaluation; the preparation of bulletins, publications, and curricular materials designed to improve instruction; and the public relations activities designed to acquaint the legislatures, communities and parents with information regarding the status and progress of special education in the respective states.

DUAL NATURE OF
STATE SUPERVISION

It should be immediately apparent that, unlike local consultant services, state supervision has a dual nature or role; that is, personnel are required by statute to carry out regulatory-supervisory tasks as well as perform consultative functions. In a sense, state personnel in the past have been somewhat handicapped by this dual function, since most authorities in educational administration are agreed that consultative service should be freed from regulatory control in order to most efficiently serve teachers. Moore and Walters (4) have stressed the point that the modern consultant or supervisor should have a "staff relationship" charged with the improvement of instruction. Use of such terms as "coordinator" or "helping teacher" in local systems has been designed to improve criticism of and objection to supervisory function by certain critical groups.

Rorer (5) is also critical of consultative service linked with regulatory control. Discussing the historical evolution of school supervisory practices this author states, "Having the authority and being held responsible for results, the tendency was strong for supervisory officers to tell the teacher both what to teach and how to teach. Hence inspectional concepts of supervision soon developed autocratic methods of handling teachers and directing the instructional activities." This authority concludes that supervision and administration are correlative, coordinate and complementary functions of education having as their common purpose the provision of all means and conditions favorable to better learning and teaching.

In the light of this modern point of view regarding the division of consultative and regulatory functions, we might raise the question as to how state department special education personnel may resolve this dual function problem to the advantage of those concerned and still perform those tasks delegated to them under state law. We might inquire, too, as to the role of the local community and the local schools in minimizing state regulatory controls, thereby strengthening the state's leadership and consultative functions. In order to resolve this issue we should first examine the competencies needed by personnel at the state level who are responsible for special services to exceptional children with particular reference to democratic principles required to establish the consultative approach to improvement of instruction.

COMPETENCIES NEEDED BY STATE CONSULTANTS

A report developed jointly by the United States Office of Education and professional workers in the field of special education, *Special Education Personnel in State Departments of Education*, (3) has attempted to outline the personal characteristics required of state department personnel in this area. It is assumed that all members of the educational profession should possess tact, patience, and an understanding of children as well as self-understanding, creativeness, resourcefulness, optimism and a high code of professional ethics. Over and above these common competencies required by all educators, however, the worker with exceptional children must be motivated by a strong interest in children who deviate from the so-called "norm" and must be both physically healthy and emotionally well-adjusted. State special education personnel especially must be physically strong to withstand the rigors of a type of work which requires constant and extensive travel, frequent night engagements, the strain of heavy responsibilities and constant appearances before parent, community and educational groups.

The ultimate goal of the state worker is equalized educational opportunites for all exceptional children, and to effectively realize these goals with groups contacted, the state supervisor must have a philosophy and operating techniques which are based upon democratic principles of group leadership and participation. His work brings him into contacts with persons from various economic and social stratas in a multitude of situations. Examples of the types of groups affected by his democratic practices are parent organizations, special teachers and other auxiliary workers, school boards, county boards, and civic and fraternal organizations. His effectiveness in the leadership role has a direct relationship to the democratic practices he brings to group discussions and meetings.

The state worker must recognize that when discussing common problems with teachers and administrators in local communities his consultative function is to maintain the common viewpoint. Group participation in curriculum development, staff policy formation, and the extension of services is encouraged in terms of felt needs, fair hearings for all discussants, and a program of action to follow. When conflicts arise the consultant serves as a catalytic agent and assists in the development of constructive processes of problem solving within the groups. According to Savage (6) consultants should participate in group discussions but remain in the background in such a manner that the group clarifies its own thinking and is made to feel that the decisions rendered are of their own for- mation. On the other hand, this author believes the special education consultant must understand that in specific situations, school personnel want direct "expert" answers, analyses, and recommendations with the opportunity and the reserved right to accept, modify or reject the suggestions and recommendations they receive.

It is obvious that because of the nature of his responsibilities, the state consultant or supervisor ought to possess characteristics which make him both socially and professionally acceptable in order that he may be effective in promoting programs with lay individuals and professional educators. Desirable personality traits of adaptabil- ity and flexibility are required to meet these social situations effectively.

Certainly one of the characteristics of any person engaged in professional work is growth and knowledge, skill and understanding in his chosen area of specialization. If the state consultant is to assume the role of leadership throughout the state he must be thoroughly informed of new developments in all fields of special education as well as in the area of specialization. His training and experience as a supervisor of special education should help him to understand the problems of administration which he encounters in regular education and help to adjust the special service to the local program with the least disruption as is possible. In order to be respected by teachers in special education he must be at least as reasonably competent in the actual teaching of such children in his specialty as any worker in a local program in his state. In order to have achieved this position the state worker must, in addition to adequate training, have had wide experience in his field. This point of view is expressed throughout the U. S. Office of Education report (3). The state consultant operates from a peculiar vantage point since through classroom observations and discussions with special teachers, the consultant obtains ideas regarding special techniques, teaching aids and devices which can be distributed to and discussed with individuals and groups. Since state special education consultants assist local specialists and special teachers rather than working directly with children they must understand the so-called "supervisory techniques." They must merit confidence through their personal competence and professional training rather than through the prestige of the position which they hold.

The U. S. Office of Education report (3) emphasizes competencies required in assisting local communities in inaugurating new programs of special education. The special consultant must be able to analyze needs, organize community surveys, determine the most proper course of action to follow and must possess the qualities of leadership to get communities started on programs. Understanding of human nature, skill in group dynamics, and adjustability are required in such situations.

Competencies are required in evaluating pupil personnel and in using psychological techniques to determine and recommend the best possible solution to individual problems of children. Too frequently the consultant's services are requested in the hope that the community may solve its problem by the exclusion of the child from school. The consultant must use his skills in determining *the best solution for the child*, and if this involves adjustment in the school program commensurate with the child's handicap, tact and understanding are required to assist school administrators, teachers and parents to accept the proper course of action to be followed.

These then are some of the competencies required of state personnel responsible for the special education of handicapped children. The writer has stressed the need for democratic personnel practices and the consultant point of view. We have by no means exhausted the competencies required to help resolve the dual nature of state supervision, but it is believed those discussed are illustrative of the "ideal" in state supervision. Nevertheless, if we set our sights high, state supervisory functions will be improved and aimed at leadership and coordinative functions while de-emphasizing the regulatory roles.

STATE SUPERVISORY
WEAKNESSES

In analyzing existing weaknesses of state supervisory practices, we might point up a number of recognized inadequacies at both state and local levels and ask ourselves what local schools can do to strengthen the state special education services and assure themselves of improved democratic supervision. The previous discussion has considered the "ideal state consultant" and our aim is to strive toward this level of competency. One area, according to the U. S. Office of Education report (3) which might bear investigation is the method of selection of state personnel for positions in special education. To what extent do civil service regulations influence decisions and determine the quality of consultant service? It may be necessary to carefully analyze the duties performed by state workers as well as the competencies required, in order that civil service requirements be up-graded in this respect.

Since state department workers must frequently learn from the "hard school of experience" many of the requirements of their position, it may be necessary for the colleges and universities preparing special education workers to evaluate their training programs to determine special courses and competencies required or greater areas of emphasis needed in existing courses so that improved preservice and in-service training of state personnel is brought about. Implementation of Public Law 85-926 should accelerate this evaluation process in at least one area of exceptionality, *i.e.*, in preparatory programs for leadership positions in the field of the mentally retarded. Through the establishment of regional graduate training centers it may be anticipated that future state consultants and directors of educational programs for the retarded, as well as others in leadership roles, will more closely approximate the "ideal" level of competency previously referred to.

There is another element to be considered in analyzing present inadequacies in state consultative services. Too frequently local school authorities and state department staffs assume that direct state staff supervision of local classroom instruction is necessary and a primary function. Beach (1) has pointed out that this concept of state consultant service is basically unsound and not in harmony with the American concept of local self-determination. Supervision of classroom instruction, in most instances, is and should be a local responsibility and state staff supervision of individual instruction, even when cleared with local authorities, sets up barriers to the consultative function. State supervisors should center their supervisory emphasis upon the strengthening of local supervisory services and more effectively utilize their time through consultative service to groups or to local school authorities, according to Beach (1). Others (2) have reiterated this point of view by stressing the fact that the supervisory process is indirect as far as influencing experienced teachers, and that it involves working with groups of teachers rather than with individuals. Furthermore, these authors believe that adult behavior is seldom permanently improved through direct appraisal and criticism.

LOCAL ADMINISTRATIVE WEAKNESSES

Local school practices strengthen or impede the state's leadership function in a number of ways. When local systems fail to maintain the minimum standards established by state departments they tend to stimulate regulatory and inspectorial aspects of state supervision while creating barriers to consultative leadership. When local school administrators and school boards are overly concerned about obtaining increased state aids without parallel improvements in special education services or when unwarranted claims for state reimbursements are made the inspectorial function frequently must be exerted.

Specific examples of these types of practices are continuing local efforts to use special services for the mentally retarded as "catch-all" units for behavioral, remedial, and emotionally disturbed children. Despite the fact that state laws specifically mention mental handicap as a criteria for service, efforts are exerted to have other types of handicap serviced by the teacher of the retarded, in some instances denying fringe and rural retarded youth the benefits of these services. Failure to maintain state recommended minimum and maximum enrollments or to maintain adequate physical facilities for special education stimulates the regulatory function. Lack of cooperative efforts on the part of local school administrators in encouraging personnel to meet minimal state certificiation requirements in special education hamper the state's effort to upgrade professional status and training. Criteria established for state reimbursement to communities with special education services are frequently over-looked in local attempts to include budget items not approvable for state aids.

These are a few illustrations of ways in which local districts develop barriers to local-state cooperative planning and coordination of services. If local areas would adhere to basic foundational criteria established by state departments, less state level inspectorial and regulatory controls would be required of state personnel and they would in turn be freed to discharge their more important functions of consultation, advising, planning, research, coordination and public relations.

SUMMARY AND CONCLUSIONS

In summary, this paper has discussed the dual nature of state department specialists in education of exceptional children and youth by examining the modern point of view regarding the "consultative" nature of state supervision. The bases and source of state administrative authority and responsibility were explored from a historical vantage point as well as the nature and extent of state control over special services and teaching personnel. The influence of technological and industrial society, greater understanding of child growth and development, and the influence of the child-centered curriculum were outlined in detail as factors affecting this changing concept of state supervision.

Competencies required by state consultants, as well as presently existing inadequacies at both state and local levels were examined in an effort to resolve the dual nature of the state supervisory function; that is, consultative, coordinative, and leadership versus inspectorial and regulatorial. The point was emphasized that the state's role is to set basic minimum foundations and exert leadership in assisting local communities in "exceeding" these minimums. Barriers to these leadership services were exemplified in illustrations of non-cooperative practices at the local level. These barriers need to be removed and more effective lines of communication opened up between state and local school officials if progress is to be made and special education is to be improved and extended.

In conclusion, the development of satisfactory units of local control through school district reorganization, and the improvement of organization and functions at the state department level through the up-grading of staff competencies will have the long range effect of improved educational services for exceptional children. The state department and local organizations must be partners in discharging this state responsibility, and when democratic principles are applied in actual practice, these more immediate and long range goals will be achieved. The results will be to the direct advantage of all concerned with our most precious inheritance, the children and future citizens of the respective states.

BIBLIOGRAPHY

1. Beach, Fred F. *The Functions of State Departments of Education*, U. S. Office of Education, Miscellaneous #12 Washington, 1950, 70p.
2. Elsbree, W. S. and Reutter, E. S. *Staff Personnel in the Public Schools*, Prentice-Hall, Inc., New York, 1954, 438p.
3. Mackie, Romaine P., and Snyder, Walter E., *Special Education Personnel in State Departments of Education*, Washington U. S. Government Printing Office, 1957. (Office of Education, Bulletin 1956, No. 6), 49p.
4. Moore, H. E., and Walter, N. B. *Personnel Administration in Education*, Harper Bros., Publishers, New York, 1955, 476p.

5. Rorer, John A. *Principles of Democratic Supervision*, Bureau of Publications, Teachers College, Columbia University, New York, 1942, 230p.
6. Savage, William W. "The Value of State Consultative Service," *Administrator's Notebook*, Vol. IV, No. 3, November, 1955, 4p.
7. *35th Biennial Report of the Superintendent of Public Instruction*, 1949-51. Issued by the State Superintendent of Schools, Department of Public Instruction, Madison, Wisconsin, 1952, 158p.

section C

special education services in sparsely populated areas

The traditional problems associated with the functional implementation of special education programs in urban districts are compounded in rural and sparsely populated areas. Problems related to organization, finance, personnel and supportive services present almost insurmountable obstacles to the adequate development of special education in these areas. Until recently, very

167

little discussion of this problem or programming of significance has been reported.

There is a paucity of published information relative to designs and strategies for special education in sparsely populated areas. One notable exception was the timely and major conference dealing with this subject which was co-sponsored in 1966 by the Western Interstate Commission for Higher Education and the Montana State Department of Public Instruction. The following article resulted from this national research conference and highlights the problem of providing special education in sparsely populated areas.

*administrative organization**

ROBERT M. ISENBERG†

The existing and traditional arrangements for administering schools in sparsely populated areas do not lend themselves readily to, and in fact generally preclude, the provision of special education services. Vast land areas, scattered population, and a low incidence of children having particular special needs become obstacles for the development of service programs requiring highly trained and scarce personnel and specialized facilities and equipment. Local school districts, large in geographic area but small in enrollment, are not an appropriate base for administering comprehensive special education programs. Continued district reorganization and consolidation will not substantially alter this lack of appropriateness. Obviously necessary is the development of new administrative patterns which can reconcile these circumstances.

BACKGROUND INFORMATION

Any exploration of new or innovative organizational approaches must take full account of certain distinct realities.

1. There is no inherent value in any organizational framework. It is nothing more than a vehicle which permits program

*Reprinted from *Sparsely Populated Areas: Guidelines for Research*, pp. 4-8, by permission of the author and the Western Interstate Commission for Higher Education, 1966.

†Robert M. Isenberg is Associate Secretary, American Association of School Administrators, National Education Association.

development. Nonetheless, there must be structure before there can be function.

2. Public education is the legal responsibility of each individual state. However much a state legislature may delegate administrative authority for programs of development and implementation, it cannot divest itself of ultimate responsibility. Where structural modifications, adaptations, or innovations go beyond present legislative provisions, additional legislative action will be required.

3. Adaptations or innovations in administrative organization for extending educational services in sparsely populated areas must be in harmony with, or at least cognizant of, educational organizational arrangements which already exist.

4. New administrative patterns for extending special education services to sparsely populated areas should be designed in such a way that they incorporate, or at least operate harmoniously with, those programs of special education which are now in operation.

5. The greater the degree of sparsity, the more likely it may be necessary to provide state level direction, coordination, and financing.

6. The development of administrative patterns within the framework of educational organization should take fully into account other public and private organizations and agencies and the services they provide. Coordination among agencies and the avoidance of duplication should have high priority.

7. The development of special education programs derives much of its thrust from other than internal administrative forces — parent groups, legislatures, private organizations, etc. Providing direction for these forces requires extraordinary professional leadership.

8. Adequate and appropriate special education programs administered in the most efficient way possible will be high cost programs. The conditions and circumstances peculiar to each state are likely to be the greatest determiner of the kind(s) of administrative pattern(s) which might appropriately be developed. It is doubtful that there is any one best way, any single uniform pattern of organization that would fit all states with equal appropriateness. Whatever type or pattern of arrangement is devised, the organizational framework within which special education programs are provided should be (a) an integral part of the state school system, i.e.,

part of the structure that provides education for all children, and (b) capable of undertaking other than special education functions.

Recognizing that the need to develop some kind of administrative organization with comprehensive special education services capability requires a multidistrict approach immediately suggests some type of regional agency. Such an agency in a sparsely settled area may be a county or multicounty area or may have no relationship to existing political boundaries other than those of the separate local school districts which comprise the service area. Degree of population sparsity, coupled with the nature of the local school districts in the area to be served, the total state financial plan for education, the special education program requirements, and the readiness to adopt new organizational patterns, provides a basis for determining how large the geographical area for regional program development might be and the degree to which this area should conform to existing political boundaries. There is much room for flexibility.

Certain desirable characteristics for a regional service agency or area special education program can be identified, however. The program should (a) be organized to serve all types of exceptional children; (b) provide or have access to a complete diagnostic team and diagnostic facilities; (c) be closely associated with all the health, welfare, and other agencies and resources of the area; (d) have the ability to provide or assume the necessary followup services for all exceptional children; and (e) provide leadership that can coordinate all the special education efforts in the area.

This concept of a regional agency or area (multidistrict) program is not to suggest that all children having special needs should be brought to a center. Most activities carried on would actually be more effective in operation in local school districts and local school buildings. What seems important if sparsely populated areas are to be served is providing leadership, administration, and coordination on an area basis so that planning, the employment and deployment of staff specialists, and program adaptation can be carried on in an efficient and effective manner.

Providing special education services in sparsely settled areas requires an administrative structure with enough flexibility to use a wide range of techniques in program implementation:

1. Moving children — full or part time.
2. Moving staff — full or part time.

3. Utilizing state institutions.
4. Utilizing foster homes.
5. Establishing small boarding homes. (The school home might be a desirable alternative to a residential school for handicapped children in sparsely settled areas — a temporary, perhaps only five days per week and nine months per year, foster home simulation.)
6. Bringing parents and children to centers.
7. Developing new modes of contact — radio, television, and telephone.
8. Providing inservice education for regular teachers and principals to permit them, with supervision, to work more effectively with children with special needs.
9. Preparing rural specialists in special education to perform this inservice education function.

Any or all of the above approaches may be utilized by a single administrative organization or by a combination of school agencies operating at different levels in the structure.

PROBLEM AREAS FOR RESEARCH

The development of administrative patterns suited to providing special education services in sparsely settled areas could be greatly facilitated by completion of certain systematic studies.

There is an absence of information regarding children living in sparsely populated areas and having special education needs.

1. Who are they? Where are they? What do they need? Are they being served now? From what sources and how are they receiving help? What about those in rural subcultures? Those who are excluded from school? Those who are out of school?
2. What is the mobility pattern for these children? Are they likely to remain in or near their home community or go elsewhere?
3. What occupational opportunities are available to them?
4. What educational program leads can be derived from such information?
5. How might such data be used in developing a program or service index that could be used in educational planning?

There is need for a serious exploration of the potential of an area program approach in selected sparsely populated states.

1. Is it feasible to create service areas with boundaries different from towns, cities and counties?
2. Is it possible to provide area direction and coordination of a program in such a way that the local school districts served are strengthened? In such a way that the program is responsive to the unique circumstances of local school districts? In such a way that a variety of approaches and techniques are used and tested? In a way that assures sufficient flexibility to meet changing needs and circumstances? In a way that makes maximum use of the services and resources of other institutions and resources — public and private agencies, colleges and universities, state education departments, etc.? In a way that a pattern for statewide development might be evolved?

There is need to explore the potential of regional programs which cut across state lines.

1. Is there merit in developing interstate planning and services? Might such an effort be gauged broadly enough to include health, welfare, and rehabilitation interests, as well as education?
2. Can strategies regarding the preparation and assignment of personnel, the utilization of certain facilities, and the conduct of research and demonstration efforts be developed?

There is need for an intensive study of existing administrative patterns for providing special education services.

1. What are the various types of area programs now in operation?
2. What are their organizational characteristics? How are functions allocated and responsibilities assigned?
3. How adequate are the programs provided? How efficient? What are the organizational strengths and weaknesses? What special problems do they encounter?
4. How do they relate to local school districts? To the state education department? To the total state system of schools?

5. Does the area nature of program operation encounter special difficulties in working with other agencies?
6. How much flexibility do they have for program adaptation? For extending special education services? For undertaking other than special education functions?

There is a particular need to strengthen state leadership in special education in states having vast areas of sparse population.

1. Can effective state leadership provide the encouragement and direction for local and area pilot projects?
2. Can a statewide pattern for service be evolved through such a procedure?

There is a need for developing a central registry of all handicapped children.

1. Is it not possible to avoid expensive diagnostic duplications when these children move from one community, area, or state to another? Can there be immediate identification of their need to be cared for in the event of the death of their parents or guardian? Do states now have such a registry?
2. Could one be organized and maintained?
3. What program contributions would access to such information have?
4. Is this a means of keeping track of those who leave residential institutions? Might such a registry be an extension of service?

section D

recurring and emerging issues

*a crisis in evaluation**

MAYNARD C. REYNOLDS[†]

About three-quarters of a billion dollars were appropriated for this year by the United States Congress to support new school programs for "educationally deprived" children. Next year the appropriation is expected to be higher. The legislative reference is to Title I of Public Law 89-10, which is the single most significant enactment within a broad pattern of legislation which has created a large and, in many ways, new federal partner in educational affairs of the United States at elementary and secondary school levels.

I wish to underline two things about this legislation and the programs it supports. The first is the emphasis upon innovation. A community which offers preschool classes, speech correction, psychological services, or other specialized programs will usually qualify for federal support if and only if the service is new. As a result, thousands of school districts are taking on new functions this year. The political leaders and the new administrators in the expanding federal educational bureaucracy are saying, in effect:

> *The school programs of the past have been held too closely to the mainstream; there has been too little change; by their very organization and emphases, schools have compounded the problems of neglected children. Create more*

*Reprinted from *Special Education: Strategies for Educational Progress* (April 1966), pp. 251-258, by permission of the author and the Council for Exceptional Children. Copyright 1966 by the Council for Exceptional Children.

†Maynard C. Reynolds is Director, Special Education, University of Minnesota.

*streams. Broaden the options. So serious is the problem
that we hereby allocate most of the federal educational
resource to the support of new programs.*

The second point of emphasis is the insistance upon program evaluation. Every project under Title I of PL 89-10 requires a report of evaluation. Many of us have not yet begun to realize the wide implications of this requirement. It certainly proposes a radical change in the habits of educators. Miles (1964, p. 657) reports that "educational innovations are almost never evaluated on a systematic basis." This conclusion is supported by recent reviews made in our two most populous states (Johnson, 1964: Brickell, 1961). The evaluation problem created as part of the new federal support program is now rising and rolling toward us and will soon reach shock wave intensity. Of course, we've always had an evaluation problem, but until now it has usually been relegated to some dark place for hiding.

A unique and rigorous test is being placed upon the schools of the United States this year. After years of talk, federal support became a reality. Planning and discussion were perfectly open for all to see for a long time, and even the time interval from authorization to appropriation on PL 89-10 was long enough to give fair warning to those who wished to hear and to plan ahead. But how well were the schools organized for change? How effectively is the shift from talk to action taking place?

I see some failure and some clear success, but mostly a barely passing performance this first year. Many problems of long standing have become visible just in trying to design and launch new services — problems such as inadequate staffing of state education offices, inadequate school district size, personnel shortages, and general inflexibility in meeting new problems. These early difficulties should stir us to help mobilize the forces necessary for improvement.

My guess is that even surpassing the present difficulties in organizing new programs will be the problems of evaluation. Little preparation has been made for this phase of present developments, and again some fundamental and longstanding problems are likely to come to surface. Failures and successes here may not be highly visible in the short range, but they can be of crucial significance in longer range.

THE PURPOSE OF EVALUATION

We sometimes think of evaluation in very threatening terms. Especially if funds for a project come by special grant from an external source do we fall easily into thinking about evaluation as a kind of final positive plea made just before the verdict on project renewal is reached. This puts evaluation into a kind of good-bad, general accounting framework.

Reflection quickly suggests the futility and even the danger of such an orientation. The most important requirement of an evaluation is that it reveal as objectively and as fully as possible what is happening as a result of the project. It should show the specific abilities or other attributes that are developing among pupils, the extent of such developments, and the interactions among pupil characteristics and other variables as the project proceeds. Out of this kind of knowledge, programs can be improved! The purpose of evaluation in education is simply to contribute to improvements in instruction — certainly not to justify projects.

A SPECIAL RESPONSIBILITY

The field of special education has a particular responsibility in this context, partly because it has been favored as an area of emphasis in recent legislation. Many of the new programs under Title I of PL 89-10, for example, are designed to serve handicapped and gifted children. But other forces also serve to bring a spotlight to special education at this time. Our field is ripe for innovation because of a new and more open attitude. We're less sure today than we were even a few years ago about the potentialities of the children in our classrooms. Perhaps we have less to be defensive about than some other fields, just because we are of a mood to admit that old base rates for educational progress aren't very stable or very impressive.

This changing outlook undoubtedly has roots in many social and economic conditions and forces. Organized parent groups, insisting that their handicapped children can and should be helped, have been a goading external force of great influence. But there has also been much ferment in the community of those who think mainly of research and theory.

Besides "Batman" reruns, we're seeing frequent reruns these days on the nature-nurture studies of the 1930's and later. Recent reviews suggest that although many of the early studies were faulty in details, the total weight of all evidence suggesting the importance of environmental determinants of functional intelligence cannot be neglected (Hunt, 1961). A few recent practical demonstrations, such as Kirk's (1958) preschool study of the influence of school programs and the price of educational neglect on the intellectual development of children, have added force to a shift in views. The view which is emerging does not ignore genetic factors, but it does encourage a more optimistic outlook concerning the extent to which the achievements of children can be influenced by particular kinds of efforts. Many of the interesting new programs in special education grow out of this optimistic framework.

A growing and more radical general influence is a resurgence of the psychology of the empty organism — the view that behavior can be understood in surface or peripheral terms. The central procedure of the behavior modifiers a la Skinner is operant conditioning, which simply involves rewarding desired behavior (or approximations of it) thereby shaping the behavior and influencing the probability of its reoccurrence. Those who are committed to this highly environ-mentalistic outlook have generated a great deal of openness and optimism. McClelland (1965) has classed them with religious missionaries in the sense that they believe so strongly that almost any human behavior can be changed if only one approaches the task with conviction, appropriate techniques, and patience. Scholars of this persuasion have great appeal to teachers, because they accept a very practical test for their ideas. That test is simply: does it work? Many new projects may be observed in special education which grow out of the specific ideas of Skinner (1953) and his associates.

The intellectual ferment also includes elements quite opposite to those of the operant conditioners — an emphasis upon central structure and processes, especially cognitive structure and processes. Those of this persuasion insist that much more is involved in understanding complex behavior than knowing about environmental contacts and reinforcement histories. (Between sensory input and responses are mediational processes of varying degrees of com-plexity.) A great many new programs are being launched in special education which have their theoretical base in theories relating to cognitive development and intellective processes.

However different and conflicting the theories may be, there appear to be a few common themes, including a more open view concerning human potentialities and a special emphasis upon the early years of life as the period of greatest modifiability. I cite these somewhat theoretical notions not because they are uniquely relevant to special education, but simply because special educators, more than other educators, have been paying attention to the theoreticians and vice versa, with the result that thinking and innovative developments in our field have been influenced markedly by theory.

Much impetus and specific forms for innovation grow from this surge of ideas. There is some danger that theorists will recruit teachers to their views prematurely and that we will get a kind of "choosing of sides" among educators. The desirable course for teachers is to proceed with the innovative developments proposed by theory, but to maintain a rigid objectivity in testing outcomes.

THE VALUES IN EVALUATION

Imbedded not very deeply in the word evaluation, yet often repressed, is the base word "value." This suggests a pause to think carefully about what it is we are trying to accomplish in our programs — what it is we value. It is not enough simply to measure what we're doing to test whether present programs are effective, nor do statistical tests of differences tell us whether differences are really important. The question is: what ought we to be doing in the schools for exceptional children? This is by no means entirely a technical question.

A bit of history shows how fickle we have been about the values represented in special education curricula for the handicapped. At various times and places we have seemed to slant our values toward vocational training, development of personality and motivation, academic skills, simple relief to parents, social adjustment, sheer happiness, or use of leisure time. We seem all too ready to let new curricula or technology sway our objectives. Today there seems to be a strong surge of interest in what has been called a kind of intellectual plainsmanship. "Find the child's weaknesses or disabilities and remedy them" is a common theme.

Let me illustrate the problem further by citing a few specific concerns about what it is we ought to accomplish. Some observers note that in present programs, retarded children tend to become outer directed or greatly sensitive to cues from other people, rather than inner directed, self-reliant, and forthright in their behavior. Do we think this is desirable for them, perhaps as a precondition to the greater degree of supervision they may require from others? Or do we regard this as a specific problem to be avoided by teaching them in ways which make them more self-reliant or inner directed? I believe we can and do influence children on this variable. What's your choice?

Should everyone learn to read, even if it involves agonizing difficulties and great sacrifices in other kinds of learning? How much time and attention should be given to teaching directly for intellectual development of the retarded? How successful do we need to be in such efforts to justify neglect of other dimensions of learning in which modifiability may be greater? Under what circumstances is it justifiable to teach children a communications system (such as manual methods for the deaf) which is usable only in special and very small social systems? How much time can we justify spending on teaching severely crippled children to walk?

These are difficult questions which must be answered in specifics, not glossed over in highly abstract terms. When we have been clear about what it is we want to accomplish, we can then proceed to teach and to put yardsticks on the operation to gauge success and to plan improvements.

THE MEASUREMENT PROBLEM

It would be a happy circumstance, of course, if all the needed technical background for this next step — measuring program variables — were well established, but unfortunately that is not the case. Indeed, we have only a dawning awareness of some problems in this sphere.

One of the difficult problems is concerned with measuring change or growth. To assess the effects of a treatment, we are often interested in changes that take place in children during a specific interval of time. Commonly we give pretests and posttests and look at the differences which individuals show during the interval as growth or change. It all seems simple, but appearance is deceiving. An indication of the problem is that on variables of interest in education we so often get negative correlations between measures of change and measures of beginning status. What is becoming clear is that instruments which are useful in measuring current status may not be useful for measuring change. The measurement of change presents its own distinct problems of reliability and validity (Harris, 1962).

The problem of measuring change can be seen most clearly at the level of evaluating individual progress. If we have repeated measures of individual children, we're likely to find that those of high achievement tend not to be changing much, and those of lowest achievement show highest gains — whether judged in raw score or grade score terms. Such observations may result simply from technical problems of measurement. Unfortunately, there are no neat solutions to this problem as it concerns individual pupils. I mention it here because there are so many misinterpretations of measurements on this point.

A closely related and equally fundamental difficulty concerns the ability of most of our present tests to differentiate among groups receiving different treatments. Almost all of the tests commonly used in the schools have been constructed by techniques which serve to accentuate differences among individuals. Thus, in the typical experimental paradigm of pretest-treat-posttest, we get wide variations among individuals on both the pretest and the posttest. For purposes of comparing one method against another, however, it would be better to have near zero mean scores and zero variability at the beginning of the experiment, with posttest results showing substantial means and variances. Tests to serve in this way would be exceedingly difficult to construct. They would need to be developed by techniques which are specific to the problem of differentiating treatment differences, rather than individual differences (Glaser, 1963).

A third closely related technical problem, one which is particularly bothersome in special education, relates to regression effect. When we select children for special programs on the basis of very high or very low performance on some measuring device, it is almost inevitable that they will tend to be less deviant on a retest, even if given the next day. Those who score low initially will go up and those who score high initially will tend, in relative terms, to score lower on the retest.

Many reports of special education research appear to show most striking treatment effects in the initial part of the study. It is difficult in such cases to justify arguing for treatment effects against the simpler hypothesis of mere regression effects. A similar observation may be made when several measures are taken on individual children. Even if tested the next day, children will tend to show improvements on their lowest scores and decrements on the variables where they initially scored high. These circumstances frequently lead to misleading interpretations of the effects of remedial programs. Fortunately, definite corrective actions can be taken to avoid such misinterpretations through use of control groups for comparison purposes.

There are, of course, many other measurement problems. For example, Guilford (1959) is undoubtedly correct in his view that present school measuring devices tend to emphasize mere awareness, retention, and single answer problem solving. We badly need to develop procedures for assessment of evaluative abilities and productive thinking of more diverse forms. If we wish to teach for abilities in this expanded domain, then we must somehow begin to assess individual and group pupil progress over a similarly expanded domain. Deep issues and problems exist which are concerned with norming, range restriction, and format of scales specially created for exceptional groups.

PSYCHOLOGICAL BARRIERS TO EVALUATION

An equally serious problem is a tendency to avoid careful evaluation of creations for which we feel special responsibility. This problem is certainly not unique to special education. Kendall (1964) has said:

> *. . . creators of experimental programs often impress one as being men of conviction who have little question about the efficacy of the changes they have introduced. They know that the courses thay have developed are the best possible under existing conditions; and in the light of this assumed fact, systematic evaluation seems superfluous (p. 344).*

Brickell's (1964) study of innovation in schools of New York state led him to this somewhat similar comment:

> *. . . design, evaluation and dissemination are three distinctly different, irreconcilable processes. The circumstances which are right for one are essentially wrong for others. Furthermore, most people prefer to work in one place, and find working in the others uncomfortable if not distasteful. People preferring different places often have an abrasive effect on each other when brought into close contact (pp. 497-498).*

A further comment from Brickell (1964) is insightful: "Almost every research specialist the writer met in a local school system seemed somehow misplaced. His desire to hold a new program steady in order to evaluate it ran headlong into the teachers' urge to change it as soon as they sensed something wrong" (p. 498).

The three phases of innovation as outlined by Brickell — design, evaluation, dissemination — make a proper sequence, but the clear fact is that almost always we have skipped the middle step. Perhaps this is because it is so difficult, expensive, and intrinsically threatening to subject our programs to test. If Brickell is correct (as I think he is) in saying that different people will often be involved in design and evaluation, then evaluative efforts may also involve personal confrontations that are threatening.

The major thesis of my remarks is that despite all the difficulties, we must proceed in all seriousness to evaluate programs. Design and evaluation must be seen not as competing activities (the latter only delaying and denying needed services), but rather as necessary parts of a sequence and broader cycles of activities designed to build programs that are dependable and worthy of our high responsibility.

SOME POSSIBLE GUIDELINES

I do not have solutions, much less tidy ones, to all of the above problems; but I would like to reflect a bit on a few possible approaches to solutions. Above all other suggestions, perhaps, is the simple one that we turn more attention, talent, and time — and the sooner, the better — to problems of evaluation. But let us proceed to a few somewhat more specific considerations.

The Questions We Ask

There has been a tendency in the recent past to over emphasize large questions when we think about evaluation. In the past decade, for example, there have been a number of studies concerned with comparing the efficacy of regular classes and special classes for retarded children. I agree with the Robinsons (1965), who say that few of these studies deserve serious review. The main difficulty with most of these studies is that they started with a group of children already in special classes and then proceeded to compare them with control groups recruited in very different ways. It is very difficult to be sure what a special class or a regular class is, yet there have been some incautious generalizations from the recent studies.

We need more patient work, biting away at processes of learning and teaching, trying to specify the variables about which we should be sensitive in teaching exceptional children. And in a gradual way, hopefully, we will reshape programs toward workable total systems. It is to be hoped that as evaluations of the new programs now being launched go forward, we will not always feel obliged to make total, summary judgments. Of course, there are occasions for the big scale comparative studies, but we will be better off with only an occasional and carefully planned big horse race.

Experimental
Design

Many of the evaluative efforts we undertake will necessarily fall short of the ideal designs which statisticians create. Sometimes the truly important problems involve people and situations which don't bend to fit the design model. The answer here is to compromise the design of studies as little as possible and to be aware of what we're doing. One particularly important requirement in studies is that we run control groups for comparison with experimental groups and that we do this with utmost care. Many of the problems which we otherwise encounter are curtailed if we do a conscientious job of setting up controls.

A serious deficiency encountered repeatedly in reports of evaluations is failure to describe in sufficient detail what the experimental variable was. To make results useful in any broad way, it is necessary to clearly and operationally define treatments; and it is helpful if description of control conditions is also given.

Development of
Measurement Techniques

In earlier portions of these remarks I've stressed the very great technical difficulties we face in attempting to measure educational outcomes. There are no quick and easy solutions here. This problem should alert us so as not to be misled into evaluation schemes biased simply by availability of particular tests. I prefer the judgments of disinterested colleagues — a kind of *Consumers Report* — to studies overly refined in design, but weak at the point of measurement.

Strong efforts should be made to develop techniques and instruments of measurement which are useful in special education. This exceedingly important activity comes up too often, just as an ad hoc effort within a broader study. Instrumentation deserves to be a well supported activity apart from specific experiments. The successful development of instruments then becomes a springboard for later application in evaluative studies.

A New
Team

The evaluation problems stressed here are those of the classroom, school, and clinic — the practical marketplace of education. Not many specialists in evaluation reside there. There are too few specialists of the kind we need anywhere. Some are in colleges and universities.

If designers and evaluators work far apart, can we expect effective collaborative work? Freeman and Sherwood (1965) suggest that the evaluator, if at a distance, can set his evaluative techniques after simple guessing about overall goals and later be told he was wrong; or "he can insist that program persons provide them (goals) in which case he should bring lots of novels to the office to read while he waits, or he can participate or even take a major responsibility for the development of the action framework." Their conclusion is that "if the researcher is going to act responsibly as an agent of social change through his evaluation research, it is probably mandatory for him to engage himself in program development" (p. 17).

In the future the schools will themselves more frequently employ evaluation specialists in addition to the use of part time consultants from universities or other agencies. All of us must anticipate new team relationships and join in constructively, defining new roles in the expanding enterprise of evaluation.

Borrowing from Friends

Many more guidelines and problems might be explored. If time were available, I would especially stress the importance of more adequate training in evaluation for all special educators and of training more specialists in the area of evaluation. The fact is that most special educators are not very sophisticated about evaluation procedures, and we will need to do all we can to upgrade ourselves and to utilize talents from neighboring fields as well. I would also stress the importance of looking to other specialties, such as agriculture, for guidance in ways of dividing up jobs of design, evaluation, and dissemination. We will probably need a few very large centers to carry out major tasks in evaluation.

Each community needs to decide for itself when its local circumstances alter the applicability of evaluative findings from other communities and when values generally held for specific programs are not acceptable. Every school district has its evaluation problems, but individual school systems will rarely be able to do large scale systematic research. Indeed, it would be wasteful for every school district to undertake systematic studies of every new program. Thus we need to plan and build, probably in concert with developments relating to other aspects of education, a variety of kinds and levels of research centers.

An Antidote for Unlimited Openness

As commented earlier, there is a great deal of openness of views in special education these days with respect to possible achievements of exceptional children. It is to be counted a gain that views are more open and positive, but there are dangers inherent in such a situation as well. The indefiniteness of the situation invites attempts at closure by the untutored and by those who would play the charlatan's role. Some will be seduced by simple charismatic appeal.

All of us must clarify for ourselves an attitude in this matter. Somehow we must be open in our views, yet realize that it is no kindness to be unrealistically optimistic in instances of specific children. It is necessary to make predictions, at least of short range, concerning particular children in order to plan for them, and sometimes what we honestly foresee is not very encouraging. How do we achieve the needed balance between openness and realism?

The key is simple honesty. In dealing with individual children, predictions and decisions must be made on the basis of present knowledge and programs. It is not relevant to the immediate problem that we and others may think that much more promising programs are "just around the corner." At the same time, we can maintain a general openness and strive to design and evaluate programs which will create the more favorable prognosis in the future.

SUMMARY

The schools of the United States are engaged in a very rapid expansion of specialized school programs. The leaders who have allocated resources to support the programs have also insisted upon systematic program evaluation. The implications of this have not really registered with us in a broad, practical way, and there is some danger that we will let evaluation procedures slip to perfunctory levels. This great challenge comes with heavy force in the field of special education, because programs for exceptional children have been favored in recent federal legislation. All of this arises at a time of great intellectual ferment relating to our work.

All of us must be concerned about the response which is given in this situation. Almost one hundred years ago, there was much eager school building for the handicapped. Theories of that time and some practical demonstrations were encouraging, but views changed and expectations of some of the leading program advocates proved to be unrealistic. Professionals deserted the field for half a century. Only very recently has there been a return to the task of educating all children, including those we serve in special ways. Much depends upon careful evaluation of the programs we are now building and upon our ability to reshape programs in accordance with the hard facts of results.

If we proceed incautiously, there is risk of coming up with seriously wrong answers. We must not put special education at risk in that way. If we proceed carefully, exceptional children will be better served. We are about to be called for an accounting. Let us do the difficult job and do it well!

REFERENCES

Brickell, H. N. The American educational system as a setting for innovation. In M. B. Miles (Editor), *Innovations in education.* New York: Bureau of Publications, Teachers College, Columbia University, 1964. Pp. 493–531.

Brickell, H. N. *Organizing New York state for educational change.* Albany: State Education Department, 1961.

Freeman, H. E. and Sherwood, C. C. Research in large-scale intervention programs. *Social Issues,* 1965, 21, 11–28.

integration and the
special class administrator*

GEORGE BRABNER†

INTRODUCTION

In education circles today, one hears much talk of integration and its converse segregation. Most of this talk is associated with certain controversial issues that are raised as a result of the presence or absence of certain minority groups in the public schools, and is typically characterized by a high degree of emotionality and often considerable fuzziness of thinking. One such minority group is the mentally retarded[1] and it is with this group that the ensuing discussion is most directly concerned.

The purpose of this paper is to examine the meaning of the term "integration," as it applies to special class programs for the mentally retarded, so that the administrator responsible for such a program, though he may disagree with the thoughts expressed in this paper, will be better able to decide for himself what integration means, who should be integrated and why, and in what ways integration can be accomplished most effectively. No attempt will be made to argue the desirability or undesirability of integration. A discussion of the pros and cons of the integration versus segregation issue, as it applies to the mentally retarded in the public schools, is

*Reprinted from *Journal of Education*, Vol. 147 (October 1964), pp. 105-110, by permission of the author and the Journal of Education, Boston, Massachusetts. Copyright 1964 by the Journal of Education.

†George Brabner is Associate Professor of Education, University of Delaware.

[1] The term "mentally retarded" is used in this paper to designate educable and trainable mentally retarded children in public school special classes.

felt to be beyond the scope of this paper although reference will be made to pertinent aspects of this controversy.

WHAT INTEGRATION MEANS

That some confusion exists, at least in the minds of special class teachers in Illinois, as to the role of the administrator in integration was indicated recently in responses to a questionnaire sent to all special class teachers of that state: "Teachers who were asked to delineate the administrator's place in the process either had difficulty in outlining any specific role, or made a blanket statement that the integration and selling of the program of special education to school and public was the responsibility of the administrator" (Goldstein, 1958).

More than likely, there is also some confusion in the minds of administrators of special education programs regarding their role, although most would probably agree that integration is a "good thing" and would be reluctant to see the dictum "Special education must be *a part of, not apart from,* the regular program." Graham (1950) relegated to the status of an empty cliché.

Webster defines integration as the "act or process of integrating," to integrate means "to unite or become united so as to form a complete or perfect whole." Segregation, on the other hand, means "to separate or cut off from others or from the general mass." "Process" is also a key word for the understanding of integration as used in this paper, but will be used to represent only one of a triad of "integrations" to which the administrator must give consideration. Perhaps more importantly he must realize that:

(1) Integration is first and foremost a *belief* upon which the "process of integration" is predicated. This belief either is or is not a part of the total school philosophy which in turn reflects the mandate of the people mediated by the board of education. If it is a part of the total school philosophy, the administrator must either subscribe to the belief, attempt to change it, using ethical procedures and established channels of communication, or resign and seek a position elsewhere.

The belief may be stated as follows: Not only are all children, regardless of race, color, creed, or handicap entitled to equality of educational opportunity in a democratic society, but in addition they are entitled to equality of opportunity for positive *social interaction,* insofar as this is feasible within the existing limitations of facilities, services, and availability of qualified personnel. Social interaction, so conceived, is viewed by the proponents of integration as an essential and not to be denied component of the total educational experience and as something to be fostered in every way possible.

(2) In light of this belief, or acceptance of integration as a philosophical tenet, an established course of action must be arrived at through a process involving the participation of all school personnel (not only professional members of the staff) coming in contact with the pupils. A copy of this policy in printed form should be disseminated to all personnel, and should also be available to any parent or other interested citizen.

This published course of action may be referred to as a "policy of integration" and serves as a readily available declaration of the school's official position, wherever any question arises as to the stand taken by the school relative to integration. The procedure outlined above is, of course, no different from the one that would be followed with respect to any general policy making, i.e., it is always desirable to have policies stated in written form and available to all affected by the policies — especially where sensitive issues are involved:

After taking into account the two major considerations enumerated above, the special class administrator is then in a position to implement a "policy of integration," but in order to do this effectively actual procedures must be formulated by the administrator and his staff in cooperation with the general school staff, procedures which will serve to stimulate and encourage the "process of integration." *The nature of the actual process of integration is as yet poorly understood and is probably a phenomenon, or more probably several phenomena, which can be most appropriately investigated within a conceptual framework derived from social psychology.* It is with this thought in mind that the following definition of the process of integration is offered. By the process of integration is meant:

> *Those social-psychological interactions, occurring spontaneously or by design in the relations of all individuals and groups whose welfare is directly affected by the total school program, which tend toward a diminution of conflict within individuals, between individuals, between individuals and groups, and between groups.*

Individuals whose welfare is directly affected by the total school program would include all school personnel, all pupils, and all parents of the pupils. It is with these individuals that the special class administrator is primarily concerned, although in the last analysis the entire community is affected by the school program, and the administrator does have a public relations function to perform with respect to the community at large. Before proceeding further, the reader may find it helpful to examine Figure 1 which depicts the interrelationships among the three "integrations" defined above.

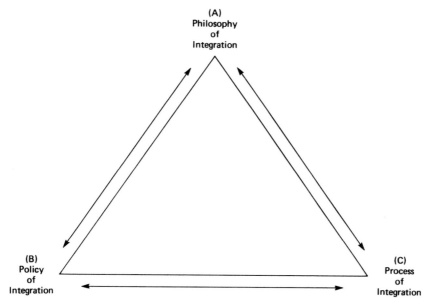

FIGURE 1. *To provide opportunity for a maximum degree of positive social interaction in the school program, steps A, B, and C are followed in that order; however, a reciprocal relationship also exists between each component of the triad in that each should be congruent with, and supportive of, the other two.*

At first glance an examination of the definition of the third member of the triad offered above, i.e. the "process of integration," may seem quite at variance with the positive connotations customarily associated with the term integration; however, it is felt that a process which successively reduces or minimizes conflict as described leads progressively to a state of greater social unity and is in that sense positive. Reduction of conflict within individuals tends to create a higher order of personality integration which in turn facilitates the individual's social intercourse with other individuals and groups.

A reduction of conflict, for example, between a group

representing the interests of gifted children and one representing the interests of retarded children may lead away from a divisive factionalism toward a common goal for both groups — perhaps toward a unified approach to the problems of all exceptional children in the school system or in the community as a whole. To the writer it seems that integration is best understood from the perspective afforded by this definition, for increasing social unity or integration should follow, at times slowly but inevitably, from those spontaneous interactions that serve to reduce conflict (e.g., something which could be as simple as a smile of consent directed toward someone uncertain as to how to proceed in a given situation), or from those interactions conceived or intentionally modified to reduce conflict, as when an administrator plans an open discussion among special staff and general staff for the purpose of airing mutual grievances or clearing up mutual misconceptions.

WHO SHOULD BE
INTEGRATED AND WHY?

Unfortunately, the term "integration," or "social integration," as opposed to mere "physical integration," as used in the speech and writing of layman and professional alike, seems to be one that labels a variety of complex behavioral phenomena without revealing much about the actual nature of these phenomena. Yet, it is with the direct or indirect influencing of the behaviors associated with the process in staff, pupils (both normal and retarded), and in the community that the administrator must be most vitally concerned, for of the three things that he has direct responsibility for integrating — the special education program, the class, and the children — the first two are, from the standpoint of integration, merely administrative devices that serve its purpose. They can be viewed as being organized to promote tolerance (?), acceptance (?), participation (?), harmony (?), or whatever may be presumed to be consonant with the school's philosophy of integration and the perceived meaning of social integration between normal and retarded children. Such social integration exists to a degree among normal children and ideally should exist to as high a degree possible between the normal and the retarded. Whether this objective is a realistic one for the mentally retarded in general or for the trainable mentally retarded specifically is a moot question.

At this point some interesting questions can be raised, e.g., admitting that integration is a "two-way street," from the standpoint of the retarded what precisely are the benefits that are derived from "contacts" with normal children? Will only desirable behavior be learned? What is the relationship between level of intelligence and socially desirable behavior? How does learning take place — through imitation? Incidental learning? Do the retarded learn well in this way? Does the better judgment of the normal child "rub off" in some way onto the retarded child? Shouldn't the learning experience which may be afforded by integration be more important for the normal children, for ultimately it is they who must learn to accept the retarded? Will the normal children merely develop a kind of "see how the other half lives" viewpoint? These are some of the questions that the administrator should keep in mind in developing his own program. They are questions which point up our ignorance of the nature of the social learning that occurs in the integration process and the need for clearer answers. It will be difficult to make intelligent decisions with respect to the integration-segregation question until some of the answers to these questions are forthcoming from the social scientist.

There are those who would contend that the very fact that the destructive effects of ridicule and teasing of retarded children by normal school children, during the school day, can be avoided in a segregated public school situation is almost sufficient reason for the establishment of that facility in preference to the integrated special class. It is argued that at least the child can be shielded from these effects during the crucial formative years. Although critics of the segregated public school may feel that such shielding is unrealistic and only forestalling the inevitable, advocates of the segregated policy might well paraphrase, by substituting the word ridicule for failure, the words of Hilgard and Russell (1950) who point out that the child does not have to be taught to accept failure by providing him with repeated failure experiences. "A better preparation for failure is to have a sufficient backlog of success experiences so that failure is not devastating" (p. 52). One eminent psychologist has suggested that the essential difference between a brave man and a coward is that the latter has been overwhelmed by a concentration of certain negative experiences whereas the former has been exposed to such experiences in more manageable doses over wider intervals of time. The above remarks should not be interpreted as necessarily suggesting any preference on the part of the writer for a segregated public school as opposed to the integrated special class for the mentally retarded. The intent is only to indicate to the reader that the administrator should remain open-minded in regard to the segregated public school versus the special class controversy. He may be committed in principle to a policy of integration, but such a commitment does not preclude his professional evaluation of educational practices of any kind.

At the present time, the special class is being endorsed by state legislatures and public school administration with few exceptions, despite the fact that there is no clear-cut evidence justifying unqualified endorsement (Kirk, 1960). It is conceivable that this national trend could be altered or even reversed at some subsequent date in light of future research findings. Where the trainable child is concerned there is even some evidence suggesting that the purported benefits accruing to these children, through membership in special classes integrated with the regular school program, are open to serious question. Kirk (1957) has summarized some of these findings. Johnson (1957) has reported evidence of a similar kind.

IN WHAT WAYS CAN INTEGRATION BE ACCOMPLISHED MOST EFFECTIVELY?

In addition to taking cognizance of some of the factors set forth earlier in this paper, and observing certain more or less obvious practices, e.g., endeavoring to minimize teasing and ridicule of the retarded, providing materials and services comparable to those of the normal children, being diplomatic in interdepartmental relations, persisting in attempts to broaden the range of social activities in which the retarded child can participate, etc., the administrator can probably do most to foster integration by gleaning insights from and keeping abreast of education and social-psychological research — particularly studies of group interaction — and by being as realistic as possible in appraising his own and his staff's efforts. For example, the process of integration occasionally receives some impetus from the very proximity of mentally retarded children to normal children, but not unusually frictions are also created which rapidly attain proportions of sufficient magnitude to negate any positive interactional effects which may have resulted. In other words, the administrator cannot conclude that the mere physical juxtaposition of special classes and regular classes, or of retarded children and normal children in the cafeteria, the gymnasium, or on the playground will eventuate, through some curious osmotic social process, in a "merging" of the special class program with the general program. This applies equally to relationships between special education staff and general education staff, although the location of an office or classroom of the former group in the vicinity of other offices and classrooms, rather than in the basement, provides at least some equality of opportunity for positive social interaction.

"Physical integration" is no guarantee, whatsoever, that positive social interaction will be generated automatically. This seems to hold for both "progressive" and "non-progressive" schools (Johnson & Kirk, 1950). The process of integration is one that does not proceed continuously and steadily toward Webster's "complete and perfect whole" without deliberate efforts by the administrator and his staff to understand the process and to facilitate it. Providing opportunity for positive social interaction and reduction in conflict requires something more than the vague feeling that retarded children should be allowed to interact with normal children because "something good" will come of it.

It is important also for the administrator to keep in mind the fact that the integration problems of the educable and the trainable child are not only quite different in many respects, but may also vary with regard to program level. For instance, the social integration of the educable retardate at the secondary level sometimes presents difficulties for the administrator which are not encountered earlier in the special class program. These difficulties are often compounded by the "normal" problems of adolescence indigenous to Western European society.

In conclusion, the public relations function of the administrator referred to earlier in the paper deserves comment. In his contacts with the public he should strive to reduce conflicts, relating to the special class program, that occur among individuals and groups. He accomplishes this by providing accurate information about the mentally retarded in general and about the special class program, specifically, through talks given to his staff and to various civic groups, by letters to the local newspapers, and in informal everyday contacts with individuals. He functions in this capacity in order to counteract the deleterious effect of misinformation and misunderstanding propagated by uninformed or hostile members of the school and the community.

REFERENCES

Goldstein, H. *A Curriculum Guide for Teachers of the Educable Mentally Handicapped.* Illinois: State Office of Public Instruction, 1958.

Graham, R. *The Educable Mentally Handicapped.* Illinois: State Office of Public Instruction, 1950.

Hilgard, E. R., and Russell, D. H. "Motivation in School Learning," *Yearbook of the National Society for the Study of Education.* 1950, 49, 36-68.

Johnson, G. O. *Research Project on Severely Retarded Children.* Albany, New
    York: Special Report to the New York Interdepartmental Health
    Resources Board, 1957.
Kirk, S. A. *Public School Provisions for Severely Retarded Children: A Survey of
    Practices in the United States.* Albany, New York: Special Report to the
    Interdepartmental Health Resources Board, 1957.
Kirk, S. A. *Research in Education of the Mentally Retarded.* Illinois: University
    of Illinois, Unpublished, 1960.

what is special about special education revisited: the mentally retarded*

HOWARD L. SPARKS† and
LEONARD S. BLACKMAN

Special education is firmly rooted in American education and has evolved, essentially, from the democratic idea of equal opportunity for all people. The ultimate goal of special education, as with all education, is to prepare children through appropriately planned programs for successful and satisfying living. Every state now has special education services for at least some segment of its exceptional student population, and many local school districts throughout the country have departments of special education. There is at least one employee in every state department of education devoting time to the problems of exceptional children (Mackie and Littlefield, 1961.)

Of all the handicapped children being trained in the public schools, the educable mentally retarded constitutes, by far, the largest group, with the exception of the speech handicapped. In 1940, there were 99,000 educable mentally retarded children enrolled in special day schools, and by 1958, the figure had increased to 218,185 (Dunn, 1962.)

*Reprinted from *Exceptional Children*, Vol. 31 (January 1965), pp. 242-247, by permission of the authors and the Council for Exceptional Children. Copyright 1965 by the Council for Exceptional Children.

†Howard L. Sparks is Consultant, Mental Retardation, Virginia State Department of Education. Leonard S. Blackman is Professor of Education, Department of Special Education, Teachers College, Columbia University.

SPECIAL TEACHERS
REQUIRE SPECIAL SKILLS

An assumption underlying the placement of educable mentally retarded children in special classes and in the special preparation of the teachers is that special class teachers require instructional skills not normally required of teachers of the regular grades. Presumably, courses in methods and materials provide the skills and a unique approach to the special child. Support, however unscientific, for this assumption has come from a variety of sources.

A major source has been the teacher competency study conducted by the U. S. Office of Education. Two methods were used in determining the skills needed by teachers of mentally retarded children. First, a committee of distinguished educators enumerated desirable skills and attitudes, and second, a group of teachers, all considered superior, rated the items as (a) very important, (b) important, (c) less important, or (d) not important. The result was a list of competencies considered important for teachers of mentally retarded children (Mackie, Williams, and Dunn, 1963).

Support has also come from principals of elementary schools and regular class teachers who have long considered the preparation of elementary teachers inadequate to deal effectively with mentally retarded pupils. In recognition of this and in support of special education, Kirk (1953, p. 141) asserts that "the development of special education is contingent upon the development of clinical teaching procedures." Clinical teaching would involve identification of specific learning problems and the application of remediation according to effective principles of learning (Kirk, 1953).

As a result of the increased demand for specially trained teachers and the availability of federal funds, colleges and universities across the country are rapidly developing programs of teacher preparation in the area of special education for mentally retarded children. In 1949, the Society of Crippled Children and Adults reported 22 colleges offering a sequence of courses to prepare teachers for mentally retarded children (NARC, 1961). The National Association for Retarded Children in 1957 reported that the number had increased to 46 and in a followup study in 1961, to 140.

SPECIAL CLASS PLACEMENT VERSUS
REGULAR CLASS PLACEMENT

In view of the increasing numbers of these children being placed in special classes, the mushrooming of teacher training programs, and the evergrowing financial support by both federal and state governments, a review of studies comparing the efficiency of regular classes versus special classes for educable mentally retarded children becomes important. The findings reveal that children in regular classes almost invariably demonstrate academic achievement superior to that of special class children. Gains, if any, from special class placement, seem to accrue in the area of personal and social adjustment.

Bennett (1932) compared 50 mentally retarded and dull-normal children placed in special classes with 50 mentally retarded and dull-normal children in regular classes. She found achievement to be significantly better for the children who remained in the regular classroom. Pertsch (1936) compared two groups matched for chronological age, mental age and intelligence quotient and found regular grade children performed significantly better academically. In addition, he found that despite the "loading" to increase motor skills and manual skills among the special class children, greater ability in these areas did not result. Personality development was higher among regular class boys, but there was no difference of personality among the girls, regardless of class placement. Elenbogen (1957), in a smaller study, found better social adjustment, more realistic vocational goals, more friends and more after school jobs among the special class children. Again, it was found that performances on standardized achievement tests were significantly better for the children in the regular classes.

Cassidy and Stanton (1959) compared 100 special class children with 94 children in regular grades and found that the regular group had higher achievement, but that the special class children had made a better social adjustment. Thurstone (1959), in a study involving approximately 1300 children, found that the children enrolled in special classes were inferior in their academic work, but again, the children in special classes were found to be better adjusted and with an increased number of friends. Baldwin (1958), in a study to determine the social position of mentally retarded children in regular public school classes, found a low degree of social acceptance among mentally retarded children in regular classes. Blatt (1958) found more social maturity and better emotional stability among special class mentally retarded children than among regular class mentally retarded children, using the New York Scales of Social Adjustment. Using the California Test of Personality, he discovered no significant differences in personal adjustment and social adjustment between the two groups. Blatt, moreover, found no significant differences in achievement between the two groups in reading, arithmetic and language.

Based upon available research findings, the evidence is decidedly in favor of placement in regular classes if evaluation is based solely on academic achievement. When the factors of social and personal adjustment are introduced, it appears from the evidence that placement in special classes may be superior to placement in regular classes.

Jordan (1961) confounds even this tentative conclusion, however, as a result of a study of 349 children in 22 secondary special classes. She found social relationships in special classes much the same as in regular classes, with low intelligent children maintaining low social positions and the more intelligent children maintaining high social positions. This indicates that educable mentally retarded children may have the same relative social position, regardless of class placement. It is therefore questionable whether special classes are accomplishing the goal of increased social and personal adjustment. Since the regular class may be more analogous to post-school life than the artificial environment of the special class, it is conceivable that optimal accommodation for mentally retarded children in school could result in post-school problems of adjustment.

The studies previously cited reveal methodological weaknesses which limit the use of their findings as justification for placing educable mentally retarded children in regular classes rather than in special classes. One major weakness was the lack of control of the teaching in the experimentation. The large number of variables in the teaching-learning process prevents an easy and quick interpretation of pupil growth without consideration of this important area, despite the numerous problem involved. A second important weakness was the lack of random assignment of children to special and regular classes to avoid the obvious problem of a priori factors militating against the achievement of the mentally retarded children in the special class.

Despite the methodological weaknesses, however, Johnson (1962, p. 66) maintains that "the reported research to date does not support the subjective evaluations of teachers and their contentions that education for mentally handicapped children in special classes is superior to that provided these children in the regular classes." He also maintains that experimental designs have been varied enough, that the criticism of comparisons on the wrong variables is not valid.

Along with the studies concerned with social adjustment and academic achievement as a function of class placement, there has been research in the area of post-school adjustment of mentally retarded children from regular and special classes (Carriker, 1957; Lapp, 1957; Porter and Milazzo, 1958). These studies have been essentially status surveys and, since little or no attention has been paid to socioeconomic status, it is difficult to interpret their relevance to school provisions. Heber recommends the following research:

> Studies are needed of the social adjustment of retarded adults in comparison with the adjustment of non-retarded adults living in comparable socio-economic conditions. Research attention must be directed to the relationship of specific educational treatments (e.g., curricula emphasizing job skill training vs. curricula emphasizing traditional academic achievement) to adult adjustment, and to the relationship of extra-personal variables (e.g. employer, co-worker, and community activities) to adult community adjustment (1963, p. 89.)

In view of the inconclusiveness of the research, the critical issue of whether we should continue to schedule special classes, with the accompanying increased costs as a result of reduced class sizes, special equipment and materials, special salary increments and the additional training required of teachers, remains unresolvable. Despite increasing national focus on the effectiveness of teaching and current attempts to separate the teaching act from the learning act for purposes of analysis (Medley and Mitzel, 1963), special education departments in colleges and universities continue to prepare special teachers and more and more school systems are creating special classes on the assumption that special preparation results in special teaching.

Quay (1963, p. 673) in a survey of the literature pertaining to educational placement of mentally retarded children, urges that as a result of the inconclusiveness of the data, " . . . teacher and pupil characteristics should be studied to determine whether certain kinds of teachers are more effective in special classes . . . " Warburton (1962) maintains that, "Behavior of teachers is as important as the behavior of children, yet only a tiny proportion of research has been directed to this problem." (p. 372)

Since the global and administrative approach to research into special class versus regular class placement of educable mentally retarded children has not been productive, it may be appropriate to attempt a more analytical approach in order to look more closely at fewer variables. Instead of involving the entire teaching-learning process, detailed study of specific segments of the special class complex could yield important results. One of the aspects worth consideration is the behavior of the teacher in clearly delineated areas as it relates to her pedagogical training.

SPECIAL TEACHER PREPARATION

A survey of the literature to determine whether the special teacher's approach to the special child actually differs from the regular teacher's approach to the normal child did not unearth a single study comparing the two teaching processes on any dimension. Hudson (1960), in an effort to delineate specific teaching techniques employed by teachers of trainable mentally retarded children, analyzed five twenty-minute protocols from 29 classrooms to obtain 43 separate techniques employed. However, there was no regular class control for comparison. Dorward (1963) reported that a study designed to determine the special skills needed by teachers of emotionally disturbed children did not identify any. However, this study was based on questionnaires completed by regular and special teachers and did not involve observations to determine the extent to which responding teachers actually practiced the items they listed as important.

A review of the literature to determine the bases of sequences of courses leading to certification as a teacher of educable mentally retarded children reveals no validation studies nor any claims for teaching the mentally retarded.

On the basis of existing evidence, it is only possible to conclude that the special education teacher has superior qualification to teach exceptional children to the degree that the concensus of intelligent and experienced special educators is accepted. Empirical proof of the validity of special preparation does not exist. Furthermore, the extent of which college teachers of special methods courses are committed to the quantitative or qualitative school of differences concerning the learning characteristics of mentally retarded children probably figures heavily in their approach. Ultimately then, there may be little uniformity among the methods courses, with some teachers assuming that children learn in ways different from the normal population and others viewing the learning of mentally retarded children as a slower but identical process.

Fields (1958) has indicated that teachers must be well informed and specially trained and suggests that thought should be given to determining what constitutes a best program of teacher preparation.

There is some evidence that a method of teaching is not particular for a specific population. Instead, that which is valuable as method is common to all teaching. Dewey, writing years ago, said:

> Strictly, speaking, method is thoroughly individual. Each has his own instinctive way of going at a thing; the attitude and the mode of approach and attack are individual. To ignore this individuality of approach, to try to substitute for it, under the name of 'general method', a uniform scheme of procedure, is simply to cripple the only effective agencies of operation and to overlay them with a mechanical formalism that produces only a routine conventionality of mental quality (1913, p. 202.)

Wyles (1959) also has an individual approach to teaching method. He asserts:

> Teaching method consists of judging each teaching situation — and there may be a thousand or more a day — and choosing at the moment the procedure deemed most likely to be successful. We are able to make the decisions intelligently and with assurance, if we have thought through our philosophy of teaching and have decided upon the function we should perform (p. 30).

Both Dewey and Wyles seem to suggest that teaching method is instinctive, creative and individual; therefore, it may not be possible to instill in a teacher a particular method of dealing with a particular population without the loss of important personal and intellectual characteristics.

In a different but somewhat related field, Fiedler (1950), comparing experts and non-experts as defined by training and experience in the Adlerian, Rogerian and Jungian schools of counseling, found that regardless of school of training, experienced counselors bore more similarities to each other than the experienced and inexperienced trained in the same school. He also found that the expertness of a therapist is most related to ability to "communicate and understand, maintain appropriate emotional distance, and to divest themselves of status concern regarding the patient" (p. 444). The Fiedler study, which indicates the appropriateness and generality of certain personality configurations, may support the individuality of teaching method suggested by Dewey and Wyles.

Barr (1958) indicates the following are personal qualities of successful teachers: resourcefulness, intelligence, emotional stability, considerateness, buoyancy, objectivity, drive, dominance, attractiveness, refinement, cooperativeness and reliability. Symonds (1955), through a correlation of principal and student ratings of teachers, found that superior teachers like children, are personally secure, well integrated and have well organized personalities.

It seems probable that some of the desirable qualities of teachers indicated by Barr and Symonds overlap those designated by Fiedler as determinants of expertness among counselors, regardless of methodological or pedagogical training.

Goldberg (1952), in a retrospective study, found that special class teachers felt they would have benefitted from additional course work in human growth and development, methods of teaching subject matter, methods of teaching reading, and a broader base in educational foundations. This poses the question of whether teachers have been forced to obtain these skills while in service, and if so, how nearly they approximate the pedagogy employed by the regular classroom teacher.

SUMMARY

There is increasing emphasis on special class placement of educable mentally retarded children and special preparation for teachers. At the same time an analysis of available evidence continues to point toward the lack of superior academic achievement and to cause some questioning of the superiority of the social environment provided by the special class.

In view of the need for determining, empirically, some of the essential differences between special and regular teaching, it is necessary to determine the extent to which special methods courses for teaching educable mentally retarded children actually result in a special approach to the special child as contrasted with the approach to a normal child by a regular class teacher. Needed research in this area, therefore, would include ecological studies comparing the "natural habitat" classroom behaviors of special and regular class teachers along some clearly defined and easily observable dimensions.

Proof must be forthcoming that there is more special about special education than the children assigned to these classes. If the null hypothesis relating to the differences between regular and special classes can not be rejected, then the field of special education, represented primarily by its teacher trainers and administrators, will be required to do some serious soul searching.

REFERENCES

Baldwin, W. E. The social position of mentally handicapped children in the regular classes in the public schools. *Exceptional Children*, 1958, 25, 106–112.

Barr, A. S. Characteristics of a successful teacher, *Phi Delta Kappan*, 1958, 39, 282–284.

Bennett, Annette. *A comparative study of subnormal children in the elementary grades.* New York: Teachers College, Columbia University, Bureau of Publications, 1932.

Blatt, B. The physical personality and academic status of children who are mentally retarded attending special classes as compared with children who are mentally retarded attending regular classes. *American Journal of Mental Deficiency*, 1958, 62, 810–818.

Carriker, W. R. A comparison of post-school adjustments of regular and special class retarded individuals served in Lincoln and Omaha, Nebraska Public Schools. *Dissertation Abstracts*, 1957, 17, 2206–2207.

Cassidy, Viola. M., and Stanton, J. E. *An Investigation of factors involved in the educational placement of mentally retarded children.* Columbus: Ohio State University Press, 1959.

Dewey, J. Method. In P. Monroe (Editor), *A cyclopedia of education*, New York: The MacMillan Company, 1913. Pp. 202–205.

Dorward, Barbara. A comparison of the competencies for regular classroom teachers and teachers of emotionally disturbed children. *Exceptional Children*, 1963, 30, 67–73.

Dunn, L. M. A historical review of treatment. In J. Rothstein (Editor), *Mental retardation.* New York: Holt, Rinehart & Winston, Inc., 1962.

Elenbogen, M. L. A comparative study of some aspects of academic and social adjustment of two groups of mentally retarded children in special classes and regular classes. *Dissertation Abstracts*, 1957, 17, 2496.

Fiedler, F. E. A comparison of therapeutic relationships in Psychoanalytic Non-directive and Adlerian therapy. *Journal of Consulting Psychology*, 1950, 14, 436–485.

Fields, H. Who makes the best teacher of mentally retarded children: a panel discussion. *American Journal of Mental Deficiency*, 1958, 58, 251–267.

Goldberg, I. I. *Guide for future development of special education programs at Teachers College, Columbia University.* Unpublished doctoral dissertation, Teachers College, Columbia University, 1952.

Heber, R. The educable mentally retarded. In S. Kirk and Bluma Weiner (Editors) *Behavioral Research on exceptional children.* Washington, D. C. The Council for Exceptional Children, 1963, p. 89.

Hudson, Margaret, An exploration of classroom procedures for teaching trainable mentally retarded children. CEC Research Monograph, Series A. No. 2, Washington, D. C., 1960.

Johnson, G. O. Special education for the mentally retarded — a paradox. *Exceptional Children*, 1962, 29, 62–69.

Jordan, June B. Intelligence as a factor in social position — a sociometric study in special classes for the mentally handicapped. *Dissertation Abstracts*, 1960–61, 214, 2987–2988.

Kirk, S. A. What is special about special education? *Exceptional Children*, 1953, 19, 138–142.

Lapp, Ester R. A study of the social adjustment of slow-learning children who were assigned part-time to regular classes. *American Journal of Mental Deficiency*, 1957, 62, 254–262.

Mackie, Romaine P. and Littlefield, L. *Special education personnel in state education departments.* Washington, D.C.: Government Printing Office 1961.

Mackie, Romaine P., Williams, H. and Dunn, L. M. Teachers of children who are mentally retarded. Washington D. C.: Government Printing Office, Bulletin 1957, No. 3.

Medley, D. M., and Mitzel, H. E. Measuring classroom behavior by systematic observation. In N. L. Gage (Editor), Handbook of Research on Teaching. Chicago: Rand McNally, 1963.

National Association for Retarded Children. *Opportunities for professional preparation in the field of education of mentally retarded children.* New York: The Association, 1961.

Pertsch, C. F. A comparative study of the progress of sub-normal pupils in the grades and in special classes. Unpublished doctoral dissertation, Teachers College, Columbia University, 1936.

Porter, R. B., and Milazzo, T. C. A comparison of mentally retarded adults who attended a special class with those who attended regular classes. *Exceptional Children*, 1958, 24, 410–412.

Quay, Lorene C. Academic skills. In N. R. Ellis (Editor), *Handbook of mental deficiency.* New York: McGraw Hill, 1963. Pp. 664–690.

Symonds, P. Characteristics of the effective teacher based on pupil evaluations, *Journal in experimental education*, 1955, 23, 289–310.

Thurstone, Thelma G. *An evaluation of educating mentally handicapped children in special classes and regular classes.* Chapel Hill: University of North Carolina School of Education, 1959.

Warburton, F. W. Educational psychology. *Annual Review of Psychology*, 1962, 13, 317–414.

Wyles, K.*Teaching for better schools.* Englewood Cliffs, New Jersey: Prentice-Hall, 1959.

part iii

federal programming and legislation

With the beginning of the First Session of the 88th Congress in 1963, legislation has been enacted which has affected the handicapped in significant ways. The articles which follow document the development of this legislation and highlight the organization, programs, trends and projected plans of the major new Bureau of Education for the Handicapped, U. S. Office of Education.

James J. Gallagher in the lead article discusses the new organizational structure of the U. S. Office of Education and its potential for helping the handicapped. Gallagher relates the organizational process to the need for a more complex model of the transmission of the kind of knowledge that can bring about innovative comprehensive educational changes.

Edwin W. Martin, Jr., outlines not only the factual development of recent federal legislation affecting the handicapped, but in a very interesting and intimate way comments on the personalities and related factors integral to its development.

Michael Marge comments on the necessity for identifying long-range goals and strategies for effective national planning for exceptional children. Marge further outlines the five major functions of the Office of Program Planning and Evaluation of the Bureau of Education for the Handicapped.

Elizabeth G. Goodman outlines six major functions related to coordination of services for the handicapped and presents a functional table of federal programs administered specifically by the Bureau of Education for the handicapped.

The fifth article, edited by Charles Meisgeier, is a two part summary of legislative highlights and a review of the major provisions of twenty-eight federal laws relating to the handicapped.

organization and
special education*

JAMES J. GALLAGHER†

There was a time not too long ago when organization and planning in our society were seen as evil things. Our heroes were the Sam Spades, Tarzans, and Jack Armstrongs, all antiorganization men who bucked the system and, through ingenuity and courage, beat the faceless representatives of organizations bent on nefarious deeds. Our thinking today still contains elements of antiorganization or antiplanning, expressed in its most extreme form in the hippies and those who would rather drop out than become involved in the system.

What has this to do with the handicapped? Just this: the entire issue of this journal is devoted to telling you about a new organization, the Bureau of Education for the Handicapped in the U. S. Office of Education. The purpose of this organization is to find ways to speed federal participation in the solutions of the educational problems of the handicapped. We at the Bureau also hope to demonstrate that the Bureau now has a greater potential to help you and the handicapped children you serve than was possible before, due to its new structure and organization.

The job of all educators, including special educators, is to find the mechanisms through which we can translate new knowledge into action at the instructional level. Only in this way can we improve our

*Reprinted from *Exceptional Children,* Vol. 34 (March 1968), pp. 485-491, by permission of the author and the Council for Exceptional Children. Copyright 1968 by the Council for Exceptional Children.

†James J. Gallagher is Deputy Assistant Secretary/Commissioner for Educational Planning, U. S. Office of Education.

services beyond a type of crafts or guild operation in which knowledge was passed on from master to apprentice in each generation.

Until very recently, we have depended upon a very simplified transmission of "knowledge into action" model in educational research and, to be blunt, it has proven to be a magnificent failure. This system provided financial support to the individual researcher who conducted his investigations and then reported his new discoveries in channels primarily designed to communicate with his professional colleagues rather than to the great mass of teachers and educators. The results of his research were then collected together, as best as possible, by college professors who presented them, in retranslated form, to embryonic teachers in the college classroom. These aspiring teachers were, in turn, expected to translate this information again to produce changed behavior in the classroom. Experience has taught us that we need a much more complex model for transmission of knowledge if we are to have any hope of producing the comprehensive educational changes that this generation desires and needs.

We have realized that the process of translating knowledge into action seems to require several rather distinct phases, each of which requires time, organization, and a constancy of purpose. The instant solutions of a Tom Swift or Jack Armstrong will not do. Table 1 shows the complex phases through which knowledge may be translated into action. If any of these phases are not adequately executed, there will likely be no lasting change in the special education program.

As the table indicates, there appear to be five major stages in the knowledge to action cycle: *research*, *development*, *demonstration*, *implementation*, and *adoption*. To take a hypothetical example, suppose research on concept formation in mentally retarded children found that these children can learn numerical concepts more efficiently through the use of concrete or tangible aids. For this information to be educationally useful beyond a college text book, it would then be necessary to *develop* a program or curriculum through which lessons could be organized and sequenced, in harmony with the research findings. Such a curriculum program would have to then be *demonstrated* on a particular group of mentally retarded children to show educators the effective interaction of this instructional program with handicapped children.

Even after this has been done there still remains the problem of convincing the local school administrator or special educator that such a program could work in his setting. Therefore, methods must

TABLE 1.

Phases of Translation of Knowledge to Action through Organizational Support

Developmental Phase	Purpose	Supporting Organizations
Research	The discovery of new knowledge about handicapped children or about those intellectual and personality processes that can be applied in these children.	These are usually research centers and institutions, often found in universities, which can provide organizational support for long range attacks on difficult research problems.
Development	Knowledge, to be educationally useful, must be organized or packaged into sequences of activities or curricula that fit the needs of particular groups of children.	Sometimes done through research and development centers which concentrate on sequencing of existing knowledge; basic setting is still the university.
Demonstration	There must be an effective conjunction of organized knowledge and child. This conjunction must be demonstrated in a school setting to be believable.	A combination of university or government and school operation required. Usually, the elementary or secondary school is the physical setting and additional resources are supplied by the other agency.
Implementation	Local school systems with local needs usually wish to try out, on a pilot basis, the effective demonstrations they have observed elsewhere to establish its viability in a local setting.	Additional funds for retraining personnel and for establishing a new program locally are needed. Some type of university, state or federal support is often needed as the catalyst to bring about this additional stage.
Adoption	To establish the new program as part of the educational operation. Without acceptance of the new program at the policy level, demonstration and implementation operations can atrophy.	Organized attempts need to be made to involve policy decision makers (i.e., school board members, superintendents, etc.) in the developmental stages so far. Items like cost effectiveness need to be developed to help make decisions.

be found to help the local special educators *implement* this new idea in their particular program, on a trial basis. Finally, there is that last crucial decision as to whether this trial program is to be *adopted* — actually become a part of the regular on-going educational program. There is many a slip betwixt these stages, as educators know.

An analogy to music in stages of progression from creation to wide acceptance might be helpful. Research in the nature of harmonics may lead to the discovery of new chord structures. Such knowledge in its own right would be of interest only to other music theorists. However, one further developmental stage might be attained by a composer who would organize such knowledge into a piece of music. Such creative work could then be demonstrated, i.e., performed in concerts or other musical programs.

For wide acceptance and use of the new music technique or chord structure there would have to be extended attempts to disseminate (i.e., implement) this music through popular media, and to see that it was readily available to the general public. Even after this occurred, great efforts at salesmanship would still be needed to gain general adoption of the new technique or method.

One need hardly point out that no one would expect the same person to perform all of these diverse musical functions, and that a very complex set of organizations is needed for every phase of the operation if the final goal of wide acceptance is to be attained. It takes well trained professionals in each operation, with the best organizational skills, to see that new ideas blossom into program actions.

The complex society is not the end of the creative individual or the brilliant thinker who cannot stand the system. His ideas can, through the presentation of new concepts or incisive criticism, cause the system to change form or direction. These people are greatly needed in our society. Anyone who has tried to produce ideas through a committee system can appreciate the wry humor in the statement that "the camel was a horse that was put together by a committee."

The individual thinker can still think and innovate and criticize, but often he cannot achieve program implementation within the highly sophisticated and complex society we now have. This must be done through complex organizations and systems. If the systems are inadequately designed, the implementation goals will not be met, regardless of the individual ingenuity or genius of its constituents.

Neither do we need to accept the belief that creative work can only be done outside the system. Some of the most innovative advances of our society have been accomplished by trying to make these systems more viable for human needs. This is often a frustrating experience requiring more stamina, tolerance, and courage than that required of the isolated critic.

BUREAU ORGANIZATION

The Bureau of Education for the Handicapped is organized in three major operating divisions which, in turn, represent three major foci for the field of special education. (See Figure 1 for complete organization.) They are:

1. *Division of Research.* Supports investigators and organizations in the discovery, organization, and sequencing of knowledge for the maximum educational benefit for the handicapped.
2. *Division of Educational Services.* Provides distribution of resources to assure that educational services for the handicapped can be initiated, expanded, or extended at the local and/or state educational levels.
3. *Division of Training Programs.* Provides support to institutions of higher learning and to state educational agencies so that programs for the preparation of special educational personnel can be supported or expanded.
4. *Bureau Office.* Provides coordination, planning, management, evaluation, and an information service for the overall program.

It is my privilege to lead this new Bureau, and to work with the outstanding group of professionals who comprise its staff. As you will read in this issue, they are addressing themselves to an amazing variety of problems and issues. With your support and assistance, they will be your representatives in Washington to help you.

Each will describe one part of our complex activity. The remainder of this article will discuss some projected goals that now have a possibility of being attained through the creation of this new Bureau.

BUREAU INTERRELATIONSHIPS

One of the great deterrents to American education has been the administrative isolation of the various component parts which bring about change. What has been learned through educational research has rarely been translated into service.

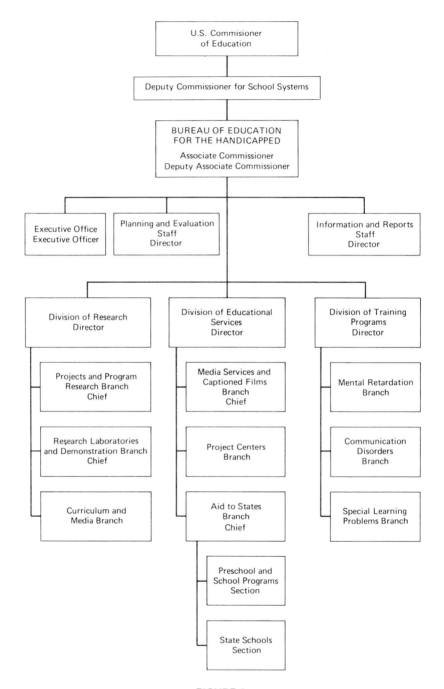

FIGURE 1.

ORGANIZATION CHART FOR BUREAU OF EDUCATION FOR THE HANDICAPPED

The need for specific skills revealed through service operations has rarely been translated into modified training programs. The new Bureau has brought together into one unit these three major components — research, training, and services. One potential advantage of this structure is that the personnel in these units share their particular expertise with one another.

For example, there are elements of training in all three of the major programs. The Division of Research possesses the potential for supporting the training of educational researchers, and the Division of Educational Services has provided support for training in their state aid and media programs. It is important that both of these programs have liaison with staff involved in the major training operations in special education.

The competencies of the Research Division are needed to aid in the design of self evaluation methods for our own programs and to channel the consequences of research findings into both the teacher training and services dimension.

Another example of an operation with broad goals and diverse functions is the network of Instructional Materials Centers, described at greater length, elsewhere in this issue (See pp. 515-519). This network of centers aims to provide for the collection, evaluation, development, and dissemination of instructional materials for special education. As such, it contains elements of research, training, and service operations. The needs of these centers are most easily served through a bureau that can provide coordination over this three dimensional operation. The Captioned Films for the Deaf Program has had Media Centers similar in many respects to the Instructional Materials Centers, but there has been little previous interrelationship or contact between them because these units were in different divisional structures in the old organization of the Office of Education.

THE BUREAU AS A
POLICY VOICE

It is difficult, from any geographic distance, to appreciate the change in the position of interests of handicapped children within the U. S. Office of Education as a result of the establishment of the new Bureau. However, there is an analogous situation that is easily understandable. If the key decisions affecting the program for handicapped children in your own local school district were in the policy hands of the director of elementary education, or the director of guidance, or an Assistant Superintendent who had no previous contact or experience with handicapped children, many predictable things could happen. Programs for handicapped children rarely flourish under such circumstances. Decisions important to the development or survival of programs are being made by people who have little professional background to make such decisions. It has usually been found that the central program operation responsibilities and decision making on programs for handicapped children at the local level are carried out more effectively under the direction of persons whose basic professional background has been in the area of the handicapped.

Much the same thing is true at the federal level. If the programs for the handicapped, or the essential policy decisions regarding these programs, are being made by persons who have had little background or experience in these areas, the decisions that are made are often unfavorable to the handicapped.

Even more disturbing for the future of education is that the special knowledge which has been acquired about the exceptional child, at such a high price, would be unavailable to the general education policy maker. As we know, interest in the mentally retarded child more than a half century ago stimulated important work on the measurement of intelligence. Interest in the emotionally disturbed child has provided us with insights into the personality development of the average child, and current work at precise educational diagnosis of serious learning disabilities possesses the potential for a more thorough understanding of the developing intellectual abilities in all children and methods for improving these abilities.

The organizational step of producing a Bureau of Education for the Handicapped has opened the door for communication between those who work with the handicapped, who have special knowledge and expertise, with other important components of the American educational community, which have too often been shielded or isolated from that knowledge. In my responsibilities as a Bureau chief, I have presented the position of our professional areas to the Association of School Boards, the staff members of the Compact for the States, and other visitors to the Office of Education, I have testified before committees of the Congress, and attend weekly meetings at the policy level of the U. S. Office of Education itself. While it is hard to measure the immediate impact of any of these meetings, it seems likely that the long range consequences can only be good for special education. Let me emphasize that these opportunities occurred not because of the nature of the Bureau Chief, himself, but because the organization demanded such meetings!

Because of the new structure, the Bureau of Education for the Handicapped provides a policy voice at a level just below that of the U. S. Commissioner of Education himself. It also assures that its programs are identifiable and not merely small component parts of much larger programs. Thus, it is much easier to identify program progress and, more important, it places the essential policy decisions regarding the operation of programs for the handicapped in the hands of persons whose backgrounds have been with exceptional children.

THE BUREAU AND INTERAGENCY COOPERATION

One of the great challenges that we face in our established organizations is that the needs of handicapped children do not stop at the boundaries of established legislation or organizations. Parents are justifiably irritated when told that this or that agency cannot deal with one part of their problem and that they have to go to another one for further service.

When I was a lad growing up in Pittsburgh, Pennsylvania, I can still remember my grandmother going out on one of her many shopping expeditions. Sometimes it was to the bakery, sometimes the grocery store, sometimes the butcher shop or drug store. Since she had 13 children she had to make many separate trips to many different kinds of places in order to take care of the numerous needs of the family. She might well have dreamed about such a place as a supermarket where all of these family needs could have been taken care of in one magnificently expensive expedition — but these changes were not destined to take place in her lifetime.

In the fields of professional services today we have many isolated shops analogous to the specialty shops of my grandmother's day: the pediatric shop, the school shop, the mental health shop, etc. A parent who is unfortunate enough to have a child who has a multiplicity of handicaps has no choice but to visit all of the shops, one at a time, and will never receive the combined benefits of the knowledge of all of the specialists in other shops.

There is a clear trend towards doing away with these separate shops. The future is going to involve much more professional interaction and many cooperative relationships between specialists and programs. This total supermarket concept for handicapped children will provide a more comprehensive and centralized set of services for the handicapped child, who will be identified at a much earlier age.

One specific example has been the cooperative efforts established between the Bureau and the Division of Mental Retardation in the new Social and Rehabilitation Service of the Department of Health, Education, and Welfare. Through these cooperative arrangements we have begun the funding of five pilot programs whereby special educators would be hired in each of the University Affiliated Centers for Mental Retardation as part of the total special education training program for that particular institution. These educators would participate in the policy decisions of the affiliated centers and play a major role in the interdisciplinary training programs established through these centers.

The staff of the Bureau is also assisting other federal agencies to design and establish more effective educational guidelines for programs which are not primarily educational, but which contain a specific special education component. Here again, the visibility and new status of the Bureau provides the basis for such contacts and arrangements.

THE BUREAU AND
FUTURE PLANNING

One of the potential advantages of the new Bureau of Education for the Handicapped is that it provides an identifiable launching pad for future developments in the education of handicapped children. When one thinks of the many unsolved problems in special education and the major new directions the field may take in the next decade, it is comforting to know that there is, within the federal establishment, a central place where federal support can be mustered and new programs can evolve.

Part of planning for the future must involve the development of some greater expertise about the nature of planning, itself. Usually, we are happy with the idea of planning in direct ratio to how close we personally are to the planning operation. The great challenge for us all is to fit a general concept of controlled societal planning into a democratic framework. It won't be easy or without considerable irritation and frustration. Still, as Gunnar Myrdal recently pointed out, the alternative to planning is not planning, and we know where that has gotten us. Most significant is the amount of lead time necessary to accomplish a societal goal, even when there has been a discovery or decision that a major effort should be launched.

Even if we made a great breakthrough in discovery — such as new ways to stimulate language development for the deaf, or new educational methods to treat children with specific learning disabilities, or in finding ways to substantially improve the intellectual performance of mentally retarded children — we must ask ourselves an embarrassing question. How long would it take to distribute such knowledge and skills throughout the country?

For instance, we still have hardly considered the problem of effective and widespread dissemination of information and skills. We have made a significant start on dissemination activities with the establishment of the Educational Resources Information Center (ERIC) at The Council for Exceptional Children in Washington, D. C. This center will provide access to research related information on exceptional children. But this is merely a very small beginning to a solution for a very large problem.

It is probable that some new systems or new structures for dissemination, not now available, will have to be developed to make sure that ideas and skills are disseminated and implemented with maximum efficiency and speed. When these determinations are made, it will be easier to concentrate interest and federal action through the established organization which deals with handicapped children, within the Office of Education.

In summary, the Bureau provides one more vital resource in the complex of organizations designed to carry out important societal goals within a complex society. It is not a substitute for good ideas, nor for honest effort at the local and state levels, nor for intelligent planning in colleges and universities. It does not guarantee that good things will happen or that good practices will prevail. However, it does provide a vehicle by which the cycle of planning, research, development, demonstration, implementation, and adoption can occur.

The full impact of this new dimension in the education for the handicapped calls for involvement and coordinated action at all professional levels. We share with you, the nation's professional leaders, the privilege of participation and the responsibilities inherent in achieving its objectives in this century.

As the President and the Commissioner have stated, the handicapped child and his family are at last earning their full share of attention from our society. Society's goals have changed as well. It is no longer satisfied to provide a smothering care with fostered over-dependency. We now seek to bring each handicapped individual to the very limit of his potential. Our goal is self realization and self sufficiency to the limits of each handicapped individual. The Bureau of Education for the Handicapped is both a symbol of that determination and a vehicle whereby such a realization can more easily be obtained.

ADDENDUM

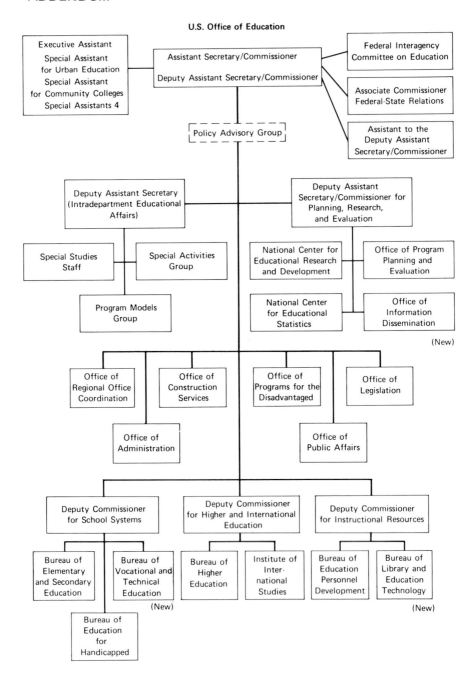

U.S. Office of Education

breakthrough
for the handicapped:
legislative history*

EDWIN W. MARTIN, JR.†

Room EF 100, in the East Front of the Capitol, is in a political sense, "no man's land." Near the Rotunda and between the House and Senate wings, belonging to neither body, it would be dissected by a line through the middle of the Capitol. In keeping with the formal ritual which is so much a part of the legislative branch, there are separate entrances into each end of the room along the rear wall so that Senators and Representatives can enter and leave through distinct passages in the direction of their chambers. In fact, however, most legislators enter through the double doors in the center of the wall nearest the middle of the Capitol. The separate exits are more likely to serve the practical rather than ritualistic rite of ducking an ardent persuader sitting in the lobby on benches near the main doors.

Twice in the less than 14 months between late October, 1966, and December 15, 1967, members of the House and Senate committees responsible for educational legislation came to Room EF 100 to form a conference committee. These conferees were charged with resolving differences in the 1966 and 1967 Elementary and Secondary Education Act amendments which, among their many purposes, promised to change dramatically the course of education for handicapped children in the United States.

*Reprinted from Exceptional Children, Vol. 34 (March 1968), pp. 493-503, by permission of the author and the Council for Exceptional Children. Copyright 1968 by the Council for Exceptional Children.

†Edwin W. Martin, Jr. is Acting Associate Commissioner of Education for the Handicapped, U. S. Office of Education.

The Senate conferees, led both years by the chairman of their Education Subcommittee, Oregon Senator Wayne Morse, and the House conferees, led by the chairman of the Education and Labor Committee (in 1966, New York Representative Adam Clayton Powell; in 1967, Kentucky Representative Carl Perkins), faced the complex task of resolving conflicting aspects of their respective versions of the same bill. In many instances, these involved complex distribution formulas and changes affecting the basic nature of programs. Inseparably bonded to these conflicts were powerful emotional and political factors, such as church-state issues, civil rights, state's rights, school busing, etc. In this context, amendments affecting the lives of the minority group known as handicapped children attracted little attention from the press. People vitally interested in the education of handicapped children, certain members of the conference committee and their staffs, professional groups and their members, and persons operating programs within the government which serve these children, worked, watched, waited, hoped, and eventually exulted over what they knew were major breakthroughs for handicapped children.

The breakthroughs of 1966 and 1967 were the high points of the legislative accomplishments of almost a decade, and of efforts toward these accomplishments of many people over a much longer period of time. The following sections present reports on the development of this federal legislation affecting education for handicapped children and reports on some of the factors which were integral to its development (See Table 1).

THE FIRST
STEP

PL 83-531 —
The Cooperative Research Act

The 531st Bill to be approved by the 83rd Congress and the President, thereby earning for itself the label "Act," was signed by President Eisenhower on July 26, 1954. It was described as "an act to authorize cooperative research in education," and it made provisions for a program of grants to be given to institutions of higher learning and to the states providing for cooperative support of educational research, surveys, and demonstrations, and for the dissemination of information derived from educational research.

One indicator of the attitudes toward federal aid to education held at that time may be found in the fact that this Act remained unfunded until 1957. That year, of the $1 million appropriated, $675,000 was earmarked to be spent on research related to education of the mentally retarded. This action of the Congressional Appropriation Committees set into being a research program which, with the help of some timely transfusions, is still alive. It also represented the first sign of recognition by Congress of the need for categorical aid for the education of handicapped children since the beginning of federal support for Gallaudet College in 1864 and the American Printing House for the Blind in 1879. In contrast to later programs initiated by new authorizing legislation, this research program was initiated through the Appropriations Committees directing the use of general funds for educational research into this specific area. The support of key men on the Appropriations Committees, particularly the late Representative John E.Fogarty from Rhode Island and Senator Lister Hill of Alabama, was to be an essential factor in almost every phase of the latter development of education legislation benefiting handicapped children.

PL 85-905 —
Captioned Films for the Deaf

On September 2, 1958, "An Act to provide in the Department of Health, Education, and Welfare for a loan service of captioned films for the deaf" was signed into law. The Captioned Films program was primarily aimed at the cultural enrichment and recreation of deaf persons, although its educational implications were apparent. Its passage in 1958 was another evidence of increasing concern on the part of the government for the welfare of handicapped persons. However, the greatest contributions of this program to the sequence of development of educational legislation were to come from later amendments in 1962 and 1965 (PL 87-715 and PL 89-258). These amendments broadened this program into an amazingly flexible and productive comprehensive instructional media program for the deaf, involving research and development, production, acquisition, distribution, and training of teachers to use media. This successful program provided a model for legislation in 1967, extending these benefits to all handicapped children requiring special education.

PL 85-926 —
Training of Professional Personnel

In its statement of purpose, PL 85-926 was "to encourage expansion of teaching in the education of mentally retarded children through grants to institutions of higher learning and to state educational agencies." Aimed primarily at training professional personnel who would, in turn, train teachers to work with mentally retarded children, PL 85-926 was perhaps the most significant of the early legislative accomplishments.

Research in education of the retarded had begun to receive support during the previous year under the general provisions of the Cooperative Research Act, but continuing support under this program was not definite, as later events were to prove. Captioned Films for the Deaf, signed four days earlier, was not primarily an educational act; its main thrust was recreational and cultural.

PL 85-926 was developed in the Congress at the same time the National Defense Education Act was under study, and they were signed by the President within a week of each other. NDEA was the landmark legislation which established federal support for individuals pursuing higher education. It established a precedent which almost simultaneously was elaborated upon by PL 85-926 to offer categorical support for education of the handicapped. With this new authority, the pace of legislative support quickened.

PL 87-276 —
Teachers of the Deaf
During the 87th Congress the next step was taken with the approval of a new Act which authorized support for training teachers of the deaf. Whereas the earlier mental retardation program focused on leadership personnel, this program appealed to Congress because of its emphasis on classroom teachers. With the establishment of programs of support for training in the areas of mental retardation and the deaf (including a spread of support from undergraduate trainees through leadership training), the momentum gathered strength for the expansion of this training authority to include other major areas of handicapping conditions requiring special education. Each new building block made the wall stronger and provided a base for new construction.

Throughout the struggle to gain passage for these programs, the forces interested in this legislation continued to grow in strength and experience. Members of Congress who were sympathetic and influential were enlisted in the cause. CEC and other groups dedicated to serving handicapped children stirred their memberships to work with the Congress. They provided testimony and other information necessary for legislative study and, above all, urged support for the new bills. Philosophical differences had to be set aside, at least temporarily, as in the instance of "oral" and "manual" groups interested in deaf education uniting behind PL 87-276.

Most importantly, handicapped children had help from people with professional expertise in legislation, who recognized that special programs were necessary, and who knew how to help them. Key members among these professionals were Patria Winalski Forsythe of the Department of Health, Education and Welfare; Jack Forsythe, Charles Lee, and Roy Millenson, professional staff of the Senate Labor and Public Welfare Committee; and Russell Derrickson, Robert McCord, and Charles Radcliffe of the House Education Committee staff. Attempts to list key figures in developing legislation will inevitably leave out too many people who have played important roles, yet it would be inaccurate in even the briefest account to fail to identify these usually anonymous people who as resources have provided strength for legislation for handicapped children. Frequently legislation needs powerful support, financially or in numbers of affected voters in order to win approval. Legislation for the handicapped has had to succeed primarily on its basic appeal for compassion, and on the efforts of its expert friends.

The momentum established as these first programs were developed, the growing strength of the "legislation for education of the handicapped team," plus the heightened public interest in handicapped children stimulated by President Kennedy, set the stage for the next phase of development.

PUBLIC LAW 88–164 AND THE DIVISION OF HANDICAPPED CHILDREN AND YOUTH

I am glad to announce at this time that we are establishing a division in the U.S. Office of Education to administer the teaching and research programs under this Act. This will be called the Division of Handicapped Children and Youth.

With these words, President Kennedy signed PL 88–164, and programs for education of the handicapped reached an administrative high water mark. The Division brought together in one unit the Captioned Films program, an expanded teacher training program, and the new research program in education of the handicapped established by PL 88–164. Dr. Samuel A. Kirk was chosen by the President to establish the Division.

A history of legislation concerning education of the handicapped must inevitably involve, to some extent, the administrative structures charged with the operation of programs. This is true because of the traditional governmental response to new programs—that is, a new program begets a new administrative unit. There is almost a one to one correlation between the level of the administrative unit formed and the degree to which the program is valued by the administration establishing it. (This pattern has been readily perceived by Congress, and upon occasion the legislative branch has indicated its interest in a program by creating, by statute, an administrative structure at the level it feels appropriate. One example, of course, is the Bureau of Education for the Handicapped, to be discussed later.) This pattern had been borne out by the development of programs in the area of special education which, by one name or another, had been a part of the Office of Education since its earliest days. For most of those years, special education was a one or two person program primarily charged with gathering and disseminating information. These programs were frequently located near the bottom of the administrative hierarchy. The first significant change in that pattern had come with the initiation of the professional training and Captioned Films programs when, for the first time, Office of Education personnel had the authority to disburse money as part of their attempt to assist in the development of educational programs for the handicapped. The financial resources increased OE's prestige and impact on the professions involved. A new division, second only to a Bureau in the Office of Education hierarchy, brought new strength and significance to the programs for which it was responsible.

PL 88- 164, Section 301 — Training Professional Personnel

Section 301 of the Mental Retardation Facilities and Community Mental Health Centers Construction Act of 1963 amended PL 85- 926. It combined the earlier training authorities for professional personnel in the areas of retardation and deafness, and authorized grants to institutions of higher education and to state education agencies. Under the new definitions of this section, personnel could be trained to provide special education, speech correction, and related services to handicapped children, i.e., "mentally retarded, hard of hearing, deaf, speech impaired, visually handicapped, seriously emotionally disturbed, crippled or other health impaired children, who by reason thereof, require special education."

The basic training legislation, PL 85- 926, has been amended twice since its major revision by PL 88- 164. In each case, the amendments have extended and increased the authorizations for training personnel, but have not changed the nature of the proven program. The most recent change in authority was enacted as part of the 1967 Mental Retardation Amendments, PL 90- 170. In this legislation, the authorization was extended through Fiscal Year 1970, and increased to $55 million. Congressional support for this vital program has been based on recognition of its effectiveness. Since its beginning, more than 32,000 awards have been made to support individuals on full or part time study.

PL 88- 164, Section 302 —
Research and Demonstration Projects in
Education of Handicapped Children

This legislation authorized the Commissioner of Education to make grants for research and demonstration projects relating to education for handicapped children to

States, State or local educational agencies, public and nonprofit institutions of higher learning, and other public or nonprofit educational or research agencies and organizations.

Later in 1965, PL 89-105 added to this authority a section permitting the construction, equipping, and operation of facilities for research and related purposes, including demonstrations, dissemination activites, and training of research personnel.

The necessity for a special research program with its own funds, specifically aimed at education of the handicapped, was demonstrated by the declining support for mental retardation under the Cooperative Research Act. In 1957, 61 percent of funds spent under this Act were spent in the area of retardation. In 1958, the amount was 54 percent. The following year the "earmarking" was removed, and by 1961, only 9 percent of the funds were being spent on projects in the retardation area. By 1963, the percentage was down to 5 (Kirk, 1966).

The message that categorical legislation was necessary to protect the interests of handicapped children was once more reinforced, and the research provisions of PL 88-164 came into being. The demonstrated operational effectiveness of the resulting program and its creative leadership has led to the rapid growth of support from $1 million authorized in 1964 to $18 million authorized for 1970.

Reorganization. Eighteen months after the Division of Handicapped Children and Youth was formed in July, 1965, it was disbanded, caught in USOE's overall reorganization which had been brought about by the giant new responsibilities which accompanied passage of the Elementary and Secondary Education Act of 1965. This action was no reflection on the Division or its leaders, Samuel Kirk and his successor Morvin Wirtz. In fact, under their leadership, the Division received a Presidential citation and a superior service award from the Secretary of Health, Education, and Welfare. (Kirk's leaving the Office of Education to return to Illinois after he completed his agreed upon stay has been immortalized in the classic pun of Representative Hugh L. Carey,

TABLE 1.

Basic Federal Legislation for Education of the Handicapped, 1957-1967

Year	Authority	Purpose
1957	Pl 83-531. Cooperative Research	Action of the Appropriations Committee earmarked for the retarded approximately 2/3 of the $1 million appropriated.
1958	PL 85-905 Captioned Films	A program of captioning films for cultural enrichment and recreation of deaf persons.
	PL 85-926. Professional Personnel	Grants for training leadership personnel in education of the mentally retarded.
1959	PL 86-158. Professional Personnel	Added authorization for support grants to institutions of higher learning.
1961	PL 87-276. Teachers of the Deaf	Grants for training basic instructional personnel in education of the deaf.
	PL 87-715. Captioned Films	Provided for the production and distribution of films.
1963	PL 88-164, Section 301. Professional Personnel	Expanded authority to train personnel for handicapping conditions not previously covered; "hard of hearing, speech inpaired, visually handicapped, seriously emotionally disturbed, crippled, or other health impaired," were added to mentally retarded and deaf.
	Pl 88-164, Section 302. Research and Demonstration	Grants for research and demonstration projects in the area of education of the handicapped.
1965	PL 89-36. National Technical Institute for the Deaf	Created a new source for higher education for the deaf.

TABLE 1 *(Continued)*

Year	Authority	Purpose
	PL 89-105. Professional Personnel and Research	Extended basic authorities, allowed development of research and demonstration centers.
	PL 89-258. Captioned Films	Expanded authority, allowed development and distribution of other media and equipment in addition to films.
	PL 89-313. State Schools	Amended Title I, ESEA to provide grants to states for children in state operated or supported schools for the handicapped.
1966	PL 89-694. Model Secondary School for the Deaf	Created a model high school in Washington, D. C.
	PL 89-750. Education of Handicapped Children (Title VI, ESEA)	Grants to states for preschool, elementary, and secondary school children; National Advisory Committee; Bureau of Education for the Handicapped.
1967	PL 90-170. Mental Retardation Amendments of 1967	Extended basic training authority, added new authority for training personnel and for research in area of physical education and recreation for handicapped children.
	PL 90-247 Amendments to Title VI, ESEA	Regional Resource Centers; Centers for Deaf Blind Children; expansion of Media Services; grants for Recruitment and Information dissemination; earmarking 15 percent Title III of ESEA for handicapped children; intramural research and contracts for research; increased funds for state schools; changes in Title VI grants-to-states formula and authorizations.

Chairman of the Ad Hoc Subcommittee on the Handicapped, who told the 1966 Convention of The Council for Exceptional Children that it was a "case of separation of Kirk and State.")

Special education, the minority group, had once more been caught in the philosophy of the greatest good for the greatest number. Under the new organization, the programs for training, research, and Captioned Films were placed in separate administrative units. Programs continued to be operated as effectively as possible, but attempts at coordination were not always successful and, in general, the new administrative structure seemed to dissipate the sense of active leadership in the national effort to improve education for the handicapped. While creation of the Elementary and Secondary Education Act indirectly contributed to a plateau in the growth of federal support for education of the handicapped in the administrative dimension, its programs did provide new support. In addition, its passage added new strength to the momentum of federal aid for education and to the concept of categorical aid for minority groups.

The Great Congress —
First Session 1965

The 89th Congress felt strongly that it had a mandate from the people to enact into law the major goals of the Kennedy and Johnson administrations. President Johnson had received 61 percent of the votes in his election the previous November, the highest percentage of votes received by any President. There were strong majorities in both houses of Congress, and the time had come to face what the President called "our ancient enemies, illiteracy, disease, poverty, and bigotry."

Of the many programs developed and approved by the Congress and the Administration — programs aimed at the cities, at the aged ("medicare"), etc., — none outranked in brilliance the Elementary and Secondary Education Act of 1965, PL 89-10. Its final passage, with its programs of assistance to children in disadvantaged areas (including handicapped children), new instructional materials, centers for innovation and research, and support for strengthening state educational agencies, was precedent shattering not only in its educational implications, but also in the brilliance of its legislative drafting and strategy which succeeded in overcoming the traditional barriers to federal aid to education.

PL 89-313 —
Aid for Education of Handicapped
Children in
State Operated Institutions

As ESEA became implemented, children with handicapping conditions shared in its benefits. Projects under Title I reached handicapped children in low income areas through local education agencies. Title III provided support for some excellent new programs under its provisions for supplemental centers and its support for innovative programs. Provisions from the other titles also offered some help. It was apparent, however, that the basic thrust of ESEA was toward the economically disadvantaged or the general educational community, and that more direct sources of support for the handicapped would be necessary.

On November 1, 1965, a major step was taken toward this goal through a provision of PL 89-313. While this law was primarily concerned with school construction assistance in major disaster areas, Section 6 of that Act amended Title I of ESEA to provide support to state agencies which were directly responsible for educating handicapped children. Until this amendment, Title I worked through local educational agencies; thus, state operated or supported schools for the deaf, retarded, etc., which were not a part of a local school district, were not eligible for Title I benefits.

This provision has had a profound impact on the educational programs in schools and institutions for the handicapped, by providing new teachers, equipment, supplemental personnel, diagnostic facilities, etc. In numerous cases, children who had been receiving only custodial care began to participate for the first time in educational training.

In addition to its educational implications, the PL 89-313 amendment may be seen as another precedent, a building block toward the total construction of categorical aid for education of handicapped children. As early legislation for training teachers of the retarded and deaf led to broader authorities, so this provision for educational services to institutionalized children paved the way toward broader provisions of service to children in day schools.

PL 89-36 — The National Technical Institute for the Deaf Act

The great educational challenge presented by deafness, the effectiveness of people interested in this area, and the success of the training and Captioned Films programs, all have combined to develop a special awareness and receptivity in Congress for educational programs benefiting the deaf. This favorable attitude has been an important component in the expansion of programs to include other areas of handicapping conditions.

For 100 years, Gallaudet College in Washington, D. C., has been the only institution in the world designed specifically to provide post-secondary education for the deaf. While Gallaudet's liberal arts program has won plaudits from educators around the world for its successes, modern society increasingly calls for people with technical and professional training. This need, coupled with declining employment possibilities for the deaf, was documented by national conferences and workshops, the Babbidge report (Advisory Committee on Education of the Deaf, 1965) to the Secretary of Health, Education, and Welfare, and by Congressional hearings.

On June 8, 1965, President Johnson signed the National Technical Institute for the Deaf Act (PL 89-36) authorizing the Secretary of Health, Education, and Welfare to enter into an agreement with an institution of higher education for the establishment and operation of a postsecondary technical training facility for young deaf adults. This agreement had subsequently been made with the Rochester Institute of Technology, in New York.

With these new programs and an expansion and extension of the authorities for the Captioned Films, training, and research programs, the first session of the 89th Congress closed. It was a session which produced new programs, extended authorities, and strengthened momentum, thus setting the stage for the next major era.

THE CAREY COMMITTEE AND
TITLE VI, ESEA

In the spring of 1966, Congress decided it was time to take a closer look at federal programs for education of the handicapped, to consolidate gains, and to build a foundation for the future. Representative Hugh L. Carey of Brooklyn, New York, was named Chairman of a Special Ad Hoc Subcommittee on the Handicapped of the House Committee on Education and Labor. A similar House of Representatives Study Committee headed by Congressman Carl Elliott of Alabama, had held nationwide hearings in 1959 and 1960, and while no legislation was forthcoming in that session of Congress, many of the items discussed became part of later Acts. Representative Carey, a prime mover in the development of ESEA, had been a supporter of programs for the handicapped, taking an active part in introducing and gaining passage of PL 89-313 and the National Technical Institute, among other programs.

For a total of nine months, the Carey Committee examined the situation, hearing witnesses from federal programs, professional groups, and state and local agencies. Over 1,000 printed pages of testimony and supplemental information comprised the record of this examination. By August the pattern was clear, and on August 4, 1966, Mr. Carey introduced the Handicapped Child Benefit and Education Act (HR 16847). Following the pattern of ESEA, it provided for grants to the states for education of children in the elementary and secondary schools, grants for the purchase of instructional materials, support for innovative programs, and policies to strengthen state departments in the special education area. In addition, it proposed: (a) expansion of the Captioned Films for the Deaf program to include development and distribution of instructional materials for all types of handicapped children; (b) new programs for recruitment and distribution of information; (c) expansion of research and training authorities; (d) a Statutory National Advisory Committee on Education of the Handicapped; and (e) as a central organizing force, a new Bureau within the U. S. Office of Education specifically for education of the handicapped.

Although this bill was received by the professions with great enthusiasm and anticipation, it was not slated to be passed. Of the thousands of bills introduced each year, only a relatively few pass through the hurdles of subcommittee and committee hearings, debate on the floor before the full House or Senate, and reconciliation of differences by a joint conference committee, to achieve final approval by each House. Among the many factors which influence the fate of a bill, perhaps the most critical is whether or not the Administration approves it, not only in concept, but in timing. Is it a planned part of the President's budget? How much will it cost? These are important practical factors to be weighed, in addition to careful analysis of its ingredients from the program operation point of view.

While the interest of the Administration in education of the handicapped was clear, the combination of cost and timing factors soon made it obvious that while the concept was approved (with the exception of the statutory bureau), the time was not ripe for full scale approval of the Carey Bill. However, within 15 months, every major feature of the Carey Bill had become part of the law, passed as amendments to the Elementary and Secondary Education Act.

PL 89–694 –
The Model Secondary School
for the Deaf Act

In its study of federal programs for the handicapped, the Carey Subcommittee was struck by the report that there was not a single high school in the country for deaf children which was comparable in quality to a first class high school for hearing children.

This fact was especially impressive in light of the recent passage of the National Technical Institute for the Deaf legislation. In addition, Gallaudet College authorities testified that only 8 per cent of deaf children attended college, as compared with over 40 percent of hearing children, and they pointed to inadequate high school education as a major factor.

Representative Carey and Senator Hill introduced and gained passage for legislation which created a Model Secondary School for the Deaf, which would be built on the campus of Gallaudet College and would serve children from the District of Columbia and nearby states. The school was planned to serve sufficient numbers of children in order to offer a full curriculum and the normal extracurricular activities of high schools. The success of this model may pave the way for future schools in varying regions of the country.

PL 89-750 — Title VI:
Education for Handicapped Children

When it had become apparent that the Carey bill would not be able to gain Congressional approval, the House had already passed its version of the Elementary and Secondary Education Act Amendments of 1966, but the Morse Subcommittee on Education of the Senate Committee on Labor and Public Welfare was just beginning its study. When that subcommittee finished its deliberations and reported the 1966 ESEA amendments, Senator Morse had successfully added a new Title VI, Education of Handicapped Children. As part of the total ESEA package, its chances of at least partial success were excellent.

The new Title proposed a program of grants to the states for the initiation, expansion, and improvement of programs for educating handicapped children in preschool, elementary, and secondary schools. It proposed to set up a national advisory committee on handicapped children for the Commissioner of Education, and it called for the creation of a bureau within the U. S. Office of Education to provide coordination and leadership for programs affecting handicapped children. This proposal to create a bureau became the center of controversy.

The Carey hearings had brought into focus the feeling among professionals that programs for the handicapped had suffered since the dissolution of the Division of Handicapped Children and Youth. Some of the most colorful aspects of the Carey hearings revolved around differences in philosophy between those setting policy for programs in the Office of Education and the Committee Chairman, whose beliefs had practically unanimous support from people in the professional fields involved. The Senate Committee's studies reinforced support for a new bureau.

Administration resistance to the bureau centered around three factors: (a) its statutory nature overruled a usual prerogative of the Executive Branch to plan its own administrative structure; (b) it could possibly set a precedent for the establishment of bureaus for other special interest or minority groups within education; and (c) it would take the research in education of the handicapped program out of the Bureau of Research, thereby undoing the organizational pattern of the Office of Education in which all research activities were under this one structure.

And so the stage was set for the first Conference Committee meeting which was referred to at the opening of this article. If the bureau was not going to be accepted by the conferees, the U.S. Office of Education would probably establish a new division, but in all likelihood the program of research in education of handicapped children would remain in the Bureau of Research. With a new bureau, education of the handicapped would reach full parity with the other programs of the U. S. Office of Education and, for the first time, specialists in education of the handicapped, would be at top policy making levels within the Office. There was debate. At the end of the first day of the conference, the general impression was that the bureau was out of consideration, but when the conference ended, Title VI was intact. Senator Morse made a strong statement on the floor of the Senate calling for quick action to establish the program. Within two months, the bureau was established by Commissioner of Education, Harold Howe, II.

THE 1967 LEGISLATIVE PACKAGE

In the jam packed first months of the Bureau's operation, the logistics of transferring people, selecting the new Associate Commissioner who in turn selected his staff, the beginning of the new Title VI grant programs, and all the necessary and intricate demands of a continuing government program tended to ˙obscure temporarily the significance of the new legislative proposals which would be part of the Administration's suggestions for 1967 amendments to ESEA. The great excitement of the previous year's hearings and the creation of Title VI and the new Bureau threatened to make new programs slightly anticlimatic.

This perspective was not shared by Bureau personnel and the HEW and Congressional legislative experts who had been developing legislation for the handicapped year by year. The Administration's proposed program to: (a) develop regional resource centers; (b) to provide support for recruitment of personnel and dissemination of information; and (c) to expand the target group of the Captioned Films program, were seen as a heightened commitment to education of the handicapped. Almost all of the previous legislation had been stimulated by Congress, not suggested by the Executive Branch. In addition, there seemed to be a readiness in Congress to move forward from last year's achievements. Congressional support in both Houses was bipartisan, Democrats and Republicans alike expressing interest in providing equal educational opportunity for every handicapped child.

The Education and Labor Committee in the House quickly approved these new provisions for the handicapped, and the bill moved to the Senate for consideration.

The bill that emerged from the Senate Committee, was approved by the full Senate, and went to the House-Senate Conference, included not only these Administration provisions, but added new ones. In all, it was the broadest program of benefits for the education of the handicapped ever to reach this legislative stage. Its provisions would affect every facet of the program of the Bureau of Education for the Handicapped: manpower, research, media, and direct support for children in the schools. In summary, it provided for the following:

1. *Regional Resource Centers.* These centers would assist teachers and other school personnel by providing education evaluation and assistance in developing specific educational programs and strategies. While providing direct services to children and parents, the basic aim of the resource centers would be to work with teachers in meeting the extraordinary challenges presented by handicapped children.

2. *Recruitment and Information.* Under this provision, grants or contracts could be awarded to develop programs for recruiting personnel into the field of education for the handicapped and related educational services. Awards could also be made for the development and distribution of information about these programs to parents, teachers, and others.

3. *Expansion of the Media Program to Include All Handicapped Children.* This new program would serve the educational needs of children who are mentally retarded, seriously emotionally disturbed, speech impaired, visually handicapped, crippled, or those having other health impairments, in addition to those deaf or hard of hearing children who are currently benefiting. The program provides for research, acquisition, production, and distribution of media, and for

training teachers and other persons in the use of educational media with handicapped children.

4. *Centers and Services for Deaf Blind Children.* This program provides for the establishment and operation of centers for deaf blind children. The centers would provide comprehensive diagnostic and evaluation services; programs for education, adjustment, and orientations; and consultative services for parents, teachers, and others working with the deaf blind. In addition, centers would include research and training programs, where appropriate.

5. *Programs for the Handicapped under Title III of ESEA.* A major source of new support for innovation and for implementation of the newest in educational knowledge in programs for the handicapped would be made available by specifying that 15 percent of Title III funds must be used for programs and projects in the area of education for the handicapped. This provision, effective in Fiscal Year 1969, would provide approximately $30 million during that year for projects which will help bridge the gap between research findings and application in everyday classroom activities.

6. *Increase in Title I Funds for Children in State Schools (PL 89-313).* Title of ESEA would be amended to provide increased support for education of children in state operated or supported schools for the handicapped. Under the new formula, states receive maximum grants on behalf of these children. This change provides approximately $9 million in additional support in Fiscal Year 1968.

7. *Research and Demonstration.* The program for research and related purposes in education of the handicapped would be extended and expanded to include authority to train research personnel, conduct research, and to award contracts for research, in addition to the current authority under which grants have been available. A new intramural authority would be used to help evaluate the effectiveness of federal programs for education of the handicapped when support for research under the grant and contract method is not practicable.

8. *Changes in Title VI Grants to States Program.* New provisions would allow Title VI grants to be made to the Department of Defense on behalf of handicapped children in schools operated by that department and to the Department of Interior on behalf of children on Indian reservations serviced by schools operated by that department. A change in the grants-to-states allocation formula provides that no

state shall receive less than $100,000 or 3/10 of one percent of the appropriation for Title VI grants to states, whichever is greater. This provision is designed to give each state a grant large enough to insure that Title VI programs in that state will be of sufficient quality and magnitude to offer a reasonable possibility of effectiveness.

PL 90-170 —
Physical Education and
Recreation for the Handicapped

While the 1967 amendments to ESEA were in the final stages of development, the 1967 Mental Retardation Amendments were passed, becoming PL 90-170. In addition to extending the 85-926 program, as noted earlier, the Act added a new Title V to the Mental Retardation Facilities and Community Mental Health Centers Construction Act of 1963. This new authority provides support for training professional personnel and for research and demonstration activities in the area of physical education and recreation with mentally retarded and other handicapped children. In language and intent, the new Title parallels the basic training and research authorities for education of handicapped children, and will provide new resources for development in this area.

Final Approval. The legislative process involved in securing passage for the 1967 ESEA Amendments progressed slowly. Finally, Congress was in the last week of its session and rumors were that ESEA would be carried over into the next session to begin in January of 1968. Protests were heard from educators around the country, who had been waiting for funds through ESEA programs until the formulas were revised by these amendments, and they wanted final decisions. People interested in education for the handicapped wanted the new programs signed, sealed, and delivered, recognizing that new legislative proposals are never secure until passed. Finally the President and Congressional leadership were able to move the bill along.

The conferees accepted every new proposal to benefit handicapped children. It was not accidental. Much hard work had been done in the nearly 12 months since the session had begun in January of 1967, and, in fact, during the past decade. The full House and Senate approved the conferees' actions, in the last half-hour before adjournment on December 15th. President Johnson's signature completed the process and the 1967 ESEA Amendments became PL 90-247.

THE
FUTURE

Throughout this discussion, we have traced the development of new authorities and programs. The separate and distinct appropriation process has not been stressed, but, in the final analysis, appropriations are "where the action is."

Converting these new authorities into successful operating programs will require support funds, not only for the grants to be awarded, but for the staff to administer the programs, to oversee their operation, and to cooperate with the grantees in evaluating their effectiveness.

While the glamour and excitement is in the new authorization bills, the power is in their funding. Beyond this, the final meaning of the legislation and the fulfillment of its promise are in the efforts of professional people, teachers, and related specialists who give it life through their successful work with children.

REFERENCES

Advisory Committee on Education of the Deaf. *Education of the deaf: a report to the Secretary of Health, Education, and Welfare.* Washington: U. S. Department of Health, Education, and Welfare, 1965.

Kirk, S. A. *Hearings. Part I.* Ad-hoc Subcommittee on the Handicapped. House Committee on Education and Labor. 89th Congress, Second Session; June 15, 1966. Washington: U. S. Government Printing Office, 1966.

planning
and evaluation
*for the future**

MICHAEL MARGE†

Throughout the history of man, there has always been an expressed need for experts who can predict the future. Each generation has had its soothsayers, astrologers, and fortune tellers. Even in modern times we still take heed of the predictions of various popular prognosticators. The reason that such prophets have existed throughout the ages is that man has a profound need to know his destiny. Man is frustrated by the uncertainty of the things to come and desires some knowledge about future events so that he will be prepared for the best or the worst. This frustration is understandable, especially as man reviews the past and the role he has played in the development of the events of history. It is then that he realizes how these events may have been altered had he known what to expect. Hindsight, therefore, has taught the lesson of the need for planning.

Though some of the information offered by the soothsayers tells what to avoid or what steps to take to alter an outcome, most of their predictions imply a fixed outcome which is destined by a divine force and which cannot be modified or prevented. Finding this type

*Reprinted from Exceptional Children, Vol. 34 (March 1968), pp. 505-508, by permission of the author and the Council for Exceptional Children. Copyright 1968 by the Council for Exceptional Children.

†Michael Marge is Director, Program Planning and Evaluation, Bureau of Education for the Handicapped, U. S. Office of Education.

of planning service unacceptable, many segments of the society have sought other means by which to predict the future for the purpose of controlling it.

A new band of soothsayers — the program planners — have come into existence. Armed with statistical techniques, research design methods, high speed electronic computers, systems of data collection, and a small crystal ball (for good luck!), they offer their services predicated on a simple thesis: man can control his destiny once he has identified all the variables related to an event and the methods for altering the variables.

Though industry and the business world have accepted the efficacy of program planning, the nation has been somewhat resistant to applying such planning to educational and social issues. It is quite clear now that if the nation is to realize substantial progress in eliminating the major educational and social problems with which we are faced, it must accept the concept of planning. In the areas of general and special education, for example, it becomes necessary to identify long range goals and a commitment to a long term strategy if we are to effectively eliminate the current pattern of patchwork programs to meet the educational needs of children.

In recognition of this problem, the Office of Education has established program planning and evaluation staffs at the Commissioner's level and in each of the bureaus to identify these goals and to develop appropriate strategies for education. In concert with the efforts of the Office of Education and other agencies interested in the education of the handicapped, The Council for Exceptional Children also has taken steps to study the future growth and development of special education.

Effective national planning involves the participation of all segments of our society interested in the problems of special education. As part of the Bureau's total planning operation, this would include the National Advisory Committee on Handicapped Children; the Bureau's review panels in research, training, and services; professional organizations concerned with the education of the handicapped; professionals from the field of special education; and authorities from medicine, psychology, sociology, anthropology, social work, business and private industry, and associations interested in the problems of providing special educational services to the handicapped. Planning, therefore, becomes a cooperative effort by the participation of a wide segment of the leadership in our nation, resulting in a better designed, more feasible, and better supported plan for the future.

PROGRAM PLANNING AND
EVALUATION FUNCTIONS

The Office of Program Planning and Evaluation for the Bureau of Education for the Handicapped has five major functions. They are:

1. The Management of the
Program Planning and
Budgeting System (PPBS)

The Program Planning and Budgeting System is a facility within the Department of Health, Education, and Welfare which assists in the development of five year projections of programs and financial plans for each of the agencies within the Department. After analyzing the current requests by the constituent agencies, the Department prepares program projections for future years. PPBS has been designed as a planning tool and as an information source. It groups funding and program results by major purposes, activities, and beneficiaries. The information is organized to identify the agency, appropriation, mode of financing, legislative authority, and the nature of the recipient to whom funds may be distributed. In addition to the classification of programs by purpose, the system distinguishes programs by the ways in which purposes are accomplished. These purposes include research and development, demonstration and testing, training of personnel, provision of services, dissemination of information, and management activities. Finally, recipients are identified according to those who will realize immediate benefits and those who will ultimately benefit from the support of the program. The results or products of programs are expressed in non-financial output indicators or measures. Such measures are related to specific program objectives and to the scope and magnitude of the problem to which a program is directed.

In essence, the Bureau, through PPBS, creates a plan which identifies the relationships among program purposes, activities, beneficiary groups, and results, projected into the future. On the basis of such information, the Bureau is better able to plan for changes in program emphasis, for the development of new legislation, and for the utilization of new strategies. However, as with all planning systems, certain precautions must be taken by the administrator in utilizing the results of the system. There is a tendency for the system to create an attitude that it is an end in itself rather than a means to support the decision making process of the administrator. As long as the planning system is recognized as a tool to provide the administrator with the best available information organized in a meaningful manner, its validity will be supported. The policy maker needs as much information as possible in order to decide on future program directions. The planning system is only one source of such information.

2. The Evaluation of Programs Administered by the Bureau

Evaluation encompasses the maintenance of an ongoing program of assessment to determine the impact of federal legislation on education for the handicapped and the accumulation and study of pertinent data on the handicapped through surveys and field studies. Before planning can be intelligently and meaningfully initiated, certain hard core data are necessary. Therefore, as part of the process of evaluation, the Bureau's Program Planning and Evaluation (PPE) staff is continuously engaged in collecting the most recent data on training, research, and services for the handicapped.

Plans for evaluation projects for 1968-1969 include the following: (a) a study of manpower needs for the handicapped and the effect of PL 85-926, as amended (Training of Professional Personnel in the Education of the Handicapped), on meeting these needs; (b) the development of an evaluation model for Title VI of the Elementary and Secondary Education Act; (c) the identification and assessment of new models of educational services for the handicapped; and (d) a study of the effect of Office of Education research and demonstration activities on the improvement of educational programing for the handicapped. In addition, short term studies of the review process of grant applications for support under the various legislative authorities administered by the Bureau will be conducted. Finally, PPE will conduct a study of the programs of support for education of the handicapped in the Office of Education and in other federal agencies to determine the government's commitment in this area of activity.

3. Development and Maintenance of a Management Information System

The Program Planning and Budgeting System is augmented by the management information system which organizes the continuous input of information related to the Bureau's operation. It collects the information about all significant aspects of the Bureau's programs and activities from application forms, letters, written reports, publications, and other sources, then stores it in appropriate categories, and assures rapid availability for use in decision making. The Bureau is faced with the need for managing its massive input of information from governmental and nongovernmental sources. Requests from the public, professional organizations, state and local educational agencies, other federal agencies, Congress, and from other sources, for descriptive information and summaries about the programs of the Bureau require a system by which data may be automatically processed. PPE has taken the necessary steps to implement the development of such a system, which should become operational in late spring, 1968.

4. Search for New Concepts and Strategies in Special Education

A fourth function is to participate with professionals in and outside of government in the search for new and promising directions in the provision of services for the handicapped, with the purpose of developing appropriate program emphases and new legislation. In the areas of professional personnel training, research, and direct services to children, the exploration for better methods, materials, and techniques in the education of the handicapped is a continuing responsibility of PPE. In recognition of this, PPE works closely with the professional community in carrying out this function.

5. Coordination of Program Activities

Coordination refers to a broad program to establish formal and informal mechanisms for the purposes of communication and cooperation among bureaus within the Office of Education and between it and other federal agencies to accomplish the common goal of quality educational programing for handicapped children. Though coordination is generally initiated by the Associate Commissioner, the maintenance of liaison with a task force or a committee has been one of the major functions of PPE.

As part of the Office of the Associate Commissioner, PPE carries out these functions — a new dimension for strengthening the Bureau with support and advice. Besides its primary responsibility to the Associate Commissioner and the Bureau operation, it offers many services to the divisions and to their respective administrative units. PPE's effectiveness is dependent upon the close cooperation of all professional staff members of the Bureau, since almost all of its projects require voluntary assistance.

In planning for the future, PPE has identified a number of long range goals and strategies which are still under advisement. One of the most prominent goals is the provision of effective educational programing and services to all handicapped children in the United States during the next decade. With the current and potentially vast resources of our nation, this goal can be accomplished. By establishing an action oriented partnership among the federal agencies, state and local educational agencies, professional organizations, institutions of higher education, and parent interest groups, all committed to the goal of services for all handicapped, the task is feasible. The population of the handicapped represents a relatively small target group when compared with other populations in need of assistance. It will require, however, a shift in national priorities so that the necessary funds, efforts, and interest are available. Besides the benefits it will bring to the handicapped child and adult, the realization of this goal will have an historical significance. Our nation will be identified as one which, in keeping with its espoused humanitarian values, can direct some of its vast resources to the assistance of a population long in need of help.

The accomplishment of this goal, as well as others in the education of the handicapped, will require a great deal of planning. The Bureau's Office of Program Planning and Evaluation is prepared to provide the necessary elements for such planning. These elements will be the result of the best available information concerning the education of the handicapped. But when such information is not available, it is hoped that we will be forgiven when we turn, as did the soothsayers of old, to our crystal ball to foretell the future.

*implementing
effective coordination
of programs
for the handicapped**

ELIZABETH M. GOODMAN†

Cooperative, coordinated effort is recognized by educators of handicapped children as an essential element of effective programing on a day to day basis. The teacher is one of a team of specialists working along with the diagnosticians, clinicians, therapists, pupil personnel staff, administrators, and parents — all hopefully harmonized in an integrated process for the development of a handicapped child. One of the major problems as we face growing coordination of programs and services is how to organize a team with amicable interpersonal relationships. When the interdisciplinary team concept prevails, group planning and deliberation, rather than the single judgment of one expert, give direction to the overall program for the child.

The child's classroom instruction is, wherever possible, carefully blended with other developmental activities. This insures consistency of direction to his total progress and sometimes results in concerted remedial therapeutic effort. With an increase in recognition that the child's personal, social, and intellectual development is dependent upon the environment of the classroom and the instruction he receives, the school plays an increasingly important role as the focal point for coordination of services. Funding for these services may

*Reprinted from *Exceptional Children*, Vol. 34 (March 1968), pp. 569-576, by permission of the author and the Council for Exceptional Children. Copyright 1968 by the Council for Exceptional Children.

†Elizabeth M. Goodman is Education Program Specialist, Program Planning and Evaluation Staff, Bureau of Education for the Handicapped, U. S. Office of Education.

originate from a variety of sources from public or private, local, state, federal, or a combination of several sources. Coordination must strengthen and support the total effort in order to meet the many needs of handicapped children. In working with handicapped children, it is important to combine as many services as possible within one facility, preferably at the school or reasonably accessible to it. The teacher of the handicapped is primarily concerned with following the prescriptions which treat the handicapped child's learning disabilities; the success of the treatment depends largely upon its coordination with related disciplines. With so many types of services needed, we must aim to achieve effective professional coordination without becoming involved in destructive or corrosive interpersonal relationships. What are some of the mechanisms to help improve efforts toward the team approach?

Coordination has six major functions which relate to planning, operation, and evaluation of programs, whether it takes place laterally or at different operational levels. It attempts to provide the following functional mechanisms for effective programing at all levels:

1. Identification of needs.
2. Identification of resources.
3. Identification of gaps.
4. Identification of unwarranted duplication.
5. Collaboration.
6. Concerted effort to meet critical needs.

With an increasing amount of federal funds becoming available for the benefit of the handicapped population, the Bureau of Education for the Handicapped is deeply interested in improving coordination. The chart on federal programs administered by the Bureau of Education for the Handicapped shows its expanding responsibility for the handicapped (Table 1). There also exist related programs administered by other bureaus of the Office of Education which could significantly benefit the handicapped. The Bureau has developed a mechanism for providing active coordination within and without the Office of Education, and for promoting the concept of the schools as a focal point for coordination of services.

Like the classroom teacher, the Bureau of Education for the Handicapped has as its ultimate goal the desire to help every handicapped child grow and develop to the maximum, in accordance with his abilities. Its professional staff is concerned with the continued improvement of educational facilities and programs for

TABLE 1.

Federal Programs Administered by the Bureau of Education for the Handicapped

Program and Legislative Authority	Purpose	Who May Apply	Fiscal Year 1968 Appropriation	Where to Apply
Elementary and Secondary Education Act, PL 89-10				
Title I, State School Support (PL 89-313)	Grants for handicapped children in state supported schools to expand and improve educational programs. (Includes acquisition of equipment and, where necessary, construction of facilities).	Eligible agencies apply through state departments of education.	$24,700,000 (estimate)	Division of Educational Services
Title III, Supplemental Educational Centers and Services. Special Programs and Projects for the Handicapped	Grants for supplementary or exemplary programs or projects designed to meet the special educational needs of the handicapped, which hold promise of solution of critical educational problems. (Not less than 15 percent of Title III funds shall be used for handicapped.)	State departments of education and local educational agencies through state departments of education (begins in Fiscal Year 1969).	0	Office of Associate Commissioner
Title VI-A, Education of Handicapped Children, Preschool, Elementary, and Secondary	Support for initiation, expansion, and improvement of programs and projects for the education of handicapped children.	Local public educational agencies apply through state departments of education.	14,250,000	Division of Educational Services

Title VI-B, Regional Resource Centers	Grants or contracts to assist in establishing regional centers to develop and apply the best methods of appraising the special educational needs of the handicapped and to assist schools, agencies, and institutions in providing programs.	Institutions of higher education, state and local educational agencies or combination within particular regions.	a	Office of Associate Commissioner
Title VI-C, Centers and Services for Deaf Blind Children	Grants or contracts to provide through model centers for deaf blind children, programs beginning in early childhood, which will enable the deaf blind to develop to their full potential (which may include construction, diagnostic and evaluative services, and consultative service for parents and teachers).	Public or nonprofit agencies, organizations or institutions.	a	Division of Educational Services
Title VI-D, Recruitment of Personnel and Information on Education of Handicapped	Grants or contracts to improve recruiting of educational personnel, and to improve dissemination of information concerning educational opportunities for the handicapped.	Public or nonprofit agencies, organizations or institutions may receive grants; public or private agencies, organizations, or institutions may receive contracts.	a	Office of Associate Commissioner

aUnfunded for Fiscal Year 1968 as of January 9, 1968.

TABLE 1 *(Continued)*

Federal Programs Administered by the Bureau of Education for the Handicapped

Program and Legislative Authority	Purpose	Who May Apply	Fiscal Year 1968 Appropriation	Where to Apply
Captioned Films for the Deaf, PL 85-905				
Captioned Films for the Deaf and Instructional Media for the Handicapped	Provides a captioned film loan service for educational, cultural, and vocational enrichment of the deaf.	State or local public agencies and schools, organizations or groups of deaf, persons involved with the deaf, individuals who are deaf and shut in at home.	$ 2,800,000[b]	Division of Educational Services
	Promotes educational advancement of the handicapped by producing and distributing educational media; includes acquisition of specialized equipment and film projectors.	State or local public agencies and schools, organizations or groups which serve handicapped, their parents, employers, or potential employers.	a	Division of Educational Services
	Provides contracts for research in use of educational and training films and other educational media for the handicapped, and for their production and distribution.	By invitation.	[b]included above	Division of Educational Services

Program	Description	Eligibility	Amount	Administration
	Grants for training persons in the use of educational media for the handicapped.	Public or other non-profit institutions of higher education for teachers, trainees, or other specialists.	[b] included above	Division of Educational Services
Handicapped Teacher Training, PL 85-926				
Training of Teachers of Handicapped Children (as amended by PL 88-164)	Grants to institutions of higher education and to state educational agencies for the training of teachers and specialists for the handicapped.	Institutions of higher education and state educational agencies are eligible for grants. Applicants for traineeships or fellowships apply to state educational agency or the participating higher institution.	$24,500,000	Division of Training Programs

TABLE 1 *(Continued)*

Federal Programs Administered by the Bureau of Education for the Handicapped

Program and Legislative Authority	Purpose	Who May Apply	Fiscal Year 1968 Appropriation	Where to Apply
Mental Retardation Facilities Construction Act, PL 88 164				
Title III, Section 302, as amended, Research and Demonstration Projects in Education of Handicapped Children	Grants and contracts to promote research and demonstration to improve the education of the handicapped. Grants for construction of research facilities.	State or local educational agencies, public or private institutions of higher education, public or private educational or research agencies, organizations, or individuals.	$11,100,000	Division of Research
Title V, Section 501, Training of Physical Education tors and Recreation Personnel for Handicapped Children.	Grants to public and other nonprofit institutions of higher education for professional training of physical education and recreation personnel for the handicapped.	Institutions of higher education.	a	Division of Training Programs

Title V, Section 502, Research and Demonstration Projects in Physical Education and Recreation for the Mentally Retarded and Other Handicapped	Grants for research and demonstration projects relating to physical education or recreation for the handicapped.	State or local educational agencies, public or nonprofit private educational or research agencies and organizations.	a	Division of Research

the children. Like the classroom teacher, it has a child centered approach focused on the growth and development of the whole child, and recognizes its responsibility for both his intellectual and social development, and his personal and vocational adjustment from preschool years into adulthood. This philosophy prevails in the administration of its programs.

The ultimate growth of the handicapped child as shown on Figure 1 is greatly dependent upon the extent and quality of effort and the amount of support given the many influences upon each stage of his development. This effort and support create a partnership administered and coordinated through federal, state, local, public, and private agencies which provide facilities, interdisciplinary services, personnel training, and research. They give continuous propulsion and momentum for the production of effective programs. Coordination takes place at various levels. Examples of some of the coordination functions performed by the Bureau, in order to keep the wheels balanced and evenly spinning, are shown in Figure 1.

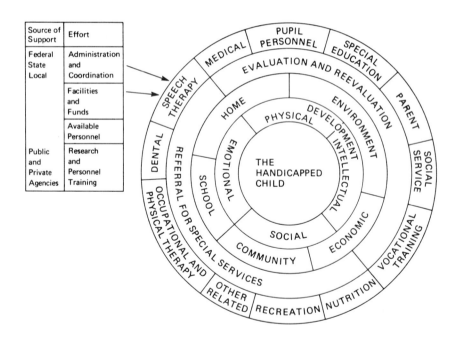

FIGURE 1.

IMPACT OF SOURCES OF SUPPORT AND EFFORT ON THE INTERDISCIPLINARY
TEAM APPROACH TO THE DEVELOPMENT OF THE HANDICAPPED CHILD

IDENTIFICATION OF
NEEDS

The Bureau's major contribution in this area is a data collection system designed to provide the information on the size and scope of problems relating to the education of the handicapped. Because of many factors, such as inadequate reporting systems, varying definitions of target populations, and incomplete information, it has been difficult to determine the extent of existing needs among the estimated five million school aged handicapped children. The Bureau staff has been cooperating with a variety of federal agencies concerned with data collection. It is concerned with developing standard terminology for school reporting and gathering information on the number and types of handicapped children, professional competencies of personnel, personnel shortages, and cost analyses to project future needs and potential capabilities. The nation's needs will be significantly clarified through the increased coordination of information provided by various state administrative and operational plans which the states submitted in order to become eligible for federal funds.

The exciting research findings in the field of cognitive development and the new knowledge accessible through the ERIC systems are giving school administrators and special educators a more realistic picture of the needs for the handicapped.

IDENTIFICATION OF
RESOURCES

The Bureau's principal activity is the conducting of ongoing functional analyses, both of various pieces of legislation and of the extent to which they may benefit the handicapped and may be combined to provide comprehensive services. Eligible recipients for grants or contracts to carry out the health, education, or welfare programs are designated in most instances as the state agencies, public and private institutions of higher education, or other nonprofit organizations. The Bureau staff examines the provisions of the laws and congressional intent, in order to provide information to individuals or groups concerned with the design of multifunded projects which combine services aimed at similar target groups. For example, a community could become skillful in packaging several pieces of funding to supplement their limited resources and concentrate on problem areas by providing well rounded, imaginative multifunded programs. The following series of steps for strengthening a program in mental retardation could conceivably (a) obtain consultative help from a state education department specialist funded through Title V of ESEA, (b) arrange an inservice special study institute through the Teacher Training Program for the Handicapped, (c) receive special materials to improve communication skills under Title III of NDEA, (d) obtain suitable library books from the school library or bookmobile which were purchased through funds of Title II of ESEA, (e) benefit from the Instructional Materials Center funded through the Research and Demonstration Program for the Handicapped, and (f) have an educational diagnostic center under Title VI of ESEA. In addition, many handicapped pupils could benefit from health services funded through the provisions of the Social Security Act programs, such as the following programs administered through state health and welfare departments.

1. *Child Welfare Services* (Title IV, Social Security Act, as amended). Needy children whose families qualify for public assistance may be provided with economic support for their health care and development. Emphasis is on rehabilitative services through social services and medical care.
2. *Maternal and Child Health Services* (Title V, Social Security Act, as amended). Mothers and children who would not otherwise receive care may be provided with health care and services. Program emphasis is the prevention of mental retardation. Special project grants may assist the mentally retarded to establish clinics with diagnostic, evaluation, counseling, treatment, education, and followup services.
3. *Crippled Children's Service* (Title V, Social Security Act, as amended). Disabled children may be provided comprehensive medical services. Program emphasis is on children with multiple handicaps or with severe physical handicaps.
4. *Medical Assistance Program* (Title XIX, Social Security Act Amendments). All needy persons whose income is insufficient to meet medical costs may be provided medical assistance. Program emphasis is on assisting people who have enough income or resources for daily living, but not enough for medical expenses.

The Bureau staff has identified related education legislation which may benefit the handicapped. Updated copies of these lists will be sent by the Bureau upon request. Some of the government agencies publish useful compilations of legislative programs which may be obtained directly from the agency or purchased from the

Superintendent of Documents, U. S. Government Printing Office, Washington, D. C. 20402. Following are four recent publications:

> *Catalog of Federal Assistance Programs.* A description of the federal government's domestic programs to assist the American people in furthering their social and economic progress, published by the Office of Economic Opportunity. It may be obtained, at no cost, from: The Office of Economic Opportunity Information Center, 1200 19th Street, N. W., Washington, D. C. 20506.
>
> *1968 Report on Federal Money for Education.* Reprint from American Education, February 1968 issue, U. S. Department of Health, Education, and Welfare, Office of Education; OE No. 11015. 15 cents.
>
> *Education '67, The Office of Education, Its Programs and Services.* U. S. Department of Health, Education, and Welfare, Office of Education; Superintendent of Documents Catalog No. FS 5:211,11006- 67. 35 cents.
>
> *Federal Research and Demonstration Programs Benefitting the Disadvantaged and Handicapped.* U. S. Department of Health, Education, and Welfare, Office of Education; Superintendent of Documents Catalog No. FS 5.235:35092. Single copies may be obtained at no cost from the Office of Education, 400 Maryland Avenue, N. W., Washington, D. C. 20202.

IDENTIFICATION OF GAPS

One of the main responsibilities of government is gathering information about the needs of all Americans, wherever they may be, and conveying these needs to the executive and legislative bodies. The Bureau of Education for the Handicapped has participated in the recent efforts to identify gaps related to education for the handicapped. This has resulted in new legislation potentially benefiting deaf blind children, and handicapped children in Interior and Defense Department Schools, as well as expanding educational media to all types of handicapped children.

IDENTIFICATION OF UNWARRANTED DUPLICATION

The various studies made by the Bureau reveal duplication and gaps in educational programs for the handicapped. Through coordination, it is possible to work with interagency groups within the government to determine ways to correct or prevent unwarranted duplication of effort. For example, the Bureau is working closely with the vocational education and rehabilitation staffs of the Office of Education and Rehabilitation Services Administration, respectively, to integrate rather than duplicate services. It has similarly established a cooperative relationship with the Children's Bureau staff regarding projects for the mentally retarded.

In the area of clinical services, especially those federal programs which may provide psychological diagnosis and therapeutic counseling, there exists the possibility for considerable duplication. The Bureau staff is working on efforts to avoid unnecessary duplication.

COLLABORATION

The federal agency staff is uniquely qualified to bring together groups representing areas of mutual concern in dealing with its broad social problems. Thus, the Bureau, representing the educational interests of the handicapped, is able to collaborate with other groups at the federal level in planning and making recommendations for the solutions of these problems. This may take the form of representation on a continuing committee such as the Interdepartmental Committee on Children and Youth, or on an interdisciplinary special task force appointed to prepare recommendations for a particular problem.

Another type of collaboration which presents a creative challenge is in the coordinated interagency multifunding approach. For example, the respective Commissioners of the Office of Education and the Rehabilitation Services Administration (formerly known as the Vocational Rehabilitation Administration), jointly sent a letter in January, 1967, to each of the state commissioners of education and state directors of vocational rehabilitation on the subject of cooperative educational and vocational rehabilitation programs for handicapped youth. This letter suggested joint conferences of appropriate staff members from the areas of vocational education, special education, and vocational rehabilitation "to stimulate new activities in those areas where service gaps for inschool disabled youth exist." They further commented:

> *It is especially appropriate at this time for education and vocational rehabilitation agencies which have not yet developed a coordinated effort to review their activities*

and investigate the advantages of a cooperative approach. The 1965 Vocational Rehabilitation Amendments have made available . . . new grant programs for the innovation and expansion of vocational rehabilitation services. . . . The 1963 Vocational Education Act and the 1966 Elementary and Secondary Education Amendments provide extraordinary opportunities for the initiation, expansion and improvement of programs and projects for the education of handicapped children and youth. The articulation of these programs prevents an unnecessary duplication of effort and facilitates an effective sequence of service to those handicapped young people in need of assistance.

The Bureau of Education for the Handicapped is working closely with these agencies to continue this effort. We are delighted to report that a few innovative programs in this area are now being carried forward. A school district in Minnesota has developed an excellent multifunded habilitation program to prepare students for gainful employment. This program involves staff of the special education office, the vocational rehabilitation division, the vocational education office, and the local cooperating high schools, with each agency sharing substantially in the expenditures.

CONCERTED EFFORT

In the future, the Bureau will be able to concentrate more and more on areas of critical need. At present its Divisions of Research, Training, and Educational Services are concentrating on cooperating in a concerted effort to speedily implement effective programs in the area of educational media for the nation's handicapped school children. It is hoped that coordinated effort on change models needed to modernize the educational practices in keeping with proven research will help to strengthen the nation's special education activities. It is further hoped that the concerted effort on personnel training will help to more rapidly decrease manpower shortages in special education.

CONCLUSIONS

This is an exciting and challenging period, with increasing new knowledge and resources available to all professionals. However, in converting these elements into effective working programs which benefit people, every sector involved is increasingly dependent upon the other. The interdisciplinary competencies at all professional levels, each of which has a contribution to the development of the handicapped child, need to be coordinated through a system of cooperation, collaboration, and concerted effort. The Bureau level can provide information, but the creativity of application, the innovations, and the utilization of resources for the younger generation constitute the challenge faced by the field.

a summary of
selected legislation
relating to
*the handicapped**

CHARLES MEISGEIER, ED.

Since 1963, major laws affecting the handicapped have been enacted at an increasing rate. Broad in scope and flexible in approach, these laws have furnished incentive and inducement to institutions and organizations to develop and expand programs and services of every variety for the handicapped. The following summary of this legislation is reprinted principally from summaries of selected legislation relating to the handicapped 1963-1967 and other more recent documents published by the U. S. Department of Health, Education, and Welfare.

PART I LEGISLATIVE HIGHLIGHTS

1. **SOCIAL SECURITY AMENDMENTS OF 1963 (P.L. 88-156)**

Between 1935 and 1963 the Social Security Act has been developed by successive amendments to provide: (1) a general base of support for the aged and disabled on the insurance principle (social security); (2) cash assistance through the State welfare

*Printed by permission of the editor. A major portion of this article was excerpted from *A Summary of Selected Legislation Relating to the Handicapped 1968* and *A Summary of Selected Legislation Relating to the Handicapped 1963-1967*, U. S. Government Printing Office.

systems to those in dire need because of age, disability or blindness or dependence of children deprived of their fathers; and (3) an extension program of project grants and formula grants to the States to support such programs as Maternal and Child Health Services, Crippled Children's Services and Child Welfare Services.

The Amendments of 1963 authorized Federal expenditures of $265 million over a five-year period beginning with fiscal year 1964; expanded maternal and child health and crippled children's services; authorized project grants to provide health care services for expectant mothers from low income disadvantaged areas; approved grants for research projects in maternal and child health and crippled children's services which might provide for breakthroughs in these programs; provided grants to the States to assist in a comprehensive planning action to combat mental retardation at the State and community level.

Under P.L. 88-641 (1964) the authority for Federal matching of payments for children placed in nonprofit private child-care institutions was extended until June 30, 1967. This law also broadened the assistance program to permit matching of payments to needy children over age 18, but under 21 if in high school or vocational or technical training programs.

Public Law 88-650 (1964) permitted a disabled worker to establish the beginning of his disability for purposes of social security protection as of the date of his actual disablement; the law also allowed States to extend from the existing 12 months up to a maximum of 36 months, the period within which specified amounts of income are exempted in determining need for aid to the blind.

The 1965 Social Security Amendments (P.L. 89-97) provided for major changes and expansions of child health and other welfare programs, and also provided the first general increase in social security cash benefits since 1958.

Of significance were the "medicare" and "medicaid" provisions of the 1965 bill. The former provided: (1) a basic program of hospital insurance, extended care and home health services for the aged, financed through social security; (2) a voluntary supplemental program covering doctors' fees and some other health services. The Medicaid Program authorized in the new Title XIX expanded the Kerr-Mills program authorizing medical assistance for the needy aged, blind, disabled and dependent children, and offered the States the option of extending medical assistance to the medically needy not in the foregoing categories.

A new section established a 5-year program of special project grants to provide comprehensive health care and services for needy children of school and pre-school age. Funds were also provided for the training of professional personnel in the care of crippled children, particularly mentally retarded children and children with multiple handicaps.

The 1967 Social Security Amendments (P.L. 90- 248) placed special emphasis upon early casefinding services for children. The Amendments increased authorizations for child welfare services and consolidated the existing child health authorizations into a single authorization. Of the total authorization, 50 percent was designated for formula grants, 40 percent for project grants and 10 percent for training and research grants for the period July 1, 1968, to June 30, 1972. Until July 1972, project grants are authorized for: (1) the reduction of infant and maternal mortality and of the incidence of handicapping conditions associated with childbearing; (2) promotion of the health of school and pre-school age children; and (3) provision of dental care to children. Beginning in July 1972, the States will be responsible for carrying on these projects. The legislation amended Title XIX, Medical Assistance, to require early identification and treatment of physical or mental problems of children. Title XIX also requires agreements for utilization and reimbursement for services furnished by agencies or institutions participating in the various maternal and child health grant and project programs under Title V of the Social Security Act. The program of Special Projects for Maternity and Infant Care was increased and extended for four years.

The 1967 Amendments also placed special emphasis on the program of research projects relating to Maternal and Child Health Services and Crippled Children's Services, and an examination of the need, feasibility, cost and effectiveness of utilizing health personnel with varying levels of training in comprehensive health care programs. The training of health personnel to work in such projects was also authorized.

2.   MENTAL RETARDATION FACILITIES AND COMMUNITY MENTAL HEALTH CENTERS CONSTRUCTION ACT OF 1963 (P.L. 88- 164)

This law provided for construction of research centers and training facilities relating to mental retardation, construction and establishment of community mental health centers, research and demonstration in the education of handicapped children, and amended P.L. 85-926 to provide training of personnel in all areas of education for the handicapped at all levels of preparation — from teacher training to the training of college instructors, research personnel, and the administrators and supervisors of teachers of the handicapped.

The 1965 Amendments (P.L. 89-105) closed a gap in the original legislation enacted in 1963 by authorizing a $224 million program of grants for staffing community mental health centers during the first 51 months of their operations with technical and professional personnel. In addition, the 1965 Amendments extended and expanded the existing grant program for training teachers of handicapped children and for research and demonstrations in the education of handicapped children.

The Mental Retardation Amendments of 1967 (P.L. 90-170), (1) extended and expanded through June 30, 1970, the programs under which matching grants are made for construction of university-affiliated mental retardation facilities and community retardation facilities; (2) established a new program of matching grants following the formula used in the Community Mental Health Centers Act to help meet the cost of initiating services in community mental retardation facilities; (3) extended until June 30, 1970, the provisions of P.L. 85-926 (as admended); and (4) provided for training of physical education and recreation personnel for mentally retarded and other handicapped children and for research and demonstration projects in these areas. The Research and Demonstration activities were extended until 1970 by the Elementary and Secondary Education Amendments of 1967 (P.L. 90-147).

3. **THE ELEMENTARY AND SECONDARY EDUCATION ACT OF 1965 (P.L. 89-10)**

This law authorized a total expenditure of $1.33 billion for fiscal year 1966, which represented the greatest legislative commitment ever made by the Federal Government to the improvement of elementary and secondary education. The law authorized $1 billion of assistance to local school agencies, to be provided through the States for use in programs to meet the special needs of educationally deprived children. It also authorized major programs to assist the States in the acquisition of library resources and textbooks; to create supplemental educational centers providing special scientific, cultural, and other educational resources; to increase educational research and to establish a series of national and regional education research laboratories; and to strengthen State educational agencies.

Public Law 89-313 amended Title I of the Elementary and Secondary Education Act to provide grants to State agencies directly responsible for providing free public education for handicapped children.

The 1966 Amendments (P.L. 89-750) amended the 1965 Act by adding a new Title VI which provided for assistance in the education of the handicapped children. To participate in the program a State must submit to the Commissioner of Education a State plan providing satisfactory assurance that funds paid to the State under this program would be expended either directly or through local education agencies solely to initiate, expand, or improve programs and projects (including pre-school programs and projects) which were designed to meet the special educational and related needs of handicapped children throughout the State. The programs and projects must be of sufficient size and scope and quality as to give reasonable promise of substantial progress toward meeting these needs.

The 1966 Amendments also directed the Commissioner of Education to establish in the Office of Education a National Advisory Committee on Handicapped Children to make recommendations to him concerning programs carried on for handicapped children by the Office of Education. The Commissioner was also directed to establish and maintain within the Office of Education a bureau for the education and training of handicapped children which would be the principal agency in the Office of Education for administering and carrying out programs and projects relating to the education and training of handicapped children, including programs and projects for the training of teachers of the handicapped and for research in special education and training.

The 1967 Amendments (P.L. 90-247) broadened and extended the existing program of services to the handicapped. A program of Regional Resource Centers was authorized which will provide testing and educational evaluation to determine special education needs of handicapped children referred to them, develop educational programs to meet those needs and assist schools and educational agencies in providing such educational programs through consultation, re-examination and re-evaluation, and technical services.

The legislation also authorized the establishment and operation of Centers for deaf-blind children. The Centers will provide comprehensive diagnostic and evaluation services; programs for education, orientation and adjustment; and consultative services for parents, teachers and others working with the deaf-blind. In addition, the legislation authorized grants and contracts for research, demonstrations and training in the area of the deaf-blind.

The 1967 Amendments also authorized a program designed to improve recruiting of educational personnel and to improve dissemination of information concerning educational opportunities for the handicapped.

The existing Instructional Media Program, which initially provided a loan service of captioned films for the deaf, was expanded to include the production and distribution of educational media for the use of all types of handicapped persons, their parents, employers, and other persons involved in the work for the advancement of the handicapped and the training of persons in the use of instructional media for the handicapped; and research in the use of educational and training films and other educational media for the handicapped.

Special earmarking of funds for the handicapped was also provided for in Title III beginning in fiscal year 1969.

The 1967 law also provided for full funding under Section 103(a)(5) of Title I for educational activities for children in State-operated or supported institutions for the handicapped.

The research activities authorized under P.L. 88-164 were extended by the 1967 law. Funds were authorized through June 30, 1970. The Commissioner of Education was given contract authority in addition to the grant authority he previously had and funds could be used for related purposes in addition to research and demonstrations. In addition, the Commissioner was permitted to directly conduct research, surveys and demonstrations in the area of education of the handicapped. See also the 1970 Amendments, page 326.

4.   VOCATIONAL REHABILITATION ACT AMENDMENTS OF 1965 (P.L. 89-333)

The 1965 Amendments improved and expanded the existing vocational rehabilitation legislation by making possible more flexible financing and administration of State vocational rehabilitation programs, including provisions to allow Federal matching of local public funds made available to the States; provided a new formula for the allotment of Federal funds among the States; encouraged the development and extension of rehabilitation services by providing a program of innovation grants to States for the introduction of new techniques and the expansion of services, particularly for the severely disabled; established a new five-year program of grants for the construction of rehabilitation facilities and workshops, including assistance for planning, expansion, remodeling, renovation and initial equipment; authorized a five-year program of grants for the staffing of rehabilitation facilities.

The 1965 Amendments authorized a new five-year program of project grants for workshop improvement, including training projects (with allowances for trainees), operational improvement projects; authorized the Vocational Rehabilitation Administration to provide technical assistance to workshops; established a National Policy and Performance Council on workshop improvement; also created a National Commission on Architectural Barriers to Rehabilitation of the Handicapped; authorized grants for research and study into personnel practices and personnel needs in the field of correctional rehabilitation; authorized project grants to public and other non-profit agencies for the expansion of vocational rehabilitation services, as well as a new two-year program of grants to States for comprehensive planning. The Vocational Rehabilitation Administration was given specific authority for intramural research. States were given wider latitude in determining rehabilitation potential of individuals.

The 1967 Amendments (P.L. 90-99), amended the Vocational Rehabilitation Act and extended and expanded the authorization of grants to States for rehabilitation services; also authorized assistance in establishment and operation of a National Center for Deaf-Blind Youths and Adults. The 1967 Amendments further provided funds for projects which would extend rehabilitation services to handicapped migrant agricultural workers.

PART II   A LEGISLATIVE REVIEW

1.   MATERNAL AND CHILD HEALTH AND MENTAL RE-
     TARDATION PLANNING AMENDMENTS OF 1963
     (P.L. 88-156)

Public Law 88-156 was enacted on October 24, 1963.

The amendments were designed to carry out a number of the recommendations made to the President and to the Nation by the President's Panel on Mental Retardation.

MAJOR PROVISIONS

Planning grants to the States: — The legislation authorized $2.2 million for grants to States for comprehensive mental retardation planning. The funds appropriated were available for fiscal years 1964 and 1965. The grants were used to determine action needed to combat mental retardation in a State, to assess resources available to develop public awareness of the problem and to coordinate State and local efforts in education, employment, rehabilitation, welfare, health and the law for the prevention, treatment and amelioration of retardation. The Federal grant could not cover more than 75 percent of the cost of the project. A minimum of $30,000 was allocated to each jurisdiction eligible to participate in the program.

Project grants for maternal and infant care: — Authorized a five-year program of grants to public health agencies for projects which would provide necessary health care for expectant mothers who were unlikely to receive such care either because they were from families with low income or for other reasons. Authorized grants totaled $110 million — $5 million in fiscal year 1964, $15 million in 1965, and $30 million each for fiscal years 1966-1968. The Federal grant could not exceed 75 percent of the cost of any project.

Increases in maternal and child health services: — Expanded the existing Federal-State program by raising to $50 million over a seven-year period, beginning with fiscal year 1964, the annual ceiling of $25 million on Federal funds.

Increases in crippled children's services: — Federal funds authorized for crippled children's services were also increased, over a seven-year period, from the existing $25 million a year to $50 million for fiscal year 1970 and subsequent years.

Grants for research relating to maternal and child health and crippled children's services: — Authorized up to $8 million per year for grants, contracts, or jointly financed cooperative arrangements for research projects related to maternal and child health and crippled children's services that showed promise of substantial contribution to the advancement of these programs.
See also P.L. 89-97 and P.L. 90-248.

2.   MENTAL RETARDATION FACILITIES AND COMMUN-
ITY MENTAL HEALTH CENTERS CONSTRUCTION ACT
OF 1963 (P.L. 88-164)

Public Law 88-164 was enacted on October 31, 1963.

This legislation authorized appropriations of $329 million over a five-year period to provide grants for: (a) construction of research centers and facilities related to mental retardation; (b) construction and establishment of community mental health centers; and (c) training of teachers of handicapped children.

MAJOR PROVISIONS

Construction of research centers and facilities for the mentally retarded: (Title I): - Part A of this title authorized project grants for the construction of public or nonprofit centers for research that would develop new knowledge for preventing and combating mental retardation.

Part B authorized project grants to assist in the construction of public or nonprofit clinical facilities for the mentally retarded, associated with a college or university which: (1) provide, as nearly as practicable, a full range of inpatient and outpatient services; (2) aid in demonstrating provision of specialized services for diagnosis, treatment, training, or care; and (3) aid in the clinical training of physicians and other specialized personnel needed for research, diagnosis, treatment, training, or care.

Part C authorized Federal grants to States to assist in the construction of specially designed public and nonprofit facilities to provide diagnosis, treatment, education, training, custodial (personal) care and sheltered workshops for the retarded. The program is administered in each State by an officially designated State agency. Allotments to States are based on population, extent of need for facilities for the mentally retarded and financial need, with a minimum allotment of $100,000 for any State.

Construction of community mental health centers (Title II): — Authorized grants to the States for the construction of public and other nonprofit community mental health centers — facilities providing services for the prevention or diagnosis of mental illness, or care and treatment of mentally ill persons, or rehabilitation of persons recovering from mental illness.

The provisions relating to allotments among the States and to the Federal share of the cost of projects are substantially the same as for construction grants for community mental retardation facilities (Part C of Title I).

Training of teachers of mentally retarded and other handicapped children (Title III): — Authorized grants to institutions of higher learning and to State educational agencies to extend and strengthen the existing programs for training teachers of mentally retarded children and deaf children and to expand these programs to include the training of teachers of all handicapped children, including the visually handicapped, the speech impaired, the seriously emotionally disturbed, the hearing impaired, the crippled and other health impaired children.

Title III also authorized grants to States and to public and nonprofit educational or research agencies for research or demonstration projects relating to the education of the handicapped.

See also P.L. 89-105 and P.L. 90-170.

3.   HOSPITAL AND MEDICAL FACILITIES AMENDMENTS OF 1964 (P.L. 88-443)

Public Law 88-443 was enacted on August 18, 1964.

These amendments extended and revised the Hill-Burton hospital construction program.

MAJOR PROVISIONS

A total of $1.34 billion was authorized for an expanded five year program of grants and loans to aid new construction, modernization, and replacement of hospitals, long-term care facilities, public health centers, diagnostic and treatment centers and rehabilitation facilities.

Project grants were authorized to assist in the development of comprehensive regional, metropolitan, or other local area plans for health facilities.

Grant programs for chronic disease hospitals and nursing homes, previously separate, were combined under the category of "Facilities for Long Term Care" with an increased annual authorization of $70 million.

States were allowed to use up to two percent of their allotments, or $50,000, whichever is less, for purposes of administration of the State plan.

Between 1948 and 1963, $12.9 billion was spent on the construction of hospitals and other health facilities; of this amount, $4.5 billion was expended in projects receiving Federal assistance under the Hill-Burton legislation, with the Federal share averaging 35 percent, or a total of $1.6 billion.

By bringing the previously separate categories of chronic disease hospitals and nursing homes into a single program, the legislation sought to overcome program and administrative problems that had arisen from attempts to plan separately for these two types of long-term care facilities in the past.

4.   SOCIAL SECURITY AMENDMENTS OF 1964 (P.L. 88-641)

Public Law 88-641 was enacted on October 13, 1964.

This legislation extended and broadened the provisions of the Aid to Families with Dependent Children Program (AFDC) by (a) continuing Federal participation in payments for children requiring foster care, and (b) authorizing AFDC payments for children up to age 21, provided they were in school.

Extended authority for Federal matching payments for children placed in nonprofit, private child-care institutions until June 30, 1967.

Broadened the definition of "dependent child" to include children in high school, or in vocational or technical training programs up to age 21.

Foster Care: — To give the States an alternative to leaving children in unsuitable homes or caring for them elsewhere without Federal participation in the costs, the Congress in 1961 enacted a temporary provision for Federal participation, under limited circumstances, in the cost of care in foster family homes. This applied to children who had been receiving aid to dependent children but who had been removed by a court from homes found contrary to the welfare of the child.

The Public Welfare Amendments of 1962 made permanent the Federal Participation in the cost of care in foster family homes and extended until September 30, 1964, the provision to include care in nonprofit, private child-care institutions so that the most appropriate facility for a particular child may be used. The 1964 law extended this provision until June 30, 1967.

Extension of Age Limit: — The provision extending the age limit from 18 to 21 years of age recognized that children may remain dependent while they are pursuing an educational program. As noted by the Senate Report, "the . . . sharp cutoff at age 18 may have the effect of forcing just those children to leave school who are most in need of a high school education or vocational training if they are to become self-sufficient and stay off the welfare rolls."

See also P.L. 88-156, P.L. 88-650, P.L. 89-97, and P.L. 90-248.

5.   SOCIAL   SECURITY   AMENDMENTS   OF   1964   (P.L. 88-650)

Public Law 88-650 was enacted on October 13, 1964.

This Law amended the Social Security Disability Insurance Program and the Public Assistance Program of Aid to the Blind.

MAJOR PROVISIONS

Amended the OASDI (Old-Age, Survivors, and Disability Insurance) program to permit a disabled worker to establish the beginning of his disability, for purposes of social security protection, as of the date of his actual disablement.

Amended Titles X and XVI of the Social Security Act and permitted States to extend from 12 months to 36 months the period within which specific amounts would be exempted in determining need under aid to the blind program.

Retroactivity of Disability Applications: — The Social Security Amendments of 1956 made benefits available to disabled workers, including those who had become disabled many years before, provided that, at the time the disability began, disability-insured status requirements were met. Subsequently a restriction on the retroactivity of disability applications became effective; the beginning of a period of disability could not be established more than 1½ years before the application was filed.

Public Law 88-650 eliminated the restriction on the retroactivity of disability applications, and permitted disabled workers to establish the beginning of a period of disability as of the date of actual disablement, even though the application for disability benefits is filed much later, as under the original disability provisions.

The Public Welfare Amendments of 1962 amended Titles X and XVI of the Social Security Act to provide that, in determining eligibility in the aid to the blind program, a State shall, in addition to the specified exempted amount of earned income — the first $85 per month plus one-half of other earned income — exempt such other amounts of income and resources for an individual who has a plan approved by the State agency for achieving self-support. The period of additional exemption could not exceed 12 months for any individual. Public Law 88-650 permitted a State to allow up to a total of 36 months for an individual who had such a State-approved plan.

See also P.L. 88-156, P.L. 88-164, P.L. 89-97 and P.L. 90-248.

6.   ELEMENTARY AND SECONDARY EDUCATION ACT OF 1965 (P.L. 89-10)

Public Law 89-10 was enacted on April 11, 1965.

The heart of this legislation was a three-year program of Federal grants to the States for allocation to school districts having children in low income families. The funds are available for projects adding to the local educational agency's programs for "educationally disadvantaged" children. This term was defined by Congress to include handicapped children. The six titles of this Act involved the following programs:

TITLE   I — Education of children of low income families

TITLE   II — School library resources, text books, and other instructional materials

TITLE III — Supplementary educational centers and services

TITLE IV — Educational research and training; Cooperative Research Act

TITLE V — Strengthening state departments of education

TITLE VI — General provisions and definitions

MAJOR PROVISIONS

The Elementary and Secondary Education Act of 1965 (P.L. 89-10) gave an enormous impetus to developing educational services for the handicapped. Title I authorized a three-year effort to encourage and support the creation, expansion, or improvement of special programs. This included the construction of facilities to meet the needs of culturally deprived children from low-income families, many of whom are diagnosed as mentally retarded or emotionally disturbed, but who actually are primarily lacking in educational experience and a sense of achievement. It is estimated that 50 percent or more of children with IQ's between 70 and 80 come from disadvantaged homes. Special teaching efforts for these children in the pre-school and early school years can make up for much of their scholastic shortcomings and possibly prevent functional mental retardation from becoming permanent.

Funds appropriated under this Act could be employed to finance home visits by teachers, counselors and social workers who, with the aid of key men and women from the neighborhood, would try to solicit parental interest and cooperation.

Once identified, the handicapped could be helped by special classes or could even be guided back into the mainstream of regular work with supplementary teaching materials designed to encourage the widest possible use of their latent physical and mental capacities. The aim would be to provide those enriching and stimulating experiences which the normal child takes for granted. An important role was reserved under *Title II* for picture books, movies, and taped records of music and simple poetry. Programmed instruction, too, will play an increasing part as suitable curricula are developed for the handicapped child. Many children receive speech and hearing services to help them overcome the barriers to learning which are related to communication disorders.

Funds were provided under this Act for refresher training for supervisors and for training and hiring teacher aides.

The handicapped, like other children, need variety in their lives, for psychological as well as intellectual reasons. This Act helped school districts provide educational summer camps or all day summer schools for mentally retarded children.

Title III of the Act recognized that one of the greatest challenges to improving educational quality for all students is the uneven distribution of scientific and cultural as well as purely "educational" facilities and resources. This inequality is particularly unfortunate for the handicapped. Among the variety of supplementary services that may make the difference between success and failure in teaching the handicapped are special instruction in science, languages, music, and the arts, and regular, easy access to museums, laboratories, art galleries and theaters. Title III opened up these opportunities to the handicapped on a fairly large scale for the first time.

Educational centers were also set up to establish model programs which could mark the beginning of wholly new approaches to teaching the culturally deprived and handicapped. Because the education of the handicapped is constantly changing, teachers in this field need to experiment with new ideas and materials and test them under actual classroom conditions. The Centers enhance such experimental teaching. The use of auxiliary teams of psychologists and social workers can be weighed, organic defects and environmental conditioning can be evaluated, and appropriate curricula and methods prepared in these special centers.

Title IV of the Act amended the Cooperative Research Act to authorize the training of research personnel and the development of improved methods of disseminating research findings to other education centers and local school districts. Private noncollegiate research organizations and professional associations were eligible to participate in this training effort.

Title V of the Elementary and Secondary Education Act authorized a five-year program to stimulate and assist in strengthening the leadership resources of State education departments.

See also P.L. 89- 313, P.L. 89- 750 and P.L. 90- 247.

7.   NATIONAL TECHNICAL INSTITUTE FOR THE DEAF
      ACT (P.L. 89- 36)

Public Law 89- 36 was enacted on June 8, 1965.

This legislation provided for a residential facility to give post-secondary technical training and education for the deaf to prepare them for successful employment. A twelve-member, ad hoc Advisory Board on Establishment of the National Technical Institute for the Deaf was appointed by the Secretary of Health, Education, and Welfare to review proposals from institutions of higher education which offered to enter into an agreement with the Secretary for the construction and operation of a National Technical Institute for the Deaf, to make recommendations with respect to such proposals and with respect to the establishment and operation of the Institute. After the Secretary had entered into the agreement, the Board would cease to exist.

The National Technical Institute for the Deaf will provide a broad, flexible curriculum suited to the individual needs of young deaf adults with potential for further education and training. Successful operation of such a technical training program for the deaf will depend upon the availability of adequately trained staff, resourceful and imaginative in meeting the challenge of the special problems involved.

MAJOR PROVISIONS

The Institute will enroll at least 200 students per year to a capacity of 600, with provisions for further expansion.

The principal objective of the Institute is the employment of the student upon his completion of the prescribed educational program.

The National Technical Institute for the Deaf will be located in a large metropolitan industrial area to serve the special needs of deaf youth from any community. The area will have a wide variety of nationally representative types of industrial activities available for training experience that will prepare the student to return home for employment. The Institute will be affiliated with a major university for the administration of its program.

The curriculum will be flexible enough to permit a variety of adaptations-tailor-made for individual students, without having to conform to traditional accreditation standards.

The program will be broad enough to include a basic remedial program, a supplementary curriculum of the social sciences and humanities, and a technical science curriculum.

In addition to serving as a practice teaching center for the training of teachers, instructors, and rehabilitation counselors for the deaf, the Institute will serve as a research facility for the study of educational problems of the deaf. The National Technical Institute for the Deaf will be an excellent proving ground for the development of new educational techniques that can be applied to all programs where deaf children are taught.

8.   SOCIAL SECURITY AMENDMENTS OF 1965 (P.L. 89-97)

Public Law 89-97 was enacted on July 30, 1965.

Funds were authorized for training professional personnel for the care of crippled children, $5 million for fiscal year 1967, $10 million for 1968, and $17.5 million for each fiscal year thereafter. The program has helped reduce the severe shortage of professional personnel to deal with mentally retarded children and children with multiple handicaps.

A five-year program of special project grants for low-income school and pre-school children has provided comprehensive health care and services for children of school age and for pre-school children, particularly in areas with concentrations of low-income families.

Grants of $2.75 million a year for 1966 and 1967 were authorized to assist States in following up and implementing the comprehensive plans to combat mental retardation that have been developed under legislation enacted in 1963.

Federal funds to the States were authorized for aid to the needy aged in mental or tuberculosis institutions, effective January 1, 1966. Mentally retarded residents of institutions benefited from this provision.

MAJOR PROVISIONS

Training of Professional Personnel for the Care of Crippled Children: — P.L. 89-97 authorized appropriations of $5,000,000 for fiscal year 1967, $10,000,000 for fiscal year 1968 and $17,500,000 for each fiscal year thereafter for grants to be used in the training of professional personnel for the care of crippled children, particularly mentally retarded children and children with multiple handicaps.

Grants have been made to institutions of higher learning for training professional personnel such as physicians, psychologists, nurses, dentists, and social workers.

Project Grants for the Health of School and Pre-School Children: — Children of low-income families have benefited from the comprehensive medical care program provided in Section 532 of the Social Security Act. In order to promote the health of children and youth, particularly in areas with concentrations of low-income families, P.L. 89-97 amended Section 532 by authorizing $15,000,000 for the fiscal year 1966, increasing to $50,000,000 for the fiscal year 1970 to provide up to 75 percent of the costs of comprehensive projects which must include screening, diagnosis, preventive services, treatment, correction of defects and aftercare, both medical and dental. The services provided under such projects are required to be coordinated with other State or local health, welfare, and educational programs for these children.

These programs have served children with a wide vareity of problems, and have contributed to the development of additional resources, especially in major population centers where there is frequently overcrowding in existing facilities.

Grants have been made to health departments, crippled children's agencies, schools of medicine and to teaching hospitals affiliated with such schools.

Changes in the Disability Program: — The requirement that a worker's disability must be expected to be of long-continued and indefinite duration was eliminated. The 1965 Amendments further provided that an insured worker was eligible for disability benefits if he had been under a disability which could be expected to result in death or which had lasted or could be expected to last for a continuous period of not less than 12 calendar months.

The 1965 Amendements provided for reimbursement from social security trust funds to State vocational rehabilitation agencies for the cost of rehabilitation services furnished to selected individuals who were entitled to disability insurance benefits or to disabled child's benefits.

The 1965 law modified the disability provisions with respect to the blind. The definition of disability was modified so that an individual would be considered disabled if he was between the ages of 55 and 65, and met the definition of "blindness" and was unable by reason of such blindness to engage in substantial gainful activities requiring skills or abilities comparable to those required in his past occupation or occupations.

The 1965 Amendments also provided an alternative insured status requirement for persons who were disabled before age 31 by reason of blindness.

Implementation of Mental Retardation Comprehensive Plans: — The "Maternal and Child Health and Mental Retardation Planning Amendments of 1963" (P.L. 88- 156), authorized, for the first time, grants to States and Territories for comprehensive mental retardation planning. The planning was collaborative and interagency in nature, with participation of agencies responsbile for services in education, employment, rehabilitation welfare, health, and the law, including both community agencies and residential programs. Funds totaling $2.2 million were made available for two fiscal years, 1964 and 1965.

Basic planning grants of $30,000 each were allocated and awarded to all the States and Territories (except American Samoa), and supplemental planning funds, totaling $579,998, were awarded to a total of 35 States and Territories for a variety of extended planning projects. These grants have made it possible for the States and Territories to begin comprehensive mental retardation planning. Close Federal-State liaison has been maintained in this effort.

P.L. 89-97 extended the grant program for comprehensive planning in mental retardation initiated under P.L. 88-156 to enable States to begin implementing their comprehensive plans to combat mental retardation. These grants are used to determine the action needed to combat mental retardation and the resources available for this purpose; to develop public awareness of the mental retardation problem and the need for combating it; to coordinate State and local activities relating to the various aspects of the problem; and to develop specific programs for implementing the recommendations of the comprehensive State plan. Appropriations of $2.75 million were made in both fiscal years 1966 and 1967, to be available through 1968, and the minimum allotment to a State was $35,000 out of each of the appropriations.

See also P.L. 88-156, P.L. 88-641, P.L. 88-650 and P.L. 90-248.

9. MENTAL RETARDATION FACILITIES AND COM-MUNITY MENTAL HEALTH CENTERS CONSTRUCTION ACT AMENDMENTS OF 1965 (P.L. 89-105)

Public Law 89-105 was enacted on August 4, 1965.

The 1965 Amendments provided for a program of grants for staffing community mental health centers during the first 51 months of their operations with technical and professional personnel.

This Act also amended prior legislation which authorized programs in the area of the education of handicapped children. The legislation extended and expanded the training activities for teachers of handicapped children, extended and expanded research authority, and added construction authority to the program of research and demonstrations in this area.

MAJOR PROVISIONS

This legislation amended two existing laws which provided funds for training of teachers of handicapped children and research and demonstration projects related to special education. The law strengthened and expanded the programs for the mentally retarded begun under prior legislation, and accelerated the national effort to provide the best possible education to mentally retarded children.

The program of training of teachers of mentally retarded and other handicapped children was extended for an additional three years. The existing law authorized the program through June 30, 1966. The 1965 Amendments extended it through June 30, 1969.

The research and demonstration program was also extended to 1969 with increased authorization for appropriations. The existing law authorized funds only through June 30, 1966. In addition, as part of the research and demonstration authority, the Commissioner of Education was authorized to make a grant to an institution of higher learning for the construction, equipping and operation of a facility for research and demonstration in the field of education of handicapped children.

Training of Teachers: — A major deterrent to the needed expansion of special education programs for our Nation's handicapped children has been the critical shortage of well-trained teachers and other related professional personnel. It is estimated that we have only one-fourth of the number of special education teachers that are currently needed.

During fiscal year 1968, 247 colleges and universities and 54 State or Territorial educational agencies were awarded grants in the training of teachers of the handicapped. About 12,000 students will receive support for either part-time or full-time study during the 1968-1969 school year.

Research and Demonstration in the Education of Handicapped Children: — P.L. 88-164 authorized a program of research and demonstration in the education of handicapped children. This program has grown from $1 million in its first year of operation to $11.1 million in fiscal year 1968. In addition to support of individual research projects, the program supports a national research and demonstration center at Columbia University in New York City and a network of 14 special education instructional material centers across the country.

See also P.L. 88-164, P.L. 90-31 and P.L. 90-170.

10.   COMMUNITY HEALTH SERVICES EXTENSION AMEND-MENTS OF 1965 (P.L. 89-109)

Public Law 89-109 was enacted into law on August 5, 1965.

The amendments extended four existing programs of the Public Health Service relating to health services; immunization, migratory worker health services, general health services, and special project grants for community health services.

MAJOR PROVISIONS

Immunization Programs: — P.L. 89-109 extended the provisions of the Vaccination Assistance Act of 1962 for three years, through fiscal year 1968, with no change in the authorized annual appropriations of $11 million. The amendments also expanded the coverage of the program to include assistance in immunization programs against measles and other diseases presenting a major public health problem. Eligible beneficiaries were changed from children "under the age of five years" to children "of preschool age."

During its three-year history, the Vaccination Assistance Act has contributed greatly to the reduction of the incidence of polio. At the time of the law's enactment, the Public Health Service estimated that only one-third of the children under five years of age had been immunized. Since its enactment in 1962, an estimated 58 million people have received three doses of oral polio vaccine and seven million children have been immunized against diphtheria, tetanus, and whooping cough. By September 1964, some two-thirds of all children under five years of age had been immunized against polio.

Since the enactment of the 1962 legislation, two measles vaccines have been developed. As other communicable diseases of childhood have increasingly come under control, there has been growing recognition of measles as a major health problem. An estimated four million cases occur each year, resulting in at least 500 deaths and in extensive complications and serious disabilities such as mental retardation, pneumonia, hearing disorders, and measles encephalitis (inflammation of the brain).

This law also authorized the Surgeon General to make grants for immunization programs against any infectious disease which can be practically eliminated through immunization with preventive agents which may become available in the future, and which he finds to represent a major public health problem. Under this authority, new immunization programs can be established without further legislative action by the Congress.

Migratory Workers Health Services: — The amendments extended for three years, through fiscal year 1968, the project grant program which provided community health services for domestic migratory agricultural workers and their families. A total of $24 million was authorized for a three-year period. Under the Migrant Health Act of 1962, the Public Health Service has assisted 60 county or multi-county projects in 29 States and the Commonwealth of Puerto Rico. Project grants have paid part of the costs in 100 counties of such public health services as immunizations, pre- and post-natal clinics, dental services, and case finding and treatment for communicable diseases. The amendments also provided that the services that may be financed with Federal assistance include necessary hospital care.

General Health Services: — P.L. 89-109 extended for one year, through fiscal year 1967, the program of formula grants for general health services authorized by Section 314(c) of the Public Health Services Act. Funds authorized for general health grants were used largely for establishing and maintaining basic health services in State and local public health organizations, such as mental health services, radiological health services, dental health services, and services for the chronically ill and aged. Under this authority, grants also were made to schools of public health for the provision of public health training.

Project Grants for Community Health Services: — The Community Health Services and Facilities Act of 1961 added Section 316 to the Public Health Service Act, establishing a program of project grants to State or local public agencies or nonprofit private agencies to finance studies, experiments, and demonstrations for the development of improved methods of providing health services, particularly for the chronically ill or aged. This authority, which would have expired June 30, 1966, was extended for one year, with no change in the annual appropriation authorization of $10 million.

See also P.L. 89-749 and P.L. 90-174.

11.   THE   HEART   DISEASE,   CANCER,   AND   STROKE AMENDMENTS OF 1965 (P.L. 89- 239)

Public Law 89- 239 was enacted on October 6, 1965.

Passage of the Heart Disease, Cancer, and Stroke Amendments of 1965 (P.L. 89- 239) marked the launching of a major assault on the Nation's three major killing diseases.

The Amendments implemented the major recommendations of the 1964 Presidential Commission to study the problems and recommend means to achieve significant advances in the prevention, diagnosis, and treatment of three disease groups which exact such a staggering toll of human life and suffering.

The principal purpose of this program was to provide the medical profession and medical institutions of the Nation greater opportunity to make available to their patients the latest advances in the diagnosis and treatment of heart disease, cancer, stroke, and related diseases. This was to be accomplished through the establishment of regional programs of cooperation in research, training, continuing education, and demonstration activities in patient care among medical schools, clinical research institutions, and hospitals.

MAJOR PROVISIONS

To accomplish these goals, P.L. 89- 239 authorized a three-year, $340 million program of grants for the planning and establishment of regional medical programs. These grants provided support for cooperative arrangements which linked major medical centers — usually consisting of a medical school and affiliated teaching hospitals — with clinical research centers, local community hospitals, and practicing physicians of the Nation. Grants have been made for planning and for feasibility studies, as well as for pilot projects to demonstrate the value of these cooperative regional arrangements and to provide a base of experience for further development of the program.

The legislation authorized appropriations of $50 million for fiscal year 1966, $90 million for fiscal year 1967, and $200 million for fiscal year 1968, the funds for each fiscal year to remain available until the end of the following fiscal year. Grants could be made to pay all or part of the cost of the planning and other activities related to establishment of the regional medical programs. Funds for renovations and built-in equipment, however, could not exceed 90 percent of the cost.

A National Advisory Council on Regional Medical Programs was appointed to advise and assist the Surgeon General in the formulation of policy and regulations regarding the regional medical programs, and to make recommendations to him concerning approval of applications and amounts of grant awards.

To assist physicians and other interested persons, the Surgeon General was directed to establish and maintain a current list of facilities in the United States equipped and staffed to provide the most advanced methods and techniques in the diagnosis and treatment of heart disease, cancer, and stroke. The Surgeon General was also directed to maintain a record of the advanced specialty training available in these institutions, along with other information he deems necessary. In order to make this information as useful as possible, the legislation requires the Surgeon General to consult with interested national professional organizations.

The Surgeon General was also required to make a report to the President and the Congress by June 30, 1967. In addition to recounting the activities carried out as a result of this legislation, the report was to analyze the effectiveness of the activities in meeting the stated objective of the regional medical programs, as well as recommendations for extension and modification of this program.

12.   CAPTIONED FILMS FOR THE DEAF ACT (P.L. 89- 258)

Public Law 89-258 was enacted on October 19, 1965.

MAJOR PROVISIONS

P.L. 89- 258 made possible a total approach to the communication problems of the deaf.

In addition to educational and training films, other educational media (including tapes, transparencies, programmed instruction, etc.) and all of the devices of modern instruction could be acquired and distributed. To use media more effectively, provision was made for the training of personnel and conduct of research.

Educational media were also made available to persons directly involved in assisting the deaf (parents, rehabilitation workers, placement officers, and actual or potential employers) as well as to the deaf themselves.

The amendments authorized an increase in appropriations from a level of $1.5 million in fiscal year 1965 to $3 million each for fiscal years 1966 and 1967, $5 million each for fiscal years 1968 and 1969, and $7 million annually thereafter.

The P.L. 89-258 amendments also provided for a National Advisory Committee on Education of the Deaf to advise the Secretary of Health, Education, and Welfare.

Basic Act of 1958 and Amendments of 1962: — The 1958 legislation (P.L. 85-905) permitted the U.S. Office of Education to purchase, lease, or accept films, caption and distribute them through State schools for the deaf or other appropriate agencies. The 1958 Act focused on the provision of recreational films. The 1962 Amendments (P.L. 87-815) included the production of captioned films, the training of persons in their use, and conducting research to improve the quality and effectiveness of production and broad utilization of the film medium.

See also P.L. 90-247 and P.L. 89-511.

13. FEDERAL ASSISTANCE TO STATE OPERATED AND SUPPORTED SCHOOLS FOR THE HANDICAPPED (P.L.89-313)

Public Law 89-313 was enacted on November 1, 1965.

MAJOR PROVISIONS

Public Law 89-313 amended Title I of the Elementary and Secondary Education Act to provide grants to State agencies directly responsible for providing free public education for handicapped children.

Students in State operated and supported schools for the handicapped have benefitted from a wide variety of services funded by this Act.

Funds authorized under this Act for fiscal year 1966 totaled

$15.9 million, for fiscal year 1967, $15.0 million, and for fiscal year 1968, $24.7 million.

See also P.L. 89-10, P.L. 89-750 and P.L. 90-247.

14.   VOCATIONAL REHABILITATION ACT AMENDMENTS OF 1965 (P.L. 89-333)

Public Law 89-333 was enacted on November 8, 1965.

MAJOR PROVISIONS

Expansion of Programs for Vocational Rehabilitation Services:— This amendment provided for a five-year incentive grant program to States and other nonprofit groups to plan and initiate a further expansion of rehabilitation programs in States which seem to have a high potential for increasing the number of persons who could be rehabilitated and employed.

The provision for comprehensive State planning has made possible an inventory and review of existing vocational rehabilitation resources. This has included analysis of the extent to which available services for the handicapped may need to be supplemented or redirected to achieve the training and placement of greater numbers of severely disabled people each year.

Rehabilitation Facilities: — One of the basic requirements for effective service to the severely disabled is to have available modern rehabilitation facilities. Under the Hill-Burton Facilities Construction Program, a substantial beginning has been made in improving rehabilitation clinics and centers associated with hospitals.

A comparable effort is needed in connection with those facilities which are primarily of a vocational nature, along with workshops in which the disabled person's work potential can be evaluated and job training given.

This legislation authorized a five-year program involving Federal assistance to plan, build, equip, and initially staff rehabilitation facilities and workshops.

Workshops for the handicapped can include such construction as may be necessary to provide residential accommodations for use in connection with the rehabilitation of these individuals.

Experimental Projects (Locally financed): — In many communities local public funds from a variety of sources such as the school systems, hospitals, and welfare departments can be made avaialble to the States to help in the rehabilitation of handicapped local residents. Heretofore, these resources ordinarily have not been used for the vocational rehabilitation of their residents.

This amendment waived certain requirements for Statewide operations and permitted Federal matching of such funds in the same manner and at the same rate as other State funds are matched. Local rehabilitation resources have been expanded, improvements made in existing services, and the numbers of disabled people given services have increased.

Innovation Projects: — Under Sec. 3 of the 1954 Amendments, State rehabilitation agencies have developed numerous projects for the extension and improvement of rehabilitation services. These projects have contributed significantly to the development of specialized programs needed in the rehabilitation of the severely disabled and other hard-to-rehabilitate cases. This amendment extended up to 5 years the time, during which the favorable rate of Federal funds for these developmental projects could be paid. The Federal rate was increased to 90 percent of cost during the first 3 years and 75 percent of cost during the next two years. At the request of the State, such payments would be at a lower percentage.

Services to Determine Rehabilitation Potential of the Disabled:— This amendment permitted Federal funds to be used to help provide vocational rehabilitation services for a period of 6 months to certain handicapped persons whose vocational capabilities could not be predicted as favorable at the outset.

In the case of mentally retarded persons and other persons with disabilities especially designated by the Secretary, the period may be extended to 18 months. During this time a more adequate evaluation of their real capacity can be undertaken. Their eligibility for more and complete help toward employment can be determined.

Workshop Improvement Programs: — Under these amendments the Secretary was able to undertake several new activities in connection with workshops. These amendments were designed to help improve the Nation's workshops as resources for the vocational rehabilitation of greater numbers of disabled persons.

The Secretary was directed to establish a National Policy and Performance Council to advise him with respect to policies and programs designed to improve workshops.

Improvement grants have been made to workshops on a project basis to help pay part of the cost of analyzing, improving, or increasing professional services to clients or improving their business operations. Project grants have been made to certain workshops to enable them to pay the cost of training services, including allowances, for handicapped persons undergoing training. The programs for grants for workshop improvements and training allowances were each authorized for a five-year period.

Research and Information: — This amendment extended the authority of the Secretary to undertake research, studies and demonstrations and to make reports upon such new knowledge. Existing authority to establish and operate a substantially augmented program of information service was supplemented.
See also P.L. 90- 99.

15. LIBRARY SERVICES AND CONSTRUCTION ACT AMENDMENTS OF 1966 (P.L. 89- 511)

Public Law 89- 511 was enacted on July 19, 1966.

The handicapped have benefitted from the provisions of this Act which added to the effectiveness and efficiency of the nation's library system.

MAJOR PROVISIONS

Part A of Title IV authorized a program to assist the States in providing library services in State institutions for inmates, patients, and residents, as well as physically or mentally handicapped students who are in residential schools for the handicapped operated or substantially supported by the State.

Federal funds may be used by the State library agency to plan and initiate programs to provide books, other library materials and library services for such students. An Advisory Council composed of representatives of eligible institutions assists the State library agency to develop its State plan under this title. The authorization was $5 million for fiscal year 1967, $7.5 million for fiscal year 1968, $10 million for fiscal year 1969, $12.5 million for fiscal year 1970, and $15 million for fiscal year 1971.

Part B of Title IV made Federal funds available to State agencies for the establishment and improvement of library services for individuals who are certified by competent authority as unable to read or to use conventional printed materials as a result of physical limitations. Such services may be provided through public or nonprofit library agencies or organizations. An Advisory Council composed of representatives of eligible agencies, acts in an advisory capacity to the State agency.

16.   MILITARY MEDICAL BENEFITS AMENDMENTS OF 1966 (P.L. 89-614)

Public Law 89-614 was enacted on September 30, 1966.

This law provided major updating of the Dependents' Medical Care Act which deals primarily with health care benefits for the dependents of active duty members of the uniformed services (the Army, Navy, Marine Corps, Air Force, Coast Guard and the commissioned corps of the Public Health Service and the Environmental Science Services Administration).

MAJOR PROVISIONS

Included in the expanded benefits authorized by this law was a financial assistance program for active duty members who have a spouse or child who is moderately or severely mentally retarded or who has a serious physical handicap.

Under this law, spouses or children with the type of conditions referred to above are eligible under a new government-sponsored program for: diagnosis; inpatient, outpatient and home treatment; training, rehabilitation and special education; institutional care in public and private nonprofit institutions and facilities and, when appropriate, transportation to and from such installations and facilities.

The law provides for a sliding scale of monthly deductibles payable by the active duty member, based upon his pay grade. Those in lowest enlisted pay grade are required to pay the first $25 each month of expenses incurred by their dependents. Four-star generals and admirals are similarly required to pay the first $250. All other active duty members with participating dependents pay amounts in between these two amounts, as determined by the Secretary of Defense and the Secretary of Health, Education, and Welfare. The law provided that the government's share of the monthly costs can not exceed $350 per month. Consequently, the active duty member in some cases has to pay an amount in addition to the deductible in order to meet the remaining difference between the government's share and the total monthly charge.

The handicapped portions of the law stemmed from recognition of the fact that payment for care, training and special education of mentally retarded and physically handicapped dependents is frequently such a drain on the financial resources of the serviceman as to make it impossible for him to maintain an acceptable standard of living.

These portions of the law became effective January 1, 1967. The Army, as Executive Agent for the Department of Defense and the Department of Health, Education, and Welfare has operated the new program for all seven uniformed services.

17. MODEL SECONDARY SCHOOL FOR THE DEAF ACT (P.L. 89-694)

Public Law 89-694 was enacted on October 15, 1966.

MAJOR PROVISIONS

Public Law 89-694 authorized the Secretary of Health, Education, and Welfare, after consultation with the National Advisory Committee on Education of the Deaf, to enter into an agreement with Gallaudet College to establish (including construction and equipment) a model secondary school for the deaf, to serve primarily residents of the District of Columbia and nearby States.

This high school, while serving primarily the needs of the National Capital Area and nearby States, will also provide a model for the development of similar programs across the country. In addition, the formulation of new educational methods and educational technology and specific curriculum offerings will contribute to the Nation's total educational program for the deaf.

It is expected that the concept of this model school will grow to the extent that every deaf high school age student will eventually have the opportunity for an education equal to that of his hearing peers and commensurate with his abilities and desires.

18. COMPREHENSIVE HEALTH PLANNING AND PUBLIC HEALTH SERVICES AMENDMENTS OF 1966 (P.L. 89- 749)

Public Law 89- 749 was enacted on November 3, 1966.

Significant and extensive Federal legislation enacted in the last three years has enabled the States to assume sizeable new functions and responsibilities in the field of health services. However, the development of coordination mechanisms has not kept pace with the growth and diversity of the Federally-aided health programs. The provisions of P.L. 89- 749 have contributed significantly to meeting this need.

MAJOR PROVISIONS

This legislation authorized a total of $24 million for a two-year program of grants for comprehensive health planning. These funds have been used to develop the intelligence and the administrative techniques necessary for such planning. The Act also authorized $62.5 million for a one-year program of formula grants to States for comprehensive public health services; a redirected, flexible support to more clearly focus health program activities on bringing services to people. Health services for the mentally retarded are among those which have been supported with these funds. An additional sum of $62.5 million was provided for a one-year program of health service developmental grants. These funds have been used to continue existing project grants, as well as to stimulate and initially support innovative health service programs, which include programs for the mentally retarded and other handicapped persons. The sum of $5 million was authorized for fiscal year 1968 for continuation of grants to schools of public health for comprehensive professional training and technical assistance in the field of public health. Temporary interchange of Federal and State personnel engaged in health-related work was authorized in this Act.

The law establishes a statutory framework for the revitalization and expansion of Federal-State-local cooperative efforts to make maximum use of national health resources, and strengthens State and local capacity and initiative by modifying existing patterns of Federal financial assistance to States. This revision of the Federal health grant structure made Federal grant funds available to States, and through them to local communities on a flexible basis, thus enabling these groups to focus on the needs of individuals and on familes in their area. Communities have been better able to provide services for maintenance of good health as well as for rehabilitation following disease. Through the support of training and the interchange of Federal and State health personnel, competency and strength necessary for planning and administration of comprehensive health services can be improved.

See also P.L. 89-109 and P.L. 90-174.

19.   ELEMENTARY AND SECONDARY EDUCATION ACT AMENDMENTS OF 1966 (P.L. 89-750)

Public Law 89-750 was enacted on November 3, 1966.[1]

P.L. 89-750 amended Title VI, Elementary and Secondary Education Act, to provide authorizations of $51.5 million for fiscal year 1967, and $154.3 million for fiscal year 1968 for the purpose of assisting the States in the initiation, expansion and improvement of programs and projects for the education of handicapped children. This includes children at the preschool, elementary and secondary school levels. A State's proportion of these funds was based on the number of children in the State aged 3 to 21 inclusive as it bears on the number of such children in all States. A special provision was made for Puerto Rico, Guam, American Samoa, the Virgin Islands, the Trust Territories of the Pacific Islands.

MAJOR PROVISIONS

A State, to participate, must submit to the Commissioner of Education a State plan which provides satisfactory assurance that funds paid to the State under this Title will be expended either directly or through local education agencies solely to initiate,

---

[1] This act renewed, clarified, and broadened programs initially authorized under PL89-10. This is probably the most significant legislation for special education enacted to this time. The act provides important new benefits for handicapped children.

expand, or improve programs and projects (including preschool programs and projects) which are designed to meet the special educational and related needs of handicapped children throughout the State. The programs and projects have to be of sufficient size and scope and quality as to give reasonable promise of substantial progress toward meeting these needs. They can include the acquisition of equipment and when necessary the construction of school facilities. The plan also must provide satisfactory assurance that to the extent consistent with the number and location of handicapped children in the State who are enrolled in private, elementary and secondary schools, provision will be made for participation of such children in programs assisted or carried out under this Title.

Public Law 89-750 required the Commissioner of Education to establish in the Office of Education a National Advisory Committee on Handicapped Children which is to make recommendations to him concerning programs carried on for handicapped children by the Office of Education. P.L. 89-750 also required the Commissioner to establish and maintain within the Office of Education a bureau for the education and training of handicapped children which is to be the principal agency in the Office of Education for administering and carrying out programs and projects relating to the education and training of the handicapped, including programs and projects for the training of teachers of the handicapped and for research in special education and training.

See also P.L. 89-10 and P.L. 90-247.

20.   HIGHER EDUCATION ACT AMENDMENTS OF 1966 (P.L. 89-752)

Public Law 89-752 was enacted on November 3, 1966.

MAJOR PROVISIONS

Student Financial Assistance: — Title IV of the Higher Education Act has helped to provide students attending colleges and universities with a program of student financial assistance opportunities. Educational opportunity grants, combined with low-interest insured loans and college work-study programs, have had a major impact in alleviating the financial burden of attending college.

The 1966 law amended the National Defense Education Act by providing for cancellation of loans made to students under this Act. Such loans made to students who later teach handicapped children could be cancelled at the rate of 15 percent of the loan for each year spent teaching the handicapped.

Teacher Programs: — Title V of the Higher Education Act of 1965 provided a variety of teacher training and preparation programs. For fiscal year 1966, $9.5 million was appropriated for the National Teacher Corps. The Teacher Corps program aims at producing more teachers specially trained to work in the slums by setting up a two-year program which prepares interns with bachelor's degrees to be teachers with master's degrees, with special academic and practical training in the character of poverty. Second, by involving colleges and universities throughout the country, it expects to perpetuate interest in special training for slum teachers long after the Teacher Corps itself is ended.

21.   MENTAL HEALTH AMENDMENTS OF 1967 (P.L. 90-31)

Public Law 90-31 was enacted on June 24, 1967.

This legislation extended the authority for grants for construction and initial staffing of community mental health centers through fiscal year 1970. It also extended the program to include funds for acquisition or renovation of existing buildings for use as mental retardation facilities and community mental health centers.

MAJOR PROVISIONS

The legislation further provided that Public Health Service grants for research, training or demonstration projects be available to Public Health Service hospitals, Veterans' Administration, Bureau of Prisons and Saint Elizabeth's Hospital, on the same terms as non-Federal institutions. Funds authorized for Center Construction for fiscal years 1968-70 totaled $180 million. The Act authorized $142 million for staffing for the 1968-70 fiscal years.

See also: P.L. 88-164, P.L. 89-105 and P.L. 90-170.

22.   EDUCATION PROFESSIONS DEVELOPMENT ACT (P.L. 90-35)

Public Law 90-35 was enacted June 29, 1967.

The intent of this Act is to coordinate Federal programs bearing on the subject of teacher education, to improve the quality of teaching and to help meet critical shortages of adequately trained educational personnel.

MAJOR PROVISIONS

The Act establishes a National Advisory Council, allows the Commissioner to make grants to or contract with State or local educational agencies, instititutions of higher education, and public and private agencies, institutions, and organizations to attract qualified persons into the field of education.

Grants for the development of elementary and secondary educational personnel are authorized under Parts C and D. Part C authorizes fellowships for graduate study leading to an advanced degree for persons who are pursuing or plan to pursue a career in elementary and secondary education or post-secondary vocational education.

Part D authorizes grants for improving the qualifications of persons who are serving or preparing to serve in educational programs in elementary and secondary schools, including pre-school and adult and vocational programs, or post-secondary vocational schools or to supervise or train persons so serving.

The new legislation, flexible in its approach and wide in its coverage, has broad implications for improving personnel preparation programs in the area of the handicapped.

23.   VOCATIONAL REHABILITATION ACT AMENDMENTS OF 1967 (P. L. 90-99)

Public Law 90-99 was enacted on October 3, 1967.

The 1967 Amendments to the Vocational Rehabilitation Act reflect a departure into several areas previously uncharted.

MAJOR PROVISIONS

Deaf-Blind Youth and Adults: — The 1967 Amendments, authorized funds for the establishment of a National Center for Deaf-Blind Youth and Adults. The Secretary of Health, Education, and Welfare was authorized (by grant or contract with a non-profit organization) to enter into arrangements to pay all or part of the cost of construction, equipment, staff, and other expenses for such a center. The deaf-blind will receive an intensive program of specialized services to prepare them for adult responsibilities, including employment wherever this is possible.

The National Center also will conduct extensive programs of research, professional training, family orientation and education, and an organized informational service for the public and interested groups and agencies. Later, with experience gained in this center, other centers may be developed at various locations in the country.

Handicapped Migratory Workers: — The plight of the Nation's migratory agricultural workers and their families has been well publicized in recent years.

To begin dealing with this situation, the 1967 changes in the rehabilitation law authorized a special system of project grants to the State rehabilitation agencies, to pay from Federal funds up to 90 percent of the cost of providing vocational rehabilitation services to handicapped migratory agricultural workers. Services also can be provided to family members, where necessary to the rehabilitation of the migratory worker. The Secretary of Labor was directed to establish the rules determining who are migratory workers for this purpose. The law also calls for coordination of this new program with other Federally-aided programs for migratory agricultural workers.

Continued Growth of the Federal-State Program: — The 1967 Amendments continued funds for the Federal-State program for another 2 years, through June 30, 1970. The amounts of Federal funds to be allotted among the States also were increased each year. From the level of $400 million which the Act authorized for the fiscal year 1968, the 1967 law increased the amounts for allotment to $500 million in 1969 and $600 million in 1970.

State Planning for Rehabilitation: — In nearly all States, extensive planning is under way by groups appointed by the Governors to measure the needs of the disabled, the resources available (rehabilitation centers, hospitals, workshops, voluntary programs, etc.) and what needs to be done to meet the needs of all the disabled who need special help.

The 1967 Amendments authorized a final year of Federal support of this Statewide planning in rehabilitation.

Residence Requirements: — Most States have traditionally required that an individual furnish proof of his status as a resident of the State before services will be furnished. In some States, this is a flat requirement; in others the requirement is modified in certain ways under certain conditions.

Long experience in rehabilitation work for the disabled has shown that this frequently is a serious burden, and often a complete barrier, in trying to reach and restore handicapped people, and that it usually works to the greatest disadvantage among the poorest of the disabled people.

The 1967 Amendments to the Vocational Rehabilitation Act required that all States agree that no residence requirement will be imposed which excludes from vocational rehabilitation services otherwise-eligible handicapped persons who are present in the State. This assurance must be incorporated into the State plan, which is subject to approval by the Secretary of Health, Education, and Welfare before Federal funds can be made available to a State. This change must be in effect in all States not later than July 1, 1969. States may introduce the change earlier if they wish.

See also P. L. 89-333.

24. MENTAL RETARDATION AMENDMENTS OF 1967 (P. L. 90-170)

Public Law 90-170 was enacted on December 4, 1967.

In October 1963, Congress passed the Mental Retardation Facilities and Community Mental Health Centers Construction Act (P. L. 88-164) to provide assistance in combating mental retardation through grants for construction of facilities which would render new and expanded services for the mentally retarded and grants to initiate new training and research programs in special education.

The Mental Retardation Amendments of 1967: (1) extended through June 30, 1970, the programs under which matching grants are made for the construction of university-affiliated mental retardation facilities and community mental retardation facilities; (2) established a new grant program to pay a portion of the costs for compensation of professional and technical personnel in community facilities for the mentally retarded for initial operation of new facilities, or of new services in a facility; (3) extended until June 30, 1970, the existing program of training in the education of handicapped children; and (4) established a new program for training and research in physical education and recreation for the mentally retarded and other handicapped children.

MAJOR PROVISIONS

University-Affiliated Mental Retardation Facilities: — Public Law 90-170 provided for the extension of the university-affiliated construction program for three additional years, or until June 30, 1970, with authorization for appropriations of $10 million for the fiscal year 1968 and $20 million each for the fiscal years 1969 and 1970. These funds may be used to pay up to three-fourths of the costs of construction of facilities providing a full range of inpatient and outpatient services for the mentally retarded which will provide the physical setting for demonstration of specialized services and for training efforts needed to alleviate the acute shortages of professional and technical personnel required to care for the mentally retarded.

The initial law was further amended by P. L. 90-170 to provide for: (1) the inclusion of persons with other neurological handicapping conditions that are related to mental retardation; (2) the inclusion of research incidental or related to the program of the facility; and (3) the use of up to 2 percent of funds appropriated to support university-affiliated facility program planning grants, not to exceed $25,000 each nor more than 75 percent of the planning costs.

Community Facilities for the Mentally Retarded: — The law extended the authority for construction of community facilities for the mentally retarded for an additional two years — through fiscal year 1970 and retained the present authorization of $30 million for fiscal years 1968 and 1969. For the fiscal year 1970 there is an authorization of $50 million.

The law authorized States to use up to 2 percent or $50,000 of the funds appropriated for the construction of community mental retardation facilities to cover a portion of the cost of administering the program at the State level. The payment of funds for this purpose could not be approved if the States spend less than their 1967 level of funds for administration.

The law required that effective July 1, 1969, State plans for community mental retardation facilities provide enforcement of minimum standards of operation of these facilities.

Staffing of Community Mental Retardation Facilities: — In order to assure the continuum of services necessary to make real progress in the treatment and rehabilitation of the retarded, adequate staff must be available to the community facilities. Total sources of funds to support the operation of community mental retardation facilities are over-burdened. Potential sponsors of community facilities are frequently unable to provide the necessary operational support.

Since a major portion of operating expenses of community facilities is for staffing, the provisions of the 1967 law which permit grants for the cost of professional and technical personnel will provide significant assistance toward meeting total operating costs, and the means for attracting qualified personnel in mental retardation. Grants were authorized to meet a portion of the costs of professional and technical personnel for initial operation of new facilities or for new services in existing facilities for the mentally retarded.

This grant program provided for a declining Federal participation over a period of 4 years and 3 months with 75 percent Federal share for the first 15 months, 60 percent for the next year, 45 percent for the next year, and 30 percent for the last year.

Staffing grants can be made for the initial operation of new facilities and new services in existing facilities. Federal funds will be used to supplement and increase, to the extent practicable, the level of State, local and other non-Federal funds for mental retardation purposes.

An appropriation of $7 million was authorized for the fiscal year 1968, $10 million for fiscal year 1969 and $14 million for the fiscal year ending June 30, 1970.

Education of Handicapped Children: — The law extended through fiscal year 1970 the authorization for the existing program of training teachers of handicapped children; $55 million was authorized for fiscal year 1970 to carry out the program.

Physical Education and Recreation Personnel for Mentally Retarded and Other Handicapped Children: —

Preparation of Professional Personnel —

The vital role of exercise, sports and games in the growth and development of all children is well recognized. Research has shown that the children who need these activities most are the ones who get the least — the physically, emotionally and mentally handicapped. They need group play for social growth, skill achievement to build a positive self-image, and vigorous fitness activities to improve strength and endurance, areas in which they lag 2 to 6 years behind normal children. Also there is increasing evidence that motor activities can influence intellectual performance, particularly of the mentally retarded.

Most educators feel that the handicapped need specially adapted programs of physical education and recreation conducted by specially trained people.

Public Law 90-170 added a new Title V, which authorized the Secretary to make grants to public and nonprofit institutions of higher learning to assist them in providing professional or advanced training for personnel engaged or preparing to engage in employment as physical educators or recreation personnel for mentally retarded and other handicapped children. Also included are supervisors of such personnel who are engaged or preparing to engage in research or teaching in fields related to the physical education or recreation of such children.

Funds authorized for training personnel under Title V for the fiscal year 1968 total $1 million, $2 million was authorized for fiscal year 1969, and $3 million for fiscal year 1970.

Research and Demonstration Projects —

Title V authorized $1 million for fiscal year 1968 and $1.5 million for fiscal year 1969 and 1970 to enable the Secretary to make grants to State or local educational agencies, public and nonprofit private educational or research agencies and organizations for research or demonstration projects relating to physical education or recreation for mentally retarded and other handicapped children.

The Secretary was also authorized to appoint panels of experts and an advisory committee consisting of seven members to assist in the administration of Title V.

See also P. L. 88-164, P. L. 89-105 and P. L. 90-31.

25.   THE PARTNERSHIP FOR HEALTH AMENDMENTS OF 1967 (P.L. 90-174)

Public Law 90-174 was enacted on December 5, 1967.

MAJOR PROVISIONS

Comprehensive Health Planning and Services: — Federal-State cooperation in health is nearly as old as the Nation. But formal, continuing Federal assistance for the development of State public health programs is much more recent; the Social Security Act of 1935 provided the first general support for State public health programs. This program was followed by others directed toward specific diseases — tuberculosis, cancer, heart disease — and earmarked for use only in State programs dealing with these problems.

The "Partnership for Health Act of 1966" removed almost all of the categorical limitations, giving the States much more flexibility in the use of Federal health grant funds. Project grants, which support targeted attacks on new or special health problems and stimulate development of new health services, were made available for the whole range of health activity.

The 1966 Act also recognized the necessity for the most effective marshalling of all health resources, public and private. It encouraged State comprehensive health planning as a means of determining needs and establishing priorities. Grants were also made available for area-wide planning projects.

The 1967 Amendments retained all of the innovative provisions of the "Partnership for Health Act," and extended them for two years, through June 30, 1970, and authorized larger expenditures. In addition, new and expanded authorities were provided for health services research and development and for improvement of clinical laboratories.

Research in Health Services: — Many efforts have been made in recent years to assure all Americans access to health services. Under the 1967 law, these efforts will be supplemented by an intensive research program to find better ways of organizing, financing and delivering health services.

Finding ways to contain medical costs, to bring all Americans into the mainstream of medical care, to increase the productivity of health personnel and facilities, are some of the purposes of research and development in health services.

To enlist the Nation's best minds and most vigorous institutions in a research and development program that encompasses every element of the health services system, a National Center for Health Services Research will be established within the Department of Health, Education, and Welfare. The Center will administer the program and disseminate carefully evaluated results to health service agencies and practitioners. It will also provide a Government-wide focal point for research in this vital area.

See also P. L. 89-109 and P. L. 89-749.

26.   ELEMENTARY AND SECONDARY EDUCATION AMENDMENTS OF 1967 (P. L. 90-247)

Public Law 90-247 was enacted on January 21, 1968.

MAJOR PROVISIONS

Regional Resource Centers: — Regional Resource Centers will assist teachers and other school personnel by providing educational evaluation and assistance in developing specific educational strategies. In addition to providing direct services to the children, parents and teachers involved — the Centers will function to disseminate modern educational approaches. Schools that do not have special programs for the handicapped (about one-half the nation's school districts) will now receive assistance to develop special education programs. Appropriations authorized for this program amount to $7.5 million for fiscal year 1968. For fiscal year 1969, $7.75 million is authorized and for fiscal year 1970, $10 million is authorized.

Centers and Services for Deaf-Blind Children: — This program provides a major breakthrough in response to the needs of thousands of children affected by the rubella epidemic of several years ago, which resulted in approximately 20,000 to 30,000 babies being born with one or more handicapping conditions. It provides for the establishment and operation of Centers for deaf-blind children. The Centers will provide comprehensive diagnostic and evaluation services; programs for education, orientation and adjustment; and consultative services for parents, teachers and others working with the deaf-blind. In addition, the Secretary may make grants and contracts for training teachers and related specialists, for research and demonstration programs, and for dissemination activities. The Act authorized an appropriation of $1 million for fiscal year 1968, $3 million for fiscal year 1969, and $7 million for fiscal year 1970.

Recruitment of Personnel and Information on Education of the Handicapped: — Under this program grants or contracts may be authorized to improve recruiting of educational personnel, and to improve dissemination of information concerning educational opportunities for the handicapped. Grants or contracts may be made to public or nonprofit agencies, organizations, or institutions. This program is intended to encourage students and professional personnel to work in various fields of education of handicapped children through developing and distributing imaginative or innovative materials, to assist in recruiting personnel for such careers, or publicizing existing forms of financial aid which might enable students to pursue such careers.

The information program is intended to disseminate information about programs, services and resources for the education of handicapped children, referral services for teachers, parents and others interested in the handicapped. Authorized appropriations for this program were $1 million for fiscal year ending June 30, 1968, and $1 million for each of the two succeeding fiscal years.

Expansion of Instructional Media Programs to Include all Handicapped Children:— This program expanded the existing program of the Bureau of Education for the Handicapped to provide, in addition to a loan service of captioned film for the deaf, the producing and distributing of educational media for the use of all types of handicapped persons, their parents, actual or potential employers, and other persons directly involved in work for the advancement of the handicapped, the carrying on of research in the use of educational media for the handicapped and the training of persons in the use of educational media for the instruction of the handicapped. Under this program, the handicapped were defined as deaf, mentally retarded, speech impaired, visually handicapped, seriously emotionally disturbed, crippled, or other health impaired persons.

Funds authorized for this program were increased from $5 million to $8 million for fiscal year 1968 and 1969, and for fiscal year 1970 the increase was from $7 million to $10 million.

Earmarking Title III of ESEA: — A major source of new support for innovation and for implementation of the newest in educational methodology related to education of the handicapped was made available by specifying that 15 percent of the funds of Title III of the Elementary and Secondary Education Act be used for these purposes. This provision, which becomes effective in 1969, is expected to provide approximately $30 million for that year on projects which will help bridge the gap between research findings and everyday classroom activities.

A change in the basic formula of Title III, effective in fiscal year 1969, will assign 75 percent of the appropriations for Title III to the States under a State plan formula. Twenty-five percent will be reserved for projects approved by the Commissioner of Education. The funds reserved for the Commissioner will be available in fiscal year 1969, for the support of new awards. In fiscal year 1970, funds reserved for the Commissioner will be used only to support the continuation costs of previously awarded projects. The intent of the new formula is to transfer control of approval for all projects to the States. The 15 percent of the funds "earmarked" for the handicapped will follow this overall pattern.

Title I Funds for Children in Institutions for the Handicapped: — The formula for support of educational activities for children in State-operated or supported institutions for the handicapped was amended to provide increased support for this program (commonly called the P. L. 89- 313 program for the handicapped). Under this law, State agencies receive a maximum grant for the children they are educating through State-operated or supported schools. In fiscal year 1968, this amendment will provide approximately $9 million in additional funds for new personnel, instructional materials, and other programs which reach into the State schools to aid the retarded, emotionally disturbed, deaf, etc., and bring education and hope to the children in these schools.

Schools for Indian Children Operated by the Department of the Interior and Defense Department Overseas Dependent's Schools in Title VI: — The Act authorized assistance for handicapped children in schools operated by the Department of Defense and Children on Indian reservations, serviced by schools operated by the Department of Interior.

Research in Education of the Handicapped: — The program for research and related purposes in education of the handicapped was extended and expanded to include authority to conduct research surveys and demonstrations and to award contracts for research, in addition to the grants which previously have been awarded. The intramural research program will be developed to support and complement the broader extramural program. The program will be designed to: assure optimum utilization of funds; study methods of improving the administration; fill the gaps in the extramural program; conduct or arrange for specific research activities and surveys which are national in scope; replicate promising activities; provide for integration of the extramural program; and allow staff members to maintain their research skills and pursue individual research interests.

The Act authorized the Commissioner of Education to contract, as well as provide grants to, private educational or research agencies and organizations. This change will allow the research program to take advantage of the expertise of private, as well as public, educational and research agencies and organizations. Also authorized was the training of research personnel. This program was extended through the fiscal year 1970, with $18 million authorized to be appropriated for that year.

Authorizations for Grants to States and Minimum Allotment to States: — The act amended the provisions of Title VI authorizing grants to States for education of handicapped children by providing that no State receive less than $100,000 or 3/10 of 1 percent of the appropriation, whichever is greater. This provision assures that each State will get a grant large enough to insure that programs will be of sufficient magnitude to be effective. The basic authorization for the grant to State programs was extended to $162.5 million for fiscal year 1969 and $200 million for fiscal year 1970.

See also P. L. 89-10, P. L. 89-750 and P. L. 89-313.

27. SOCIAL SECURITY AMENDMENTS OF 1967 (P. L. 90-248)

Public Law 90-248 was enacted on January 2, 1968.

MAJOR PROVISIONS

Advisory Council on Health Insurance for Disabled Beneficiaries to be Established: — The existing law made health insurance protection under social security (medicare) available to persons aged 65 and over. Under the 1967 amendments, the Secretary of Health, Education, and Welfare was directed to establish an advisory council to study the question of providing health insurance for disabled beneficiaries and report its findings and recommendations to the Secretary by January 1, 1969.

Child Welfare Services

Over one-half million children benefit each year from the services of professional child welfare workers with public agencies. Whenever possible, these workers enable children to stay in their own homes. They do this by counseling families on their problems, arranging for visiting homemakers, training mothers in homemaking and child-rearing, providing day care for children whose mothers must work, and in other ways.

When home care is impossible, child welfare workers arrange for foster or adoptive homes. They arrange special care for physically and mentally handicapped children, and help youngsters who have been discharged from institutions.

The 1967 Amendments authorized an increased appropriation for child welfare services. Additional Federal aid will enable States and communities to provide more help to more children, particularly children in need of foster care.

Projects for Experimental and Special Types of Child Welfare Services: — State and local agencies need to strengthen their ongoing programs by trying different methods of providing services and testing them.

The 1967 legislation amended the child welfare research and demonstration authority of the Social Security Act to: make possible dissemination of research and demonstration findings into program activity through multiple demonstrations on a regional basis; encourage State and local agencies administering public child welfare services programs to develop and staff new and innovative services; and provide contract authority to make it possible to direct research into neglected and vital areas.

Improvement of Child Health

Early Casefinding and Treatment of Handicapping Conditions in Children: — The number of children served under the crippled children's program has more than doubled since 1950.

Less than half the children served have orthopedic handicaps;

the rest include mental retardation, epilepsy, hearing impairment, cerebral palsy, cystic fibrosis, heart disease and many congenital defects.

The 1967 Act authorized grants to State crippled children's agencies to assist them to extend and improve services for locating crippled children and for providing medical, surgical, corrective and other services for children who are crippled or who have conditions which may lead to crippling. State crippled children's agencies use their funds to locate handicapped children, to provide diagnostic services, and then to see that each child gets the medical care, hospitalization, and continuing care by a variety of professional people that he needs.

The 1965 Amendments to the Social Security Act required the States to make their services available to children in all parts of the State by 1975. In addition, the costs of the program were greatly increased beginning July 1, 1967, when hospital services must be paid for in accordance with reasonable cost.

The 1967 Amendments consolidated the existing separate authorizations into a single authorization and allocated 50 percent of the total authorization for formula grants, 40 percent for project grants and 10 percent for research and training. The consolidated authorization is $250,000,000 for 1969, increasing to $350,000,000 for 1973, and for each fiscal year thereafter.

One purpose of the 1967 legislation was to intensify the States' efforts to reach crippled children early and to give them the help they need.

The 1967 Amendments required the States to include in their plans a description of ways to increase casefinding so that diagnostic services and appropriate care and treatment can be given. Intensified casefinding procedures can be carried out through schools, day care centers, well-baby clinics, nursery schools, Head Start centers, etc. Birth certificates can be checked for reports on congenital malformations.

The legislation amended Title XIX, Medical Assistance, to require screening and treatment of children and arrangements for use and payment where appropriate of agencies administering maternal and child health services, services for crippled children, maternity and infant care projects or projects providing health services for children and youth.

Maternal and Child Health Services: — The 1965 Amendments to the Social Security Act required that States make maternal and child health services available to children in all parts of the State by

1975. This will mean extension of the program into cities, and into additional rural counties, many of which have only rudimentary programs. These Amendments also required payment of reasonable cost for hospital services, effective July 1, 1967. Both of these requirements add substantially to costs of the program.

States use Federal funds, together with State and local funds, to pay the costs of conducting prenatal clinics where mothers are examined by physicians and get medical advice; for visits by public health nurses to homes before and after babies are born; for well-baby clinics where mothers can bring their babies and young children for examination and immunizations, where they can get competent advice on how to prevent illness and where their many questions about the care of babies can be answered.

These services have been instrumental in the reduction of maternal and infant mortality, especially in rural areas. Funds are used to make available physicians, dentists, and nurses to the schools for health examinations of school children. They are also used for immunizations.

The 1967 Amendments to the Social Security Act should help the States move toward the goal of extending maternal and child health services so that they will be reasonably available to children in all parts of a State by July 1, 1975. This would include the provision of preventive health services for more mothers and children. The greater availability of services should contribute to further reduction of infant and maternal mortality.

The 1967 Amendments, which consolidated the maternal and child health program and crippled children's services into one program, also increased the authorization for appropriations. The legislation also includes safeguards against reduction in the amounts of State and local funds provided for maternal and child health and crippled children's programs.

Special Projects for Maternity and Infant Care: — These projects are offering high quality care to high risk maternity patients and medical and intensive nursing care for prematurely born and other high risk infants. They have brought maternity clinics into the neighborhoods where the patients live and made available a broad spectrum of diagnostic and specialists consultation services.

Research in Maternal and Child Health and Crippled Children's Services: — Present and anticipated manpower requirements for medical personnel in obstetrics and pediatrics are such that comprehensive child health care on a wide scale will not be feasible unless ways are found to extend the services of such personnel.

The 1963 Amendments to the Social Security Act established a research grants program in Title V to support studies "which show promise of substantial contribution to the advancement . . . " of maternal and child health services or crippled children's services and authorized an annual appropriation up to $8,000,000. The appropriation for fiscal year 1968 was $5,900,000.

This legislation broadened the language to give emphasis to projects concerned with the need for feasibility, cost and effectiveness of health care programs making use of personnel with varying levels of training and to training of health personnel for work in comprehensive health care programs.

Amendments to the Disability Program

Benefits for disabled widows and widowers: — The 1967 Amendments provided for benefits to disabled widows (including surviving divorced wives) and disabled dependent widowers after attainment of age 50.

Insured Status for workers disabled while young: — The 1967 law extended to all workers disabled before age 31 — regardless of the nature of their disability — the alternative insured-status requirement provided under the existing law for workers disabled by blindness before age 31.

Extension of retroactivity of disability application: — The 1967 law provided a longer period of time after termination of disability for the filing of a disability freeze application by an individual whose mental or physical incapacity was the reason for his failure to file a timely application.

See also P. L. 88- 641, P. L. 88- 650 and P. L. 89- 97.

28. VOCATIONAL REHABILITATION AMENDMENTS OF 1968 (P. L. 90- 391)

Public Law 90- 391 was enacted into law on July 7, 1968.

MAJOR PROVISIONS

Grants to States for Vocational Rehabilitation Services: — The amendments extend through fiscal year 1971 the authorizations for appropriations for Section 2 grants to States for vocational rehabilitation services. Prior to the new amendments there were authorizations through fiscal year 1970. $700 million is authorized for allotment among States in 1971. The Federal share is increased to 80 percent, effective fiscal year 1970.

Establishment of Minimum Allotments to States: — To increase efficiency, expand rehabilitation services and reach a greater number of clients, a base of $1 million has been fixed under Section 2 to assist States in achieving these goals.

Construction of Rehabilitation Facilities: — The amendments provide that Section 2 funds may be utilized for new construction as well as expansion and/or alteration of existing buildings. A limitation of 10 percent of Section 2 allotments has been established for financing new construction. A "maintenance of effort" provision is included to assure that other services presently provided under Section 2 will not be diminished.

Private Contributions for Construction or Establishment of Facilities: — This law authorizes the use of voluntary funds for construction as well as for establishment of a public or nonprofit rehabilitation facility.

Grants to States for Innovations: — The amendments extend the program of grants to States for innovation of vocational rehabilitation facilities. The Federal share in these projects is 90 percent for the first 3 years and 75 percent for the fourth and fifth years. Appropriation authority is extended with authorizations of $3.2 million for 1969, $6 million for 1970 and $10 million for 1971.

Grants to States for Special Projects: — The amendments extend the authorization for specialized projects in the areas of research, demonstration, expansion and training of rehabilitation personnel. The authority for projects under this section is expanded to include: (1) projects for rehabilitation service to the mentally retarded; (2) projects with industry for training the handicapped; (3) grants for training manpower for agencies serving the handicapped; and (4) grants for developing new career opportunities for the handicapped. Appropriation authority is extended with authorizations of $80 million for 1969, $115 million for 1970 and $140 million for 1971.

State Plan Requirements: — Public Law 90-391 makes a number of modifications in State plan requirements for participation in the vocational rehabilitation program. The principal ones are:

(1) Waiver of the "sole agency" and "statewideness" requirement. This authorizes State vocational rehabilitation agencies to share funding and administrative responsibility with other State agencies.

(2) Statewide planning — This provision proposes that a plan requirement specify that a State vocational rehabilitation agency conduct a continual planning operation as part of its regular program and that such planning be financed under Section 2.

(3) Construction — A requirement is made that if a State plan includes provision for construction of rehabilitation facilities, it must not contemplate construction when the Federal payment exceeds 10 percent of the State's allotment. In addition, Federal standards and the Hill-Burton matching rates applicable to construction in Section 12 of the Vocational Rehabilitation Act will be applicable to new construction with Section 2 funds.

Evaluation of the Vocational Rehabilitation Program:— Provision is made for ongoing evaluation of the vocational rehabilitation program. The purpose of such evaluation is to insure proper program development through focusing on areas of special needs.

Rehabilitation Facilities Construction and Staffing: — Public Law 90-391 extends the program for rehabilitation facilities construction and staffing as provided for in Section 12. This program enables public and private non-profit organizations to expend Federal funds for part of the costs of building new facilities, acquiring existing structure, purchasing land and expanding and renovating current facilities.

The program also enables newly constructed rehabilitation facilities to utilize Federal funds to acquire necessary staff to implement programming. Federal funds for staff are available on a declining scale for 4 years and 3 months, beginning with 75 percent during the first 15 months and decreasing to 30 percent during the last 12 months.

Appropriations authority is extended with authorization of $10 million for fiscal year 1969, $20 million for fiscal year 1970, and $30 million for fiscal year 1971.

Vocational Evaluation and Work Adjustment: — Public Law 90- 391 establishes a program to serve the disadvantaged (including youth of school age with mental or physical disabilities), as well as persons who have behavioral problems, are gross under-achievers, or are socially maladjusted as a result of environmental deprivation.

The focal point for the program will be a vocationally-oriented rehabilitation facility, since the availability of work for clients undergoing evaluation and adjustment is a most important element in many cases. Such a facility may be operated by a State vocational rehabilitation agency, or by a voluntary agency under contract from the State agency.

President's Committee on Employment of the Handicapped:— Public Law 90- 391 increases the limitation on the amount authorized to be appropriated for the work of the President's Committee on Employment of the Handicapped from $500,000 to $1 million.

29. ELIMINATION OF ARCHITECTURAL BARRIERS TO THE PHYSICALLY HANDICAPPED IN CERTAIN FEDERALLY-FINANCED BUILDINGS (P. L. 90- 480)

Public Law 90- 480 was enacted into law on August 12, 1968.
This Act is designed to ensure that certain buildings financed with Federal funds are so designed and constructed as to be accessible to the physically handicapped.

MAJOR PROVISIONS

The Federal Government has recognized for some time the need to rehabilitate and employ as many of the physically handicapped as possible. These people constitute a tremendous asset of our country which is not being fully utilized. Early recognition of this need led to the establishment of a Presidential Committee on Employment of the Handicapped in 1947. In addition, in 1965 the National Commission on Architectural Barriers to Rehabilitation of the

Handicapped was created and its report "Design for All Americans" was transmitted on January 8, 1968, to Congress. P. L. 90- 480 is a response to the recommendations made in the report.

Public Buildings-Accessibility to Physically Handicapped: — The term building means any building or facility (other than a privately-owned residential structure or buildings on a military installation designed and constructed for able-bodied military person-nel) intended for public use must be accessible to the physically handicapped.

Standards: — In order to ensure that physically handicapped people have access to and use of buildings, structures and facilities subject to this Act, appropriate standards will be developed by the Secretary of Health, Education, and Welfare in consultation with:

> The Administrator of General Services;
> The Secretary of Housing and Urban Development; and
> The Secretary of Defense.

Applicability: — Every building designed, constructed or al-tered, after the effective date of standards issued under this Act, must be in compliance with these standards.

Waiver: — The Administrator of General Services, the Secretary of Housing and Urban Development and the Secretary of Defence, with respect to standards relating to their agencies, may under certain conditions waive a standard when it is deemed necessary; surveys may also be conducted to ensure compliance with such standards.

30. ESTABLISHMENT OF NATIONAL EYE INSTITUTE (P. L. 90- 489)

Public Law 90- 489 was enacted into law on August 16, 1968.
This law established a new Institute in the National Institutes of Health, known as the National Eye Institute, which is responsible for conducting and supporting research for new treatment, cures and training relating to blinding eye diseases and visual disorders.

MAJOR PROVISIONS

Establishment of National Eye Institute: — P. L. 90- 489 adds a new Part F to Title IV of the Public Health Service Act, providing for the establishment of a National Eye Institute. The Secretary is authorized to establish a National Eye Institute which will conduct and support research relating to blinding eye diseases and visual disorders, including research and training in special health problems and requirements of the blind.

Establishment of an Advisory Council: — The new legislation provides for establishment of an Advisory Council to advise, consult with, and make recommendations to the Secretary on matters relating to the activities of the Institute.

Functions of National Eye Institute: — P. L. 90-489 specifies the functions of the National Eye Institute.

P. L. 90-489 changed the name of the National Institute for Neurological Diseases and Blindness to the "Institute for Neurological Diseases." However, subsequent legislation (P. L. 90-639) again changed the name of that Institute to the "National Institute of Neurological Diseases and Stroke."

31.   WHITE HOUSE CONFERENCE ON AGING (P. L. 90-526)

Public Law 90-526 was enacted into law September 28, 1968.

This law provides for a White House Conference on Aging to be called by the President of the United States in 1971.

MAJOR PROVISIONS

The purpose of the White House Conference on Aging is to stimulate joint efforts by the Federal Government, the States and their citizens to develop recommendations and plans for action which will serve the purposes of:

    a)   assuring middle-aged and older persons equal opportunity with others to engage in gainful employment which they are capable of performing;

    b)   enabling retired persons to enjoy incomes sufficient for health and for participation in family and community life as self-respecting citizens;

    c)   providing housing suited to the needs of older persons and at the prices they can afford to pay;

    d)   assisting middle-aged and older persons to make the

preparation, develop skills and interests, and find social contacts which will make the gift of added years of life a period of reward and satisfaction;

e) stepping up research designed to relieve old age of its burdens of sickness, mental breakdown, and social ostracism; and

f) evaluating progress made since the last White House Conference on Aging, and examining the changes which the next decade will bring in the character of the problems confronting older persons.

The President of the United States is authorized to call a White House Conference on Aging in 1971 in order to develop recommendations for further research and action in the field of aging. The Conference shall be planned and conducted by the Secretary of Health, Education, and Welfare.

A final report of the White House Conference on Aging shall be submitted to the President not later than one hundred and twenty days following the date on which the Conference is called. The findings and recommendations of the report shall be made available to the public.

The Secretary shall, within 90 days after the submission of the final report, transmit to the President and the Congress his recommendations for the administrative action and the legislation necessary to implement the recommendations contained in the report.

Advisory Committee: — The Secretary is directed to establish an Advisory Committee of 28 members to the White House Conference on Aging.

Authorization: — For the purposes of carrying out a White House Conference on Aging, the sum of $1,900,000 is authorized.

32. HANDICAPPED CHILDREN'S EARLY EDUCATION ASSISTANCE ACT OF 1968 (P. L. 90- 538)

Public Law 90- 538 was enacted into law on September 30, 1968.

This act will: support experimental preschool and early education programs for handicapped children which show promise of promoting a comprehensive and strengthened approach to the special problems of such children, including activities and services designed to encourage the intellectual, emotional, physical, mental, social and language development of handicapped children; encourage the participation of the parents of these children in assisting the professional educators in the development and operation of such programs; and acquaint the community with the problems and potentials of its handicapped children.

MAJOR PROVISIONS

Program Authorized: — The Act enables the Commissioner of Education to make grants or contracts to public and private nonprofit agencies for the development and implementation of experimental programs. These grants will be distributed on a broad geographical basis throughout the Nation. This does not mean that there necessarily must be a single program in each State. It is even conceivable that some States will combine their resources and develop regional centers.

The model preschool program should stimulate all areas of the handicapped child's development including his emotional, physical, intellectual and social needs. In fact, the report of the House Committee on Education and Labor on this measure urged that programs encompass not only all disabilities, but all age groups from birth to 6 years of age.

The portion of the Act dealing with participation of parents has two major purposes: (1) to provide the parents with counseling and guidance on how they can effectively respond to the special needs of their handicapped children; and (2) to provide supportive supplementary programs which will aid parents in better coping with problems as they arise.

Another aim of the Act is to acquaint the community with the problems and potentials of handicapped children. This feature is included in the belief that society, including educators, too often underestimates the capacities of these children and, as a result, often limits their opportunities to develop and function as constructive members of our society.

The Act directs that each program be coordinated with the local school system in the community being served. Dissemination of information, inservice training and other aspects of the model programs will be designed to encourage the development of successful early education programs throughout the State and neighboring areas. Where possible, new demonstration programs will be established in settings so that they may be used for the training of teachers, speech pathologists and audiologists, clinicians, psychologists, physicians, and other supportive personnel whose contributions are required in affecting good early childhood education of the handicapped.

The Act provides for a Federal share of up to 90 percent of the cost of a project. The non-Federal share may be in cash or in kind. The requirement of a non-Federal share is designed to encourage a commitment of community and other public and private agencies to the success of the programs through tangible involvement from the program's inception.

Evaluation: — P. L. 90- 538 authorizes the Commissioner to provide, either directly or through contract with independent organizations, a thorough and continuing evaluation of the effectiveness of each program assisted. Each program will be expected to include in its planning an evaluation component to help in the continuous improvement of the program. In addition, the Commissioner is expected to provide an overall evaluation of the total program once it has had time to become operational.

The evaluation aspect of this legislation is important in that it is advantageous for the educational community to compare programs which are both effective and ineffective so that successful approaches can be replicated and ineffective attempts can be avoided.

Definition of Handicapped Children: — Handicapped children for the purposes of this Act are defined as: mentally retarded, hard-of-hearing, deaf, speech impaired, visually handicapped, seriously emotionally disturbed, crippled, or other health-impaired children who by reason thereof require special education and related services.

Appropriations Authorized: — The Act authorizes the appropriation of $1 million for fiscal year 1969, $10 million for fiscal year 1970, and $12 million for fiscal year 1971. The sums appropriated for the first year will be used primarily as planning funds for demonstration projects. It is estimated that the $1 million will support the planning phases for these centers.

33. HEALTH SERVICES AND FACILITIES AMENDMENTS OF 1968 (P. L. 90- 574)

Public Law 90- 574 was enacted into law on October 15, 1968.

The Amendments extend five existing programs and authorize one new program relating to health services. The Amendments extend: the Regional Medical Program; the Migrant Health Program; the Hill-Burton Hospital Facilities and Construction Program; and the Solid Waste Disposal Act. P. L. 90–574 authorizes a new program for the treatment of alcoholics and narcotic addicts in Community Mental Health Centers.

MAJOR PROVISIONS

Regional Medical Programs: — This program was established in 1965 to assist the Nation's health resources in making available to all Americans the advances of medical science against heart disease, cancer, stroke and related diseases.

In addition to extending the basic authorities of the Regional Medical Programs for two years, the new Act provides that up to one percent of the appropriation for any fiscal year beginning with 1970 may be used by the Secretary for evaluation of the program. The Act makes clear that Regional Medical grants can be awarded to a combination of Regional Medical Program agencies for carrying on a Regional Medical Program.

A new authority will permit grants to any public or private nonprofit agency or institution for services which will be of substantial value and use to any two or more Regional Medical Programs. Another authorizes the use of funds to permit the full participation of Federal hospitals.

Migrant Health: — Prior to the enactment of the migrant workers health law in 1962, few of the Nation's migrant families received anything more than emergency health care. Today, 115 migrant health projects are in operation in 36 States and Puerto Rico, serving approximately 300,000 people. All projects provide sanitation workers and health education programs. The 1965 extension of the migrant health act added hospitalization services, and funds became available for this purpose in 1967.

For the migrant who is unable to secure medical care on his own and is ineligible for public assistance, these projects are virtually the sole source of health services.

The 1968 amendments continue the program for an additional two years, with authorizations of $9 million and $15 million, which should permit a significant increase in services.

Hospital Construction and Modernization: — Since 1946 Federal assistance has been given to States and their communities in the construction of hospitals and other health facilities under the Hill-Burton Act. As a result of that construction, facilities for medical care are being made accessible to individuals in communities across the country.

The new legislation provides for a one year, $295 million extension of the current Hill-Burton Hospital Facilities and Construction program which was to expire as of June 30, 1969.

Rehabilitation of Alcoholics and Narcotics Addicts: P. L. 90-574 authorizes a two-year grant program for building and staffing facilities for preventing and treating alcoholism, using the same types of mechanisms as provided in the Community Mental Health Centers Act.

The new legislation also amends the Community Mental Health Centers Act by authorizing the construction, staffing, and the training of personnel for facilities for the treatment of narcotic addicts, as well as related surveys and demonstrations, but subject to limitations comparable to those in the existing Community Mental Health Centers programs. The new legislation also provides for use of 1 percent of Community Mental Health Centers' funds (including funds under the new provisions on alcoholism and narcotic addiction) for evaluation of the program.

Section 402 of the Narcotics Adult Rehabilitation Act of 1966, which provided for programs for the rehabilitation of narcotic addicts, is repealed.

34.   HIGHER EDUCATION AMENDMENTS OF 1968 (P. L. 90-575)

Public Law 90-575 was enacted into law on October 16, 1968.

This law extends and revises the National Defense Education Act of 1958, the Higher Education Facilities Act of 1963, the Higher Education Act of 1965, the International Education Act of 1966, and related acts.

MAJOR PROVISIONS

Student Financial Assistance: — The Commissioner of Education, under the new law, is authorized to make grants or contracts with institutions of higher learning to enable them to develop and carry out a program of Special Services for Disadvantaged Students. These programs of special services are for students who are enrolled in or accepted by the institution receiving the grant and who, by reason of deprived educational, cultural, or economic background, or physical handicap, are in need of such services to help them initiate or continue their post-secondary education.

The new amendments transfer the Upward Bound program

from the Office of Economic Opportunity to the Office of Education in fiscal year 1970. Upward Bound is a demonstration program which provides intensive and concentrated educational opportunities to disadvantaged and impoverished youth.

Loan Forgiveness: — The 1966 Higher Education Law amended the student loan forgiveness provisions of the National Defense Education Act by providing for cancellation of loans made to students who later teach handicapped children. The rate of cancellation was 15 percent of the loan for each full year spent teaching the handicapped. The 1968 amendments extend this forgiveness feature for two additional years. The loan forgiveness provisions shall apply only to loans made prior to July 1, 1970.

Acquisition of Equipment to be Used in Programs for Educationally-Deprived Children: — P. L. 90- 575 authorizes grants to local educational agencies for the acquisition of equipment and materials designed to meet the special educational needs of educationally-deprived children.

35.   VOCATIONAL EDUCATION AMENDMENTS OF 1968 (P. L. 90- 576)

Public Law 90- 576 was enacted into law on October 16, 1968.

This law amends the Vocational Education Act of 1963. It retains the comprehensive State grant provision on a continuing basis and authorizes new programs for 5 years. The law authorizes appropriations of $355 million for fiscal year 1969, $565 million for fiscal year 1970, $675 million each for fiscal years 1971 and 1972, and $565 million for fiscal year 1973. These authorizations are for State Vocational Education Programs and Research and Training in Vocational Education. There are also special authorizations for certain categorical programs.

MAJOR PROVISIONS

State Advisory Councils: — This legislation provides that any State which desires to receive a grant under this title for any fiscal year shall establish a State Advisory Council. The responsibilities of this council shall include:

(1) Advising the State Board on the development of, and policy matters arising in, the administration of the State plan.

(2) Evaluating vocational education programs, services, and activities assisted under this title and publishing and distributing the results thereof.

(3) Preparing and submitting through the State Board to the Commissioner of Education and to the National Council an annual evaluation report which evaluates the effectiveness of vocational education programs, services and activities and recommends such changes as may be warranted by the evaluations.

This legislation specifies that State Advisory Councils shall include as members persons who have special knowledge, experience or qualifications with respect to the special educational needs of physically or mentally handicapped persons.

National Advisory Council on Vocational Education: — Public Law 90-576 creates a National Advisory Council on Vocational Education. This Council shall:

(1) Advise the Commissioner concerning the administration of, preparation of general regulations for, and operation of programs supported under this title.

(2) Review the administration and operation of vocational education programs under this title.

(3) Conduct independent evaluations of programs carried out under this title and publish and distribute the results thereof.

This law specifies that the Council shall include in its membership persons who are experienced in the education and training of handicapped persons.

Definition of Handicapped: — These amendments define handicapped as follows:

"The term 'handicapped', when applied to persons, means persons who are mentally retarded, hard-of-hearing, deaf, speech impaired, visually handicapped, seriously emotionally disturbed, crippled or other health impaired persons who by reason thereof require special education and related services."

Designation of State Funds for Programs for Handicapped Persons: — This legislation provides that at least 10 percent of each

State's allotment of funds appropriated for any fiscal year beginning after June 30, 1969, shall be used only for vocational education for handicapped persons who, because of their handicapping condition, cannot succeed in the regular vocational education program without special educational assistance or who would require a modified vocational education program.

Training of Teachers of the Handicapped: — Public Law 85- 926 is amended to permit relevant agencies and institutions other than higher education and State agencies to receive grants to enable them to participate in the education of professionals to work with the handicapped. Examples of such institutions and agencies could be the university-affiliated facilities for the mentally retarded, regional educational laboratories, State institutions and agencies related to mental health.

36.   NATIONAL CENTER ON EDUCATIONAL MEDIA AND MATERIALS FOR THE HANDICAPPED (P.L. 91- 61)

Public Law 91- 61 was enacted on August 20, 1969 and amends an earlier law, P.L. 85- 905. It provides for establishment, construction and operation of a National Center on Educational Media and Materials for the Handicapped.

MAJOR PROVISIONS

The Center will provide a continuing production source for special materials. It will be available to the Bureau of Education for the Handicapped as a centralizing agency for its many media activities.

The Center will develop specific material and media for the Model Secondary School for the Deaf located in Washington, D. C.

The Center will be a central communication link in a system involving the following activities of the Bureau of Education for the Handicapped: Regional Media Centers for the Deaf; Instructional Materials Centers; the Educational Research Information Center project; Language Instruction to Facilitate Education; curriculum projects under way in research; and a distribution network for captioned films.

Construction of a specially designed facility which will provide the necessary environmental controls for specialized media will be possible under this act. This facility will be available for training senior scholars, media specialists and professional personnel as well as teachers of the handicapped.

Authorization for the Bureau of Education for the Handicapped to contract with profit making as well as nonprofit organizations offering resources to perform the specific tasks of the center is provided in this legislation.

Authorizations of $12.5 million for fiscal year 1971, $15 million for fiscal year 1972, and $20 million for fiscal year 1973 and each year thereafter is provided in the law.

37. THE EDUCATION OF THE HANDICAPPED ACT (P.L. 91-230) (Elementary and Secondary Education Assistance Programs Extension)

Public Law 91-230 was enacted April 13, 1970. The new law extends and amends The Elementary and Secondary Education Act of 1965.

Title VI of the bill creates, as a separate act, the "Education of the Handicapped Act," which constitutes a single statute authorizing programs in the Office of Education specifically designed to meet the special educational needs of the handicapped. The "Education of the Handicapped Act" replaces the provisions in present law enacted as (1) Public Law 85-905, (2) Public Law 85-926, (3) titles III and V of Public Law 88-164, (4) title VI of Public Law 89-10, and (5) Public Law 90-538. Title VI does not replace those parts of titles I and III of Public Law 89-10 and of Public Law 88-210 relating to the education of the handicapped.

MAJOR PROVISIONS

The Education of the Handicapped Act provides for —

Part A — General Provisions

a) a bureau within the Office of Education for the education and training of the handicapped;

b) a National Advisory Committee on Handicapped Children;

c) funds for the acquisition of equipment and the construction of facilities;

Part B — Assistance to States for Education of Handicapped Children

a) grants to states to assist them in the initiation, expansion, and the improvement of programs for the education of handicapped children;

Part C — Centers and Services to Meet Special Needs of the Handicapped

a) grants and contracts to support regional centers designed to appraise the special educational needs of handicapped children and to provide services to assist in meeting such needs;

b) funds to support centers to meet the special needs of deaf-blind children;

c) funds for the development and carrying out of experimental pre-school and early education programs for handicapped children;

d) research to identify and meet the full range of special needs for handicapped children;

e) development or demonstration of new, or improvements in existing, methods, approaches, or techniques, which would contribute to the adjustment and education of such children;

f) training (either directly or otherwise) of professional and allied personnel engaged or preparing to engage in programs specifically designed for such children, including payment of stipends for trainees and allowances for travel and other expenses for them and their dependents;

g) dissemination of materials and information about practices found effective in working with such children;

h) thorough and continuing evaluation of the effectiveness of the above programs;

i) a new program of grants and contracts to support research training and model centers to meet the special needs of children with specific learning disabilities is authorized.

Part D — Training Personnel for the Education of the Handicapped

a) grants to institutions of higher education and other
    nonprofit institutions and agencies to assist them —

    (1) in providing training of professional personnel to
         conduct training of teachers and other specialists in
         fields related to the education of handicapped chil-
         dren;

    (2) in providing training for personnel engaged or prepar-
         ing to engage in employment as teachers of handi-
         capped children, as supervisors of such teachers, or as
         speech correctionists or other special personnel pro-
         viding special services for the education of such
         children, or engaged or preparing to engage in
         research in fields related to the education of such
         children; and

    (3) in establishing and maintaining scholarships, with
         such stipends and allowances as may be determined
         by the Commissioner, for training personnel engaged
         in or preparing to engage in employment as teachers
         of the handicapped or as related specialists.

b) grants to state educational agencies for programs for
    training personnel engaged or preparing to engage as
    teachers of handicapped children or as supervisors of
    special teachers;

c) grants or contracts to improve recruiting of educational
    personnel and to improve dissemination of information
    concerning educational opportunities for the handicapped;

d) the training of physical educators and recreation personnel
    for handicapped children.

Part E — Funds for

a) research and demonstration projects in the education of
    handicapped children;

b) research and demonstration projects in physical education
    and recreation for handicapped children.

Part F — Funds for Instructional Media for the Handicapped

a)   captioned films and educational media for handicapped;

b)   a national center on educational media and materials for the handicapped.

Part G — Special Programs for Children with Specific Learning Disabilities, through Grants and Contracting Authority for

a)   research relating to the education of children with specific learning disabilities;

b)   professional or advanced training for educational personnel who are teaching or preparing to be teachers, or who are preparing to be supervisors;

c)   establishing and operating model centers for the improvement of education of children with specific learning disabilities.

SELECTED DEFINITIONS

The term "handicapped children" means mentally retarded, hard-of-hearing, deaf, speech impaired, visually handicapped, seriously emotionally disturbed, crippled, or other health impaired children who by reason thereof require special education and related services.

The term "children with specific learning disabilities" means those children who have a disorder in one or more of the basic psychological processes involved in understanding or in using language, spoken or written, which disorder may manifest itself in imperfect ability to listen, think, speak, read, write, spell, or do mathematical calculations. Such disorders include such conditions as perceptual handicaps, brain injury, minimal brain dysfunction, dyslexia, and developmental aphasia. This term does not include children who have learning problems which are primarily the result of visual, hearing, or motor handicaps, of mental retardation, of emotional disturbance, or of environmental disadvantage.

part **iv**

national
perspectives
and trends

The perspective of special education services is always different at different levels. Few meaningful school enumerations of exceptional children, special education programs, or staff have appeared in the literature. Definition and identification are constant problems in demographical studies of special education.

For several decades the United States Office of Education has collected and distributed statistics on the status of the handicapped. The report that appears first in this chapter is a collection of nationwide statistical information by Romaine Mackie and others that reflects trends in the education of exceptional children. The report includes the number of pupils by type of handicap, the number of administrative units in local public schools having a special education program, and the number of teachers and speech correctionists. The next article, which is excerpted from part of a report of a Department of Health, Education, and Welfare Task Force, examines the nature and extent of handicapping conditions and clearly points out the massive proportions of this problem. The final article in this chapter is a unique and comprehensive view of special education services and trends in selected large city school districts. The results of this survey conducted by Richard Slater are summarized and presented in five different sub-sections including: Administrative Structure, Geographical Location, Specialized Diagnostic Services, Special Education Programs, and Financial Structure.

statistics on special education in the united states: 1948-1966 *

ROMAINE P. MACKIE
in collaboration with JOHN DAVIS,
PATRICIA HUNTER and FRANCES MULLEN
(FRANCES P. CONNOR, ED.)

This report on special education focuses upon the quantitative advances between the years 1948 and 1966 in: pupil enrollments by area of exceptionality; number of public school systems and public and private residential schools; and the number of special educators and speech and hearing specialists employed. The report includes Office of Education statistics for 1963, not formerly published, and Office of Education estimates for 1966 made on the basis of earlier studies. The findings are encouraging because they show marked progress in providing educational opportunity for exceptional children. They reflect the deepening faith of the nation's citizenry in the value of special education. They further reflect the accomplishments of special educators and attest to the increased contributions of colleges and universities in the field of special education.

The Office of Education has included in its surveys all public school systems in the United States, all school programs in public hospitals for the mentally ill, and all known public and private

*Reprinted from *Special Education in the United States: Statistics 1948-1966* (Teachers College Series in Special Education, F. P. Connor, ed.) by permission of the editor and the Teachers College Press. Copyright 1969 by the Teachers College Press, Teachers College, Columbia University.

residential schools for the blind, the deaf, the mentally retarded, and the emotionally disturbed and socially maladjusted including the delinquent. It does not include nonpublic day schools. (See method of study for scope of survey, Appendix B.)

Pupil
Enrollment

The advance in pupil enrollment in special education during the past two decades has been almost beyond anticipation. The reported enrollment in 1963 was slightly more than 1,666,000 and the estimates for 1966 about 2,100,000. More than 90 per cent of these pupils are in local public schools and less than 10 per cent in residential schools. Comparison of enrollments in day and residential schools by area indicates that the largest proportion of emotionally disturbed and socially maladjusted, and deaf children in special education are in residential school programs. In contrast, by far the largest numbers of mentally retarded children in special education were reported to be in day school programs.

A genuine narrowing of the gulf between the number of children estimated to require special education and the number receiving it has occurred. Even so, many American children in need of some form of specialized programs still do not have access to them. It is believed that about 10 or 12 per cent or about 6,000,000 of the school age population would benefit from some form of special education. The percentage of children requiring special education in relation to those receiving it varies considerably from one area of exceptionality to another.

Nursery school and kindergarten programs for various types of exceptional children, although still relatively few, are developing at a rapid rate. The Office of Education attempted for the first time in the 1963 survey to systematically secure figures on nursery school and kindergarten enrollments for all areas of exceptionality. The public day schools reported about 33,000 exceptional children in kindergarten and nursery school programs. Speech-impaired children comprised the largest number. The public schools were also providing preschool special instruction for several thousand children classified as hearing-impaired, crippled, or having special health problems. Both the residential schools for deaf and socially maladjusted showed a rapid percentage rise in enrollment of pre-school pupils, although the actual number is not high.

The report also shows a continued rise in enrollment of handicapped pupils in special education for those of the youth age group.

School
Systems
A remarkable increase in the number of public school systems with special education programs occurred between 1948 and 1966. More than one-half of the nation's school districts now either maintain their own special education programs or provide for such programs through cooperative arrangements with other school districts. This brings the opportunity for special education to far larger numbers of pupils in their homes or neighboring communities.

Special
Educators
The number of teachers and speech and hearing specialists working directly with exceptional children increased substantially during the period covered by this report. In view of the nationwide shortage of special education personnel, this increase is one of the most gratifying findings of the survey. By 1963, there were more than 71,000 special teachers and speech and hearing specialists in public day schools and private residential schools. It was estimated that by 1966, the number was more than 82,000. Of the public day school teachers, the largest number was engaged in the instruction of the mentally retarded; in the residential schools the largest number worked with the emotionally disturbed and socially maladjusted. Since 1948, the greatest percentage increases of special educators in the *public schools* have taken place in the areas of the gifted and the speech-impaired. In almost all areas, the increase in public school special education personnel has been larger (as was the increase in pupil enrollment than that in the residential schools).

SOME
IMPLICATIONS
The statistics contained in this report have high significance as a basis for future planning. They are being made

available at a time when new and powerful forces are at work in American education and when major improvements are expected of all schools. The concept of the handicapped child's right to suitable educational opportunity is now reaching out to all children who have special needs such as the environmentally deprived, migrants, and children of cultural minority groups. The population of the traditionally conceived handicapped child overlays that of many of other disadvantaged children. It is urgent that this fact be recognized in planning school programs both within and outside of special education. Due to improved conditions in American education, it is possible that many children who formerly would have required special education for the handicapped will now be able to make their way in some of the streams of general education. New concepts call for distinction between those who are handicapped by capacity, such as blindness or deafness and those who are only functioning as handicapped due to their environments. Their educational treatment must also be differentiated.

In addition to the nationwide efforts of local and state communities to serve all pupils, the Elementary and Secondary Education Act of 1965, with its amendments, is making a signal impact on the quality and availability of programs for all kinds of different children. Many innovations and creative activities are under way which may affect — and even alter — some concepts in the education of the handicapped. All six titles of the Act are aimed at bringing improved schooling to those who need something different or something in addition to the usual program. Noteworthy are: early identification and follow-up of children who are culturally deprived especially those in the ghettos; curriculum innovations; closer community-school coordination; improved use and selection of teachers and other school personnel.

Change is occurring in all American education. Special education is bound to change with the times. Even now, under close scrutiny are such matters as terminology and classification of pupils and professional standards for personnel. The ever-present quest for suitable curriculum and teaching materials is at a high pitch. These are but examples. The report presented here does not treat such problems, but it is hoped that as a statistical report it will provoke many questions.

Thus, in viewing this report it should be thought of as a bench mark against which to measure programs for the handicapped and also in relation to other humanitarian movements within general education. It is hoped that this quantitative report will serve as a basis for mutual planning both by special and general educators, so that all different children may soon have the individual and group education opportunity which will best liberate their talents and prepare them for life. . . .

TABLE 1. Pupil Enrollments in Special Education,

Area of Exceptionality	Total			
	1948[1]	1958[2]	1963[3]	1966[4]
1	2	3	4	5
Total	439,656	975,972	1,682,351	2,106,100
Visually handicapped, total	13,366	18,557	21,531	23,300
Blind	— —	— —	9,066	9,200
Partially seeing	— —	— —	11,661	14,100
Not reported separately	— —	— —	804	— —
Hearing-impaired, total	26,948	35,986	45,594	51,300
Deaf	— —	— —	21,894	23,500
Hard-of-hearing	— —	— —	21,684	27,800
Not reported separately	— —	— —	2,016	— —
Speech-impaired, total	182,344	494,137	802,197	989,500
Speech-impaired	181,856	489,644	704,185	— —
Speech and hearing not reported separately	488	4,493	98,012	— —
Crippled and special health, total	47,227	57,230	64,842	69,400
Crippled	21,115	29,339	26,538	29,500
Special health problems	19,124	23,077	30,684	39,900
Not reported separately	6,988	4,814	7,620	— —
Emotionally disturbed and socially maladjusted	37,800	65,620	79,587	87,900
Mentally retarded	108,440	251,594	431,890	540,100
Upper range	— —	— —	— —	— —
Middle range	— —	— —	— —	— —
Not reported separately	— —	— —	— —	— —
Gifted	20,712	52,269	214,671	312,100
Other, total[5]	2,819	579	22,039	32,500
Severe learning disability	— —	— —	13,434	19,800
Brain-injured	— —	— —	2,472	3,600
Culturally restricted	— —	— —	4,380	6,500
Not reported by area of exceptionality	2,819	579	1,753	2,600

[1] Includes 48 states and the District of Columbia — Martens, Elise H.; Harris, Catherine; and Story, Robert C. Statistics of Special Schools and Classes for Exceptional Children, 1947-48, Washington: U.S. Government Printing Office, 1959.

[2] Includes 48 states and the District of Columbia — Mackie, Romaine P.; Williams, Harold M.; and Hunter, Patricia P. Statistics of Special Education for Exceptional Children and Youth, 1957-58, Washington: U.S. Government Printing Office, 1963.

by Area of Exceptionality: 1948 to 1966

In Local Public Schools				In Residential Schools			
1948[1]	1958[2]	1963[3]	1966[4]	1948[1]	1958[2]	1963[3]	1966[4]
6	7	8	9	10	11	12	13
377,615	889,560	1,570,370	1,978,900	62,041	86,412	111,981	127,200
8,216	11,660	13,962	15,400	5,150	6,897	7,569	7,900
529	2,898	4,405	5,300	——	——	4,661	3,900
7,464	8,643	9,529	10,100	——	——	2,132	4,000
223	119	28	——	——	——	776	——
13,977	21,616	28,551	32,700	12,971	14,370	17,043	18,600
3,514	6,473	6,612	7,500	——	——	15,282	16,000
9,914	13,150	20,219	25,200	——	——	1,465	2,600
549	1,993	1,720	——	——	——	296	——
182,344	494,137	802,197	989,500	——	——	——	——
181,856	489,644	704,185	833,400	——	——	——	——
488	4,493	98,012	156,100	——	——	——	——
47,227	57,230	64,842	69,400	——	——	——	——
21,115	29,339	26,538	29,500	——	——	——	——
19,124	23,077	30,684	39,900	——	——	——	——
6,988	4,814	7,620	——	——	——	——	——
15,340	28,622	30,871	32,200	22,460	36,998	48,716	55,700
86,980	223,447	393,237	495,100	21,460	28,147	38,653	45,000
——	205,243	361,263	——	——	——	18,898	——
——	16,793	30,022	——	——	——	18,689	——
——	1,403	1,952	——	——	——	1,066	——
20,712	52,269	214,671	312,100	——	——	——	——
2,819	579	22,039	32,500	——	——	——	——
——	——	13,434	19,800	——	——	——	——
——	——	2,475	3,600	——	——	——	——
——	——	4,380	6,500	——	——	——	——
2,819	579	1,758	2,600	——	——	——	——

[3] *Data based on a 1963 status study of special education, Romaine Mackie, director. Includes 50 states and the District of Columbia.*

[4] *Estimated by the National Center of Educational Statistics and includes 50 states and the District of Columbia.*

[5] *These categories reported under "other" were not included in the questionnaire sent to the schools, but were frequent write-in replies. In view of the large response, the figures might have been much larger if the data had been requested.*

TABLE 2.

Pupil Enrollments in Special Education in Relation to
Need, by Area of Exceptionality: 1966

Area of Exceptionality	Estimated Number of Children in Need of Special Education[1]	Estimates of Prevalence (Per Cent)[2]	Estimated Enrollment 1966	Per Cent Enrolled
1	2	3	4	5
Total	6,025,000	12.0	2,106,100	35.0
Visually handicapped, total	50,000	.1	23,300	46.6
Blind	16,000	.033	9,200	57.5
Partially seeing	34,000	.067	14,100	41.5
Hearing-impaired, total	301,000	.6	51,300	17.0
Deaf	50,000	.1	23,500	47.0
Hard-of-hearing	251,000	.5	27,800	11.1
Speech-impaired	1,757,000	3.5	989,500	56.3
Crippled	377,000	.75	$29,500^2$	7.8^2
Special health problems	377,000	.75	$39,900^2$	10.6^2
Emotionally and socially maladjusted, total	1,004,000	2.0	87,900	12.0
Mentally retarded, total	1,155,000	2.3	540,100	46.8
Upper range	1,005,000	— —	475,300	47.3
Middle range	150,000	— —	64,800	43.2
Gifted	1,004,000	2.0	312,100	31.1
Other	— —	— —	32,500	— —

[1] Based on school age population of 50,749,000 as estimated in Projections of Educational Statistics to 1974-75, OE-110030-65, Circular 790. Washington: U.S. Government Printing Office, 1965.

[2] Figures and percentages are based on the number of children enrolled in local public schools and do not include those in residential institutions or in independent hospitals.

TABLE 3.

Number of Public School Systems Operating Special Education Programs and
Percentage of Programs in Each Area of Exceptionality: 1948-1966[1]

*Total No. of Public School Systems Operating
Special Education Programs:*

Year	Total
1966	6,711
1963	5,560
1958	3,641
1948	1,459

Year	Blind		Partially Seeing		Deaf		Hard-of-Hearing	
	No.	%	No.	%	No.	%	No.	%
1966[2]	543	8.1	604	9.0	268	4.0	681	10.1
1963	467	8.4	564	10.1	293	5.2	653	11.7
1958	340	9.3	498	13.6	335	9.2	607	16.6
1948	39	2.6	240	16.4	122	2.8	261	17.8

Year	Speech-Impaired		Crippled		Special Health Problems	
	No.	%	No.	%	No.	%
1966[3]	3,397	50.6	— —	— —	— —	— —
1963	2,730	49.1	1,289	23.1	1,135	20.4
1958	1,618	44.4	1,408	38.7	1,190	32.7
1948	455	31.1	959	65.7	549	37.6

Year	Emotionally Disturbed and Socially Maladjusted		Mentally Retarded		Gifted	
	No.	%	No.	%	No.	%
1966[2]	875	13.0	6,003	89.5	595	8.9
1963	726	13.0	4,879	87.7	462	8.3
1958	478	13.1	3,005	82.5	240	6.6
1948	90	6.1	729	50.0	15	1.0

[1] *See Table 7 for types of public school systems included in the survey.*

[2] *Estimates for 1966 were compiled by the National Center for Educational Statistics of the U.S. Office of Education.*

[3] *Data showed no clear trend on which to base an estimate for 1966.*

TABLE 4. Pupil Enrollments by Level of Instruction in Local

Area of Exceptionality, by Type of School	Nursery Schools and Kindergartens			
	1948[2]	1958[3]	1963[4]	1966[5]
1	2	3	4	5
Public School System				
Total	— —	5,226	33,201	50,000
Blind and partially seeing	— —	307	279	300
Deaf and hard-of-hearing	— —	986	2,212	2,500
Speech-impaired	— —	1,551	26,729	42,300
Crippled and special health problems	— —	1,228	2,030	2,500
Emotionally disturbed and socially maladjusted	— —	2	123	300
Mentally retarded	— —	996	1,252	1,400
Gifted	— —	155	505	700
Other[8]				
Severe learning disability	— —	— —	— —	— —
Brain-injured	— —	— —	30	— —
Culturally restricted	— —	— —	41	— —
Not reported by area of exceptionality	— —	1	— —	— —
Residential Schools				
Total	— —	2,508	3,331	3,800
Blind and partially seeing	— —	860	420	100
Deaf and hard-of-hearing	— —	1,547	2,060	2,400
Emotionally disturbed and socially maladjusted	— —	101	851	1,300

[1] *This table does not include pupils not reported by level of instruction, which in 1963 amounted to about 134,484 children.*

[2] *Includes 48 states and the District of Columbia — Martens, Elise H.; Harris, Catherine; and Story, Robert C.* Statistics of Special Schools and Classes for Exceptional Children, 1947-48, Washington: *U.S. Government Printing Office, 1959.*

[3] *Includes 48 states and the District of Columbia — Mackie, Romaine P.; Williams, Harold M.; and Hunter, Patricia P.* Statistics of Special Education for Exceptional Children and Youth, 1957-58, Washington: *U.S. Government Printing Office, 1963.*

Public Schools and in Residential Schools: 1948-1966[1]

Elementary Schools				Secondary Schools			
1948[2]	1958[3]	1963[4]	1966[5]	1948[2]	1958[3]	1963[4]	1966[5]
6	7	8	9	10	11	12	13
307,051	701,128	1,108,415	1,356,900	50,486	148,516	335,483	448,000
6,924	8,520	8,968	9,200	1,325	2,426	2,869	3,100
11,893	14,358	19,017	6,300	2,173	3,360	4,989	6,000
173,246	444,138	683,151	842,100	9,068	39,674	70,692	89,300
24,133	38,933	42,402	44,500	5,614	11,013	17,476	21,400
12,151	18,519	14,330	36,600	3,156	7,838	11,162	18,700
76,624	147,005[6]	237,720[6]	292,100	12,518	51,104[7]	107,825[7]	141,900
4,080	19,808	86,257	126,100	16,632	32,159	116,815	167,600
— —	— —	9,948	— —	— —	— —	2,703	— —
— —	— —	2,001	— —	— —	— —	205	— —
— —	— —	3,523	— —	— —	— —	580	— —
— —	9,847	1,098	— —	— —	942	167	— —
— —	30,828	35,485	38,300	— —	21,912	31,952	38,000
— —	4,252	4,669	4,900	— —	1,651	2,035	2,300
— —	9,433	9,923	10,200	— —	2,916	4,867	6,000
— —	17,143	20,893	23,200	— —	17,345	25,050	29,700

Includes 50 states and the District of Columbia. Data based on a 1963 status study of special education conducted by the Office of Education

Includes 50 states and the District of Columbia. Data estimated on the basis of previous studies.

Pupils reported as housed in elementary schools.

Pupils reported as housed in secondary schools.

These categories reported under other were not included in the questionnaire sent to the schools, but were frequent write-in replies. In view of the large response, the figures might have been much larger if the data had been requested. (See Appendix B.)

TABLE 5. Pupil Enrollment in Programs Operated by Local Public

Area of Exceptionality	Total	Full-Time in Special Class or in Special Day School
1	2	3
Total	1,570,370	456,145
Visually handicapped, total	13,962	5,975
Blind	4,405	1,950
Partially seeing	9,529	4,021
Not reported separately	28	5
Hearing-impaired, total	28,551	10,274
Deaf	6,612	5,435
Hard-of-hearing	20,219	3,689
Not reported separately	1,720	1,150
Speech-impaired, total	802,197	— —
Speech-impaired	704,185	— —
Speech and hearing	— —	— —
Not reported separately[3]	98,012	— —
Crippled and special health problems, total	64,842	27,386
Crippled	26,538	15,336
Special health problems	30,684	9,304
Not reported separately	7,620	2,746
Emotionally disturbed and socially maladjusted, total	30,871	15,780
Emotionally disturbed	9,677	3,456
Socially maladjusted	11,769	6,170
Not reported separately	9,425	6,154
Mentally retarded, total	393,237	339,596
Upper range	361,265	310,108
Middle range	30,022	27,723
Not reported separately	1,950	1,765
Gifted	214,671	49,624
Other, total	22,039	7,509
Severe learning disability[4]	13,434	1,917
Brain-injured[4]	2,472	1,479
Culturally restricted[4]	4,380	3,555
Not reported by area of exceptionality	1,753	558

[1] *Data based on a 1963 status study of special education conducted by the Office of Education.*

[2] *Includes instruction in a regularly scheduled special class or by a special, itinerant, or resource teacher together with some time in a regular class.*

Schools by Type of Program Organization: 1963[1]

Part-Time in Special Programs and Part-Time in Regular Class[2]	In Home Instruction	In a Hospital, Sanitorium, or Convalescent Home	In Residential School	Not Reported by Type of Program
4	5	6	7	8
986,509	28,229	5,965	4,092	89,430
7,426	136	20	12	392
2,242	56	17	12	128
5,164	77	3	— —	264
20	3	— —	— —	— —
17,744	71	15	— —	447
960	49	12	— —	156
16,233	22	3	— —	272
551	— —	— —	— —	19
802,197	— —	— —	— —	— —
704,185	— —	— —	— —	— —
— —	— —	— —	— —	— —
98,012	— —	— —	— —	— —
7,417	20,296	5,269	192	4,282
1,746	4,822	1,796	78	2,760
5,420	13,207	1,948	114	691
251	2,267	1,525	— —	831
8,136	1,271	641	3,843	1,200
4,450	916	313	52	490
2,732	189	142	1,960	576
954	166	186	1.831	134
40,862	6,375	— —	45	6,359
40,135	6,217	— —	45	4,760
600	150	— —	— —	1,549
127	8	— —	— —	50
89,510	— —	— —	— —	75,537
13,217	80	20	— —	1,213
10,799	— —	— —	— —	718
924	35	— —	— —	34
825	— —	— —	— —	— —
669	45	20	— —	461

[3] All enrolled in a speech and hearing program are assumed to be part-time although it is recognized that a small number may be in self-contained special classes.

[4] These categories were not included in the questionnaire sent to the schools, but were frequent write-in replies. The figures might have been much larger if the data had been requested.

TABLE 6.

Residential Schools by Type of Control and
Receipt of Public Funds: 1963[1]

Residential School by Type of Control[2] and Receipt of Public Funds by Private Institutions	(Number of Institutions and Enrollment by Area of Exceptionality)									
	Total		Blind		Deaf		Emotionally Disturbed and Socially Mal-adjusted		Mentally Retarded	
	Number of Institutions	Enrollment	Number of Institutions	Enrollment	Number of Institutions	Enrollment	Number of Institutions	Enrollment	Number of Institutions	Enrollment
1	2	3	4	5	6	7	8	9	10	11
Total	738[4]	111,981	55	7,569	75	17,043	409	48,716	224	38,653
Residential schools under public control	443	88,418	42	5,813	46	12,412	265	38,870	108	31,323
Residential schools under nonpublic control: some public funds received for school programs	146	14,043	12	1,711	20	3,760	83	5,949	35	2,623
Residential schools under nonpublic control: no public funds received for school program	141	8,860	1	45	8	731	58	3,634	77	4,450
Residential schools under nonpublic control: no information on public funds received for school program	8	660	- -	- -	1	140	3	263	4	257

[1] Data based on a 1963 status study of special education conducted by the U. S. Office of Education.

[2] Questionnaire specified administrative control as legal control not financial support or licensing authority.

[3] Questionnaire specified any public funds (local, county, or state) received for the operation of an education program.

[4] The figures on number of residential schools are not mutually exclusive. They cannot be added vertically or horizontally. The numbers include 25 institutions reporting school programs for two categories of handicapped — 14 in blind and deaf: and 11 in emotionally disturbed and socially maladjusted and mentally retarded.

TABLE 7.

Number of Public School Systems Operating a Program for
Pupils by Type of Administrative Unit: 1963[1]

Area of Exceptionality	Type of Administrative Unit[4]			
	Total[3]	Local Public School Districts	Intermediate School Districts	Other
1	2	3	4	5
Blind	467	415	36	16
Partially seeing	564	503	44	17
Deaf	293	261	20	12
Hard-of-hearing	653	586	51	16
Speech and hearing program	2,730	2,432	263	35
Crippled	1,289	1,175	95	19
Special health problems	1,135	1,060	65	10
Emotionally disturbed	552	513	28	11
Socially maladjusted	236	213	21	2
Mentally retarded	4,879	4,543	284	52
Gifted	462	435	17	10
Other[2]				
Severe learning disorder[2]	97	91	5	1
Brain-injured[2]	128	112	6	10
Culturally restricted[2]	15	15	— —	— —
Not reported by major area of exceptionality	31	28	2	1

[1] Data based on a 1963 status study of special education conducted by the Office of Education.

[2] These categories were not included in the questionnaire sent to the schools, but were frequent write-in replies. The figures might have been much larger if the data had been requested.

[3] These figures should not be totaled, as many school districts operate a special program in more than one area of exceptionality.

[4] Types of administrative units are described in the questionnaire. (See Appendix D.)

TABLE 8.

Residential School Pupils, Teachers, and Public and Nonpublic
Schools Which Participate in Cooperative Programs
with Local Public Schools: 1963[1]

Type of Institution in Area of Exceptionality	Pupils				Teachers		Residential Schools	
	Enrolled in Education Programs Who Do Not Live in the Institution		Living in the Institutions but Receiving More Than Half Their Formal Instruction Outside the Institution		Teachers Employed by Local Public Schools Who Teach in Residental Schools			
	Number of Institutions	Enrollment	Number of Institutions	Enrollment	Full-Time	Part-Time	Reporting a Cooperative Program	With Double Session Instructional Programs
1	2	3	4	5	6	7	8	9
Total	207	4,340	128	1,131	359	45	87	187
Visually handicapped, total	43	766	8	33	1	2	1	1
Public	35	455	5	15	- -	2	- -	1
Nonpublic	8	311	3	18	1	- -	1	- -
Hearing-impaired, total	62	2,030	3	19	7	2	3	- -
Public	39	921	1	7	- -	2	2	- -
Nonpublic	23	1,109	2	12	7	- -	1	- -
Emotionally disturbed and socially maladjusted, total	38	368	93	967	278	27	71	112
Public	18	167	37	193	126	12	39	99
State training schools	1	35	8	69	50	4	6	51
Schools in mental hospitals	16	86	27	109	47	8	28	39
Other	1	46	2	15	29	- -	5	9
Nonpublic	20	201	56	774	152	15	32	13
Mentally retarded, total	64	1,176	24	112	73	14	12	74
Public	18	233	8	22	50	4	4	64
Nonpublic	46	943	16	90	23	10	8	10

[1] Data based on a 1963 status study of special education conducted by the
U. S. Office of Education.

TABLE 9.

Number of Special Educators by
Area of Exceptionality: 1948 to 1966[1]

Area of Exceptionality Taught	Number of Teachers		
	1948[2]	1963[3]	1966[4]
1	2	3	4
Total	16,234	71,029	82,000
In local public schools	10,308	59,557	69,400
In residential schools	5,926	11,472	12,600
Visually handicapped, total	1,594	2,750	3,000
In local public schools	659	1,423	1,600
In residential schools	935	1,327	1,400
Hearing-impaired, total	2,734	4,373	4,700
In local public schools	704	1,646	1,800
In residential schools	2,030	2,727	2,900
Speech-impaired in local public schools	1,256	6,675	7,800
Crippled and special health problems, total	1,542	2,351	2,500
In local public schools	1,488	2,351	2,500
In residential schools	54	— —	— —
Hospital and home instruction in local public schools	— —	10,272	12,800
Emotionally disturbed and socially maladjusted total	2,308	7,928	9,000
In local public schools	609	3,290	3,800
In residential schools	1,699	4,638	5,200
Mentally retarded, total	6,178	27,916	32,300
In local public schools	4,970	25,136	29,200
In residential schools	1,208	2,780	3,100
Gifted in local public schools	622	8,395	9,900
Not reported by area of exceptionality	— —	369	— —

[1] Special educators reported include teachers of handicapped children and speech-correctionists. Other special educators, such as supervisors, college staff, and researchers, are not included.

[2] Includes 48 states and the District of Columbia — Martens, Elise H.; Harris, Catherine; and Story, Robert C. Statistics of Special Schools and Classes for Exceptional Children, 1947-48, Washington: U. S. Government Printing Office, 1959.

[3] Includes 50 states and the District of Columbia — Data based on a 1963 status study of special education conducted by the Office of Education.

[4] Includes 50 states and the District of Columbia — Data estimated on the basis of previous studies.

TABLE 10. State Estimates of Special Education

State	Blind	Partially Seeing	Deaf	Hard-of-Hearing[2]	Speech and Hearing Program	Crippled
Totals	5,300	10,100	7,500	3,378	1,011,322	29,500
Alabama	14	10	8	0	1,110	170
Alaska	4	0	34	0	747	27
Arizona	57	57	69	0	5,548	118
Arkansas	0	43	0	0	1,329	109
California	1,534	1,019	1,706	0	131,060	3,588
Colorado	54	125	118	109	15,142	356
Connecticut	199	152	8	26	8,766	356
Delaware	8	35	21	0	820	180
Florida	274	321	62	0	9,518	41
Georgia	89	273	56	89	8,221	192
Hawaii	92	40	184	325	3,084	342
Idaho	8	37	0	159	646	139
Illinois	336	1,000	111	114	62,988	0
Indiana	56	190	12	0	29,613	1,328
Iowa	13	117	19	95	35,056	482
Kansas	55	65	0	10	8,551	159
Kentucky	0	136	66	45	3,557	338
Louisiana	26	89	60	0	12,000	568
Maine	0	8	0	0	1,316	0
Maryland	36	451	0	359	19,939	174
Massachusetts	58	375	167	0	27,404	406
Michigan	241	746	227	130	71,644	3,864
Minnesota	160	113	408	56	18,972	535
Mississippi	0	3	0	0	1,254	18
Missouri	17	121	273	192	21,557	393
Montana	0	0	0	0	199	5
Nebraska	6	34	0	12	4,177	132
Nevada	18	67	8	57	1,369	194
New Hampshire	0	16	1	0	693	14
New Jersey	191	166	250	215	33,126	669
New Mexico	1	0	0	0	783	50
New York	316	0	668	13	141,557	4,070
North Carolina	32	9	0	0	19,865	289
North Dakota	11	0	0	0	3,331	12
Ohio	244	747	1,109	118	39,434	1,183
Oklahoma	27	44	25	53	7,233	156
Oregon	89	45	114	29	8,780	717
Pennsylvania	275	1,772	342	553	96,282	3,001
Rhode Island	7	166	3	32	4,140	165
South Carolina	2	0	0	0	1,933	156
South Dakota	0	0	0	0	2,129	98
Tennessee	37	252	105	0	11,469	914
Texas	306	331	674	0	49,013	1,460
Utah	0	67	58	115	7,865	69
Vermont	4	64	4	41	170	36
Virginia	81	217	0	227	11,753	532
Washington	218	419	302	160	32,418	365
West Virginia	23	5	7	2	1,874	48
Wisconsin	51	107	221	0	30,371	559
Wyoming	0	0	0	0	1,516	6
District of Columbia	30	49	0	42	0	717

[1] Estimates for 1966 were compiled by the National Center for Educational Statistics of the Office of Education.

Enrollments in Local Public Schools: 1966[1]

Special Health Problems	Emotionally Disturbed and Socially Maladjusted	Mentally Retarded	Gifted	Other	State Totals
39,900	32,200	495,100	312,100	32,500	1,978,900
77	0	3,385	108	0	4,882
243	16	228	182	17	1,498
74	151	3,846	0	152	10,072
74	31	2,060	21	32	3,699
3,813	3,006	61,644	26,567	3,034	236,971
202	154	4,798	484	156	21,698
112	422	5,919	915	425	17,300
0	0	1,357	0	0	2,421
798	804	11,346	919	812	24,895
40	84	7,111	802	85	17,042
110	339	2,061	1,941	342	8,860
125	0	1,002	375	0	2,491
515	0	14,453	2,985	0	82,502
286	770	7,650	2,189	778	42,872
494	309	8,116	1,313	311	46,325
133	115	2,848	1,086	117	13,139
527	10	4,473	925	10	10,087
15	187	4,063	851	189	18,048
0	0	862	100	0	2,286
666	161	23,336	1,869	162	47,153
0	612	12,192	3,027	618	44,856
926	8,534	29,708	37,586	8,612	162,218
235	927	8,224	1,748	936	32,314
2	0	1,222	0	0	2,499
80	347	18,987	2,534	351	44,852
0	0	697	294	0	1,195
25	31	1,381	562	32	6,392
101	263	1,683	48	266	4,074
0	0	607	301	0	1,632
698	1,346	17,216	694	1,357	55,928
32	104	2,153	0	105	3,228
22,188	25	46,651	80,702	25	296,215
1	135	12,459	105,852	137	138,779
0	0	613	0	0	3,967
1,473	1,027	26,136	14,101	1,035	86,607
602	270	3,719	0	272	12,401
0	315	4,645	2,792	318	17,844
465	1,571	53,279	3,089	1,585	162,214
81	277	1,900	781	280	7,832
87	21	3,435	2	22	5,658
160	11	825	682	12	3,917
786	130	10,658	233	132	24,716
858	1,462	23,189	1,686	1,475	80,454
606	12	2,269	176	13	11,250
214	0	51	0	0	584
512	1,702	7,143	1,398	1,717	25,282
1,023	5,194	10,340	1,817	5,241	57,497
106	50	1,767	0	51	3,933
0	84	11,873	2,798	85	46,149
0	0	471	569	0	2,562
335	1,191	9,049	4,996	1,201	17,610

[2] These figures differ from figures in other tables in this report because they include only those hard-of-hearing children estimated to be enrolled in special classes, either full-time or part-time.

TABLE 11.

Estimated Number of School Age Children
(5-17 Years) in Need of Special Education: 1966[1]

Area of Exceptionality	Estimates of Prevalence (Per Cent)	Estimated Need 1966
1	2	3
Total	12.0	6,025,000
Blind	.033 ⎫ .1	16,000
Partially seeing	.067 ⎭	34,000
Deaf	.1	50,000
Hard-of-hearing	.5	251,000
Speech-impaired	3.5	1,757,000
Crippled	.75	377,000
Special health problems	.75	377,000
Emotionally disturbed and socially maladjusted	2.0	1,004,000
Mentally retarded	2.3	1,155,000
Gifted	2.0	1,004,000

[1] *Since there are no current nationwide studies on which to base firm estimates of prevalence in each area of exceptionality, a variety of sources have been used, including information from state education.*

report of hew task force on handicapped children and child development*

U.S. DEPARTMENT OF HEALTH, EDUCATION, and WELFARE

INTRODUCTION

The term "handicap" is not easily defined. In general terms, it describes an individual's disability in performing major life functions. Standards of performance however, vary between groups and cultures and the range of human capabilities spans a wide spectrum of behavior. Specifying the boundaries between normal and limited activity therefore, is a complex task. The problem becomes especially difficult when an individual is only marginally incapacitated in several major functions or more severely disabled in only one function.

Because of these considerations, a universally agreed upon definition of handicap has not yet been developed. From an operational standpoint however, an arbitrary, working definition setting forth the broad parameters of our concern would seem to be in order.

Toward a Definition

For the purposes of this Task Force Report:

"A handicapped child or youth is one who because of physical, intellectual or emotional impairment, is significantly hindered from

*Excerpted from, "Report of the Task Force on Handicapped Children and Child Development, U. S. Department of Health, Education, and Welfare," 1967.

learning, working, playing, adapting to the expectations or demands of society, or doing the things other children or youth of his age can do. Among the factors that may contribute to handicapping are: (1) constitutional deficiencies; (2) an acquired disease, injury, or condition; or (3) social-environmental deprivation or trauma. For some, the handicap may be manifested in one major area of life function, whereas for others, several functions may be involved.

These criteria apply to adults as well, with the major area of dysfunction evident in social-personal relationships and employment."

Broadly speaking, any disadvantage confronting the individual that makes the attainment of success more difficult would conceivably be defined as a handicap. But in a complex society such as ours the determinants of success are varied and complex. They include such factors as innate or acquired skills, social opportunity, the impact of life experiences on the developing child and the state of the economy, to name but a few. Nor can we disregard the less tangible but often equally compelling circumstances of the social heritage into which the child is born, or of fortune and fate.

Clearly, the individual who is significantly impaired intellectually or physically, or who suffers from an emotional or psychiatric disorder is handicapped. Presumably his disability affects — in greater or lesser degree — his participation in those functions essential to his self-fulfillment. Given remedial help or treatment, or special training to compensate for his disability his chances for the full development of his capacities may be markedly improved.

SIGNIFICANCE OF
THE PROBLEM

Handicapping conditions among children and youth in this country rank as a major national health, social, educational and economic problem:

— An estimated 50 million Americans have physical, intellectual or emotional handicaps that to some degree limit their ability to carry on major life functions. Approximately 13.5 million of this number are children and youth. Approximately 8 million persons have more than one handicap (See Table 1). Still more suffer from chronic conditions or impairments that impede optimal functioning and require special attention or treatment, but do not limit activity.

— In fiscal year 1966, the Federal Government obligated an estimated $3.5 billion for programs for the handicapped, about $2.65 billion of which was for income maintenance and the remainder for research, training, construction and special services.

The expenditures by States and localities are far in excess of this amount, including over $1.2 billion in matching funds.

— The Nation is denied billions of dollars of economic output because of the underachievement, underproduction and/or the complete or partial incapacity of the handicapped.

— The human anguish and anxiety resulting from handicapping conditions is a source of possible family disruption and a strain on family resources that blights the future of millions of American families. An estimated 40 to 50 million people live in families where there is a handicapped child or youth.

Scope of the Problem

Precise data on the incidence and prevalence of handicapping conditions in the United States are not available. A number of factors are responsible for this situation:

1. There are no universally accepted definitions of what constitutes a handicap or uniform standards of behavior by which it can be objectively measured.
2. Mechanisms have not yet been developed within the hospitals, treatment facilities, schools, agencies and other critical centers for a unified and standard procedure for casefinding, identification and reporting.
3. Techniques and resources for the detection and diagnosis of the more subtle forms of disability vary considerably between States as to quality and quantity.
4. Certain conditions that are associated in the public mind with feelings of stigma or shame or that are thought to deny the handicapped person access to employment or other benefits, tend to be grossly underreported.

While these limitations urge caution against overreliance on statistical data currently available, the gap between services and needs, fact and opinion, and training resources and needed manpower is very great. Even a markedly increased effort at all levels of government and by voluntary associations is unlikely to bridge these gaps for years to come.

By whatever criteria are applied — personal unhappiness, family stress, social and educational costs, economic loss — the problems of the handicapped in our society are massive. Only through a vigorous national effort, directed toward every critical point of impact will significant solutions be achieved.

TABLE 1.

Estimated Prevalence of Handicapping
Conditions in the United States
1965

	All Ages	Children and Youth
Mental Illness & Emotional Disorders (1,2)*	18,000,000	5,000,000
Mental Retardation (3)	5,700,000	2,280,000
Visual Impairment-Severe (4)	1,099,000	65,000
Legally Blind.	(411,000)	— — — —
Hearing Impairment-Severe (4)	327,000	41,000
Speech Defects (4)	1,200,000	730,000
Orthopedic Impairments (4)	3,031,000	250,000
Neurological Disorders (5)	11,000,000	5,100,000
Including:		
Epilepsy	(1,500,000)	(1,000,000)
Cerebral Palsy	(600,000)	(350,000)
Multiple Sclerosis	(250,000)	(50,000)
Muscular Dystrophy	(250,000)	(200,000)
Parkinsonism.	(400,000)	(— — — —)
Minimal Brain Damage	(7,000,000)	(3,500,000)
Other.	(1,000,000)	(— — — —)
Allergic Disorders (4)	866,000	158,000
Anemia & other diseases of blood forming organs (4)	189,000	10,000
Heart Conditions (4).	2,970,000	33,000
Rheumatic Fever & other diseases of circulatory system (4)	608,000	29,000
Respiratory Diseases (4)	842,000	47,000
Digestive System (4)	1,613,000	51,000
Genitourinary System (4)	766,000	42,000
Diseases of Muscles, Bones & Joints (4) . . .	3,350,000	37,000
Paralysis, Complete or Partial (4)	758,000	114,000
All other impairments (4)	755,000	236,000
All other chronic conditions (4)	5,525,000	261,000
TOTAL	58,599,000**	14,484,000**

*Numbers in parenthesis identify sources of data listed in original report p. 70-71.
**These figures represent numbers of conditions, not persons. A proportion, not
precisely known, have more than one handicap.

The National Health Survey has applied different criteria for
assessing limitations in major life functions, according to broad age
groupings. For the preschool child, major limitation is defined as the
inability to take part in ordinary play with other children or a
limitation in amount or kind of play most children routinely engage

in. For the school age child, it is the inability to go to school or to attend full time or the need for a special school or special teaching. The limited adult is one who cannot work at a job or business or else is restricted in the amount or kind of work he can do, needing special aids, more rest, etc. Similar criteria are applied to housewives.

Based on these criteria, over 16.6 million persons are handicapped to a *significant* degree. It should be stressed, however, that certain conditions such as mental retardation, emotional disturbance and minimal brain dysfunction tend to be vastly underreported. Parents of retarded children, particularly those who are culturally and socially deprived, frequently do not think of their children as handicapped. The child with minor emotional or neurological impairment is seldom reported because he generally attends regular classes, even though he has a learning disability or behavioral problem.

— An alarming 39 million (estimated) people have chronic or permanent defects resulting from disease, injury or congenital malformations. Generally, these individuals — of whom about 6.5 million are under age 24 — have decreased ability to perform various functions, particularly those of the musculoskeletal system and sense organs. While most of these defects, except when they occur in severe form, do not impede the capacity to learn, work or play (Figure 1), the effects on the individual's self-image, personality growth and optimal development may be detrimental.

Vision and hearing disorders are not only prevalent in childhood, but are significant adult disabilities. Three out of four blind persons are over 40 years of age and the prevalence rates for hearing impairments rise from a low of 8.1 per 1000 for children under 17 to a high of 120 per 1000 for those age 45 and over. By contrast, speech defects occur more frequently in the young, accounting for 64 percent of the conditions reported. These conditions occur twice as frequently in families with incomes under $2000 as compared to those in the $7000 and over group.

— The incidence of congenital malformations, while difficult to precisely determine, represents a significant source of handicapping conditions, involving approximately 2.5 million persons with varying degrees of disability. Among infants weighing more than 5.5 pounds, it is also the leading cause of death in the first month of life. Included in this category are orthopedic impairments, cleft palate, hydrocephalus, spina bifida, congenital heart disease and numerous others. About 30 percent of the caseload in the crippled children's program consists of congenital malformations, including 25,000 per year with congenital heart disease.

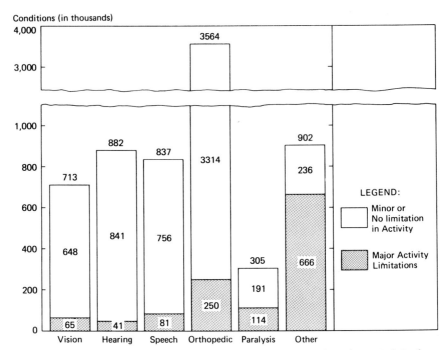

This figure clearly reveals the degree to which common impairments interfere with major life functions.

FIGURE 1.

SELECTED IMPAIRMENTS AMONG CHILDREN AND YOUTH

— Emotional disorders are among the more prevalent handicapping conditions of childhood. In 1963, 31,000 persons under age 24 were admitted to mental hospitals. Both the first admission rates and the resident population rates for this group have increased at an accelerated pace during the last decade. This is especially true for children age 10-14; a twofold increase in the general population since 1950 has witnessed a sixfold increase in the mental hospital population. An estimated 10 percent of public school children are emotionally disturbed and in need of psychiatric guidance. At least 250,000 children with psychiatric disorders receive services each year at mental health clinics and 500,000 appear before the courts each year for antisocial acts.

The incidence of delinquency and suicide among adolescents is a source of continuing concern.

— Mental retardation is a developmental disorder of childhood. About 400,000 are so retarded that they require constant care or supervision or are severely limited in their ability to care for themselves and to engage in productive work. The remainder (5 million) are mildly disabled, and in many instances can achieve partial or total economic self-support. They are heavily concentrated among families with poor education and low incomes.

Approximately 250,000 (80,000 children) are cared for in public and private residential institutions. Rates for first admission of retarded children to institutions have shown a gradual increase during the last decade.

— Selective Service statistics reveal a significant incidence of handicapping conditions in youths age 18-26. As reported in One-Third of a Nation, recent studies indicate that if the entire male population of draft age were examined, about one-third would be disqualified from military service. The "overall" rejection rate is computed to be 14.8 for medical reasons, 11.5 mental, 1.5 medical and mental, and 3.5 other. Clearly, rejection from military service is not synonymous with handicapping in civilian life.

Differentials in rejection rates among States, however calcu-lated, are striking. Particularly is this true for the mental test rejectees, with rates ranging from as little as 3 percent in some States (Mountain, Great Plains, Far West), to more than 50 percent in others (Southeastern region). These variations are highly correlated with educational and cultural deprivation and the racial and ethnic backgrounds of the populations within these States.

Many medically impaired youths, particularly the more severely handicapped, never reach the induction center. Thus, among those disqualified by the Local Draft Boards, almost 85 percent of the psychiatric disorders are either mentally deficient (54%) or psychotic (31%); of the neurological diseases, 81 percent are either cerebral paralysis (40%) or epilepsy (41%); and unilateral blindness, repre-sents 70 percent of all disqualifications for eye defects.

In this brief overview, the nature and extent of handicapping conditions stands forth clearly as a problem of massive proportions. The chronic conditions and impairments which afflict today's children are often the handicaps of tomorrow's adults. But the numerical aspects of the problem are only one of the significant dimensions. Qualitative components are equally important. Some of these considerations are touched upon in the following sections.

special services and trends in large city school districts*

RICHARD SLATER†

The following tables are excerpted from a report of a survey conducted in August, 1965, by Richard Slater. The purpose of the survey was to ascertain the types and characteristics of Special Services or Pupil Personnel Services offered in school districts of 100,000 or more scholastics.

Questionnaires were sent to eighteen of the nineteen school districts (excluding Houston) in this category and fifteen or 83.3% of the school systems responded, representing a total of 2,145,925 scholastics. The article summarizes the results in the areas of (a) administrative structure, (b) geographical location of special services administration, and (c) specialized diagnostic services provided by sampled school districts.

A. ADMINISTRATIVE STRUCTURES

1.   Present Status

The chart shown on page 359 identifies selected departments and/or functions related to special services and the major administrative sections to which they may be assigned.

*Reprinted from *The Results of Survey Conducted to Ascertain the Present Status of the Various Departments of Special Services and the Future Trends of These Departments in School Districts of 100,000 or More Scholastics, The Long Range Study Report VI, The Division of Special Services, Part II* (December 1965), pp. 10-24, by permission of the Houston Independent School District. Copyright 1965 by the Houston Independent School District.

†Richard Slater is Associate Deputy Superintendent, Curriculum, Educational Research, and Program Development, Houston Independent School District.

			ADMINISTRATIVE DIVISION RESPONSIBLE				
Department or Function	Curriculum	Business	Research	Secondary Education	Elementary Education	Special Services (PPS)	Others
Attendance		7.7%	7.7%			76.9%*	7.7%
Census		21.4%	35.8%			28.6%**	14.2%
Transfer				20.0%	20.0%	46.6%**	13.4%
School Health Services	7.7%					61.5%**	30.8%
Psychological Services	21.4%			7.1%	7.1%	57.3%**	7.1%
Special Education	26.7%			13.3%	13.3%	33.4%*	13.3%
Counselors, Elementary	10.0%			10.0%	20.0%*	60.0%	——
Counselors, Secondary	14.4%			21.4%*		50.0%	14.2%
Counselors, Vocational	9.1%			9.1%**		63.6%	18.2%
City-Wide Testing Program	20.0%			33.3%		33.3%*	13.4%
Educational Research	18.8%			62.5%		12.5%**	6.2%

*Asterisk indicates Houston Independent School District throughout this article.

2.   Trends

    a.   Greater emphasis on better attendance, early identification of pupils with problems. This will involve a larger attendance staff, more counselors, more special education programs and more psychological personnel.

    b.   Expanded Health Services to include more aspects of a total public school health program.

    c.   Increased educational research which will be reflected in improved methodological and technological approaches to learning.

    d.   Data processing will enter into areas that deal with guidance, curriculum, and many other areas of academic and vocational education.

B. GEOGRAPHICAL LOCATION OF SPECIAL SERVICES ADMINISTRATION

1.   Present Status

    Listed below are the three most used geographical approaches to administration.

a.	One centrally located unit*	33.3%
b.	Two geographically located units	6.7%
c.	More than two units geographically located throughout the school district	60.0%

2.   Trends

    a.   Interest in decentralization, incorporating the district plan, is on the increase.

    b.   Where decentralization is now in operation, the approach of retaining one department head as the administrator in charge for the total school district with assistants assigned geographically appears to be the better plan. An example would be one administrator in charge of the total district's special education program with an assistant in each sub-district of the total school district.

C. SPECIALIZED DIAGNOSTIC SERVICES PROVIDED BY SCHOOL DISTRICTS

1.   Present Status

Below are listed the most common diagnostic services now offered by school districts.

	Yes	No	Consultant
a. Individual psychological testing	93.8%*	— —	6.2%
b. General medical examination	56.2%	31.2%*	12.6%
c. Neurological examination	6.7%	60.0%*	33.3%
d. Audiological examination	75.0%*	6.2%	18.8%
e. Psychiatric examination	20.0%	26.7%	53.3%*
f. Ophthalmological examination	33.3%	40.0%*	26.7%

2.   Trends

   a.   Diagnostic services are expanding, and include cardiac examinations, epilepsy, and tubercular examinations.
   b.   Because of the rapid assembly line approach to physical examinations of children which are not depicting health problems that interfere with learning, there is a trend for larger school districts to offer these services to these children rather than using another governmental agency.

D. SPECIAL EDUCATION PROGRAMS
(Types, per-pupil cost, and geographical locations)

The following special education programs are the most common programs found in the public schools. The percentages reported for each type of program and geographical location indicate the present status of 83.3% of the school districts of 100,000 or more scholastics responding to this question.

The per pupil cost for each program represents the average cost for the eight school districts responding to this particular item.

Per Pupil Cost and Geographical Location of Special Education Programs in Fifteen School Districts of 100,000 or More Scholastics — 1967

S. Ed. Area	Per Pupil Cost	No Such Program			Neighborhood Schools			Centrally Located			Integrated Schools			Segregated Schools		
		Pre. S.	Elem.	Sec.	Pre. S.	Elem.	Sec.	Pre. S.	Elem.	Sec.	Pre. S.	Elem.	Sec.	Pre. S.	Elem.	Sec.
Blind, P.S.	$1,336	75.0%	—	12.5%	8.3%	25.0%	37.5%	16.7%	62.4%	43.7%	—	6.3%	6.3%	—	6.3%	—
Deaf	$1,648	42.9%	—	18.8%	7.1%	17.6%	18.8%	28.6%	35.3%	37.4%	—	29.4%	12.5%	21.4%	29.4%	12.5%
EMR	$ 871	100.0%	—	6.2%	—	53.3%	50.0%	—	46.7%	31.2%	—	—	6.3%	—	7.1%	6.3%
TMR	$1,212	92.3%	14.3%	26.7%	7.7%	14.3%	13.3%	—	35.7%	26.7%	—	—	—	—	5.6%	6.2%
ED	$1,411	100.0%	22.2%	50.0%	—	16.7%	12.6%	—	38.8%	18.8%	—	—	6.2%	—	—	—
Neuro-Logical	$1,486	92.9%	28.6%	71.5%	—	7.1%	—	—	57.2%	21.4%	—	—	—	7.1%	7.1%	7.1%
Ortho	$1,431	83.4%	5.6%	25.0%	—	—	6.2%	8.3%	33.2%	18.8%	—	5.6%	6.2%	8.3%	50.0%	37.6%
Mult.-Hand.	$1,486	78.6%	40.0%	50.0%	—	—	—	14.3%	33.3%	28.6%	—	—	—	7.1%	20.0%	21.4%
Speech	$ 154	100.0%	—	20.0%	—	86.7%	73.3%	—	13.3%	6.7%						
Home Bound	$1,366	—	6.7%	—												
Hosp.	$1,117	—	13.4%	—												

COMMUNITY OPERATED AGENCY

TMR (E - 28.6%)   ED (E - 16.7%)   ORTHO (E - 5.6%)   MULT (E - 6.7%)
     (S - 33.3%)   (S - 6.2%)   (S - 6.2%)

E = Elementary   S = Secondary

Total number of students enrolled in all of the school district returning this questionnaire (217,000*)

2,145,925

Total number of students enrolled in all of the special education programs of these same school districts (7,100*)

215,252

Percentage of students enrolled in these special education programs (3.2%*)

10%

E. FINANCIAL

1. Present Status

   a. State reimbursement of special services personnel.

      The following lists contain the most commonly reimbursed special services personnel.

	Yes	No.
(1) Special Education teachers	100.0%*	
(2) Special Education administrators	60.0%	40.0%*
(3) Counselors, Elementary	36.4%	63.6%*
(4) Counselors, Secondary	60.0%*	40.0%
(5) Counselors, Administrators	50.0%	50.0%*
(6) Psychologists	60.0%	40.0%*
(7) Psychologists, Administrators	60.0%	40.0%*
(8) Nurses	*	100.0%
(9) Nurses, Administrators		100.0%*
(10) Medical Doctors		100.0%*
(11) Medical Administrators		100.0%*

   b. Special Services Personnel Salary Schedules

      The following salary schedules for the most commonly employed special services personnel are the average monthly salaries of the school districts completing this question.

1. *Special Education Teachers*

    (a)   Minimum monthly salary, B.A. $544
                                         ($532)   Maximum monthly salary, B.A. $878
                                                                                        ($799)

    (b)   Minimum monthly salary, M.A. $577
                                         ($563)   Maximum monthly salary, M.A. $940
                                                                                        ($911)

    (c)   Minimum monthly salary, Ph.D. $604   Maximum monthly salary, Ph.D. $1048

    (d)   Number of months employed (9)   9.8

2. *Counselors*

    (1)   Minimum monthly salary, B.A. $N/E[2]   Maximum monthly salary, B.A. $N/E

    (2)   Minimum monthly salary, M.A. $588
                                         ($541)   Maximum monthly salary, M.A. $945
                                                                                        ($889)

    (3)   Minimum monthly salary, Ph.D. $611   Maximum monthly salary, Ph.D. $1043

    (4)   Number of months employed (10)   10.0

3. *Psychologists*

    (1)   Minimum monthly salary, B.A. $ *[3]   Maximum monthly salary, B.A. $ *

    (2)   Minimum monthly salary, M.A. $680
                                         ($559)   Maximum monthly salary, M.A. $972
                                                                                        ($906)

    (3)   Minimum monthly salary, Ph.D. $787   Maximum monthly salary, Ph.D. $1087

    (4)   Number of months employed (11)   10.3

[1] (   ) indicates Houston's Salary Schedule.
[2] N/E none employed.
[3] *only 3 employed at the B.A. level.

2.   Trends

Financial (as reported by administrators completing this question)

Salary schedules for specialists are beginning to be developed throughout the country. In the special service division, salary schedules for specialists seem to include generally, counselors and school psychologists. For school psychologists, the special salary schedule makes provisions for employing a psychologist at the Bachelor's degree level, a differentiation for students beginning public school work with a Master's degree, and a third classification for psychologists with a Master's degree with experience in a public school setting.

Salary differentials were also noted for special education teachers, however, not to the extent that they were noted for counselors and psychologists.

part V

the special
education
administrator

The role of the individual who has responsibility for directing programs for exceptional people is by definition a special education administrator. He may function primarily at the local, state, or federal level. Relatively few statements or studies can be found that deal directly with the preparation, professional standards, or function of the special education administrator.

This chapter begins with a statement by Leo Connor that proposes a method for the preparation of special education administrators that cuts across traditional handicapping areas. Robert Henderson then leads the reader to a review of preparation programs in special education administration in all fifty states and projected needs in the field of administration and supervision of special education. Because of the wide variation of organizational structures for the administration of special education in school systems throughout the United States, the Council for Exceptional Children issued guidelines for the preparation of administrators and supervisors of special education. These areas of professional competence are presented in the chapter. Ray Graham and others detail another brief checklist highlighting the qualifications, professional preparation, and experiences necessary for the person who is responsible for the special education program in the public school system. Meisgeier and Sloat present a comprehensive survey of related literature in this area. The final article is an application of the simulation technique as a training approach in a special education administration workshop developed by Daniel Sage.

preparation programs for special education administrators*

LEO E. CONNOR†

Abstract: To create a true profession of special education, as distinct from a loose confederation of educators of various exceptionalities, has been the dream of leaders in the special education field. While a few colleges and universities endeavor to fashion a preparation program for teachers which cuts across traditional handicapping areas, a method is proposed through the preparation of special education administrators, rather than administrators of any one exceptionality area. Based upon a baccalaureate program outside the special education field and a master's degree stressing teaching experience in one area of exceptionality, the suggested minimum program of preparation for administrators in special education is three years of successful teaching experience and 30 graduate semester hours beyond the master's degree. The doctorate in administration of special education remains the most desirable goal.

In executive positions, "the guys who really get things done are the ones with fire in their bellies" (Moynihan, 1964, p. 4).

Research in educational administration "has not been grounded sufficiently in theory to provide data which are predictive of the behavior of phenomena" (Griffiths, 1959), p. v).

*Reprinted from *Exceptional Children*, Vol. 33 (November 1966), pp. 161-166, by permission of the author and the Council for Exceptional Children. Copyright 1966 by the Council for Exceptional Children.

†Leo E. Connor is Superintendent, Lexington School for the Deaf, New York City.

Universities which prepare general school administrators have recently shifted from the study of how to be an administrator to the study of administration. The science, the technology, and the research findings concerning administration are being stressed, with a consequent deemphasis on the art, traditional functions, and recognized characteristics and practices of successful administrators. The effects of such a shift of emphasis are evident in the upgrading of membership requirements by the American Association of School Administrators (1958), the raising of university standards for the preparation of educational administrators (American Association of School Administrators, 1961), and the increased interest in the research and theory of this field (Griffiths, 1959). Thus, the emerging trend is the substitution of scholarship for know how.

Lipham (1964) indicated that regular themes had been developed by recent research investigations of administrative behavior, dealing with organizational roles, measurement of personality variables, study of cultural and individual values, interpersonal perceptions, and assessments of leadership qualities. Campbell and Faber (1961) stressed the central motifs that had borne the main weight of past and present attempts at building administrative theories: decision making, efficiency matrices, problem solving, social systems, stress and community pressures, leadership concepts, human relations, organizational charting, and power structures.

A major doubt exists as to whether these general administration research and theory activities and the movement toward higher standards and upgraded requirements are sufficiently reflected within the special education field or in the universities providing advanced degrees and leadership programs for the exceptional. A review of the literature in special education seems to confirm this critical surmise, although CEC's activities in professional standards and the U. S. Office of Education's stimulation grants to universities promise increased attention to the topic.

SPECIAL EDUCATION
LITERATURE

Kirk (1957) outlined ten problem areas of doctoral level study and indicated the standards held at the University of Illinois for teacher educators, researchers, and administrators in special education. The basic requirements for admission for advanced students included a master's degree, a teaching certificate in one of the areas of exceptionality, two years of teaching experience, and successful performance on a battery of tests. The doctoral program was described, with prospective administrators deviating from the generalized activities only in courses in general educational administration.

Gallagher (1959), as chairman of a committee of CEC's Teacher Education Division, provided a broader base of support for a recommended advanced training program for special education leaders when he compiled the agreements of the heads of seven special education departments offering doctoral degrees. While the items of admission requirements, program structure, and skill areas did not differ essentially from Kirk's, the minimums outlined were more comprehensive and detailed.

> ... the committee has suggested that the doctoral training program for Administration and Teacher Training are very similar and differ mainly in the character of the practicum experience obtained. The Research student has a different training program and the tendency toward flexible requirements suggests that individual programs may have to be designed for persons interested in this field (p. 104).

The specific skills mentioned for administrators are knowledge of supervision of elementary and secondary schools, understanding of theory and practice of American educational administration, legal basis of school administration, and school finance and business management.

Connor (1961) described skills and areas of knowledge necessary for special education administrators. Although this was essentially a textbook approach, the items of administrative structure, functions, and duties were interrelated to indicate present practice, informational gaps, and potential research areas. Strongly urged was the development of more effective and suitable university training programs, with equal emphasis given to general and special education administrative fields to help special educators meet the increasingly complex challenges and pressures in administrative positions.

The Council of Administrators of Special Education in Local School Systems (Tudyman, 1961) prepared a summarized list of standards for directors of special education. Listed were 11 competencies (e.g., personnel, program development, fiscal planning, and legal aspects), as well as the kinds of university courses and educational experiences necessary to achieve them.

Connor (1963) indicated the bases and characteristics of a theory of special education administration, describing the core of knowledge in special education administration as the organizational patterns and processes, skills and competencies, values and traditions, functions and patterns, and theories and research available in the literature. The article called for basic courses in the traditional functions of special education administration (e.g., transportation, finance, personnel, and legal provisions), as well as advanced seminars to study the problems and issues of this emerging field.

Milazzo and Blessing (1964) surveyed the university preparation programs for special education directors and supervisors and outlined a comprehensive set of program guidelines, improvements, and higher standards. Citing deficiencies in current practice, they pinpointed weaknesses in the preparation of present professional personnel, the inconsistency of the university response, and the need for specific training and experience in administrative endeavors. Although 40 universities claimed preparation programs for directors and supervisors of special education, only 8 had a sequence of general administrative courses and practicum in addition to special education administrative offerings.

Cain (1953) reviewed the period from 1944 to 1953 and indicated the sparsity of research in special education administration. He noted that the highlights of materials published prior to 1953 were the U. S. Office of Education's competency study of personnel, outlining suggestions for state and local directors of special education; Graham and Engel's summary of administrative principles in the *49th Yearbook* of the National Society for the Study of Education; and Haitema's guide for administrative research needed in special education.

Baer's (1959) review of the subsequent five year period of administrative research in special education required only 3 pages of a 185 page publication. The research topics of his chapter included legislation, instructional planning and staffing, community and parent relations, and utilization of buildings. No studies on the preparation of special education administrators were reviewed for this half decade. Voelker and Mullen (1963) could not locate any research between 1959 and 1963 concerning the preparation of leadership personnel in special education. Willenberg (1966) described several obstacles which might account for the "paucity of specific research on administration of special education" (p. 134).

In summary, the present state of knowledge indicates the need for more information regarding incidence, definitions, finances, organizational techniques, decision making, power structures, leadership qualities, curricular effectiveness, political activity, personal values, selection of personnel, preparation patterns, and community influences.

The foregoing review of relevant surveys of research, committee reports, and articles dealing with administration of special education programs reflects an intermittent and slow rate of interest in specifying and upgrading standards of preparation. A few current activities are portents of the immediate action needed to create new insights and consensus regarding the nature of administrative functions and objectives.

CURRENT ACTIVITIES

In the third year (1965) of PL 88-164, the U. S. Office of Education announced that fellowships would be available for preparation in special education administration, as well as in the disability categories. The provision of these stimulation grants to evolve varied preparation patterns for administrators throughout the United States should result in new and creative trends for subsequent advanced students, as well as employment of full time university personnel specializing in special education administration.

A regional attempt has been initiated by the Southern Regional Education Board to define and delineate the areas of competency needed by special education administrators. After a series of meetings involving national consultants; university personnel; and local, state, and residential administrators, position papers will be published as guides to southern universities for the development of leadership preparation programs.

The Council for Exceptional Children (1966) has published a series of policy statements which detail proposed professional standards in all areas of exceptionality, including advanced graduate programs and administration and supervision. A national conference considered the statements, while subsequent regional meetings began their dissemination. The Council has dedicated itself to a realization of these adopted standards. Their impact upon state certification regulations and university preparation programs is expected to result in substantial improvement of preparation programs for all special education personnel.

ROLE OF ADMINISTRATOR

The mainstream of special education is an instructional program for handicapped and gifted children and the unwanted and uncomfortable pupils in the regular classes. The goals of its leadership must be, first, to carry out the mandates of the American people in the educational development of exceptional children and, second, to overcome or mitigate the peculiar problems of its own existence — the differences in children which make them eligible for special education.

The administrator of such unusual enterprises must be experienced in dealing with these educational problems and with the community's reluctance to spend more money or to make concessions regarding traditional values of normalcy and academic success. He should be a person of considerable knowledge, for every science and modern movement has an immediate impact upon his work with the handicapped and gifted, usually by making it harder for his charges to make their way in the world. He must be ready for trials and pressures, because gains for the atypical are never made easily.

If educational leadership is to be at the center of social improvement, then the best possible education of children must be provided through the creation of community and school conditions under which this goal can be achieved. The chief administrator has, among other functions, those of manager, instructional leader, technician, financier, legislator, psychologist, politician, and educationalist. Preparation programs must provide opportunities and insights into all of these practical areas of endeavor.

Since the role of an administrator in any school concerns leadership involving teachers, other staff members, parents, and the community, the major emphasis in the preparation for such positions will be directed toward a depth study of the field of education, together with a cross section of the behavioral and social sciences.

GUIDELINES FOR PREPARATION PROGRAM

When the preparation program for special education administrators is based upon the twin foundations of general education administration and its relationships to special education, many discussion questions are readily answered.

The general education field of administration has set its entrance requirements and its minimum preparation standards as two years of graduate study at an accredited institution of higher learning (American Association of School Administrators, 1958). Is it possible, then, that the field of special education can prepare administrators of any national stature or accepted competence at the master's level? It seems clear that special education administrators need preparation at universities with already recognized and accredited departments of general education administration. Since The National Council for Accreditation of Teacher Education (NCATE) has been selected by the American Association of School Administrators for this accrediting role, the distinguishing between qualified and unqualified universities is readily evident. Henceforth, only universities with NCATE approval for their program of educational administration should develop programs for special education administration.

The national trend to prepare for a professional field at the master's level also delimits the direction of special education activities and throws the emphasis upon administration into a postmaster's or sixth year program. Thus, the potential administrator of special education may have a baccalaureate degree in liberal arts, general education, or any field other than special education.

The master's degree work should be in a teaching field of special education and will vary in length and specifics according to prior preparation. Leaders in many exceptionality areas indicate the need for at least a year and a summer or two to acquire the necessary knowledge and skills for their specialty. Student teaching in general education (if not taken previously) and in special education will add to the usual one year period for a master's degree in special education.

It has been proposed that the first year of teaching in special education become known as the internship under the coordinated sponsorship of the university and a local school program. An additional two to three year period of successful teaching experience should be completed as a prerequisite for administrator certification. The special teacher will have completed, meanwhile, the necessary academic and practicum program of advanced graduate study in special education administration.

SPECIFIC PREPARATION
PROGRAM

The sixth year of graduate work in special education administration requires an emphasis upon professional competencies, as contrasted to research skills. This distinction appears to be a vital and valid one, and the tendency of some university programs to value research procedures and statistical studies while neglecting the increasing knowledge and sophisticated techniques of influencing human behavior is an unfortunate trend.

Conscious and rigorous selection of special education teachers for administrative preparation is necessary if special education is to grow beyond the substandard policies apparent at all levels of past selection practices. Only graduate students who have completed preparation programs in special education will be eligible to enter the sixth year level to major in special education administration. The Ed. D. degree, as the highest professional goal, is the proper final objective for future special education administrators, while the Ph. D. will distinguish the aim of research orientation for other special education leaders.

Special education administrators could be certified for their positions at the M. A. plus 30 semester hours level, with a minimum of three years' teaching experience while they continue their work toward an Ed. D. degree.

All special education students at the postmaster's level should have a core of courses in common. In addition, administrative majors in special education would have a core of courses in common with general education administration majors. Further, special education administration majors at the postmaster's level would benefit from advanced course seminars and practicum in their own particular specialty and its concomitant areas of interest (e.g., for the deaf, concomitant areas might be mental retardation, neurological problems, and audiology). Finally, administrative majors in special education would require advanced courses that would cut across all the exceptionality areas.

Practicum requirements would include an internship in both an area of administration (such as supervision, residential programs, curriculum development, or state department work) and a broadly based program of special education involving several exceptionality groups.

The following suggested outline, using semester hours, illustrates the preparation principles described in this article.

MINIMUM PROGRAM FOR
SPECIAL EDUCATION ADMINISTRATION

(M. A. + 30 graduate semester hours)

1. B. A. or B. S.

a.   Liberal arts or
b.   Education (not special education) or
c.   Any nonprofessional field of study

2. M. A. or M. S.

a.   Based upon B. A. or B. S. in liberal arts or other nonprofessional field of study, at least a 40 to 50 hour graduate program, including:

1) Student teaching with nonhandicapped and exceptional children
2) 24 semester hours in special education
3) 12-18 semester hours in education

or

b. Based upon B. A. or B. S. in education, at least a 30 hour graduate program, including:
1) Practice teaching with exceptional children
2) 24 semester hours in special education
3) 6 semester hours of advanced study in behavioral and social sciences

3. Experience

a. One year teaching internship and
b. Two to three year period of successful teaching experience with exceptional children

4. Postmaster's Program
(30 graduate semester hours)

a. Fundamentals of administration (12 semester hours)
1) General education administration (6 semester hours)
2) Special education administration (6 semester hours)
b. Administrative internship (up to 6 semester hours, at least 1 semester full time)
c. Advanced study of an exceptionality (6 semester hours)
d. Concomitant fields (6 semester hours)

CERTIFICATION
REQUIREMENTS

The field of special education has several examples of national certification standards (American Speech and Hearing Association, Conference of Executives of American Schools for the Deaf, American Instructors of the Blind). The exceptionalities not covered by minimum standards must also receive attention, and consistent statements of requirements should characterize the entire field. In certain areas of exceptionality, the national standards now in effect need revision to meet modern conditions or strengthening in their educational emphasis because of the generalized orientation of their parent organization.

State education departments and/or other legally constituted bodies probably will retain the right to license, but the professional organizations of many fields have indicated the necessity and the pathway to upgrading personnel standards through establishing national statements of requirements for minimum competence at levels such as classroom teachers, administrators, college teachers, and researchers.

Certain premises underlie the requirements which are outlined in state certification statements. The following list is abridged and amended from a New York State Education Department (1965) publication:

1. Certification requirements establish minimum standards for entrance to specific positions.
2. Certification requirements serve as guidelines for development of collegiate programs of instruction.
3. Certification requirements relate to the functions performed, rather than to the title assigned by local school authorities.
4. Local school authorities have the right and the responsiblity for establishing patterns of organization for administrative positions.
5. Colleges and universities have responsibility for developing strong programs to prepare prospective administrators for their roles in the schools.
6. A permanent teaching certificate and teaching experience are prerequisites for administration positions.
7. Local school authorities and universities may establish requirements in excess of the minimum certification requirements.

AREAS OF FURTHER STUDY

Data concerning the status of special education administrators, their pressures and attitudes, and the changing condition of their jobs are urgently needed. Conspicuously absent in the special education literature have been reports, even of doctoral studies, which throw new light upon the basic questions of who should be a special education administrator, what the current attitudes are of special education administrators toward their problems, or what community and national trends affect the administration of special education programs.

Mullen's (1958) compilation of organizational information, Wisland and Vaughan's (1964) listing of critical areas of concern, and Edwards' (1964) and Chalfant's (1965) studies of state administrative patterns are examples of the handful of isolated materials within the past decade that are utilized by administrative students to analyze trends and formulate principles of modern special education administration.

Techniques which can be transferred to special education problems are available from the behavioral sciences. Even closer at hand are the replication of designs and instruments from general education administration. Possible topics include the following.

Personnel

What kind and how many special personnel are required for an effective special education program? When should cost factors influence the employment of additional or different personnel? What is the most effective ratio of special education administrators and supervisors to teachers? What are the ingredients for the initiation of a special education program? What principles influence the selection, promotion, or reassignment of special education personnel? What is the best process for selecting special education administrators?

Decision Process

Is the administrative decision process similar to that utilized in curriculum work and financial or research areas? Is decision making in special education affected by factors different from those which exist in general education or administration of any field? Are special education administrators more effective as generalists in special education? What are the criteria of success in administrative decisions?

Methods and Materials

Would a national testing center for special education materials be feasible? Have any large scale research studies compared the accomplishments of various methodologies for exceptional children? What evaluative instruments are available for determining the value of new materials? Can critical incident studies evaluate reactions to varied approaches in specific learning situations?

REFERENCES

American Association of School Administrators. *Something to steer by.* Washington, D. C.: Author, 1958.

American Association of School Administrators. *Commitment to excellence.* Washington, D. C.: Author, 1961.

Baer, C. J. Organization and supervision of special education. *Review of Educational Research*, 1959, 29, 566- 570.

Cain, L. General problems and administration of programs for exceptional children. *Review of Educational Research*, 1953, 23, 391- 399.

Campbell, R. F., and Faber, C. F. Administrative behavior: theory and research. *Review of Educational Research*, 1961, 31, 353-367.

Chalfant, J. C. Factors related to special education services in Illinois. Unpublished doctoral dissertation, University of Illinois, 1965.

Connor, L. E. *Administration of special education programs.* New York: Teachers College, Columbia University, 1961.

Connor, L. E. Preliminaries to a theory of administration for special education. *Exceptional Children*, 1963, 29, 431-436.

The Council for Exceptional Children. *Professional standards for personnel in the education of exceptional children.* Washington, D. C.: Author, 1966.

Edwards, S. A. Indices of community readiness for special classes for the educable MR in Kentucky. Unpublished doctoral dissertation, Columbia University, 1964.

Gallagher, J. J. Advanced graduate training in special education. *Exceptional Children*, 1959, 26, 104-109.

Griffiths, D. E. *Research in education administration.* New York: Teachers College, Columbia University, 1959.

Kirk, S. A. A doctor's degree program in special education. *Exceptional Children*, 1957, 24, 50-52, 55.

Lipham, J. M. Organizational character of education: administrative behavior. *Review of Educational Research*, 1964, 34, 435-454.

Milazzo, T., and Blessing, K. The training of directors and supervisors of special education programs. *Exceptional Children*, 1964, 31, 129-141.

Moynihan, D. P. In *Carnegie Corporation of New York Quarterly*, 1964, 12 (4), 4-5.

Mullen, F. Staffing special education in 34 large cities. *Exceptional Children*, 1958, 25, 162-168.

New York State Education Department. *Certification requirements for administrative and supervisory positions.* Albany: Author, 1965.

Tudyman, A. Standards committee report. In *Proceedings of the annual convention of The Council of Administrators of Special Education in Local School Systems.* Washington, D. C.: The Council of Administrators of Special Education in Local School Systems, 1961. Pp. 19-21.

Voelker, P., and Mullen, F. Organization, administration and supervision of special education. *Review of Educational Research*, 1963, 33, 5-19.

Willenberg, E. Organization, administration and supervision of special education. *Review of Educational Research*, 1966, 36, 134-150.

Wisland, M., and Vaughan, T. Administrative problems in special education. *Exceptional Children*, 1964, 31, 87-89.

preparation of administrators and supervisors of special education*

ROBERT A. HENDERSON†

         The preparation of administrators and supervisors of special education began with a course at Teachers College, Columbia University, in New York, in 1906. A few other universities followed suit, and added a single course — usually to be taken as an elective when something more suitable was not available that semester.

         Most of the students who were able to get the one course in administration of special education usually took it during the summer session, as few if any universities had a faculty member who was qualified to, or desired to, teach a course in administration. The qualified, well prepared, experienced administrator of special education needed on the university staffs were out in the field as working administrators — and at salaries which made them "untouchables" from the university's standpoint.

         Thus we found ourselves a few years ago with the need and opportunity to prepare some administrators and supervisors, but lacking the programs to effect the pre-service preparation in even the strongest special education departments of our largest universities. Even the impetus of PL 85-926, with each state having two graduate fellowships to prepare "leadership personnel for the mentally retarded," university programs just did not change dramatically. However, with the extension of PL 85-926 to all areas of the

*Presented at the 46th Annual CEC Convention, April 17th, 1968. Reprinted by permission of the author and the Council for Exceptional Children.

†Robert A. Henderson is Chairman, Department of Special Education, University of Illinois.

TABLE 1.

Current and Projected Distribution of Leadership Personnel

Type of Leadership Personnel

Category:	Currently Employed		Estimated Total Needed		Estimated Increase	
	Number	% of Total	Number	% of Total	Number	% of Total
Directors	1243	32.47	2442	24.84	1199	19.97
Principals	653	17.06	1025	10.43	372	6.21
Coordinators	491	12.83	1266	12.88	775	12.90
Supervisors	624	16.30	2602	26.46	1978	32.94
Consultants	644	16.82	2040	20.75	1396	23.25
Others	173	4.52	457	4.64	284	4.73
TOTALS	3828	100.0%	9832	100.0%	6004	100.0%

Locale of Employment

Category:	Currently Employed		Estimated Total Needed		Estimated Increase	
	Number	% of Total	Number	% of Total	Number	% of Total
Local Public School Districts	1775	46.37	4745	48.26	2970	49.47
Intermediate/Coop. Programs	503	13.14	2141	21.77	1638	27.28
Residential State Schools	637	16.64	1160	11.79	523	8.71
State Offices of Public Instruction	355	9.27	800	8.16	445	7.41
Private Schools	558	14.58	986	10.02	428	7.13
TOTALS	3828	100.0%	9832	100.0%	6004	100.0%

handicapped by the amendments contained in PL 88-164, a separate category of administration and supervision programs was established, with a special ad hoc committee developed to evaluate proposals for funding. The first committee — wisely, I believe — took the stand that programs of preparation for administrators should not be a stepchild of the institution's program, but must represent an identifiable program of study at the advanced graduate level with a qualified, experienced staff member devoting his major efforts to that program exclusively. Under these standards, only four applicants were funded the first year, FY 1965. In addition, six other institutions were encouraged to build their programs to an acceptable level by the award of program development grants that year. In the coming year (FY 1968) 15 universities will be awarding fellowships to about 30 advanced graduate students in this area.

The USOE ad hoc panel meeting in December, 1966 wondered about the proliferation of new programs, and about their geographical distribution. At the panel's request the Institute for Research on Exceptional Children, University of Illinois, undertook a nation-wide study of the current status and projected needs in the field of administration and supervision of special education. Dr. Kenneth Wyatt, now Coordinator of State Plans and Administration for the Bureau of Education for the Handicapped, USOE, was project director for this study, which obtained data from all 50 states.

The table seen here summarizes current and projected numbers of special education leadership personnel by type of position and by employment agency. You will note that while the increase in directors is impressive (from 1243 to 2442), they will actually be decreasing in terms of proportion of directors to the total leadership personnel required. Principals of special schools also show a drop, while coordinators are seen holding their own. Consultants and supervisors, on the other hand, will gain both in terms of total numbers and the proportion of positions which they hold. This would seem to verify the prediction: that as school district reorganization plus formation of multi-district cooperative programs for exceptional children produce larger, more efficient units, the need for several all-purpose directors decreases, but conversely, the need for supervisors of particular phases of the program increases as the number of specialists in a given program permit such a supervisor to be employed.

The right hand half of the table shows the current and projected employment locales for special education leadership. Here too we see a changing picture: proportions dropping in public and private residential schools, and in state offices. Intermediate, cooperative district programs and single school districts will show the major increases.

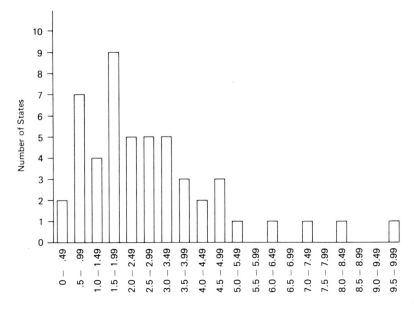

FIGURE 1.

DISTRIBUTION OF STATES ACCORDING TO THE PERCENT OF THE TOTAL PUBLIC SCHOOL POPULATION ENROLLED IN SPECIAL EDUCATION PROGRAMS

The underlying assumption to all these data, of course is that we have not met the needs of all exceptional children. Taking the USOE report of number of exceptional children served, and census data of public school enrollment, we see that most states are providing three percent or less of their school children with special educational services. The near-ten percent state is North Carolina, and achieves this status by enrolling an unusual proportion of children in programs for the gifted. If prevalence estimates have any validity, most of the states have a long way to go before meeting the needs of exceptional children. This, therefore, adds credence to the estimates of administrative personnel needed.

As we approach the goal of meeting needs, a shift in type of personnel needed is seen. Combining the directors, principals and coordinators as "administrative" positions, we can see the relative change compared to the supervisor and consultant who are combined as "supervisory" in this figure. While today the administrators

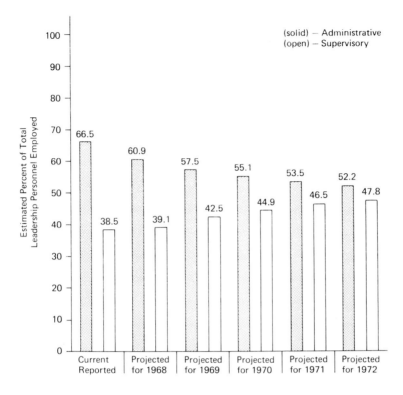

FIGURE 2.

**REPORTED AND PROJECTED RATIOS BETWEEN SPECIAL EDUCATION ADMINIS-
TRATIVE AND SUPERVISORY PERSONNEL EMPLOYED IN LOCAL, COUNTY,
AND COOPERATIVE PUBLIC SCHOOL PROGRAMS**

outnumber the supervisors by 2 to 1, it is estimated that in just 5 years they will be about even. This is not to say that the director of today does not provide supervisory services, nor that the supervisor of special classes does not perform administrative tasks relating to bus schedules, etc. As larger units come into being, however, specialization of function will inevitably take place — and the clearest trend for these data is that the supervisory function now exercised by the administrator in the smaller districts will be removed and assigned to a supervisor whose role will be less ambiguous and contradictory.

If indeed this does occur, we will find supervisors of a radically different variety than now available. Too often "supervisor" equals "junior administrator," with differences between director and supervisor limited to scope but not activity. Since positions labelled as "supervisor" carry this connotation, and are many times seen as stepping stones to positions of director, they are seldom sought by "master teachers." These individuals want close contact with the classroom and are repelled by administrative duties.

When and if sufficient specialization occurs, it should be possible to employ these master teachers as supervisors in the true sense of the term. Tasks now assigned to supervisors, such as bus schedules, budget and inventory, etc., would go instead to an administrative assistant working under the director or as a coordinator. The supervisor would have improvement of the curriculum as primary responsibility, and would spend most of his time in the classroom demonstrating the use of new materials or techniques, or freeing the teacher to visit another class of children with similar problems. In-service education and curriculum development would thus be a continuous, integrated function of supervision.

From what we know of personality differences and role expectations, the budding administrator will not be the person to fill this kind of supervisory role. Conversely, the master teacher will reject "promotion" if the new position involves assuming administrative responsibilities. Thus, the supervisor of tomorrow will have a new role. Even in small districts where all administrative personnel wear several hats, it will be possible to seduce the master teacher into assuming the supervisory role by (1) maintaining the separation of function and (2) combining part-time teaching instead of administrative duties, with the supervisory position.

Another problem facing universities preparing administrators and supervisors in this field is the extreme variation existing between states. The problems in providing special educational services for exceptional children will vary considerably due to the population density and urban nature of the population. A state with a growing population will be building schools while a decreasing population requires re-districting to enable consolidation of school population sufficient to provide special services.

Will the character of the educational needs differ between states such as Minnesota and Washington and Mississippi? Remember Kirk's definition of what is special about special education: regular plus special. Thus in a state where regular education is failing 2/3 of its young men, special education will have an immensely greater problem than in a state where strong regular education exists — so much so that entirely different patterns of special educational services may be needed, and thus extra special preparation for the administrators placed in charge of such programs.

What of the financial differences between states? Will the special education administrator in Mississippi have any more problems in finding qualified teachers than his colleagues in California? With the shortage of teachers of exceptional children, certainly the salary differential and the public school revenue receipts per pupil will make teacher recruitment extremely difficult where the differences are double and even triple within a few hundred miles. The director of special education in Delaware — either at the local or state level — faces an entirely different set of financial problems than that faced by his counterpart in Nebraska. With the development of Title III centers for diagnosis and remediation of learning disability problems, would you think the Director in Montana or North Carolina is more concerned about how he can get the children needing this service to the centers?

All of this reminds us that education is a state responsibility and that while the federal government has injected considerable financial assistance in the past few years, enormous differences between states still exist which basically effect programs for exceptional children. We may well need to analyze the effect of these differences to determine whether special elements are needed in programs preparing administrators for states with extremely sparse, non-urban population characteristics.

What are some other implications for programs preparing administrators and supervisors of special education programs. Obviously the first is quantitative: many more administrators and supervisors will be needed in the future, and our training programs are producing only a few. Equally obvious is the fact that as the size of administrative units increase, and the director's role becomes more clearly defined, the preparation of directors will need to extend beyond a summer session course or two. As larger proportions of exceptional children are provided with special educational services, control of larger proportions of the public school's funds and personnel will be delegated to the director of special education. With such increased power will come increased responsibilities. Thus increases in the quality of programs to prepare administrators in this field are mandatory.

The role of the director of special education is unique in the public school administrative structure. He usually serves in the dual capacity of staff and line administrator. Unlike most administrators he has direct contact with a variety of community agencies, with state and federal programs which directly or indirectly effect the children whom he serves. State and federal legislation is of immediate concern, and therefore he must devote some of his energies and attention to this area. Teaching techniques and materials are only now beginning to be identified as truly special. But how to separate the valuable from the expensive gimmick? Thus the director needs to know and through such applied research will we be able to rise above the folklore of "promising practices" and testimonials, to objective validation.

To be able to do this we need to review the content and process of programs of preparation for special education administrators. Skills in interpretation of research findings and in developing and conducting action research programs must be included. Perhaps most important, we need to develop a respect for the application of the scientific method to administrative problems. The director which we prepare today will need to provide leadership in objective study of tomorrow's problems, either through organizing and conducting research projects himself, or through cooperative programs with university staffs. Our university programs, in turn, need to provide practicum opportunities during the period of preparation. This means too that our present directors must recognize this future requirement and supply the needed action research projects so that realistic practicum facilities are available as an integral part of the preparation programs.

In this same area of concern, we need to develop internships in local, state and national offices providing services to exceptional children. The complex and myrid responsibilities of an administrator of special education cannot be appreciated without close continuous contact for a substantial period of time. Only through year-long, full time, internships can the necessary skills and techniques be acquired before assuming direct responsibilities as a director.

While it may be possible to acquire some sophistication in the range and score of activities of an administrator through course work and simulation techniques, only through experience in the real world of school administration can the impact of the responsibilities and duties assigned to a special education administrator be sufficiently experienced so as to become integrated into the behavior patterns of the neophyte director or supervisor.

In summary, the pattern of preparation of administrators and supervisors seems to be evolving as follows:

1. The number of adequately staffed, comprehensive programs to prepare administrators and supervisors has increased dramatically in the past few years, mainly due to the stimulus of PL 85-926, as amended.
2. As a corollary to this, the number of personnel being prepared still falls far short of the anticipated demand, and thus additional programs are needed.

3. Wide variance on a number of educationally significant factors between states suggest that preparation for posts in sparsely populated areas may need to be different from that of wealthy, densely populated states.
4. As the size of the administrative unit becomes larger, greater differentiation of roles will occur, with three patterns of personnel clearly needed: (a) the Director of Special Education with overall responsibility for the educational program of up to ten percent of the children in the schools; (b) supervisors of particular phases or categories of children; and (c) administrative assistants specializing in such tasks as inventory control, bus scheduling, etc.
5. There is a clear trend for integration of school systems and preparation programs in recruitment and preparation of special education administrators and supervisors. Practicum stations and internships in local, state and national settings will shortly become the *sine qua non* for entry into the profession.

special education administration and supervision — a review of relevant literature*

CHARLES MEISGEIER† and

ROBERT SLOAT

An historic work conference centering a-round the theme "Common and Specialized Learnings, Competencies, and Experiences for Special Education Administrators" was held in March, 1969, at The University of Texas at Austin. Attending this conference were coordinators of special education programs, professors of special education, and doctoral students from 17 of the nation's major universities with programs in this area funded by the United States Office of Education. In addition, outside organizations such as the University Council for Educational Administration (UCEA), The Council for Exceptional Children (CEC), the Council of Administrators of Special Education programs (CASE), the National Association of State Directors of Special Education (NASDSE) were represented at the meeting. The group met to identify and delineate problems and issues related to the training of special education administrators and to devise ways by which the member universities of the newly developed Consortium could effectively communicate and exchange information. The group further concentrated on mechanisms for developing inter-university research, criteria for training programs, mechanisms for assessing the effectiveness of programs, and overall, for facilitating the broader

---

*Printed by permission of the authors.

†Charles Meisgeier is Coordinator, Special Education Administration Programs, The University of Texas at Austin. Robert Sloat is Assistant Professor of Special Education, Florida Atlantic University.

utilization of resources within each university which has relevance for training and research.

The concept of a consortium made up of member universities preparing administrators of special education resulted from the recent and extensive growth of programs for training administrators of special education under the stimulus of federal funding. The new Consortium of Universities Preparing Administrators of Special Education has for the first time focused major attention on preparation programs for administrators and supervisors. Leadership positions in the field have been in existence for at least four decades, but the administration and supervision of special education as a particular and vital aspect of the total area has received little attention and there is a paucity of studies relating to this area in the literature.

HISTORICAL OVERVIEW

As early as 1928 Ayer and Barr (1928) found that 16 major cities employed 29 supervisors and six directors of special instruction. Their study involved 44 cities with populations of over 100,000 offering public school special classes. According to Connor (1963) the first college course for administrators of special education was offered at Teachers' College. Columbia University, about 1906-1907. Despite this early beginning, Baker reported in 1944 that with the exception of a very few special schools, the administration of special education was in the hands of regular school administrators. A later article by Haitema (1947) discussed needed research in terms of attitudes, effectiveness of programs, existing weaknesses, and patterns for state and community programs, but made no mention of personnel.

In the early 1950's an apparent change was reported by Cain (1953) who indicated that supervision in teaching in special education was developing interest and that some research inroads were beginning to be made in administration, supervision, and teaching. By 1955 Mackie and Engel (1955) reported an extensive study of local special education leadership personnel. However, Baer (1959) in reviewing research in this area contained his review to three pages, and mentioned nothing about preparation or research directly related to supervisors or administrators of special education programs. In 1960 Howe (1960) indicated that only one other study could be found in the literature from 1953 to 1959 which dealt directly with the administration of special education. While Federal recognition of the needs of special education developed widespread interest and emphasis in terms of research and teacher training, the problems of organization, administration, and supervision received little attention from researchers.

Voelker and Mullen (1963) reported a great deal of research on the evaluation of classes; however, they were surprised to find so few studies conducted in the area of supervisory leadership. Willenberg (1966) in his review of educational research reported that "the paucity of specific research on administration of special education continues to plague the reviewer (p. 134)." Willenberg reported studies by Wisland and Vaughn (1964), and Milazzo and Blessing (1964) which reflected an interest in local special education leadership personnel. Interest and activity picked up during the period 1966 through 1969 when at least ten dissertations were completed relating to the area of special education administration. The Council for Exceptional Children in 1966 published 43 pages of abstracts which contained four pages specifically devoted to "Administration." Included were articles dealing with the preparation of special education leadership personnel. In 1969 The Council for Exceptional Children again published a major review entitled *Administration of Speical Education Programs* in which not one of its 81 abstracts dealt with either the preparation, task, or overall job responsibilities of local educational leadership personnel. In the same year Reynolds (1969), in the latest issue of *The Review of Educational Research* devoted to exceptional children, indicated the programs for exceptional children had doubled or tripled during the past two or three decades, but for the first time during this period *The Review* contained no section dealing with the administration and supervision of these numerous programs.

COMMON AND SPECIALIZED LEARNINGS FOR SPECIAL EDUCATION LEADERS

Over forty years ago Ayer and Barr (1928) commented that "owing to the special nature of instruction offered in connection with the classes. . . it was necessary from the beginning to place them in charge of special teachers. . . special subjects. . . soon led to special supervision (p. 31)." Wyatt (1968) has estimated that by 1972 full-time public school special education leaders will increase by 157 percent. Connor (1961) as well as Ayer and Barr have indicated that specialized instruction for exceptional children has resulted in the need to prepare specialized leaders for the field.

Connor stated that "Special education programs are but a division of the larger administrative field of instruction, different from and yet part of elementary and secondary schools (p. 22)." He pointed out the ideal twin base for the preparation of special education directors; that is, specialized administrative experience and general administrative knowledge.

This concept of common and specialized learnings has been long recognized by general education administration personnel. The University Council for Educational Administration (UCEA) had, during the early 1950's, expressed the belief that there was a common base for the training of all educational leaders regardless of the type of educational leadership position held. They indicated (Miller, undated) that there are "concepts, knowledges, and skills common to all educational administration and those which are special or unique to a given position or level of the school system." They pointed out that there were no hard and fast boundaries between these two types of learning. Carlson (1953) emphasized the concept of common learnings and Culbertson (1953) developed a list of content for all administrators and supervisors and indicated that common processes included communicating, making decisions, handling morale, and coping with change.

Culbertson pointed out that underlying the common elements specialized content was necessary (a) when the administrator performs a unique function, (b) when the contextual knowledge to be applied differs, and (c) when the characteristics of the person served differ.

The necessity for flexibility within preparation programs in order to meet individual needs, was more recently emphasized by Morphet, Johns, and Reller (1959). Graduate training in special education was studied by a committee of CEC, and Gallagher (1959) reported that the committee suggested additional training beyond the basic coursed in special education in the areas of:

1. Knowledge of skills and supervision of elementary or secondary schools.
2. Understanding of theory and practice of American educational administration.
3. Legal basis of school administration.
4. School finance and business management (p. 107).

The view that special education administrators need to be conversant with the various facets of general education administration was further reinforced by Connor (1963). He indicated that general educational administrative knowledge should be "at least equal" to the emphasis on specialized techniques. The necessity for common and specialized preparation was again emphasized by Milazzo and Blessing (1964) who suggested that trainees "would be required to have a comprehensive understanding of general education administration and/or supervisory functions as well as the related aspects of the relationships of special education to general education (p. 131)." In addition to a common core in the area of special education the previous writers suggested a differentiated core including general educational administration and supervision and an internship experience.

SPECIALIZED PREPARATION PROGRAMS FOR SPECIAL EDUCATION ADMINISTRATORS AND SUPERVISORS

In discussing doctoral programs in special education, Kirk (1957) indicated that administration of local and state programs was one of the three major types of leadership positions in the field, although he did not dwell specifically on the preparation of administrators. Kirk further pointed out that other courses should be required in addition to special education courses. In a 1966 review of much of the literature relating to the preparation of special education leadership personnel, Connor (1966) indicated that in terms of administration more information is needed "regarding incidence, definitions, finances, organizational techniques, decision-making, power structure, leadership qualities, curricular effectiveness, political activity, personal values, selection of personnel, preparation patterns, and community influences (p. 163)." Connor suggested guidelines for a preparation program, certification requirements, and areas for further study. He pointed out that funds provided for the training of administrators through the provisions of P. L. 88-164 would contribute to the growth of this type of preparation program.

The National Association of State Directors of Special Education (NASDSE) conducted a study dealing with leadership training programs. Reporting on this study, Milazzo and Blessing (1964) stated that 174 of the 224 colleges and universities offering special education course sequences responded to the questionnaire concerning their programs. Forty colleges and universities reported programs for the preparation of administrative and supervisory personnel. However, there were a number of between-school and within-level preparation differences found. Only one-fourth included courses in either general or special education administration, and only 16 offered full-time course work. In two studies of the subject-curricular emphasis of federally funded programs in special education administration Henley (1967; 1969) found major differences between the institutions. Of the eleven institutions studied in 1967 he found:

1. A wide variety of courses were offered including courses in general education administration, law, finance, public relations, and plant planning, and courses in the field of business.
2. Program emphasis within each institution varied greatly and many unique patterns were found within individual university programs.

Some of the more specific findings of his 1969 follow-up study reported at the Consortium meeting included:

1. A range in the reporting institutions of from one to nine courses in educational administration.
2. Eleven required courses in research and statistics but no more than four required courses in such areas as psychology, educational psychology, sociology, group dynamics, or the culturally deprived.
3. All utilized local school districts or state departments of education as intern settings, but one-fourth or less provided experiences at either USOE, professional associations, regional centers, university departments of special education, or public and/or private residential schools.
4. Only two institutions differentiated between administrators and supervisors in terms of separate types of preparation programs.
5. Only one developed a special course in the supervision of special education and only nine required a minimum of at least one course in supervision of instruction.

In suggesting a possible reason for the lack of program content agreement, Willenberg (1964, 1966) and Sage (1968) indicated that there are no basic tools for instruction in special education administration and/or supervision and no guidelines associated with the training programs.

PERCEPTIONS OF LOCAL EDUCATION AGENCY DIRECTORS OF SPECIAL EDUCATION

The differentiation between special education administration and supervision was made almost twenty years ago by Graham and Engel (1950) when they indicated that supervisory type individuals assumed both administrative and supervisory responsibilities. Several years later, Mackie and Engel (1955) were able to differentiate between special education leaders with administrative and those with supervisory type job responsibilities, and it has been predicted by Wyatt (1968) that by the year 1972 there will be as many purely supervisory as purely administrative special education personnel. Most of the studies dealing with leadership personnel in special education between 1955 and 1968 tended to dichotomize this group in terms of their being either purely or primarily administrative types, although Graham (1956) and Brown (1967) discussed the special education director's job in terms of administrative, supervisory, and coordinating functions. Erdman (1961) supported the idea that the director of special education had the responsibilities for administrative, supervisory, and coordinating functions. However, most writers and researchers in the field have perceived the special education director as either purely or primarily an administrator.

This concentration on administration is evident in several recent studies. Department heads of university special education programs, state directors of special education, and professors of school administration were questioned by Hodgson (1963) in an attempt to define the scope of special education. He found that the three groups generally agreed in terms of supporting the traditional classification system. However, he questioned only "administrative" type personnel and this may have influenced his results. In discussing the unique role aspects that separate the special education administrator and supervisor from the classroom teacher, Reger pointed out only unique aspects of administration and did not mention supervision. Schwabe in his survey of Missouri special education discussed the state's public school organization only in terms of administration. Wisland (1962) distinguished between directors and supervisors although he did not discuss this duality in terms of the problems of administration and supervision, thus precluding the possibility that directors' tasks and/or problems were primarily supervisory in nature. Voelker (1966), Leonard (1966), Taylor (1967), Kothera (1967), Courtnage (1967), Hill (1967), and others conducted their studies on the assumption that directors were primarily administrators. Only

Marshman (1965) and Wyatt (1968) suggested that the position may be primarily or purely supervisory.

A number of writers in the field have indicated that the role function of special education leadership personnel is dependent upon such factors as leadership and teaching experience, maturity of position, professional preparation, socio-economic status of the school district, types of credentials held, and size of school district. The size of the district is by far the most frequent characteristic studied and although a substantial number of researchers have found a high relationship between tasks and skills and size of organization, others have found size not to be a significant influence in role responsibility and specific task emphasis (Wisland, Vaughn, Sage, Howe, Leonard, Wyatt, Taylor, Milazzo and Blessing, Courtnage, Richardson, and Mackie and Engel).

TASKS AS A MEANS OF IDENTIFYING AND DESCRIBING ROLE FUNCTIONS

Sage (1968b) pointed out that the major means utilized by those interested in constructing a conceptual scheme for framework for describing the job responsibilities of school administrators has been through the differentiation of tasks. Harris (1963) distinguished between tasks on one hand being goals of the organization and competencies being a composite of skills possessed by people. However, tasks, competencies, and problems are often perceived as juxtaposed and used interchangeably in special education. The list of .Willenberg's (1964) problems of special education administration are found on lists of competencies of CEC (1966) with slightly modified wording. (Therefore, in terms of the remainder of this review competencies, problems, activities, and tasks will be considered to be tasks or job responsibilities of special education leadership personnel.)

SKILLS NEEDED CONCEPT

Although the recent literature in both general and special education administration contains a good deal of discussion of the tasks, activities, and job responsibilities of leadership personnel, discussions of the skills used by these leaders in completing their task assignments, have been somewhat neglected. Education as a field has adopted many of the practices and concepts born in the area of business, but the "skills needed" concept, first discussed by Katz (1955) has received little attention. Harris (1963) pointed out that within each of Katz's three major classes of skills (human, conceptual, and technical) there reside many different specific skills which tend to cluster together under these three basic skills and that these are the basic skills of leadership. Davis (1958) indicated that education had moved from the human, to the technical and was in its present stage of conceptual development. Connor (1961) mentioned the three skills, but did not eleborate on them in terms of special or general education leadership tasks. More recently Purrington (1968) added administrative skills to the three previously mentioned by Katz in a study of how supervisory skills facilitate or hinder system functioning. He found that effective handling of the four skill areas was related to competencies. Sage (1967, 1968b) appears to have been the only major researcher in special education who has employed this concept when he developed a matrix consisting of the skills and the four major parts of the job of educational administration. (This will be discussed in greater detail later in this chapter.)

TASKS OF SPECIAL EDUCATION LEADERSHIP PERSONNEL

Although the director of special education assumes an important role as a program leader and molder of human opinion, very few studies, according to Howe (1960), had been conducted concerning his role prior to 1954. He indicated that a basic question in the field revolved around the types of tasks being performed by individuals responsible for the leadership of public school special education programs. He stated that an important beginning was made when the U. S. Office of Education published a study of special education directors and supervisors in local school districts (Mackie and Engel, 1955).

The study by Mackie and Engel has been used as a basic reference in a number of articles pertaining to the roles of special education leadership in the public schools (Howe, 1960; Voelker, 1966; Kothera, 1967). The purpose and rationale of the study as stated in the introductory comments can be generalized to be the purpose of many of the recent task studies of educational leadership personnel. The authors stated that "this deepened understanding 'of elements which contribute to effective leadership' is needed by directors and supervisors themselves as a basis for measuring their own competency; by school systems as a basis for the selection of directors; by colleges and universities offering professional preparation for special educators as a basis for the development of curriculums (p. 2)."

The authors surveyed 103 directors (administrative type) and 50 supervisors (supervisory and/or consultant type) of special education leaders in various sized school districts. Functions performed, types of pupils served, competencies needed, professional experience, supervisory-teacher relations, and other areas were studied. The authors also utilized the services of a committee of twelve leaders in the field. This committee perceived the special education leader as engaging in tasks in eleven different competency areas including:

1. Personal competencies.
2. Administration and leadership.
3. Evaluation and development of programs.
4. Teacher recruitment and selection.
5. Motivating professional development of staff.
6. Supervision.
7. Budget and finance.
8. Research.
9. Coordination with community agencies.
10. Legislative procedures.
11. Public relations.

The committee indicated that the director (administrative type) directs, guides, integrates a well-organized and highly complex program of special education and guides the supervisors, while the supervisor assists and guides teachers to carry out an effective program. In their study, Mackie and Engel found that the most highly valued ability of the director is the ability to give leadership to the entire special education program, to select qualified staff, to relate the special education program to the regular school, and to cooperate with parents, while the most highly valued ability of the supervisor is the knowledge and skill necessary to consult with teachers about methods, teacher-pupil relationships, social and emotional needs of children, and to work with parents (pp. 46- 47). In their conclusion, the authors emphasized that "the effective leader is one who has a wide range of distinctive competencies in addition to those required for directing and supervising a program for handicapped children (p. 46)." However, they did indicate that directors and supervisors do have different kinds and degrees of competencies.

Voelker (1966) summarized the findings of the Mackie and Engel study and pointed out that the directors' time was divided among four major areas: (1) administrative duties including preparing and reviewing reports and budgets, interviewing applicants, setting criteria for membership in special class, and consultation with state and federal personnel and parents, school administrators and community agency representatives occupied 37 percent of his time; (2) supervisory and consultative duties including working directly with teachers and in curriculum planning and consultation with physicians, school nurses, curriculum supervisors, and regular class teachers and supervisors occupied 28 percent of his time; (3) direct services to children including testing, counseling, teaching, home visits, arranging clinic appointments, job placements, and follow-up occupied 13 percent of his time; and (4) miscellaneous duties including public relations, in-service training of teachers, study, and research occupied the remaining 22 percent of his time (pp. 95- 96).

Following the Mackie-Engel study and within recent years, a number of writers in the field became interested in the tasks and/or job problems faced by special education directors. Some authors spoke of the director in terms of his supervisory type tasks; however, most discussed him as being either primarily or purely an administrator. In these studies the main concern was with within-group problems and task delineation; that is, little mention was made of the task similarities of special and general education leadership personnel. However, several writers have discussed between-group studies; that is, those comparing the director's tasks to those of general educational personnel. Notwithstanding, implied in these studies was the belief that the director was primarily an administrator.

WITHIN-GROUP STUDIES
AND STATEMENTS

Although Graham (1956) emphasized that the director had varied roles and that he had administrative, supervisory, and coordinative functions, he pointed out that the director "is directly connected in his responsibilities to the chief administrative officer superintendent and is an extension of that official (p. 8)." Wisland (1962) and Wisland and Vaughn (1964) discussed a study involving the identification of problems of special education administrators and supervisors in terms of eight major administrative areas, listing the ten most significant problems experienced by these personnel. Voelker (1966) discussed eleven different task areas of the director in terms of overall administration of·special education. Willenberg (1964) outlined ten general task area problems which should be studied in relation to "special education administration." Fogle (1967) who spoke as a school administrator listed twenty statements and indicated that a training program should be based upon these. Taylor (1967) surveyed 78 administra tors of special education in unified school districts in an attempt to determine the role of the administrator of special education classes. The majority of the individuals held the title of director and reported that they participated in special education administrative and supervisory practices, even though only five held supervisory credentials and sixty percent held general administrative certificates. Taylor recommended specific training in administration, but made no mention of training in supervision.

Connor (1961), in outlining the "Administrative Functions" of special education, spoke of the leader as being an administrator, although he did point out that "some of the generally accepted responsibilities of (special education) supervisors will be considered under the administrator's functions (p. 11)." Brown (1967) in the belief that the director's functions were cross-lined over both administrative and supervisory areas listed the administrative, supervisory, and coordinative features of a good special education program and emphasized that a study be conducted to determine the values to be placed on each of these types of services within a school system.

Within-group studies and statements dealing with the "supervisory" functions of the special education leader comprise only a small percentage of the literature in the field primarily because, as previously indicated, the major emphasis has been upon "administrative" functions. Henderson (1967) distinguished between the two types of individuals by pointing out that as districts grow in size and hire additional personnel, specific tasks are assigned to administrators while others are delegated to supervisors. However, he implied that an understanding of the supervisory type position is essential because with the growth of the field, the present primarily administrative position of the director will eventually be handled by two individuals; the director as an administrator and a supervisor. Henderson, as did Wyatt (1968), pointed out that although in 1967 "administrators outnumber the supervisors by two to one," by 1972 the numbers will be equal.

Baumgartner and Lynch (1967) listed ten tasks of supervisors, many previously found on lists of tasks of administrators of special education. The most extensive study of directors of special education in terms of their being supervisory type individuals was conducted by Marshman (1965). The purpose of his study as stated in his introduction was "to synthesize, gather, and reorganize information relative to the job of Director of Special Education in order that a reasonably valid description of that job may result (p. 3)." Basing his study on the tasks developed by Harris (1963) he attempted to provide this job description based primarily upon supervisory responsibilities. He listed 91 responsibilities or sub-tasks under eleven major supervisory task areas, administration being one of these task areas. In general, Marshman found that the director's responsibilities span both supervisory and administrative areas. In conclusion, he indicated that:

> The Director of Special Education is an educational leader with many and varied responsibilities. The basis for his professional behavior is a body of specialized knowledge which he uses to create a general education program for a specialized clientele. To do this he interacts with the entire spectrum of the school system. His responsibility is not confined to academic areas, to curriculum, or to instruction, or even to administration. He must coordinate a variety of services — psychological, vocational, transportation, etc. Expenditure of funds, to be properly coordinated, requires his specialized knowledge. Organizing this job into a meaningful description is no small task (p. 31).

BETWEEN-GROUP STUDIES

Recent emphasis in special education administration and supervision has been upon comparing the tasks and job responsibllities of special education directors with those of general education leadership personnel. However, these general leaders have been primarily of the administrative type. Angellotti (1967), in studying the administrators of programs for the emotionally disturbed in Michigan, distinguished between principals on one hand and directors, coordinators, and supervisors of special education on the other in terms of what they perceive to be their most important responsibilities. Although he found some differences, he pointed out that in general there were areas of commonality. Hill (1967) developed the "Administrative Task Inventory" (ATI) which contained 55 specific administrative tasks. In administering the ATI to only directors of special education and superintendents of schools he found little disagreement between the two groups. Courtnage (1967) also used superintendents and directors as his sample comparison groups. He found strong agreement between the groups regarding their attitudes toward the internal responsibility and issues of special education administration. He also found that size of district did not influence his findings.

Edgington (1968) studied "The Administration and Supervision of Programs for the Educable Mentally Retarded." He surveyed five types of individuals in public school systems in California including:

(1) assistant superintendents, (2) principals, (3) psychologists, (4) teachers, and (5) directors of special education. (Supervisory type individuals were not included in the study.) He found differing opinions concerning the problems faced by these personnel, but that these problems were not unique to special education. Huddle and White (1969) circulated a questionnaire to special education directors, school administrators, and "doctoral students in special education administration." In this questionnaire they attempted to obtain opinions as to the nature of special education and the position of the director and they listed 28 tasks specifically oriented to special education. Individuals completing the questionnaire were asked to rate the tasks in terms of their degree of importance. (The results of this study, although not yet available, will provide additional information concerning the perceptions of doctoral students concerning the role functions of special education directors.)

TASK AND SKILL
GROUP STUDIES

The growing concern for a clearer delineation of the role and task responsibilities of special education personnel resulted in the creation of the Professional Standards Committee of The Council for Exceptional Children. In 1966, after a number of years of intensive work, the committee issued its report (CEC, 1966a). In the introductory comments in the section entitled "Administration and Supervision." The Committee indicated that "the functions of administrators and supervisors, though complementary, are different. . . this initial effort attempts to foster leadership preparation of value to the individual who has both administrative and supervisory assignments (pp. 48-49)." The Committee outlined fifteen major areas of professional competence ("areas of knowledge") and 79 administrative and supervisory tasks or functions which are dependent upon those knowledges.

Sage (1967, 1968b) utilized the CEC list of 79 tasks in an attempt to ascertain if special education administration can be differentiated from general education administration. He employed a twelve cell matrix consisting of Katz's (1955) three types of skills (human, conceptual, and technical) which was superimposed over the four major jobs of the educational administrator. These are: (1) improving educational opportunities; (2) obtaining and developing personnel, (3) maintaining effective interrelationships with the community, and (4) providing and maintaining funds and facilities. Sage reported that this matrix had previously been developed and used by researchers in educational administration to describe the proportion of time spent in task emphasis of elementary school principals. By comparing the results of this study (Hemphill, Griffiths, and Fredrickson, 1962) to the task emphasis ratings of thirty-seven special education administrators, all members of the Council of Administrators of Special Education (CASE), Sage found a number of "striking differences." Although total skill emphasis was similar, he found differing emphases within the four job task areas.

Sage then submitted the CEC competency list to twelve doctoral students in "special education administration" and asked them to classify the 79 tasks into the twelve cells. He found that, on the basis of percentage classification, the emphasis within the professional standards report was on technical type skills. Differences between the CASE members' percentage of time ratings and the task placement of the doctoral students was due primarily to the within human and technical column placement. He also found, as did Kothera (1967), contrary to the findings of Leonard (1966), Wisland (1962), Wisland and Vaughn (1964), Courtnage (1967), and others, that size of district was a variable which contributed to the results. Small district CASE members placed greater emphasis on conceptual rather than technical type skills. However, he did not attempt to differentiate among the CASE members or the doctoral students as to whether they perceived the specific tasks of the director's job to be primarily either administrative or supervisory. The 37 CASE members were only described in terms of size of school district.

Newman (1968) employed a different classification of tasks to describe the role responsibilities of special education directors. Employing the POSDCORB (planning, organizing, staffing, directing, coordinating, reporting, and budgeting) taxonomy she asked "special education administrators" to rank the importance of tasks within each of the seven areas. She found differences in ranking based upon such variables as specialized training and teaching experience. The most outstanding differences were found in the directing function which she defined as "making decisions and serving as the leader of the enterprise." This function may be perceived as one employing conceptual skills.

Kothera (1967) gathered 815 problems encountered by special education directors. These problems were listed by the directors as they occurred over a four-week period. He found only a small percentage of these problems could be superimposed over either the Wisland-Vaughn (1964) or Mackie-Engel (1955) problem and competency lists. As a result he developed a list of 20 problem areas (19 plus one entitled "no category") in which he found 95 percent of the 815 problems could be placed. He then extracted a list of 100 "Most Relevant Problems" from the 20 problem areas. In his recommendations, however, he stated that "the data produced by this study indicated differences between areas of special education administration. These differences should be investigated further (p. 53)."

A recent study by Sloat (1969) was designed to answer two questions concerning special education leadership personnel in Texas. The answer to the first question, "Is the special education leader's role different from that of general education administrative and/or supervisory personnel?" was obtained by comparing the task perceptions of these three public school leadership types. The second question, "Is there more than one type of special education leader?" was answered through the use of a hierarchal clustering technique which isolated two distinct types of special education directors, one whose task importance perceptions were juxtaposed to a majority of general education leaders and one whose self-ratings of task-skill importance was different from other educational leaders.

Sloat found that special education leaders were somewhat younger than the other two groups and had less leadership experience. Almost two-thirds in this study had special education teaching experience and more had experience in secondary rather than elementary schools. As a group they had more frequent contacts with many different types of professionals from other areas of education both within and outside their own school districts. Approximately half were males and the majority had been awarded at least a master's degree and had completed additional academic course work beyond this degree. They held more teaching certificates than either administrators or supervisors, but held few administrative and/or supervisory certificates.

The special educators in Sloat's study perceived all types of administrative and supervisory tasks to be important in relation to their jobs. However, their importance ratings of supervisory type tasks were not significantly different from those of general education supervisors, thus supporting the contention of Wyatt (1968) and Marshman (1965), and contrary to what has been implied in the literature, that public school special education leadership personnel tasks may be more analogous to supervisors vis-a-vis administrators.

The analysis of the task-skill perception ratings as previously indicated revealed two distinct groups of special education leaders. The first group was entitled "Special Education-Unique" (U) denoting the uniqueness of their task-skill importance scores. Members of this group perceived all tasks to be very important and in their clusters they outnumbered the administrators and supervisors, who also rated all the tasks as being vital, by almost three to one. The second group was entitled "Special Education-Combination" (C) denoting a similarity of task-skill perceptions with over 75 percent of all administrators and supervisors included in the study. The C group was further sub-divided into two groups, those with very low task-skill scores (CL) and those with higher scores (CH), but still significantly lower than the perceived task importance scores of the U-type leaders.

Sloat reported that the U-type leader might be considered to be a generalist in special education; that is, one who perceives his job to be equally important in all facets of job responsibilities in public school leadership positions. He tends to be older but has had less total professional preparation beyond the master's degree plus additional courses than the C-type leader. He appears to be more secure in his position and is not status oriented at least in terms of his desired title and in his perceptions of the nature of special education. He has had more experience in special education and his position has tended to be in existence for a longer period of time. He works primarily in small and/or medium-sized school districts and engaged in frequent contacts with high level administrators within his district and representatives of both universities and state departments. These closer contacts may be a result of either the size of his district or his perceptions of the importance of his tasks or a combination of both.

The C-type leaders' perceptions of their tasks being more closely aligned to a majority of the administrators and supervisors tends to support the contention of Howe (1960) who indicated that there existed a group of special education leaders who could not be differentiated from general education leaders. However, although the CL groups' task perceptions were generally homogeneous, the CH groups' perceptions of the importance of their tasks was highest in those tasks identified as being primarily supervisory.

The CH-type leaders tended to prefer titles which would place them on the assistant superintendent or director level. These leaders were generally employed in larger districts, but had only slightly larger special education programs than those districts employing U type leaders. Twenty percent of the CH leaders held doctorates. Members of this group, being younger than the U-type leaders, had, in terms of actual years, less total teaching and leadership experience although this difference was not significant. They had more frequent contacts with the pupil personnel director in their districts and with members of the lay public than CL-type leaders, but with the exception of these association and task perception differences they were very much like the members of the CL group.

On the basis of the results of the study Sloat recommended that in addition to the conducting of a more extensive replication study in order to verify some of the basic assumptions and results, modifications should be considered in university preparation programs. These would include greater emphasis placed upon the training of potential public school special education leaders to both use and understand supervisory techniques. It was also suggested that efforts should be made within all educational leadership training programs, either through formal courses, seminars in sensitivity type experiences, or in field training, through which leadership personnel can develop the human skills which are essential for the successful completion of many tasks.

REFERENCES

Angellotti, A. T. An investigation into the factor influencing the administration of programs for the emotionally disturbed — Michigan. Unpublished doctoral dissertation, Wayne State University, 1967.

Ayer, F. C., and Barr, A. S. *The organization of supervision.* New York: Appleton, 1928.

Baker, H. J. Administration of special education. *Review of Educational Research*, 1944, 14, 209-216.

Baumgartner, B., and Lynch, K. D. *Administering classes for the retarded: what kinds of principals and supervisors are needed?* New York: John Day, 1967.

Brown, F. M. The extent which desirable administrative, supervisory and coordinating services are provided in local special education programs in Alabama. Unpublished doctoral dissertation, University of Alabama, 1967.

Cain, L. F. General problems and administration of programs for exceptional children. *Review of Educational Research*, 1953, 23, 391-399.

Carlson, R. O. Common learning for all administrators. In D. J. Leu and H. C. Rudman (Editors), *Preparation programs for school administrators: common and specialized learnings.* East Lansing: Michigan State University, 1953.

Connor, L. E. *Administration of special education programs.* New York: Bureau of Publications, Teachers College, Columbia University, 1961.

Connor, L. E. Preliminaries to a theory of administration for special education. *Exceptional Children*, 1963, 29, 431-436.

Connor, L. E. Preparation programs for special education administrators. *Exceptional Children*, 1966, 33, 161-167.

The Council for Exceptional Children, National Education Association. *Professional standards for personnel in the education of exceptional children.* Washington, D. C., 1966.

Courtnage, L. E. School administrators' attitudes and opinions concerning public school responsibility in providing education for exceptional children. Unpublished doctoral dissertation, Colorado State College, 1967.

Culbertson, J. Common and specialized content in the preparation of administrators. In D. J. Leu and H. C. Rudman (Editors), *Preparation programs for school administrators: common and specialized learnings.* East Lansing: Michigan State University, 1953.

Edgington, H. J. The administration and supervision of programs for the educable mentally retarded. Unpublished doctoral dissertation, University of Southern California, 1968.

Erdman, R. *Educable mentally retarded in elementary schools: administration of special education in small school systems.* Washington, D. C.: The Council for Exceptional Children, 1961.

Fogle, D. The view from school administration. Paper presented at the 45th Annual Council for Exceptional Children Convention, St. Louis, March 29, 1967.

Gallagher, J. J. Advanced graduate training in special education. *Exceptional Children,* 1959, 26, 104–109.

Graham, R. *A guide — directing the education for exceptional children in a local school district.* Springfield, Illinois: Office of the Superintendent of Public Instruction, 1956.

Graham, R., and Engel, A. M. Administering the special services for exceptional children. *The Education of Exceptional Children,* Forty-ninth Yearbook of the National Society for the Study of Education, Part II. Chicago: University of Chicago Press, 1950. Chapter 2, pp. 18–27.

Haitema, J. S. Adminstrative research necessary for special education. *Journal of Educational Research,* 1947, 60, 628–637.

Harris, B. M. *Supervisory behavior in education.* Englewood Cliffs, N. J.: Prentice-Hall, 1963.

Hayakawa, S. I. *Language in thought and action.* New York: Harcourt Brace, 1964.

Hemphill, J. K., Griffiths, D. E., and Fredericksen, N. *Administrative performance and personality.* New York: Bureau of Publications, Teachers College, Columbia University, 1967. Cited by D. D. Sage, 1967, 1968b.

Henderson, R. A. Preparation of administrators and supervisors of special education. Paper presented at the 46th Annual Council for Exceptional Children Convention, New York, April 17, 1968.

Henley, C. E. Designing a college program in special education administration. Paper presented at the 46th Annual C.E.C. Convention, New York, April 17, 1968.

Henley, C. E. A national perspective-preparation programs in special education administration. Paper presented at the National Conference of The National Consortium of Universities Preparing Administrators of Special Education, Austin, Texas, March 21, 1969.

Hill, R. A. Tasks of the special education director as defined by superintendents of schools and by directors of special education. Unpublished doctoral dissertation, University of Georgia; 1967.

Hodgson, F. M. Special education —facts and attitudes. *Exceptional Children,* 1964, 30, 196–201.

Howe, C. E. Roles of the local special education director. Paper presented at the 38th Annual Council for Exceptional Children Convention, Los Angeles, April, 1960.

Huddle, D. D., and White, C. R. Letter and questionnaire addressed to all doctoral candidates in special education administration, Indiana University, School of Education, January 2, 1969.

Katz, R. L. Skills of an effective administrator. *Harvard Business Review,* 1955, 33, 33–42.

Kirk, S. A. A doctor's degree program in special education. *Exceptional Children,* 1957, 24, 50–52, 55.

Kothera, R. J. A criterion and set of reality based problems for simulation in special education administration. Unpublished doctoral dissertation, University of Kansas, 1967.

Leonard, C. E. An analysis of the graduate courses of selected special education administrators. Unpublished doctoral dissertation, The University of Nebraska Teachers College, 1966.

Mackie, R. P., and Engel, A. M. *Directors and supervisors of special education in local school systems.* Bulletin No. 13, Office of Education, Washington, D. C.: U. S. Government Printing Office, 1955.

Marshman, L. R. Job description for director of special education, Jefferson township school district. Unpublished paper, The University of Texas at Austin, January, 1965.

Milazzo, T. C., and Blessing, K. R. The training of directors of special education programs. *Exceptional Children*, 1964, 31, 129-141.

Miller, V. *Common and specialized learnings for educational administrators* UCEA position paper, Columbus, Ohio: The University Council for Educational administration.

Newman, K. S. Tasks of the administration of programs of special education in selected public school systems with pupil populations between 13,000 and 30,000. Unpublished doctoral dissertation, Arizona State University, 1968.

Reger, R. The view from school psychology. Paper presented to the 45th Annual Council for Exceptional Children Convention, St. Louis, March 29, 1967.

Reynolds, M. C. Foreword, *Review of Educational Research*, 1969, 33, 4.

Richardson, E. J. Administrative policies and practices of programs for the educationally handicapped in selected school districts of Southern California. Unpublished doctoral dissertation, University of Southern California, 1968.

Sage, D. D. *The Development of Simulation Materials for Research and Training in Administration of Special Education.* Final Report, OEG 1-6-062466-1880, Office of Education, Bureau of Education for the Handicapped, November, 1967.

Schwabe, Gladys J. The nature of administrative organization for the education of children with exceptionalities in the public schools of Missouri. Unpublished doctoral dissertation, University of Missouri, 1967.

Sloat, R. S. Identification of special education and other public school leadership personnel through task and skill area delineation. Unpublished doctoral dissertation, The University of Texas, 1969.

Taylor, F. D. The position of administrator of special education in unified school districts of California. Unpublished doctoral dissertation, University of Southern California, 1967.

Voelker, P. H. Administration of special education in local school systems. *Proceedings of the second colloquium on exceptional children and youth.* The University of Texas, 1966, pp. 94-100.

Voelker, P. H., and Mullen, F. Organization, administration, and supervision of special education. *Review of Educational Research.* 1963, 33, 5-19.

Willenberg, E. P. Administration of special education: aspects of a professional problem. *Exceptional Children*, 1964, 31, 194-195.

Willenberg, E. P. Organization, administration, and supervision of special education. *Review of Educational Research*, 1966, 36, 134-150.

Wisland, M. V. The identification of the major problems of directors and supervisors of special education in the thirteen western states. Unpublished doctoral dissertation, Colorado State College, 1962.

Wisland, M. V., and Vaughn, T. D. Administrative problems in special education. *Exceptional Children*, 1964, 31, 87-89.

Wyatt, K. E. Current employment and possible future needs for leadership personnel in special education. Unpublished doctoral dissertation, University of Illinois, 1968.

functions of the director of special education*

STATE OF ILLINOIS,

SUPERINTENDENT OF PUBLIC INSTRUCTION

INTRODUCTION

During the past few decades a changing social philosophy has pointed to an awareness of and a responsibility for each individual within a democratic society. The impetus for this development has come from many sources — national, state, and community, from professional as well as lay groups and parents. Because schools are an agency of the people, this emphasis on the individual has brought about changes within the school philosophy and, therefore, changes in the approach to learning within the classroom.

Compulsory education laws not only imply the right of every child to an education but also make school attendance obligatory. The present cross section of school age children in any district includes those with exceptionalities of ability and disability: children, both gifted and disabled or handicapped, with exceptionalities, differences and problems; children with dual or multiple handicaps as well as children with deviations which are temporary and which may benefit by remedial teaching. These children are in every school and at all age and grade levels.

Classroom teachers are trained observers of children and their behavior. They recognize the need for special skills in teaching the child with impaired hearing, with a speech problem, with a visual or

*Reprinted from *A Guide — Directing the Education for Exceptional Children in a Local School District,* 1956, by permission of the Superintendent of Public Instruction, State of Illinois.

involved physical impairment, with a reading disability, with neurological disorders, with social and emotional problems, with mental limitations. They also recognize that special skills are needed in teaching the child who is gifted. This awareness by teachers, principals and other school personnel has led to the development of special programs so that educational needs of all children may be met.

The educator who is interested in a program that meets individual needs should remember that exceptional children have differences that may vary greatly in degree and kind. In developing classes and services that include and provide for children with the more serious differences, the school does not want to interpret or use these services to separate these children from the general school program. Rather the special services make it possible for exceptional children to keep their identity with the total group.

In organizing and conducting the school so that this premise is realized, the following principles and procedures will need to be observed:

Any educational program to be successful must be accepted and integrated into the whole school plan.

Every child merits consideration as a total child.

Marked individual differences increase the need for individual planning and help.

Every child must be accepted by and integrated into the total social plan of the school.

Locating, examining, and programming exceptional children is involved and includes some considerations not necessary for other children.

The use of resources within the community and the school which have an unusual and different application to the exceptional child involves the development of unique professional relationships and procedures.

Conferences which are held to establish relationships and to give consultation to parents of exceptional children require skills, techniques, and procedures different in degree from the usual parent-teacher or parent-principal conference.

The accentuated needs of the exceptional child, whether his differences be physical, emotional, or mental, require modifications and adaptations to the curricula.

Equipment and educational materials unusual to the regular program will need to be carefully selected and supplied.

Transportation, rest, lunch and other special facilities which do not fit into the regular plans for the entire school require additional provisions for the atypical child.

Teachers must be selected and properly assigned. If State reimbursement is to be given, specific qualifications must be met.

Meeting the needs of children with accentuated differences requires the extending and correlating of in-service programs with outside agencies as well as with school resources.

The very nature of these children's problems and some of the unusual phases of their total program necessitate some different, detailed and additional records and reports.

Continuous planning and evaluation for special education include considerations common to all school organization. The differentiating factor is that special education deals with the planning for children who must be diagnosed and provided for in keeping with their exceptionality.

When an administrator considers these principles, he realizes the need for delegating some of these responsibilities to a person competent to direct such a complex program.

In determining the position of the director of education of exceptional children in a local school district, it is necessary to define the position in terms of his place in the school organization, his responsibilities and the carrying out of those responsibilities.

A director of education for exceptional children is a staff member of the school system who is delegated certain responsibilities for administering, supervising and coordinating all educational programs and facilities for atypical children. He is directly connected in his responsibilities to the chief administrator officer and is an extension of that official because his functions reach into practically every phase of the school program. The director functions within the administrative framework as established by the superintendent of schools to carry out these responsibilities.

A district must consider when to employ a director, how to establish the position and what qualifications are required.

When the school system and the community have become aware of their responsibility to ALL children and have the desire to serve exceptional children, consideration of the appointment of a director can be justified.

This position is established by official action of the local board of education upon recommendation of the superintendent of schools. Consultation with the state division of education for exceptional children in regard to the selection and employment of a director is often helpful.

The person directing the program of special education must be adequately trained and possess educational experiences and personal qualifications which enable him to give leadership to a desirable program.

SECTION I

CONSIDERATIONS IN ESTABLISHING THE POSITION

Any public school district which contemplates employing a director of special education will need to consider the range and scope of its existing or proposed special education facilities. The employment of a director may be considered in any one of the following situations:

A district having no special programs but being aware of the need and having the desire to develop a program for the education of exceptional children.

A district providing special programs only in one or two areas of special education, such as in speech correction and visiting counselor service, but having the desire to develop an extensive special education program.

A district providing special programs for large numbers and kinds of exceptional children and needing leadership to bring about direction, continuity, coordination and consistency.

The problem of the three districts is quite dissimilar. In determining when to employ a director, the district must consider its readiness, the number and kinds of programs to be provided and the political and geographical areas to be served.

CRITERIA FOR ESTABLISHING THE POSITION

The Readiness of a District

The philosophy of the local administrative officials and their interpretation of the communities' responsibility to exceptional children needs to be determined before a decision is made to establish the position. This philosophy must include plans for a permanent and expanding special education program.

In districts with no programs or districts with one or two programs, a director could be expected to provide leadership and guidance in developing a readiness for needed programs among the staff, the board of education and the community. From a time standpoint, the director should be able to bring to bear upon the inauguration and operation of the program all of his attention, energy and special training.

In districts with many programs readiness for a special education program may have been developed without the help of a director. The problem of readiness in this instance is related to the readiness of the regular and special staff and the administration and the board of education to *accept* the establishment of the position of a director.

The decision to employ a director should be made only after consideration has been given to the duties and functions of the director and to the place of the director in the total school organization, the reassignment of responsibilities that will be occasioned by establishing the position and the contribution that the director should be able to make to the total school program.

The Number and Kinds of Programs to be Provided

Although the position of a director may be considered by the readiness of a district, from a practical point of view some consideration must be given to the number and kinds of programs to be provided. When a program represents a minimum departure in organization, curricula and methodology, the need for administrative and supervisory personnel is usually based on the time required by the number of teaching units. The different kinds of programs which a director will administer must also be considered.

Each program for exceptional children has its own special problems and techniques, and good administration and supervision implies special training and experience. It is impossible to specify an arbitrary number of teaching units as a criterion without respect to the kinds of programs. It seems conservative to point out, however, that if a district plans to provide complete programs in several areas of exceptionality and these areas include special classes in two areas as well as speech correction, homebound, psychological, and/or visiting counselor services, and the total number of units equals eight or nine, then that district has a full time position for a director. Some indication of the number of units may be gained through the application of tables of incidence of exceptional children in relation to total school population. It has been estimated that from 10-12 percent of the children of school age are exceptional to the degree that special services are needed. (See appendix.)

In projecting the total school population in a given community it will be necessary to include an estimate of the number of children who may be transferred to the public school from private and parochial schools in the community. More definite information may be secured by actually conducting a survey.

After the number of children to be served has been established, the next step will be to determine the number of special personnel needed.

These criteria have been approached from the point of view of justifying the position of a director. Some attention must be given to the number and kind of units that a director can adequately and efficiently administer and supervise. A director should have the same prerogative of other administrator in determining this number. Any district that considers the establishment of the position of a director should recognize that additional special supervisory assistance may have to be provided as the program develops.

The Political and Geographic Area to be Served

If the school population does not justify individual programs, two or more districts may cooperate in setting up programs to meet their combined needs. If such mutual planning is done, it is essential that the director be made administratively responsible to only one district.

Transportation of children from other districts becomes a factor at this point. The "safe" distance to be traveled by the pupils will suggest the geographic area to be covered. This "safe" distance varies for individual children in different geographic areas. Here, again, the director may give practical assistance in working out these problems.

ESTABLISHING THE
POSITION OF DIRECTOR

After the criteria for establishing the position have been considered, three steps are necessary in taking action:

Use of Consultant
Service

Any district planning a special education program or employing a director will receive help by contacting the Illinois Director of the Education of Exceptional Children, the Office of the Superintendent of Public Instruction. Consultation with this resource will give clues to proper organizational procedures. Arbitrary standards are difficult to establish with reference to school size, area, population, number or programs. But the general evaluation of the need and scope of the local situation will be better understood after one or more conferences with the state director. Many problems not presently apparent may be suggested in such a conference, and many difficulties may be resolved.

Board
Action

The local school board is responsible for establishing the position of local director. The usual resolution by the board should include the organizational status of the position.

Employment of
the Director

Following the consideration of the qualifications of a director, the board should employ a director in accordance with the employment procedures of the local district.

STAFFING AND EQUIPPING THE
OFFICE OF THE DIRECTOR

In making a decision to establish the position of director, a district should make plans for supplying office space and facilities commensurate to the functions of the position. Items to be considered will include provision for adequate secretarial and clerical help.

Location of
Office

Office facilities should be in or near the school administrative or central office and near other special education services. Preferably, it should be on the first floor since many parents will be visiting the office bringing their exceptional children with them for evaluation and planning. A convenient ground level entrance will be serviceable to such patrons.

Equipping the
Office

The environment of the office should be pleasant and conform with the accommodations afforded other administrative personnel. The office should be equipped to meet the needs of this particular service. Provisions should be made for the storage of records and pupil accounting forms, space for typing and mimeographing and for small group conferences, a professional library, a private telephone outlet, besides the usual equipment to be found in such an office.

To provide for the needs of a special office, a suitable budget item must be included in the annual school budget. It should not only provide for office needs but include travel allowance for the director and his staff, and the establishment of a petty cash fund.

Only when these various items have been considered will the school administration have a reasonable expectancy that the work of the director will progress smoothly and effectively.

SECTION II

THE FUNCTIONS OF
THE DIRECTOR OF
SPECIAL EDUCATION

Establishment of a certain number of classes and adding a number of special educators to the school staff does not constitute a department or division of special education. A department or division of special education exists only when an acceptable philosophy of education of exceptional children is being practiced; when uniform practices and procedures are being followed; when planned, developmental, ongoing programs are provided; when records are cumulative and provide for continuous evaluation; when channels of communication which allow, and necessitate, team work are established; when the various members are well acquainted with each others' work; when all special programs are being continuously evaluated in terms of meeting present and future needs of exceptional children; when consideration is always given to the impact of a single school policy on special education; when all special personnel *feel* that they have the identity with a department that is an integral and vital part of a school system. The entity of a department is developed and assured only to the extent that the foregoing provisions are satisfied.

The functions of a director of special education are broad in scope "within the established policies of the school district." The superintendent of schools delegates to the director the administration, supervision and the coordination of special education. In order to carry out these delegated responsibilities, the director must have his duties classified so that he will neither neglect certain responsibilities, nor assume others that are not his.

ADMINISTRATIVE FUNCTIONS

The role of the director in the development of educational policies within the total school merits emphasis. Policies derived from an educational philosophy which includes special education provide the basis for the organization of curriculum, practices and procedures to implement the philosophy of providing for individual differences.

Responsibilities for Developing Policies

The director has a contribution to make in the development of total school philosophy. He should be charged with the responsibility for seeing that adaptations are made of all school policies to the needs of the department and suggesting changes or exceptions which will need to be made in implementing the policies.

The director should be responsible for providing leadership in the development of policies which are unique to the department of special education. These policies, which may involve the six areas listed below, relate to pupil and personnel problems not covered in general school policies:

Pupil personnel — (e.g., referral and placement of children in special programs, special transportation, dismissal and transfer of cases)

Class organization and management — (e.g., classroom organization, curricula, promotion of pupils, grouping, consistency of practices and procedures from school to school in each program, teacher and pupil records)

Cooperative arrangements with other districts and agencies — (e.g., enrollment of non-resident pupils, arrangements for sharing information and services)

Recommendations of qualified personnel to the superintendent

Public relations in line with general school policy

Development of new programs and extension of existing programs

The director has the responsibility for consulting with other administrators in the school and for calling regularly scheduled special education department and sectional meetings.

The director must have access to the superintendent of schools or such persons designated by him in charge of instructional services to secure his counsel regarding any changes in policy.

Responsibilities for Establishing Special Education Programs

The director must know the legal requirements involved in establishing programs.

He serves as an administrative leader in guiding the district through the readiness stages in the establishment of programs.

He initiates and revises screening programs for the continuous identification of children who need special education or services.

He helps maintain and promote improvement in the standards of existing programs. He reports to the superintendent those conditions which must be changed, advises him in the establishment of new programs and approves any changes in the facilities, location or organizational structure in any area of special education.

He is available for screening, interviewing and recommending applicants for positions in the special education program, who meet the state certification requirements.

Responsibilities in Placement of Children

The director has responsibility for the development of uniform procedures of referral, securing medical reports, psychological examinations, placement, and dismissal of children in special classes.

Most decisions concerning placement of an eligible child in a special class are cooperatively derived. In those cases where there is not complete agreement, the decision rests with the director to whom this responsibility has been delegated.

The director is responsible for the development of uniform

procedures for the establishment of case loads for speech correction-ists, visiting counselors, the teachers of homebound and hospitalized children and psychologists.

Responsibilities for Schedules of Special Teachers

In most school districts speech correction-ists and visiting counselors serve more than one school. In some instances they share the same room with other special services and personnel. The director is responsible for developing special person-nel schedules which assure privacy of facilities and the opportunity to carry on effective programs.

Responsibility for Completion of State Forms

The director is responsible for the initiation of the "Application for Conditional Preapproval" of the various programs required by the State each year.

The director is responsible for submitting information necessary for making out the State claims for reimbursement.

Responsibility for Pupil Accounting and Records

When classes are located in regular school buildings, the methods of reporting attendance that is in use usually satisfies attendance requirements of State claims. It is necessary for teachers of homebound students to keep accurate attendance records.

The same cumulative records that are used in the school system with some adaptations are used in special classes. Additional and detailed individual case records are required.

A coordinating file, a system of records which contains essential identification information on each child in each area of special education, is very helpful to the director.

Responsibility for Teacher Accounting

The attendance of special education teach-ers who are housed full time in one building should be reported by the building principal. The attendance of all special education personnel who are itinerant or part-time in several buildings should be reported by the principal of the school which is the home base.

In line with the general school policy, the director may have the responsibility for excusal of teacher absences and for securing substitute teachers.

Responsibilities for Transportation

It is the responsibility of the director to work with those in charge of transporting children who are in special classes.

The director is responsible for the arrangements of safe and adequate transportation.

The director is responsible for approving bills for transportation when other than school bus is used.

The director develops arrangements and contracts for transportation and tuition with neighboring districts who desire to enroll students.

Responsibility for Establishing Channels of Communication

From an organizational point of view the various areas of exceptionality — the speech impaired, the hard of hearing and deaf, the partially sighted and blind, the orthopedically handicapped, those with social-emotional problems, the mentally retarded, the gifted, those with brain damage and those with reading difficulties — may each be thought of as sections of a department. The director is responsible for establishing channels of communications in and between the sections and makes himself available to his staff as well as other school personnel.

The director holds regularly scheduled department meetings. These meetings facilitate the development of channels of communication between sections within the department and between the department and the superintendent and the total school system. They serve as a means for disseminating general information which should be of interest or concern to the entire department, and they clarify and implement the development of policies and procedures.

The director holds regularly scheduled meetings with each section of the department. These meetings provide a means for developing procedures, curricula, and practices, as well as a method for the evaluation of personnel.

Responsibilities and Evaluation of Personnel

The director consults with principals, supervisors, and the superintendent in evaluating staff personnel. The director's recommendations should be considered in determining whether a teacher goes on tenure. The director recommends and approves any promotions within the department.

The director of the department is concerned with the selection of staff who are personally and professionally acceptable to the department and school system. He is familiar with the nature of various teacher training programs. He has the responsibility for obtaining applications, interviewing applicants, and recommending appointments to the superintendent or the personnel director.

Responsibilities for Equipment and Instructional Supplies

Most school systems have an established procedure for the requisitioning of supplies and equipment. Within this policy the director is responsible for establishing a procedure which allows for his approval but does not impede the processing of a requisition.

The director is responsible for maintaining a permanent inventory of equipment purchased for special education.

The director administers procedures for the maintenance and control of all items of special equipment in compliance with the general policies of the district.

Responsibilities for Planning and Appraisal of the Total Program

The director is responsible for continuous re-evaluation and appraisal of the special education program.

He seeks new and better ways of improving: channels of communication, the curricula, materials and equipment, scheduling of classes, the inservice and pre-service training of teachers, record system and the evaluation procedure.

He utilizes basic research for better ways of meeting current and future needs.

He is continuously projecting plans for extension of existing services in terms of needed facilities and personnel and procedures as the need of the program may justify them.

He stimulates interest in the staff and school in the study of new programs.

He develops techniques of communicating to the superintendent, board of education, special and general staff, and the community what is happening and what should be happening in special education.

Some Considerations for Integration of Special Education in the Total School Organization

The director formulates certain principles that guide him in his relationships with other administrators, special and regular teachers, lay and professional groups.

The director uses vision, tact, initiative and courage in developing new procedures and in working through the many problems of relationships.

He applies to adults the principle of "taking 'people' where they are and going on from there."

He recognizes that success of a specific program is largely dependent on its acceptance and his ability to work effectively with other staff members.

He understands that disapproval of a plan for children may stem from a failure in communication, or from a fault in the plan, rather than from a rejection of the principle involved.

The director is aware that it may be necessary to delay temporarily a plan when it involves a principle that is misunderstood.

The director recognizes that his philosophy and leadership will permeate the total school system.

SUPERVISORY FUNCTIONS

The director of special education has a responsibility for promoting programs that lead to the growth and improvement of exceptional children and the personnel in special education. In carrying out these functions he provides leadership in developing curricula, materials and methods for meeting the needs of exceptional children; in improving the physical environment, in assisting the teacher in classroom organization, pupil evaluation and diagnosis; in developing a parent education program; and in stimulating and motivating leadership among his staff.

While many of the supervisory functions of the director will coincide with the general policies of the school, the director will be confronted with special problems in providing an adequate program for exceptional children. To this degree the director will need to be creative in delineating new procedures, while at the same time he works for the integration of the program within the total school. The director's supervisory functions includes the following activities:

424   THE SPECIAL EDUCATION ADMINISTRATOR

Fostering Professional
Growth

The director uses the individual approach in fostering professional growth through classroom visitation; individual conferences; encouraging professional reading and attendance at professional meetings; encouraging advanced study; participating in community activities; visiting programs in other school districts; and participation in general school activities.

The director uses the group method in fostering professional growth through staff meetings of an entire department or sections of a department; case conferences; workshops; general faculty meetings; parent-teacher association meetings; curricular development projects.

The director fosters professional growth in the orientation of new teachers to the whole system, to special education and to general policies and procedures.

Evaluating
Personnel

In addition to day by day contacts with the teacher which lead to continuous evaluation, the director provides for periodic formal evaluations which are developed during a conference with the teacher and eventually placed in the school files.

The director considers the principals' evaluation and the state consultants' recommendations regarding the effectiveness of special education personnel.

Criteria for evaluation of special education personnel will include: the teacher's ability to plan and implement the individual child's program; evidence of improvement of habits, skills and attitudes of children; understanding of a child's particular difficulty and responsibility for long range planning as well as day by day preparation. His ease of communication with the director, professional growth and enthusiasm, use of new teaching aids and summary reports are considered in evaluation.

The degree of acceptance and understanding of the program in the school system and the community's acceptance and understanding of the program may reflect an evaluation of special personnel.

Relationships and morale within the buildings where special services are provided should be considered in evaluating personnel.

Parental reaction and cooperation must be considered in evaluation.

Serving as a
Resource Person

The director fulfills the supervisory function of a resource person by: setting up educational goals and programs for individual children; procuring and developing materials; adapting methods, techniques, and materials to individual children; improving instruction and classroom organizations; grouping of pupils to facilitate learning, recommending changes in the curriculum; improving physical environment in the classroom, conferring with parents.

Building Staff
Morale

An important supervisory function of the director in cooperation with the principal is the development of staff morale. This is done through stimulating and encouraging personnel by giving recognition for outstanding work, encouraging leadership and independence in their work and in professional organization, conveying a sound philosophy, considering individual differences of staff, encouraging creativity and experimentation, supporting personnel in carrying out their professional responsibilities and conferring with teachers.

COORDINATING
FUNCTIONS

The effectiveness of a department of special education is contingent upon the coordination of the various areas of special education, the integration of special education into the total program of the school, and the optimum use of community and state resources. The director of special education furnishes leadership and works closely with school personnel, community agencies, and state personnel representing special education.

School
Personnel

The director works closely with school personnel in developing policies pertaining to special education, scheduling and allotment of time of special education personnel in a building, determining the location of a special class and adequate working conditions in a building for special education personnel, assisting in the selection and requisition of equipment and materials.

The director has a coordinating function by assisting in the identification of children in need of a special class placement or special services through setting up, conducting and cooperating in screening programs; arranging for diagnostic studies; and securing information necessary for determining eligibility and admissibility of children for special class placement or for receiving special services.

The director coordinates with school personnel by arranging for transportation, setting up and presiding at case conferences and following up on recommendations and decisions, interpreting the special education program and clarifying procedures for obtaining special education services, determining the readiness of a child from a special class to be integrated into a regular class, and participating in teachers' meetings and serving on various school committees.

Community
Agencies

In working with community agencies, the director is coordinating with school personnel by interpreting special education services available in the school, sharing information on individual children, becoming acquainted with the services rendered by an agency, establishing referral procedures to a community agency and considering recommendations made by an agency, participating actively in community organizations.

State
Personnel

The director works closely with persons representing the Office of the Superintendent of Public Instruction, Division of Education for Exceptional Children, by planning for official visitation of the state consultant by presenting plans and outstanding problems to the consultant prior to the time of visit and by assisting the consultant in scheduling his time to the best advantage of all concerned.

The director utilizes the consultative service of state personnel by obtaining recommendations regarding immediate problems, evaluating the existing program, assisting in making long range plans, interpreting the need for additional special education services to school personnel and parents.

The director considers the recommendations made by the consultant in the evaluation of an area visited and the feasibility of carrying out the recommendations for improvement, discusses with special education personnel in a specialized area evaluations and recommendations made following a visitation and makes plans to improve the program, discusses with building principals the consultant's recommendations for improvement in special classes and keeps the consultant informed of progress or improvements in a specialized area.

SECTION III

ORGANIZATIONAL AND PROFESSIONAL RELATIONSHIPS

To enable the director to carry out his duties, specific working relationships must be established with school personnel and allied professional groups in the school and community.

RELATIONSHIP WITHIN THE SCHOOL

The establishment of a good working relationship within the school system provides a basis for the director's work with regular and special school personnel and parents.

The Superintendent

The director of special education is directly responsible to and confers with the superintendent concerning policies and decisions relating to special education. He has regularly scheduled conferences and prepares written reports, in addition to sharing information and understanding. Conferences should be held both before and after written reports are presented.

The director keeps in mind in reporting to the superintendent the purpose and type of report, the necessity of brevity and conciseness, the inclusion of pertinent data to substantiate all recommendations, frankness in identifying and making recommendations concerning weaknesses in the program, and considerations for long term as well as current action.

Among the type of reports usually preceded by a conference with the superintendent are the following: regular monthly reports, annual reports, special reports pertaining to critical problems affecting the program, or pertaining to new developments or outstanding features of a program; reports and recommendations concerning personnel; reports presenting needs for further development and recommendations for meeting needs; budget proposals; reports pertaining to legislation; state consultants' reports; reports on research; and reports and recommendations evaluating candidates for positions.

The
Principal

School administration policies recognize that the principal is the administrator in his particular building. The superintendent will interpret the general school policies to the principal and the director. This will include those policies related to special education. All personnel in special education, including the director, when working in a specific building, are responsible to the principal of that school. The principal and director must have a clear understanding and acceptance of the relationship which must be developed to facilitate the effective operation of special education in each building.

Unless the related functions of each are clearly understood, there will be apparent overlapping of functions. On the one hand it should be remembered that the director is a representative of the chief administrator of the district in implementing and interpreting certain policies pertaining to special education in the district. The director will be alert in seeing that his procedures and practices in any building have the approval of the principal. On the other hand the principal will remember that the director has certain skills and understandings basic to his appointment that result in his being given responsibility for the over-all policies of special education in the district. The principal will, therefore, be alert to his responsibility for giving all aid to the director in seeing that those policies are effectively carried out in his building. Only as this relationship is clearly understood will the special program be correctly integrated into the total program of the building.

The position of director may be established by a Board of Education, the functions may be described by the Superintendent, and relationships may be described in bulletins in terms that are acceptable and understandable to principals and director, but relationships must be developed between people. Although this booklet recognizes the importance of the principal's role in facilitating the fulfillment of the director's responsibilities, the focus is on those procedures which the director will need to recognize or initiate in establishing a working relationship.

Major changes in a special education program in a school should be planned with the principal. The director is responsible for interpreting and clarifying referral procedures to the principal. Referrals to outside agencies are discussed with the principal. All referrals for special education services should be channeled through the principal, who is responsible for seeing that health history forms and referral blanks for the psychologist and visiting counselor are completed.

Each assignment of special education personnel to a particular building is discussed with the principal of the building.

Scheduling of special education services and classes is arranged cooperatively with the principal of the building.

Case conferences, following a diagnostic study of the child by the psychologist, are set up cooperatively by the director and principal of the building. The principal is responsible for notifying all personnel on his staff who are concerned with the child or family and who he feels should attend the conference. The principal shares the responsibility for decisions derived at case conferences and the follow-up.

The principal consults with the director at any time in regard to problems involving special education personnel, children in special classes or parents of these children.

The principal, together with the director, is responsible for recommending a physical set-up, materials and equipment conducive to a good special education program.

Working out problems of transportation for special classes becomes the joint responsibility of the director and principal.

The
Classroom Teacher

The classroom teacher is the key person in identifying and referring children who are in need of special education services.

The director serves as a consultant to the classroom teacher in regard to children who may be in need of a special class placement or service. Arrangements for this consultation should be planned with the principal. The director in cooperation with the principal interprets policies related to all areas of special education to the teacher.

The director sees that the classroom teacher receives, when possible, professional service requested of special education personnel.

The director includes the regular classroom teacher in the planning of an educational program for the atypical child and provides help in understanding the problems of the exceptional child who is being integrated into his program.

The director with the principal, the special teacher, and the regular teacher evaluates the readiness of an exceptional child to be integrated into a regular classroom program.

The Special Teacher and
Other Special Education Staff

Personnel in special education are considered members of the staff of the particular schools where they are assigned as well as members of the special education department and are directly responsible to the principal while working in that particular building. They attend building meetings and general teachers meetings. In addition they meet with the special education department personnel and have regular meetings with the director in their own specialized areas. The director has a responsibility for the quality of service given by special education personnel.

The Special
Class Teacher

The director is responsible for initiating, planning, and conducting staff meetings; conducting workshops; arranging for visitations; encouraging attendance at professional meetings; helping individuals plan their own long-range programs for professional growth and development; and encouraging personnel to engage in professional writing and research.

The director acts as consultant for the improvement of the curriculum and assists the teacher in working out programs for individual children. This includes not only the curriculum while the child is in the special program, but also plans for his return to the regular class and follow up with the regular class teacher.

He assists the special teacher in determining what referrals should be made.

The director arranges case conferences for the purpose of sharing with the special teacher information concerning new children admitted to his class.

The director plans an effective parent education program with the special teacher and helps deal with problems involving parents.

He assists in setting up a system of keeping records and in making out requisitions for special equipment and materials.

The director plans conferences with the principal, special teachers, regular teachers, and other school personnel for the purpose of planning ways of integrating the exceptional child in a regular class and in the school. He orients new teachers to the school system and particularly to the special education program.

The Teacher of
the Homebound

The director has conferences with the classroom teacher and other school personnel for the purpose of sharing information (1) that the teacher of the homebound will know as much about the child as possible before she begins work with him, (2) that the classroom teacher will have information before the child is returned to the regular grade.

The director helps the teacher of the homebound plan a program for each individual child and assists in obtaining teaching materials, school records and supplies.

The director obtains information from the child's doctor from time to time which enables the teacher of the homebound child to understand better the handicapping condition and to adjust her instruction to fit the needs of the pupil.

The director helps the teacher of the homebound child with problems involving parents.

The Speech
Correctionist

The director helps the correctionist carry out survey procedures for locating cases.

The director assists the correctionist in interpreting the speech correction program to school personnel and parents.

The director works with the correctionist to improve the system of records and in reporting pupil progress to parents, teachers and principals.

The director acts as a consultant with reference to reporting to and working with parents.

The director has regularly scheduled conferences with the correctionist for the purpose of discussing and improving service.

The director plans with the principal so that the correctionist has an adequate physical set-up and educational materials for working with children.

The Visiting
Counselor

The visiting counselor utilizes case work methods to help children make a better adjustment to school. The director assigns visiting counselors to buildings and assists in interpreting the service to state personnel.

He develops an in-service training program for counselors.

The director supervises the establishment and operation of an adequate system of record keeping.

He helps the counselor make plans for particular children with whom the counselor is working.

The director orients new counselors to the public school system.

He plans with the principal for adequate physical facilities and materials to aid the visiting counselor in working with children.

The
Psychologist

The psychologist is a specialist in the evaluation of intellectual, emotional, social and educational development and adjustment. He has the responsibility for making decisions as to eligibility of children for special classes, for interpreting clinical findings to parents and school personnel and for serving as consultant to the classroom teacher.

The director shares with other school personnel the responsibility for selecting cases for referral to the psychologist and obtaining information necessary to make a complete diagnostic study.

The director arranges for and presides at staff conferences which follow the psychological examination of a child and together with the principal includes all personnel who are concerned with the child. After the staff conference the director makes referrals to outside agencies when the need is indicated.

He helps to interpret the services of the psychologist to lay people and school personnel.

He plans with the principal for suitable facilities, supplies and necessary materials in the buildings where the phycologist is testing.

Supervisors of Specific Areas
of Special Education

Some districts have felt a need for supervisors in some areas of special education. Such supervisors are responsible to the director of special education. While the supervisor is not an administrator, he does make recommendations which may lead to administrative action.

The director plans with the supervisor assignments of special education personnel in buildings, setting-up regular staff meetings and in-service training programs, and interpretation of the program to lay people and school personnel.

The director, supervisor and principals discuss the service rendered in a school and the effectiveness of special education personnel in a building.

He conducts regular conferences with the supervisor concerning solutions to problems and ways of improving the specialized area.

He discusses any changes in procedures in other areas or new developments which may have a bearing on the particular area.

Other School Personnel

In many schools there are music, art, physical education and other consultants. The director's relationship with these school personnel includes making known to the special education personnel the function of these specialists, conferring with these specialists to enlist their help in assisting special class teachers in their particular areas of competence, interpreting the particular handicap and needs of the exceptional child to the consultant.

Schools often have directors of instruction, research, curriculum, elementary education and secondary education, who are interested in the over-all functioning of the schools. They are interested in how special services and special classes fit into the total program of the school. The director of special education confers with them on such matters as interpretation of the various areas of special education, procedures for referral, integration of handicapped children in the regular classes, evaluation of special services rendered, curriculum studies, problems and improvements in the special education program, research requiring joint efforts, orientation of regular and special staff to the school system and recruitment of special teachers.

The state special education department, consisting of a director and consultants in specific areas, is responsible for determining whether the various programs in special education are meeting the standards established under the law. It has a major responsibility for assisting local personnel in the improvement and further development of special education.

The local director of special education assumes the responsibility for establishing a working relationship with state personnel; completing applications for pre-approval, which are routed through the local superintendent's office to the county superintendent, and thence to the State Division of Education of Exceptional Children,

Department of Public Instruction; requesting visitation of consultants to discuss ways of improving programs; setting up plans for official visitations; submitting credentials of candidates for positions in special education to state consultants for approval; participating on committees and programs appointed by the state director.

The
Child

Meeting the needs of the individual child who may profit from special education programs is the ultimate goal of special education. The director is responsible to the child in the following ways; providing methods of identifying the child who may be in need of special services or a special class placement; arranging for systematic collection of data with reference to the individual child which will form the basis for diagnosis and for the formulation of an educational plan for that child; arranging for transportation to a special class and for the services from outside agencies when deemed necessary.

The
Parents

Children usually receive special services and are placed in special classes with the knowledge and consent of parents or guardians. Parents, guardians and school personnel have a common interest in the educational growth and welfare of the child. The director shares responsibilities in relation to parents and guardians.

He interprets directly or arranges for other school personnel to interpret the needs of the child as revealed through careful analysis and diagnosis.

He informs parents about services available for exceptional children in the school system and outside agencies; sets up procedures for reporting to parents on the progress of their child; encourages special education personnel to confer with parents regarding particular problems of the child; confers with parents concerning admission to or dismissal from a special class; provides guidance, council and resources of staff for parent groups or organizations.

Health
Services

Many schools have their own nursing staff, while others rely on the Public Health Nurse from city or county staffs. In each case a cooperative working relationship is developed.

The director has regular meetings with nurses to discuss common problems. He cooperates in setting up screening programs for locating children who may have need of programs in special education and has the responsibility of working out procedures and cooperative relationships relative to the health service for exceptional children.

RELATIONSHIPS WITH ALLIED PROFESSIONAL PERSONNEL AND GROUPS

The director of special education has a responsibility for leadership in coordinating those services within a community that have a bearing on the problems of the child in the school. The director has knowledge and understanding as well as acceptance of all the disciplines which these agencies represent. A clear-cut plan of procedures helps avoid duplications and misunderstandings. The director establishes working relationships with these professional groups and personnel.

Professional Groups

The director needs to know what clinics exist within his community and to understand their functions. He needs to know which social agencies exist in the community, who are the personnel in charge and the types of service each agency is set up to offer. The director works with law enforcing agencies but avoids situations which may tend to identify him or his staff as "law enforcing persons."

In each instance the relationships involve developing sound, acceptable referral policies and procedures; cooperating in providing for reciprocal invitations to staff meetings; cooperating in interpretation and integration of plans of parents and children; establishing policies concerning interviewing children in school.

Professional Personnel

The director needs to know and to interpret the ethics and practices that exist within the specialized areas of the medical profession. He understands and respects what the church can and cannot do for certain children and families. In developing relationships with other professional personnel, the director is concerned with acceptable referral policies and procedures.

He develops procedures which avoid the possibility of several people contacting the same person for the same information.

He interprets special education to professional personnel to bring about a more nearly complete understanding of exceptional children's needs, abilities and limitations.

He attempts to bring about a reciprocal sharing of information which will contribute to total planning for a child and ensure confidentiality of shared information.

PUBLIC
RELATIONS

The director of education for exceptional children assumes a major responsibility for the public relations program involving special education and adheres to the overall policies of the school regarding public relation plans and procedures. In school systems where there is a director of public relations, the director of special education works closely with this person and cooperatively develops a public relations program for special education. The director should be well-informed regarding public relations plans in all areas of the school and promotes them for the whole system as well as for the special education program.

To inform the patrons of the school system of the current developments and of the need for future development and improvements in the program, the director utilizes various methods and techniques. Here are listed some of the different types of media to be used in working out a public relations program:

Newspapers

The wise use of the newspaper serves an important part in a public relations program. The newspaper offers an excellent medium and provides a permanent record of special education activities. The local newspaper staff may be invited to make a tour of the schools and observe special education activities. Conferences should be scheduled with reporters to keep them informed of new developments in the program. Guidance in choosing pictures of activities which will interpret special education to the public should be given to photographers.

The director is further concerned with obtaining parental permission when pictures are taken of children and clearing all stories or editorials on special education with the school superintendent.

Radio and Television

Radio and television offer a method to reach a large number of people. The effect of these two media can be greatly broadened by advance notices to the public of the hour and time such programs are scheduled as well as some information regarding the nature of the program.

In this area the director suggests panel type programs or informal discussions of a specific area or problem. He should encourage parents and professional persons from other disciplines to participate on such programs along with special education personnel.

He utilizes teacher-pupil demonstrations to show special methods and secures parental approval prior to a child's appearance on television.

Community Groups

Community organizations are a functional part of the community. It is well to keep them informed of the work being done in the schools. Strong support for the special education program can be built with influential and interested community leaders.

With these groups the director participates in programs regarding special education, arranges for visitations to the schools and participates on committees and in community projects to increase understanding and support of the program.

Social Agencies

Many professional people are extremely interested in special education. They want to know the resources available for exceptional children and to make wise use of these facilities. The council of social agencies is in an excellent position to interpret the program.

To aid in this interpretation, the director plans visitation tours of special education classes and interprets their services; invites agencies to discuss policies in which they are involved; informs agencies regarding radio and television programs that might be of interest; notifies them relative to new or expanded special education programs; and expresses appreciation for their assistance and cooperation.

Parent-Teacher Associations

The PTA groups can be invaluable in sensitizing parents to individual differences and the need for special education for children who are exceptional. The PTA is one of the strongest supporters of special education.

In working with this group, the director cooperates in developing in the PTA council and the school PTA's a special education committee and serves as its advisor.

He makes himself and the staff available for PTA programs to give a balanced picture of all areas of special education which will include providing films, panels, demonstrations and visitations for the PTA council and special committees.

The director emphasizes the contributions made by both regular and special education to the welfare of all children and is an active PTA member as he serves on committees.

School Personnel

Interpreting special education to regular education personnel is vitally important, since it is the classroom teacher who identifies and refers the exceptional child for special service.

The director encourages teachers to visit special education classes and provides an easily accessible library of professional books and periodicals on exceptional children.

He makes available demonstrations, visitations, films and programs for administrators, supervisors and teachers and assists in the orientation of new personnel to the school.

The director reports statistical material, improvements and developments in the program to the superintendent, the board of education and other interested school personnel.

He participates in social activities which include all school personnel.

administration and supervision — cec professional standards for personnel in the education of exceptional children*

WILLIAM GEER†

The superintendent of schools is the chief administrative officer of a school district. He is responsible for providing appropriate learning experiences for all the children of the school district, including those with additional or variant educational needs. In small school districts, the superintendent may of necessity assume responsibility for directing the special education program. As the size of the district increases and the special education program becomes increasingly complex, it usually becomes necessary to delegate authority and responsibility for this aspect of the school program. This extension of the superintendency is then charged with the identification of unusual learning needs of children and the initiation and expansion of the necessary special education services.

The organizational structure for the administration of special education varies in school systems throughout the United States. There seems to be no single pattern which has emerged out of these organizational arrangements. In the past, persons designated to direct the programs of special education have been assigned different titles. These have included such titles as the director or supervisor of special education, coordinator of special education, consultant for special education, and assistant superintendent in charge of special education.

*Reprinted from *Professional Standards Project Report* (April 22, 1966). pp. 48-52, by permission of the author and the Council for Exceptional Children. Copyright 1966 by the Council for Exceptional Children.

†William Greer is Executive Secretary of the Council for Exceptional Children.

Special education has a jurisdictional responsibility for both elementary and secondary instructional programs. In addition, it often includes aspects of special services and district-wide operational as well as consultative responsibilities. The person who heads special education within the school system should have sufficient authority to carry out all of the responsibilities encompassed in the line and staff functions outlined later in this statement. This means that he should be at such an administrative level as to have opportunity to influence policies and develop the procedures by which progress can be carried forward. He should have access to and be able to utilize the full range of school services. Furthermore, it is imperative that he be fully prepared as a leader in special education and take the initiative in keeping his knowledge and skills upgraded.

The responsibilities of the administrator of special education will vary with the size and type of program. In some cases, the administrator may have total responsibility for the administration and supervision of all of special education. In others, he may be responsible for the administration of special education but may delegate all or part of the responsibilities for supervision. In these instances, persons with only supervisory responsibilities should have the professional competencies required of those in the area(s) served. At the state level, the administrator of special education may have total responsibility for all of special education and in addition may have direct or indirect responsibilities for state operated residential and special day school facilities.

The functions of administrators and supervisors, though complementary, are different. We are just entering a period when recognition is given to the need for specialized preparation of such leadership personnel. The trend is given impetus by increased school district reorganization, new state legislation encouraging the employ-ment of administrative and supervisory personnel, new federal legislation for the preparation of administrators and supervisors, etc. These have increased the need for a definition of separate functions and related competencies of administrative and supervisory personnel in special education, the certification of such separate positions, and/or the accreditation of institutions preparing persons for each of these positions.

Although later it may be possible to differentiate between the specific training requirements of special education administrators and supervisors, this initial effort attempts to foster leadership prepara-tion of value to *the individual who has both administrative and supervisory assignments.*

PREPARATION
PROGRAMS

To solve his problems, the administrator calls upon his knowledge of education, special education, psychology, sociology, political science, economics, the communication skills, and other behavior sciences. There is scarcely any field which does not have its point of contact with the school administrator's function.

Since the program of special education is an integral part of the educational effort of the community, the administrator of special education must have completed such preparation as will give him a broad background in general education. He must have knowledge of and appreciation for the objectives and operational procedures of the general school program. In addition, he must have such advanced preparation as will equip him to meet the educational and other school related needs of children with communication disorders, with special learning needs, and with behavioral disorders, and to meet newly emerging educational needs of children and youth.

The administrator must acquire the knowledge and skill necessary to carry out the various functions described in the succeeding section. It will be necessary to organize some of the content included in the various areas of professional competence into formal coursework. However, the nature of much of the content is such that it will be essential to utilize problem solving seminars, using simulated situations and materials and actual problem solving situations through practicum and internships. While the introduction to content in such areas as developing a research climate, redirecting pressures toward positive action, public relations, etc., may be included in coursework, the strengthening, of these understandings will come through seminars, practicum, internships, reports and professional writings, conferences, and committee responsibilities.

Broad practical experiences should be included in preparation in view of the differing responsibilities of administrators of special education as related to the size of the school system, the stage of development of the special education program, the changing role of the administrator of special education, whether employment is at the state or local level, etc. Since such experiences may be provided during the practicum and internship periods, it becomes important to distribute them at the state, county, and local levels of school organization.

It is suggested that the preparation program be not less than six years. The institution offering specialized professional preparation in this area should have the program necessary to provide the competencies specified in this statement.

Additional consideration of preparation in this area is found in the Chapter, Doctoral Programs in Special Education.

MAJOR AREAS OF PROFESSIONAL COMPETENCE

To determine the content which should be included in a program for the preparation of administrators and supervisors of special education, two approaches were combined. First, the major administrative and supervisory functions necessary for the effective operation of special education programs at either the state or local level were identified. Second, the major areas of knowledge necessary to carry out these basic functions were considered.

The following outline presents the resulting 15 areas of knowledge and the various administrative and supervisory functions which are dependent upon these knowledges. The quality of leadership which implies creative effort as well as efficient performance of routine activities should be demonstrated in these functions. It is recognized that this is not an exhaustive listing of either areas of knowledge or functions.

The 15 areas of content are not intended to infer course titles; neither is the outline to be interpreted as a recommendation for the combination of content into course organization or sequence.

1. UNDERSTANDING OF TOTAL EDUCATIONAL PROCESS

a.   Provide leadership and develop working relationships between regular and special education personnel
b.   Philosophy
  (1)   Develop a statement of philosophy which reflects the needs of exceptional children and is consistent with that of the total school system and acceptable to the community
  (2)   Promote understanding and acceptance of this philosophy in the school and community
c.   Provide for the continuous assessment of the special education needs of the pupil population and supply this information to administrative officers for program planning and budgetary purposes
d.   Policies and procedures
  (1)   Develop policies and procedures which reflect the philosophy

    (2) Continually evaluate and modify policies and procedures based on new knowledge and changing needs

e.   Participate as a member of the total school system

f.   Represent employer at various meetings

2. KNOWLEDGE OF SCHOOL ORGANIZATION AND ADMINISTRATIVE PRACTICES

a.   Provide for effective organization and administration of special education programs within and among school districts, including cooperative arrangements and residential programs where indicated

b.   Determine class size and case load

c.   Develop schedules for special educational personnel

d.   Employ sound personnel and office management principles with professional or nonprofessional persons

e.   Insure effective staff utilization

f.   Develop procedures for selection and inventory of books, equipment, supplies, and other instructional materials

g.   Develop appropriate record and report forms

h.   Prepare reports to superintendent, board of education, and others

i.   Develop appropriate publications, brochures, and other materials

3. KNOWLEDGE OF VARIOUS ADMINISTRATIVE PROVISIONS

a.   Provide for continuing placement, replacement, and dismissal

b.   Provide for ancillary services

c.   Provide for adequate guidance, placement, and follow-up services

d.   Assess transportation needs

e.   Determine best transportation means

f.   Arrange appropriate transportation schedules

g.   Provide necessary personnel to insure safety of children

4. KNOWLEDGE OF FISCAL PROCEDURES

a.   Maintain inventories

b.   Prepare budgets with supportive data

c.   Develop and process forms and reports

d.   Administer local budget

e.   Administer state reimbursement program

f.   Administer federally funded programs

5. KNOWLEDGE OF
CURRICULUM DEVELOPMENT AND
METHODOLOGY

a. Provide for appropriate methodology of teaching various exceptional children
b. Develop appropriate curriculum guides, courses of instruction, and methods
c. Plan for continuous evaluation of and experimentation with curriculum and methodology
d. Develop publications, brochures, and other materials
e. Utilize appropriate resource and consultant help

6. KNOWLEDGE OF
SUPERVISORY PRACTICES AND
THEORY AND TECHNIQUES OF
STAFF DEVELOPMENT

a. Identify needs for and conduct inservice training
b. Develop channels of communication (for example, staff meetings, individual conferences, "brain storming sessions," and seminars)
c. Make recommendations on groupings and organization for instruction
d. Provide for the improvement of instruction through classroom visitation and consultative services to personnel
e. Develop appropriate publications, brochures, and other materials
f. Develop and implement a state plan for federal programs for preparation of professional personnel

7. KNOWLEDGE OF
PSYCHOEDUCATIONAL AND
OTHER DIAGNOSTIC PROCEDURES

a. Develop procedures for identifying children for program
b. Determine eligibility
c. Evaluate pupil progress
d. Refer to appropriate agencies
e. Interpret medical, psychological, and other reports
f. Develop appropriate publications, brochures, and other materials
g. Maintain appropriate pupil records
h. Assist other personnel (teachers, principals, etc.) in techniques for the identification of children with special needs

8. KNOWLEDGE OF
PERSONNEL PRACTICES

a. Plan for recruitment, placement, and transfer of teachers
b. Assist in evaluating personnel
c. Identify persons for promotion possibilities
d. Provide consultative service on personnel problems
e. Build staff morale
f. Maintain personnel records

9. KNOWLEDGE AND UTILIZATION OF
COMMUNITY ORGANIZATIONS AND RESOURCES

a. Refer to appropriate agencies
b. Coordinate relationships between special education programs and other related agencies
c. Encourage and assist cooperative planning and development of centers for preparation of special education personnel

10. ABILITY TO IDENTIFY, DEFINE, AND
INFLUENCE THE POWER STRUCTURE
BOTH WITHIN AND OUTSIDE EDUCATION

a. Knowledge and techniques in directing group thinking and action
b. Establish effective working relationships with the various individuals and groups with consideration for both stated and unstated principles and purposes

11. KNOWLEDGE OF
PUBLIC RELATIONS

a. Carry out a continuous program of community education to professional and lay public
b. Develop appropriate publications, brochures, and other materials
c. Promote interest and understanding of special education through speeches, publications, news releases, etc.
d. Establish provision for the interpretation of special programs to parents of exceptional children
e. Establish channels of communication between the school and the home

12. KNOWLEDGE OF SCHOOL LAW AND LEGISLATIVE PROCESSES AND THEIR IMPLEMENTATION

a. Develop rules and regulations to implement special education legislation
b. Comply with and enforce state standards for program operation and certification
c. Stimulate the development of needed legislation and work toward accomplishment of this legislation
d. Operate programs as set forth by various school laws

13. KNOWLEDGE OF SCHOOL PLANT PLANNING AND UTILIZATION

a. Plan for initiating and providing appropriate physical environment in coordination with total school program
b. Plan for physical environment and needs of all children and staff

14. KNOWLEDGE OF RESEARCH TECHNIQUES AND PROCEDURES

a. Possess knowledge and ability to apply current research
b. Conduct and apply the findings of meaningful research and studies
c. Create a research climate
d. Identify sources and requirements for funding and implementation of research projects
e. Cooperate with universities and other research centers

15. KNOWLEDGE OF PROFESSIONAL RESPONSIBILITIES TO THE FIELD

a. Stimulate interest in special education as a career
b. Work with preparation centers of various personnel in special education by providing practicum experiences (observation, demonstration, participation, student teaching, supervision-administration internship)
c. Hold membership and participate in appropriate professional organizations

d.   Stimulate local participation, in partnership with others, in the development of personnel with administrative and supervisory responsibilities
e.   Evaluate college and university sequences in the preparation of special education personnel for certification purposes

the seats game — an experimental instrument*

DANIEL D. SAGE†

School programs for exceptional children have experienced tremendous growth during the past two decades. As in many other aspects of the educational community, growth has been accelerated by the input of federal funds. From the modest beginning in 1958 under Public Law 85-926, authorizing an appropriation of one million dollars for personnel preparation, subsequent amendments have extended and increased authorizations covering both research and demonstration, and personnel training, until the amount for the award year beginning September, 1969, totals 37.5 million dollars.

The proliferation of public school programs concurrent with this stimulation has created increasing attention to the need for competent administrative personnel to provide leadership at all levels and in a wide variety of organizational structures. This need is felt in the local school system, cooperative programs covering broad geographic areas, the state education agencies, various federal offices, and in both public and private residential schools. The administrative roles range from rather specific or circumscribed responsibilities for supervision in a single area of exceptionality to broad involvement with comprehensive services for a wide variety of exceptional children.

*Reprinted from *Selected Convention Papers, 46th Annual CEC Convention, New York City, New York, April 14-20, 1968*, pp. 194-203, by permission of the author and the Council for Exceptional Children. Copyright 1968 by the Council for Exceptional Children.
†Daniel D. Sage is Assistant Professor of Special Education, Syracuse University.

While it is clear, therefore, that no single job description can approach adequate coverage of the field encompassed by the term "Administration of Special Education," an attempt to respond to the need has been manifested in the inclusion of an "Administrative Area" in the federally supported training programs in special education. Program development grants have been awarded to encourage university training programs in this area, and post master's degree fellowships available have been increased so that during the 1967-68 academic year approximately 61 administrative fellows are studying in special education departments of 12 colleges and universities with approved funded programs, while an additional 26 fellows, whose awards were granted through State Departments of Education, are studying at a total of 19 institutions.

In considering this rapid increase in program development, it is immediately apparent that there is a lack of the basic tools and guidelines generally associated with training programs. As Willenberg (1964) has pointed out, "After more than a half century of public school programs for exceptional children, there is still no single source of comprehensive information providing a rationale, structure, and process for the administration of special education programs. Colleges and universities are preparing leadership personnel without the basic tool of such instruction — a textbook on the subject." To this time there remains a lack of clearly defined criteria for selection of training personnel in this field, an established curriculum for such training, and, perhaps most crucial, a lack of validated description of the competencies required in the administration of special education which are discriminable from those inherent in any other type of administration.

SIMULATION AS
AN APPROACH

Recognizing the need for both an instrument for studying administrative behavior and a vehicle for conducting a meaningful training program for students already enrolled, the author has developed a set of materials utilizing the simulation model and pertaining to one of the many roles subsumed under the general term, Administration of Special Education. The development of the materials, which came to be known as the "Special Education Administration Task Simulation (SEATS) Game," was supported by a grant from the USOE, Bureau of Education for the Handicapped (Sage, 1967). The choice of the simulation model was predicated on the belief that the study of administrative behavior in actual situations imposed severe difficulties due to the impossibility of providing either standardized or controlled conditions. Further, as a training approach the success of simulation has been documented by Culbertson (1960), Hemphill, Griffith and Fredricksen (1962), and by Weinberger (1965). A previous endeavor dealing with the application of simulation to special education administration was reported by Ray L. Jones (personal communication) in which the basic "Whitman School" material of Hemphill, Griffith and Fredricksen (1962) was modified to include an integrated program for the deaf. This material has been utilized in workshops focusing on the problems related to the administration of such programs. However, the orientation is from the viewpoint of the elementary principal rather than from that of the central office administrator and is limited to that one type of special education program.

The conclusions drawn by Weinberger (1965), in his evaluation of the simulation approach, pointed out the chief strength as being "high student involvement and motivation; provision for skilled practice in a real, but controlled situation; opportunity to compare administration behavior; and a change to test theories on real problems." The weaknesses reported were largely concerned with technical aspects of the utilization of materials. Recommendations for improved use of simulation included the provision of feedback on consequences of decisions made, particularly by a branching programed system of either a machine or manual type; the provision of greater realism through filmed problems in which the participant is a part; telephone recording and playback systems which would reduce the unrealistic amount of written responding which has been necessary in existing systems; the provision for administrative team approaches and group decisions. In the development of the SEATS Game the provision for such improvements was seen as a major objective. It was also considered necessary to orient the materials to a specific role which would have greatest applicability to the field in general, either through the selection of a role which exists in greatest frequency in the field or a type which carries the greatest degree of common elements with other roles so as to provide for maximum transfer.

High priority was also placed on the production of materials which would permit maximum utilization of the particular advantage of the simulation concept, i.e., realism within a standardized and controlled practice setting. The aim was to allow students and practitioners in the field to assume a role in a simulated special education directorship in a school district with given characteristics, in which they could react to problem situations presented in a standardized manner. In order to gain maximum realism, a simulated environment was created with sufficient background information so that participants could play the role to the hilt.

An additional prerequisite to the relevant utilization of simulation in a training program was the development of an assessment instrument for measurement of change in participants as a function of exposure to the training program, as well as a system for recording and classifying the responsive behavior of participants during the actual training process. An experimental edition of materials designed to reach these objectives is described below.

THE SEATS GAME

The SEATS Game consists of both background material and task inputs demanding problem solving activity. The materials utilize both written and audiovisual media with the major input of tasks taking the form of a communication in basket, supplemented by telephone calls, filmed classroom observations, and role played conferences. The content was selected with the objective of broad sampling of situations confronting the director of special education in a medium sized and typically organized administrative structure involving a comprehensive program of special education services.

The background material was designed to provide a realistic framework from which decisions and actions could be determined. Information is provided to establish both factual data and general feeling tone in order to enhance the participants involvement in the problem situations. Unlike previous school district simulations, the environment for the SEATS Game was not taken directly from any existing locality, but represents a composite of a number of real places and organizations. This composite resulted in a school district of sufficient size to guarantee the existence of children of all types of exceptionality, yet too small to permit independent operation of programs for some of the low incidence types of handicaps, and therefore, requiring cooperative arrangements which are characteristic of many actual special education organizations, and which constitute a major source of the problems peculiar to special education.

In recognition of the fact that community socioeconomic conditions have influence on the development of special education, the background materials were contrived so as to present issues for consideration most representative of those facing the greatest number of persons in the field. State laws and administrative regulations were simulated to represent a composite of those to be found in states occupying a high average position in terms of sophistication and development at the state level, but leaving noticeable room for growth and improvement.

The background material introduces the participant to the role of "Lee Blank" who has just accepted a newly created position as Director of Special Education in the Dormit Central School District (so named to befit its status as a "bedroom" community) in the suburbs of the city of Metropolis, an industrial seaport of a half million population in Jackson County, state of Lafayette.

An orientation packet contains a term paper entitled "Cultural Influences on the Development of Special Education in the Dormit Central Schools" which provides basic information as to the current status of the program and its relationship to the main stream of education in the district. Another document is the "Special Services Handbook" which serves as a guide to policies and procedures currently in effect dealing with the program, while a third document entitled "Education of Handicapped Children in the State of Lafayette" establishes the legal framework within which Lee Blank and the Dormit School District must operate. Other written material in the orientation packet welcomes Lee Blank to the district, provides updating information as to program statistics and personnel, requests an evaluation of the present status, and invites some preliminary goal setting.

A slide set with a tape recorded commentary to be used with participants after they have had an opportunity to study the written material serves to reinforce both the cognitive and affective impact of the orientation packet. Maps, organization charts, and program descriptions supply the role player with basic factual data approximating that which newcomers in an actual position would have. The audiovisual media, including taped conversations between significant colleagues in the environment and in which Lee Blank is a passive participant, exposes the role player on the affective level to the social psychological environment.

The task materials utilize a variety of media, with the written communication in basket (letters and memoranda) carrying the major load. Additional problem input is provided through telephone calls which Lee Blank receives from various teachers, administrators, parents, and ancillary professionals, posing a variety of problems on which decisions as to processing must be made. Assistant Instructors role play the initiator of these telephone conversations, following an introductory script with a general outline of alternative branches to follow depending on Lee Blank's response to the initial situation.

Materials are provided to initiate two case conferences in which Lee Blank must moderate a discussion between significant personnel concerned with reaching a decision as to the placement of certain children in the special education program. Additional audiovisual input is provided by 16 mm films of actual classroom instruction in five different settings involving five types of handicapped children. In each observation, participants are expected to practice observation skills, to carry out an evaluation of what they have seen, and to complete a written statement and/or a live supervisor teacher conference about the observation.

UTILIZATION IN A TRAINING WORKSHOP

Various parts of the SEATS Game had received informal testing during their development with students in seminars in administration of special education during the academic year. The total package was utilized for the first time in a two week workshop during Summer Session 1967. Twenty-one graduate students who had either recently assumed or expected in the near future to assume responsibility in an administrative position in special education were enrolled in the workshop. The group represented considerable experience in education, though with two, this had been limited to experience as school psychologists. Eighteen had previous experience in general classroom teaching, sixteen in special education teaching, but only four had had experience in general educational administration. Nine had previous experience in special education administration but in only two cases was this experience for more than four years.

In terms of previous training, all were trained to a certification level in either elementary education, special education, or school psychology. Most had some previous training in special education, with thirteen having considerable training (22 semester hours or more). Previous professional training in school administration was much less in evidence with only eight having any training and none of these over 21 semester hours.

The workshop content was organized to deal with issues in the administration, supervision, and coordination of special education programs in public school districts. The group met for 5½ hours daily for nine days and the SEATS Game was used as the central core of the entire workshop. Lectures and discussions dealing with specific topics were interspersed within the five packets and activities of the SEATS Game in a manner which permitted maximum correlation between the formal topic and the simulated situations. Content of specific lecture discussions included such topics as "Varying Roles in Administration of Special Education," "Organizational Structure for Administration," "Criteria for Evaluation of Adequacy of Services," "Supervisory Relationships Under Shared Responsibilities," "Observation and Analysis of Classroom Behavior," "Physical Facilities for Special Education," "Pupil Placement Procedures" and "Ancillary Services to Instruction".

Two instructors and a number of parttime research assistants were involved in the presentation of formal material, the handling of responses to written and oral aspects of the SEATS Game, and the leading of the feedback discussions which followed each of the five packets on which the participants worked when role playing the Director of Special Education.

A special instructional communications facility in the Newhouse Communication Center at Syracuse University was utilized for this workshop and provided particular advantages for the SEATS Game. The room contains desks with individual telephones for up to 25 participants. The telephones are tied to an internal dialing system and to two tape recording decks so that two telephone conversations can be monitored and/or recorded simultaneously from a control booth adjacent to the room. In this manner, the instructors who role played the "Significant Others" in the simulated environment were able to call each participant sequentially, interrupting his work on the written items of the in basket and presenting with an optimum degree of realism the kinds of problems which the telephone brings to all administrators. Over the period of the workshop each participant received at least eight of the twelve possible telephone calls included in the SEATS Game. As a part of the feedback discussion after each work session the staff was able to select certain phone conversations for playback to the total group for analysis and illustration of possibilities inherent in a variety of alternative reactions.

This facility also permitted showing of films, recording of group conferences involving committee decision making, and the recording of live teacher supervisor conferences which followed the classroom observation films, utilizing "simulated teachers" who role played the teacher who had been observed on film.

Of primary consideration in the entire activity was the maintenance of optimum realism for the participant while achieving maximally complete data recording of all behavior for research purposes in the analysis of the simulation game as an instrument in studying administrative behavior.

EVALUATION

In the development of the SEATS Game, a number of approaches to analysis were considered and attempted on an experimental basis. The scope of this article does not permit discussion of all these procedures. However, the instrumentation utilized to measure the effects of the workshop warrants description.

A behavioral choice test, with two alternate forms had been prepared to be used as a pre- and posttest in such training situations. The test followed a simulated written communication format. Four written communications are addressed to a director of special education, coming from a subordinate (teacher), superordinate (superintendent), and extraorganizational persons (two parents in different relationships to the director), posing a variety of problems to be handled. A series of possible alternatives for handling each of the problems is presented with the subject required to indicate his degree of agreement or preference for each alternative by checking a Likert type scale for each alternative. The 44 items of each test were initially developed and organized into subscales to assess the emphasis placed by the respondent on ten interpersonal relationship dimensions in problem solving.

The theoretical construct on which the test is based lies in the hypotheses that in his interactions with others in the performance of his job, the special education administrator is required to utilize in comparison with other educational administrators:

1. Greater involvement with groups of persons (Team) rather than with one person at a time or in independent activity
2. Greater involvement with persons representing disciplines or professions other than instruction (Multidisciplinary) and, therefore, relatively less involvement with activity limited to instructional personnel only
3. Greater involvement with persons on the same level of the administrative hierarchy (Horizontal) and, therefore, relatively less involvement with subordinates and superordinates
4. Greater involvement with persons in other departments of the administrative organization (Interdepartmental) and, therefore, relatively less involvement with persons within an immediate department
5. Greater involvement with persons who are outside the administrative organization (Extraorganizational), both lay and professional individuals and organizations.

The basis for these hypotheses and a more extensive analysis regarding them are reported elsewhere by Sage (1967), but the use of the pre- and postforms of the test in connection with this workshop served as one indication of behavioral change over a treatment period.

An additional vehicle for assessing the value of the SEATS Game took the form of an opinionnaire to be completed by subjects at the close of the workshop. This was designed to get at such factors as the relative values of each part of the simulation game, the degree of realism provided by the materials, the amount of time and emphasis placed on each part, the instructional approaches used in conjunction with the materials, and an overall subjective appraisal of the entire workshop.

RESULTS

The effects of the utilization of the SEATS Game in this training workshop can be considered under two general categories, (a) the objective data from the pre- and posttest scores and (b) the subjective responses to the opinionnaire.

While the validity of the ten scales of interpersonal relationship dimension is open to question and will require further study, the overall change from pre- to posttest of the workshop group as compared to the control group provides evidence that the workshop experience did indeed bring about change in the way participants approach the solution of problems.

Responses to each item of the test could range on the Likert type scale from 1- 5, with a 3 indicating neutral or intermediate level of preference for a particular alternative. On the pretest it was found that both the workshop and the control group made choices which averaged on the "stronger preference" side, with the total test mean for the workshop being 2.47 and for the control group 2.59. These differences between the groups are nonsignificant. As Table 1 illustrates, only one of the subscale scores, the same scale for each group, yielded a mean beyond the neutral position of 3.00.

Upon posttesting, the resulting mean scores for each group were compared to the pretest and the differences in means subjected to a t test for correlated measures. As Table 1 indicates, the change in mean score on the total test from 2.47 to 2.84 for the workshop group was significant at the .01 level. Likewise, seven of the subscale changes were significant at the .01 level and two more were significant at .05. By contrast, the control group showed no significant change of mean on the total test, one subscale change significant at the .01 level, and one at the .05 level.

TABLE 1.

Mean Scores on Pre- and Posttesting
by Scales and Total Test

Scale	Control Group (N-10)			Workshop Group (N-21)		
	Pretest X	Posttest Y	t	Pretest X	Posttest Y	t
Independent	3.50	3.10	1.33	3.27	3.69	2.42*
Dyadic	2.57	2.72	.83	2.58	3.26	5.44**
Team	1.87	2.05	1.25	1.58	1.95	2.31*
Intradepartmental	1.90	1.83	.30	1.82	2.41	4.96**
Interdepartmental	2.22	2.57	2.07	2.12	2.55	4.10**
Extraorganizational	2.42	2.62	2.14	2.13	2.54	4.78**
Multidisciplinary	2.19	2.94	5.45**	2.02	2.71	6.17**
Instructional	2.46	2.58	.66	2.37	2.82	4.66**
Horizontal	2.50	2.65	.52	2.69	3.00	1.98
Vertical	2.36	2.77	2.33*	2.35	2.97	5.29**
Total Test	2.59	2.70	.84	2.47	2.84	5.32**

Significant at .05 level.
**Significant at .01 level.*

Scrutinizing the direction of the change scores which were significant leads to some interesting conclusions. It was found that contrary to expectations the workshop experience did not cause participants to be more prone to choose avenues of interpersonal relationships which were consistent with the aforestated theoretical constructs regarding the administrative role in special education. That is, they did not show stronger preference for team interactions, interdepartmental interactions, extraorganizational interactions, multidisciplinary interactions, etc. Instead, they showed a definite change toward a neutral position throughout the test, indicating less strength of preference for any of the alternatives.

This change is interpreted as an indication that participants became more cautious in committing themselves to any alternative avenue of interaction and more prone to consider multiple ramifications of an issue and, perhaps, to delay judgement. In this regard, it was noted that the participants took much longer to respond to the posttest, even though practice with the familiar format should have allowed more rapid response. When questioned about this, subjects were quick to acknowledge that the workshop experience had caused them to consider more carefully all of the issues involved and to be less certain of shooting from the hip.

The opinionnaire, which was completed by participants anonymously at the end of the workshop, consisted of 15 items, 10 of which pertained specifically to the simulation approach with the remaining ones dealing with more general aspects of the workshop. A summary of the responses to the opinionnaire would indicate that almost all of the participants felt that the use of the SEATS Game had been a highly appropriate and valuable approach. Most felt that the in basket items were outstandingly or fairly realistic and that the proportion of emphasis on simulation within the workshop had been optimal. There was an expression of feeling that greater time could have been spent on followup discussion of the simulation activities but that the distribution among the various types of activities comprising the SEATS Game had been appropriate. It was felt that a greater emphasis on the oral communication situations and role playing in group conferences would have been desirable and that more time to devote to study of background material prior to attempting problem solving would have been desirable also. However, no one suggested that there had been too much of any one thing, so to extend time on any one activity would necessitate adding time to the total workshop.

Most felt that the classroom observation films, the role playing of group case conferences, and the telephone calls had been valuable and a realistic or very realistic experience. The minority who considered these situations somewhat unrealistic still attested to their value within the framework of training. There was unanimous agreement that the overall value of the workshop was extremely worthwhile. Responses to an open ended item at the end of the opinionnaire were highly lauditory, and suggested ways of extending the total time for future workshops in order to go into greater depth on some aspects of the total experience. The group was also unanimous in its expression that the daily schedule had been satisfactory and that the 5½ hour day had not been too long, given the variety and flexibility of activities that were included.

From the point of view of the instructional staff utilizing the materials, there was confirmation that the aspects having greatest value were those involving live feedback such as the face to face conferences, both group and dyadic, and the phone calls. Unfortunately, these are also the activities which impose the greatest complication in terms of time and staff utilization for groups even as small as 20 participants. Evaluation of the tape recordings of these aspects, which was largely subjective due to having only crude and limited analytic systems for this material, suggested that these activities were providing an anxiety producing but generally appreciated opportunity for the participants to play a role in which communication and awareness of the other person were the key factors in coordination, mediation, and persuasion. It was clear that the pressure existing in these situations influences responses on the part of the participants which are worthy of analysis on many more dimensions than those which have been developed thus far for using the SEATS Game as a research tool.

Fielding difficult problems coming from difficult people was seen by most subjects as a much needed and rarely available experience. One effect of the experience is perhaps best demonstrated by the comment one participant added to the end of the opinionnaire form stating:

> *I know I'm a good EMR teacher and because I've been asked by my Administration to help new teachers, I'm willing. I also know — this course helps me to make up my mind — I do not care to be a Lee Blank. However, I have gained insight into administration and the problems involved.*

The implication of this statement, when one considers the manner in which many persons move into the ranks of administration, may be of unforeseen relevance for the application of simulation procedures to training programs.

CONCLUSIONS

The findings from this application of simulation to a special education administration training workshop, when one considers the reports of previous uses of the technique, are certainly not surprising. It would seem that the simulation game is a "sure fire" technique, particularly when confronted by persons who are relative novices to the field. The significance of its contribution at this point lies in the fact that the materials described herein may provide a vehicle for training and an instrument for behavioral research in a field so far lacking in directly relevant tools. There is no question that the vehicle is at this point crude, but it is a beginning. On the assumption that the basic process of administration in special education would vary only slightly from that in other administration and can, therefore, depend upon using general administrative knowledge as a foundation, the additional specific content and specialized approaches provided by the type of workshop and materials described herein may do much toward preparing personnel to fill the role.

REFERENCES

Culbertson, J. A. Simulated situations and instruction: A critique. *Simulation in administrative training*, Columbus, Ohio: The University Council for Educational Administration, 1960.

Hemphill, J. K., Griffiths, D. E., and Fredericksen, N. *Administrative performance and personality*. New York: Bureau of Publications, Teachers College, Columbia University, 1962.

Sage, D. D. *The development of simulation materials for research and training in administrators of special education*, Final Report, OEG-1-6-062466-1880, Office of Education, Bureau of Education for the Handicapped, November 1967.

Weinberger, M. J. The use of simulation in the teaching of school administration. Unpublished doctoral dissertation, Teachers College, Columbia University, 1965.

Willenberg, E. Administration of special education: Aspects of a professional problem. *Exceptional Children* 1964, 31, 194-195.

part VI

facilities
and
technology

Although increasing in scope, depth, and impact, little of significance has been published relative to innovative facilities and technology in special education until quite recently.

The increasing impact that the new technology could have on special education through the student-subject matter interface is discussed in the first article of this section by Edward Blackhurst. The new federal developments relating to "Educational Media and the Handicapped Child" are discussed by John Gough and James McCarthy, presenting an overview of the federally sponsored Special Education Instructional Materials Center Network.[1]   James Wolf presents a series of traditional guidelines on education specifications for the design of effective facilities for special education. The last article presents priorities for action from the 1967 report of the National Commission on Architectural Barriers, appointed by the Secretary of Health, Education, and Welfare.

[1] A new name for the Network which more appropriately reflects the collaborative efforts of the Instructional Materials Centers (IMC's) and the Regional Media-Centers for the Deaf (RMC's) is a recent outcome. The Instructional Materials Center Network was rechristened the Special Education IMC/RMC Network. The Special Education IMC/RMC remains essentially a communication system, providing special educators and others with ready access to materials and information.

technology in special education — some implications*

A. EDWARD BLACKHURST†

Abstract: This paper illustrates the impact that technology could have on special education through the introduction of the student-subject matter interface concept. Various devices are described that could possibly be constructed to meet the unique needs of different types of exceptional children.

Tondow (1964) has pointed out the versatility of computers and has advocated their application to special education. He suggests that computers could be used for a variety of purposes including diagnosis of learning difficulties, motivation, tailoring instructional materials to specific needs, and planning programs for various types of exceptional children.

At the present time, computer based instructional facilities are technologically feasible. However, the major problem in their application is the determination of the appropriate display and response mechanisms which would be used in conjunction with computers (Glaser, Ramage, and Lipson, 1964). Glaser, et al. (1964) have coined the term, *student-subject matter interface*, to describe any device that is used by the student in interaction with subject matter.

*Reprinted from *Exceptional Children*, Vol. 31, 1963, pp. 440–456, by permission of the author and the Council for Exceptional Children. Copyright 1963 by the Council for Exceptional Children.

†A. Edward Blackhurst, Director, Regional Special Education, Instructional Materials Center, University of Kentucky.

The purpose of this paper is to suggest some applications of the student-subject matter interface concept to special education. Considerations will be given relative to the programming of information and various physical designs of an interface for different types of exceptional children. Certain problems will be delineated that could possibly be ameliorated through the application of various types of interface devices.

THE VISUALLY HANDICAPPED

Visually handicapped children can be generally described as those whose visual deficit, after correction, interferes with learning. For educational purposes, two major categories are common: (a) the partially seeing, whose vision can be corrected to such an extent that ink print can be employed for their education; and (b) the blind, who cannot use vision to acquire education.

Current educational materials for seeing children are adapted for the partially seeing in the form of large type printing and/or through the use of low vision aids. Since there is no evidence to support the notion that partially seeing children differ from seeing children in educational achievement (Nolan, 1963), it can be assumed that educational programs for seeing children could be modified, as suggested above, through the use of an interface and be useful with the partially seeing.

An interface incorporating the cathode ray tube could provide a means for the magnification of materials. Materials of instruction could be programed in such a fashion that the student would immediately be able to control the size, contrast, and brightness of the image to fit his individual needs. Conventional instructional materials would receive wider usage than at present simply by televising and enlarging them. This would enable the student to read most books with a minimum of difficulty. Any aural programs for normal children could be used without modification.

Careful consideration should be given to the physical aspects of the interface itself. For example, green chalkboards are recommended for the partially seeing. It may be that reading materials should be projected in negative on a green background rather than the conventional black and white image. Children with severe visual limitations may need to be quite close to the interface console. The display mechanism, then, would have to be adjustable so that the child could choose the viewing angle at which he is most comfortable. The console itself should be of a light, neutral color with a dull finish. If the console consists of a keyboard and viewing screen, it may be necessary to mount the keyboard on either side of the screen to allow the child to get close to the screen without hindering his ability to operate the keyboard. External lighting should be carefully controlled for those who are sensitive to glare. Lighting controls, which would be operated by the learner, could be built into the interface console.

Instructional programs for the blind will of necessity be aural, tactile, and olfactory in nature. Enc and Stolurow (1960) have shown that materials presented aurally can be comprehended at speeds faster than the average oral reading rate. Information could thus be compressed and programed on audio tape. An automatic selection device could be constructed which would enable the student to make selections of appropriate materials and regulate the rate for playback. A large variety of programs could be made available by providing a central tape library and broadcasting station. Each student would be provided with a receiver and earphones. These programs could be used individually or entire classes could use them in much the same way as they would a radio broadcast.

Reading instruction could be programed on computer operated braillewriters. The student would be presented with a braille stimulus to which he would respond orally. Aural reinforcement or correction would be given with the student making the appropriate corrections as necessary.

Punched tape that is phonetically coded activates the keyboard of a stenotype machine that has recently been developed at the Massachusetts Institute of Technology (*Medical Tribune, 1964*). A blind person can be taught to read at speeds of 300 to 400 words per minute by feeling the movement of the keys with his fingers. Once the learner has become proficient in the operation of this device, conventional programs requiring reading could be adapted for the blind.

Mathematical concepts are most difficult for the blind to learn. The abacus is typically used in teaching arithmetic to the blind. Perhaps programs could be developed for its use. A modified Cuisenaire program could be structured with the manipulation board for instruction in algebra and geometry. "The manipulation board . . . is a surface capable of providing information concerning the identity and orientation of specific items located on its surface. This device would have the capability of providing information regarding patterns or arrangements of specific items . . . which can then be interpreted by associated equipment in accordance with a particular program" (Glaser, et al., 1964, p. 124). Equipment controlled three dimensional models would also be of value. Blind children could respond to the programs either orally or by using the typewriter. In fact, instruction in the use of both the braillewriter and the conventional typewriter would prove very amenable to programing.

The blind depend to a large extent on olfactory cues when traveling from place to place. A device that emits different odors could be used for training in olfactory discrimination. This would be a valuable adjunct to mobility training since the student would be able to experience many different olfactory sensations in the controlled environment of the classroom or training area. Devices designed for teaching auditory discrimination would likewise be valuable for training in readiness activities and mobility.

Parts of an interface, such as switches, that the blind child must manipulate would have to be either labelled in braille, be of various shapes and sizes, or be constructed in such a manner that auditory cues are made available in the form of click stops.

THE CEREBRAL PALSIED AND PHYSICALLY DISABLED

For purposes of this discussion, the cerebral palsied and physically disabled are grouped together since their educational problems are related to the physical aspects of an interface, even though they are two entirely different disability groups that require separate educational considerations. Programs designed for normal children could often be applied to these groups; however, adaptations will be necessary in making provisions for manipulations of an interface and for overt responses in cases in which an oral response is impossible.

In cases of bilateral amputations or where the learner has no use of his arms and hands, it will be necessary to design the console in such a manner that it can be manipulated by the feet, toes, or other parts of the body, Photoelectric cells could be utilized so that responses could be made by moving the head to break a beam of light.

In a personal communication, Godfrey D. Stevens, University of Pittsburg, suggested the possibility of a specially designed electric typewriter. A revolving wheel on which different letters are inscribed could be connected with an electric typewriter. For example, the quadraplegic could hold a triggering mechanism in his mouth. When the appropriate letter on the wheel appears below an indicator, the learner could activate the typewriter by applying pressure with his teeth on the triggering mechanism. This device could also be used by those who are less severely disabled by activating the triggering device with any functional part of their body.

Due to poor muscle coordination, children with cerebral palsy may have extreme difficulty manipulating various types of switches, buttons, and knobs that would appear on an interface console. It is suggested that response mechanisms take the form of recessed push buttons. The child could then locate the appropriate button, hook his finger over the edge of the hole, and depress the button. This would eliminate inefficient motions which might result in the activation of the more conventional types of switches thus recording an incorrect response. This technique is similar to that which has been successfully used to enable cerebral palsied children to use the standard typewriter. Templates are placed over the typewriter keyboard to reduce the possibility of the child inadvertently depressing the wrong key.

THE DEAF AND
HARD OF HEARING

Educational provisions for children with auditory disabilities are dependent on their ability to communicate. Two educational programs are common — one for hard of hearing children and the other for deaf children.

Deaf children are generally three to four years educationally retarded (Kirk, 1962). A contributing factor to this educational retardation may be that a large amount of school time is spent in developing speech, language, and speechreading (lipreading) skills. It is possible that automated instruction might be an important factor in improving educational achievement in this group of children.

Researchers in this field have been primarily interested in the processes and disorders of hearing rather than the effects of the hearing disability on school achievement and adjustment of the individual (Quigley, 1963). This preoccupation with disability provides educators with little information on which to base instructional programs. However, deaf and hard of hearing children have certain needs that could be met by programing and by adaptations of the student-subject matter interface.

Since the deaf child lives in a world of auditory language deprivation, it is difficult for him to acquire general language efficiency. An interface programed for language instruction would be valuable for the education of the deaf. Some preliminary work has been done in this regard. Stuckless and Birch (1964) studied the efficacy of programing for the development of written language in the deaf. They found that grammar could be taught through programed instruction in less than half the time that traditional teaching methods required. They also found that the grammar of adolescent deaf children, in whom language had been previously established, could be significantly improved through programing.

The development of speech is important for the deaf child if he is to be able to communicate efficiently with hearing persons. Since the deaf child cannot effectively utilize auditory feedback in developing speech, other cues must be employed. In considering a design for an interface that would produce adequate speech, the child would be presented with a visual stimulus which he would pronounce. Utilizing the visible speech cathode ray tube translator, the oral response could be transformed into a graphic pattern. A graph of the correct response could be superimposed on the student's response for purposes of comparison. Different phonetic sounds could be paired with visual symbols. If the stimulus is mispronounced, the appropriate symbol would appear as a cue on the display mechanism. The learner would then pronounce the stimulus until a correct response is elicited.

Speechreading, or lipreading, is another important communication need of children with auditory disabilities. Speechreading is dependent on the child's ability to analyze, in a meaningful way, various lip and facial movements produced in the act of talking. The child must learn to read all configurations of lips and facial expressions. An interface could be programed to display representative facial types pronouncing the same or different words and phrases. This would be helpful in teaching discrimination in speechreading.

In classroom situations, a communication problem is presented when a student responds to the teacher's questions. Very often, the other members of the class either misinterpret or do not understand the response.

This situation could possibly be remedied by using the graphic pattern detector (Glaser, et. al, 1964). The student could write his response at his desk and have it appear on a screen for the cognizance of the entire class.

The interface concept could also be applied to the hard of hearing. The majority of these children do not differ from hearing children in intelligence or school achievement and should be educated in the regular classroom (Streng, 1953). It is sometimes necessary, however, to provide special instruction in communication. These children need training in speech, language, and speechreading.

The programs described may be applicable to the hard of hearing with the exception that amplified auditory signals could be added to the visual cues. Programs designed for children with normal hearing could be utilized. An interface that would provide training in auditory discrimination would be helpful to the hard of hearing since many of these children need assistance in interpreting sounds.

CHILDREN WITH BEHAVIOR DEVIATIONS

Children with behavior deviations are generally described as being either socially maladjusted or emotionally disturbed. These are generic terms which encompass various types of rather complex anomalous personal behaviors. It is not within the scope of this discussion to dwell on descriptions of different behavior deviations; but rather to provide a rationale for innovations in the design of student-subject matter interfaces.

These children have difficulty with interpersonal relationships. This is particularly true in the typical classroom situation in which the child must interact with the teacher and his classmates. The resulting problems generally lead to ineffective learning — if indeed learning takes place at all. It seems likely that an automated interface, being impersonal, would appeal to such children and possibly be more effective than the teacher.

Quay (1963) advocates the use of programed instruction for the withdrawn child because it is highly structured, can require simple responses, and allows for a maximum of correct responses. In programing for the withdrawn child, it would be wise to use branching techniques to keep anxiety producing, incorrect responses to a minimum.

Teaching machines are also advocated by Quay (1963) for the acting out child. Instruction should be programed to provide more repetition than the ordinary child would receive. Quay states that these children are novelty seekers and as such, proposes the use of ". . . teaching machines which provide not only the correct answer as the reinforcer but at the same time light up, ring bells, and perhaps even shoot fireworks" (p. 30). The implications for the stimulus change capabilities of certain interfaces are quite apparent.

THE MENTALLY RETARDED

Heber (1961) states that "Mental retardation refers to subaverage intellectual functioning which originates during the developmental period and is associated with impairment in adaptive behavior" (p. 499). The mentally retarded are generally classified in two groups for purposes of education: (a) the educable mentally retarded (EMR), who generally have IQ scores between 50 and 75 and can obtain functional literacy but will have learning difficulties in the regular grades, and (b) the trainable mentally retarded (TMR), who have IQ scores between 25 and 50 and cannot obtain functional literacy, but will be able to attain self-help skills, limited social skills, and minimal economic efficiency.

Since the differences between retarded and normal children are primarily intellectual in nature, few specific problems in the physical design of the interface should be encountered. The most important concern should be in the programing of information for an interface. Therefore, the bulk of this section will deal with considerations in programing for the retarded.

Lorene Quay (1963) reports that there are qualitative and quantitative differences between the learning characteristics of the trainable retarded and normal children. On the other hand, Quay states that the educable retarded may learn some tasks in the same fashion as normal children but may differ in the way in which they learn others. This implies that, although some would require modification, programs that are designed for normal children could be used without modification for the EMR. Stolurow (1961) supports this notion. He states that wide ability ranges could be served by a single program provided that the learner has obtained the minimum level required for the program and that adequate provision for review is made. In addition, an interface might be adaptable so that different instructional techniques could be used with different students, depending on their performance during training. Branches could be built into programs to account, in part, for individual differences (Coulson and Silberman, 1962). Stolurow (1960) lists two additional implications in programing information for the mentally retarded: (a) The size and number of steps may be the same for both the retarded and normal. (b) An interface for the mentally retarded should be designed to provide for overt responses.

The education of the mentally retarded is intended to make provisions for individual differences. An interface that is designed to yield information regarding the performance of the retarded on learning tasks would provide educators and psychologists with valuable information, related to their learning characteristics, that would have implications for instructional practices. Thus, a major function of an interface would be as an experimental device that could control teacher variables, apply different motivational techniques, be used to study various aspects of learning, and provide a record of the subject's performance on the assigned tasks (Jenson, 1962).

More research is needed before additional suggestions can be made regarding programing information for an interface to be used with the mentally retarded. However, present understanding of the learning behavior of the mentally retarded may have implications for programing. Methods advocated by most teachers include the use of meaningful materials, conscious assistance in transfer of training, repetition of concepts in a wide range of situations, verbal mediation of concepts, spaced rather than massed practice, overlearning, and immediate reinforcement. Although many of these learning principles apply to normal children, all a₁ ₋f particular importance to the education of the retarded and should be considered in programing specifically for them.

Studies have not shown that the learning characteristics of brain injured children differ from those of retarded children with other etiologies (Lorene Quay, 1963). However, some educators believe that special teaching techniques should be utilized with brain injured retarded children. Strauss and Lehtinen (1947) proposed three principles for the education of brain injured children: (a) Reduce the space in which the learning situation takes place. (b) Control distracting stimuli. (c) Information to be learned should be presented so that it receives the child's full attention.

Gallagher (1960) proposed that the brain injured child should be provided with an individual tutor for the most effective education. An interface could be constructed to incorporate both of these views. The interface could be located in a student office that is free from distracting stimuli and could be constructed in such a manner that attention would be focused only on the display and response mechanisms.

Classical conditioning is quite effective in training the TMR and programs could be developed along the lines of this methodology. O'Connor and Hermalin (1963) have shown that conditioning can be used effectively in training the TMR to read simple words. Programs could be developed for teaching a protective reading vocabulary following a classical conditioning paradigm. For example, the word, danger, would appear on the display mechanism. The child would hear the word pronounced and would, in turn, be required to pronounce it. He would then receive a reward. This process would be repeated until the child responds to the written word without hearing the pronounciation. Pictures of dangerous situations incorporating danger signs could be used as stimuli in order to place the concept in its proper context.

Clarke (1958) lists several principles, based on research conclusions, that are applicable to the training of the TMR. Among these, (a) meaningful visual incentives should be employed; (b) tasks should be divided into their simplest components; (c) correct movements should be stressed; (d) tasks should be over learned; (e) emphasis should be on accuracy rather than speed; (f) learning should be spaced rather than massed; and (g) verbalization of concepts the child learns should be stressed for effective learning. These principles should be considered when developing programs for the TMR.

Training programs for the TMR often culminate in their placement in a sheltered workshop. The tasks performed in these workshops are manual in nature. Interface devices could be developed to provide training in manual manipulation and neuromuscular integration.

LEARNING DISABILITIES

Perhaps one of the more valuable functions of an interface would be as a tool for the diagnosis and remediation of learning disabilities. "A learning disability refers to a retardation, disorder, or delayed development in one or more of the processes of speech, language, reading, writing, arithmetic, or other school subjects resulting from a psychological handicap caused by a possible cerebral dysfunction and/or emotional or behavioral disturbances and not the result of mental retardation, sensory deprivation, or cultural or instructional factors" (Kirk, 1962, p. 263). A child is classified as having a reading disability if, for example, he has the intellectual capacity to learn to read, but does not learn with ordinary instruction.

A computer operated interface could possibly be designed to diagnose learning disabilities. All available information concerning various learning disabilities could be stored in the computer. The interface would be programed to administer a battery of diagnostic tests and record the results. The computer would then analyze these results on the basis of the stored information and make a diagnosis of the specific learning disability and suggest a program for its amelioration. Special programs would be designed to remedy different learning disabilities.

THE MENTALLY ADVANCED

The mentally advanced, or gifted, are one of the nation's greatest resources. Capable of being future leaders, they constitute the raw materials for building a greater nation and a more advanced civilization. It is the function of the school to provide activities that will bring the special abilities of the mentally advanced to fruition.

Enrichment is usually part of the educational program for the mentally advanced. This is the process of expanding the curriculum to provide additional educational opportunities for gifted children (Good, 1959). This is not an easy program for teachers to manage because they often ". . . do not have the time or, in some cases, the knowledge and skills to provide all the enriched experiences a gifted child needs" (Kirk, 1962, p. 65). Since these limitations do not apply to an interface, it would be valuable in providing enrichment for the gifted.

Acceleration, in the form of grade skipping, is another instructional modification used with the gifted. This practice sometimes produces problems because the accelerated student often has not mastered all of the skills taught in the grade which he skipped. A library of interface programs of various basic skills could be established. If a child was scheduled, for example, to skip third grade, the second grade teacher could employ the third grade interface programs during the school year. The child would thus be better prepared to enter fourth grade, as the interface program would provide assurance that he would not have missed third grade material.

One of the perplexing problems in education is that of the underachieving gifted child. Since many of the mentally advanced will be our future leaders, failure to develop their potentials is a waste of natural resources. One of the methods proposed by Kirk (1962) for ameliorating this situation is through the use of tutors. An interface would be especially valuable in such instances since it functions in a one to one relationship with the learner.

Previously in this paper, variations in interface design and programing considerations were proposed for the purposes of adaptation to various disability groups. This approach is not necessary when dealing with the gifted since they have few, if any, physical or mental disabilities that would warrant similar proposals. However, there are several characteristics of the mentally advanced that should be brought to the attention of the designer of instructional programs. These characteristics may have some bearing on the method of presentation, and content of programs designed for their use. Among these, Kirk (1962) states that gifted children (a) learn faster than the average child, thus requiring less repetition to learn the same material; (b) have superior reasoning ability enabling them to see relationships and grasp ideas more readily; (c) have a large vocabulary and good verbal ability; (d) have a broad fund of information; (e) have insatiable curiosity; (f) have wide ranges of interests; and (g) are generally observant. Student-subject matter interfaces, properly designed and programed, could show great value when used with the mentally advanced.

CONCLUSION

An attempt has been made to illustrate some ways that technology could be used in special education through the application of the student-subject matter interface concept. The notions presented here merely serve as a springboard for further thinking. The only limitations imposed are the lack of ingenuity and the sophistication of technology. While the preceding discussion may seem unrealistic to some, special educators deal with exceptional children and, in so doing, should seek exceptional devices to assist them in the performance of their task.

REFERENCES

Blackhurst, A. E. The student-subject matter interface in special education. In R. Glaser, W. W. Ramage, and J. I. Lipson (Editors), *The interface between student and subject matter.* Pittsburgh, Pennsylvania: The University of Pittsburgh, Learning Research and Development Center, 1964, pp. 157-169.

Clarke, A. D. B. The abilities and trainability of imbeciles. In Ann M. Clarke and A. D. B. Clarke (Editors), *Mental deficiency: the changing outlook.* London: Methuen and Company, 1958. Pp. 309-333.

Coulson, J. E., and Silberman, H. F. Automated teaching and individual differences. In W. I. Smith and J. W. Moore (Editors), *Programmed learning: theory and research.* Princeton, New Jersey: D. Van Nostrand, 1962. Pp. 207-217.

Enc, M. A., and Stolurow, L. M. The effect of two recording speeds on learning. *New Outlook for the Blind,* 1960, 54, 39-48.

Gallagher, J. J. *The tutoring of brain-injured mentally retarded children.* Springfield, Illinois: Charles C. Thomas, 1960.

Glaser, R., Ramage, W. W., and Lipson, J. I. (Editors) *The interface between student and subject matter.* Pittsburgh, Pennsylvania: The University of Pittsburgh, Learning Research and Development Center, 1964.

Good, C. V. (Editor), *Dictionary of education.* New York: McGraw-Hill Book Company, 1959.

Heber, R. A manual on terminology and classification in mental retardation. Monograph supplement to *American Journal of Mental Deficiency,* 1961, 64.

Jensen, A. R. Teaching machines and individual differences. In W. I. Smith and J. W. Moore (Editors), *Programmed Learning theory and research.* Princeton, New Jersey: D. Van Nostrand, 1962. Pp. 218-226.

Kirk, S. A. *Educating exceptional children.* Boston, Massachusetts: Houghton Mifflin, 1962.

Nolan, C. Y. The visually impaired. In S. A. Kirk and Bluma B. Weiner (Editors),

Behavioral research on exceptional children. Washington, D.C.: The Council for Exceptional Children, 1963. Pp. 115-154.

O'Connor, N., and Hermalin, B. *Speech and thought in severe subnormality.* New York: MacMillan Company, 1963.

Quay, H. C. Some basic considerations in the education of emotionally disturbed children. *Exceptional Children,* 1963, 30, 27-31.

Quay, Lorene C. Academic skills. In N. R. Ellis (Editor), *Handbook of mental deficiency.* New York: McGraw-Hill Book Company, 1963. Pp. 664-690.

Quigley, S. P. The hard of hearing. In S. A. Kirk and Bluma B. Weiner (Editors), *Behavioral research on exceptional children.* Washington, D.C.: The Council for Exceptional Children, 1963. Pp. 155-182.

Stenotype machine aids blind to read. *Medical Tribune,* 964, 5 (6), 30.

Stolurow, L. M. Teaching machines and special education. *Educational and Psychological Measurement,* 1960, 20, 429-448.

Stolurow, L. M. *Teaching by machine.* U. S. Office of Education Cooperative Research Monograph, 1961, No. 6 (Whole No. OE-34010).

Streng, Alice. The child who is hard of hearing. *Exceptional Children,* 1953, 19, 223-226.

Stuckless, E. R., and Birch, J. W. Programed instruction in written language for the deaf. *Exceptional Children,* 1964, 30, 296-303.

Strauss, A. A., and Lehtinen, Laura E. *Psychopathology and education of the brain injured child.* Volume 1. *Fundamentals and treatment.* New York: Grune and Stratton, 1947.

Tondow, M. Computers in special education — an introduction. *Exceptional Children,* 1964, 31, 113-116.

educational media
and the handicapped child*

JOHN A. GOUGH†

General educators have asked, "What is so special about special education?" A partial answer to this question is that education is primarily a process of communication between the learner and his society. The handicapped child frequently has a breakdown in the ability to participate in this process of communication. Breakdown in the normal communication system may be a direct result of a physical impairment in the sensory system which interferes with the transmission and reception of the communication signals. On the other hand, it may originate outside of the child and be the function of the attitudes which surround him in his environment. This may be the case when the handicapped person is seen primarily as someone who is handicapped and only secondarily as a person. Much of special education is concerned with expanding communication skills, expanding the environment of the orthopedically handicapped child through field trips or vicarious experiences, enriching the communication process of the deaf child, and expanding the world of the blind child through auditory and tactile experiences.

Educational media provide a vehicle for special education to expand and enrich the sensory world of the handicapped child in

*Reprinted from *Exceptional Children*, Vol. 34 (March 1968), pp. 561–564, by permission of the author and the Council for Exceptional Children. Copyright 1968 by the Council for Exceptional Children.

†John A. Gough is Chief, Media Services and Captioned Films Branch, Division of Educational Services, Bureau of Education for the Handicapped, U. S. Office of Education.

such a way that it both expands his real world and enhances the store of experiences upon which he can build his communication skills. This is accomplished by providing the tools and materials to implement learning and bridge the communication gaps existing in the experiences of handicapped children.

A special effort to overcome one of the most severe of all communication problems — that of the deaf child — began with the founding of Captioned Films for the Deaf in 1958. When the Bureau of Education for the handicapped was established, this program became the Media Services and Captioned Films Branch. It brought to the Division of Educational Services a wide background of experience in media research, training, and services.

These services include distribution of educational films and other media through more than sixty depositories, the operation of four Regional Media Centers for the Deaf, film and filmstrip production, and research and training in the use of media for the deaf. In addition, the Media Services and Captioned Films Branch provides a loan service of recreational films to the adult deaf, averaging some 2,500 showings per month.

OTHER MEDIA
ACTIVITIES

Funds distributed through programs now administered in the Aid to States Branch of this Division have been used extensively for purchase of educational media. State supported schools for the handicapped and local programs have shared in these acquisitions.

Efforts are currently under way to establish a Branch on Curriculum and Media in the Division of Research. Projects supported by this branch could be comprehensive studies and evaluation of media and curriculum, resulting in multimedia approaches combined with traditional materials. Possible evolution of a project might be the following sequence: first, development and evaluation by the Curriculum and Media Branch; second, revision and production by the Media Services and Captioned Films Branch; and finally, dissemination through local purchase for use in projects supported by the Aid to States Branch.

During the summer of 1967, Associate Commissioner James J. Gallagher established a bureau committee to study the special problems of coordination of media activities by the various programs in the bureau. To further emphasize the importance of media in education of the handicapped, the National Advisory Committee on Education of the Handicapped recommended that a special task force of consultants be established to aid the inhouse group in the study of media utilization for the handicapped. In 1967, Congress further accented the importance of media when it amended the ESEA by enlarging the educational portion of the Captioned Films Act to embrace all handicapped children.

Although the level of funding authorized in the amendment is not proportional to the increase in population covered by the Act, the basic concept of extending media services to all the handicapped is recognized as consistent with continuing Bureau thinking. Future expansion of educational technology for the handicapped may be expected to grow from this beginning. What are some of the basic problems to which a comprehensive media program may address itself?

Among the more important are the following.

1. *Lack of services.* Many handicapped children are not now receiving educational services of any kind. Others get only token or minimal services.
2. *Teacher shortage.* Despite the increased effort to train more teachers for the handicapped, the shortage remains acute.
3. *Insufficient preschool and parent training.* There is ample evidence to show that an early start in school and heavy involvement of parents in the educational program are very basic needs of handicapped children. Thus far, success in providing these services has been extremely limited.
4. *Lack of opportunity for continuing education for the handicapped.* Handicapped children often get only the rudiments of an education during their years of formal schooling. They need special opportunities to learn in later years.

INDIVIDUAL PUPIL INSTRUCTION

In the not too distant future, satellite communication systems may be used to reach the handicapped child who is geographically isolated and the homebound or preschool child for whom there is no local program available. New techniques which can turn the home television set into a teaching machine through the use of self contained cartridges will be realized in the near future. This device may be used on a limited basis this year to provide both lessons for the child and counseling for the parent.

New materials designed for the handicapped and presented in new modes will permit greater individualization of instruction. If the handicapped child can work with materials that are within his grasp, at a rate appropriate to his capacities and within a presentation system that is patient and prompt to correct his errors, and rewards his successes, he will be freed of many of the limitations of the traditional classroom of the past. Media can expand the learning experience so that it is not limited to the classroom or to the school day.

Media offer new avenues for self expression. Working with the disadvantaged children, social workers have found that allowing them to create their own movies with a motion picture camera has opened new vistas to these youths and given them new outlets for self expression that will make substantial changes in their personalities and self images. On a limited basis, deaf children have had similar experiences. Improvement of self image, motivation, reduction of egocentricity, and changes in child parent relationships are some of the outcomes that can emerge from such experiences.

As the learning process for the handicapped child involves these new activities, value systems will undoubtedly tumble. Through a wide imaginative use of educational technology in a systems approach to education, handicapped children may be freed from the lockstep of traditional education and will be allowed to develop skills that are compatible with their potentials.

Today most special educators are faced with a shortage of program materials that can meet the needs of their children. Instructional materials designed for the handicapped are not readily available: in fact, we are little better off than "Old Mother Hubbard." An urgent need exists for us to move forward quickly and pragmatically to fill this void. To be sure, our pragmatic efforts need to be carefully controlled so that quality programs are developed. This requires creative and talented persons working with the special educator to bring the best of education and technology together.

TEACHER
SHORTAGE

In relation to teacher shortage, educational media offer important dividends. For instance, when well planned self instructional materials are designed and packaged, their use will not require so much attention from a highly trained teacher. The problem of the teacher will be to analyze the needs of the child and suggest particular programs from the array of possible choices. At this point, an assistant teacher, subprofessional, or assisting parent may take over and give the child such adult supervision as he may need until he proceeds to a point where the teacher's more expert help is again needed. This approach could have a substantial effect in reducing the present teacher shortage. Current notions as to appropriate class size for handicapped children might be changed and the intensive labor requirements reduced. This is not necessarily to suggest that costs would come down. The costs of educational media are not insignificant. If we go to computer assisted instruction, the costs may be very high unless these devices are used by large numbers of children. As this and other technological advances are contemplated, cost benefit ratios will have to be studied.

It seems fairly obvious, however, that some of the innovations which can be utilized to improve the training of professionals and subprofessionals for the handicapped would include the following:

1. Improvement of methods courses by filming or tape recording expert teachers at work in the classroom to demonstrate particular principles or theories.
2. Tape recording of the trainee at work in the practicum so that he may have an opportunity to observe his own strengths and weaknesses.
3. Skill development training for individual study by the trainee.
4. Production of films or tapes that will be useful in recruiting more trainees and those of higher potential.
5. Dissemination of inservice training materials which will help to upgrade the work of many who are presently serving but have inadequate training.

PARENT COUNSELING

As teachers of the handicapped, we often fail to appreciate the importance of parents and the difficulties which they face. Meeting with them frequently consumes what we consider as our own leisure time and may bring us into contact with difficult problems which we do not know how to solve and would like to consider as not being a part of our job. Here again, media can help. Materials can be developed to help parents understand their responsibilities, to acquaint them with available resources, and to give them training in specific skills that they can practice in order to fulfill their role with maximum effectiveness. Similarly, the teacher can gain better insight into the problems of the child at home and the kinds of teacher-parent-child relationships which are desirable from all three points of view. Films, tapes, and all the paraphernalia in the world cannot take the place of direct consultation, of course, but they can do much to lay the groundwork and establish the primary understandings that will greatly enhance personal contacts.

CONTINUING EDUCATION

Significant programs can be launched to assist the handicapped in continuing education after they leave school. Special programs can be developed to be used with television and radio that meet these peoples' needs for additional information on health and social problems. Educational films and records can be designed for individual and small group viewing. Special programs may be developed to expand employment opportunities.

The handicapped person who finds a role in which he is a contributing member of society helps to develop in the public an awareness of his value as a person. As the public is aroused and becomes aware of its responsibilities to the handicapped, the greater handicapping factors of misunderstanding and indifference will tend to disappear.

Educational media may enable a nation, which is capable of placing a man on the moon, to narrow the gap between the normal child and the handicapped child by narrowing the communication gaps that exist today.

an overview
of the imc network*

JAMES J. McCARTHY†

The Instructional Materials Center Network for Handicapped Children and Youth (IMCNHCY) is a federation of regional Instructional Materials Centers (IMC's) whose primary client is the special educator and whose region of service is the continental United States, Hawaii, Alaska, Puerto Rico, and the Virgin Islands. Although there is a lag between the Network's accomplishments and aspirations, this gap is closing at a rapid rate as new service and research roles are being assimilated. The Network can be a boon to special educators who know how to use it and what it can do for them.

To many special educators hearing about it for the first time, the Network may seem to be a complicated monolith which is sprung suddenly full blown from the impersonal council of the omnipresent federal government and which really has little personal value for them. Nothing could be further from the truth.

The purpose of this article is to dispel this concept by providing an overview of the Network's development. It should be stated at the outset that the Network is designed to become a permanent organization locally controlled and locally funded. It is to serve and be guided by special educational personnel to help them better serve handicapped children. Network services are, or will be, available to every special educator in the United States.

*Reprinted from *Exceptional Children*, Vol. 35 (December 1968), by permission of the author and the Council for Exceptional Children. Copyright 1968 by the Council for Exceptional Children.

†James J. McCarthy is Associate Professor of Education, Department of Counseling and Behavioral Studies, School of Education, University of Wisconsin, Madison.

HISTORICAL
PERSPECTIVE

The Network consists of 14 Instructional Materials Centers (IMC's) and CEC-ERIC. Each regional Center is developing regional satellite centers, which may be stationary or mobile and have simple or elaborate service structures, depending on local needs, resources, and commitments. In some cases, Centers are hundreds of miles away from clients in their region and a satellite center is the only means of providing personalized service.

The IMCNHCY has a federal advisory board which is developing an information storage and retrieval system and a system of communication and coordination whereby all parts may be articulated. It is analagous to a corporation in which the stockholder is the special educator.

The beginnings of the Network were quite unelaborate, although they did contain the seeds of the growing and evolving structure seen today. That a Network such as this could develop was, I feel, foreseen in the beginning. What was not foreseen was the spectacular and unprecedented growth of a new type of major and permanent element in special education which appears to be a uniquely American contribution.

In 1964, two prototype IMC's were funded by the U. S. Office of Education under PL 88-164, Title III. President Kennedy's Task Force on Rehabilitation and Education had originally conceived the idea of Instructional Materials Centers in Special Education from its inspections of overseas nations. Traditionally, continental special educators have made more of their own instructional materials than have their American counterparts and many European special educators are actually certified to teach because, in part, of their skills in materials production. The midtwentieth century attitude in the United States seemed to be that commercial America had the resources to design and produce instructional materials in special education and that this task, properly executed, required expertise and resources (e.g., advanced psychology and learning courses, statistics and experimental design, and production facilities) not available to teachers. Moreover the teacher was considered a practitioner, not producer; his or her time was to be actively spent in the teaching role. The teacher was seen as analogous to the physician who uses surgical instruments and drugs, but doesn't usually design, create, or test these things.

Although the President's Task Force did not specify the nature of IMC's, the prevailing American attitudes in special education strongly suggested directions. The original IMC's would collect extant instructional materials in or related to special education; catalog, loan, store, and retrieve such materials; consult with teachers and student teachers; publish acquisition lists and informational pamphlets; hold inservice meetings; help others who wished to initiate their own Centers; and even attempt to produce an item or two. They promised attempts at materials evaluation and design.

Within 2 years, these prototype Centers had demonstrated that they could prepare themselves to provide needed services in special education. However, they had not convincingly demonstrated the ability to design, evaluate, or produce instructional materials. In addition, though various experiments had been tried (e.g., mail order materials borrowing), the prototype Centers' services were restricted to a relatively small geographical region. Certainly, for the Centers to be of value, services needed to be extended to wider areas. Thus, in 1966, 8 additional regional Centers were funded, bringing to 10 the number in existence at that time.

Although every regional Center will eventually be locally funded, the initial years were largely funded by federal dollars. The government's mounting investment resulted in considerable planning at the federal level which, in retrospect, can be viewed as the next developmental stage of the Network. In 1966, a meeting of Center directors was held in Madison, Wisconsin. At that time, an organization was formed (later called the IMCNHCY), and a chairman was elected. Simultaneously, an IMC Advisory Committee was formed with the U. S. Office of Education.

At this time:

1. Definitive service regions for each Center were agreed upon in order to avoid overlap and to identify parts of the country yet unserved.
2. Each Center declared those areas of handicap for which it would process instructional materials (e.g., mental retardation, visual impairment, etc.) according to the competencies of its staff. This knowledge made it possible to refer client requests to appropriate Centers should the Center originally queried not stock the desired materials.

Through the establishment of more regional Centers, the number of special educators reached with services increased; however, this still represented a small percentage of the total. It was apparent that hundreds more of these Centers would be needed to cover the country adequately, and this was patently impossible. The solution came from the IMC Advisory Committee, which advised:

1. The regional Centers should assist in establishing satellite centers within their respective regions, adequate in size and scope to collectively service all clients in their regions. These centers would eventually be locally funded, locally controlled, responsive to local needs, and related to respective regional Centers. This last point is critical for it allowed great economies. It meant that expensive consultation, assistance with inservice training, search and retrieval of information on materials, and other services were freely available to each satellite center which could, therefore, retain a fairly small staff and a locally responsive collection of materials with the assurance of help from the regional Center when special needs arose.
2. Evidence of regional preplanning must be required of proposals for regional Centers from areas of the country not yet covered, so that parts of large states (or several small states) would agree upon how their entire region was to be served.

Thus, by 1968, 14 IMC's collectively service the entire country. About eighty satellite centers have been established and 300 to 400 professional staff persons are devoting all or a portion of their time to operating this system. A major problem has now become one of alerting special education personnel to the availability of these services.

THE FUTURE
OF THE NETWORK

The Network is an evolving structure and can be responsive to emerging needs. Its directors and advisory board meet periodically to assess progress and plan the future. The present stress is upon:

1. The rapid development of satellite centers. When these are established, special educators can receive all their services in or through these local centers. These centers, in turn, can act as sensors to detect current needs and transmit them through the Network to the Bureau of Education for the Handicapped, U. S. Office of Education. For purposes of training, materials evaluation, and activities yet unforeseen the completed Network will provide a remarkable communi-

cation instrument with the individual special educator at one end, the federal government at the other, and all other levels of the profession plugged in somewhere between those two terminals.

2. Increased coordination among regional Centers. To sense the urgent need for precise intercenter coordination, one need only contemplate the value of (a) joint production of inservice training sessions, (b) uniform publications, (c) cooperative exchange of staff and materials among Centers, and (d) the need to speak as one with commercial producers, foreign nations, and others who are interested in the Network. Obviously, attempts at research and evaluation, materials design and evaluation, and data storage and retrieval are also enhanced through close intercenter coordination. Accordingly, this coordination is of great current importance. Steps to achieve it include the appointment of a Network coordinator and uniform procedures in reporting, data retrieval, and abstracting.

3. Stress on local funding. It is clear that as the Network grows, the federal government will find it increasingly difficult to support. No estimates of yearly costs are yet available for the Network operation, but an estimate of close to $5,000,000 of federal and local funds is not an unrealistic figure for present operational costs.

4. Initiation of materials design and evaluation procedures. In the last analysis, materials design and evaluation are the *raison d'etre* of IMC's. They were designed for this purpose and are, accordingly, uniquely suited to it. Yet, to date, these processes have not developed apace with other Center activities. The scientific development of instructional materials and their objective evaluation present the most difficult and demanding challenge of all to the Network.

It is important to understand that the teacher is the primary client, that he or she can receive help by contacting her Center director, and that the range of service available is not highly restricted. Indeed, a client may ask for a type of assistance never contemplated and a Center may decide to incorporate such service into its routine. Thus, the Network needs the teachers' help to grow and diversify; teachers need the Network's help to serve handicapped students more adequately. And such help is literally theirs for the asking.

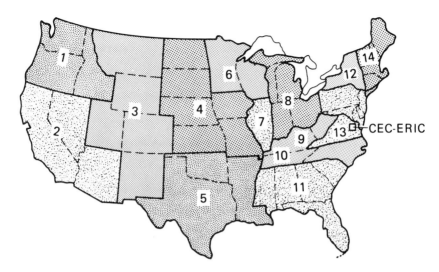

CEC-ERIC

Key to IMC's, with Regions Served

1. University of Oregon, Eugene: Alaska, Hawaii, Idaho, Oregon, Washington

2. University of Southern California, Los Angeles: Arizona, California, Nevada

3. Colorado State College, Greeley: Colorado, Montana, New Mexico, Utah, Wyoming

4. University of Kansas, Lawrence: Iowa, Kansas, Missouri, Nebraska, North Dakota, South Dakota

5. University of Texas, Austin: Arkansas, Louisiana, Oklahoma, Texas

6. University of Wisconsin, Madison: Minnesota, Wisconsin

7. Illinois State Department of Public Instruction, Springfield (The two Illinois Centers are located at Springfield and Chicago.): Illinois

8. Michigan State University, East Lansing: Indiana, Michigan, Ohio

9. University of Kentucky, Lexington: Kentucky, North Carolina, Tennessee, West Virginia

10. American Printing House for the Blind, Louisville, Kentucky: National reference center for visually handicapped

11. University of South Florida, Tampa: Alabama, Florida, Georgia, Mississippi, South Carolina, Puerto Rico, Virgin Islands

12. New York State Department of Education, Albany (The three New York Centers are located at Albany, Buffalo, and New York City.): New York

13. George Washington University, Washington, D.C.: Delaware, District of Columbia, Maryland, New Jersey, Pennsylvania, Virginia

14. Boston University, Boston, Massachusetts: Connecticut, Maine, Massachusetts, New Hampshire, Rhode Island, Vermont

☐ CEC-ERIC Clearinghouse on Exceptional Children and Network Coordinator's Office, Washington, D.C.

FIGURE 1.
INSTRUCTIONAL MATERIALS CENTER
NETWORK FOR HANDICAPPED
CHILDREN AND YOUTH

physical facilities guidelines for handicapped children*

THE PHYSICALLY HANDICAPPED

General Considerations

It is estimated that five children in every 1,000 are crippled to the extent that they need to be in a special class.[1] This group may include the orthopedically handicapped, cardiac conditions, epileptics, the severely injured and others. Some children may need physical therapy, occupational therapy and speech correction. Other children may require special building adaptations, rather than treatment.

Location.

1. Special classes should be conducted in a building that houses regular classes of children of the same ages and grades.
2. Classroom should be located on the first floor.

---

*Reprinted from the December issue of *School Management* magazine with permission of the author and the publisher. This article is copyrighted. ©1967 by CCM Professional Magazines, Inc. All rights reserved.

†James M. Wolf is Coordinator of Special Education, Division of Schools, Balboa Heights, Canal Zone.

[1] Prevalence figures of handicapped children are difficult to document and should be viewed with great caution. Even the experts disagree, not only as to how many are handicapped but as to what is a handicap.

3. Classroom should be located close to an entrance door, to the lunchroom and to other general use rooms.
4. Classroom should connect to the physical therapy room.

Size.

1. Size of classroom depends upon age of children and type of handicaps.
2. Sixty square feet of floor space per child allows for movement of wheel chairs, walkers and other equipment.
3. For a maximum enrollment of 15 pupils, a room 26- by 38-feet to 30- by 50-feet is recommended.

The U.S.A. Standards Institute (formerly the American Standards Assn.) has developed "American Standards specifications for making building and facilities accessible to and usable by the physically handicapped."[2] Its recommendations should be followed in building facilities for physically handicapped children.

Construction.

1. Classroom should have two doors, one near front, one near back.
2. If only one door is planned — unwise from a fire safety standpoint — it should be near the back, so children can be taken out for therapy without disturbing the whole class.
3. Chalkboard should be low. Bottom edge: 24 inches from floor.
4. Chalktray, built with a strong curved edge, can serve as handrailing. For older children who need more support, a vertical bar is better. It should be placed at right and left edge of chalkboard.
5. Chalkboard can be built so it can be raised or lowered. The reversible chalk and tackboard also aids.
6. Classrooms should contain as many cork and peg boards as possible.
7. Durable door should be a minimum width of 36 to 40 inches, equipped with kick plates.
8. Doors should have automatic door checks that keep the door open for wheel chairs and crutch walkers.

[2] Order from U. S. A. Standards Institute, 10 East 40 St., New York, N. Y. 10016. Refer to Standard No. A117.1 — 1961. $2.

9. Doors to outside corridors should have glass areas arranged so that children clearly see other side.
10. Thresholds to outside and inside doors should be kept at a minimum – eliminated completely, if possible.
11. Long grasping bars, rather than door knobs, are preferred.
12. Classroom sink should be accessible from three sides. (A sink in the classroom is imperative.)
13. Faucets should be of the delayed, self-closing type.
14. Separate toilet facilities for boys and girls should be adjacent to the classroom. Toilet facilities are a must for preschool and primary grades. They may be located off the corridors for intermediate and upper-grade children, usually toilet-trained.
15. Toilet cubicles should be large enough to accommodate a wheel chair. Provide grab bars, too.
16. A drinking fountain in the classroom is desirable. It should be accessible for those in wheel chairs.
17. Color and control of stimuli for classroom should be handled sensibly and with moderation.
18. Facilities for rest are needed within the room or in a separate rest room, with sufficient space for cots.
19. Floor should have nonskid surfaces. Rubber tile is satisfactory.
20. Warm floors are essential.
21. Elevators must be provided if all facilities are not on one floor.
22. Storage and cupboard space should have sliding doors.
23. Lighting should conform to best modern practice.
24. Walls with a smooth finish are best.
25. Ceilings should be acoustically treated to prevent noise and strain.
26. Handrails should be recessed or without sharp corners.
27. Electrical outlets should be located every 10 feet.
28. Low windows permit easy vision to the outside.
29. Entrances to the building should be carefully planned, so that children can be loaded and unloaded without exposure to weather. In cold climates, a loading room containing a ramp, and so designed that wheel chairs may be rolled directly into buses, is extremely important.
30. Ramps should follow American Standards for slope: not more than five percent.

Equipment.   Adjustable seats and desks,

tables of varying sizes to accommodate body clearance for wheel chairs and relaxation chairs, stand-up table, chairs on rollers, folding screen to segregate child who needs quiet, cots within the classroom, filing cabinet with lock, easels, portable reading racks, weighted "doll buggy" to slow down spastics and make walking easier, record player, piano, typewriters.

PHYSICAL THERAPY PROGRAM

Location.

1. The physical therapy room should connect by door with the classroom for physically handicapped.

Size.

1. The size of the physical therapy unit will depend on the number of children to be enrolled, type of handicaps and frequency of treatment.
2. The maximum load for one physical therapist is an average of 15 children per day.
3. The size of the therapy room will also depend on what auxiliary facilities, such as a gymnasium, are available, and to what extent hydrotherapy will be used.
4. Usually, a room of large-classroom size, for heat, light and muscle coordination treatments, is indicated in most public school settings.

Construction.

1. Adequate storage for crutches, braces, football helmets, sand bags, etc., should be provided.
2. Electrical outlets should be located three to four feet above the floor between treatment tables and in each individual treatment space. Receptacles should be of the grounding type.
3. Wall space should be as unbroken as possible, to place equipment.
4. When a small tank room for hydrotherapy is indicated, the tank should be approximately 8- by 12- feet, and four feet deep.

5. Tank room should be equipped with hoist, for lifting children.
6. A physiotherapist's office is vital.
7. Opening off this office should be a room or rooms for clothing, lockers, dressing space, showers, lavatory and water closet.
8. Heat controls should be arranged to permit a temperature of 85 degrees in swimming pool and up to 95 degrees in treatment room and tank.

Equipment. Full-length mirror, stall bars, parallel bars, mats, steps (varying risers), stand-up table, stabilizer, rubber mat (25 feet minimum for crutch walking), treatment tables, walkers, tricycles, relaxation chair, pulleys.

OCCUPATIONAL THERAPY PROGRAM

Location.

1. The occupational therapy room should be readily accessible to the physically handicapped child. In smaller programs, it may be part of a two-room suite (occupational therapy and physical therapy), divided by office, toilet and clinic rooms.

Size.

1. The size of the occupational therapy room will vary, depending on the program and the children served.

Construction.

1. Work counter should be built-in, with staggered heights for different age groups (30- and 26- inches high).
2. Provide plenty of storage space for toys, table trays, feeding boards and other equipment.
3. If a separate arts and crafts program is developed, a larger facility is needed to accommodate woodworking equipment, looms, tables, etc. Tool racks must be built-in.
4. If not located near a cafeteria, where separate food service instruction can be accomplished, then this facility must be

added. Kitchen facilities should be available in the training room.

Equipment. Arts and crafts equipment, work bench, tools, loom, stand-up table, record player, coordination boards.

Related Facilities.

1. Larger programs may need a brace shop for making minor repairs.
2. Cafeteria is best operated family-style. Provide a special room for food service training.
3. Physical education: medium-sized gymnasium (50- by 70- feet) opening on to play area may be indicated.
4. Play area should have both grass and hard-top surfaces in sun and shade.

THE DEAF AND
HARD OF HEARING

General
Considerations

Children who have severe hearing losses, resulting in language and speech deficiencies, can profit from special education classes in a regular school. Some deaf children, however, may require a more specialized service of a state residential school. Generally, about three percent of the school population is found to have hearing difficulties. The number and degree of handicaps among these children with hearing difficulties vary according to school and general populations, and local conditions.

Location.

1. Locate facilities in a quiet section of the building — removed from street noises, sources of vibration from machinery and heating systems, etc.
2. Locate classrooms near rooms for children whose hearing is normal.
3. Whenever possible, and to whatever extent possible, integrate children with hearing impairments into regular classes. For this reason, it is best to place primary group youngsters with the regular primary section, intermediate group near their contemporaries, and older children with their peers.

Size.

1. Provide a classroom for eight to 10 children.
2. Although there are fewer children enrolled in this program, their varied activities necessitate a regular-sized, or even larger, classroom.

    Multiple grade room: minimum space — 65 square feet per child.

    Pre-school and primary: minimum space — 65 square feet per child,

    Elementary: minimum space — 45 square feet per child.

    Secondary: minimum space — 35 square feet per child.
3. A small, soundproof room, adjacent to the special classroom, is desirable for audiometric testing. It should connect to classroom and hall.

Construction.

1. Classroom should be acoustically treated.
2. Special floor covering is needed, to deaden sounds.
3. All surfaces should have non-glare finishes and special sight-saving illumination should be provided to relieve eye strain and fatigue. (Eyes are used excessively in lip reading.)
4. Provide controlled heating and ventilation. Air conditioning witn humidity control is recommended in areas of high humidity.
5. Plan electrical outlets to accommodate tape recorder, record player, audiometer and group amplifier.
6. Installation of a ceiling microphone is useful.
7. Space appropriately located receptacles around room, to receive jacks for special amplification equipment.
8. If individual hearing aids are used with group amplifier, then magnetic loop should be installed in room.
9. Install large, clear, eye-level, 3- by 6-foot mirror on wall.
10. Provide ample storage space.
11. Supply adequate chalkboards and bulletin boards — more than is recommended for regular classrooms.

Equipment. Basic classroom equipment and furniture, movable children's desks, portable or permanent rack for headsets, desk amplifier, auditory training unit, audiometer (standard, pure tone), tape recorder, teaching materials.

THE PARTIALLY SIGHTED

General Considerations

Approximately one in 500 children of school age is partially seeing. Two different plans are usually followed in providing for these children: itinerant teacher plan and/or the special class plan.

Special Class Plan

Location.

1. Since a wide geographic area will be served, the special class must be placed in a centrally located school.
2. It should be located convenient to transportation resources.
3. Experience indicates that, wherever possible, second-floor rooms are preferable, since it is easier to eliminate or minimize glare from various types of ground surfaces such as snow, concrete, etc.

Size.

1. A regular-sized classroom, or larger, is recommended.
2. The room is a combination study room, workshop and library that must accommodate children of varied grade levels. (Preferably, not more than four grades should be represented in the class.)
3. Sixteen pupils is recommended as maximum enrollment.
4. Approximately 50 square feet per child is needed.

Construction.

1. Storage space must be ample to provide for the oversized materials and special materials.
2. Bookshelves, 18-inches high and 24-inches deep, should be installed.
3. Plenty of electrical outlets are needed for special equipment.
4. Windows should never be placed in the front of the room. Instead, they should be installed along the side.

5. Care should be taken to prevent direct sunlight from entering the room at undesirable angles.
6. Such architectural features as overhangs and louvers should be considered for glare control.
7. When prismatic directional glass brick is used, the lower sections of the windows should be clear glass.
8. Daylight may be controlled by placing two light-buff or light-gray translucent shades at each window. Rollers of these shades are to be placed at center of window — one directly below the other. The space between them should be covered by opaque metal bar. Shades should be wide enough to prevent streaks of light from the sides.
9. Either incandescent or fluorescent illumination is satisfactory if it is correctly installed, controlled and maintained. Incandescent light should have a luminous bowl to blend with ceiling.
10. Switches should be arranged to light separate areas of room.
11. The size and spacing of lights should be arranged so that no shadow spots appear on ceiling; no marked variations in lighting various parts of room are seen; and no shadows are cast by hands on work areas.
12. Ceiling should be white; walls, light pink; woodwork, dull finish; floors, light-colored, dull-finished; chalkboards, light green or gray; bulletin boards, light in color.
13. Desirable reflectances of room surfaces: ceilings — white, 85- 80%; walls — pastel tints, 60- 50%; furniture — light-colored, 50- 30%; chalkboards — light green, 20- 15%.

Itinerant Teacher Plan

Location.

1. The itinerant teacher plan calls for two types of housing:
A small office in a central location from which a teacher can work. A storage closet is required — a minimum 60 square feet, with shelf space for over 100 large-type books and other special equipment. The usual office equipment will be needed.
In each building the teacher visits, there is need for a small room (150 to 200 square feet) where the teacher works with individual pupils.

THE
BLIND

General
Considerations

In the population of school-age children, approximately one in 5,000 is blind. Day classes for blind children in public schools are conducted, of necessity, in larger population centers. The blind, like partially sighted pupils, usually spend part of the day in regular classes.

Location.

1. The braille classroom is a homeroom or resource room for blind children and is located in a regular school building.
2. The classroom should be located where there is a minimum amount of noise, but near regular classes, to facilitate integration of blind pupils.

Size.

1. The classroom should be of standard size or larger.
2. Children of three or more grade levels may be enrolled in the class. Six to eight pupils are considered an adequate enrollment, since the blind require more individual attention than the partially sighted.

Construction.

1. The room should have the same standards of lighting as a sight-saving classroom.
2. All standards in a correct visual environment, such as white ceilings, walls of light tints, and absence of glare, should be observed.
3. An abundance of well-organized shelf space is needed.
4. Electric outlets should be adequately spaced. Some floor outlets may also be advisable.
5. Bulletin boards are needed, but not as much as in a regular class.
6. A small listening cubicle or area is indicated.
7. Acoustical treatment is desirable to reduce noise made by pupils.

Equipment. Adjustable desks with large tops to accommodate both braille books and writing materials, library tables and chairs, bookcases large enough for braille literature, cork bulletin boards instead of the usual chalkboards, radio, talking book machine, braille writers, recorder, wooden relief map (preferably a sectional map of the United States, if only one is provided), braille relief maps of all countries, large relief globe, typewriters, Dictaphone or Ediphone, braille dictionary.

Braille books, corresponding, as nearly as possible, to those used in the regular classes; braille word cards and phrases for beginners; braille weekly magazines; slates and styli; paper for braille writing.

Counting blocks, arithmetic slates (if desired), arithmetic splints; measuring cups, bottles and pitchers; braille rulers, large clock face marked in braille, geometric forms (cubes, spheres, cones, etc.), sewing materials (self-threading needles, needle threader, regular needles).

Handwork materials: scissors, raffia, reed, plastic lacing, leather-craft goods, modeling clay, paste, crayons, construction paper, kindergarten beads, looper clip frames.

Edited ink-print copies of all braille books for the use of the teacher (edited means that books, when transcribed into braille, have explanatory markings in the ink-print copy), small chalkboard for children with some vision, white canes of varying lengths (the length of the cane depends upon the heighth of the child, his length of stride, length of arm and where it is to be used).

THE EDUCABLE
MENTALLY RETARDED

General
Considerations

It is estimated that from 1 to 3 percent of the school-age population is mentally retarded and in need of special class placement. A school district usually does not have enough mentally retarded children to organize classes for them at each grade level. Classes are frequently organized on the primary, intermediate, junior high and senior high school levels. Educable mentally handicapped pupils are like normal children in most ways. Classes for these children should be placed in a building where there are grades that serve children of the same age. Such children should have the same privileges of recreation periods, assemblies, art, music, library, physical education and other activities as have all children.

Location.

1. Facilities should be located in a regular school, where a modified activity-type program can be given.
2. The classroom should be in a desirable location and not, as too often happens, be a cast-off.
3. To facilitate integration with other students, the primary class should be located adjacent to the primary department, the intermediate class a part of the elementary grades, and the advanced group with the junior and senior high school.

Size.

1. Class enrollment should approximate one-half of an average size class. A maximum enrollment of from 10 to 15 in the primary level, 15 at the intermediate level, and 15 to 18 at the advanced level is usual.
2. A classroom 1½ times as large as a regular classroom is desirable. Sixty square feet per child, or 1100 to 1200 square feet, is very adequate.
3. When there is more than one classroom in a building, a special suite for the mentally retarded is desirable. Two classrooms separated by a common workroom is popular.
4. It is important to have these classes removed from distracting and disturbing features of the school.
5. Approximately 15% to 20% of the classroom's total space may be used for manipulative skills.
6. Another 15% to 20% of each classroom should be used for a library and science center.

Construction.

1. Thirty to 40 feet of bulletin and chalkboards should be allowed.
2. Primary and advanced classes need more bulletin board space. Intermediate classes need more chalkboard space.
3. There should be separate toilets for boys and girls, connected with the classroom, at the primary level.
4. Color harmony should be considered for the walls and ceiling.
5. Windows should be low enough for children to see out without straining. East or west exposure is best.

6. Adequate storage is essential.
7. A kitchen unit in the classroom is very desirable at junior-senior high school levels.
8. Counter areas are needed for displays and work space.

THE TRAINABLE
MENTALLY HANDICAPPED

General
Considerations

The program for trainable mentally handicapped youngsters focuses on helping these children care for themselves personally, become better adjusted socially and to be useful in the home or a sheltered environment. A homelike environment is preferable to a strict schoollike class.

Location.

1. A self-contained classroom in a regular elementary building is sometimes recommended. The classroom should be close to an exit and semi-isolated from regular activities.
2. A house is sometimes urged as a physical plant for these children.

Size.

1. Experience indicates a maximum class size of about eight to 10 pupils.
2. From 900- to 1200- square feet is recommended.
3. If a house is used, then one room should be large enough to provide space for physical activities.
4. The physical features of the classroom should be flexible enough to provide for a variety of arrangements of furniture and equipment.

Construction.

1. Bulletin boards and chalkboards are needed, but less than the amount used in a regular classroom.
2. Flooring soundproofing, illumination and decoration should be like all well-designed classrooms.
3. A kitchenette is desirable; since lunch is served in the classroom, this permits instruction in eating habits.
4. Give special attention to adequate storage space.

SPEECH CORRECTION PROGRAMS

General Considerations

Approximately seven to 10 percent of elementary school students (slightly lower in secondary schools) have speech difficulties that require the services of a correctionist. A school building with an enrollment of 1000 or more usually needs a full-time speech correctionist and a permanent speech room. In a building with a smaller enrollment, the correctionist is usually an itinerant teacher and comes two or three times a week. It may be necessary to share the speech room with other specialists in smaller schools. If so, it should be reserved exclusively for the speech correctionist during the time scheduled for this program. If the work of the speech correctionist takes him to several buildings, a centrally located office should be provided as a home base.

Location.

1. The speech room should be centrally located to permit children to go quickly and easily to and from class.
2. For younger children, a location near the classrooms is sometimes desirable. A major portion of the children treated will be under 10.
3. The speech room may be a part of a suite which contains a waiting room and separate rooms for itinerant workers such as psychologists and school social workers.
4. Put it in a quiet area of the building, away from distracting noises. If the room cannot be located away from noise -producing areas, it should be sound-treated.

Size.

1. The speech room should be about half as large as the space planned for the deaf (see page 494) — seldom will more than five or six people be in the room at any one time. About 250 to 400 square feet are adequate.

Construction.

1. Follow the requirement of classrooms for the deaf, for construction of the speech room. (see page 494).
2. If the speech program is large and there are a number of

speech rooms, one should be soundproofed to insure accurate audiometric testing.
3. Windows should be high enough to eliminate distracting stimuli.
4. Adequate electrical outlets are needed to accommodate record player, tape recorder, audiometric and amplification equipment.
5. Thirty feet of open shelves are desirable for storage and display of books, games and toys.
6. Room should be acoustically treated.
7. Room should be well lighted to 8C - 100 foot candles.
8. Include controlled temperature and ventilation. Air conditioning with humidity control is essential in areas of high humidity.
9. Provide a mounted chalkboard, mirror and bulletin board − none smaller than three or four feet.
10. A lavatory bowl is useful in all speech rooms.

Equipment. Tables and chairs suitable to size of children, adult chairs (available for parent teacher conferences), teacher's desk, locked filing cabinet, audiometer (standard, pure tone, portable), portable tape recorder, portable record player, auditory training unit, appropriate teaching materials, telephone (it is sometimes necessary and time saving to discuss, over the telephone, confidential information with medical and non-medical specialists or to talk with parents), typewriter, secretarial services necessary for typing reports and letters.

THE EMOTIONALLY HANDICAPPED

General Considerations

Two plans are generally followed in providing services for children who have social and emotional problems: a full-time class is conducted by a special teacher and itinerant services are provided by school social workers. Estimates of the number of children needing counseling, casework or some form of therapy range from six to eight percent of the total school population. Only a small percentage of the school population will have social and emotional problems so severe as to require a full-time special class.

Social Work Program

Location.

1. The prime requisite for a visiting counselor's or social worker's room is privacy. The room should also be located in a quiet area of the building. If distractions cannot be eliminated, room should be soundproofed.
2. Location on the first floor is recommended, so the room is easily available to the parents, teachers and children in the primary grades.
3. Rooms should be near administrative offices and other special services.

Size.

1. For one school social worker, the minimum-sized office is 10 by 15 feet.
2. The school social worker rarely sees more than one child at a time.
3. Some large school districts which have several school social workers may provide a large office as the central office for all workers.

Construction.

1. Door should be solid — no clear glass.
2. Proper lighting, ventilation and heating are essential.
3. Color should be restful but gay.

Special Classroom

General Considerations. At the present time, planning for the rehabilitation of emotionally disturbed children is experimental.

Location.

1. A classroom, largely self-contained, should be on the ground floor and should be as isolated from the other classrooms as possible.

Size.

1. Experience to date indicates that the number of children per teacher should be about six to 10. A classroom of regular size is adequate.

Construction.

1. Usual features of a well-designed classroom are desirable.
2. A drinking fountain and toilet should be connected to the classroom.
3. Ample counter work and display space, with sink, should be provided.
4. An alcove, offset from the classroom, should provide rest facilities for students, with some isolation.

PSYCHOLOGICAL EXAMINATION PROGRAMS

General Considerations

1. Each school should incorporate at least one small room for psychological testing and counseling. Any child needing this service can then obtain it in his own school building.

Location.

1. The examining room should be on the ground floor, out of main traffic area, and yet easily accessible.
2. It should be located away from distracting noises. If this is not possible, then it should be soundproofed.

Size.

1. A room 10- by 15- feet is adequate for testing.
2. The room may be used, by preset plan, with other specialists.

Construction.

1. Provisions may be made for these rooms to have one-way observation windows.

2. Walls should be painted a restful color that does not stimulate or distract.
3. The room should be well-lighted: 80- to 100- foot candles.
4. The doors should be of solid material. No clear glass.

design for
*all americans**

CHARLES MEISGEIER†

The following article is excerpted from a
report of the National Commission on Architectural Barriers appointed by the Secretary of Health, Education, and Welfare in April,
1966, and published by the Department in December, 1967. A
checklist of publications relating to architectural planning for the
physically handicapped appendixed to this report is included in the
annotated bibliography.

PRIORITIES
FOR ACTION

The modern man-made environment is de-
signed for the young and healthy. Yet almost everyone, sooner or
later, is handicapped by a chronic or temporary disability or by the
infirmities of old age. By designing for the ideal human body, we bar
real people from getting an education, earning a living, becoming a
part of active community life. More than 20 million Americans are
built *out* of normal living by unnecessary barriers: a stairway, a
too-narrow door, a too-high telephone. At the right moment, their
needs were overlooked. In time, the last vestiges of such thoughtlessness will disappear from the American scene. To speed the Nation

*Printed by permission of the author as extracted from *Design for All
Americans, A Report of the National Commission of Architectural Barriers to
Rehabilitation of the Handicapped*, Department of Health Education, and
Welfare, 1967.

†Charles Meisgeier is Coordinator of Special Education Administration, The
University of Texas at Austin.

toward that goal, the Commission offers a series of recommendations in this report. Those of major importance for immediate action are:

1. Enactment of Federal legislation requiring that all new public buildings and facilities which are intended for use by the public must be designed to accommodate the elderly and the handicapped if any Federal funds are used in their construction.
2. Issuance of an Executive order to apply accessibility standards to new construction and directing all Federal agencies to plan and budget for feasible changes in their existing buildings and facilities.
3. Enactment or revision of State legislation to require that State and local buildings constructed with public funds meet accessibility standards and to include strong enforcement provisions.
4. Revision of all building codes so that industries, shops, and other privately owned structures used by the public will be built for accessibility in the future and so that, when existing buildings are renovated, feasible improvements in accessibility will be made.
5. Assignment of responsibility and resources to specific units of Federal, State, and local governments to administer the accessibility legislation, to conduct and/or support research and demonstrations, and to work with voluntary, professional, business and industrial organizations to the end that all buildings and facilities used by the people of every community will be readily accessible to elderly and handicapped people.
6. Expansion of public and privately supported education and information programs so that no longer, merely through thoughtlessness, will millions of citizens be unable to use buildings, parks, and other facilities.

THE SENSITIVITY GAP

A recent public opinion poll revealed that 64 percent of the American people had not thought enough about how the handicapped manage to get around in their communities to realize that a serious problem exists. They were unaware that:

The greatest single obstacle to employment for the handicapped is the physical design of the buildings and facilities they must use.

One out of 10 persons has some disability which prevents him from using buildings and facilities designed only for the physically fit. Among this one-tenth of the population are 2 million children with orthopedic handicaps; millions of adults who are enfeebled by age or who have heart disease, arthritis, deafness, blindness, and other chronic disabilities. Over and beyond the handicapped one-tenth of the Nation are the millions temporarily disabled by accidents who could return to school or work sooner if buildings were designed for accessibility.

In every community, virtually all of the buildings and facilities most commonly used by the public have features that bar the handicapped.

The most common causes of inaccessibility are due entirely to failure to think of the needs of the handicapped at the design and planning stage.

They include:

Steps and curbs

Inaccessible elevators

Steep and narrow walks; gratings in walkways

Doors that are too narrow, revolve, or are hard to open

Lack of parking spaces reserved for the handicapped and designed for their use

Lack of accommodations for wheelchairs in theaters, stadiums, and other public gathering places

Too-narrow aisles in cafeterias, restaurants, libraries, auditoriums, etc.

Too-small public toilet stalls and telephone booths

Too-high telephones, drinking fountains, vending machines, light switches, fire alarms

New facilities built and equipped to accommodate the handicapped cost little or no more to construct than buildings designed only for the able bodied.

Many old buildings could have some of their barriers removed at nominal cost.

A fresh reservoir of competent employees can often be tapped or new customers obtained by adding just a few accessibility features such as:

Hand rails

A ground-level main entrance or ramp

Steps that are rounded instead of squared at the edges

Doors that open automatically

Raised letters and numbers on doors and in elevators so that the blind can read them

Danger signals equipped with light as well as sound so that the deaf will be warned

An open booth with a low-placed telephone

One or more wide toilet stalls with grab rails

Nonslip flooring

Many improvements made to accommodate the handicapped also add to the safety and convenience of the able bodied.

Any building can be made accessible to the handicapped with little or no loss of space and without detracting from its usefulness for the able bodied.

THE RISING COST OF THOUGHTLESSNESS

In both human and dollar terms, this Nation will pay an ever-increasing price if it continues to create an environment in which only the able bodied can thrive.

Every year, 100,000 babies are added to the population who are born with the kinds of defects that will require them to use crutches, braces, or wheelchairs all their lives. In the past, fewer such babies lived. For those who did, and for other handicapped children, special and costly institutions, schools, and classrooms were constructed. The University of Illinois has found that 60 percent of its handicapped students attended special grade and high schools or grew up in institutions for the handicapped.

The inhumane and costly practice of treating children with handicaps as an isolated group will have to be expanded unless accessibility is made an integral part of all design

Every year, the traffic toll mounts. It is estimated that at the present time there are about 125,000 paraplegics in the United States. During the next 10 years there will be increasing numbers of traffic accident victims who become permanently disabled.

The number of war veterans who must use wheelchairs is also increasing, both because the nature of the war in Vietnam — with its landmines and boobytraps — results in proportionately more crippling wounds and because medical advances enable more men to live. In World War I, only 400 men with wounds that paralyzed them from the waist down survived at all, and 90 percent of them died before they reached home. In World War II, 2,000 paraplegics lived and 1,700 of them are alive today.

If these and other seriously disabled Americans are to have a real future, the wheelchair — not the athlete's leg — must become the gauge of accessibility.

In spite of the half billion tax dollars invested annually in the vocational rehabilitation of the disabled, hundreds of disabled men and women find their path to independence blocked by man-made barriers. Their arduous efforts to qualify for work were in vain and the aid they received only added to their frustration.

Every day, 1,000 Americans pass their 65th birthday and enter the period when strokes, arthritis, and other crippling impairments are most likely to occur.

No rehabilitation gains that can be anticipated in the foreseeable future will be sufficient to prevent the size of the accessibility problem from mounting.

Because of the obstacles we have put in their way, the handicapped today are a hidden population. Only the most intrepid risk the dangers and suffer the discomforts and humiliations they encounter when they try to live a normal, productive life. Most of the handicapped are out of sight. Will we continue to put them out of mind — to forget about the child with cerebral palsy, the housewife with muscular distrophy, the student with multiple sclerosis, the worker who had to retire because of a stroke, the amputee from Vietnam?

These people live among us. They have hopes, talents, ambitions like the rest of us. Their number is growing every day.

part **vii**

international
perspectives

Few authors have centered their attention on special education at the international level. The World Confederation of Organizations in the Teaching Profession has recognized the need for leadership in the international development of special education and has established a Committee on Education of Handicapped Persons. The International Society for the Welfare of Cripples (ISWC) has also played a key role. The ISWC Committee on Education of Handicapped Persons sponsored a major survey of special education programs in twenty-one western European countries. Drs. Wallace Taylor and Isabelle Wagner Taylor devoted two years to the research and writing of the report. In this emerging area, the reader has an opportunity to review a variety of types of organizations and systems of administration that have developed in special education practices in Western Europe.

Ronald Gulliford in his article offers a comprehensive outline of the organization of special education in England and a consideration of a number of areas in which international cooperation could be productive.

the organization
and administration
of educational services *

WALLACE W. TAYLOR † and
ISABELLE W. TAYLOR

In the last 150 years education in Europe
has increasingly reflected the dynamic influences of the Industrial
Revolution and of nationalism. The Industrial Revolution resulted in
compulsory education laws and the delegation to the school of duties
which up to this time had been assumed by the home and the
Church. The spirit of nationalism has tended to equate more and
better education with national power, and therefore has made
government, usually at the national level, responsible for seeing that
the educational objectives of the State were accomplished.

The educational systems that have developed in response to the
demands for more and better schooling have sooner or later accepted
responsibility for handicapped children. Liberty, equality, and
fraternity have in time come to apply to the handicapped as well as
to the normal, and the first efforts to assist them to compensate for
their disabilities came from the same social and economic forces that
culminated in the French Revolution. There was no charter for the
disabled in the Declaration of the Rights of Man, but the aspirations
manifested there were to find outlets in broad social and humanitarian ventures that eventually included the handicapped.

*Reprinted from *Special Education of Physically Handicapped Children in
Western Europe*, Chapter 1, pp. 3-17, by permission of the authors and the
International Society for Rehabilitation of the Disabled. Copyright 1960 by the
International Society for Rehabilitation of the Disabled.

†Wallace Taylor is Professor of Education, State University of New York,
College of Education, Albany. Isabelle Taylor is Chairman, Department of
Psychology, Russell Sage College, Troy, New York.

Before the eighteenth century, health services like educational services were primarily individual and family concerns, with the Church assisting in some instances by giving aid to the indigent. Growing scientific knowledge and widespread acceptance of the idea of progress led to cooperative provision for those medical services beyond the means of most families, usually by religious and voluntary societies but in some instances by governmental agencies.

Realization of the inter-relationship between health and education came slowly, and is still imperfectly understood. Even in the rehabilitation of handicapped children the development of an understanding of the complementary functions of medicine and education was very gradual.

Similar stages in the development of special education are thus found in the twenty-one countries of western Europe: (1) a belief in the desirability of compulsory education for all; (2) recognition of the desirability of extending educational advantages to the handicapped; (3) a parallel development of educational and health services, with problems arising concerning the integration of these services; and (4) a steady trend for local, provincial, or national governments — or all three in cooperation — to take over the services and institutions which had been established and maintained by private individuals, voluntary organizations, and religious groups. This occurred when the need for services reached a magnitude such that only governments could command the resources necessary to provide them on a scale commensurate with the national interest.

The problems of special education in Europe are basically the same as the problems of educating handicapped children in the United States and Canada. The most striking difference is the slower progress made in most European countries toward the achievement of solutions. This slower progress is caused by a variety of factors: (1) the complexities of large numbers of political subdivisions, languages, and cultures; (2) a less uniform degree of industrial development; (3) the interruption of normal progress resulting from depression, two world wars, and reconstruction; and (4) the added burden of personnel shortages and damage to facilities and programs during World War II.

A variety of types of organization and systems of administration has developed in Europe in response to the historical development and social and economic needs of each country.

Authority for the administration of services may be completely centralized in the capital as in Greece, or left to local governments as it is in Germany and Switzerland. In Greece any action must come from the appropriate ministry, with local authorities having no power except to petition the capital. In the Federal Republic of Germany, on the other hand, the states have full autonomy in educational matters, in both regular and special schools. The same is true of the cantons in Switzerland, although medical care, particularly in the areas of tuberculosis and industrial accidents, is shared with the cantons by the Office of Public Health in the Ministry of Internal Affairs.

With these two exceptions, responsibility for the education of the handicapped is vested in a variety of national ministries; corresponding departments administer programs at the provincial and communal levels. Titles vary, sometimes because of a genuine difference in function, and sometimes simply because of differences in terminology. The Ministry of Education (variously called the Ministry of Public Instruction, National Education, Church and Education, and Education, Arts, and Sciences) is involved in every country.

The Ministry of Social Welfare (or Social Administration, Social Affairs, Public Assistance) shares this responsibility with the Ministry of Education in eleven of the twenty-one countries, and the Ministry of Health (or Public Health) in the same number. However, only six countries have both ministries for social affairs and for public health. Many of the smaller nations have never had a separate ministry of health, and therefore incorporate such concerns in other ministries. For example, Norway has a Directorate of Health Services under the Ministry of Social Affairs (just as there is a Directorate for Special Schools under the Ministry of Church and Education). The Netherlands has a combined Ministry of Social Affairs and Public Health.

The Ministry of Labor has some responsibility for the handicapped in six countries, usually in the fields of employment services and vocational training and rehabilitation. In England, Northern Ireland, and Scotland the Ministry of Labor assumes many of the functions that would be allocated to a Ministry of Social Welfare in many other countries.

The Ministry of the Interior (or Home Affairs) in Austria, Sweden, and Switzerland has some responsibility for certain medical services. The Ministry of Pensions and National Insurance in England and in Northern Ireland performs functions similar to those of the Invalidity Insurance Court in Denmark. Italy has a combined Ministry of the Interior and Public Assistance.

In Belgium and in Greece the Ministry of Justice is included; in Belgium this ministry places handicapped children in appropriate special institutions, whereas in Greece the Ministry of Justice is preparing legislation for crippled children, with the aim of making education compulsory for them, and of protecting them from exploitation. In the Netherlands the Ministry of Defense is represented on the Rehabilitation Council along with other ministries.

The general pattern has been for the Ministry of Social Welfare or the Ministry of Health to have primary responsibility for the handicapped during the period when welfare considerations were uppermost. As educational opportunities developed, there was usually a move to rest at least part of the responsibility with the Ministry of Education. This trend has been accelerated by the popular demand that education costs be accepted as a national rather than local responsibility. Functions of Ministries of Education have therefore been expanding, and it has frequently proven more economical to administer all types of special education within this administrative organization.

For example, a 1949 law in Poland transferred to the Ministry of Education (under the Division of Special Schools and Child Care) all activities of the Ministry of Labor and Social Welfare connected with the special care of children and youth. Only in Portugal today is special education almost entirely under the jurisdiction of the Ministry of Social Welfare, a reflection of the still limited educational provisions for the handicapped in that country.

The lodging of administrative responsibility for the blind and deaf with the Ministry of Social Welfare, while allocating programs for other groups of the handicapped to the Ministry of Education, is a reflection of the historical evolution of programs of services. Since the blind and deaf were usually provided for first in this historical sequence, the welfare concept generally placed them under the jurisdiction of the Ministry of Social Welfare, or the medical-care emphasis assigned them to the Ministry of Health. Groups like the orthopedically handicapped or the cerebral palsied, for whom provisions are relatively recent, tend to come under the Ministry of Education since their needs are more frequently recognized as educational.

An example of this continuing distinction in administrative responsibility for the blind and deaf and for other groups is found in Greece, where the Ministry of Education has charge of all special education except for teacher salaries and maintenance for teachers and pupils in the schools for the blind and deaf, which are financed by the Ministry of Social Welfare. Also in Denmark instruction in schools for the blind and deaf is still under this ministry, though it consults with the Ministry of Education in these matters since the latter Ministry has charge of all other special schools.

In several countries problems have arisen from the division of responsibility among the ministries of education, social welfare, and health. Services for the handicapped would be more effective if there were greater centralization of such services, or at least better coordination of the programs for which different ministries are responsible. Usually educational provisions are under the Ministry of Education, welfare provisions under the Ministry of Social Welfare, and medical treatment under the Ministry of Health, in countries where there are three ministries with these titles. Handicapped children need all three types of services, and frequently they need them at the same time.

In different countries arrangements for coordination and allocation of responsibility follow a variety of patterns. In Poland the division is made in terms of age; the care and rearing of children is the responsibility of the Ministry of Health up to the age of 3, of the Ministry of Education from 3 to 18 years of age, and of the Ministry of Labor and Social Welfare from age 16 to age 18.

In Belgium, the Ministry of Public Health and the Family pays subsidies for hospitalized children, and supervises the National Foundation for Child Welfare, a semi-autonomous organization chiefly concerned with delicate children. The Ministry of Public Instruction has a division of special education under the Department of Elementary Education and a division for special vocational education under the Department of Technical Education. The Ministry of Social Affairs administers two special funds — the Fund for the Crippled and the Fund for Schooling. The Ministry of Justice places handicapped children in appropriate institutions.

In France the responsibility is divided between the Ministry of National Education and the Ministry of Public Health and Population, and between various other public and private agencies. The Ministry of Public Health administers and supervises the public institutions for the blind and deaf, whereas private institutions for these groups are under the control of the "département" or province where they are located. The examinations for the teaching personnel of the four schools for the blind that are either departmental or municipal are under the control of the Ministry of National Education. The Ministry of Public Health administers the examinations which teachers of the deaf must pass in order to be certified. The teacher education program is determined by the Ministry of National Education, but the program of instruction for the children themselves is determined by the institutions concerned, and controlled by the Ministry of Public Health. In this ministry there is a special bureau in charge of the education of deaf-mute children, and another for the administration of social aid to them. For many years now the blind in France have been trying to get their schools placed entirely under the Ministry of National Education in order to secure uniform regulations concerning such matters as programs of studies and rules governing admission of pupils.

An example of how a complex administrative organization may affect a particular special school is that of the Waldschule Rehabilitation Center for Handicapped Children at Wiener-Neustadt in Austria. The responsibility for supervision is assigned to the director of the Education Department of Lower Austria, but six other provinces participate in the administration and financing of the school according to an agreement based on the number of handicapped children coming from each province. These provinces are represented on the Advisory Board which meets twice a year, and which includes representatives of the provincial government and federal Ministry of Social Administration.

In Denmark until 1920 both general education and the care of children and youth were entrusted to the Ministry of Education. At that time the care of needy children and youth was placed under the jurisdiction of the Ministry of Social Affairs. All school education, including special schools and classes (except for the blind and deaf, and for homebound and hospitalized children), was left with the Ministry of Education.

Arrangements for coordinating the services of various ministries serving the handicapped are illustrated by English practices. The Chief Medical Officer of the Ministry of Health is also the Chief Medical Officer of the Ministry of Education, and physicians on the staffs of both ministries are responsible to him. Employment services provided by the Youth Employment Board, industrial rehabilitation units, and vocational training centers are under the Ministry of Labour and the Ministry of Education jointly.

In many countries there are special administrative bodies created within the framework of a particular ministry, or supported by a ministry, which serve the needs either of the handicapped as a whole or of a particular group of the handicapped. The functions served vary from more limited to very broad ones.

In Belgium a privately organized but tax-supported group called the National Committee of Coordination for the Handicapped Child has established sixteen centers for the crippled in the Flemish part of Belgium. There is also a Specialized Office of Vocational Orientation which likewise represents a combination of private and official sponsorship. A Commission of Public Assistance which provides for indigents sometimes pays the cost of medical care and of prostheses. The National Committee of Home-Care Services of Catholic Charities provides regional clinics and home-care services approved by the Ministry of Public Health and the Family; the Catholic Charities organization also sponsors the Commission of Organizations for the Ill and Handicapped.

In Denmark, there is a Handicapped Persons Division in the Ministry of Social Affairs, which administers the Public Assistance Act and supervises the institutions and services providing the care. Also responsible to the Ministry of Social Affairs are several special boards for those with sensory handicaps: the Board for the Blind, the Board for the Practically Blind, the Board for the Deaf, and the Board for the Hard of Hearing. The Director of Welfare Services for the handicapped is chairman of each board, which includes representatives of the schools in question, parents' councils in these schools, and the related voluntary association. The Invalidity Insurance Court is the central disability authority, and administers the financial assistance provided through the Social Insurance Act, particularly with reference to vocational training.

In England the National Assistance Board has a network of local offices, and provides for those with permanent disabilities. The Youth Employment Board serves both normal and handicapped youngsters.

In Finland the Ministry of Social Affairs, through a State Medical Board, assigns handicapped children to vocational schools and hospitals. A semi-autonomous Central Board of Education responsible to the Ministry of Education administers finances as they relate to both regular and special schools.

A Permanent Conference of the ministers of education in the various states of Germany has been organized to coordinate state educational programs. Special education comes under a committee of this Permanent Conference.

In Greece, a National Rehabilitation Board has been formed on the basis of a recommendation from a 1956 WHO survey. There are also two governmental offices relating to rehabilitation, one in the Ministry of Social Welfare for supervising rehabilitation services, and another in the Ministry of Labor concerning vocational rehabilitation.

In Norway, under the Ministry of Church and Education, there is a Directorate for Special Schools. In Sweden, under a similar ministry there is a Board of Education within which there is a section for special education headed by the Director of Special Schools, in addition to a Board of Vocational Education. Under the Swedish Ministry of the Interior a Medical Board is responsible for the medical care of school children, and the Ministry of Social Affairs has an Employment Board responsible for vocational training and placement.

In Spain under the Ministry of Education are two agencies concerned with special education: the National Society of Special Education and the "Patronato de la Infancia Anormal." In addition, a Special Education Commission has been created to study the problems of special education.

The Yugoslav Educational Council discusses common problems in the various republics, including those relating to special education, and coordinates their educational efforts.

In addition to this division of responsibility, administration of programs may be further complicated by the necessity of taking into account the provisos under which trust funds were established. The original bequests have usually been supplemented by government funds, but in many cases the operating boards continue to be autonomous. For example, in Belgium there is the Special Assistance Fund (once called the Common Fund) for the care and education of mentally and physically handicapped children; it replaces a number of separate communal and provincial funds. There is also a Fund for the Crippled, a Fund for Schooling, and a new Fund for the Training, Rehabilitation, and Reclassification of the Handicapped, based on a 1958 law.

In Greece needy and handicapped children are aided by the Royal Fund, which resulted in 1956 from the merger of two separate government funds called the Queen's Fund and the King's Fund. In the Netherlands a Sick Fund provides for ill or handicapped children up to their twenty-seventh year. Added to these are many private funds, allocated either by private groups or by a combination of official and voluntary representatives.

Although in most countries provisions for handicapped children are made separately from those for normal children, England in 1944 (and Scotland in 1945) instituted the policy of guaranteeing equality of educational opportunity for all children. Under the basic education law, it became the duty of Local Education Authorities to furnish special educational treatment as a part of their general duty to provide elementary and secondary schools to suit the varying ages, abilities, and aptitudes of pupils attending them. The Local Education Authorities were also charged with the responsibility of ascertaining which pupils needed special treatment.

The decision to remove a child from his home and place him in a special institution may be made by an official agency for this purpose. In Denmark, a Child Welfare Committee performs this function for children under 18 who are deaf and dumb, speech handicapped, or crippled or deformed. In Poland the Provincial Boards of Education investigate the needs for child care and supervise the correct placement of children needing special care and special education.

Special schools have varying degrees of autonomy in the determination of curricula. In Austria, Greece, and Sweden, both private and public schools, including special schools, must follow official educational programs determined by the Ministry of Education. In most countries an attempt is made to keep the curriculum in special schools as similar as possible to that in regular schools, with only those modifications necessitated by a particular kind of handicap or a lengthening of the time allowed for covering the material as in the case of the blind and deaf. England and Scotland recommend that the curricula be the same except for additional emphasis on art and music in special programs, because of their social and therapeutic value.

In a few countries authorities on the provincial or municipal levels determine the content of curricula. In Germany educational provisions are the responsibility of individual states. In Switzerland the cantonal and municipal educational authorities determine programs of special education. In Yugoslavia the 1958 General Law on Education provides that school curricula in the various republics be determined by the respective republican councils of education.

The certificates or diplomas given to special teachers are issued by the national government in only two countries, France and Sweden. In all other countries they are issued by the special school or institute providing the training program.

The inspection of special schools is undertaken by the national Ministry of Education in sixteen of the twenty-one countries. Portuguese special schools are inspected by officials of the Ministry of Social Welfare, except for some private schools chartered by the Ministry of Education. In France responsibility is divided between the Ministry of National Education and the Ministry of Public Health and Population. In Austria all schools are supervised by full-time inspectors appointed by the Ministry of Education except the thirty-five special schools in Vienna, for which the municipality appoints a special inspector. Only in Germany, Switzerland, and Yugoslavia is there any decentralization of authority for inspection services; in Germany they are appointed by the state Ministries of Education, in Switzerland by education officials in each of the cantons and municipalities, and in Yugoslavia by the Council of Education in each republic. Efforts are made in several countries to choose inspectors who have had previous experience as special teachers.

It is impossible to estimate the amount of money spent on special education, particularly when there is a division of responsibility on various governmental levels within a particular country. An estimate of the total amount spent by all agencies in the field of special education is even more difficult to obtain because of the multiple sources of financial aid involving numerous voluntary agencies, and the complex variety of subsidized services.

The extent of the financial responsibility assumed by the central government varies from almost complete financing to limited subsidies. It may be practically complete, as in Norway, where all special schools are State schools, and where the government pays all expenses except in a few instances where the local government (commune, county, or parish) is required to pay a fixed amount. In Sweden, where some special schools are run by voluntary organizations, most of the costs of special education are still paid by the government. In Denmark the government pays the expenses of educating and training handicapped children not only in official institutions but also in approved private establishments, and half the teachers' salaries. A more common pattern is that found in Finland, France, and Poland, where the financing of programs of services for the handicapped child is shared by federal and local authorities and by voluntary associations. In Finland the government owns and operates the six schools for the deaf and the two schools for the blind, whereas other schools are operated and financed by voluntary groups with some government subsidies.

Varying policies are followed with reference to the plant and operating costs of the schools. In Austria the government pays for the administration, inspection, and salaries in all public schools, including special schools, and for the buildings and maintenance costs of institutions for secondary and higher education. But the municipality provides the buildings and maintenance for all public primary schools, including special schools, though a few private schools furnish their own. Norway provides the buildings for both private and public special schools, as well as their maintenance. Northern Ireland provides for the external maintenance of schools, as well as their equipment. In Ireland the government gives a partial subsidy for the costs of heating and cleaning school quarters, and for special equipment in schools for the blind and the deaf; also grants are given to defray up to two-thirds the cost of building and equipping new schools. In Spain the government pays half the costs of constructing special schools, while the municipalities furnish the sites; the State also provides the major proportion of the equipment and operational costs.

An example of the sharing of expenses for capital construction is that of the School Foundation for Cripples in Finland, a school for 120 orthopedically handicapped children. The site for a new building was given by the municipality of Helsinki, while the national government granted an interest-free loan for the building itself.

It is a common practice for the central government to pay the salaries of teachers at least in the public special schools. These salaries are paid in full by the government in Austria, England, France (in the national institutions), the Netherlands, Ireland, Norway, Poland, Luxembourg, Scotland, and Sweden. Payments are often made through the local education board or council. Austria also pays the costs of special classes, including the teachers' salaries, when classes reach 15 in size. Similarly the government in Belgium pays a teacher's salary when the number of children taught reaches 15 in an establishment classified as a social welfare institution. In Greece the salaries of teachers in schools for the blind and the deaf are paid by the government. In Italy, these salaries are paid in addition to those for teachers in special classes and centers for the crippled. In Portugal the government pays salaries for teachers in all sanitaria and welfare establishments.

In other countries the government pays a part of the salaries. In Denmark, the government pays half the cost of teachers' salaries in public and private schools, and all direct expenses in training special teachers. In Spain the government pays the larger share of salary expenditures in special schools, whereas in Switzerland, where the cantons assume most of the responsibility for both regular and special education, the federal government contributes only a small subsidy and the cantons and municipalities a larger share. Similarly, special teachers' salaries in Poland are paid from a combination of government budgets on the national, provincial, and county levels.

In some instances where the central government pays the salaries of teachers in public institutions, there may be partial subsidies for salaries and other expenses in private schools, as in England, where the Local Education Authority can pay, with grants from the Ministry of Education, private school fees which have been approved by this Ministry. Partial subsidies are also available for private schools in Greece and in Portugal.

In Germany and Yugoslavia, these salaries are paid on the provincial level. In Yugoslavia however, it may be either the republican Executive Council or the local government.

Even when the government pays teachers' salaries in special schools, a distinction is frequently made between these instructional services and medical or therapy services, the cost of which may be borne by voluntary groups.

Transportation costs for handicapped youngsters receiving education or treatment are paid in various ways. In few countries do authorities feel that provisions are adequate. Some countries have laws making it mandatory for the government on the national or local level to provide transportation for handicapped youngsters attending the regular schools or day special schools or receiving out-patient treatment in clinics and hospitals, but these laws are not always enforced. For example, in Belgium the law requires that public authorities provide transportation when an educable handicapped child lives more than 4 kilometers from school, the costs to be apportioned in this way: five-eighths paid by the national government, one-eighth by the provincial government, two-eighths by the commune where the child resides. But since the law, passed in 1958, is not yet fully in effect, many parents still pay for such transportation or are assisted by voluntary organizations.

Transportation services are more frequently found in the larger cities, where the municipal government either provides the transportation itself or pays for the costs of using existing facilities. For example, the city of Vienna provides three special school buses to transport orthopedically handicapped children to and from special day schools, while all other handicapped children have free transportation in public conveyances such as streetcars and buses for themselves and an attendant.

It is a common practice throughout Europe to provide special tickets or reduced rates on public transportation such as street cars, buses, and trains for the handicapped, especially for traveling to and from their homes for vacation periods. Sometimes the special rates are also given to the parents as well, and to a guide or companion for the handicapped child when one is necessary.

Parents and voluntary associations still assume responsibility for the transporting of handicapped children in many countries. Insurance companies sometimes pay such costs for the children of members, and special private funds such as a polio fund may in other instances pay part or all of the costs.

Assistance given to parents in meeting the costs of special treatment and education for handicapped children, whether given by official or voluntary agencies, is commonly based on some kind of means test, except in a few countries like Denmark. Parents are expected in most countries to share the costs, but they rarely pay more than a small fraction of the total expenses involved in caring for and educating their handicapped children. In Poland, for example, medical care and tuition in a special school are free, but parents are expected to pay for the maintenance, depending on their income. On the average, Polish parents pay about 20 per cent of the total cost of their child's maintenance. At the same time there are private Polish institutions for the epileptic and the crippled where full maintenance is provided.

Even in Switzerland where parental responsibility is stressed to a greater extent than in most other countries, the parents are often aided by grants from voluntary organizations like Pro Infirmis or its member associations, some of which are in turn subsidized by the cantons to give such grants. Some cantons have special funds for medical care, and every canton provides scholarships for vocational training.

Legislation has followed the general pattern of providing first for the blind and deaf, later for the war-injured and/or job-injured, and only more recently for the crippled as such, and for other groups of the handicapped. For example, it was only within the last decade that amendments to the Child Welfare Law in Finland have extended benefits to victims of polio, tuberculosis of the bones and joints, pulmonary tuberculosis, and rheumatoid arthritis. A 1957 decree in Belgium arranged to pay for the treatment and education of cerebral palsied children less than 14 years of age, with an IQ above 60.

The handicapped youngster looking for work is sometimes benefited by preferential legislation allotting the handicapped a certain proportion of jobs. In Austria the blind and those physically handicapped in accidents have the same employment rights as veterans. A 1958 law in Belgium requires that enterprises employing at least 20 persons must employ a certain number of handicapped persons registered with a government placement body. The Scottish government has established a 3 per cent quota of handicapped persons to be employed in business and industry, and reserves certain kinds of work for the handicapped, such as "Passenger Electric Lift Attendant" and "Car Park Attendant."

Special education developments in a particular country may depend in part on the encouragement given by favorable legislation to certain groups. For example, in Belgium in recent years there have been established a disproportionate number of classes for the physically handicapped as compared with the mentally retarded. This results from the fact that subsidies for the instruction of the mentally retarded are less generous than those for the crippled; therefore the tendency has been to classify children as "physically handicapped" whenever possible.

In some countries the adequacy of services for the handicapped varies considerably from one part of the country to another. In Italy, for example, some municipal governments such as that in the commune of Milan have assumed more responsibility than the national government for the handicapped; the services in Milan are said to represent the highest level of development of any program of public services for the handicapped in Italy. In Yugoslavia it is reported that there is a more unified approach to the problem of handicapped children in Serbia than in the other republics.

The medical and welfare provisions that are often an important supplement to the educational provisions for handicapped children are in most countries financed at least in part by some form of national social welfare or sickness or disability insurance program. In a few countries, like Ireland, the Netherlands, and Norway, membership is compulsory for the general public, but in most countries membership is optional. Even in this case a large percentage of the population enroll (e.g. 45 per cent in Yugoslavia, 60 per cent in Spain, 70 per cent in Switzerland). Coverage varies in its comprehensiveness. In Austria, for example, the insurance program does not cover congenital handicaps or prolonged rehabilitation treatment, the costs for which are left to provincial welfare organizations. Switzerland has instituted in 1960 a more comprehensive program of invalidity insurance to replace the earlier program.

Many European governments provide special family allotments, some of which make allowance for handicapped children in particular. The allotment is frequently extended to a later age in the case of handicapped youngsters, as in Austria where the age limit is 21 for normal children and 25 for the handicapped. Also in Finland the age limits are 16 and 17 respectively. The allotment may be given for each child, as in Austria, Finland, Northern Ireland, and Yugoslavia, or for each child except the first, as in Ireland and Norway.

In some cases the allotment is given for a particular kind of handicap. In Belgium crippled youngsters 14 to 21 years of age receive special compensation. In France special payments go to deaf children less than 15 years old with a permanent loss of capacity of 80 per cent. In Germany there is an extra allowance, over and above an ordinary family allowance, when there are blind children under the age of 16. In Greece and Italy special allotments are given for children crippled during World War II; Greece extends this coverage to children with disabilities resulting from causes associated with the War, but possibly producing postwar injuries, such as mines and hand grenades.

Practice varies in making the family allowance or special child disability allowance dependent on a means test. The French provision for deaf children does depend on need, but Irish provisions do not when the child is under 16.

Handicapped children who are also orphans usually receive the same benefits as non-handicapped orphans, if there are special provisions for this group. For example, in Poland all schools and institutions are free for orphans, and when they complete their school education they receive a grant to help them make a start in life.

In those countries where special provisions are made for children who were orphaned in World War II, handicapped and normal children are usually treated alike.

It is a common practice throughout Europe for the costs of education, treatment, special equipment, prostheses, etc., for the handicapped to be shared by voluntary organizations, even when there are official sources of financial aid. Some of these societies are devoted to physically handicapped persons in general, such as the national veterans' associations and the Red Cross, and others to the orthopedically handicapped as an inclusive group, such as the Rotary Club. Still others are concerned with specific groups such as the blind or deaf, and those with polio, tuberculosis, epilepsy, heart conditions, or more recently, cerebral palsy. Some organizations are devoted only to members and families of members, such as national insurance companies, whereas others do extend their help beyond their membership lists.

Although in every country the earliest provisions for the handicapped were made by voluntary organizations or private individuals, the government — whether national, provincial, or municipal — has assumed increasing responsibility for the handicapped. In some countries the national government has taken over these private ventures, and made them free public institutions financed entirely by the State, as in the case of the schools for the blind and for the deaf in Finland and in France. More frequently, however, the State has subsidized them increasingly, while leaving their administration in the hands of the sponsoring organization, as in Greece.

Usually the subsidized private institution is operated by a voluntary, welfare, non-profit group. The sponsoring organization may be lay or religious. Yugoslavia is the only country in which there is a policy of no government subsidies for the special education efforts of religious groups.

The proportion of services provided for the handicapped by religious organizations has steadily declined in most countries. Although in Belgium 90 per cent of institutions for the handicapped are still operated by Catholic orders, and religious groups also provide many special schools in France, Germany, the Netherlands, and Portugal, there has been a general increase in lay voluntary and government services. Only Belgium, the Netherlands, and Germany now report that they have separate voluntary organizations for the handicapped based on religious affiliation.

Thus voluntary organizations, with an increasing proportion of non-denominational sponsorship, continue to provide important services for the handicapped in every European country. In Switzerland 80 per cent of the special schools are still operated by voluntary groups, and in the Netherlands, 83 per cent. But even where these private organizations operate few of the special schools they provide many other services. In Norway, where all the special schools are state owned, many voluntary organizations have directly and indirectly served the handicapped child. In 1956 almost half the Norwegian population were members of four major associations — the Norwegian Red Cross, the Women's Public Health Association, the Norwegian National Tuberculosis and Public Health Association, and the Norwegian People's Relief Association. In addition there are many other organizations devoted to a single category such as those for the blind, the protection of hearing, cancer, cripples, tuberculosis, polio, the deaf, arthritis and rheumatism, cerebral palsy, and diabetes.

The range of services provided by voluntary organizations is often very wide. They arrange conferences and lectures for special teachers, parents, or the general public. They organize exhibits, such as those for the painting and sculpture by the deaf. They provide recreational opportunities for the handicapped, which may consist of specific parties or of clubs and recreation centers. They often provide vocational guidance, placement, and follow-up services. They organize work for the homebound. They provide library services, or publish journals of interest to special educators, to the general public, or to a particular group of handicapped children. They provide financial aid and legal information.

Cooperation among various voluntary organizations working for the handicapped has resulted in many instances in important social advances. For example, the combined efforts of various medical, social, and educational institutions in Belgium resulted in the passage of a law in 1958 concerning the vocational training, rehabilitation, and social reclassification of the handicapped.

Education of the general public is thus in some cases an important function of volunteer groups. They can inform the general public about health matters, convince public organizations of the value of new preventive or curative health measures, and emphasize special educational and welfare needs of the handicapped. Often their convictions are demonstrated through the medium of pioneering experimental work in the institutions they maintain.

Closely related to this process of educating the general public is the research carried on by private groups. Although there are some government sponsored programs of research in a few countries like

Austria, France, Poland, and Scotland, in most countries the major research in the field of special education is still conducted by private individuals, universities, and voluntary organizations. An outstanding example is the work of the Ewings at Manchester University in England concerning the education of the deaf. It seems that more research is devoted to the problems of the deaf than to any other group of the handicapped.

These varied contributions that voluntary societies are making to the provisions for the handicapped in every European country are usually coordinated with official agencies serving the handicapped. In addition the voluntary groups maintain close relationships with similar interest groups in other countries, or with related international organizations such as the World Council for the Welfare of the Blind, the World Federation of the Deaf, and the International Society for the Welfare of Cripples.

Effective administration of programs of services in some instances, as in Belgium, has been difficult to achieve because of the rivalries between various voluntary groups working for the handicapped, some of which may feel they have a vested interest in welfare and educational activities for a particular category of handicapped persons. It is understandable that duplication and overlapping of facilities, with the persistence of uneconomical multiplicity of small institutions and centers, may occur because of the haphazard way in which such establishments emerge in the early stages of special education development in most countries.

European authorities in the field of special education recognize that many improvements and changes are needed in order to increase the efficiency with which services for handicapped children are organized and administered.

More specific information is needed about present methods of financing special education services. Data are needed concerning the per-pupil costs of education for various categories of handicapped children. Also necessary are summaries of the various formulas used for sharing costs among the localities, provinces, and national government. Basic programs described in terms of minimum permissible expenditures for each category of disability would furnish incentives for local communities to improve their programs, especially with regard to equipment. Furthermore such detailed information, would better enable various countries to profit from each other's experience, adapting techniques and findings to their individual situations.

It is generally felt that services for the handicapped would also be more efficient if there were greater centralization of authority, preferably in the Ministry of Education. This would make possible a kind of over-all planning and regulation that is at present very difficult to achieve in many countries. Problems such as those related to curricular development, transportation for handicapped pupils, adequate compensation for special teachers, improved teacher preparation, better integration of medical and educational provisions for the handicapped, financing of programs, and equalized opportunities for various kinds of handicapped persons can be approached more systematically when viewed in terms of the total picture in a given country. The research necessary to the solution of such problems might be planned and directed through some central agency.

In every country attempts have been made to realize these objectives. Solutions will of course differ in details because of the differences in historical background and in cultural and political development in European countries, but there is widespread recognition of broad common objectives in the administration of programs of services for handicapped children.

special education in england*

RONALD GULLIFORD†

Following is an outline of the organization of special education in England and a consideration of a number of areas in which international cooperation could be productive.

TYPES OF SPECIAL EDUCATION

Present arrangements for special education stem from the Education Act of 1944 which gave the local education authorities (of large towns and countries) the duty of finding out which children in their area suffer from any disability of mind or body and of insuring that they received special education in special schools or in other ways. Ten categories of handicapped children were specified: blind, partially sighted, deaf, partially hearing, educationally subnormal, epileptic, maladjusted, physically handicapped, speech defective and delicate. (The gifted are not included because we consider them to be well cared for by grammar schools.)

The *educationally subnormal* correspond to the American term educable retarded. The definition of educationally subnormal was

*Reprinted from *Selected Convention Papers, 46th Annual International CEC Convention, New York City, New York, April 14-20, 1966*, pp. 171-175, by permission of the author and the Council for Exceptional Children. Copyright 1968 by the Council for Exceptional Children.

†Ronald Gulliford is Senior Lecturer in Education, University of Birmingham, England.

deliberately made a broad one, referring to children who were educationally retarded on account of limited ability or because of other conditions, in order to get away from rigid IQ criteria and from the prewar certification of pupils as mentally defective or feeble-minded. The result is that they range in IQ from 50 to 85 (sometimes higher), and there is a lot of consideration given to deciding what criteria should apply.

The *maladjusted* category was a new one in 1944. Their education was first mainly given in small boarding schools which combined a family atmosphere with a therapeutic approach. Day schools and classes have been developing, although the provision does not match the need. The majority of *epileptic* children are of course in ordinary schools, but there are six schools for severe problems requiring specialized education and medical treatment. The majority of *speech defective* children are in ordinary schools but there are several boarding schools for aphasic children. There is a wide range of day, boarding and hospital schools for the *physically handicapped*.

Of possible interest is the *delicate* category. Originally open air schools for delicate children were started in the early 1900's for children whose health had suffered from poor social and health conditions in industrial urban areas. With improved health and welfare the number of such children has declined and the vacant places have been used as an extra facility for children with a variety of conditions such as minor maladjustment, educational retardation, social disadvantages, or other needs not appropriately met by other special schools.

Trainable retarded children are at present the responsibility of local health departments who provide for them in training centers; others are in hospitals for the subnormals. There are moves afoot which make it likely that the trainable will come under Education and become a part of special education. There has already been a trend to set up assessment classes for borderline retarded children of 5 to 8 years as a means of deciding the degree of educability before placement in training center of special school.

Delinquent children may be sent to boarding schools approved and supervised by the Home Office. Most large towns have remedial teaching, home teaching and language teaching for immigrants.

Two supporting services are the School Health Service, which plans an important part in the identification of handicapped children and in child guidance, school psychology and speech therapy (the latter two laboring from shortage of personnel), and school welfare services; and the Youth Employment services.

The larger authorities (London, Birmingham, Manchester, etc.) provide schools and classes for each of the handicaps but areas with smaller populations may arrange for some groups of handicapped children to go to schools in neighboring authorities or to boarding schools; of the 76,466 pupils in special schools, 20,898 are in boarding schools. The majority of schools are run and financed by local authorities out of local taxes supplemented by government grants. There are a number of schools run by private organizations (especially for blind, physically handicapped and maladjusted children), although the fees are paid by local education authorities. The vast majority of pubils are educated at public expense; there is very little private special schooling. Medical examinations and treatment are provided by the School Health Service and by the National Health Service.

Special training and certification for teachers is only obligatory at present for teachers of the deaf and the blind, although many colleges and universities provide training courses in special education. Training consists of a year of full time study three to five years after initial teacher qualification, with the teachers being paid full salary by their local authorities. Just under half the teachers in special education are men.

ISSUES FOR
COOPERATIVE PLANNING

The population is small enough and the geography compact enough to aim at comprehensive provision for all who really need special education. One of the questions in which we could fruitfully cooperate internationally is how much special provision to make for different groups of handicapped children. The survey by the Wood Committee in 1929 is acknowledged to be one of the more reliable estimates of the prevalence of mental defect. At present Professor Tizard of London University is directing an interdisciplinary research in which whole age groups of children in the Isle of Wight are carefully screened for disabilities — not only the major ones but the less obvious disabilities affecting learning. Information from this study should provide a basic measure of the minimum provision needed in other areas. For example, in this relatively rural area with few large towns he has come up with an incidence of maladjustment of 6 percent.

But it is one thing to know the expected incidence of disability; it is another thing to set up the machinery for ensuring early identification. Public health departments of local authorities already operate observation registers listing all children born at risk and these are followed up by pediatricians and infant welfare doctors. This increases the chances of detecting sensory and physical handicaps as early as possible in the preschool period. We need to develop a second tier of identificatory procedures in the first school years in order to ensure the early detection of disabilities which become apparent in an educational setting. Present procedures used in Britain are routine school medical examinations, visual and audiometric screening and referral by headteachers (school principals). But we know that some children are identified much later than they should be; there are variations in the competence of schools to identify children and there are variations between areas, notably between the North and South of England. In England, children start school at five years of age, and by the time they reach the age of seven, teachers have a fairly intimate knowledge of them. It would be useful to develop a systematic use of teachers' observations of their pupils supplemented by a sample of children's performances on several critical tasks in order to identify children who are obviously going to need special help and those who are likely to need special help. It seems especially important to identify educable retarded children, maladjusted children and children with learning difficulties. Many school systems do in fact screen children at about age 8, but it would be preferable to screen them by the end of the seventh year. In England, it is unlikely that there will be enough experts with the time to perform this initial screening but with professional guidance, the teachers' contribution to this process could be made more systematic, objective, and reliable. In a recent survey of 11,000 seven year olds, headteachers were asked to specify whether in their opinion the child needed some form of special education. The teachers had no difficulty in classifying 5 percent as likely to need special help and were undecided about another 3.5 percent.

A second issue that lends itself to international cooperation is the organization of special education. The English system is based on the special school. Thus 45,000 educationally subnormal children attend special schools and this represents 0.7 percent of the total school population of children from 5 to 16. There is a larger number of retarded children receiving some form of special teaching in ordinary schools but these arrangements are less well organized and supervised. There are special classes in ordinary schools for partially sighted, partially hearing, maladjusted, and delicate children. However, there is an important need for special schools in a system of special education as a center where a variety of resources and specialties can be focused. In England, the need is felt to develop a special class system complementary to special schools, and this is one area in which American experience would be helpful. A related problem is how to ensure the satisfactory integration of the exceptional child into ordinary schools and regular classes. We all pay lipservice to the belief that wherever possible the handicapped child should be integrated, but it is not so easy to ensure that the school and the teachers have sufficient insight, knowledge and the appropriate attitudes to do this adequately.

One of the problems which confronts special educators at the present time is the many children who don't fit neatly into official classifications. Research into disability distinguishes various neurological disabilities, clumsy children, language disorders, autistic children and other kinds of specific disorders, sometimes seen as separate groups from the major handicaps, and sometimes as problems occurring in all of them. Distinct educational programs and environments are specified for them; parent pressure groups add to the demand. If a country is trying to develop a comprehensive system of special education and its resources are strained to provide for the major needs, just how far should it go in differentiating provision for subgroups of exceptionality? Maybe the answer depends on the existing method of organization, and within special schools perhaps it is possible to meet special needs by setting up classes. Perhaps also the answer depends on demographic factors, and it may be possible in large urban areas to cater for many distinct needs, but in thinly populated areas special classes and schools will have to continue to cater for a spectrum of disability by individualizing treatment as far as they can. In England, this problem is before us in the educationally subnormal schools which inevitably include the socially disadvantaged, the maladjusted and retarded, the neurologically impaired, the borderline trainable, the noncommunicating child, and children with mild physical and sensory disabilities. The question of the possible value of separate schools for the cerebral palsied and for spina bifida children is also under discussion. There is a distinct trend in English thinking towards the notion of a comprehensive special school which provides for a variety of handicaps, and for more liaison and interchange between specialists in different areas. There is need for much discussion of such issues which are very relevant to the situation of countries where special educational development is just getting under way.

Another issue for cooperation is in planning preschool education for exceptional children. It would be superfluous to argue the case for early education of the handicapped. In England there is a fair provision for the preschool deaf and for the physically handicapped. For a long time English pre nursery schools (run publicly for children between the ages of three and five) have taken a number of handicapped children, especially the emotionally disturbed and those with delayed language and speech. Day nurseries run by the Health Department have also taken a few children, including the mentally retarded. There is strong public pressure for public nursery schools to be provided much more extensively, especially for socially disadvantaged children. Also middle class parents have banded together and are running their own play groups, often including a handicapped child. We also have a preschool specifically for handicapped children acting as a diagnostic center and counseling service. These developments suggest other possibilities for the highly desirable preschool education of exceptional children. This again is a growing point in special education in which international interchange would be beneficial.

There are of course many other issues in curriculum planning and special methods worthy of cooperation, and the idea of international cooperation in planning special education could be a fruitful one. There is nothing more stimulating to thought than finding that someone else does something different from you -- unless it is trying to unravel how something which appears to be the same in two countries (like deafness!) is yet different. As far as Britain is concerned, we already make much use of American textbooks and research reports. It is to be wished however that there were more interchanges between personnel such as those offered by the CEC conventions; that is one reason we of the Association for Special Education were glad to welcome a large contingent at our 1966 Conference in London (as well as a contingent from Russia). But conference interchange is not enough nor is communication between University personnel. There could be more reciprocal visits between administrators and teachers. Also, it would be helpful to know more about European special education. There surely would be benefit in more thorough comparison of the ways different countries tackle similar problems.

There are, however, some important qualifications to make about the values of international cooperation in special education. One can't really understand another system without having real understanding of the sociocultural differences, the different political and administrative framework, the history of the educational system and particularly its aims and general philosophy. For example, the amount that we in England can learn from what Americans are doing in compensatory education is open to question. England certainly has socially disadvantaged children and some of their problems are comparable. But, one difficulty is to assess how similar the problem really is in social and educational terms, and another is to assess how far American methods and techniques are applicable in a different cultural and educational setting. Certainly, the evaluation of different systems of special education is an important field of study, in the light of all the relevant differences between societies. Comparative Special Education would be not just an academic exercise but a valuable foundation for the inevitable expansion of special education in undeveloped countries.

part VIII

special education personnel: characteristics, preparation, staffing, and research

There is considerable and recurring interest in the area of special education personnel, but with limited accompanying research. The questions are obvious even in this relatively new teaching area. What are the personnel and situational forces crucial to selecting special education as a vocational choice, and how can we identify people with outstanding potential for achievement in special education? As understanding of the relationships of vocational choice and behavior to personality, personal development, social psychology, and related areas increases, so in turn should this foster an increased number and variety of empirical studies and theoretical formulations in the area of personnel for special education.

Charles Meisgeier, whose paper begins this chapter, presses for identifying and quantifying characteristics of individuals which set them apart as successful in their student teaching of mentally and physically handicapped children. As one of the first significant multivariate approaches to this problem, Meisgeier identifies three characteristic and unique patterns of successful special class teachers. He also raises the question of the relationship of regular class teaching to special class teaching. He notes that "no prior regular class teaching experience" was found to be significantly related to effective special class teaching. Reginald Jones provides a comprehensive review of major research in the field and suggests a need for systematic research programs. Louis Schwartz proposes a preparation program for the clinical educator which would encompass diagnostic and remedial skills for learning difficulties presented by exceptional children. Additionally, he discusses the knowledge gap between exceptionality and teacher education curricula and problems associated with shortages of personnel and the qualitative aspects of special education.

Frances Mullen analyzes data from a Chicago Public School study on special education staffing and policies in 34 large cities. Pupil-teacher ratio, class size, policies, and finance are compared among these cities. She suggests some measure of the comparative extent to which a city meets the educational needs of its exceptional children may be obtained by calculating the percentage of all elementary pupils in that city who are in special classes or schools. Mullen hypothesizes that a city with a generous staffing policy with respect to elementary class size should be generous in its staffing policies for special education and suggests a crude index of generosity from the data of this study.

James B. McDonald, in the concluding article, notes an increasing number of teacher education studies appearing in the literature but that these are better called innovations rather than systematic research. He essays two major avenues for developing experimental programs for the education of teachers.

the identification of
successful teachers of mentally
or physically handicapped children*

CHARLES MEISGEIER†

Abstract: To accomplish the purpose of identifying and quantifying characteristics which contribute to successful student teaching of mentally and physically handicapped children, five dimensions of human behavior were investigated. Three characteristic patterns of successful student teaching experiences emerged from the investigation. The successful student teachers (a) were well adjusted, emotionally stable, and able to encounter difficult special class situations: (b) possessed physical energy, vitality, and enthusiasm necessary to meet special classroom demands; (c) obtained high scores on measures of scholastic achievement and ability.

Although many studies have been made of the characteristics of regular class teachers, there is an overall lack of empirical information concerning the characteristics of effective special education teachers. One dimension recurrently subjected to scrutiny is the early selection of students who, for various reasons, aspire to teach mentally or physically handicapped children. With the exception of one major study conducted over ten years ago (Mackie,

*Reprinted from *Exceptional Children* (December 1965), pp. 229- 235, by permission of the author and the Council for Exceptional Children. Copyright 1965 by the Council for Exceptional Children.

†Charles Meisgeier is Coordinator, Special Education Administration Programs, The University of Texas at Austin.

Williams, and Dunn, 1954) there is a paucity of information regarding either the characteristics of teachers of mentally or physically handicapped or the prediction of effective teaching of these children.

PURPOSE OF THE STUDY

The purpose of this study was (a) to identify and quantify the characteristics that might contribute to successful student teaching of mentally or physically handicapped children and (b) to establish criteria for the selection of prospective teachers of these children. To accomplish this, five dimensions of human behavior were investigated to determine the relationship, if any, to successful student teaching of handicapped children. The five areas were: (a) scholastic aptitude, (b) scholastic achievement, (c) educational (vocational) interest, (d) personality, and (e) attitudes toward children and toward teaching.

METHOD

The 41 subjects included in this investigation were student teaching in special classes for either mentally or physically handicapped children. With the exception of one 30 year old subject, the students ranged in age from 20 to 24 years, with a mean age of 21 years. The mean IQ of the group was 122 with a standard deviation of 7.07. The students were undergraduates in their junior or senior years from seven colleges offering training programs for students preparing to become teachers of mentally or physically handicapped children.

Test Battery

The sources of information consisted of (a) academic transcripts, (b) admission records, (c) a battery of seven selected instruments, and (d) the criterion measure — the *Evaluation Record for Teachers of Handicapped Children* (ERTHC). The test battery completed by each student consisted of the following seven instruments: Otis Gamma Test of Mental Ability Form E_M (OGT); Personal Information Blank (PIB); Sixteen Personality Factors

Questionnaire, Form C (16 PF Test); Thurstone Temperament Schedule (TTS); Gordon Personal Inventory (GPI); Educational Interest Inventory (EII); Minnesota Teacher Attitude Inventory (MTAI). The OGT was administered to each student either in groups at the colleges by a member of the staff or individually by the cooperating teacher; the remainder of the tests were administered by mail.

The PIB and ERTHC were developed particularly for use in this investigation. The PIB provided information pertaining to the student's reasons for entering special education, the age when the choice was made, and the student's satisfaction with the choice. Items pertaining to the choice of vocation were included in six major areas of influence; personal, educational, professional, occupational, social, and miscellaneous.

The ERTHC, a new criterion measure, was developed to measure the effectiveness of student teachers of mentally or physically handicapped children. A cumulative rating on the ERTHC was made by the cooperating teacher and the college supervisor.

The *Teaching Evaluation Record* by Dwight Beecher (1953) formed the basis for the new evaluation instrument. After critical analysis by a panel of teachers and a panel of professors, 19 inappropriate items of the original 32 Beecher items were deleted, and the remaining 13 items were modified in varying degrees to meet the particular needs of this study. Nine completely new items were added, making a total of 22 items on the experimental form of the new instrument. Several hundred items from six major sources formed the basis for the modification of the Beecher items and for the construction of the new ones.

After examination of the experimental form by the panel of teachers and professors, a competent jury of experts reviewed the instrument and further modifications were made. The final form of the new instrument (ERTHC) contained 20 items. The reliability of the new instrument is .82.

Several techniques, including a factor analytic study of observer ratings, were used to determine the best possible way to administer the criterion measure. The factor analysis and varimax rotation indicated that the loading of the Composite ERTHC (composite rating of college supervisor and cooperating teacher) on the Performance Factor (F3) was significant beyond the .01 level. These results, combined with analysis of the degree of saturation of the criterion variable, indicated that the Composite ERTHC was the most useful criterion variable.

RESULTS AND
CONCLUSIONS

Successful student teaching in special classes is correlated with observable criteria which can be measured objectively. Nineteen predictor variables measuring five dimensions of human behavior were found to be significant at or beyond the .05 level. The five measured dimensions were: (a) scholastic aptitude, (b) scholastic achievement, (c) personality traits, (d) educational (vocational) interests, and (e) teacher attitudes. Thirteen of the correlations were significant at the .05 level and six were significant at the .01 level. The coefficients of correlation of the 19 significant predictor variables with the criterion measure are indicated in Table 1.

Considerable evidence was found to indicate acceptance of the five hypotheses of the investigation, and thus all five were accepted. Conclusions one to six summarize the findings pertaining to the five hypotheses.

1. A positive, significant relationship was found between scholastic aptitude and successful student teaching of mentally or physically handicapped children. The correlation between the OGT and the measure of successful student teaching was positive and significant beyond the .05 level.

2. A positive, significant relationship was found between scholastic achievement and successful student teaching of mentally or physically handicapped children. Four measures of college achievement — the All College Cumulative Grade Point Average (CGPA), CGPA Psychology, CGPA Special Education, and the CGPA General Courses — were significantly correlated with the measure of successful student teaching beyond the .05 level. The correlations of the All College CGPA and General Education CGPA to the criterion measure resulted in positive correlations significant at the .01 level. It is interesting to note that only the CGPA in "professional education" courses failed to produce a significant correlation, although it did load highly with the others in the factor analysis.

   Indirect measures of achievement such as background or experience were found generally to be unrelated to successful student teaching of handicapped children. Of the ten background experience measures, only two resulted in significant correlations. The correlation of the number of

TABLE 1.

Coefficients of Correlation of 19 Predictor
Variables with the Criterion Measure of
Successful Student Teaching
(Composite ERTHC)

	Predictor Variable	Correlation with Criterion Measure
6	Otis Gamma Test of Mental Ability	.36*
10	Gordon Personal Inventory — Vigor	.43**
15	Thurstone Temperament Schedule — Dominant	.34*
16	Thurstone Temperament Schedule — Stable	.36*
24	16 PF Test F Enthusiastic, Talkative (Surgency)	.32*
26	16 PF Test H Adventurous (Parmia)	.37*
27	16 PF Test I Tough, Realistic (Harria)	—.42**
29	16 PF Test M Conventional, Practical (Praxemia)	—.30*
35	16 PF Test Q_4 Phlegmatic, Composed (Low Ergic Tension)	—.31*
36	Minnesota Teacher Attitude Inventory	.41**
40	Educational Interest Inventory — Elementary Teacher	—.39*
42	Educational Interest Inventory — Elementary Principal	—.36*
47	Educational Interest Inventory — Researcher	.33*
49	Cumulative Grade Point Average, All College	.43**
50	Cumulative Grade Point Average, Psychology	.39*
51	Cumulative Grade Point Average, Special Education	.37*
53	Cumulative Grade Point Average, General College Courses	.49**
56	Number College Courses — General Education	.37*
60	No *Student* Teaching Experience in Regular Class	.40**

Correlation significant at the .05 level.
**Correlation significant at the .01 level.*

general courses completed, with the criterion measure, was
significant beyond the .05 level. Prior student teaching
experience in a regular class was not positively related to
successful special class teaching. The correlation was
significant beyond the .01 level.

3. A significant relationship was found between various
measures of personality and successful student teaching of
mentally or physically handicapped children. Eight significant measures of personality were found on the three
personality instruments used in the study. These measures
and significant subscales were: (a) the GPI — Vigor (V);
(b) The TTS — Dominant (D), Emotionally Stable (E); and
(c) the 16 PF Test, Form C — Enthusiastic (F), Adven-
turous (H), Realistic (I), Practical (N), Stable (Q_4).

4. A significant relationship was found between three measures of educational (vocational) interest and successful student teaching of mentally or physically handicapped children. These measures were on the EII. The significant subscales were Elementary Teacher, Elementary Principal, and Researcher.

5. A significant relationship was found between certain attitudes toward children and teaching, and successful student teaching of mentally or physically handicapped children. The correlation between the MTAI and the criterion measure was significant beyond the .01 level.

6. By factor analysis, it was determined that the measures of scholastic achievement were the most highly associated with successful student teaching of mentally or physically handicapped children.

7. Three patterns of successful student teachers of mentally or physically handicapped children emerged from this investigation. All three patterns were characteristic of the successful student teacher. They were found (a) to be well adjusted, emotionally stable, able to successively encounter the many trying situations that arise in a special class, (b) to possess the physical energy, the vitality and enthusiasm necessary to meet the demands of special class teaching, and (c) to obtain high scores on measures of scholastic achievement and general ability or intelligence and to possess a favorable attitude toward teaching and children. These three patterns and subpatterns were: *Pattern 1* — Achievement-Ability-Attitude; *Pattern 2* — Personal Adjustment-General Emotional Stability; (a) Experimenting (b) Sociable (c) Composed (d) Emotionally Stable; *Pattern 3* — Dynamic Energy: (a) Energetic (b) Responsible (c) Realistic.

8. The student teachers of mentally or physically handicapped children differed markedly from other college students and from students preparing to teach in other fields on selected measures of personality, interest, and attitude. Comparisons of the mean scores of the student teachers with published norms on the GPI, 16 PF Test, MTAI, and EII indicated that the student teachers possessed relatively unique characteristics. Thirty of the 40 comparisons resulted in differences significant beyond the .05 level.

On the GPI, the student teachers were compared with a norm group of college students and significant differences were noted on all five of the scales (Cautiousness, Personal Relations, Original Thinking, Vigor, and Total Score). A similar comparison with college students on the 16 PF Test indicated significant differences on ten of the scales (Factors A, B, C, G, H, I, M, Q_1, Q_2, Q_4). On the MTAI, comparisons were made on nine norm groups selected as being most like the study group. Out of the nine comparisons, seven were significantly different at the .01 level. There were no significant differences for beginning education juniors on the "Secondary nonacademic" group or for "Experienced Elementary Teacher." Significant differences were found on eight subscales of the EII. No significant differences were found on either the Elementary Teacher scale or on the Supervisor scale.

9. Personal, educational, and professional experiences or desires comprised the major components influencing the student's decision to enter the field of special education.

    The student teachers in the present investigation indicated that they entered the field primarily because of personal reasons. Few indicated they had become interested in special education because of high school counseling programs. The challenge of the field, the desire to help the handicapped, visits to special classes, schools or hospitals, and the opportunities for jobs caused by teacher shortages were some of the choices most frequently checked by the students as influencing their decision to become teachers of mentally or physically handicapped children. No clear cut patterns were observed, nor was any systematic recruitment procedure discernible. Rather, there seemed to be a haphazard combination of accidental, unrelated experiences responsible for their choice.

10. Two multiple regression equations computed for testing and use in future studies concerned with the problem of predicting successful teaching of mentally or physically handicapped children resulted in multiple R's of .62 and .72 significant beyond the .01 level.

11. The multiple regression with parsimony process was utilized in each case to determine the one regression equation with maximum prediction value and minimum number of independent predictor variables. The first multiple regression analysis included the variables from Factor 3 (the achievement-performance factor), and all 19 of the significant predictor variables were employed in a second analysis

regardless of factor loadings. This was done since the significant variables before factor analysis could be considered more complex than the variables only loading in the achievement-performance factor. Thus, it would be expected that a higher multiple R would result from an analysis of the 19 variables than would result from an analysis utilizing only the variables from a common factor such as Factor 3. This expectation was verified by the results. The contribution to the variance of the five variables was significant beyond the .01 level for each equation.

Equation One. Computed on Factor 3 variables resulted in a multiple R of .62 and the following equation:

$$Y = .089\,X_1 - 10.8493\,X_2 + 2.6571\,X_3 + 2.5796\,X_4 + 7.9294\,X_5 + 55.719$$

where:

Y = Criterion Measure—Composite ERTHC
X_1 = Adjusted MTAI Score
X_2 = CGPA All College
X_3 = CGPA Psychology Courses
X_4 = CGPA Special Education
X_5 = CGPA General Education

Utilization of Equation One would result in a prediction about 22 percent better than what probably would occur by chance.

Equation Two. Computed on 19 significant variables plus the remaining Factor 3 variables resulted in a multiple R of .73 with the following equation. The five variables in the equation measured personality, attitude, and scholastic achievement.

$$Y = .4458\,X_1 - .5998\,X_2 + .0679\,X_3 + 2.9799\,X_4 + .6657\,X_5 + 44.223$$

where:

Y = Criterion Measure — Composite ERTHC
X_1 = 16 PF Test—Subscale F (enthusiastic)
X_2 = 16 PF Test—Subscale I (realistic)
X_3 = Adjusted MTAI Score
X_4 = CGPA General Education
X_5 = Number of General Education Courses

The standard error of R is .042 indicating that the obtained R probably will not vary more than .11 from the population value of R. Utilization of Equation Two would result in a prediction about 32 percent better than what probably would occur by chance.

Though results for both equations indicate little room for doubt that a genuine significant multiple correlation exists in the population, caution must be exercised in applying these equations to larger groups since this investigation is the first of its type on the prediction of success of special class teachers, and as such, has many exploratory aspects. However, it is quite likely that the identified factors will appear with some consistency in future studies.

CHARACTERISTICS AND QUALIFICATIONS OF STUDENT TEACHERS

The results of this investigation have some explicit implications relative to the characteristics and qualifications of student teachers of mentally or physically handicapped children. Throughout the long process of selection, guidance, and training, certain patterns should become apparent if the students are to be effective in the classroom. The findings indicated that student teachers of mentally or physically handicapped children are a relatively unique group of individuals with characteristics different from those of other college students and other education students. However, their interests and attitudes are most like elementary teachers.

Three significant characteristic-qualification patterns of successful student teachers of mentally or physically handicapped children emerged from this study which are applicable to a selection and recruitment program. By projecting these results it can be concluded that prospective teachers of mentally or physically handicapped children should possess the following characteristics.

Pattern 1

Achievement — Ability — Attitude. Prospective teachers should possess high ability (intelligence), a good attitude toward children and teaching, and should be good students with high grades in college preparatory courses.

Pattern 2

Personal adjustment — General emotional stability (experimenting, sociable, composed, emotionally stable). Prospective teachers of mentally or physically handicapped children should be well adjusted and emotionally stable in order to be able to effectively deal with the adjustment problems of parents and the emotional and social needs of the children. The following personality characteristics are important aspects of this pattern:

> Experimenting. They should be adventurous, experimenting, impulsive, ready to try new things.
>
> Sociable. They should be responsive, friendly, cheerful, and sociable.
>
> Composed. They should be composed, unannoyed at leaving a task unfinished. They should possess an even disposition and be able to remain calm in a crisis.
>
> Emotionally Stable. They should be abundant in emotional response, able to face people and grueling emotional situations without fatigue. They should be emotionally stable and free from various nervous and instability symptoms.

Pattern 3

Dynamic energy (energetic, responsible, realistic). Prospective teachers of mentally or physically handicapped children need to be vigorous and energetic in order to be able to effectively meet the physical, mental, and emotional demands of the special classroom. They should be realistic, practical, and responsible since many times they are left on their own with little help and inadequate supervision, and thus need to have a maximum capacity for self direction. The following characteristics are important aspects of this pattern:

> Energetic. They should be vigorous, energetic, enthusiastic, talkative, expressive, alert, and extroverted.
>
> Responsible. They should be responsible, independent, leaders, and organizers. They should enjoy promoting new projects and influencing others.
>
> Realistic. They should be practical, logical, and able to keep a group operating on a practical and realistic basis.

REGULAR CLASS TEACHING – A PREREQUISITE?

The results of the investigation also raised the question of the relationship of regular class teaching to special class teaching. "No prior regular class teaching experience" was found to be significantly related to effective special class teaching. The implications of such findings need no elaboration.

The question of whether or not regular classroom experience should be a prerequisite for the special class teacher has been discussed and debated for many years. Tenny (1954) was interested in this problem and expressed a series of objections to the concept that the recruitment of special class teachers should be limited to those who have had teaching experience in the regular classroom. In contrast to Tenny, Lord and Kirk indicated that in general " . . . teachers of exceptional children should first obtain education and experience in teaching normal children . . ." (Lord and Kirk, 1950, pp. 104-105). Lord and Kirk did, however, list a number of practical limitations to this requirement.

As part of the U. S. Office of Education study (Mackie, Williams, and Dunn, 1957), an inquiry form was sent to the participating educators on which they noted the amount of classroom experience they considered as necessary and desirable for teachers of mentally retarded children. The results indicated that the responding groups generally favored some teaching experience in the regular classes. The college instructors generally were satisfied with less regular class teaching than were the other groups. The results would seem to indicate that further study of this problem in detail might cast some interesting light on this question.

RECOMMENDATIONS FOR FURTHER RESEARCH

Several possibilities for further research result from this study. They include the following:

1. A study should be made on a large sample of students preparing to be teachers of mentally or physically handicapped children to test the prediction equations resulting from this investigation.
2. There is a need for further detailed study of the criteria for measuring the effectiveness of teachers and student teachers of mentally or physically handicapped children.
3. A study should be made of (a) the relationship of regular class teaching experience to student teaching in a special class and (b) the relationship of regular class teaching experience to successful teaching of mentally or physically handicapped children in the field.
4. A large scale study of the problem of predicting successful teaching of mentally or physically handicapped children should be made over a long period of time involving hundreds of teachers. Such a study should delineate the

differences, if any, between teachers of physically handicapped children and teachers of mentally handicapped children as well as any variation in characteristics resulting from sex differences of the teachers.

REFERENCES

Beecher, D. E. *The teaching evaluation record.* Buffalo, New York: Educators Publishing Company, 1953.

Berry, J. R. *Professional preparation and effectiveness of beginning teachers.* Coral Gables, Florida: University of Miami, 1960.

Cattell, R. B., Saunders, D. R., and Stice, G. *Handbook for the sixteen personality factor questionnaire — forms A, B, and C.*

Cook, W. W., Leeds, C. H., and Callis, R. *Minnesota teacher attitude inventory — manual.* New York: Psychological Corporation, 1952.

Gordon, L. V. *Gordon personal inventory — manual.* Yonkers, New York: World Book Co., 1956.

Lord, F. E. and Kirk, S. A. The education of teachers of special classes. In *The Education of Exceptional Children,* Forty-ninth Yearbook of the National Society for the Study of Education, Part II. Bloomington, Illinois: Public School Publishing Company, 1950. Pp. 103-116.

Mackie, Romaine P., Williams, H. M., and Dunn, L. M. *Teachers of children who are mentally retarded.* Office of Education Bulletin No. 13. Washington, D.C.: U. S. Government Printing Office, 1954.

Otis, A. S. *Otis quick-scoring mental ability tests: new edition gamma test: E_M.* New York: Harcourt Brace and World, Inc., 1954.

Ryans, D. G. *Characteristics of teachers: their description, comparison, and appraisal.* Santa Monica, California: System Development Corporation, 1962.

Symonds, P. M. *A manual of instructions for the educational interest inventory.* New York: Bureau of Publications, Teachers College, Columbia University.

Tenny, J. W. Preparing teachers of mentally handicapped children. *American Journal of Mental Deficiency,* 1954, 566-572.

research on the special education teacher and special education teaching*

REGINALD L. JONES†

Abstract: Research on the special education teacher and special education teaching was reviewed, and several unpublished studies reported. The need for systematic research programs in this area was highlighted. Such programs would (a) explore individually classes of variables that might have some usefulness in explaining attraction to special education teaching, (b) combine the most promising of these variables into a model which would maximize the explanatory power of the individual variables, and (c) test the predictive efficiency of the model using certain experimental techniques.

There is at present widespread concern about the shortage of special education teachers (Cruickshank and Johnson, 1958; President's Panel on Mental Retardation, 1962; Western Interstate Commission on Higher Education, 1960). The best estimates indicate a need for some 200,000 teachers, 55,000 in the field of mental retardation alone. To adequately staff classrooms

*Reprinted from *Exceptional Children*, Vol. 33 (December 1966). pp. 251–257, by permission of the author and the Council for Exceptional Children. Copyright 1966 by the Council for Exceptional Children.

†Reginald L. Jones is Professor, Psychology and Education, Ohio State University.

for the mentally retarded in the next decade, it has been estimated that 6,000 teachers must be added each year to the pool of already available specialists. It is highly unlikely that all needed teachers of the retarded or of other exceptionalities will be attracted, although increased funds for training do make it probable that relative numbers will increase. It does not appear feasible, from a practical standpoint, to subsidize all special education teachers needed. Clearly, alternative solutions must be explored.

A program of research inquiring into a variety of concerns related to special education teaching as a career field may be most fruitful in the long run. An exploration of such areas as the image of special education teaching and exceptional children held by high school students and others, the standing of special education in the occupational structure, the characteristics and satisfactions of practicing special education teachers, the occupational desires of adolescents and the extent to which these desires are perceived as being satisfied by special education teaching, the relative attractiveness of special education teaching compared to other fields, and the interactions among these and other variables would seem to contribute substantially to our understanding of the reasons why small numbers have been attracted to special education teaching.

OVERVIEW

There has been a paucity of research on the characteristics of special education teachers themselves and on the motivations underlying the choice of special education teaching as a career field. Some work (Gottfried and Jones, 1964) has been done on stated reasons for becoming a special education teacher. However, there appears to be little published research on the standing of special education teaching in the occupational structure (i.e., the relative attractiveness, prestige, etc. of special education teaching compared to other kinds of teaching or other occupations) or on the images of special education teachers held by presently employed or prospective candidates of this occupational area. A few studies (Billings, 1963; Guskin, 1963; Horowitz and Rees, 1962; Perrin, 1954) have been done on attitudes toward certain exceptionalities and on the correlates of such attitudes. The personality traits possessed by special education teachers have also been studied.

A variety of studies (Kilpatrick, Cummings, and Jennings, 1964; Super, Starishevsky, Matlin, and Jordan, 1963; Tiedeman and O'Hara, 1963) in closely related areas, as in occupational psychology, provides a number of suggestive leads bearing on our concerns here. However, except in one or two instances, these leads have not been pursued.

RESEARCH FINDINGS

Experience

Lord and Wallace (1949) reported that the influence of friends and relatives, as well as actual contact with exceptional children, was related to the decision to become a special education teacher. These findings were confirmed by Gottfried and Jones (1964) and by Meyers (1964). It is well to note in the three studies just cited that, while there is some evidence that preteaching experience is related to a decision to teach exceptional children, such knowledge by itself does not advance theoretical formulations seeking to account for attraction to special education teaching. Unexplained are the reasons why some individuals having such experiences elect to work in other occupational areas or why some without such experiences elect to work in special education. As Gottfried and Jones (1963) note in their discussion of the experience variable:

> One could presume that not all observers of the handicapped neighbor would choose to enter a field involving work with handicapped. One could assume that only those observers whose psychological-motivational makeup made them sensitive to the stimulus situation (handicapped neighbor) were greatly affected. Some observers appropriately motivated would have entered the field whether or not they had a handicapped neighbor. The determination of the relative contribution of psychological need structure and situational structure to career choice requires considerable further investigation (p. 14).

Johnson (1964) developed a comprehensive questionnaire designed to assess experience with the exceptional as a variable that might be predictive of attraction to special education teaching. The rationale of his investigation was that the length, time, and type of contact with the exceptional might have much greater explanatory usefulness than might knowledge only of whether the respondent had some kind of unspecified contact with an exceptional person. Unfortunately, Johnson was unable to procure a large enough sample of teachers of exceptional children to make a thorough analysis of his questionnaire. However, the instrument has been thoroughly pretested and is now available for use in studies in which experience or contact with the exceptional may be a variable.

Preferences

Several studies (Badt, 1957; Jones and Gottfried, 1962; Meyers, 1964) of preferences for teaching exceptional children have been reported. These studies reveal that certain teaching specialties have greater attractiveness than do others; generally, specialties involving work with the emotionally maladjusted, the mentally gifted, and the mentally handicapped are rated highly attractive.

Three studies inquired into how preferences among various teaching specialties were interrelated. The first study (Jones and Gottfried, 1962), which compared only special education fields with themselves, identified several interest clusters. One cluster, bipolar in nature, consisted of interest in teaching the educable mentally retarded on the one hand and interest in teaching the mentally gifted on the other. A second bipolar cluster consisted of the hard of hearing and the partially seeing on one pole of the continuum and the severely mentally retarded on the other. A third cluster was composed of certain preferences for teaching deaf, blind, delinquent, and emotionally disturbed children. The subjects of the study were naive college students (of both sexes) in education.

Three methodological questions relating to the generality of the results have been raised: (a) The sexes were combined in undetermined proportions. Since there are sex differences in interest in the special education fields, any analysis combining the sexes runs the risk of yielding unclear results. (b) The population included subjects who were largely unfamiliar with the characteristics of exceptional children. Therefore, they may not have clearly understood what is involved in teaching such children. Hence, their responses could have been little more than random in nature. (c) The technique of cluster analysis is crude, with a certain subjectivity involved at critical points in the computational process.

These questions led to a second study, presently unpublished, designed to remedy the aforementioned problems: (a) only females were included as subjects; (b) experienced teachers (both in regular and special classes), students enrolled in special education, and students enrolled in regular education training programs served as subjects; and (c) the technique of factor analysis (principal components analysis, varimax rotation) was used in data analysis.

The results revealed some overlap in the results of the study involving cluster analysis and the factor analytic study. The patterns of relationships were sharpened in the latter study.

A third and unpublished study of preferences identified patterns of interest related to preferences for teaching intellectually exceptional (gifted and retarded) and certain of the more common specialties (e.g., kindergarten, secondary English, or foreign languages). Factor analysis uncovered meaningful relationships among the variables. Also, there was considerable consistency in the patterns for four samples of subjects. Of special interest was a factor of preference for teaching educable mentally retarded children, found in all samples. This factor suggested that preferences for teaching the various levels of mentally retarded children (i.e., elementary, junior high school, and senior high school) were seen as belonging together and also different from other teaching specialties. A second factor of interest, usually bipolar in nature, consisted of the elementary teaching specialties on the one hand and the secondary specialties on the other, with the exception that teaching of the retarded at the secondary level never loaded on the secondary pole of the factor, while preferences for teaching elementary level retarded children did load on the elementary pole of the factor.

Why the concern about interrelationships among preferences in the special education teaching areas? Studies of preferences for special education teaching were undertaken following the assumption that, if interests in certain areas are closely related, there is the possibility that a common core of variables might explain attraction to these areas. If this should be the case, we need not study each area of exceptionality separately for purposes of isolating crucial variables. Much time and energy are saved, and a more powerful conceptual model is developed.

Personality

Several studies (Cawley, 1964; Garrison and Scott, 1961; Jones and Gottfired, 1966b) have been done on personality characteristics of presently employed teachers or prospective teachers of exceptional children. One methodological shortcoming of these investigations is their failure to use teachers of nonexceptional children or persons employed in other occupations as contrast subjects. Thus, while a given group of traits may be seen as characteristic of teachers of a given exceptionality, they may be in reality no different from those possessed by persons employed in a wide variety of seemingly diverse occupations.

In another unpublished study, Gottfried and Jones identified a number of personality variables differentiating satisfied from dissatisfied teachers of the educable mentally retarded. Satisfied teachers were found to score significantly higher on the teacher preference schedule subtests nondirective and preadult fixation and significantly lower on the orderliness subtest. The results could not be generalized to all teachers of the educable mentally retarded, since an analysis of variance indicated that level of satisfaction and teaching level (i.e., elementary or secondary) interact, often obscuring differences between satisfied and dissatisfied groups at each level.

Jones and Gottfried (1966a) explored psychological need variables for the purpose of differentiating persons expressing interest in or actually preparing for one area of special education from those interested in teaching in another. Again, a number of differentiating noncognitive variables were identified, many of which, on logical grounds, seem reasonable. Unfortunately, this study possesses the same methodological shortcoming mentioned previously: it presents no evidence supporting the view that the particular psychological needs identified as being related to a preference for teaching any one exceptionality are uniquely related to preferences for teaching that exceptionality.

Garrison and Scott (1961) identified certain psychological needs differentiating prospective teachers of the exceptional from those of others. A methodological shortcoming of this study is its lumping together of teachers of a variety of types of exceptional children. Certain evidence on preferences for teaching exceptional children (Cawley, 1964; Jones and Gottfried, 1962) suggests that entirely different factors may be operating in determining preferences for teaching one exceptionality as opposed to preferences for teaching another; exceptional children cannot be considered a single group.

Indeed, recent studies (Jones and Gottfried, 1965; Jones, Gottfried, and Owens, 1966; Semmel and Dickson, 1966) indicate that some differentiation among exceptional persons is made, depending upon the degree and kind of interpersonal contact required. Thus, one may accept any given exceptional person in one situation, but not in another. More to the point, Jones and Gottfried (1966b), using samples of teachers of exceptional and nonexceptional children, found rather clear agreement in the assignment of the degree of prestige enjoyed by the various specialties subsumed under special education.

The studies just cited suggest that special education teaching may attract persons having characteristics different from those in other occupational areas and also that some differentiation is made among exceptional children as individuals to be interacted with or to be taught.

Prestige

Prestige was one variable which seemed to have usefulness in explaining attraction to special education teaching. To date two studies in this area have been completed. The first (Jones and Gottfried, 1966b) presented a comparison of the perceived prestige of certain special education teaching areas and regular class teaching. The results revealed that special education teaching carried higher prestige than regular class teaching and also that certain differential perceptions of prestige occurred among the various specialties subsumed under special education teaching; teachers of the blind, the gifted, the emotionally disturbed, and the severely mentally retarded were seen as possessing especially high standing.

The second study (Jones, 1966) presented data on the rated prestige (using a point scale) of certain special education areas compared to regular class teaching and a wide specturm of other occupational specialties, using a high school population. The purpose of this study, consisting of over ·200 subjects and 64 occupations, was to determine how certain special education areas compared with a full range of occupational areas, rather than regular class teaching only, in rated prestige. The results reported in the present paper consist of only 24 occupations and 50 subjects (25 boys and 25 girls in their junior or senior year of high school). The data of Table 1 reveal the overall perceptions of the prestige carried by a given specialty, and they also reveal the differential occupational perceptions of boys and girls. These perceptions are especially apparent where the teaching occupations are concerned. The teaching occupations in virtually all instances are rated lower in prestige by boys than by girls.

A Multivariate Approach

Any understanding of the dynamics underlying attraction to special education teaching will require consideration of a number of variables. To capture the richness of the interrelationships, it will be necessary to plan and conduct studies utilizing a multivariate approach. The study of single variables may be valuable in preliminary explorations. However, there is always the possibility that complex interactions underlie the phenomena under study. These interactions are not uncovered by the study of single variables in isolation.

The fruitfulness of the multivariate approach has been revealed in a study by Johnson (1964). The essential procedure of the Johnson experiment involved the building of hypothetical teaching situations which included elements of the work situation which a previous analysis had suggested to be promising. The elements included for study were (a) the label (e.g., educable mentally retarded), (b) prestige and salary, and (c) certain characteristics of

TABLE 1.

Rated Prestige of Certain Special Education Teaching
Specialties and Other Occupational Areas

Occupation	Combined Average Rating	Girls	Boys
College and University Teacher	8.06 (1)	8.40 (1)	7.78 (1)
Mayor of Large City	7.44 (2)	7.48 (2)	7.40 (2)
Architect	7.22 (3)	7.28 (3)	7.16 (3)
Airline Pilot	6.54 (4)	6.32 (12)	6.76 (4)
Junior College Teacher	6.48 (5)	6.56 (8)	6.40 (5.5)
Teacher of Severely Mentally Retarded	6.48 (6)	7.20 (4.5)	5.76 (11)
Newspaper Columnist	6.38 (7)	6.36 (10.5)	6.40 (5.5)
Teacher of Secondary School Educable Mentally Retarded	6.32 (8)	7.01 (6)	5.64 (12)
Teacher of Secondary School Gifted	6.28 (9)	6.72 (7)	5.84 (9)
Teacher of Secondary School Science	6.24 (10)	6.36 (10.5)	6.12 (8)
Teacher of Secondary School English	5.97 (11)	6.40 (9)	5.44 (13)
Building Contractor	5.86 (12)	5.56(14.5)	6.36 (7)
Teacher of Elementary School Gifted	5.84 (13)	6.28 (13)	5.40 (14)
Teacher of Elementary School Educable Mentally Retarded	5.68 (14)	7.20 (4.5)	4.16 (18.5)
Insurance Agent	5.45 (15)	5.14 (16)	5.80 (10)
Teacher of Elementary Grades 4-6	5.04 (16)	5.56 (14.5)	4.56 (16)
Teacher of Elementary Grades 1-3	4.88 (17)	5.00 (18)	4.76 (15)
Teacher of Nursery School and Kindergarten	4.62 (18)	5.12 (17)	4.12 (20)
Teacher of Secondary Home Economics (girls) and Industrial Arts (boys)	4.23 (19)	4.84 (19)	4.40 (17)
Plumber	3.96 (20)	3.76 (20)	4.16 (18.5)
Taxi Driver	3.60 (21)	3.08 (21.5)	3.04 (21)
Streetcar Motorman	2.76 (22)	3.08 (21.5)	2.22 (22)
Sharecropper	2.02 (23)	3.04 (23)	1.02 (23)
Shoe Shiner	1.19 (24)	1.06 (24)	1.32 (24)

Note: rank order in parentheses.

the children to be taught (for example, their need for sympathetic understanding).

It was thus possible to build hypothetical job descriptions in which a variable was absent or present in varying degrees and in which each variable could be studied both singularly and in combination with others. In responding, the subject indicated the strength of his interest in the hypothetical positions by checking a nine point rating scale. Two of the hypothetical positions are presented below:

A position is offered to you to teach a group of educable mentally retarded children who have no special needs for sympathetic understanding. This is a position of average salary and prestige in the community.

I would   *would not*

9	8	7	6	5	4	3	2	1

like a position teaching this group of children under the circumstances cited above.

A position of above average salary and prestige is offered to you to teach a group of children who need considerable sympathetic understanding. This is a group of educable mentally retarded children.

I would   *would not*

9	8	7	6	5	4	3	2	1

like a position teaching this group of children under the circumstances cited above.

For any given exceptionality, 10 different hypothetical positions (including the variables in various combinations) were developed. It was thus possible, using analysis of variance techniques, to isolate the combinations of variables leading to greatest attraction to a given area of special education teaching. And by developing the same kinds of hypothetical situations describing the teaching of nonexceptional children as were used to describe the teaching of exceptional children, it was also possible to isolate aspects of special education teaching which serve to heighten or diminish its attractiveness compared to regular class teaching.

Data obtained on a small and select group of students revealed statistically significant differences in degree of interest in teaching exceptional and nonexceptional children related to prestige and salary and to certain psychological characteristics of the children to be taught. Where teaching of exceptional children was concerned, prestige and salary were not always critical variables. The study needs replication. The intent in this section has been merely to point out the need for a multivariate approach in the study of preferences for special education teaching and to indicate the work that has been undertaken using this approach.

SUMMARY

A three pronged research program has been suggested in this paper: (a) delineation of the status of certain areas of special education teaching as occupational areas, the images held of these areas and their practitioners, and the relationship of the images of special education teaching compared to the images of other occupations; (b) a delineation of the actual unique characteristics and experiences possessed by special education practitioners, as compared to persons in other occupational areas; and (c) a meshing of data obtained from the two analyses above, taking account of the interactions among variables where appropriate.

When put into proper long range perspective, the aim of a total research program would be to (a) explore individually classes of variables that might have some usefulness in explaining attraction to special education teaching, (b) combine the most promising of these variables into a model which would maximize the explanatory power of the individual variables, and (c) test the predictive efficiency of the model using certain experimental techniques. If certain crucial variables predictive of interest in special education teaching are identified with some precision, it should be possible (a) to include these variables in certain communications (e.g., films and written messages) to maximize interest in special education teaching, and (b) to predict the characteristics and backgrounds of individuals most likely to be attracted to this vocational area and hence receptive to the communication.

Data of the type presented in this paper represent only the first level of analysis in a multiphased research program. Once crucial variables are identified, it will be necessary to demonstrate their practical value, a step taken only recently (Meisgeier, 1965).

REFERENCES

Badt, Margit I. Attitudes of university students toward exceptional children and special education. *Exceptional Children*, 1957, 23, 286-290, 336.

Billings, Helen K. An exploratory study of the attitudes of noncrippled children toward crippled children in three selected elementary schools. *Journal of Experimental Education*, 1963, 31, 381-387.

Cawley, J. F. Selected characteristics of individuals oriented toward mental retardation. Paper read at The Council for Exceptional Children, Chicago, April, 1964.

Cruickshank, W. M., and Johnson, G. O. *Education of exceptional children and youth.* Englewood Cliffs, New Jersey: Prentice Hall, 1958.

Garrison, K. C., and Scott, Mary H. A comparison of the personal needs of college students preparing to teach in different teaching areas. *Educational and Psychological Measurement*, 1961, 21, 955-964.

Gottfried, N. W., and Jones, R. L. Some observations on background factors associated with career choices in the teaching of exceptional children. Paper read at The Council for Exceptional Children, Philadelphia, April, 1963.

Gottfried, N. W., and Jones, R. L. Career choice factors in special education. *Exceptional Children*, 1964, 30, 218-223.

Guskin, S. L. Measuring the stereotype of the mental defective. *American Journal of Mental Deficiency*, 1963, 67, 569-575.

Horowitz, Leola S., and Rees, Norma S. Attitudes and information about deafness. *Volta Review*, 1962, 64, 180-189.

Johnson, M. R. An experimental investigation of some dimensions underlying preferences for teaching exceptional children. Unpublished master's thesis, Fisk University, 1964.

Jones, R. L. Special education teaching in the occupational structure: a factor analytic study. Paper read at The Council for Exceptional Children, Toronto, April, 1966. ·

Jones, R. L. and Gottfried, N. W. Preferences and configurations of interest in special class teaching. *Exceptional Children*, 1962, 28, 371-377.

Jones, R. L., and Gottfried, N. W. The Social distance of the exceptional. Paper read at American Psychological Association, Chicago, September, 1965.

Jones, R. L., and Gottfried, N. W. Psychological needs and preferences for teaching exceptional children. *Exceptional Children*, 1966, 32, 313-321.(a)

Jones, R. L., and Gottfried, N. W. The prestige of special education teaching. *Exceptional Children*, 1966, 32, 465-468.(b)

Jones, R. L., Gottfried, N. W., and Owens, Angela. The social distance of the exceptional: a study at the high school level. *Exceptional Children*, 1966, 32, 551-556.

Kilpatrick, F. P., Cummings, M. C., and Jennings, M. K. *The image of the federal service.* Washington, D.C.: The Brookings Institution, 1964.

Lord, F. E., and Wallace, H. M. Recruitment of special education teachers. *Exceptional Children*, 1949, 15, 171-173.

Meisgeier, C. The identification of successful teachers of mentally or physically handicapped children. *Exceptional Children*, 1965, 32, 229-236.

Meyers, C. E. Realities in teacher recruitment. *Mental Retardation*, 1964, 2, 42-46.

Perrin, Elinor H. The social position of the speech defective child. *Journal of Speech and Hearing Disorders*, 1954, 19, 250-252.

President's Panel on Mental Retardation. *A proposed program for national action to combat mental retardation.* Washington, D.C.: U. S. Government Printing Office, 1962.

Semmel, M. I., and Dickson, S. Connotative reactions of college students to disability labels. *Exceptional Children,* 1966, 32, 443-450.

Super, D. E. Starishevsky, R., Matlin, N., and Jordan, J. P. *Career development: self concept theory.* New York: College Entrance Examination Board, 1963.

Tiedeman, D. V., and O'Hara, R. P. *Career development: choice and adjustment.* New York: College Entrance Examination Board, 1963.

Western Interstate Council on Higher Education. *Teachers of exceptional children for the west.* Boulder, Colorado: Author, 1960.

an integrated
teacher education program
for special education —
*a new approach**

LOUIS SCHWARTZ†

Abstract: Preparation of the clinician educator, capable of providing diagnosis and remediation of the variety of learning difficulties presented by exceptional children, is proposed in an integrated teacher education curriculum for special education. The gap between accumulated knowledge regarding exceptionality and existing teacher education curricula is discussed, along with problems posed by shortages of personnel and increasing concern over the qualitative aspects of special education. Courses in the integrated sequence are described, and limitations noted.

Dramatic advances on the local, state, and federal levels in the education and rehabilitation of exceptional children and youth have produced challenging issues for the professional workers in the field. Dynamic changes in population, patterns of service, and the explosion of knowledge in the helping disciplines have posed conflicting problems presented by rapidly changing concepts and current practices. The enormous expansion of health, education, and welfare programs concerned with exceptional children and youth has identified special education and rehabilitation

*Reprinted from *Exceptional Children*, (February 1967), pp. 411-416, by permission of the author and the Council for Exceptional Children. Copyright 1967 by the Council for Exceptional Children.

†Louis Schwartz is Professor of Special Education, Florida State University, Tallahassee.

needs more completely, highlighted the need for professional personnel, and focused attention upon the need for a systematic refinement of existing information in order to bridge the gap between the rapidly increasing knowledge about problems in special education and the ensuing implications for the exceptional individual in the classroom.

One of the most crucial issues paralleling this period of growth is the increased concern for the numerical and qualitative aspects of teacher preparation required for the various categories of exceptionality. Although considerable effort has been devoted to increasing our supply of teachers, little attention has been placed upon the nature and extent of their preparation in terms of the changing population, patterns of service, and the growing accumulation of knowledge concerning learning and rehabilitation.

Kirk (1965) summarizes the recent decade of developments in the education of the handicapped and raises several basic issues related to the preparation of professional personnel.

> *Under the pressure of extreme shortages of professional personnel, a major issue becomes whether to (a) focus on immediate needs in terms of the numbers of special educators without regard to quality; (b) concentrate on quality in the preparation of professional personnel, even though it may mean a decrease in the numbers thus prepared; or (c) find a radically new method of accomplishing both goals at the same time (p. 102).*

The teacher education program proposed herein is an attempt to approach the problem posed by Kirk through an integrated sequence (including five traditionally separate fields of exceptionality) into one unified curriculum for the preparation of teachers of exceptional children.

BACKGROUND AND APPROACH

Finding a radically new method is not a formidable obstacle; however, translating current trends into a new curriculum structure and attempting to break from the bounds of tradition initially at the college level and eventually in the public school poses serious challenges at both the leadership and managerial levels.

Notwithstanding the many significant barriers blocking the path of change, the essential problem is translating current knowledge about (a) the changing population of exceptional children, (b) existing services in special education and rehabilitation, and (c) evolving conceptualizations about the nature and process of special education into curriculum format.

A brief review of the literature has been selected to highlight the fundamental theme, namely, that every teacher is a diagnostician (Laycock, 1934) capable of providing for the variety of learning and behavior problems presented by exceptional children without regard to separate etiological categories.

The conceptualization of an integrated teacher education curriculum evolving about a core is neither unique nor radical, and finding substantial support from the literature is fruitful. However, moving away from such traditional labels as mental retardation, deaf or hard of hearing, blind or partially seeing, physically limited, or socially and emotionally maladjusted on an implementation level presents almost insurmountable barriers.

On the national level, Davens (1965) traces the changing pattern of health services for the handicapped in our country and highlights the trends brought about by increased interdisciplinary and inter-agency efforts.

> *During the next five years, there are likely to be further trends toward broadening the definition of handicapped children and toward the organization of services and facilities to permit an integrated approach to the whole child, regardless of the number, type, or combination of handicaps he presents (p. 53).*

New Jersey (Commission on the Education of the Handicapped, 1964) appears to be moving toward the implementation of an integrated approach to the education of the handicapped by recommending the following:

> *Education needs so identified should be met without any delimitation based upon arbitrary categorization or presumed causation of the manifest educational disability. School laws and regulations which arbitrarily discriminate between children on the basis of a medical classification rather than educational need should be revised or combined and the best features of each made accessible to all (p. 8).*

This changing conceptualization of patterns of service for the handicapped has not evolved overnight. Special education has traditionally concerned itself with the individual learning needs of children; however, programs and services organized to meet these needs often have neglected to insure the attainment of this objective.

Sporadic expressions of concern over the apparent paradox between principle and practice in special education have been expressed in the literature, particularly during the period of rapid growth of programs and services of the past decade. Lord (1956) stated:

> *Rehabilitation does not begin its thinking with disability categories. It begins with individuals and plans in terms of individual needs. It defines needs carefully and established priorities for meeting those needs. . . . We seem to be bogged down in services to categories and with somewhat of an overemphasis on assumed differences between the children we serve. . . . We tend to specialize our services rather than attempt to make them comprehensive and inclusive. We continue to do this in spite of the fact that we are dealing with heterogeneous groups to which we have fixed our little disability labels. We seem to cherish the labels and even safeguard them as our individual private field of operation. Special Education is bigger than mere classifications; bigger than labels, categories, and teachers' credentials. Special Education for the handicapped has one major objective — maximum habilitation or rehabilitation of the individual child. The individual child and his constellation of particular needs is our focus of primary attention (p. 342).*

Criticism of the growing number of voluntary agencies springing up in response to the variety of disability categories identified during the past twenty years was perhaps best expressed by Hill (1959), former Chief of the Section on Exceptional Children and Youth, U. S. Department of Health, Education, and Welfare, when he stated:

> *In so far as education is concerned, special education has developed illogically and unrealistically, just as have voluntary health agencies and clinical services, around the isolation of supposedly discrete entities of disabilities . . . rather than in terms of learning problems. . . . The conclusions of these observations must be that clinical*

classifications have little relation to learning disability, and that there is no such thing as a typical example of any type of child. . . . However, the differentiation in programming must be undertaken on the basis of needs and learning characteristics rather than in terms of arbitrary classification (pp. 298–299).

Essentially, the fundamental issue appears to evolve around the changing concept toward learning handicaps presented by children, rather than specific categories of disability, and implementing this idea into programs and services.

Kirk and Bateman (1962) have most recently reawakened interest in this approach to the education of exceptional children in stressing the need for the educator to diagnose the specific learning problems indicated by the behavioral symptoms and then provide subsequent remediation, without regard to etiological factors.

Laycock (1934), thirty years earlier, had urged special educators to seriously consider every teacher a diagnostician.

As education has become increasingly scientific so the business of the teacher has likewise increasingly become that of a diagnostician, and nowhere has this been more evident than in the field of special education. The diagnostic point of view has been both the cause and result of special education. It has been the cause since only a keen appreciation and understanding of the problems of those who deviate from the typical have given rise to special education; and it has been the result since the problems of special education can be solved only by the use of the diagnostic method (p. 47).

Although there have been many similar expressions of interest in the diagnosis and remediation of learning disabilities, moving forward from philosophy and principle to actual program implementation has eluded the practitioner in the field; and for several years the dialogue has continued on the theoretical level. Kaya (1961), Levine (1961), and Reynolds (1962) are among those who have attempted to translate the changing concepts into a program format.

Fermentation of these ideas, despite the continued urging within the profession, has failed to produce some direction or even an outline for the change being advocated. Perhaps the educational lag presents too formidable an obstacle between knowledge and innovation. Programs and services for the handicapped continue to develop by the categories; in fact, additional discrete diagnostic labels have emerged into separate new areas of exceptionality. Naturally, teacher education curricula in special education have reflected the continuous development of separate fields of specialization, i.e., mentally retarded, physically limited, deaf, blind, etc.

ASSUMPTIONS

A curriculum for preparing the teacher as diagnostician requires a radical departure from traditional categories of exceptionality, with new emphasis on the psychoeducational aspects of special education. Ultimately, the diagnosis and remediation of learning disabilities, regardless of etiological categories, are dependent upon (a) a clinical assessment of the characteristics of the learner; (b) a pedagogical analysis of the task, the material, the techniques, and the teacher; (c) interaction among these factors; and (d) utilization of existing personnel and agencies. All of these factors, planned and organized to maximize individualized instruction for the exceptional child, appear to be the evolving conceptualizations regarding special education in the current and future decades.

The challenge at hand is bridging the gap between knowledge and practice into a planned and meaningful sequence of academic and clinical laboratory experiences within the confines of a college curriculum pattern for special education. The proposed integrated teacher education program for special education represents an initial attempt at innovation.

PROPOSED INTEGRATED
TEACHER EDUCATION CURRICULUM

Setting

The translation of current knowledge and trends into a curriculum pattern for the preparation of teachers of exceptional children is proposed within the framework of the existing curricula pattern established by the New Jersey Department of Education for the six state colleges. It should be noted that Trenton State College as early as 1917 conducted a two year program for teachers of the mentally subnormal and deaf. In 1959, part time graduate programs in these two fields were offered to meet the needs of the growing number of teachers of the handicapped in New Jersey. The year 1961 marked the introduction of two undergraduate majors (mental retardation and the deaf) for full time students. A new graduate program for teachers of the socially and emotionally maladjusted was recently approved, stimulated by a U. S. Office of Education program development grant, and initiated in 1966.

The college currently participates in the fellowship program for the preparation of professional personnel in the education of the handicapped under provisions of PL 85- 926 as amended in the three separate fields previously mentioned. This year marked the establishment of a child study and demonstration center on the college campus under provisions of Title III of the Elementary and Secondary Education Act of 1965. Designed primarily as a teacher education facility, the center will involve the exceptional child, teachers, and teacher trainees in the diagnostic remediation process common to all children with learning difficulties.

The proposed integrated undergraduate sequence in special education is dependent upon the clinical facilities, demonstration, practicum, and student teaching opportunities in a variety of existing local residential and day schools serving exceptional children and youth. It is anticipated that this revision will replace the current undergraduate majors in mental retardation and the deaf and avoid separate major sequences in the future. Furthermore, articulation between the new program and existing graduate specialization will require continued study and subsequent revision.

Objectives

The fundamental theme of the proposed program is based upon the assumption that the preparation of the teacher of exceptional children as an educational diagnostician and tactician requires the planned integration of a formal course of study with a variety of observational and practicum experiences: (a) normal child growth and development; (b) deviations in physical, psychological, educational, and social development; (c) clinical child study practices and procedures for the diagnosis and remediation of learning disabilities; (d) remedial programs and services within the clinic, special classes, and regular classroom; (e) special class teacher as an educational diagnostician and tactician; and (f) interdisciplinary team approach.

While disregarding traditional labels, the proposed program retains the basic New Jersey certification requirements for each area and, in addition, focuses on the common core of learning handicaps present in all categories. Specifically, the proposed program offers in separate and integrated courses all the required certification areas with additional emphasis on child study, learning disabilities, and remediation.

Table 1 illustrates the four year distribution of semester hours, with the specialized professional sequence of 53 semester hours containing the integrated approach.

Limitations

Many significant limitations become readily apparent with any such major departure from well established patterns. Serious consideration has been given to the following issues emerging from the proposal:

1. Feasibility of submerging individual identity of traditionally separate categories of exceptionality, i.e., legislation, fund raising, etc.
2. Difficulty in utilizing existing college personnel in the implementation of the program.
3. Existing practicum and laboratory facilities currently organized by separate disability groups.
4. Problems of teacher placement.
5. Usual barriers to innovation and change within college, state departments of education, and local school districts.
6. Continuous debate over graduate versus undergraduate preparation for special education.
7. Opportunity for demonstration and research of concepts, structure, operation, and results of innovation.

Recognizing the various obstacles to innovation within the academic community and implications of the change for the practitioner in the field should caution any hasty or uncritical acceptance of the proposal. Nevertheless, a renewed dialogue over the apparent discrepancy between current practices and curricula design would liberate constructive forces toward the reduction in the gap between knowledge and practice.

CONCLUSION

The enormous expansion of health, education, and welfare programs dealing with disability has identified rehabilitation needs more completely, highlighted the need for professional personnel, and focused attention upon the need for a closer coordination than ever between rehabilitation and related services. All of these factors pose demands for a volume and level of

TABLE 1.

Semester Hours in Proposed Special Education Curriculum

College Year	General Education	Basic Professional	Specialized Professional	Free Electives	Totals
First[a]	28	0	4	0	32
Second[b]	14	6	11	3	34
Third[c]	4	6	22	0	32
Fourth[d]	2	3	16	9	30
Totals	48	15	53	12	128

[a]*Survey of Exceptional Children and Youth I and II (4 semester hours). Integrates the certification areas of introduction to education of the handicapped and psychology of the handicapped. Provides orientation to the educational and psychosocial aspects of exceptional children and youth in terms of philosophy, history, nomenclature, classification, incidence, characteristics, etiology, special educational provisions, and current issues. Study of physical, sensory, mental, emotional, and social deviations.*

[b]*Child Study of Exceptional Children (5 semester hours). Integrates the certification areas of orientation in psychological tests, audiometry and hearing aids, and counseling, vocational guidance, and rehabilitation services for the handicapped. Provides orientation to the roles and processes of assessing individual differences of exceptional children and youth, with emphasis on the utilization of existing interdisciplinary and interagency resources and current evaluative techniques. Includes visits to campus, local community clinics, and centers.*

Orientation to Learning Disabilities (6 semester hours). Understanding the nature and needs of exceptional children in terms of the variety of learning impairments (a) developmental: health, motor, sensory; (b) communication: language, speech, hearing (covers anatomy and physiology of the ear and speech mechanisms); (c) behavioral: social, emotional; (d) intellectual: perceptual and cognitive; and (e) adaptive: later life.

[c]*Teaching Exceptional Children in the Elementary School (6 semester hours). Adapting the general principles and practices of teaching reading, arithmetic, language arts, social studies, arts, and crafts for children with learning impairments. Organizing and modifying the curricula from primary through intermediate levels for exceptional children.*

Diagnosis and Remediation of Learning Disabilities I and II (10 semester hours). This course integrates the certification areas of reading disabilities, teaching language to the deaf, teaching speech and speech-reading to the deaf, braille, and auditory training. Includes analysis of the concepts and techniques of diagnosis and remediation of learning impairments of exceptional children. Part I will stress evaluation and Part II will develop remedial techniques.

Occupational Laboratory (4 semester hours). Interdepartmental course— special education and industrial education and technology. Exploration of the world of work through actual experiences with the processes, tools, and materials of the various occupational families, i.e., industry, commerce, service, and agriculture.

performance, for a degree of planning, ingenuity, coordination, and understanding that will challenge the conservation and rehabilitation of our human resources as it has never been challenged before.

Programs and services that have arisen over the past several hundred years may be governmental, private, and voluntary. Patterns of service vary markedly; some are for designated types of disabilities, some for definite age groups, and others for certain types of services. This structure of community services was built largely without blueprints. Organizations and agencies have been created to meet the needs seen at a particular time. Many of our public and private health, welfare, educational, and recreational agencies have been established with little or no regard to those already existing and or in terms of the actual need.

The selection, collation, and synthesis of existing concepts into a new integrated teacher education program for special education is recommended as an approach to the rapidly growing body of knowledge concerning learning disabilities and remediation. "Every teacher a diagnostician," suggested over thirty years ago, is not radical or innovative today; however, bridging the gap between concept and practice appears to present many realistic limitations.

Connor (1964) offers a challenge for change to special educators,

> With teacher educators' focus on liberation through preparation for assumption of responsibility in approaching educational tasks, special education's revolution will be toward restructuring of most teacher education programs and reviewing the patterns of teacher placement, supervision and professional regard generally (p. 395).

Footnotes continued from Table 1.

Audiovisual Education (2 semester hours). Curriculum utilization of audiovisual materials, mastery of many types of audiovisual devices and equipment, principles of operation, possibilities for utilization, techniques for evaluation of materials and equipment, knowledge and skills in the production of simple audiovisual materials.

[d]*Special Education Practicum (8 semester hours). This course integrates the certification areas of curriculum, methods, and materials for teaching the mentally retarded, physically limited, deaf or hard of hearing, blind or partially seeing, and socially and emotionally maladjusted. Observation and participation in selected demonstration classes of exceptional children and youth and various maturation levels. Field work during summer session.*

Student Teaching (8 semester hours).

REFERENCES

Commission on the Education of the Handicapped. *The education of handicapped children in New Jersey 1954-1964* Trenton, New Jersey, New Jersey Department of Education, 1964.

Connor, Frances P. The sword and the spirit. *Exceptional Children*, 1964, 30, 393-401.

Davens, E. View of health services for mothers and children. *Children*, 1965, 12, 47-54.

Hill, A. S. The status of mental retardation today with emphasis on services. *Exceptional Children*, 1959, 25, 298-299.

Kaya, E. A curricular sequence based on psychological processes. *Exceptional Children*, 1961, 27, 425-428.

Kirk, S. A. Educating the handicapped. In *White House Conference on Education.* Washington, D. C.: Superintendent of Documents, U. S. Government Printing Office, 1965, 100-107.

Kirk, S. A., and Bateman, Barbara. Diagnosis and remediation of learning disabilities. *Exceptional Children*, 1962, 29, 73-78.

Laycock, S. R. Every teacher a diagnostician. *Exceptional Children Review*, 1934, 2, 47.

Levine, S. A proposed conceptual framework for special education. *Exceptional Children*, 1961, 28, 83-90.

Lord, F. E. A realistic look at special classes — extracts from the president's address. *Exceptional Children*, 1956, 22, 321-325, 342.

Reynolds, M. C. A framework for considering some issues in special education. *Exceptional Children*, 1962, 28, 367-370.

research designs for assessing teacher education programs in special education*

JAMES B. MacDONALD†

Research in any phase of teacher education is not presently noted for its productivity. An increasing number of studies may be noted in the literature, but the vast majority of these are better called innovations with some evaluative criteria applied, rather than systematic research. In fact, the profession knows little about program effectiveness that has been gained by careful research procedures. There are at least three reasons for this.

Climate and Competence of Teacher Educators and Institutions

Teacher education institutions have by and large been characterized by a climate of ideological commitment. As such, they have been resistant to so called objective examination of their programs. The commitment of the profession has been such that practices hard won from experience are not easily tested or manipulated in a research context because of a fear that harm may be done to a generation of children should tested practices prove less effective. In other words, research involves risk taking, and teacher educators have not been overly acceptant of the process of deliberate risk taking. This phenomenon might be called hardening of the ideological arteries.

Further, universities and colleges as a whole have not been

*Reprinted from *Exceptional Children*, (April 1966), pp. 213–220, by permission of the author and the Council for Exceptional Children. Copyright 1966 by the Council for Exceptional Children.

†James B. McDonald is Professor of Education, University of Wisconsin.

especially open to program research. Although many scholars appear to feel free to manipulate children's programs and public school teachers' behavior, university staff members in turn have tended to hold to a concept of academic freedom which precludes manipulation of content and teacher behavior at the college level. As a consequence, the climate for program research in teacher education has not been one that encourages activity.

Also, teacher educators, as a whole, have not experienced a great deal of research training. Thus, the necessary attitudes and skills for research are generally lacking in the profession. This, of course, further complicates attempts at program research.

Problem of
Teacher Effectiveness

A second reason for difficulties in teacher education research pertains to the problem of the criterion variable(s). There is a general lack of agreement about what good or effective teaching entails. This is especially noticeable in two aspects of the problem — the specification of theoretical models and the selection of measuring instruments.

The confusion in the theoretical realm is noted quite readily if one looks at studies on research in teaching. Bellack (1965), for example, looked at teaching from the perspective of games. Thus, he examined teaching in terms of the effective utilization of moves and rules in the classroom setting. The nature of teacher solicitation and moves provides one framework for looking at effective teacher performance.

Fattu (1965), on the other hand, conceptualized teaching as problem solving. He asserted that only about one-third of a teacher's activity is of a professional nature, in the sense that it involves special training to solve problems. The remainder of his time is clerical, custodial, and generally amenable to common sense operations. The problem solving is related to such things as programing decisions, diagnostic decisions, and motivational decisions.

Maccia (1965) and Flanders (1964), however, see teaching as a process of influence. Although their specific conceptualizations vary considerably, a good teacher by Flanders' orientation tends to be viewed as one who is indirect in his influence; while in Maccia's terms a person whose influence brings about rule governed behavior on the part of children is effective.

Many other positions are available. There are, in fact, almost as many theoretical positions as there are researchers (Bellack, 1963). It is apparent, then, that no general agreement on productive theoretical models for viewing teaching is in existence.

Perhaps even more disturbing is our lack of confidence in the validity of measuring instruments. Thus, even when researchers agree, for example, that understanding of individual differences is crucial for good teaching, there is a possibility that we could not produce a universally acceptable measure of the understanding of individual differences.

Our operational definitions or measurement problems leave much to be desired, both in terms of their validity and in terms of their scope of concern. It often appears that the things or qualities measured most validly tend to be those aspects of concern with least generality and potential significance. Thus, the hypotheses we test and the data we collect are both open to constant and considerable criticism.

Programs in teacher education should be based upon some theoretical model of teaching and some specification of effective teaching. Although the problem of translating a theoretical model into a prescribed series of experiences still exists, there is assuredly little hope of intelligent prescriptions without the model. Thus, new experiments in teacher education are in need of theoretical models and in need of operational definitions that can be used to assess the outcomes of the programs.

Problems of Design

A third set of problems arises through the lack of an adequate research design. What research we have done in teacher education has been predominantly characterized by what Stanley and Campbell (1963) have called quasi-experimental and pre-experimental or evaluative designs, as well as survey and descriptive studies. Frequently, these designs have been used without awareness of their limitations. Thus, the hoped for outcomes are not achieved, because the design was inadequate for the task at hand.

The major portion of what follows will be devoted to an examination of the problem of design. However, it will be important to remember that the conditions which stimulate research, the theoretical bases for research, and the measurement problems in research cannot be solved by better designs alone.

THE FUNCTION OF DESIGN IN RESEARCH

The function of design in research is essentially to provide a logic for control. Design is, in other words, primarily a logical technology. As was suggested earlier, a research study of little significance can be well designed, or data of little validity can be carefully controlled.

A design functions to assure the validity of the results of a specific study and to provide some basis for generalizing the results of other situations. These design functions Stanley and Campbell (1963) refer to as the internal and external validity factors of design.

Internal Validity

The appraisal of internal validity raises questions of control such as:

1. Did anything outside the program happen to its subjects during the research period which could account for the results?
2. Would the results have happened anyway, regardless of the experimental program — perhaps due to maturation?
3. What effect has the testing itself had on the outcome? For example, do pretests themselves provide learning experiences which affect the outcome?
4. What effect has variation in conditions of observation or assessment between pretests and posttests had upon the outcome?
5. What effect has statistical regression toward the mean had on the outcome?
6. What effect has the specific process of selection of subjects had on the outcome?
7. What effect has the mortality, or loss of subjects from groups, had on the outcome?
8. What effect has interaction between any and/or all of the above had on the outcome?

External Validity

When concerned about how generalizable results may be, provided they have internal validity, one may pose such questions as:

1. Has there been any interaction between testing and treatments, so that results are predicated not only upon the new program, but also upon the research procedures?
2. Has there been any special effect due to the interaction of the treatment and the selection of subjects? How representative are the subjects?

3. What effects have the special arrangements in program and the students' awareness of being in an experiment had on the generalizability of the results?
4. What effect has the unit of research, e.g., classroom groups, had on the outcome?

It is immediately apparent that the control of all these logically invalidating variables is indeed a difficult task. Nevertheless, whether a design can control all these factors or not, it is necessary at least to be aware of any potential weaknesses in control. Fortunately, the problem of control is not simply one of logic. Many times we can assume control of at least some of the internal and external validity variables by the nature of the research being done.

For example, if our research plan included the provision of experience for preparing teachers to apply electric shock selectively to autistic children, we might assume with reasonable assurance that our students have not had much prior experience with similar activities, and thus, the chances of anything occurring outside the program which would facilitate this learning and invalidate results are not great. In other words, the nature of the experiment itself may indicate that some control problems need not be of crucial concern.

Thus, in cases where the absence or presence of some behavior can be assumed to be predicated almost solely upon program experiences (such as the teaching of a sign language to teachers of the deaf), then there may be no direct corollary (as in the case, for example, of testing two different sign languages) to be controlled. In this case, it is plausible to assume that results which accrue from the introduction of this added element for which there may be no direct extra program behavioral corollary have been plausibly controlled.

COMMON RESEARCH DESIGNS

Preexperimental or Evaluative Design

The simplest common design is evaluative in nature. A group of students is selected, pretested, given an experimental program, and retested to see what progress has taken place. What this essentially represents is a rigorous evaluation of a program. It should be obvious that many control questions are left in doubt.

Thus, if we test students on their knowledge of mental retardation, then put them through a series of experiences and retest them, gains may be due to any number of circumstances other than the instructional procedures. Would they have shown as much progress without instruction? Have there been any TV specials, newspaper publicity, or other media coverage of the same subject which could help account for the growth? Did the pretest stimulate learning? Are results due to the specific nature of *this* program, or just to the fact that students have had *some* program?

Control Group Designs

The most powerful control techniques in design are the development of a control group or groups combined with the use of randomization procedures for selecting subjects. Thus, from a population of, say, 60 preservice exceptional education teachers, two groups of 20 each might be drawn by random sampling. One group, the experimental, would be given the new program, course, or experience. The second group would not receive the experimental treatment. Pretests and posttests would be given both groups, or in some cases posttests only might be given. These procedures would logically provide for experimental control of all the internal validity factors.

A more sophisticated design involves four groups and is called the Soloman Four Group Design. In this procedure, four groups are drawn randomly from a population. The first two receive pretests and posttests, with one group getting the experimental treatment as indicated above. A third group receives the treatment with no pretest, and the fourth group receives the posttest only. This design allows one to parcel out the effects of pretests and treatments from the total process. In most situations of program research, the four group design is difficult to manage administratively. The predominant experimental designs utilized are two group designs.

Quasiexperimental Designs

The problems of ongoing programs and the social situation of staff cooperation and school policy often make the pure experimental designs difficult to manage. There are a number of program designs called quasiexperimental by Stanley and Campbell (1963) which can be utilized under these circumstances. What I believe to be some of the promising ones for program research will be mentioned here.

The nonequivalent control group design is one common variant. The difference between this design and the pure control group is that students are not assigned randomly to groups. Thus, two classes selected by regular college or university procedures may be utilized in which pretests and posttests are given and one group receives a special treatment. Although a nonrandom assignment is weaker than the randomized procedure, there is usually no special reason to believe (except in homogeneous grouping situations) that a nonrandom assignment is necessarily related to factors which affect the experimental variable. Consequently, this design can be a very useful one.

A single modification of the evaluative design makes possible even greater control than the nonequivalent control group. If all students must receive the same program, it is possible to assign them, prior to testing, by randomized procedures into two groups (not necessarily separate physically). The first group is pretested, then all receive the new program, and the second group is then posttested.

A multiple time series design also has program promise. This procedure might be illustrated by breaking a population into two groups (e.g., two classes). Then repeated measures are taken over a period of time and an experimental treatment inserted somewhere in the middle for one group (for example, a special observation experience). Comparison can then be made with nonequivalent groups and also before and after the treatment with the experimental group.

Nonexperimental Designs

There are also a whole host of nonexperimental designs. These designs have, in fact, been the most prevalent (along with the evaluation design) in educational research. I would like to mention briefly three such patterns: the case study, the survey, and the job analysis.

A study by Mackie, Kvaraceus, and Williams (1957) illustrates the survey approach. Seventy-five teachers of socially and emotionally maladjusted children were presented with a list of competencies to rank in order of importance. The results of this opinion survey are irrelevant here, but the use of this list of competencies as a basis for building a teacher education program would be an illustration of a survey method. This would be fraught with difficulties. At best, this list could serve as a source of hypotheses for experimental or quasiexperimental testing.

Job analysis is a further elaboration of the survey procedure. The difference here is that, instead of asking the teachers, the investigators might identify good and poor teachers and then observe the behaviors or competencies which distinguish them. This procedure does provide insight for teacher education, but it does not assure that the competencies of the good teachers are amenable to teacher education. This design also is essentially most useful as a basis for generating hypotheses to be tested by more rigorous designs.

A case study approach could entail, for example, the careful depth recording of characteristics, experiences, and behaviors of students in a teacher education program. After the students have been followed into teaching, it would then be possible to look for patterns of characteristics that distinguish the competent from the less competent. These patterns could then be developed in some program format involving selection, experiences, and qualities which would be tested experimentally.

The major characteristic of nonexperimental designs is that they are primarily useful for developing hypotheses and experimental patterns to be tested. They are not nearly powerful enough in their control factors to base innovation in programs upon them with any assurance of worth. Unfortunately, much of the teacher education research in special education has been of this character.

A WORD ABOUT ANALYSIS

The analysis of results obtained by testing a sensible hypothesis placed in a well controlled design with data gathered by valid and reliable instruments must still be analyzed for its significance. The full cycle of research involved (a) an hypothesis, (b) the collection of evidence, and (c) the making of inferences from the evidence. All three are set within the logic of a research design. I shall not attempt to deal here with statistical analysis per se, except to make three general comments.

First, and foremost, a design should be selected with a statistical procedure for analysis in mind. It is often the case that statistical procedure can dictate other general design characteristics. There is nothing quite as frustrating and often times wasteful, as designing a study, collecting data, and then trying to identify an appropriate statistical technique. One is well advised to build one's analysis procedures in the planning stages.

Further, statistical analysis itself does not prove anything, in the common sense use of the term. Analysis as a part of design is an inferential process. It is a process which, in essence, provides greater assurance that the inference one makes about the effectiveness of the experimental program is most probably correct. The inference itself, however, is a human judgment based on the probabilities of error that are tested statistically. Statistical analysis is a tool for helping justify inferences and is only as valid as the sum total of a total design and study.

A third suggestion for those who are not statistically inclined or who are mathematically unsophisticated is the exploration of the possibility of utilizing nonparametric statistics. Siegal (1956) has written a lucid and usable book which sets forth the principles and procedures of nonparametric statistics in a highly sensible and understandable form. With the availability of many expert statisticians and/or the use of nonparametric statistics, there is essentially no reason to fear research because of its statistical procedures.

A POTENTIAL ILLUSTRATIVE
TEACHER EDUCATION STUDY

The analysis of classroom interaction reported by Gallagher and Aschner (1963) might serve as a basis for developing a teacher education study. Gallagher and Aschner's report dealt with the investigation of productive thought in gifted children. Following the work of Guilford (1959), Gallagher and Aschner examined, among other things, the kind of thinking called for by questions teachers ask children, and the kinds of answers children give. Questions and answers were categorized as (a) cognitive memory, (b) convergent, (c) divergent and (d) evaluative. Among other things they found that teachers vary considerably but tend to focus on cognitive memory and convergent questions and that by and large children respond in kind. Thus, teachers get the kinds of thought in answers that they attempt to elicit.

One can sensibly argue that good teaching, in the sense of eliciting productive thinking on the part of students, should consist of many questions which elicit divergent and evaluative responses, as well as cognitive memory and convergent thinking. And since teachers apparently do not tend to ask for these higher level responses, it could be argued that they need to be made aware of the possibilities of asking other kinds of questions and be provided with opportunities to practice the development of skill in a wide repertoire of potential questioning behaviors.

Provided one accepts the reasoning involved, the next step would be the development of a viable procedure for developing awareness and skill in questioning which would increase the production of divergent and evaluative responses in children. One such procedure might well be the development of a special field experience for students. Over a specified period of time (for example, one semester), students could be given a practicum in teaching which involved discussion of questioning behavior, the variety of possibilities, and the desirability of eliciting divergent and evaluative thinking. Twice a week one student in the group would be given an assignment which involved the teaching of a group of children. The student would provide plans for the rest of the class, then teach the children while the other members of the class watched over closed circuit television. Each session could be videotaped and played back if desirable. The student teacher would then discuss his lesson with the class and the instructor could help sharpen the analysis of questioning behavior.

To test the efficiency of this program procedure, a random sample of 50 students would be drawn from the total pool of preservice personnel and placed into two groups of 25 by further random sampling. Each student in both groups could be videotaped at the beginning of the semester, and a team of observers categorize their questions and the pupil responses. The experimental group would then engage in the special procedure described above, while the control group engaged in a participation experience with class discussion of problems they were encountering. At the end of the semester each student in both groups would be videotaped again and the same assessment procedures utilized.

An analysis of covariance could now be utilized to assess whether the change in questioning behavior (i.e., the evaluation of more productive thinking on the part of students) had occurred in the experimental group's performance. If the differences were statistically significant between groups, we might then plausibly infer that the special treatment was indeed effective and build it into the regular program.

TWO APPROACHES TO
TEACHER EDUCATION RESEARCH

In conclusion, I should like to indicate briefly what I see to be two major avenues for developing experimental programs for the education of teachers. These alternative positions might best be called macroteaching and microteaching approaches. They represent two dramatically different approaches to the attempts to identify specific competencies in teaching, which are then practiced by teachers with careful and appropriate supervision and continuous feedback until students have mastered these competencies.

The Stanford program is characteristic of this approach and is, in fact, the source of the term microteaching. Bush and Allen describe the process in the following way: "The micro-teaching clinic allows (ed) candidates to practice relatively small, discrete technical skills with intensive supervision, immediate critique, and opportunity to repeat the practice session, if necessary" (p. 5).

Teachers in their initial phases develop skill with small groups of children in such competencies as varying the stimulus situation, precueing student responses, eliciting student participation, controlling participation, and conducting reflective questioning. After gaining the security of these skills, students proceed to regular student teaching and other course work with emphasis upon developing a flexible and reflective use of the basic skills in actual decision making and performance.

Macroteaching, on the other hand, is predicated upon beginning with highly general or global qualities of teaching. A broad organizing framework is presented and then continually refined throughout the program by the application of the framework and the analysis of its implication in a variety of specific contexts.

Macdonald and Zaret's study of openness and flexibility in teaching is a case in point. They found in a previous study (1965) that reasonably accurate predications of student success in teaching could be made very early in the teacher education program on the basis of the judgment of experienced university supervisors, based upon what they felt was a global or general impression. Following up this global concept, they analyzed teaching transcripts in a second study in terms of opening versus closing behavior (mainly verbal) on the part of teachers and the concomitant opening and closing responses of children. They were able to reliably categorize teachers' and pupils' behavior in this manner. The open teacher phases (transaction oriented) led to searching, experimenting, evaluative, and divergent student behavior, whereas the closing teacher (role or task oriented) led to cognitive memory, parroting, and stereotyped responses on the part of children.

The suggestion growing from this research for teacher education programs is that the possibility of building from the general to the specific, rather than from the specific to the general as in the microteaching procedure, is a second theoretical style for constructing program models. More important, what both approaches suggest is the necessity for systematic rationales for teacher education which, in turn, can be formed into a research design and tested experimentally.

The need for research in special education programs is glaringly apparent from Blatt's (1966) review of research on the preparation of special education personnel in the February, 1966, Review of Educational Research:

The following review may indicate that there has been remarkable little change since 1959 in the status of research on the preparation of special education teachers. Little experimental work has been completed; there is, in fact, a scarcity of any systematic study of the problem, whether historical, descriptive, or experimental (p. 151).

Blatt Summarized his review in the following manner:

A survey of the literature between 1959 and 1965 concerned with the preparation of special education personnel disclosed no experimental studies and few investigations of any kind that could be classified as systematic research. The few descriptive studies completed fall into the opinionnaire-questionnaire category. In contrast with the general development of research programs in special education due to the tremendously increased support now provided by federal agencies and private foundations for both research and graduate education, the total impact of findings reported here is somewhat disappointing (pp. 158-159).

It is my opinion that this is something of an understatement, and that although research is difficult and risky it is still the best single approach to the development of better teacher education programs and consequently improved instruction for children.

REFERENCES

Bellack, A. The language of the classroom. In Macdonald and Leeper (Editors), *Theories of instruction.* Washington, D. C.: The Association for Supervision and Curriculum Development, NEA, 1965. Pp. 100-113.

Bellack, A. (Editor) Theory and research in teaching. New York: Bureau of Publications, Teachers College, Columbia University, 1963.

Blatt, B. The preparation of special education personnel. *Review of Educational Research,* 1966, 36 (1), 151-161.

Fattu, N. A model of teaching as problem solving. In Macdonald and Leeper (Editors), *Theories of instruction.* Washington, D. C.: The Association for Supervision and Curriculum Development, NEA, 1965. Pp. 62-87.

Flanders, N. A. Interaction analysis in the classroom: a manual for observers. Ann Arbor: University of Michigan, 1964. P. 43.

Gallagher, J., and Aschner, Mary Jane. A preliminary report on analyses of classroom instruction. *Merrill-Palmer Quarterly,* 1963, 9, 183-194.

Guilford, J. P. Three faces of intellect. *American Psychologist,* August, 1959.

Maccia, Elizabeth. Instruction as influence toward rule governed behavior. In Macdonald and Leeper (Editors), *Theories of instruction.* Washington, D. C.: The Association for Supervision and Curriculum Development, NEA, 1965. Pp. 88-99.

Macdonald, J., et al. A research oriented elementary education student teaching program. Milwaukee: University of Wisconsin, 1965.

Macdonald, J., and Zaret, Esther. A study of openness in teaching. Milwaukee: University of Wisconsin.

Mackie, Romaine, Kvaraceus, W. C., and Williams, H. C. Teachers of children who are socially and emotionally maladjusted. Washington, D. C.: U. S. Office of Education. 1957.

Siegal, S. *Non-parametric statistics.* New York: McGraw-Hill, 1956.

Stanley, J., and Campbell, D. T. Experimental and quasi-experimental design for research on teaching. In American Educational Research Association, *Handbook of research on teaching.* Rand McNally and Company, 1963.

part iX

annotated
bibliography

organization,
supervision,
administration of
special education

The material for the annotated bibliography was collected from numerous sources. In the process of the authors' search for significant material several thousand articles and books were abstracted. Bibliographies compiled by others were carefully reviewed. After review, the majority of the references were eliminated. The resulting annotated bibliography contains the publications most relevant to Special Education Administration, Organization and Supervision. A key and cross reference can be found at the end of the bibliography.

1. [A]* ABRAHAM, WILLARD. *The Slow Learner.* New York: The Center for Applied Research in Education, Inc., 1964.
   The problem of the slow learner is considered. The role of the school under the following topics — (1) organization and administrative structure, (2) current practices, (3) promotion and grading, (4) special classes, (5) curriculum, (6) teaching techniques, (7) costs, and (8) teacher qualities.

2. [F&L] ACKERMAN, PAUL. "Analysis of State Legislative Provisions for the Education of Children with Learning Disabilities."
   A summary of a review of state legislation for exceptional children as this legislation relates to programs for children with learning

*Bracketed letters refer to the key designations at the end of the Bibliography.

disabilities. It was concluded that changes in most states' legislation will have to occur before efficient programs for the remediation of such disabilities may be effected.

3. [AP] *Adapted Physical Education Program.* 1968 Report. Pittsburgh, Pa.: Pittsburgh Public Schools, Pennsylvania, Office of Research, 1968, 22 pp.
   A program to provide individualized physical education for students who could not participate in regular physical education programs. Administrative considerations are included.

4. [P] ADLERBLUM, EVELYN D. *Selection Procedures in Preparing Teachers for Emotionally Disturbed Children.* Washington, D. C.: Council for Exceptional Children (April 1966), 142-146.
   Program objectives and desirable personal competencies of teachers of the emotionally disturbed are discussed relative to the New York University teacher preparation program. Teacher candidates are selected on the basis of a multiple criteria process including a written narrative paper, individual interviews, and classroom observations.

5. [AP] *Administration of Boarding Homes for Handicapped Children, Policies and Procedures.* Madison, Wisconsin: Wisconsin Department of Public Instruction, Madison. Bur. Hand. Children, 1966, 8 pp.
   Provisions of Wisconsin statutes for enrollment in special classes and responsibilities of the Bureau of Handicapped Children and other agencies are listed. Planning procedures and reimbursements for boarding care and social service are specified.

6. [AP, AG] *Administrative Guide in Speech Correction.* Jefferson City, Missouri: Missouri State Department of Education, Jefferson City, 1964, 54 pp.
   Written primarily for school superintendents, principals, speech clinicians, and supervisors, this guide outlines the mechanics of organizing and conducting speech correction activities in the public schools. Specifications for a speech correction room, all equipment, and supplies are presented.

7. [AP, AG] ALLEN, AMY and VIRGINIA BAKER. *Slow Learning Children in Ohio Schools.* Columbus, Ohio: Ohio State Department of Education, Columbus, 1962, 115 pp.
   In this bulletin "slow learning" refers to children in the 50-75 IQ range. Eligibility for special classes is discussed, including a description of the testing program and an explanation of the IQ concept. Samples of forms used in communication with parents and district applications for special classes are included. Learning characteristics of slow learning children are briefly described. This bulletin, intended for teachers and administrators, outlines an instructional program.

8. [AT,O] ALLEN, LOUIS A. *Management and Organization.* New York: McGraw-Hill Book Company, 1958, 353 pp.
   The author identifies two basic types of organizational structures: functional and divisional. The first, according to Allen, results in excessive centralization; and the second is a vehicle for decentralization. Line-staff relationships are discussed at length.

9. [F & L] ALPREN, MORTON and CHARLOTTE HOHENSTEIN. "A Survey of Provisions for the Gifted," *Exceptional Children* (May 1960), 26:492-494.
   Existing legislation, permissive legislation, curriculum specifications, and teacher certification are discussed. Notations on the specific types of bills passed for different states are included.

10. [O] ALPRIN, STANLEY J. "The Effect of Organizational Patterns on Programs for Trainable Children in New Jersey Public Schools," *American Journal of Mental Deficiency* (November 1960), 45:376-380.
    Factors that influence the quality of instructional programs for trainable children are discussed. Advantages of multi-unit centers and one-room school plans are compared. The relationship of organizational patterns to curriculum, supervision, and parent education is described.

11. [AP, AG] ANDERSON, JEAN L. *Guide for Records and Reports for Speech and Hearing Programs.* Indianapolis: Indiana Department of Public Instruction, 1965, 32 pp.
    A rationale for record keeping and reporting is presented along with a comprehensive set of forms. Forms are available to cover all situations in diagnosis and progress, communication to other professional people, and communication to parents.

12. [AP, AG, PP, F & L] ANDERSON, JEAN L. *A Guide to the Establishment of a Speech and Hearing Program.* Indianapolis: Indiana Department of Public Instruction, Division of Special Education, 1965, 7 pp.
    The following steps necessary for establishing speech and hearing programs in Indiana are described — determine the need, prepare the community, learn about state regulations, secure a therapist, provide adequate facilities and equipment, secure consultative services, plan the program (including locating the children), and apply for state approval and reimbursement.

13. [AP, AG] ANDERSON, ROBERT M., et al. *Provisions for the Education of Mentally Retarded Deaf Children in Residential Schools for the Deaf.* Pittsburgh, Pa.: Pittsburgh University, School of Education, 1966, 134 pp.
    An investigation of the education of mentally retarded deaf (MRD) children in residential schools for the deaf. The study's aim was to

describe policies and procedures for admission, special academic and vocational provisions, and qualifications of classroom teachers. Additional purposes were to estimate prevalence of MRD children and to assess adminstrative attitudes toward instructional organization.

14. [AG] ANTHONY, ROBERT N. *Planning and Control Systems: A Framework for Analysis.* Boston: Division of Research, Graduate School of Business Administration, Harvard University, 1965, 180 pp.

The author discusses three main topics: strategic planning, management control, and operational control. Even though the term "management control" emphasizes the control aspects, planning is inherently associated with it. Although they are not specifically regarded as part of planning and control, two other topics merited consideration in the study of planning and control systems. These are information handling and financial accounting.

. 15. [A, S] APPELDOORN, HELEN. *Realistic Approaches to Supervision and Administration of Special Education.* Washington, D. C.: Council for Exceptional Children, 1963, 4 pp.

This article touches briefly the area of philosophy of special education. Of major concern to the author is the overworked director of special education. She feels that the director should place a great deal of responsibility with the supervision of various programs to free the director for work in any special area. Guiding principles for supervisors are also presented. Within this area is an appeal to look at general education. These principles are salient facts the supervisor should be aware of. One of these facts is the idea that all school personnel should be aware of the supervisor's duties and responsibilities. The functions of the supervisor are also discussed through the use of a list. The selection of supervisors with reference to characteristics needed is discussed. An appeal is also made for evaluation of programs.

16. [O, R] APPELL, MELVILLE J. and BERNARD KINSELLA. "The Coordinating Group on Mental Retardation of Monroe County, New York," *American Journal of Mental Deficiency* (July 1962), 67:14-20.

A study of the development of a coordinated community effort to work out a comprehensive plan of services for the mentally retarded, beginning with the organization of a pre-planning body with power to recommend — not to act.

17. [A, S, R] ARGYRIS, CHRIS. *Executive Leadership: An Appraisal of a Manager in Action.* Hamden, Conn.: Archon Books, 1967, 139 pp.

This book is a report of research sponsored by Cornell University to help practicing executives in understanding leadership concepts. In the first part of the book, the distinguishing features of the executive as a leader are described by comparing the researcher's impressions of the executives' leadership characteristics with the executives' own impressions. To describe the effects of this leader on his twenty supervisors (which constitutes the second part of this book), Argyris observed the behavior of these supervisors to determine whether behavior changed because of the leader's absence or presence; he then relates the behavior of these supervisors to a leadership pattern. Problems faced by the supervisors in adapting to the leader are discussed. Appendices giving research methods and problems under investigation constitute Part IV.

18. [AP] AYERS, GEORGE E. *Proceedings of a Symposium on Habilitating the Mentally Retarded (Mankato, Minnesota, February 11, 1967).* Mankato, Minnesota: Mankato State College, School of Education, 1967, 51 pp.

The conference was designed to strengthen communication and cooperation between special education and vocational rehabilitation planners and practitioners, and thus to contribute to the process of habilitating the mentally retarded.

19. [AP] BAGLEY, R. B. "Serving Children with Handicaps in a Rural State," National Committee for Children and Youth, Montgomery, Alabama, September 1963, 4 pp.

The history, clientele, responsibilities, and needs of the State Crippled Children's Service are described. The agency, designed to help with medical, educational and social problems of crippled children, tries simultaneously to aid the children in reducing their handicaps; in advancing educationally during physical rehabilitation; and in adjusting emotionally to handicaps, family, and community relations. The Crippled Children's Service Programs were at first mainly orthopedic but now serve almost all handicapping conditions. Programs vary from state to state. State and volunteer agencies cooperate in trying to help as·many children as possible without duplication of services.

Needs in Alabama, typical of the needs of other states, are for additional nurses, physical therapists, and medical social workers; for more camping and recreational facilities for the handicapped; for more workshops for the severely handicapped; and for the establishment of clinics to serve the multiple handicapped.

20. [A] BAKER, HARRY J. "Administration of Special Education," *Review of Educational Research* (June 1944), National Education Association, Washington, D. C., 14:209- 216.

Discusses views which school administration takes in special education administration including the mental hygiene of teachers and administrators, teacher training and qualifications, costs and financing, vocational guidance and placement, and several brief resumes of surveys and studies made in these areas.

21. [O] BANGHART, FRANK W. *Educational Systems Analysis.* New York: MacMillan Company, 1969.

> This text furnishes educational administrators with an orientation to systems technology. The author has organized the material into four sections which provide the reader with a complete introduction to systems analysis. The first three sections are descriptive, offering the non-mathematically trained administrator resource material which will enable him to apply systems techniques to education; the fourth is technical and permits the graduate student and interested administrator to acquire a more comprehensive understanding of systems analysis.

22. [A, AP] BARBE, WALTER B. *Psychology and Education of the Gifted: Selected Readings.* New York: Appleton-Century-Crofts, 1965, 534 pp.

> An overview of educational and psychological literature concerning the gifted is presented in 55 papers with editorial comments. Special programs to help develop and encourage giftedness, such as acceleration, enrichment, and homogeneous grouping are described and evaluated; current issues and needed research are considered.

23. [O] BARNARD, CHESTER I. *The Functions of the Executive.* Cambridge, Mass.: Harvard University Press, 1938, 334 pp.

> Barnard's observations of skilled executives and his own experience as an executive led him to develop a more complete statement of the executive process than had been done. The behavior of organizations and the people in them, especially executives is dealt with.

24. [A, AT] BARON, GEORGE, et al. (ed.). *Educational Administration: International Perspectives.* Chicago, Ill.: Rand McNally & Co., 1969.

> The papers reproduced here represent the most current thinking on theoretical and practical educational administration, based on the proceedings of the first International Intervisitation Conference organized by the University Council for Educational Administration. Emergent trends in educational administration are presented by contributors from five English-speaking countries: Australia, Canada, New Zealand, the United Kingdom and the United States.

25. [P] BARRETT, RICHARD S. *Performance Rating.* Chicago, Ill.: Science Research Associates, Inc., 1966, 166 pp.

> This book is intended to aid managers in evaluating performance of all personnel. Barrett describes techniques for improving performance ratings through the training and supervision of the raters.

26. [P] BARSCH, RAY H. *A Concept for Tomorrow: The Parent Counselor.* Washington, D. C.: Council for Exceptional Children, 1963, 5 pp.

> Parents should be acquainted with the principles of learning and the obligations and techniques of child rearing. The professional

specifically conceived to fulfill such an obligation is a parent counselor. The parent counselor would function as a member of the staff of the special education department of a community school system and carry a full-time responsibility for the development of parent counseling relationships. Specific special classes would be assigned to this counselor and the parents of the children in each class could be organized into counseling groups. The author lists several advantages of a program of parent counseling. The professional characteristics of the parent counselor are also discussed.

27. [AG] BATTEN, J. D. *Developing A Tough-Minded Climate for Results.* New York: American Management Association, 1965, 350 pp.

The author makes it clear that "tough-minded" does not mean brash or aggressive behavior, but refers to a manager's ability to develop a course of action which produces results by working with and through people. A manager should evaluate his own strengths and weaknesses, then he should determine where and how he plans to go in terms of objectives and available resources. Batten also recommends that a manager isolate key jobs in his realm of operations and staff them with effective subordinates. Another key to obtaining successful results is communication. Subordinates should be informed of the overall management philosophy and all pertinent information regarding the total organization activities. A manager should be a counselor to his subordinates, but not an all-knowing adviser.

28. [A, PP] BAYES, KENNETH. *The Therapeutic Effect of Environment on Emotionally Disturbed and Mentally Subnormal Children.* Montreal, Quebec: Society for Emotionally Disturbed Children, 1967.

Current research and thought on the effects of architectural form and color in the treatment of emotionally disturbed and retarded children are surveyed in this publication. The need for research is clarified, methods and problems are discussed, and proposals for future research are provided.

29. [AP, R] BEALS, LESTER, PATRICIA SIMMONS, and FRANK BLACK. "Administrative Implications of a Study of Gifted Students," *Bulletin of the National Association of Secondary School Principals.* Washington, D.C.: National Education Association (1965), 49:83–91.

This article gives reflections on previous counseling that had been conducted with gifted students. The implications of this counseling is reviewed. Suggestions are offered to improve counseling based on the responses given by the former students. Also given are suggestions for the classes that the gifted are attending. There is a plea by the former students for more vocational counseling and more attention from the counselor and suggestions are offered that could alleviate this situation.

30. [F & L] BECKER, R. J. and S. HELPERIN. "The ABC's of Implementing Titles I, II, III of the Elementary and Secondary Education Act of 1965 (PL 89-10)," *American School Board Journal* (1965), 151:5-9.

States the purposes and eligible activities provided in these three titles. States the roles of the Office of Education and state education agencies in implementing the legislation. Adequate information is outlined concerning the authorization of funds, evaluation requirements, and how the state must plan and coordinate its function with that of the public schools.

31. [AP] BELINKOFF, CORNELIA. "Community Attitudes Toward Mental Deficiency," *American Journal of Mental Deficiency.*

Discusses observations made of parent attitudes when a project with a name including "Mental Retardation" was presented and one in which the name was changed to Special Education Research Project. There was a more definite hesitation in the first and participation increased in the second.

32. [AG, O] BENNIS, WARREN G. *Changing Organizations: Essays on the Development and Evolution of Human Organization.* New York: McGraw-Hill Book Company, 1966, 223 pp.

Approaching organizational-change behavior from a behavioral science viewpoint, Bennis shows how knowledge developed from behavioral sciences can help managers direct change processes and achieve effectiveness in their organizations. T-groups and sensitivity training are discussed. Section IV-B of this monograph is a list of books relating to development and training.

33. [A, P] BENSBERG, GERALD J., Jr. *Job Families in Mental Retardation.* Bethesda, Md.: National Institute of Mental Health, 1966.

Three jobs are explained in which personnel work under the supervision of a fully qualified person — teaching assistants in educable mentally retarded classes (not aides), trainable class teachers, and behavior shaping technicians. Additional needs could be met by training personnel for the development and coordination of community programs.

34. [AG, AT] BERLO, DAVID K. *The Process of Communication: An Introduction to Theory and Practice.* New York: Holt, Rinehart & Winston, Inc., 1960, 318 pp.

This is a discussion of the role of language in human behavior. Berlo identifies and describes factors affecting communication and their results. The discussion of the communication is based on an inter-disciplinary approach to the study of human behavior. Central concepts of the communication process, particularly the concept of meaning, are developed in a multi-dimensional fashion. This book would be of interest and value to all persons who wish to begin a systematic study of the communication process.

35. [AG]   BILLS, ROBERT E. "Education Is Human Relations," *New Insights and the Curriculum Yearbook 1963*. Association for Supervision and Curriculum Development (1963), National Education Association, Washington, D. C., 165-187.

> A discussion of conversation as an individual method of relating to other persons, barriers to conversation, listening and understanding as therapy, openness to an experience, closedness to experience, how teachers vary in openness, and how the relationship the teacher achieves with his students determines the degree of development the students will experience.

36. [AP] BINDMAN, ARTHUR J. and LEWIS B. KLEBANOFF. "New Programming for the Mentally Retarded School Child in Massachusetts," *American Journal of Mental Deficiency* (March 1960), 64:875-880.

> Causes of the changes in the programs for mentally retarded school children in Massachusetts, problems and needs of the program, and methods for gaining acceptance for the program.

37. [O, A]   BINGHAM, DALE S., et al. "Program Organization and Management," *Journal of Speech and Hearing Disorders*, Monograph Supplement 8 (June 1961), 26:33-49.

> Data concerning the organization and management of public school speech and hearing programs, "focusing . . . upon broad aspects of overall speech and hearing program organization;" details of local programming, reporting and record keeping practices, and program financing.

38. [P] BISHOP, VIRGINIA E. *School Vision Screening; Policies, Procedures, Practices*. Chester School District, Pennsylvania, 1967, 46 pp.

> The reactions of 18 special educators to the county and city level vision screening programs in Pennsylvania are presented, along with the responses of 44 school nurses to a questionnaire concerning the vision screening practices and procedures in Chester County, Pennsylvania.

39. [P] BLACK, JAMES M. *Developing Competent Subordinates*. New York: American Management Association, 1961, 128 pp.

> The central thesis is that a company's comparative position and a manager's chances for success improve by developing competent and self-reliant subordinates. Formal training programs are not sufficient to develop the full potential of subordinates; a continuous training and development climate is essential for employee growth. In the last chapter the author gives guidelines for effective use of manpower in a competitive economy.

40. [S] BLACK, MARTHA E., et al. "Supervision of Speech and Hearing Programs," *Journal of Speech and Hearing Disorders*, Monograph Supplement 8 (June 1961), 26:22-33.

A review of the duties of supervisors of public school speech and hearing programs, a summary of current practices in the administration of these programs, and a description of personnel.

41. [AG] BLACKHURST, A. EDWARD. "Technology in Special Education — Some Implications," *Exceptional Children* (May 1965), 31:449-456.
Illustrates the impact that technology could have on special education through the introduction of the student-subject matter interface concept. Various devices are described that could possibly be constructed to meet the unique needs of different types of exceptional children.

42. [O] BLAIR, MARY A. "Administrative Organization of the Day Class," *Volta Review* (June 1960), Alexander Graham Bell Association for the Deaf, Washington, D. C., 62:22-24.
This article explains how emphasis should be placed on the contiguity of nursery school and vocational placement. Classes should be in the same building with normal children. Selection of students should be done by a screening committee. Parent cooperation should be nurtured.

43. [AP] BLESSING, KENNETH R. *Cooperative Programming*, CEC Monograph. Washington, D. C.: Council for Exceptional Children, 1969.
Presents an approach to cooperative planning of programs for exceptional children outlining the role of various resource agencies and organizations.

44. [A, P] BLESSING, KENNETH R. (ed.) *The Role of the Resource Consultant in Special Education.* Washington, D. C.: Council for Exceptional Children, 1969, 127 pp.
Chapters by selected authors on the resource consultant's role in the various fields of special education.

45. [P] BLESSING, KENNETH R. "A State Department-University Approach in Providing Internship Experiences for Prospective Leadership Personnel in Special Education," *Exceptional Children* (January 1966), 305-309.
Depicts one cooperative state-university approach to implementing federal directives for preparing supervisors and directors of special education programs for exceptional children in state and local school systems. Internship experiences which are provided graduate students in the state's special education section, in the field, and in intermediate, county, and city school systems are outlined. The underlying theme is the need for sound theoretical and course work background in the administration and supervision of special education services, coupled with broad practical internship experiences in supervision and administration. Additional needs for the extensive consideration of issues and problems involved in special education programming are indicated.

46. [A] BLESSING, KENNETH R. "The Function and Role of the Modern State Department in Providing Special Education Services for Exceptional Youth," *Exceptional Children* (April 1960), 26:395-400.

The purpose of this article is to consider the functions and role of the modern state department of education, specifically in its provision of special educational services for exceptional children. The bases and source of state administrative authority and responsibility are explored from an historical point of view as are the nature and extent of state control over special services and teaching personnel. Modern day supervisory authority is seen as a "consultative function."

47. [A, R] BLESSING, KENNETH R. "A Survey of Public School Administrators' Attitudes Regarding Services for Trainable Retarded Children," *American Journal of Mental Deficiency* (November 1959), 64:509-519.

A questionnaire method was employed to survey the attitudes of Wisconsin school superintendents concerning trainable programs in operation within their school districts since 1951. The program is relatively new. They found about eight pupils enrolled in each half-day unit. Superintendents felt the present state department policies regarding minimum and maximum enrollment were satisfactory. They felt trainable children were the public schools' responsibilities; they felt teachers should have extensive training to educate the retarded. They felt the school districts are justified in using public school buildings for trainable groups along with regular classes, as well as several other points. In all, the survey showed a greater all-around acceptance of trainable programs by superintendents.

48. [AP] BLOOM, JEAN L. "A Private Approach to Programming for the Rehabilitation Needs of Exceptional Children in High School," *Selected Convention Papers, 41st Annual CEC Convention, Philadelphia* (April 1963), 25-27.

Discusses New York's plan for homebound high school students. The screening process is presented in outline form. A detailed summary of the program is also presented. Some implications for further planning of a new program are given. The goal of this project is to provide a setting to offer homebound adolescents educational, social psychotherapeutic, group, and work experiences not otherwise available to them.

49. [L, F] BOGGS, ELIZABETH M. "Implications for the Mentally Retarded in the Elementary and Secondary Education Act of 1965," *Mental Retardation Newsletter* (June 1965), Council for Exceptional Children, Washington, D. C., III

Discusses in detail Public Law 89-10, under Titles I, II, and III. Also discusses the Cooperative Research Act and ways to get grants.

50. **[P, AP, PP]** BOHNAM, S. J., Jr. *Program Standards for Special Education and Legal Dismissal from School Attendance.* Columbus, Ohio: Ohio State Department of Education, Division of Special Education, 1966, 61 pp.

In outline form this guide presents the program standards approved by the Ohio State Board of Education in August 1966 for 13 special education programs and for legal dismissal from school attendance. The following topics are considered — general standards, eligibility for services, class size and student age range, housing, equipment and materials, program organization and content, and teacher qualifications.

51. **[AG]** BOWER, MARVIN. *The Will to Manage: Corporate Success Through Programmed Management.* New York: McGraw-Hill Book Company, 1966, 276 pp.

Systematic strategic planning is the primary essential of a programmed management system. This type of planning forces a manager to face current and anticipated programs. Only after planning is done can management develop standards, policies and guidelines for carrying out the plans.

52. **[AP]** BOWLING, WILLIAM C. "Day Classes for the Deaf-Covina Plan," *Volta Review* (January 1967). Washington, D. C.: Volta Bureau, 69:54-58.

Describes the Covina School District program for hearing impaired children started eight years ago. The program has grown steadily both in size and services offered. The program includes an aide for each special teacher and a consultant who works with all teachers in the program so there is a continuity from level to level and school to school.

53. **[AG]** BOWMAN, DONALD M. and FRANCIS M. FILLERUP (eds.). *Management: Organization and Planning.* New York: McGraw-Hill Book Company, 1963, 148 pp.

This small book is a collection of articles written by six well-known educators and practitioners who support the idea that an organization's success depends upon how effectively the planning functions are performed. Two of the articles are especially pertinent to the planning process.

54. **[A]** BRABNER, GEORGE. "Integration and the Special Class Administrator," *Journal of Education* (October 1964), 147:105-110.

The special class administrator has the primary responsibility of providing current accurate information regarding the handicapped to his staff, co-workers, and the community at large. In this way it is hoped that conflicts, occurring as a result of attempting to integrate special classes for the retarded with the regular school program, will be reduced. The purpose of the article as stated by the author was not to explore the feasibility of integration. The administrator should maintain an open minded professional viewpoint in considering segregation versus integration. At the same time he must work within the framework of established school policy. Desired changes in policy should be brought about in a professional, ethical manner.

55. [AG] BRANCH, MELVILLE C. *Planning: Aspects and Applications.* New York: John Wiley & Sons, Inc., 1966, 333 pp.

Project planning, city planning, corporate planning, and military planning are considered in this book. The first and third of these types of planning would seem to be of value to vocational rehabilitation administrators. Quantification, people, objectives, and effects are also discussed.

56. [A, R] BROWN, KENNETH W. "An Administrative Survey of the Special Education Program in Oakland County, Michigan," *Dissertation Abstracts* (1961), 22:1477-1478.

Included in the report of a study of special education programs designed to indicate the quality of professional practices observed in classrooms were the criteria on which teachers of special education were rated and recommendations made by specialists in the field.

57. [A] BROWN, RAY E. *Judgment in Administration.* New York: McGraw-Hill Book Company, 1966, 225 pp.

From his own experience and from observing many administrators, the author writes about "judgment" which he feels is central in administration. Factors which contribute to poor judgment are divided into nine groups and discussed in nine chapters.

58. [O, AP, AG] BRYAN, J. N. *Building a Program for Superior and Talented High School Students.* Chicago: North Central Association of Colleges and Secondary Schools, 1964, 90 pp.

This recent publication of the North Central Association offers guidelines in setting up and maintaining programs for gifted high school students. There are chapters on identification, guidance, motivation, and administrative and curricular provisions. The four chapters have been organized around basic assumptions and procedures that have been effectively used. The second section discusses the part that can be played by boards of education, administrators, and teachers in setting up and maintaining programs for the gifted.

59. [A, S] BURTON, WILLIAM H. and LEO J. BRUECKNER. *Social Supervision: A Social Process.* New York: Appleton-Century-Crofts, Inc., 1955.

The authors show how the principles of democracy, findings of science and implications of trends within our social order may be utilized in a theory of supervision.

60. [A, O] *Business Systems.* Cleveland: Systems and Procedures Association, 1966.
    This book is specifically designed as textbook material for upper division or graduate level business administration programs. The text is a comprehensive, in-depth presentation of business systems including such topics as management, organization, systems functions and analysis, information retrieval, operations research, and administrative work measurement and forms.

61. [AP, S] CALVERT, DONALD R., et al. "A Program for Aphasic Children," *The Volta Review* (February 1966), 68(2):144-149.
    Discusses supervisor's responsibility for admitting and dismissing children, aiding in transfer of language to the home, aiding in proper educational placement after dismissal, and obtaining additional help for the children as needed.

62. [A, R] CAMPBELL, RONALD F. and RUSSELL T. GREGG. *Administrative Behavior in Education.* New York: Harper & Row, Publishers, 1957.
    A symposium sponsored by the National Conference of Professors of Educational Administration synthesizes and interprets the research and experience relating to factors influencing administrative behavior and looks into future development of educational administration. Selected readings for each chapter.

63. [A] CANFIELD, BERTRAND R. *Public Relations: Principles, Cases, and Problems.* 4th ed. Homewood, Ill.: Richard D. Irwin, Inc., 1964, 622 pp.
    Explains the nature and history of public relations; public relations needs of the corporate public and their practices to deal with employees, stockholders, and consumers; public relations of nonprofit and governmental organizations; public relations of organizations having international operations; and the media of public relations communications are among the topics discussed in this work.

64. [AP, P] CAROLLO, ELIZABETH, et al. *An Emerging Program for Emotionally Disturbed and Neurologically Impaired Pupils in the Warwick Public Schools, Grades 1-6.* Warwick School District, Rhode Island, 1966, 50 pp.
    Admission policy, administration of both types of classes, and the duties of the teacher and teacher's aide are described. Relationships with parents, the principal, supportive personnel, student teachers, and non-teaching personnel are discussed.

65. [AP, R] CARR, DOROTHY B. "Tele-teaching: A New Approach to Teaching Elementary and Secondary Homebound Pupils," *Exceptional Children* (November 1964), 31:116-118.
    Tele-teaching is a system by which groups of homebound children are given fulltime instruction via the telephone. The present report

was an attempt to appraise an experimental program of tele-teaching in Los Angeles. The 26 children in the study made satisfactory educational progress according to follow-up evaluation of semester grades and interviews with pupils, their parents, tele-teachers, and regular school teachers. Recommendations to further improve tele-teaching are also included.

66. [A, R] CARR, JOSEPHINE. "Administrative Problems in the Education of the Deaf," *American Annals of the Deaf* (September 1966), Intelligencer Printing Company, Ill.: 552–557.

This is a study concerning the problems of administrators. Forty problem statements were written up and sent as a questionnaire to many areas of the country to identify the kinds of problems to be found. The most significant problem is finding adequate personnel. The study corresponds closely with a study done by Wisland and Vaughn in the same area (Wisland, M. V. and T. D. Vaughn, "Administrative Problems in Special Education," *Exceptional Children* (1964), 31:87–89).

67. [A, O] CARVER, THOMAS J. and FRED D. CARVER. *Organizations and Human Behavior: Focus on Schools.* New York: McGraw-Hill Book Company, 1969.

The general purpose 'of this book is to provide the student of educational administration with a series of essays on organizational life, essays not available up to the present under one cover. These readings should complement the more traditional points of view of educational administration.

68. [O, AT] CARZO, ROCCO, Jr. and JOHN N. YANOUZAS. *Formal Organization: A Systems Approach.* Homewood, Ill.: Richard D. Irwin, Inc., 1967, 591 pp.

Examples, case studies, and models are used to illustrate concepts of systems design and systems operations. Concepts of traditional theory and behavior patterns in organizational life are discussed at length.

69. [A, F & L] CASHMAN, PHILIP G. *Fiscal Program Relative to Instruction and Training of Mentally and Physically Handicapped Children* (September 1965), Memorandum to Superintendents of Schools from the Assistant Commissioner of Education, Division of Special Education, The Commonwealth of Massachusetts, Boston, 3 pp.

A statement of the Department of Education's reimbursement and total cost programs relative to the instruction, training, support, and transportation of physically handicapped, mentally retarded, and emotionally disturbed children.

70. [AG, R] CASSELL, JOHN T. "A Study to Develop a Guide for Use in

Establishing or Evaluating Special Programs for the Mentally Handicapped," *Dissertation Abstracts* (1958), 19:999.

> A study designed to meet the needs of school personnel in the establishment or operation of a special class. Twenty-six specific recommendations are made. Evidence showed that the suggestions of authorities and the suggestions of special class teachers were very similar. Supervisors of special classes are untrained and unfamiliar with problems of special classes for the mentally retarded.

71. [A] *The Changing American Scene as It Relates to Health, Education and Welfare Services for Visually Handicapped: An Institute for Executives and Board Members of Agencies Serving Visually Handicapped Persons in Region I (Amherst, Massachusetts, April 19–21, 1967).* New York: American Foundation for the Blind, 1967, 37 pp.

> The proceedings of a conference of executives and board members of agencies serving visually handicapped persons consider social welfare programing and practice. Summaries are provided for discussions on the roles of the government and voluntarism in service provision, board and executive responsibility for problem solving, and implications for administrative practice.

72. [A] CHARTERS, W. W., et al. *Perspectives on Educational Administration and the Behavioral Sciences.* Portland, Oregon: Center for the Advanced Study of Educational Administration, Univ. of Oregon, 1965.

73. [AP, O] *Child Welfare League of America Preliminary Statement on Social Work Service for Children in Their Own Homes. A Document in the Child Welfare League of America Standards Series.* New York: Child Welfare League of America, 1968, 75 pp.

> Published as a preliminary statement rather than as standards, the document outlines the development of social work service for children in their own homes and provides a definition of the service. Further information is presented on social work practice in providing the service, and on intake, continuing service for parents, working with the child, and use of other services and resources. The following are also detailed: organization and administration of social agencies providing social work service, and community organization, all for children in their own homes. Eighty-eight references are cited.

74. [AG, P] CLAVERING, R. and B. ALPER. *How to Say What You Mean.* New York: American Management Association, 1966, 85 pp.

> This is a programmed instruction course in language skills for employees and supervisors; it can be used on an individual or group basis. The course is structured around twelve rules of good writing. An instruction manual and pre-test and post-test booklets are provided.

75. [P, R]   CLELAND, C., et al. "The 'Hawthorne Effect' in an Institution in Transition," *American Journal of Mental Deficiency* (March 1962), 66:723-728.

    Report of a study to determine the Hawthorne effect of attention on a systematic basis on staff and patients from the top management in an institution which was making a transition from the care of one type of patient to the care of another type of patient.

76. [AG] CLOPPER, DONALD. *Exceptional Children, Administrative Guide for Speech Correction Programs in Local School Districts.* Commonwealth of Kentucky Educational Bulletin, (1963), 31(9):50 pp.

    This bulletin lists guidelines for developing and administering a speech correction program, with emphasis on the relationships between the following agencies — state department of education, local school district, speech correctionist, classroom teacher, and parent. The duties of the local school superintendent, principal, and supervisors are discussed.

77. [AP, P, AG]   CONNER, FRANCIS P. *Education of Homebound or Hospitalized Children* (Teachers College Series in Special Education). New York: Teachers College, 1964.

    Focuses on the educational and professional preparation of teachers, the educational setting, program content, and problem areas of the homebound child. Appendices present teaching methods and materials, particularly in the area of science. A bibliography of 140 references is included.

78. [AG, PP] CONNER, FRANCIS P. "Safety for the Crippled Child and Child with Special Health Problems," *Exceptional Children* (1962), 28:237-244.

    Ways in which a child's physical handicaps may affect his safety and limitations and modifications of external environmental factors which are necessary to promote his safety are discussed. General guidelines for fostering safety are also listed.

79. [A]   CONNOR, LEO E. "Preparation Programs for Special Education Administration," The Council for Exceptional Children, Washington, D. C. (November 1966), 33:161-166.

    After surveying the literature concerning administrators in special education the author presents a method proposed through the preparation of special education administrators. This proposal is based upon a baccalaureate program outside the special education field. Also included is a master's degree stressing teacher experience in one area of exceptionality. The suggested minimum program of preparation for administrators in special education is three years of successful teaching experience and thirty graduate semester hours beyond the master's program. The author also discusses the role of the administrator and surveys the certification requirements.

80. [A, F & L] CONNOR, LEO E. "Preliminaries to a Theory of Administration for Special Education," *Exceptional Children* (May 1963), 29:431–436.

Educational administration is the art and science of leadership for all school programs — for special education administration a theory should be developed. This theory should have characteristics including descriptions of the general administrative process; explanations of administrative behavior; predictions for the future; economy, including daily activities, financial and community factors; and skills in decision-making.

81. [A, AP] CONNOR, LEO E. *Administration of Special Education Programs* (Teachers College Series in Special Education). New York: Teachers College, Bureau of Publications, Columbia University, 1961.

This monograph discusses the major problems in the area of special education relative to program administration and offers solutions developed by successfully operated programs. The text includes sections on administrative structure, functioning, and problem areas that will effect special education program administration such as finances, personnel shortages, and program needs for the multiple handicapped child.

82. [F & L] CONNOR, LEO E. "C.E.C.'s Federal Legislative Activities," *Exceptional Children* (November 1961), 38:135–139.

Legislative activity can "bridge the gap between the theory and ideals of special education and the practitioner (teacher and administrator)." Unresolved questions concerning CEC were posed, guidelines for delineating the CEC legislative program (one of CEC's most "engrossing and stimulating areas of endeavor") and CEC's basic assumption relative to special education and legislation were given.

83. [A] COPELAND, MELVIN T. *The Executive at Work.* Cambridge, Mass.: Harvard University Press, 1951, 278 pp.

The nature of top level executive leadership is discussed in an entertaining, informative style. Illustrations from the author's experience are included.

84. [P] COTTER, KATHARINE C. *The Preparation of Teachers of Emotionally Disturbed Children: Roles of State Departments of Education and Teacher Education Institutions.* Reprinted from *The Catholic Educational Review* (October 1966), 64: 457–469.

The rapidly growing commitment of public schools to the education of emotionally disturbed children raises two important questions regarding the kinds of preparation their teachers receive. The first concerns the requirements of the state departments of education; the second, the kinds of programs offered by colleges and universities engaged in preparing these teachers. These are discussed and some general recommendations are made.

85. [A, P]   CRAWFORD, HUGH A. and WILLIAM V. VAN DUYNE. *Final Report of Day-Care Rehabilitation Center for Emotionally Disturbed Adolescents.* Providence, Rhode Island: Rhode Island Division of Vocational Rehabilitation, 1965, 116 pp.

> In this 5-year demonstration project, emotionally disturbed adults and adolescents received treatment at a day-care rehabilitation center. Patient selection, admission criteria, and referral procedures are discussed. Day-care staff descriptions include the hospital superintendent, director, assistant director, home economist, paint shop supervisor, bookbinder, woodworking instructor, school teacher, homeworker, social worker, psychologist, DVR coordinator, and counselors. The inservice training program for rehabilitation counselors is described. The philosophy of day-care, the evolution of its theoretical framework, and the attitudes of the staff toward the program at this center are discussed.

86. [A, AP, AG] CRAWFORD, WILLIAM L. and JACQUE L. CROSS. *Work-Study Programs for Slow Learning Children in Ohio Schools, Guidelines.* Columbus, Ohio: Ohio State Dept. of Education, 1967, 58 pp.

> Developed for educators who are concerned with and share the responsibility for work study programs for slow learns (IQ 50 to 80) at the secondary level, the guide presents program policies and practices current in the state of Ohio. Administrative responsibility in work study is discussed with reference to attitude, interpreting the program, involvement in the program, implications for curriculum development, considerations where work study programs overlap school districts, considerations for multiple work programs within a school district, and the role of the State Department of Education in work study. Conclusions and recommendations are made, and a 23-item bibliography is included.

• 87. [A]   CRICK, MARJORIE (ed.). *Proceedings of the Annual Convention of the Council of Administrators of Special Education* (April 1963), The Council for Exceptional Children, Washington, D. C.

> Diagnosing administrative problems in special education, and diagnosing supervisory problems in special education are both discussed.

88. [P. R] CRUICKSHANK, WILLIAM M., et al. *The Preparation of Teachers of Brain-Injured Children. Syracuse University Special Education and Rehabilitation Monograph Series 8.* Syracuse, New York: Syracuse University Press, 1968, 203 pp.

> To prepare teachers to work with brain-injured and hyperactive children, a training program leading to a master's degree was developed. Follow-up studies were done of all teacher graduates. Results indicated that local school systems should be more basically involved in the training process.

89. [A] CUTLIP, SCOTT M. and ALLEN H. CENTER. *Effective Public*

Relations. 3d ed. Englewood Cliffs, N. J.: Prentice-Hall, Inc., 1964, 512 pp.

> The authors discuss the nature and the concepts of public relations within a management framework, and they describe public relations as a four-step process: fact finding, planning, communicating, and evaluating. Different tools of communication are given, such as the printed word, the spoken word, image, and staged events. Also described are the public relations needs and practices of different types of organizations, such as business, social and welfare, management, and educational organizations.

90. [AG] DAILEY, CHARLES A. and FREDERICK C. DYER. *How to Make Decisions About People.* West Nyack, N. Y.: Parker Publishing Co., 1966, 223 pp.

> This work is particularly useful as a guide for making hiring decisions. The human relations approach is the basis for the analysis of interview results and the use of feedback. The book also uses the "how to do it" approach in covering a variety of areas such as the analysis of promotional potential, forecasting people's behavior, using the decision-making cycle, stress in decision-making, and analyzing facts about people. This work attempts to dispel some of the mystique surrounding the study of human behavior.

91. [AT, O] DALE, ERNEST. *Management: Theory and Practice.* New York: McGraw-Hill Book Company, 1965, 743 pp.

> Different types of managers, the ways in which they carry out their functions of management, and theories related to these functions and methods are explained. Contributions of writers in the management field, formal theories of corporations, practical aspects of the top executive's position, and the impact of computers are discussed.

92. [A] DALTON, MELVILLE. *Men Who Manage: Fusions of Feeling and Theory in Administration.* New York: John Wiley & Sons, Inc., 1959, 318 pp.

> Dalton conceives this book primarily as "an analytical record of interplays between compromising situations and compromising managers in commercial and industrial settings." The study focuses on conflicts between those managers who rely on method and procedure to get a job done and those who can adapt official directives and expediencies. In Dalton's words, "this book is thus a study of compromises among key individuals and groups in a rational organization, and the human structures on compromise."

93. [AP] DANIELS, ARTHUR S. and EVELYN A. DAVIES. *Adapted Physical Education, Principles and Practice of Physical Education for Exceptional Students. Second Edition.* New York: Harper & Row, Publishers, 1965.

The three purposes of this book are (1) to show how physical education activities may be adapted for exceptional students at all levels of school, (2) to serve as a practical guide to physical education personnel who wish to work for full development of each student, and (3) to serve as a text for students in training, teachers, and therapists. Part Three considers a number of administrative-organizational topics. Selected bibliographies follow each chapter.

94. [A, R] DARRAH, JOAN. *Diagnostic Practices and Special Classes for the Educable Mentally Retarded: A Layman's Critical View.* Washington, D. C.: Council for Exceptional Children, 1967, 5 pp.

Since cited research indicates that placement of the educable mentally retarded does not produce greater learning, improved social adjustment, or more constructive participation in society, the justification for maintaining such classes is questioned. The responsibility for justification of the special-class system is placed with the professionals in special education at colleges and universities whose future research can evaluate the effectiveness of education for the retarded.

95. [A, P, S] DAVIS, DONALD E. and NEAL C. NICKERSON, JR. *Critical Issues in School Personnel Administration.* Chicago, Ill.: Rand McNally & Co., 1968.

This text is based on the premise that a new approach to the employment and utilization of teachers is necessary to prepare today's children for the future. It proposes means for measuring teaching effectiveness and documents the need for professional development programs to improve effectivenesss of teaching staffs. The book provides school boards with a rational basis for achieving better education through negotiations with teacher groups.

96. [AT, AG] DAVIS, KEITH. *Human Relations at Work: The Dynamics of Organizational Behavior.* 3d ed. New York: McGraw-Hill Book Company, 1967, 559 pp.

The subject matter of this book is organizational behavior, more popularly known as human relations. The author integrates concepts proposed by McGregor, Maslow, Whyte, and others in explaining the theory of organizational behavior. Autocratic, participative, and free-rein management styles are discussed. Nine cases are given as exercises in understanding problems of organizational behavior. A list of selected readings, keyed to chapters in the book, is included.

97. [O] DAVIS, RALPH C. *The Fundamentals of Top Management.* New York: Harper and Brothers, 1951, 825 pp.

Planning, organizing, directing and controlling are the management functions given thorough treatment in this work which is aimed at the top level of management. A need for developing a philosophy of

management and the key role of executive leadership are emphasized.

98. [A, F & L]   DAY, O. L. "How to Get Tax Money for Educating
Exceptional Children," *Exceptional Children* (April 1960), 26:442.
Boards of education are encouraged to assess the feelings of their
communities in regard to spending tax money for the education of
exceptional children — perhaps with a community survey.

99. [AP] DELMO, DELLA-DORA. "The Culturally Disadvantaged: Educational Implications of Certain Socio-Culture Phenomenon," *Secondary
Schools Today: Readings for Educators* (1965), 155-162.
The problems of the large cities are discussed with relationship to
changing social patterns; i.e., a rapid influx of lower class groups into
the central city. Failure rates are discussed as in teacher-pupil
relationships. The author attempts to solve the problem of teaching
the culturally deprived children and makes a plea for better
community planning groups. Statistics are also offered on amounts
of income in the family as it relates to success in school.

100. [AP, R] DeMICHAEL, SALVATORE G. (ed.). *New Vocational Pathways
for the Mentally Retarded.* Washington, D. C.: American Personnel and
Guidance Association, 1966, 52 pp.
These papers were presented at the Abraham Jacobs Memorial
Symposium sponsored by the American Rehabilitation Counseling
Association of the American Personnel and Guidance Association
Convention, Minneapolis, April 1965. The five selections deal with
predictive studies of vocational adjustment, vocational preparation
during school years, work-study programs, longitudinal follow-up
studies of community adjustment, and political and cultural factors
influencing services in Europe and the United States.

101. [AG] *Departmental Guide, Special Education Department, Abilene Public
Schools, 1966-1967.* Abilene Public Schools, Texas, Special Education
Department, 1966, 79 pp.
Special programs of the Abilene, Texas, schools are described with
emphasis on pupil eligibility for services, purposes of the programs
and general and specific procedures used in instruction. Sources of
information used in individual psychological evaluations, certification requirements for teaching in Texas, and bibliographies for areas
of exceptionality are also included.

102. [PP, F & L] *Directory for Exceptional Children.* Boston: Porter Sargent,
Publisher, 1969.
A reference to facilities for those who are retarded, maladjusted or
physically handicapped and who require special programs, care or
treatment. Descriptions list services offered, admission policies, costs

and specialized instruction and care for more than 3600 schools, homes, hospitals, treatment and training centers, psychiatric and guidance clinics.

103. [A, S, P] DOOHER, M. JOSEPH and ELIZABETH MARTING (eds.). *Selection of Management Personnel.* 2 vols. New York: American Management Association, 1957, 906 pp.

Volume I of this two-volume work consists of a collection of articles pertaining to the selection of managerial personnel; in Volume II the editors study company practices used in the selection of managers. The editors believe that qualifications necessary for an executive are significantly different from those necessary for a supervisor.

104. [AG] DRUCKER, PETER F. *The Effective Executive.* New York: Harper & Row, Publishers, 1967, 178 pp.

Executive effectiveness has several facets, but Drucker believes that effectiveness can be learned. To become effective, an executive must move from the procedural aspects of his work to the conceptual aspects and from the mechanical to the analytical aspects. Drucker differentiates an executive from a "non-executive" on the basis of performance: an executive has the ability to get the right things done at the right times, while the "non-executive" will be found "doing the things."

105. [A, P] DUMAS, NEIL S. (ed.). *Management and Personnel Abstracts.* Regional Rehabilitation Research Institute, College of Health Related Professions, University of Florida, Gainesville, Florida, 1968, 110 pp.

This monograph is a collection of 1,000 abstracts of articles related to operations research, computers, management and business. There are a large number of articles abstracted in this monograph which are pertinent to the problems faced by vocational rehabilitation agencies. These articles deal with such topics as recruitment, selection and training of new professional and clerical personnel, purchasing and use of data processing equipment, development of programs, and administration of research and demonstration projects.

106. [O, P] DUNHAM, ARTHUR. *Community Welfare Organizations: Principles and Practices.* New York: Thomas Y. Crowell, Publisher, 1958, xiii + 480 pp.

This text is intended as a basic analysis and discussion of the principles and practices of community welfare organizations. The major emphasis of the text is on (1) introductory material on welfare organizations, (2) programs and agencies, and (3) the community welfare organization at work-practices, personnel, and records.

107. [A, F & L] DYBWAD, GUNNAR. "Administrative and Legislative

Problems in Care of Adult and Aged Mental Retardates," *American Journal of Mental Deficiency* (March 1962), 66:716-722.

Program needs of mentally retarded adults and the necessity to convey to all citizens, and especially to legislators, the reasons that mental retardation is a great public problem are discussed.

108. **[AP, R]** EDMUNDS, EDWIN RAY. "Services Offered to Exceptional Children in 217 Missouri Public Schools," *Dissertation Abstracts* (1960), 20:3149-3150.

The report of a normative study designed to compare services for exceptional children in Missouri with services which a panel of experts described as being necessary for the education of exceptional children.

109. **[AG]** *Educating the Highly Able, a Policy Statement.* Baltimore, Maryland: Maryland State Department of Education, 1962, 50 pp.

The document constitutes a policy statement for use in Maryland schools. Teachers and counselors are assigned a key role in identifying the highly able. The roles of the teacher, principal, and some views on administrative arrangements are described.

110. **[AP, AG]** *Educating Visually Handicapped Pupils.* New York: New York City Board of Education, 1967, 108 pp.

Educational programs available to blind or partially blind children in New York City are described in this illustrated bulletin. Procedures for school placement, organization of special classes, and enrollment statistics are discussed. The roles and responsibilities of the guidance and supplementary services, the administration, and the supervisory personnel are examined.

111. **[AP, F & L]** *Education of the Blind.* Des Moines, Iowa (April 1963), 1-11.

A complete report on the education of the blind in public schools of Des Moines, Iowa, covering (1) history of blind programs in public schools, (2) need for the program, (3) how the needs are being met, (4) proposed program for 1963-64, (5) transportation, (6) estimated cost, and (7) future program.

112. **[A]** "The Education of Blind, Deaf and Aphasic Pupils," Chapter 69, *Powers and Duties of the Department of Education,* Department of Education, The Commonwealth of Massachusetts, Boston, 4 pp.

The powers and duties of the Department of Education as they pertain to the education of blind, deaf, and aphasic pupils are covered.

113. **[A, AP]** *Educational Programs for Gifted Pupils: A Report to the California Legislature.* California State Department of Education, Superintendent of Public Instruction, Sacramento, (January 1961), 1-272.

Identification of pupils, evaluation of pupil achievement, characteristics of the population, evaluation of pupil programs, administration
operations of programs, evaluation of specific programs.

114. [AP] *Educational Services for Handicapped Children.* University of the
State of New York (1963), 1-3.

The methods which are used by the education department of New
York University for encouraging the developmental services for
handicapped children are discussed. Schools that provide for the
emotionally disturbed are specifically discussed.

115. [AG, O]　EHLERS, HENRY and GORDON C. LEE. *Crucial Issues in
Education.* New York: Holt, Rinehart & Winston, Inc., 1964, 262-299.

Discusses meeting needs of pupils: (1) reduced sizes of classes, (2) a
systematic testing program revealing status and growth in basic
intellectual skill and ability, (3) a permanent record folder,
(4) teacher and student personal contact plus parent contact,
(5) grouping, (6) difficulty of books, (7) same teacher over a long
period of time, (8) high school level honor programs. Also discusses
three ways to help talented children: acceleration, enrichment, and
selected classes. Resumés including attitudes toward gifted children,
overlooking gifted children, fostering development of creativity and
intelligence, and teachers' openmindedness toward the gifted.

116. [A, S, AP] ELSBREE, WILLARD S. *Elementary School Administration
and Supervision,* 3d ed. New York: Van Nostrand Reinhold Company,
1967.

The third edition devotes special attention to the following areas:
the computer as an administrative tool; instructional technology; the
future of elementary school organization, administration and supervision; the growing emphasis on pre-elementary school education;
and the changing role of the elementary school principal. The text
provides an updated bibliography, revised statistics, and new tables
and illustrations to clarify the most recent innovations in education.

117. [S]　ENGLAND, JUNE P. *Inspection and Introspection of Supervision in
Special Education.* Washington, D. C.: The Council for Exceptional
Children (March 1964), 39-45.

Inspection of special education programs is discussed. Supervisory
tasks and the benefits and problems that arise when this functional
supervisory system is implicated are listed. The role of the state, the
intermediate office, and the local district and their responsibilities
are discussed.

118. [A, O]　ERDMAN, ROBERT L. *Administration of Special Education in
Small School Systems.* Washington, D. C.: The Council for Exceptional
Children, 1-60.

The selection of children, class organization, related organizational problems, curriculum and program, description of three successful special education class programs and sample forms are discussed.

119. [AP, O] ERDMAN, ROBERT L. *Educable Retarded Children in Elementary Schools,* Washington, D. C.: The Council for Exceptional Children, 1961.

The development of a program for the educable mentally retarded, the selection of children for the program, the organization of classes, related organizational problems, curriculum and program, and a description of three successful special class programs are discussed in this monograph.

120. [AP, A, O] ESKRIDGE, C. S. and D. L. PARTRIDGE. "Vocational Rehabilitation for Exceptional Children Through Special Education," *Exceptional Children* (1963), 29:452-458.

Texas' program has a sequential preparation of materials which leads to an orderly outcome of employment for its educable mentally retarded students. The program has a definitive curriculum tract, with seven sequential levels of development in lieu of the traditional twelve grades. A plan for vocational rehabilitation assistance was formulated to implement the program. Leadership from the school's principal was enhanced by the full-time vocational adjustment coordinator, who is a certified teacher for retarded children. The program has gained much community attention and support and has experienced marked success.

121. [A] EVARTS, HARRY F. *Introduction to PERT.* Boston: Allyn and Bacon, Inc., 1964, 112 pp.

This paperback book provides a simplified, yet thorough explanation of PERT (Program Evaluation and Review Technique) network techniques. The application of PERT to management planning is shown. The book provides a glossary of terms, a bibliography and in an appendix, IBM 709 and PERT computer operations.

122. [A, S] EYE, GLEN G. and LANORE NETZER. *Supervision of Instruction: A Phase of Administration.* New York: Harper & Row, Publishers, 1965.

Concentrates on the purposes, patterns, processes, participants and products of the program for supervision of instruction. Provides a plan for developing a complete, balanced supervisory program, applicable to both general and special supervision in kindergarten through grade 12. Defines the functions and interrelationships of the various positions involved in the supervision of instruction, identifying teachers as participants in the supervisory process. Presents a theory of supervision for developing a practical program and suggests in the form of illustrations techniques for applying the theory and selecting the practices.

123. [AP, AG] FALLS, CHARLES W. *Criteria for Special Education Programs in Nebraska Schools.* Lincoln, Nebraska: Nebraska State Department of Education, 1966, 44 pp.

This administrator guide contains the full statement of laws and rulings for the establishment and operation of special education programs in Nebraska. For each type of handicap, definition, admission criteria, teacher qualifications, procedure for establishing program, and reimbursement information is provided. School psychological services and other agencies dealing with exceptional children are listed.

124. [AG, R] FARBER, BERNARD. "Family Crisis and the Decision to Institutionalize the Retarded Child," *Research Monograph* (April 1966), The Council for Exceptional Children, Washington, D. C., 1:1–66.

The investigation focuses attention on the nature of the family crisis which arises from the presence of a retarded child in the home and attempts to delineate the factors which determine the decision of parents to place their severely retarded child in an institution. Considerations in counseling parents are clarified.

125. [A, O] FAYOL, HENRI. *General and Industrial Management.* Translated by Constance Storrs. London: Pitman Publishing Company, 1949, 110 pp.

A basic book of management in which five functions of administration: planning, organizing, commanding, coordinating, and controlling are identified and described. Well-known principles of management were formulated and described by Fayol.

126. [AG] FEARON, ROSS E. *Guidelines for Speech Therapy in the Public School.* Farmington, Maine: Farmington State College, 1967, 11 pp.

Prepared for public school personnel, this booklet uses a question-answer format to explain public school speech and hearing services. Speech disorders and speech therapy are defined. The need for the services of the speech and hearing specialist and classroom speech improvement programs in the public schools is discussed. An outline suggests how a program might function, including information on the case load, parental role, scheduling, and physical requirements of the speech room.

127. [A] FEINBERG, MORTIMER R. *Effective Psychology for Managers.* Englewood Cliffs, N. J.: Prentice-Hall, Inc., 1965, 224 pp.

Feinberg provides constructive help in understanding the development, motivation, persuasion, and counseling of subordinates. He offers behavioral and psychological concepts in a simplified narrative. Among the broad topics which he discusses are controlling and using executive drive, managing executive tensions, obtaining better results through counseling and coaching, motivating subordinates, and developing the art of constructive criticism. This book should be helpful to both top executives and those who train supervisory personnel.

128. [AT] FIELDLER, FRED E. *A Theory of Leadership Effectiveness.* New York: McGraw-Hill Book Company, 1967.

This book presents a new theory of leadership effectiveness. The theory attempts to relate leadership style to group performance and to show how group performance depends on organizational characteristics as well as on leadership style. It states the concept that leadership performance is not only dependent on the leader, but also on the favorableness of the situation for the leader. People vary as to their leadership capacities, but the author theorizes that one can teach leaders how to avoid situations in which they are likely to fail and that one can modify organizational and situational factors to enable leaders to succeed.

129. [A, S]   FIELDS, HAROLD. "Examination for the Post of Director in Special Education," *The Clearing House* (May 1961), 35:533–537.

In New York City a system of tests has been devised for placement of directors of special education. A candidate is advised on the duties of the position and then is given questions involving situations in these areas. Following written tests, an interview is given, the purpose being to observe pattern of speech, ability to organize thinking, personality and familiarity with problems he might face. The next test is leading a conference discussion group within which are representatives of various school levels, counselors and others associated with the handicapped. The final two areas considered are determination of physical fitness and an examination of eligibility and past record. Decisions of tests lie in the hands of specialists of the fields.

130. [AP] FIELDS, HELEN W. "How New York City Educates Visually Handicapped Children," *New Outlook for the Blind* (December 1961), 55:337–340.

Four services available as supportive devices for children are (1) resource classrooms in elementary, junior high, and high schools, (2) itinerant teaching services, (3) classes for the emotionally disturbed blind child, and (4) classes for mentally retarded blind. Basic criterion for placement is whether the child's visual handicap is an impeding force in his total school adjustment. Healthy competition is encouraged. In addition to this program for education of the visually handicapped, progress was made toward a program for public education for the blind who, because of their serious disturbances, multiplicity of problems or additional handicaps, cannot be contained within established braille programs.

131. [P] FLEEMAN, PAUL G. "Predicted Special Education Teacher Needs in the Public Schools of Missouri 1960-61 through 1970-71." *Dissertation Abstracts* (1961), 22:1464.

    A report of methods used to predict the number of special teachers needed in the state for a certain period and also the number of special teachers needed in certain areas which the state helps to finance.

132. [O] FLIPPO, EDWIN B. *Management: A Behavioral Approach.* Boston: Allyn and Bacon, Inc., 1966, 511 pp.

    An analysis of the objections to traditional management and the behavioral-approach contributions of psychologists and sociologists are presented. The author believes that behavioral and traditional approaches to management should be merged to form a general theory or philosophy.

133. [A, P] FORD, GUY B. *Building A Winning Employee Team.* New York: American Management Association, 1964, 111 pp.

    The author presents crucial concepts of personnel administration in such a way that the line manager can acquire a sound understanding of this vital staff function. Ford clearly explains how a personnel department functions to aid the operating executive. The development and training aspects of the managerial function are emphasized. Overall, this compact work deals in ways to effectively harness and channel human energy toward accomplishing organizational objectives with a minimum of organizational friction.

134. [AG, PP, P] FOWLES, BETH. "Considerations for Design and Planning an Elementary School for Handicapped Children and Normal Children." *Cerebral Palsy Review* (January-February 1961), 22:3-11.

    A detailed description of essential considerations for a building and transportation for elementary school children. A less detailed description of the roles of teachers and therapists is also given.

135. [AP] FRAENKEL, WILLIAM. "Planning the Vocational Future of the Mentally Retarded." *Rehabilitation Literature*, National Society for Crippled Children and Adults.

    Current trends in community programming, the adult in the community, and total programming are discussed.

136. [A] FRAMPTON, MERLE E. and ELENA D. GALL. "Educational and Administrative Problems," Chapter III, Section 2, volume 1, in *Special Education for the Exceptional.* Boston: Porter Sergeant, Publisher, 1955.

    Changes in curriculum construction to meet the needs of exceptional children, special curricula, problems arising from speech deficiencies, problems of physical education and recreation for the handicapped, segregation and nonsegregation, rural problems, and transportation are the topics discussed in this chapter.

137. [O]   FRAMPTON, MERLE E., et al. *Forgotten Children — A Program for the Multihandicapped.* Boston: Porter Sargent, Publisher, 1969.
Answers need of many in the field of special education to improve the condition of the multihandicapped child. Presents recommendations for new programs and facilities, and an enlightened discussion of the need for teacher training in all areas of the multihandicapped.

138. [A, O, AP]   FRANKLIN, MARION P. *School Organization: Theory and Practice.* Chicago, Ill.: Rand McNally & Co., 1967.
Gives a concise view of vertical and horizontal school organization for the elementary school, junior high school, and high school. Contains 70 readings by recognized authorities who focus attention on the various ways to group students. Vertical grouping arrangements are presented: graded, multigraded, and nongraded classes. Horizontal arrangements such as the self-contained classroom, departmentalization, team teaching and ability groups are presented.

139. [A, AP]   FRANSETH, JANE and ROSE KOURY. *Survey of Research on Grouping as Related to Pupil Learning.* Washington, D. C.: Office of Education, Bureau of Elementary and Secondary Education, 1966.
The research that has been done in the area of grouping in the classroom and school system is explored. Nationwide studies on grouping practices in the elementary school are reviewed. Ability and heterogeneous grouping (broad, medium, and narrow range classes, and the Joplin Plan) are compared, and varieties of ability grouping are explored. The effect of ability grouping on achievement motivation is reviewed with reference to superior and low ability students. The range of individual differences, group situations as they influence the individual learner, the nongraded concept, and the need for flexibility in grouping are treated.

140. [P]   FRENCH, JOSEPH L. "Preparation of Teachers of the Gifted," *Journal of Teacher Education* (March 1961), 12:69-72.
Surveys courses for the gifted offered in 66 colleges. Summarizes the outlines and objectives of the courses.

141. [A] FRENCH, WENDELL. *The Personnel Management Process: Human Resources Administration.* Boston: Houghton-Mifflin Co., 1964, 624 pp.
Personnel management is conceived as a network of interrelated, dynamic processes and systems within the organization. The recruitment, selection, utilization, and development of human resources are described from the viewpoint of the total organization. Current personnel practices and significant personnel research are summarized.

142. [A, O]   FUSCO, GENE C. "Pupil Personnel Service Programs: Organization and Administration," *School Life* (September 1961), 44:28-29.

The report of a study of pupil personnel service programs, designed to aid administrators in planning such programs. The recommendation to adapt pupil personnel service programs to the changing needs of pupils is made.

143. [AP, O, R] GALLAGHER, JAMES J. *Research Summary on Gifted Child Education.* Springfield, Ill.: Illinois State Office of the Superintendent of Public Instruction, Department of Program Development for Gifted Children, 1966, 169 pp.

Research is summarized and analyzed in this revision of the author's 1960 *Analysis of Research on the Education of Gifted Children,* which was used as a guide in the construction and implementation of the Illinois Plan for Program Development for Gifted Children. Information is provided on identification and definition and on characteristics of gifted children. Consideration of intervention includes research design and stresses three areas of intervention: the administrative, instructional, and adjunctive.

144. [S] GALLOWAY, JAMES R. "Strategies and Tactics in the Supervision of the School Programs in Rural or Sparsely Settled Areas," *Special Education: Strategies for Educational Progress,* (April 1966), 203-206.

The monumental task of providing adequate educational opportunities and also the problems of providing special educational services in sparsely populated areas are discussed.

145. [O] GARDNER, BURLEIGH B. and DAVID G. MOORE. *Human Relations in Industry: Organizational and Administrative Behavior.* 4th ed. Homewood, Ill.: Richard D. Irwin, Inc., 1964, 479 pp.

The dynamics of human behavior within a formal organization, the interpersonal relations, individual adjustment, the tendency of individuals to distort communications, status, hierarchy, and leadership are discussed in this "classic" study of human relations.

146. [A] GARDNER, RAY. "The Effectiveness of Cooperative Area Administration for Special Education in Suburban Areas," *Selected Convention Papers 41st Annual CEC Convention, Philadelphia.* (April 1963), The Council for Exceptional Children, Washington, D. D., 87-89.

This paper deals with the development of a growing personal awareness of the effectiveness of cooperative area administration for special education. It was not until the fall of 1961 that full cognizance of the effectiveness of cooperative area administration made its imprint. The author states that two major facts became evident: (1) variation in the quality of cooperative programs which appeared sometimes to leave some children with less than maximum development of potential, and (2) much inconsistency between complementary programs. To illustrate this point, contrasts are described between any two of eight districts offering services to the deaf and hard of hearing. Some insights gained as the results of establishment of an advisory council were listed.

147. [AP] GARDNER, WILLIAM J. and HERSCHEL W. NISONGER. "A Manual on Program Development in Mental Retardation," *American Journal of Mental Deficiency* (January 1962), 66:iv, 1-192.
Considers program needs and program developments in mental retardation. Includes goals in helping the mentally retarded, guidelines in program development, role of government in mental retardation programs, identification, diagnosis, treatment, and parent counseling, role of day and residential care and training facilities, program development in communities, community planning, and keys to future progress.

148. [A] GARVUE, ROBERT J. *Modern Public School Finance.* New York: The MacMillan Company, 1969.
This book establishes the interrelationship of cultural, political, and economic forces as they relate to the financing of American public education. The book traces past decision-making theory and practice and discusses possible new standards and future techniques. The text retains, throughout, the point of view that American society has the processes and resources available to demand the quality of education needed to improve the American form of democracy.

149. [A, AP, F & L, O] GEARHEART, BILL R. *Administration of Special Education: A Guide for General Administrators and Special Educators.* Springfield, Ill.: Charles C. Thomas, Pub., 1967.
Presents an overview of the total special education program, discusses problem areas, financial structure, significant trends and federal-state-local relationships.

150. [F & L] GEER, WILLIAM; LEO CONNOR; LEONARD BLACKMAN. "Recent Federal Legislation Provisions and Implications for Special Education," *Exceptional Children* (May 1964), 30:411-421.
Impressions of possibilities for exceptional children under P. L. 88-164, the Mental Retardation Facilities and Community Mental Health Centers Construction Act of 1963; P. L. 88-210, the Vocational Education Act of 1963; and P. L. 88-204, the Higher Education Facilities Act of 1963. Attention is also given to the implications of P. L. 88-156, Maternal and Child Health and Mental Retardation Planning Amendments of 1963; and P. L. 88-214, the Manpower Development and Training Act.

151. [A] GEIGLE, RALPH C. and LORENZO ZEUGNER. "Special Education Center," *American School Board Journal* (December 1961), 143:18-20.
The description of a special education center and the program for

exceptional children in Reading, Pennsylvania. A detailed description and illustrations of the building are included.

152. [AT] GETZELS, JACOB W., et al. *Educational Administration as a Social Process: Theory, Research, Practice.* New York: Harper & Row, Publishers, 1968.

This text presents a history of theoretical approaches to administration and describes in detail a particular theoretical model. Getzels et al. demonstrate the value of administration theory to research and practice.

153. [F & L] GIAMO, ROBERT N. "Legislative Process in the Area of Special Education," *Exceptional Children* (May 1962), 28:451–454.

A paper presented by a member of the House of Representatives to the Columbus Convention of CEC outlining problems of and procedures for the passage of special education legislation and the reasons for legislative and other kinds of opposition.

154. [AP] GIBBONS, HELEN. "Safety for the Child Who is Visually Impaired," *Exceptional Children* (March 1961), 28:147–150.

The role of the school in the safety of exceptional children is discussed relative to the roles of the school nurse, the administrator, the classroom teacher, and the special teacher. Guidelines to home safety are presented. The cooperation of the school and the home must be effective in order to provide a safe environment.

155. [AP] GILMAN, ESTER and MARIAN C. HUNTER (eds.). *Handbook for the Operation of a Program for Teaching Homebound or Hospitalized Children.* Washington, D. C.: Council for Exceptional Children, 1967.

This handbook discusses program guidelines and curriculum for teaching homebound or hospitalized children. The major emphasis is on program structure rather than specific teaching techniques.

156. [AP, P] GINGLEND, DAVID, and KAY GOULD. *Day Camping for the Mentally Retarded.* New York: National Association for Retarded Children, 1962, 59 pp.

Emphasis in day camping for the mentally retarded is placed on mental health, physical development and coordination (both motor and muscular) social adjustment, and language and intellectual development. Included are samples of a camp budget, staff responsibilities, communications to parents, and application and progress report forms. An 18-item bibliography is included.

157. [A] GOFFMAN, ERVING. *Stigma.* Englewood Cliffs, N. J.: Prentice-Hall, Inc., 1963, 147 pp.

A review of writings on stigma (bodily signs which expose something unusual and/or bad about an individual) with a multitude of examples of stigmatized individuals and their reactions to social acceptance and nonacceptance. Personal identity, social identity, ego identity, and control of identity information (giving or withholding information concerning one's stigma) are dealt with in essays in the book.

158. [AP, O] GORE, BEATRICE S. "Looking Ahead for Cerebral Palsied Children," *California Journal of Secondary Education* (1950), 25:357-361.

Discusses the present policy of bringing pupils with cerebral palsy handicaps into regular classrooms as much as possible and the necessity of the teachers' understanding the nature of these difficulties and the best means to meet them.

159. [AP, O] GOTTWALD, HENRY L. "A Special Program for Educable — Emotionally Disturbed Retarded." *Mental Retardation*, American Association on Mental Deficiency (December 1964), 2:353-359.

Describes the philosophy, organization, and function of a special facility for the emotionally disturbed retarded person. Due to the increasing number of these people, it is felt that a new facility is needed for them.

160. [AG] GRAHAM, RAY (comp.). *A Guide — Directing the Education for Exceptional Children in a Local School District.* Springfield, Ill.: Office of the Superintendent of Public Instruction, State of Illinois, 1961.

This publication presents local school district superintendents with guidelines for determining a need, establishing, and staffing an office for a director of special education. Administrative, supervisory and coordinating functions of the special education director are outlined along with organizational and professional relations of the director within the school system and local community.

161. [F & L] GRAHAM, RAY. "Responsibility of Public Education for Exceptional Children." *Exceptional Children* (January 1962), 28:255-259.

The responsibility for education of children is a state function. Local school districts derive their authority from the state. Today all states have some lesislation which defines these responsibilities of local districts for the education of exceptional children. This legislation has come about piecemeal, often resulting in special programs which are separate and distinct from the total school program. The status of special education will be enhanced when we have reached a point where special education programs and exceptional children are accepted by the local community and Board of Education as an integral part of the public school program. One way to achieve integration is to strive for balanced special programs; i.e., programs which coordinate the special classes with the regular classes at all levels of instruction.

162. [A, F & L, PP] GRAHAM, RAY. "Safety Features in School Housing for Handicapped Children." *Exceptional Children* (March 1961), 27:361-364.
Considers such things as saving money by cutting construction costs which result in safety hazards; physical construction for emergency situations; and the responsibility of teachers and other faculty members to keep their heads in an emergency. Emphasizes safety in special schools as a part of the teaching-learning process.

163. [A, S, O] GRAHAM, RAY and ANNA M. ENGEL. "Administering Special Services for Exceptional Children," Chapter II in *Education of Exceptional Children: Forty-ninth Yearbook.* Chicago, Ill.: National Society for the Study of Education, University of Chicago Press, 1950.
After stating that the area of greatest responsibility for the success of any educational program rests in the administration, Graham and Engel discuss the objectives of special education, the principles of administration and supervision in special education, and the organization of special education programs at the local and state levels.

164. [A] GREGORY, HUGO H. "State Approval and Accreditation of Public Schools," *ASHA: A Journal of the American Speech and Hearing Association* (May 1961), 3:145-147.
Accreditation programs were evaluated in terms of developing a legal basis, underlying purposes, responsibilities, administration, and methods of revision.

165. [AT] GRIFFITHS, DANIEL E. *Developing Taxonomies of Organizational Behavior in Educational Administration.* Chicago, Ill.: Rand McNally & Co., 1969.
Seven authors provide educational administrators with guides for taxonomic methodology in Educational Administration. The articles furnish guides to help prepare administrators, to synthesize present knowledge of educational administration, and to encourage new research. The final chapter offers a synthesis and conclusions, identifying areas where research is meager and indicating areas where additional inquiry will be most fruitful.

166. [AT] GRIFFITHS, DANIEL E. *Administrative Theory.* New York: Appleton-Century-Crofts, Inc., 1959, vii + 123 pp.
The purpose of this book is to write an "interim statement" setting forth the present understandings of Educational Administration

theory. Major emphasis is on a theoretical definition and review of eight theories of administration; some assumptions and concepts of a theory of administration; and a description of the decision-making process in formal organizations.

167. [A] GRILLO, ELMER V. *Control Techniques for Office Efficiency.* New York: McGraw-Hill Book Company, 1963, 273 pp.

Grillo presents various techniques by which a manager can improve the operational effectiveness of an office. This is "how to do it" book. Illustrations of forms and reports and examples of their actual application to typical problems are included. Comprehensive descriptions are given of how to install and use a wide selection of control techniques applicable to both routine and non-routine office work.

168. [A] GROSS, BERTRAM M. *The Managing of Organizations: The Administrative Struggle.* 2 vols. New York: The Free Press, 1964, 971 pp.

The historical, philosophical and social background of administrative theory and the revolution in administration comprise the first nine chapters. Discussions of people in organizations and their performance, management decisions, communication within organizations, planning, activating and evaluating are also presented.

169. [A, F & L, AP] *Guidance Handbook for Special Education Programs, A Plan for Initiating, Building, Implementing, and Conducting Programs for Exceptional Children with Guidelines for Following Legal Requirements and Developing District Philosophy and Objectives.* Fresno County Schools, California, 1966, 87 pp.

For each exceptionality area, this document outlines a statement of legislative intent, services available through the office of the County Superintendent of Schools, initiating of a district program, building a district program, implementing and conducting a district program, and evaluating a district program. The appendix charts salient points in the state legislative codes and lists sources of information and services.

170. [AG] *Guidelines, County Plan for the Provision of Special Education Programs for Exceptional Children and Youth.* Tallahassee, Fla.: Florida State Department of Education, 1968, 33 pp.

Intended for county school boards of public institutions, this booklet provides guidelines for special programs.

171. [AG, AP] *Guidelines for Implementation of the Pilot Program for Emotionally Disturbed Children, a Supplement to the State Plan for Special Education.* Austin, Texas: Texas Education Agency, 1965, 8 pp.

In 1965–66, 14 school districts established 20 classes in schools, mental health centers, and hospitals for emotionally disturbed children (ages 6–17). Outlined are definitions and characteristics of emotionally disturbed children, purposes of the the program, minimum plant facilities, related personnel, eligibility requirements, class size and age grouping, teacher certification, and finance.

172. [AG, AP] *Guidelines for Implementation of the Program for Minimally Brain-Injured Children, a Supplement to the Administrative Guide and State Plan for Special Education.* Austin, Texas: Texas Education Agency, Division of Special Education, 1965, 6 pp.

Texas state standards for special classes for minimally brain-injured children include study of the child by a placement committee and psychological reevaluation of the child every three years. Criteria for admission to special education classes and minimally brain-injured classes, instructions for establishing and operating special education classes, and records to be kept.

173. [AP, AG] *Guidelines of Programs of Special Education in Alaska.* Juneau, Alaska: Alaska State Department of Education, 1966, 32 pp.

Six areas of exceptionality served by public school programs are presented, including mentally retarded both educable and trainable, blind and partially sighted, deaf and hard of hearing, orthopedically or neurologically handicapped, emotionally disturbed, and multiple handicapped. Procedures for establishing special education programs are discussed in detail, and explicit directions for submitting applications to the state department are included.

174. [AP, AG] *Guide to Practices and Procedures for the Slow Learning Program in the Elementary Schools.* Cincinnati, Ohio: Cincinnati Public Schools, Division of Special Education, 1965, 11 pp.

Procedures for administering a modified curriculum program for slow learners (IQ 50 to 75) in the elementary grades are outlined.

175. [AP, AG] *Guide to Practices and Procedures for the Slow Learning Program in Secondary Schools.* Cincinnati, Ohio: Cincinnati Public Schools, Division of Special Education, 1965.

An outline of the educable mentally handicapped (IQ range 50 through mid 70's) program in the Cincinnati Public School presents placement procedures, courses recommended for grades 7 through 12, the work experience program grading and promotion procedures, and requirements for opening new classes.

176. [A] GULLICK, LUTHER and L. URWICK (eds.). *Papers on the Science of Administration.* New York: Institute of Public Administration, Columbia University, 1937, 195 pp.

A collection of papers written by outstanding pioneers in the field of administration. Papers of the editors are included.

177. [A] HABERMAN, MARTIN. "Leadership in Schools Serving the Educationally Disadvantaged," *The National Elementary Principals.* Washington, D. C.: National Education Association (1964), 44:20–24.

Three fundamental aspects of educational leadership which are distinctly incumbent on the school administrator serving in an educationally disadvantaged environment are (1) his willingness to participate in educational change, (2) his ability to exert moral leadership, and (3) his influence on the social matrix of the community. A discussion follows each of these areas. There is an attempt to indicate five important components of the teacher's self-concept and to relate these components to the administrative behavior which foster or impede their development. There is also an attempt to relate the administrator's personal attributes to his basic modes of action. There is also an attempt to focus on selected factors which seem fundamental to teacher success and to show a few of the ways in which such factors interact with the administrator's behavior and personality.

178. [A] HAIRE, MASON. *Psychology of Management.* 2d ed. New York: McGraw-Hill Book Company, 1964.

Deals with basic psychological issues in business problems: wages organization, leadership, communication, etc. The book focuses on some principles of behavior underlying modern industrial practice and considers organization theory and new thinking about business and psychology. It aims to give a pattern and coherence to the psychological underpinnings of managerial practice in dealing with behavior.

179. [AT] HALPIN, ANDREW W. (ed.). *Administrative Theory in Education.* Danville, Ill.: Interstate Printers and Publishers, Inc., 1958.

This book illuminates the role of theory in educational administration. Major emphasis is on theoretical constructs as they relate to the administrative process, problem-solving, and organizational behavior.

180. [AG] HANEY, WILLIAM V. *Communication and Organizational Behavior: Text and Cases.* Rev. ed. Homewood, Ill.: Richard D. Irwin, Inc., 1967, 533 pp.

This book examines the communication process in the context of human behavior in an organizational setting. Haney begins by discussing the organizational framework within which the communication process takes place. In Part II he relates the behavioral aspects of communication, emphasizing perception and innovation. A bibliography on communication, organizational behavior, and related areas is provided.

181. [A] HARDWICK, CLYDE T. and BERNARD F. LANDUYT. *Administrative Strategy and Decision Making.* 2d ed. Cincinnati: South-Western Publishing Company, 1966, 642 pp.

Traditional concepts of bureaucracy, committees, discipline, chain-of-command, morale, leadership, human relations, motivation, and responsibility are discussed; but the uniqueness of the book is due to the authors' discussion of "administrative strategy."

182. [P] HARING, NORRIS G. and GEORGE A. FARGO. "Evaluating Programs for Preparing Teachers of Emotionally Disturbed Children," *Exceptional Children* (November 1969), 36:157—162.

This article presents the premises from general education that have important implications for direct evaluation of professional trainees, teachers, and training programs in special education.

183. [O] HARPER, ERNEST B. and ARTHUR DUNHAM. *Community Organization in Action: Basic Literature and Critical Comments.* New York: Association Press, 1959, 543 pp.

The purpose of this book is to "cream off" the literature of National Conference Proceedings, periodicals, and pamphlets. The text provides a concise, historical overview of community welfare organizations from 1900 to 1958. Emphasis is given to organizational practices, personnel, and program development.

184. [S] HARRIS, BEN M. *Supervisory Behavior in Education.* Englewood Cliffs, N. J.: Prentice-Hall, Inc., 1963, xviii + 557 pp.

This text deals with theory, research, and evolving concepts which have practical implications for supervision in the public schools. A functional definition of supervision is presented, central issues and problems of instructional supervision are discussed, and research is reviewed which has implications for supervision in practice.

185. [A, PP, P] HARRIS, BEN M. and WAILAND BESSENT. *In-Service Education: A Guide to Better Practice.* Englewood Cliffs, N. J.: Prentice-Hall, Inc., 1969, xvi + 432 pp.

The authors present a theoretical framework and analysis of their "laboratory" approach to in-service program planning and design. The text describes a series of in-service sessions with directions for adapting these for similar groups. Problem solving laboratory sessions are described in detail. The final portion of the text includes materials for use in designing in-service programs based on the authors laboratory approach.

186. [S] HARRISON, RAYMOND H. *Supervisory Leadership in Education.* New York: Van Nostrand Reinhold Company, 1968.

This text emphasizes the role of the supervisor as a dynamic leader whose primary function is to promote improvement in classroom instruction. The text is divided into three parts: Part I is keynoted by two chapters that define supervision in terms of the contemporary educational scene, stressing the skills and understanding required of the modern supervisor; Part II lists and analyzes the various functions performed by most supervisors; Part III deals at length with one of these functions, that of assisting teachers with persistent problems.

187. [AP] HAVIGHURST, R. J. "Educationally Difficult Student: What the Schools Can Do," *The National Association of Secondary School Principals Bulletin*, (1965), 49:110-127.
  "Difficult" students can be grouped as the socially disadvantaged, the mentally handicapped, and the privatist nonconformer. The socially disadvantaged are described in terms of family characteristics and social group characteristics of their families. The mentally handicapped are described in terms of mental deficiency. An entirely different kind of "educationally difficult" student is described as one with doubts about his own identity, the quality of his society, and his subsequent rebellion in supporting society. He prefers to lead a life of private asocial activity. The author presents guides for educational programs that hopefully reach these educationally difficult students.

188. [AG] HAVIGHURST, R. J. *The Public Schools of Chicago.* Chicago, Ill.: Chicago Board of Education, 1964, 499 pp.
  Chapters IV, V, IX, and Supplement E deal with definitions of and programs for exceptional children. Background information is given, and administrative organization, research and evaluation, and curricula for special education are discussed. In Supplement E, the report of a survey of the program of special education in Chicago and recommendations for improvement are presented.

189. [AP, AG, PP] HAY, LOUIS and SHIRLEY COHEN. *Perspectives for a Classroom for Disturbed Children.* New York: New York City Board of Education, Junior Guidance Classes Program, 1967, 4 pp.
  Guidelines are presented for the constructive use and arrangement of the classroom to contribute to the growth of learning and living together of emotionally disturbed students. Size, location, and other aspects of the room are discussed in view of the special needs of the disturbed child.

190. [AG, AP] HAYDEN, EUGENE J. *Special Education for Handicapped Children.* Detroit, Michigan: Detroit Board of Education, 1965, 33 pp.

A brief, general description is presented of the program for the handicapped children of the Detroit Public Schools. Information is also provided on a program for foreign children, transportation of physically handicapped and trainable mentally handicapped students, and vocational rehabilitation.

191. [A] HAYNES, W. WARREN and JOSEPH L. MASSIE. *Management: Analysis, Concepts, and Cases.* Englewood Cliffs, N. J.: Prentice-Hall, Inc., 1961, 526 pp.

Chapter I relates the development of management thought by presenting some scholars' contributions in seven areas or "seven streams of thought on management." Management theory is presented in odd-numbered chapters and excerpts from related literature are presented in even-numbered chapters. Managerial duties as functions of motivation, decision-making, policy-making, planning, and control are discussed in detail.

192. [A, P] HECKMAN, I. L., JR. and S. G. HUNERYAGER. *Management of the Personnel Function.* Columbus, Ohio: Charles E. Merrill Books, Inc., 1952, 718 pp.

Articles by well-known writers in the personnel management field are compiled under the basic functional areas of personnel administration: staffing, training, and development, wage and salary administration, performance appraisal, communication, discipline and grievances, and labor relations and collective bargaining. Other articles relate to general topical areas such as leadership, human relations, and personnel management; while still others pertain to specific tools of personnel management such as job analysis, job evaluation, interviewing, and testing. A bibliography of personnel management is included.

193. [AP, AG] HENSLEY, GENE, and DOROTHY P. BUCK (eds.). *Cooperative Agreements between Special Education and Rehabilitation Services in the West. Selected Papers from a Conference on Cooperative Agreements (Las Vegas, Nevada, February, 1968).* Boulder, Colorado: Western Interstate Commission for Higher Education, 1968, 44 pp.

Five papers discuss cooperative work-study agreements between schools and vocational rehabilitation services in the western states. Areas discussed include the advantages of cooperative agreements, the forms and disadvantages of third party agreements, basic concepts of the programs, and an outline form to use when applying for matching funds; the relationship of special education, rehabilitation and cooperative plans, programs, and agreements are included.

194. [AP, AG, R] HERRING, LEWIS H. *Provisions and Procedures for the*

Rapid Learner in Selected Texas Junior High Schools. Austin, Texas: Texas Study of Secondary Education, 1962, 31 pp.

The study attempted to survey the administrative, guidance, and curriculum practices employed by selected junior high schools in the state of Texas, and to compile the findings of the research in such a manner that other teachers confronted with the rapid learner in the junior high school might have a tangible source of provisions and techniques used by successful teachers.

195. [A] HEYEL, CARL (ed.). *The Encyclopedia of Management.* New York: Reinhold Publishing Corp., 1963, 1034 pp.

With subjects arranged alphabetically, the articles cover the scope of management from "accounting" to "workmen's compensation." The editor asserts that by referring to this reference work the uninformed reader may acquire the basics of a subject — objectives, scope, mode of attack, potentials with respect to his organization, sources of further information — and will be in a position to ask the right kind of questions of specialists and technicians within or without his organization.

196. [AG] HEYEL, CARL. *Organizing Your Job in Management.* New York: American Management Association, 1960, 208 pp.

This book is addressed to executives who have "too much work and too little time." Heyel provides useful insights into managing a volume of work, and gives attention to such matters as worries and tension, problems of delegation, efficient handling of committees and conferences, and personal efficiencies.

197. [A] HICKS, CHARLES B. and IRENE PLACE. *Office Management.* New York: Allyn and Bacon, Inc., 1956, 548 pp.

The purpose of this book is to present fundamental principles and successful practices in the field of office management. Major emphasis has been placed on work simplification, the human element, supervision of office workers, and the planning, organizing and controlling of office work. Problems and cases are presented at the end of each part.

198. [AT] HILLS, RICHARD J. *The Concept of System.* Eugene, Oregon: The Center for the Advanced Study of Educational Administration, University of Oregon, 1967, 20 pp.

Hills' work begins with an explanation of the minimum essentials of the concept system. He proceeds then to the consideration of refinements on the basic concept, including general conclusions and implications.

199. [F & L]   HINKLE, VAN R. "Legal Rights of the Mentally Retarded," *American Journal of Mental Deficiency* (November 1958), 63:501-505.
The history of civil and criminal liabilities of infants, children and mentally retarded persons is traced and needed changes in jurisprudence are cited.

200. [A, O]   HISKEY, MARSHALL S. and VERNON HUNGATE. *Planning for the Mentally Handicapped Children in Nebraska Public Schools*, 1957, 23 pp.
This booklet contains a detailed description of organization and administration.

201. [A, O]   HODGSON, FRANK M. "Special Education — Facts and Attitudes," *Exceptional Children* (January 1964), 30:196-201.
The Los Angeles Board of Education in 1960 supported a study, national in scope, to secure data relative to the (a) definition, (b) function, (c) organization, and (d) administration of a special education program. A questionnaire technique was employed to poll special education specialists, state department of education personnel, and professors of school administration relative to the four areas under study. The scope of special education included by definition a listing of 15 areas. In determining the best way of organization five plans were presented: segregation, partial segregation, cooperative, resource room, and itinerant teaching.

202. [A, O, P, R]   HOLLISTER, WILLIAM G. and STEPHEN E. GOLDSTON. *Considerations for Planning Classes for the Emotionally Handicapped.* Washington, D. C.: Council for Exceptional Children, 1962, 30 pp.
This outline was written for the purpose of assisting school staffs to effect more comprehensive planning and to aid teacher educators to broaden their programs of preparing teachers to work with emotionally disturbed children. The authors hope that it will stimulate research personnel to develop extensive evaluative and comparative studies.

203. [O] HOLLOWAY, WILLIAM J. "Special Educational Services Provided by Intermediate School Districts in Standard Metropolitan Areas," *Dissertation Abstracts* (1961), 22: 1487.
There is a lack of universal agreement concerning the philosophy, functions, and organization, and therefore, the value of intermediate schools. A study was designed to determine the extent of special educational services in 80 metropolitan areas in 19 states. Special education was one of the services where the greatest activity occurred.

204. [A]   HOLOWINSKY, IVAN Z. "Special Child or Retarded Child? Some

Special Problems of Class Placement," *Training School Bulletin* (November 1963), 60:118-122.

A number of problems related to placement of a child in a public school special class are dealt with. Validity of psychological evaluations, eligibility of a sub-normal child for a special class placement and the difference, if any, between functional and actual retardation are discussed. The article points to a lack of uniform criteria related to special class placement. The consensus is that a child should be placed in an educational environment where he could profit most. The author emphasizes that the validity of psychological evaluation also depends as much upon the skill of the examiner as it does upon standardized tests.

205. [O, AG] HOLT, E. E. "The Organization of Pupil Services," *Guidelines for Ohio Schools*, 1964, 4-11.

Provides guidance for (1) the identification of pupil services, their major activities, and individual services to children, to school staffs, and to the community at large; (2) the general organization of a total program of pupil services; and (3) the identification of items to be considered in the establishment of evaluative criteria for programs of pupil services.

206. [AG, R] Houston Independent School District. *Long Range Study Report VI*, The Division of Special Education (December 1965), 1-24.

This study was divided into two major sections: (1) Review of the Present Status of the Division of Special Services, and (2) Trends Identified in the Results of a Survey Conducted to Ascertain the Future Needs of the Division. Four major trends emerged: (1) need for early identification of children with problems, (2) expansion of health services, (3) increased methodological and technological research programs, and (4) utilization of data processing.

207. [A, P, AP, AG] *How Michigan Serves the Mentally Handicapped, Facts about the Administration of the Michigan Program.* Lansing, Michigan: Michigan State Department of Education, 1966, 6 pp.

Provisions for educable and trainable mentally retarded children include: (1) educable special classes, (2) consultants who work with educable mentally retarded children enrolled in regular classes, (3) trainable special classes, and (4) intermediate school district programs for trainable mentally retarded children.

208. [A] HOWE, CLIFFORD E. "Administration," Chapter 12 in *Behavioral Research on Exceptional Children*, Samuel A. Kirk and Bluma B. Weiner, Editors. Washington, D. C.: The Council for Exceptional Children, 1963.

Reports surveys and exploratory studies in administration of special education and inclusive prevalence studies. Substantial behavioral research studies in the area of administration and supervision of special education are needed. Some suggestions for projects and research problems are suggested.

209. [O] HUDSON, OLIVER. "Implications for the Initiation of Work Programs in Local School Districts," *Special Education: Strategies for Educational Progress*. Washington, D. C.: The Council for Exceptional Children (April 1966), 56-61.

Presents the Montgomery County Plan in the Dayton, Ohio, area for the children who are educable mentally retarded. The local school districts are responsible for the implementation of the program. A detailed summary of the program is presented including the philosophy of the program, educational planning problems, needs, solutions, post-school programs, advantages of a work program, organization of an educational work experience program, recommendations for graduations, job areas where slow learners may be placed; duties of teacher, diagnostician, guide and coordinator, and recommendations are offered.

210. [A] HUTCHINSON, LINN, CLIFFORD E. HOWE, and WARREN O. MENDENHALL. "Standards for Directors of Special Education," *California Administrators of Special Education*. Washington, D. C.: The Council for Exceptional Children (no date).

The California Administrators of Special Education (CASE) carried out a study via questionnaire, to determine current standards for directors of special education programs. The questionnaire was submitted to each department head of special education in the fifty states and Washington, D. C. A brief summary of the results of this study is given.

211. [P] IRWIN, RUTH B. "The Professional Education of Speech Clinicians in Public Schools," *Exceptional Children* (February 1965), 31:291-296.

The professional education of speech clinicians who work in the public schools is influenced by the requirements for certification by state departments of education and by the American Speech and Hearing Association. The professional competencies needed by speech clinicians in the public schools are essentially no different from those needed by clinicians who work in other settings. All clinicians need basic information about normal communicative processes, and professional information and skills in speech disorders. In addition, the clinician working in the schools will need some orientation to public school procedures.

212. [P] JAMES, KATHERINE GIDDINGS. "The Preparation of Teachers for the Gifted in the Elementary Schools with Special Reference to Southern Connecticut State College," *Dissertation Abstracts* (1961), 21:3005-3006.

The necessity for school programs for gifted children and for teachers trained to guide and challenge them is established. Desirable teacher characteristics and important elements in the education of teachers of gifted elementary students are discussed.

213. [A, O, AP]   JARVIS, OSCAR T. *Elementary School Administration.* Dubuque, Iowa: W. C. Brown Company, 1969.
    Investigates several facets of principalship, treats controversial issues in principalship, surveys issues in curriculum, and presents vital factors in devising an appropriate organizational framework for the elementary school. The readings provide basic information about many aspects of the elementary school principalship for the student of administration and the practicing administrator.

214. [A] JENNINGS, EUGENE E. *The Executive: Autocrat, Bureaucrat, Democrat.* New York: Harper & Bros., 1962, 272 pp.
    Jennings describes the essential characteristics of the executive's role in society. He describes three basic styles of executives: autocratic, bureaucratic, and democratic. The problem an executive faces today is not to decide which style to choose among these three but to select ingredients from each style so as to construct his own effective style in a changing social and organizational environment.

215. [AG] JEROME, WILLIAM T., III. *Executive Control: The Catalyst.* New York: John Wiley & Sons, Inc., 1961, 275 pp.
    The author lays the groundwork for his discussion of executive control by identifying some of the reasons for a control system: the complex and ever-changing nature of the society, the growth of multiplant-multiproduct operations (which, incidentally, is applicable to the multiservice nature of vocational rehabilitation agencies), and the trend toward decentralization of operations and decision-making. Three approaches to the evaluation of an enterprise and its management are discussed. The section dealing with the use of the internal audit, reviews the firm's operations by its own independent appraisal department. The discussion on the "system of executive control" is the most significant in the book.

216. [AP] JONES, J. W. and ANNE P. COLLINS. "Trends in Program and Pupil Placement Practices in the Special Education of Visually Handicapped Children," *The International Journal for the Education of the Blind* (1965), 14:97-100.
    School programs for the visually handicapped show an interesting change from a high percentage of special classes in 1946 to a very small percentage of children segregated in special classes in 1963. Resource rooms and itinerant teaching plans are used in a majority of programs. Teachers in both residential and local school programs

work with both blind and partially seeing children in combination units, and increasing numbers of programs include visually handicapped children with additional problems. The ability to use printed materials rather than the degree of visual acuity is the basis for classification in most schools.

217. [A] JONES, MANLEY H. *Executive Decision Making.* Rev. ed. Homewood, Ill.: Richard D. Irwin, Inc., 1962, 560 pp.
    Short-term and long-term goals and ways of achieving these goals should be the beginning of decision-making. Other steps in decision-making are discussed. After making decisions, the executive must gain acceptance of and implement his decision.

218. [AP] JONES, REGINALD L. "Research on the Special Education Teacher and Special Education Teaching," *Exceptional Children* (December 1966), 33:251–257.
    Research on the special education teacher and special education teaching is reviewed and several unpublished studies are reported. The need for systematic research programs in this area is highlighted. Such programs would (a) explore individually classes of variables that might have some usefulness in explaining attraction to special education teaching, (b) combine the most promising of these variables into a model which would maximize the explanatory power of the individual variables, and (c) test the predictive efficiency of the model using certain experimental techniques.

219. [AT] JORDAN, THOMAS E. "Conceptual Issues in the Development of a Taxonomy for Special Education," *Exceptional Children* (September 1961), 28:7–12.
    A definite taxonomy is needed and a comprehensive taxonomy will occur when special education has developed a comprehensive data language. Curriculum can acquire construct validity, as opposed to the face validity of many current procedures, when it employs taxonomic refinements. A comprehensive taxonomy can restore the unity of theory and practice and lead to a sophisticated pedagogy. This in turn implies professionalization of practitioners of special education.

220. [AP] JUBENVILLE, CHARLES P. "A State Program of Day Care Centers for Severely Retarded," *American Journal of Mental Deficiency* (May 1962), 66:829–837.
    A description of child-centered and parent-centered community day care centers for severely retarded individuals in Delaware.

221. [A] JUCIUS, MICHAEL J. and WILLIAM E. SCHLENDER. *Elements of Managerial Action.* Rev. ed. Homewood, Ill.: Richard D. Irwin, Inc., 1965, 496 pp.

The authors provide a perspective of management from behavioral and personal as well as functional points of view, thus giving a multi-dimensional picture of a manager. A considerable section of the book relates to what are commonly understood to be the personnel management aspects of every manager's job.

222. [A] JUDSON, ARNOLD S. *A Manager's Guide to Making Changes.* New York: John Wiley & Sons, Inc., 1966, 186 pp.

The conflict between employees' need for security and the organization's need to make changes in order to survive and to remain vital is discussed. Behavioral, psychological, and social effects of change; seven factors which can affect an employee's attitude toward change; and approaches which managers can use to minimize resistance and implement counter-measures are presented.

223. [O] Kansas State Department of Public Instruction. *Some Organizational Considerations of Elementary Classrooms for Educable Mentally Retarded* (no date given).

Discusses space needs, location, areas of pupil concentration, furniture, and equipment.

224. [A] KARNES, MERLE B. "The Slow Learner: Administrative Plans that Help," *NEA Journal* (October 1959), 48:22-23.

Discusses the basic principles for planning for the slow learner. Points discussed are early identification by use of cumulative child history, teacher observations, etc.; selection of teachers who are really interested; making teachers feel they are needed and are contributing; a program instructing the child in functional skills; inservice training to orient teachers to problems; acceptance of program by staff; acceptance by parents and community; staff conducted research; systematic sequential program from kindergarten through high school; a marking system which takes child's abilities into consideration; programming to let child advance at his own pace but as near the same chronological age as peers; additional guidance and counseling; and flexible grouping.

225. [AP, AG, S] KATZ, DAVID, and HARVEY E. WOLFE. *Teaching Brain Injured Children, a Handbook for Teachers and Supervisors.* Brooklyn, New York: Board of Education of the City of New York, Publication Sales Office, 1967.

Intended for teachers and supervisors of brain injured children, the handbook describes the educational practices and the theoretical bases for the program in New York City. A section on program organization and administration considers such matters as class size, location, materials, hours, transportation, emergency procedures, visitors, classroom routines, teacher attire, scheduling, planning, and articulation.

226. [AT] KATZ, DAVID and ROBERT L. KAHN. *The Social Psychology of Organizations.* New York: John Wiley & Sons, Inc., 1966, ix + 498 pp.

Origin of this text is the research program on human relations in organizations launched by Rensis Likert in 1947. Major emphasis of text is to extend the description and explanation of organizational processes with a shift toward a collective level of conceptualizing organizational behavior within an open-ended theoretical construct.

227. [AG, R] KELLEY, FRANCIS J. *Toward a Working Typology of Delinquent Children.* Boston: Training Center in Youth Development, Law-Medicine Institute, 1965, 27 pp.

The lack of consensus among medical-legal authorities as to the meaning of delinquency and the management of delinquent children is described. This conflict is general in that the legal definition emphasizes behavior and action while the psychological definition emphasizes the endopsychic conflict and need motivating the behavior. Emphasis is placed upon the psychological types who may commit delinquent acts. Different writers describe different types of delinquents. Too often these writers generalize to all delinquents the conclusions derived from work with a biased sample.

A review of 10,000 case histories lends support to a five-part taxonomy which suggests that psychotic, neurotic, organically deficient, character disordered and normal children may come in conflict with the law. This conclusion lends support to the need for effective diagnosis and varied treatment approaches to delinquency. Any group of delinquent children is heterogeneous.

228. [AP, A, F & L, AG] KELLY, ELIZABETH M. *The New and More Open Outlook for the Mentally Retarded.* Washington, D. C.: University of America Press, 1966, 139 pp.

The proceedings of this 1965 Workshop on Mental Retardation are presented as a collection of nine papers and summaries of three seminar discussions. Papers included "The Impact of Federal Legislation on Development of Comprehensive Progress for the Mentally Retarded" by Elizabeth M. Boggs, and "The Administration of a School Program for the Mentally Retarded" by Kuhn Barnet.

229. [AP] KENT, ALICE A. "Rationale for Educating Hearing Impaired Children in Programs Integrated with Regular Public Schools," *Selected Convention Papers, 42nd Annual CEC Convention,* Chicago, Illinois (March 1964), 62-63.

The author believes that the education of hearing impaired children can be helped in the early stages of their educational career. Integration does not have to take place with regular classrooms in academic endeavors but with non-academic classes. Gym classes, art classes, field trips and athletic contests are among a few endeavors that the hearing impaired may take part in. Parents' attitudes and community attitudes are discussed in regard to this program.

230. [A] KIMBROUGH, RALPH B. *Political Power and Educational Decision-Making.* Chicago, Ill.: Rand McNally & Co., 1964.

> This book delves into underexplored areas of educational administration: the political role of educators in influencing educational policies and legislation, and the nature of the decision-making process. A useful guide for educational administrators, leaders, and teachers, this text is also suitable for courses or seminars dealing with the political leadership and public relations responsibilities of educational administrators.

231. [A, AP, AG, O] KIRK, SAMUEL A. *Special Education for Handicapped Children, First Annual Report of the National Advisory Committee on Handicapped Children.* Washington, D. C.: Office of Education, 1968.

> In accordance with Title VI of Public Law 89–10, the National Advisory Committee on Handicapped Children must make recommendations to the Commissioner of Education and review the administration and operation of the provisions of the Law administered by him, with respect to handicapped children, including their effect on improving the educational attainment of such children. The report of the Committee's work includes a summary of its views and recommendations and an explanation of its report. A review of current organization and progress of the Bureau of Education for the Handicapped is provided, along with an organizational chart.

232. [A, P] KIRK, SAMUEL. "Rearranging our Prejudices," *Selected Convention Papers, 41st Annual CEC Convention,* Philadelphia (April 1963), 121–125.

> Discusses three stages of growth in special education in this century. Presents a brief summary of the history of administration and how it has developed in recent years. Discusses the present status of special education classes and offers some thoughts on fast accreditation for teachers and the effects they might have on children. Effective teaching procedures must be developed because the future of special education rests with its teachers and their teaching methods. The author believes that teachers should have salaries commensurate with their abilities.

233. [AP, AG, O] KLEIN, GENEVIEVE (ed.), et al. *COVERT (Children*

Offered Vital Educational Retraining and Therapy) Project, Year I. Tuscon, Arizona: Tuscon Public Schools, 1967, 27 pp.

COVERT School was designed to initiate, compare, and evaluate educational approaches to the problems of emotionally disturbed children. The school's philosophy, location and physical plant, and organization (cooperation, coordination, admission and dismissal procedures, and implementation planning) are described.

234. [A] KNEZEVICH, STEPHEN J. *Administration of Public Education.* 2d ed. New York: Harper & Row Publishers, 1969.

Reflects the impact on educational administration of the schools' increasing involvement in social issues, growing teacher militancy, the increasingly active role of the federal government in educational policy-making, and the technical revolution. The Second Edition covers both fundamental concepts and substantive material of administrative process, decision-making, negotiations, innovations, technologies, theory, models, systems, and more traditional concerns, documented by recent research data and literature. Particularly emphasizes systems analysis.

235. [A] KNEZEVICH, STEPHEN J. and JOHN G. FOWLKES. *Business Management of Local School Systems.* New York: Harper & Row, Publishers, 1960.

A practical approach to the problems of financial management of schools. Illustrations are drawn from actual school situations, and frequent references are made to the writings of practicing school business officials. The book bridges the gap between public school and other governmental accounting and auditing. Stresses the similarities and differences between private and public business management problems.

236. [AP, AG, P]   KOLSTOE, OLIVER P. and ROGER M. FREY. *A High School Work-Study Program for Mentally Subnormal Students.* Carbondale, Ill.: Southern Illinois University Press, 1965.

Characteristics and needs of the mentally handicapped and the organization of a 4-year high school work-study program for these students are described for teachers and work-study supervisors. Appendices include a suggested curriculum for a 4-year program and sample employer analysis.

237. [A] KOONTZ, HAROLD (ed.). *Toward a Unified Theory of Management: A Symposium.* . . New York: McGraw-Hill Book Company, 1964, 273 pp.

The first chapter is a reproduction of Koontz's article "Making Sense of Management Theory" which caused a controversy between management theorists and practitioners. The controversy led to a symposium held to reach some general agreement of what management theories are and to decide whether a unified theory of management might be reached. Koontz presents eleven papers presented at the symposium. The last chapter is Koontz's summary of the symposium.

238. [O] KOONTZ, HAROLD and CYRIL O'DONNELL. *Principles of Management: An Analysis of Managerial Functions.* 4th ed. New York: McGraw-Hill Book Company, 1968, 637 pp.

This book is organized along the lines of these functions of management: planning, organizing, staffing, directing, and controlling. Contributions of behavioral scientists to management and advanced techniques of planning and control are presented.

239. [A, F & L] KRUGMAN, MORRIS. "An Administrator Speaks on Current Trends in Special Education in New York City," *Exceptional Children* (January 1962), 28:245–248.

The following developments throughout the country were described: (1) changes in attitudes toward exceptional children, (2) future legislation, (3) emphasis on prevention, and (4) many exceptionalities covered in special education. The importance of CEC federation conferences and other meetings of persons in the field of special education was stressed. These meetings provide the groundwork where the above issues can be discussed.

240. [A, AP, AG, P, O] *The LaGrange Area Department of Special Education Handbook.* LaGrange Area Department of Special Education, Illinois, 1966, 35 pp.

Policies of the department are listed. Functions of the director, secretary, and coordinator-supervisor are listed in detail. Qualification for admission to special education classes, goals of these classes, and information about existing classes are presented. Descriptions of programs of psychological services, social work services, and prevocational services are included.

241. [A] LAIRD, DONALD A. and LEANOR C. LAIRD. *The Techniques of Delegating: How to Get Things Done Through Others.* New York: McGraw-Hill Book Company, 1957, 195 pp.

The Lairds examine delegation, an integral part of management, in both its social and psychological contexts. They discuss skill in delegating, and deciding what and when to delegate, and illustrate their concepts with vivid and candid examples. The clarity with which this book is written is evidence of the authors' training as psychologists.

242. [AP] LAKE, ERNEST G. and MALCOLM W. WILLIAMS. "Facilities for a

Pilot Orthopedic Program," *American School Board Journal* (December 1960), 141:15-18.

> A detailed description of the facilities for serving physically handicapped children and the principles agreed upon by the board of education during the planning stages for the facilities.

243. [A] LAMM, JESSE MAYO. "A Manual for the Administration of Recreational Programs for Mentally Defective Children in State Institutions for Mental Defectives," (Part One: The Research; Part Two: The Manual, Recreation for the Mentally Retarded), *Dissertation Abstracts* (1961), 22:196.

> In order to develop a manual for the administration of recreational programs for mentally defective children, a study was made to determine the recreational needs which influence recreational programs.

244. [A] LARSON, RICHARD and JAMES L. OLSON. "A Method of Identifying Culturally Deprived Kindergarten Children," *Exceptional Children* (November 1963), 30:130-134.

> One system of identifying factors thought to be significant to the education of culturally deprived children is presented. Factors include language development, self-concept, social skills, and cultural differences. They are factors which can be described in terms of behavioral characteristics appropriate to curriculum planning.

245. [AG]   LAUBER, ELLYN B. "Special Classes: Grading and Evaluating," *Training School Bulletin* (December 1954), 51:185-195.

> A comprehensive discussion of different types of grading systems for special classes. Letters of evaluation from teachers to parents are recommended, and a list of specifics which should be considered in writing these letters is given.

246. [A, R] LEARNED, EDMUND P., DAVID N. ULRICH, and DONALD R. BOOZ. *Executive Action.* Boston: Division of Research, Graduate School of Business Administration, Harvard University, 1951, 218 pp.

> This book is addressed to business executives and to those interested in the practical aspects of business administration. The study deals in human terms with problems of effective coordination within an organization. The authors' thesis is that working with people is at the core of the administrative process and of an executive's daily experience and that an executive team should be small enough to permit frequent face-to-face contact among its members. Effective coordination should be sought through improving each executive's willingness and ability to coordinate human efforts. Numerous executive actions were analyzed during the research on which this work is based.

247. [A] LEAVITT, HAROLD J. *Managerial Psychology: An Introduction to Individuals, Pairs and Groups in Organizations.* 2d ed. Chicago, Ill.: The University of Chicago Press, 1964, 437 pp.
>The scope of this book and something of the author's style are indicated by the titles given to the four principal sections:
>
>I.   People One at a Time — The Units of Management;
>II. People Two at a Time — Problems of Influence and Authority;
>III. People in Threes to Twenties — Efficiency and Influence in Groups;
>IV. People in Hundreds and Thousands — Problems of Organizational Design.
>
>Thus it is evident that Leavitt considers behavioral problems which confront managers from the smallest to the largest organizations. This readable book is augmented by thought-provoking questions for each chapter which are disarming in their simplicity and practicality.

248. [A] LEMKE, B. C. and JAMES DON EDWARDS (eds.). *Administrative Control and Executive Action.* Columbus, Ohio: Charles E. Merrill Books, Inc., 1961, 795 pp.
>This book contains more than 70 articles which offer a variety of approaches to the subject of administrative control. The articles are grouped to provide the reader a basic understanding of the control function, its applications, and skills and techniques needed to control an enterprise's activities.

249. [A] LERBINGER, OTTO and ALBERT J. SULLIVAN (eds.). *Information, Influence, and Communication: A Reader in Public Relations.* New York: Basic Books, Inc., Publishers, 1965, 513 pp.
>The authors have compiled a collection of articles related to public relations and communication which describe the nature and scope of public relations functions. The articles discuss the political, economic, and social spheres in which public relations is conducted. Articles also relate to the value system in public relations and consider such issues as ethics, privacy, and social responsibility.

250. [A] LESLY, PHILIP (ed.). *Public Relations Handbook.* 3d ed. Englewood Cliffs, N. J.: Prentice-Hall, Inc., 1967, 940 pp.
>The latest edition of this pioneering handbook, first published in 1950, is the work of 37 contributors. The scope of public relations, how an organization uses public relations, the techniques of communication, and organizing the public relations effort are some of the major topics. The volume sets forth essential principles, proven techniques and step-by-step instructions for planning, initiating, and maintaining a public relations program. A bibliography and glossary are provided.

251. [AG] LEVIN, RICHARD I. and CHARLES A. KIRKPATRICK. *Quantitative Approaches to Management.* New York: McGraw-Hill Book Company, 1965, 365 pp.

> PERT (Program Evaluation and Review Technique) and CPM (Critical Path Method) are dealt with in this book. It is written in simple terms and uses everyday examples to illustrate the techniques. A comprehensive bibliography is provided.

252. [R] LEVINE, SAMUEL. "A Proposed Conceptual Framework for Special Education," *Exceptional Children* (October 1961), 28:83-90.

> Proposes a conceptual framework from which hypothetical propositions were reduced relative to the personal and social development of individual with physical and/or mental deviations. The general attitudinal set by which society conceptualizes such deviations are referred to as defining attributes. "Criterial attributes" are specific to the particular individual's assessment of his abilities, interests, and aspirations. A scheme for assessing the strength of these attributes was presented using the concept of psychological and social distance as a criteria measure of social interaction.

253. [A, O] LIKERT, RENSIS. *The Human Organization: Its Management and Value.* New York: McGraw-Hill Book Company, 1967, 258 pp.

> Complete trust and confidence between superiors and subordinates is only one of the many characteristics of the best system of management discussed. Management systems of departments and divisions may be evaluated by a questionnaire that is presented. The importance of measuring the "human assets" of an organization is stressed.

254. [A, S] LIKERT, RENSIS. *New Patterns of Management.* New York: McGraw-Hill Book Company, 1961.

> Intended for persons concerned with the problems of organizing human resources and activity and written especially for those actively engaged in management and supervision. The focus is largely on the problems of business enterprises. The book presents a newer theory of organization based on the management principles and practices of managers who are achieving the best results in American business and government. It draws also upon research done in voluntary organizations.

255. [O] LILLYWHITE, HERALD. "Organizing a Hospital Program for Communicative Disorders," *Journal of the American Speech and Hearing Association* (May 1961), 3:139-145.

> Reasons for the establishment of programs in hospitals to diagnose and treat problems related to a specific problem (e.g., diagnose and

treat hearing, speech, and language problems of cleft palate patients) and program personnel requirements are discussed.

256. [O] LONGENECKER, JUSTIN G. *Principles of Management and Organizational Behavior.* Columbus, Ohio: Charles E. Merrill Books, Inc., 1964, 676 pp.

Managerial functions, social aspects of behavior within organizations, and the impact that economic and social environments have on decision-making are discussed.

257. [AP] LORD, F. E. and ROBERT M. ISENBERG. "Cooperative Programs in Special Education," *NEA, The Department of Rural Education, and CEC* (1964), 1-60.

Presents a brief history of the development of special day classes for the handicapped. The detailed approaches to developing area programs and the problems encountered in setting up programs are discussed. The organization, development, and certain characteristics of a sound program are related. The scope of educational programs for exceptional children along with the inability of a majority of local school systems to provide such programs for themselves is also presented. Administrative policies of ongoing successful programs are also discussed.

258. [P] MACDONALD, JAMES B. "Research Designs for Assessing Teacher Education Programs in Special Education," *Exceptional Children* (April 1966), 213-220.

Theoretical positions on teacher effectiveness are presented with reference to the researcher. An examination of the problem of research designs and common research designs are also presented. Analysis of results along with a potential illustrative teacher education study are presented. Definitions and examples are presented pertaining to macro-teaching and micro-teaching. The lack of research on the preparation of special education personnel is pointed out. This article suggests the necessity for systematic rationales for teacher education which in turn can be formed into a research design and tested experimentally.

259. [F & L] MACKIE, ROMAINE P. "Converging Circles—Education of the Handicapped and Some General Federal Programs," *Exceptional Children* (January 1965), 31: 250-255.

The advances made through congressional legislation and attempts to provide insight into federal activities that concern all handicapped children and youth. Four people-oriented federal activities are discussed.

260. [AG] MACKIE, ROMAINE P. "Education of Exceptional Children: Program, Progress, Problems," *School Life* (July 1962), 44:10-12.

A discussion of road blocks which have stood in the way of establishing programs for the education of exceptional children — shortage of qualified special educators, shortage of organizers and supervisors of special education, and the lack of knowledge on how best to provide instruction for these children. A survey of current studies that include education of all types of exceptional children and studies in more specialized areas is included.

261. [A] MACKIE, ROMAINE P., et al. *Special Education in the United States: Statistics 1948–1966.* (Teachers College Series in Special Education, F. P. Connor, ed.). New York: Teachers College Press, Teachers College, Columbia University, 1969.

The report is intended by the author to be a quantative presentation of statistical data relative to special education in the United States. It is the authors purpose to provide data that may serve as a foundation for future evaluations and influence educators in reexamining trends and issues in special education.

262. [A] MAIER, NORMAN R. *Problem-Solving Discussions and Conferences: Leadership Methods and Skills.* New York: McGraw-Hill Book Company, 1963.

Methods of leadership in management are changing . . . the practice of these new kinds of management requires free discussion and a new kind of conference. The text asserts that conference leadership is becoming a science. The book observes that people enjoy group problem-solving when the conference climate is appropriate, and that the resources of a group exceed those of any one individual. How to use the resources to improve the end product rather than let them lead to interpersonal conflict is the central theme of the book.

263. [A] MAILICK, SIDNEY and EDWARD H. VAN NESS (eds.). *Concepts and Issues in Administrative Behavior.* Englewood Cliffs, N. J.: Prentice-Hall, Inc., 1962, 201 pp.

This is a collection of articles dealing with administrative organization, decision-making, communication, human relations, and authority.

264. [AG] MANDELL, MILTON M. *The Selection Process: Choosing the Right Man for the Job.* New York: American Management Association, 1954, 512 pp.

Various sources of recruitment and methods of selection are described. The methods and values of interviewing are discussed, including a detailed analysis of the interview process. The value of psychological testing to determine an applicant's potential abilities and weaknesses are discussed; one chapter is devoted to the use and relevance of various specific tests.

265. [AP, AG] *Manual for Psychological Evaluation of Children for Placement in Special Classes, a Handbook for Administrators, Local Placement Committees, Psychologists, Psychometrists, and Teachers of Exceptional Children.* Montgomery, Alabama: Alabama State Department of Education, 1965, 24 pp.

Minimum evaluation of children with mental, physical, or emotional disabilities who are being considered for special class placement should include psychological evaluation, physical evaluation, a family profile, and an academic record. Regulations for psychological evaluation, referral procedure for the teacher, and placement committee membership are presented.

266. [AP, AG, O] *Manual of Standards for Rehabilitation Centers and Facilities.* Evanston, Ill.: Association of Rehabilitation Centers, Inc., 1965, 114 pp.

A 5-year project to specify standards of rehabilitation centers and facilities resulted in three publications. This manual includes the characteristics and goals of rehabilitation facilities. The standards for organization, services that should be provided, personnel included, records and reports, fiscal management, and the physical plant are described.

267. [A] MARCH, JAMES G. (ed.). *Handbook of Organizations.* Chicago, Ill.: Rand McNally & Co., 1965, 1247 pp.

The editor of this scholarly tome identified his "simple" objective: "to summarize and report the present state of knowledge about human organizations." One evidence of how well the 32 contributors have succeeded may be the author index which, even with a two-column format, requires 25 pages. The editor concludes his Introduction: "We think the study of organizations and human behavior within organizations is important. We also think it is fun."

268. [AP] MARSHALL, JAMES E. and BETTY M. BERRY. *Planning for Visually Impaired Children in Kansas,* 1962, 5-24.

Discusses the children who may be served in Kansas, plus the nature of the services that are provided for them. Also discusses the professionals available for the supervision of these services. Also discusses the amount of reimbursement and the resources available to such programs.

269. [AP] MARTINSON, RUTH A. "The California Study of Programs for Gifted Children," *Exceptional Children* (March 1960), 26:330-343.

A report of a three-year study conducted under the sponsorship of the California State Department of Education including evidence of the merit of special education planning for gifted pupils and reports from teachers who participated in the program.

270. [A] MAYNARD, HAROLD B. (ed.). *Handbook of Business Administration.* New York: McGraw-Hill Book Company, 1967, various paging.
This massive work is designed to serve the needs of practicing managers and those who aspire to become (better) managers. In addition to the initial 31 chapters which relate to organization, general management, and common concerns of all managers, the sections most relevant to managers of vocational rehabilitation organizations are titled: Accounting and Control (9 chapters), Management of Human Resources (22), Managing External Relations (8), Office Administration (6), Systems and Data Processing (7), and Tools and Techniques of Management Decision-Making and Control (7).

271. [A] MAYNARD, HAROLD B. (ed.). *Top Management Handbook.* New York: McGraw-Hill Book Company, 1960, 1236 pp.
This book "contains an exposition written by sixty different authors, all of whom are top managers themselves, of what it is that they do while they are managing." It is a discussion of the art and science of managing written from the standpoint of personal experience.

272. [AP, P, F & L, O] MAYO, LEONARD W., et al. *A Proposed Program for National Action to Combat Mental Retardation: Report to the President*
The national plan for combating mental retardation presents recommendations concerning research and manpower, treatment and care, education and preparation for employment, legal protection and development of Federal, State and local programs.

273. [A] McCLEARY, LLOYD E. and STEPHEN P. HENCLEY. *Secondary School Administration: Theoretical Bases of Professional Practice.* New York: Dodd, Mead and Company, Inc., 1961.
This textbook treats in depth the forces, functions, and responsibilities that shape the character of leadership for secondary schools.

274. [AG] McCONKEY, DALE D. *How to Manage by Results.* Rev. Ed. New York: American Management Association, 1967, 144 pp.
Practical techniques for developing, initiating, and administering a management-by-results program in which a manager analyzes the production from his department and sets the expected performance. Case studies of organizations using this concept of management are presented.

275. [AP] McDOWELL, J. B. "The Philosophy and Objectives of Catholic Special Education," *The National Catholic Education Association Bulletin* (1961), 58:374-381.

A Catholic philosophy of special education, which extends into the classroom for all children, is outlined in terms of educational, societal, and spiritual objectives. A special education program is not an educational oasis. It looks to and into every phase of the program with the hope that some children may move from one part to another and find help, a basic program, and certain values and ideas. Special education also seeks to pull the parents into the inescapable need to share responsibility with the schools for implementing the programs.

276. **[A]** McGAHAN, F. E. *Administrative Aspects for Identifying and Programming for the Minimally Brain-Injured and/or Perceptually Handicapped Child in the Educative Process.* Galena Park Public Schools, Texas (no date), 5 pp.

> The protocol for the inclusion of the perceptually handicapped and/or minimally brain-injured child in the Galena Park Schools is herein described. Such children usually behave with a significant degree of hyperactivity, dissociation, and have a short attention span. Specific data (including medical history, psychological test results, school history, the record of the placement committee decision, and the parent request for the child's placement in these classes) must be present before a child can be placed in a class. Effort is made to detect children early via an annual preschool clinic. Specialized equipment and instructional aids are provided to present the best possible learning situation.

277. **[AP]** McGAHAN, F. E. *Early Detection and Programming for Children with School Adjustment Problems.* Galena Park Public Schools, Texas (1962), 10 pp.

> The Galena Park Special Program is an effort on the part of the school administration to detect, at the earliest time, any student problem which may lead to difficulties in school adjustment. All phases of pupil personnel services are placed under one coordinator to expedite services to the child in difficulty. Early detection of potential problem children is facilitated via a preschool clinic. All children who will be entering the first grade in the fall visit the spring clinic with one or both parents. An effort is made to detect health problems as well as to assess the child's social maturation. All families concerned are contacted by telephone, and an appointment is made at the rate of 15 to 20 children per half hour. Visual screening, audiometric evaluations, dental evaluations, and social-emotional readiness evaluations and assessments are performed by qualified personnel. At least 12 different stations with as many attendant personnel are required for the most efficient functioning of the clinic. Once the child enters the first grade he may advance by several routes, depending upon the judgments of the evaluators. He

may advance regularly, pass through special transitory classes, or be detained a year to permit more adequate adjustment to the school situation.

278. [AT] McGREGOR, DOUGLAS. *The Human Side of Enterprise.* New York: McGraw-Hill Book Company, 1960, 246 pp.

This well-known work presents a newer theory ("Theory Y") of management believed to be more congruent with the findings of sociological and psychological research than the "traditional" theory ("Theory X") of management. The implicit assumptions of Theory X are that people inherently dislike work, shy away from responsibility, and consequently must be controlled directly or indirectly in order to get work done. The basic assumptions of Theory Y are that man desires to work, is self-directing and self-controlling and accepts responsibility. The book is devoted to showing the implications of Theory Y for certain managerial activities.

279. [A, P] MEGGINSON, LEON C. *Personnel: A Behavioral Approach to Administration.* Homewood, Ill.: Richard D. Irwin, Inc., 1967, 688 pp.

Three basic assumptions underlie the argument of this book: administration is a human administration; all administrative functions must include all of the interpersonal relationships in the total work environment; and although economic and physical resources are important, they are relatively less important than human resources. The manager-employee relationship exists in the total milieu of the work place. Personnel management is management by reference to the overall organization objectives which motivate everyone to contribute to the attainment of these objectives.

280. [P] MEISGEIER, CHARLES. "The Identification of Successful Teachers of Mentally or Physically Handicapped Children," *Exceptional Children* (December 1965), 229–235.

To accomplish the purpose of identifying and quantifying characteristics which contribute to successful student teaching of mentally and physically handicapped, five dimensions of human behavior were investigated. Three characteristic patterns of successful student teaching experiences emerged from the investigation. The successful student teachers (a) were well adjusted, emotionally stable, and able to encounter difficult special class situations; (b) possessed physical energy, vitality, and enthusiasm necessary to meet special classroom demands; (c) obtained high scores on measures of scholastic achievement and ability.

281. [A, P, AP] MEISGEIER, CHARLES H. and ROBERT SLOAT. *Common and Specialized Learnings, Competencies, and Experiences for Special*

Education Administrators. Austin, Texas: University of Texas at Austin Press, 1970, 115 pp.

Proceedings of the National Conference of the Consortium of Universities Preparing Administrators of Special Education. Presents current issues relative to common and specialized learnings, competencies and experiences for special education administrators.

282. [AP, AG] *Mental Retardation Facilities Construction Plan. Second Annual Report.* Augusta, Maine: Maine Committee on Problems of the Mentally Retarded, 1967, 87 pp.

Developed in conjunction with the plan for comprehensive state and community action to combat mental retardation, the Maine Mental Retardation Facilities Construction Plan is designed to be integrated with other health facilities and to serve the needs of the mentally retarded. The advisory council and the state agency in charge are described. The following are also detailed: state organization, departmental agreement, state committees having interest in mental retardation planning, the agreement with the Health Facilities Planning Council, and responsibilities of the Maine Committee on Problems of the Mentally Retarded.

283. [A] MERRILL, HARWOOD F. (ed.). *Classics in Management: Selections from the Historic Literature of Management.* New York: American Management Association, 1960, 446 pp.

Selected samples from the writings of sixteen "master" contributors to the development of management thought.

284. [AT, A] MERRILL, HARWOOD F. and ELIZABETH MARTING (eds.). *Developing Executive Skills: New Patterns for Management Growth.* New York: American Management Association, 1958, 431 pp.

This book combines the theoretical and practical aspects of management development programs and also gives the experiences of various organizations in establishing effective management development programs. Articles in the first part of this book deal with such important topics as planning for executive development, sound organization as a factor in management development, the organizational climate for management, the functions of top management, and measuring executive performance by set standards. The second part of this volume contains 14 case studies of management development programs used by leading business firms.

285. [P] MEYERS, C. E. "Realities in Teacher Recruitment," *Mental Retardation* (February 1964), Vol. 2.

Consists of questionnaire responses secured from 288 education students and 106 present teachers of the retarded. There were no distinguishing characteristics that could be suggested for the teacher of the mentally retarded.

286. [AP] MEYERS, MARVIN L., Director. *The Community Centered Program for Mentally Retarded and Seriously Handicapped Persons.* Colorado Department of Institutions, Division of Mental Retardation, Denver, 4 pp.

Colorado was one of the first states to develop a total inter-agency approach for aiding the retarded and handicapped. The state has 14 community centered programs in operation in many areas of the state. Approximately 900 persons were trainees in the program for fiscal year 1965-66. History and progress, scope of the program, participation by the state, eligibility, and forecast for the future are covered.

287. [AP, P, AG, O] *The Michigan Program for the Education of Emotionally Disturbed Children.* Lansing, Michigan: Michigan State Board of Education, Department of Education, 1966, 34 pp.

To assist school systems in setting up classes for the emotionally handicapped, the legal basis for state-approved (Michigan) programs is identified, state rules and regulations are reviewed, and relationships to other school and community services are indicated. Included are programs and their goals and administrative definitions and procedures.

288. [P] MILAZZO, TONY C. and KENNETH R. BLESSING. "The Training of Directors and Supervisors of Special Education Programs," *Exceptional Children* (November 1964), 31:129-141.

A presentation of a point of view on the training of administrators of special education, a survey of current practices involved in such training, and a statement of goals adopted by NASDSE in this area. It is expected that this presentation will stimulate further needed discussion by those concerned with quality leadership in special education.

289. [AG, R] MILLER, CECIL ROSCOE. *Psychological Characteristics of Young Adult Cerebral Palsied Industrial Workshop Trainees.* Doctor's Thesis, University of California (1964), 378 pp.

A study was made to assess the psychological characteristics of young adult cerebral palsied industrial workshop trainees. The study found that in a test-retest experiment, the subjects did not change significantly. A consistent pattern favored subjects who previously had attended regular schools in some improvements, some shop skills, and apparent motivation. Some subjects were representative of the "I tried" syndrome: dramatizing effort rather than striving for accomplishment. The fact that a few subjects were successfully placed in industry suggests that a more thorough investigation be made to develop highly individual and complex tests suited to the cerebral palsied.

290. [A] MILLER, DAVID W. and MARTIN K. STARR. *Executive Decisions*

and Operations Research. Englewood Cliffs, N. J.: Prentice-Hall, Inc., 1960, 446 pp.

The relationship between decision-making processes and operations research is discussed, and explanations for the use of operations research tools to solve problems are given.

291. [A, AP] MILLER, DONALD Y. and RICHARD H. DANIELSON. *Work-Study for Slow Learners in Ohio, Selected Training Materials for Use in Ohio Institutes on Work-Study Programs.* Columbus, Ohio: Ohio State Board of Education, Division of Special Education, 1965, 105 pp.

Vocational education and work study programs for educable mentally handicapped pupils are discussed in relation to the functions of the Vocational Rehabilitation Administration, the establishment and administration of a program, planning the curriculum, forming community relationships, and the evaluation, placement, and followup of students.

292. [A] MILLER, VAN. *The Public Administration of American School Systems.* New York: MacMillan Company, 1965, 580 + xi pp.

The purpose of this book is to provide a text for an initial course in school administration. The book provides a basis for developing one's own thinking about school administration in general. Major emphasis of the text is on philosophical basis for education in America, public school organizations and communication flow, administrator tasks and the nature of administration.

293. [A, R] MINER, JOHN B. *The School Administrator and Organizational Character.* Eugene, Oregon: The Center for the Advanced Study of Educational Administration, University of Oregon, 1967, 90 pp.

A concurrent validity study of school administrators for the purpose of establishing selection procedures for school administrators. Potential predictor variables were correlated with the administrators' job performances. The study summary stressed organizational character. The results of the study are presented in both narrative and tabular forms.

294. [P] MORIN, ARLINE. "Waukegan Finds Advantages in the Itinerant Teacher Plan," *Sight Saving Review* (1960), 30:33-35.

Concerns visually handicapped children placed in regular classrooms who progressed well with the extra help of the special teacher who visits them periodically. Stated ten advantages of the itinerant teacher plan.

295. [A, O] MORPHET, EDGAR, et al. *Educational Organization and Administration: Concepts, Practices and Issues.* 2d ed. Englewood Cliffs, N. J.: Prentice-Hall, Inc., 1967, 569 + xii pp.

This present edition, representing a major revision, draws upon the behavioral sciences and recent research findings to provide a sound theoretical basis for the concepts, practices, and issues discussed and analyzed in later parts of the text. In this edition, theories pertinent to educational organization and administration are presented and applied to practice.

296. [AP, R] MORSE, WILLIAM C., et al. *Public School Classes for the Emotionally Handicapped: A Research Analysis.* Washington, D. C.: Council for Exceptional Children, 1964, 142 pp.

All special classes serving the emotionally handicapped in the United States were located and mailed questionnaires. Site visits and intensive data were secured. Data concerning origin and operation of programs, general characteristics of pupils, classroom conditions and operations, and major statistical findings were presented and discussed.

297. [P] MULLEN, FRANCES A. "The Teacher Works with the Parent of the Exceptional Child," *Education* (February 1960), 80: 329-332.

Teamwork between the home and school is basic for effective service to any child, but especially the exceptional child. Each can help the other to understand the child more fully and to meet daily problems. The teacher's responsibility is to note symptoms of the child's exceptionalities. She is also aware of the symptoms and causes. Frankness in discussion of the child is needed to make the parent face up to all possibilities. Counseling is a long term project. Other sources of help besides the school are available. The school tries to get the family to the professional who should take over the treatment and counseling of the child. Group techniques for working with parents, especially groups such as PTA and others, as well as mass media such as radio, TV, etc., should be used.

298. [P] MULLEN, FRANCES A. "Staffing Special Education in 34 Large Cities," *Exceptional Children* (December 1958), 25: 162-168.

Report of a study of pupil-teacher ratios and of class size in programs for exceptional children in large cities.

299. [A] MYERS, THELMA J. "Survey of Opinions of Indiana Elementary School Principals Regarding Special Classes for Educable Mentally Retarded," *Dissertation Abstracts* (1962), 22:3044-3045.

Principals who had and principals who did not have provisions for educable mentally retarded children in their schools were asked their opinions as to physical location of facilities, education of special education teachers, and whether professionals or non-professionals were more likely to instigate programs.

300. [AP] National Association of Secondary School Principals. "The Education of Handicapped and Gifted Pupils in the Secondary Schools," *Bulletin*

of the National Association of Secondary School Principals (January 1955), 39: 1-162.

>Exceptional youth (a challenge to secondary education) is defined and types of exceptionalities and programs for them are described. The history of the special education movement from 1817 is traced. A section of the work discusses the problem of exceptional children in rural areas.

301. [A] National Society for Study of Education. "Basic Facts and Principles Underlying the Education of Exceptional Children," Chapter I in *Education of Exceptional Children*, Forty-ninth Yearbook. University of Chicago Press, Chicago, 1950.

>The problem of education for exceptional children and the responsibility of public education to educate *all* children are defined. Sections of this work include: a brief history of early special education, changing concepts in special education, enrollment in 1947-48, essentials of a well-rounded program, and a discussion of coordination of school and community resources.

302. [A, AP, O, AG] *New Techniques in Diagnosis and Appraisal and Implication for Therapy for All Public School Children with Communication Disorders, Proceedings of a Special Study Institute (Montgomery, Alabama, October 4-6, 1967.)* Montgomery, Alabama: Alabama State Department of Education, 1967, 95 pp.

>A special study institute, sponsored by the Alabama State Department of Education, convened for the purposes of (1) discussing the most efficacious means of speech therapy program organization, (2) exploring new techniques of speech problem identification, prognosis determination, and therapeutic sequence development, and (3) studying the role of the speech therapist in relation to the total public school program.

303. [AG] NICHOLS, RALPH G. and LEONARD A. STEVENS. *Are You Listening?* New York: McGraw-Hill Book Company, 1957, 235 pp.

>A central topic in this book is that listening is critical to the communication process and that listening is an important part of an administrator's job. After establishing a case for listening, the authors give techniques to improve listening skill. The book is addressed to practicing administrators and is stripped of confusion and complicated theories in order to provide a condensed and well-written guide to the art of listening.

304. [A] OBERMANN, ESCO C. *Coordinating Services for Handicapped Children*, CEC, NEA (1964), 65 pp.

>This could be valuable to the administrator as it sets forth guidelines for action in areas such as cooperation among voluntary organiza-

tions, coordinating services at intermediate levels, comprehensive diagnostic and treatment centers, special education and vocational rehabilitation. The mechanics for organizing group activities and coordinating these groups to obtain maximum potential are discussed.

305. [O, P] *An Opportunity for Dignity through Work, an Occupational Training Center for the Mentally Handicapped. Final Project Report.* Palos Park, Ill.: Lt. Joseph P. Kennedy School for Exceptional Children, 1966, 82 pp.

The project was designed to prepare mentally handicapped persons for work in the community and to utilize and strengthen community resources. Included were relevant data and discussion on problems of establishing and operating a sheltered workshop, such as recruitment and responsibilities of staff and trainees, acquisition and completion of work orders, counseling and placement of trainees, and development of a pay scale for trainees.

306. [AT] ORR, K. N. "Toward a Theory of Public School Special Education," *Teachers College Journal* (1964), 35: 181-185.

In trying to bring the specialized services for exceptional children into a part of the regular program in the school, the question is raised about how the field can be a part of the total program of the school when each area of exceptional children is, for all practical purposes, apart from the other areas which are striving to provide the needed specialized services. It is pointed out that there exists a commonality in terms of problems of administering both special and regular programs. A more defined theoretical base for specialized services in which hypotheses are formulated and tested would increase and improve specialized services for exceptional children in public schools. Five major and basic assumptions germane to the area of special education for the exceptional are presented.

307. [O, P, S] *Partially Seeing Program, 1966-1967.* Gurnee, Ill.: Lake Co. Special Education District, 1967, 21 pp.

This administrative outline of the partially seeing program in Lake County, Illinois, presents the duties and responsibilities of the two itinerant teachers and their immediate supervisors. The program's philosophy, goals, history and placement in the county's organizational structure are presented. The itinerant teacher's administrative responsibilities are listed.

308. [AP] PASSOW, HARRY A. *Educating the Gifted.* Cambridge, Mass.: New England School Development Council, 1961.

Identification, factors affecting talent development, current programs for the gifted, guidance needs of the gifted, who shall teach gifted and future needs of the gifted are discussed.

309. [AP] PASSOW, HARRY A. and MIRIAM L. GOLDBERG. "The Talented Youth Project: A Progress Report 1962," *Exceptional Children* (January 1962), 28: 223-231.

>   This is a report of a study sponsored by the Talented Youth Program which was initiated in 1953. This program listed as its purposes: (1) to initiate and conduct studies of the nature of talent and its role in modern American life, (2) to experiment with and study programs for the talented, and (3) to summarize and interpret past and current research for schools. The program developed and tested a guide which secondary schools can use to appraise their own educational programs for the talented.

310. [AP] PASSOW, HARRY A., et al. *Planning for Talented Youth: Considerations for Public Schools,* Bureau of Publication, Teachers College, Columbia University (1955), 1-84.

>   The historical overview is presented along with program modifications, studies of giftedness, present needs, definition of talent, basic considerations, identifying the talented, administrative adaptations, and evaluating a program for the talented are discussed.

311. [P, R] PATE, JOHN EDWARD. "Practices and Opinions Regarding Pre-Service Preparation for Teachers of Emotionally Disturbed Children," *Dissertation Abstracts* (1961), 21:2207-2208.

>   The report of a study done to describe the status of graduate collegiate programs for the pre-service preparation of teachers of emotionally disturbed children and to develop a proposal for a teacher-education program in this specialization.

312. [AG] PAYNE, BRUCE. *Planning for Company Growth: The Executive's Guide to Effective Long-Range Planning.* New York: McGraw-Hill Book Company, 1963, 316 pp.

>   This clearly written book tells how to organize for long-range planning, how to set long-range corporate objectives, and how to fit short-range objectives into a long-range plan. The author states that business should not be stimulated to action only by outside influences; rather, in order to grow, a business should initiate action and thereby exert greater control over its future.

313. [O] PEABODY, ROBERT L. *Organizational Authority: Superior-Subordinate Relationships in Three Public Service Organizations.* New York: Atherton Press, 1964, 163 pp.

>   Peabody contrasts functional authority and formal authority, explaining that both are necessary if goals and objectives are to be attained. Variations in the exercise of these two types of authority are reflected in studies of an elementary school, a public welfare agency branch office and a municipal police department.

314. [AG]   PEARCE, DAVID W. "Facilities for Teaching Blind Children," *American School Board Journal* (August 1961), 143:16-19.

    A member of an architectural firm describes an expansion building program in detail.

315. [A]   PERRY, JAMES H. "Administrative Provisions for the Gifted," *Selected Convention Papers, 41st Annual CEC Convention,* Philadelphia (April 1963), 187-189.

    Even though a variety of disciplines is generally utilized in establishing recommended criteria for the identification and selection of bright students, it remains the function of administration to promulgate such criteria. Administration must also accept the responsibility for their use and to provide proper interpretation at all levels of school and community life affected by the proposed program. This article warns the administrator of the dangers involved in assuming that one administrative technique is always sufficient to the needs of all children. The ultimate responsibility for a special school program rests with the administration. The ultimate success of the program will depend upon how efficiently that responsibility is delegated and applied.

316. [A, P] PIGORS, PAUL and CHARLES A. MYERS. *Personnel Administration: A Point of View and a Method.* 5th ed. New York: McGraw-Hill Book Company, 1965, 837 pp.

    As the title of this book indicates, what is presented are the authors's views of personnel administration and a method for making it operative in an organization. The control function in personnel administration under these different managerial philosophies is discussed. The authors also focus their attention on the individual in the organization and treat such topics as motivation, individual goals, and teamwork. Each of the skills needed for diagnosing organizational health is given detailed treatment. Pigors and Myers also discuss the concepts of development and utilization of human resources. The book concludes with some 19 illustrative cases, keyed to the earlier chapters which afford the reader a chance to apply the authors' methods and to develop his own analytical skills.

317. [O]   A *Planning Study for a Cooperative State-Wide Orientation and Mobility Program for the Blind in Oregon: Project Report.* Portland, Oregon: Multnomah School District Number 1, 1968, 71 pp.

    An introduction on blindness is followed by a summary of the initial planning grant proposal for cooperative statewide orientation and mobility program for blind children. Background, development, and utilization of mobility-orientation training are discussed in conjunction with educational programs.

318. [O] *Policies and Procedures, Bureau of Socially Maladjusted Children.*
Department of Special Education, Chicago Public Schools (August 1965).
Organization of social adjustment facilities, admission of pupils to
social adjustment centers, class size, teacher qualifications, identification of adjustment problems, index of offenses committed, pupil
adjustment problems, and agencies available for service.

319. [AP, P] *Policy and Procedure for a Vocational Education Work-Study
Program for Severely Mentally Retarded Pupils.* Santa Cruz, Calif.: Santa
Cruz County Office of Education, 1966, 53 pp.
The Santa Cruz County Program for Vocational Education of
trainable mentally handicapped students is outlined in terms of the
staff and their responsibilities. Sample forms are illustrated. A
second section of the document presents information to assist local
school systems in the preparation of applications for a vocational
education work-study project under the Vocational Education Act
of 1963 (P.L. 88-210).

320. [O] POLLERA, MARIE. "Organizing a Day Care Program for Severely
Cerebral Palsied Children," *Cerebral Palsy Review* (July-August 1962),
23:5-8.
A brief account of what was happening in the day care program in
the Cerebral Palsy Association of Western New York, Inc. Criteria
for admission, objectives of the program, and recommendations to
others who might be interested in establishing a similar program are
discussed.

321. [AP, R] PORTER, JOSEPH BERNARD. "An Analysis of Problems in the
Administration of Special Education Programs in Connecticut," *Dissertation Abstracts* (1961), 21:1824.
A description of the programs for physically and mentally handicapped and for those with defective speech in Connecticut and data
concerning these programs. Data from the chief state officers in
48 states were analyzed.

322. [F & L] *Practices of Salary Differential Payment to Special Class Teachers
of the Mentally Retarded in Iowa Public Schools.* Des Moines, Iowa: Iowa
State Department of Public Instruction, 1965, 36 pp.
During 1963-1964, 418 special classes for educable mentally
retarded (EMR) and 70 classes for trainable mentally retarded
(TMR) children were sponsored by 141 school districts and 57
county boards of education in Iowa. County boards and school
districts sponsoring these programs responded to a state questionnaire on salary differentials paid to teachers. Results showed that 58
percent of the districts sponsoring EMR classes paid salary differentials while 19 percent paid a differential to teachers of TMR classes.

323. [A] PRESCOTT, ELIZABETH. *A Pilot Study of Day-Care Centers and Their Clientele.* Washington, D. C.: U. S. Government Printing Office, 1965, 46 pp.

    The study considered what alterations in child rearing environment occur for children placed in group day-care, and what effects family background and the emotional climate of the center have upon extent of alteration. Additional data concern ethnic groups and their standards, the interviewers, and the centers' clientele, personnel, emotional climate, and programs. Conclusions stress the director's role and the discrepancy between standards and practices.

324. [P, A, O] *Proceedings of International Conference on Oral Education of the Deaf. Volume 1 (Northampton, Massachusetts, June 17-21, 1967; New York, New York, June 22-24, 1967).* Washington, D. C.: The Alexander Graham Bell Association for the Deaf, Inc., 1967.

    Educational papers deal with administration and organization of programs in the public schools and schools for the deaf on city and state levels. Teacher training and preparation of professional administrative personnel are also treated.

325. [P] *Professional Standards for Personnel in the Education of Exceptional Children.* Washington, D.C.: The Council for Exceptional Children (April 1966), 1-66.

    The background and preparation programs (for both student and faculty) are discussed relative to holding positions in the areas of the deaf, hard-of-hearing, gifted, mentally retarded, physically handicapped, and behavioral disorders. The requirements for preparation in administrative and supervisory positions in these areas are also discussed.

326. [O] *Program Description for Special Education.* Lansing, Michigan: Michigan State Board of Education, 1966, 29 pp.

    Guidelines cover the planning and operation of educational programs for handicapped children. Procedures are stated for developing services for those with hearing, visual, or physical handicaps and the homebound or hospitalized. Information is provided on procedures for determining the need for services, eligibility requirements, suggestions for various types of programs, teacher requirements, case loads, equipment, counseling services, and state aid.

327. [A, O] *A Program of Education for Exceptional Children in Oklahoma.* Oklahoma City, Oklahoma: Oklahoma State Department of Education, Division of Special Education, 1968, 114 pp.

    The guidelines for the establishment or improvement of services for students who need special attention cover law and state board regulations, teacher qualification and certification, and state and local administrative responsibilities. Listings are given of the role and qualifications of the visiting counselor, special services for home-bound students, provision for guidance services, and the role and qualifications of directors of special education.

328. [O, AP, PP] PRONOVOST, WILBERT L., et al. *The Horace Mann Planning Project; A design for a Comprehensive Center and Educational Program for Communicative Disorders.* Boston, Mass.: Boston Public Schools, 1966, 112 pp.

The purpose of this project was to develop recommendations and plans for program, personnel, and facilities for the new Horace Mann Center for the Deaf as a replacement for an expansion of the present school.

329. [A] *Pupil Personal Services.* Tacoma, Wash.: Tacoma Public Schools (December 1965), 15 pp.

A directory of functions, staff, referral procedures and admission criteria for pupil personnel services in the Tacoma Public Schools.

330. [AG] REDFIELD, CHARLES E. *Communication in Management: The Theory and Practice of Administrative Communication.* 2d ed. Chicago, Ill.: The University of Chicago Press, 1958, 314 pp.

In the first part of this book Redfield shows the significance and scope of and gives seven guiding principles for effective administrative communication and points out methods for transmitting information upward, downward, and horizontally. Part II deals with downward and outward communication by administrators; and the third part discusses various media used in transmitting information upward and inward. The final part deals with horizontal communication in which Redfield identifies two principal activities: clearance and review, and the conference process. The author provides an annotated bibliography at the end of each chapter.

331. [AD, P] *Report of a Committee for a Comprehensive Plan for Hearing Impaired Children.* Springfield, Ill.: Illinois Commission on Children, 1968, 80 pp.

The results of a study to formulate an overall plan utilizing and coordinating existing services for hearing impaired children are reported. The definition, classification, incidence, and prevention of hearing impairment and the orientation of professional personnel are discussed.

332. [O, F & L] *Report on Operation and Results of Special Educational Programs for Educationally Handicapped Minors.* Sacramento, California: California State Department of Education, 1967, 23 pp.

Upon a listing of both favorable areas and problems, recommendations were made to provide a current apportionment of state funds for all handicapped programs; initiate a grant program for teacher training in special education; evaluate current provisions of the school housing aid to exceptional children; provide state reimbursement for excess expenses (equitable funding of learning disabilities groups and extraordinary transportation costs).

333. [A] *Reporting Pupil Progress in Special Classes for the Mentally Retarded. Special Education Curriculum Development Center; An Inservice Training Program.* Des Moines, Iowa: Iowa State Department of Public Instruction, 1968, 72 pp.

An attempt to improve procedures for reporting the progress of mentally handicapped children in special classes, the guidelines state considerations related to the intent and design of report cards and describe a survey of 188 report cards used in special classes. Four sample report cards are included, which are designed to cover identification information, academic progress, personal and social progress, and subjective information.

334. [O, PP, P] *Review of Special Education Programs, Guides to Special Education in North Dakota, Volume 1.* Bismarck, North Dakota: North Dakota Department of Public Instruction, 1967, 47 pp.

Special education programs for each type of handicapped child are described in terms of organization, admission criteria, class size, equipment, teacher qualifications, and state participation. Additional special education personnel, their qualifications, and their responsibilities are listed.

335. [AP] REYNOLDS, MAYNARD C. "A Crisis in Evaluation," *Special Education: Strategies for Educational Progress* (April 1966), 251-258.

Allocation of federal funds for education carries with it a responsibility to receiving agencies for evaluation of innovative programs. The article places heavy emphasis on the need for careful program planning and urges the development of evaluation techniques and personnel to utilize these techniques effectively as criterion measures in the formulation of sound teaching-learning programs for exceptional children. The point is made to reshape programs in accordance with the hard facts of results. Incautious generalizations from studies are also discussed.

336. [AP] REYNOLDS, MAYNARD C. "A Framework for Considering Some Issues in Special Education," *Exceptional Children* (March 1962), 28:367-370.

A summary of special education programs is presented in the form of a hierarchy ordered according to increasing specialization. A broad range of services is important and children should be placed in programs of no more special character than absolutely necessary. To serve "in-between" children, such as the trainable, new patterns of interaction among a variety of agencies will be necessary.

337. [AP] REYNOLDS, MAYNARD C. "The Responsibility of the School for Trainable Retarded Children," *Exceptional Children* (September 1962), 29: 53-56.

A report of the methods used by Minnesota for allocating the public responsibility for trainable mentally retarded children and their parents, utilizing the best resources available.

338. [AP] RICE, JOSEPH P. "Screening, Examining and Programming for Gifted Pupils," *Secondary Schools Today: Readings for the Educators* (1965), 182-191.

Submits procedures to be used in setting up an extensive program for the mentally gifted. Screening and examining the pupils are discussed in detail. Ethics are also discussed. A plan for enrichment and detailed programs of acceleration are given. Also describes a total program in detail and gives steps to follow when planning a program.

339. [A, P, F & L] RICH, ANNETTE LOUISE. "The Status of Teachers of the Educable Mentally Retarded," *Dissertation Abstracts* (1961), 22: 127-128.

The report of a study of the supply of and demand for teachers of the educable mentally retarded, professional background of teachers, state requirements for special certification to teach the mentally retarded, and state legislation pertaining to these. A major obstacle for school administrators is the lack of qualified teachers for educable mentally retarded classes.

340. [A] RICHARDS, MAX D. and PAUL S. GREENLAW. *Management Decision Making.* Homewood, Ill.: Richard D. Irwin, Inc., 1966, 564 pp.

Since the author's philosophy is that the ability to make decisions is the fundamental part of management, he feels that decision-making is a basic approach to understanding management. A behavioral viewpoint is used for explaining leadership, organizational design, and the behavior of individuals and groups.

341. [P] ROGGE, WILLIAM M. "The Illinois Plan — A Strategy for Educational Change," *Special Education: Strategies for Educational Progress,* NEA, CEC, (April 1966), 36-38.

A model program is being built to nurture educational change in Illinois. The model has three components: demonstration, inservice training, and the recruiting and training of persons who perceive themselves as change agents. The program has developed a method to seek out, evaluate, and demonstrate innovations that might be of worth in program development for gifted children. These three components are discussed. There is a brief entry about the amount of financing involved.

342. [A, O] ROSS, MURRAY G. *Community Organization: Theory, Principles, and Practices.* 2d ed. New York: Harper & Row, Publishers, 1967, 290 + xiv pp.

The purpose of this book is to set forth a conception of community organization processes to describe its nature and outline principles which facilitate its development. An extensive bibliography is included.

343. [A, PP, P] *Rules and Regulations to Govern the Administration and Operation of Special Education.* Springfield, Illinois, 1964, 81 pp.

Rules and regulations for special education programs in Illinois are reviewed. Given for each handicap are a definition, establishment of educational facilities, types of services, admission to programs, eligibility of pupils, enrollment, supervision, case records, curriculum, physical plant, equipment and instructional materials, and qualifications of personnel. Rules and regulations are also provided for psychological services, transportation of exceptional children, administrators and supervisors.

344. [A] *Rules and Regulations-Special Education.* Superintendent of Public Instruction, State of Illinois, Springfield (July 1964), Special Education Publication 564, 81 pp.

Illinois state rules and regulations for the establishment and administration of special education programs. They were designed for each area of special education in an attempt to provide the framework for quality programs.

345. [A] RUSALEM, HERBERT. *Guiding the Physically Handicapped College Student. T C Series in Special Education.* New York, N. Y.: Columbia University Teachers College, 1962.

The ramifications of working with physically disabled college students (including physically handicapped, deaf, hard of hearing, blind, and partially sighted) is explored in this booklet and procedures are suggested to improve educational service for them. Chapter 1 discusses the increasing enrollment of physically handicapped students in colleges and universities. Philosophical concepts related to the admission of these students and related literature concerning physically handicapped students in colleges and universities are presented. Chapter 2 describes some of the facilities necessary for the physically handicapped student. Factors such as readers for the blind, elevators for the non-ambulatory student, and other related information are discussed. The next three chapters present the admission policies, curricular and extracurricular activities, and counseling programs needed for the physically handicapped college student. The last chapter provides the resources available for personnel serving the handicapped student — local, state, and national agencies, as well as professional organizations and journals. A 68-item bibliography is included.

346. [O, P] RUSSELL, TOMMY. *A Study of the Development of the Program for Exceptional Children in Alabama, with Emphasis on the Education and Professional Status of Teachers of Exceptional Children.* Doctor's Thesis, University of Alabama (1963), 1035 pp.

This study, conducted in Alabama, found that the most frequent type of teaching situation was the ungraded or multi-grade class in a regular day school for mentally retarded children, but that some schools organized in this way accept children with various kinds of handicapping conditions (second most frequent). The third most frequent type of teaching situation was special day schools for mentally retarded children. Progress was noted in types and availability of records. From this study increases in the number of special education teachers completing degrees and basic endorsement requirements was found. The number of institutions offering a sequence of courses in one area of special education also increased.

347. [A] SAGE, DANIEL D. *The Development of Simulation Materials for Research and Training in Administration of Special Education. Final Report.* Syracuse, New York: Syracuse University, 1967, 219 pp.

Materials utilizing a simulated environment approach were developed, produced, pilot tested, and evaluated to determine their usefulness as media for training programs and for behavioral research in the process of administration of special education. Instruments for evaluating the materials consisted of a test used before and after treatment to assess behavioral change, a category scoring system to assess performance during the training sessions, and a participant opinionnaire.

348. [A, PP, P] SALVADOR, VIRGINIA, et al. *Special Education Committee Report.* Vancouver, Washington: Vancouver Public Schools, 1966, 51 pp.

In order to provide guidelines for special education teachers, this pamphlet discusses the philosophy and objectives of special education and the interaction of special and regular classes. Types of rooms in operation, the duties of the special services personnel, identification and placement procedures, methods of evaluation including grade records and graduation diplomas, procedures to be followed in ordering materials, and schedules of staff meetings are described.

349. [F & L, A] SANDERS, DONALD, CLAUDE STANTON, and ANNE WELCH. *Administrative Procedures for the Special Education Program.*

Colorado State Department of Education, Office of Instructional Services (July 1965), 1–81.

Specific definitions are given of the (1) educationally handicapped, (2) educable mentally handicapped, (3) physically handicapped, crippled, and vision, (4) speech handicapped, and (5) homebound. There is also a definition offered for a supervisor and administrator of special education along with qualifications and certification needed by these people. Reimbursement procedures are also discussed. Legal provisions are discussed along with the Boards of Cooperative Services Act of 1965 and the Handicapped Children Educational Act of 1965. Transportation and maintenance are also discussed. Responsibility for submission of forms for approval of programs is discussed along with sample forms.

350. [A] SANDERS, JOSEPHINE P. "Administrative Responsibility in Programs for Trainable Mentally Retarded," *Exceptional Children* (December 1960), 27:196–201.

The administrator is responsible for the selection of pupils and the problems which arise concerning his various selections. Includes a list of criteria which should be used when selecting this person for special education. A definition is also introduced for the trainable mentally retarded.

351. [S] SARTAIN, AARON QUINN and ALTON WESLEY BAKER. *The Supervisor and His Job.* New York; McGraw-Hill Book Company, 1965, 464 pp.

The authors have addressed this book to three classes of readers: those who aspire to be supervisors, those who are currently employed as supervisors, and those who manage first-line supervisors. The central theme of the book is that effective supervision consists not primarily of what the supervisor does, but rather how he is viewed by his associates. The authors discuss such topics as work simplification, development and compensation of subordinates, counseling, communication, discipline, and evaluation of subordinates.

352. [A] SAVAGE, WILLIAM W. *Interpersonal and Group Relations in Educational Administration.* Glenview, Ill.: Scott, Foresman, and Co., 1968.

An introduction to the interpersonal forces and processes with which school administrators must deal. Discussion of techniques as well as theories provides a practical background for the complex human relations problems encounted. Up-to-date bibliographies are included.

353. [A] SAYLES, LEONARD R. *Managerial Behavior: Administration in Complex Organizations.* New York: McGraw-Hill Book Company, 1954, 269 pp.

A manager's job consists of three basic elements. First, he is a participant in a work flow which relates him both inside and outside the organization. Second, he is a leader who is not only responsible for directing subordinates but also for responding to them when they seek aid or representation. Third, he is a monitor of the work systems. These three elements are discussed at length by Sayles.

354. [A] SCHARDEIN, RAYMOND. "Administrative Practices and Facilities of Training Programs for Trainable Mentally Retarded Youths," *Dissertation Abstracts* (1959), 19:1978–1979.

355. [AP] SCHEERENBERGER, R. C. "Communication Needs and Programs in the Field of Mental Retardation." Washington, D. C.: The Council for Exceptional Children (April 1966), 72–75.
Informs the reader of program development and materials available to interested persons. The trend of administration today is discussed. Areas the administrator must be concerned with are outlined but not discussed. The need for regional centers capable of collecting and storing special education material, testing its adequacy and distributing information relative to its availability and utilization is discussed with mention of the "Winnower."

356. [AG] SCHELL, ERWIN H. *The Technique of Executive Control.* 8th ed. New York: McGraw-Hill Book Company, 1957, 357 pp.
This work is intended as a guide to executive life in a work environment and deals with problems an executive faces in his administrative career. Topics discussed include the executive attitude and morale; associational relationships with superiors, subordinates, and peer groups; and creativeness on the part of the executive.

357. [S] SCHMITT, PHILIP J., et al. *Supervisors and Supervision of Teachers of the Deaf.* Urbana, Illinois: Illinois University, Institute for Research on Exceptional Children, 1968, 192 pp.
Data from 258 supervisors of teachers of the deaf who replied to a self administered questionnaire yielded information on the nature of supervisory programs. Results indicate a need for more supervisors, improvement in the quality of supervision, setting of standards for supervisory personnel, and professional consideration of these problems.

358. [AP, P] SCHOLL, GERALDINE T. *Teacher Preparation for Visually Handicapped Children: A Look into the Future.* Ann Arbor, Michigan: Michigan University, 1967, 6 pp.
The paper reviews trends in education and considers their impact on educational programing and the implications for teacher education. Stress is placed upon the growing professionalism of teachers in

determining educational needs and placement and the high incidence of multiple disabilities demanding new programs.

359. [AP] SCHONELL, F. J., et al. (eds.). "The Slow Learner-Segregation or Integration," *Educational Research* (February 1963), 5:146–150.

The *Slow Learner* is a symposium in which educators from several countries describe practices and express opinions on whether slow learning children should be educated in separate schools or integrated as far as possible within ordinary ones. Contributions come from Australia, Canada, Denmark, Great Britain, Holland, Japan, New Zealand, Russia, Sweden, and the United States. Practices vary widely. In the U. S. the emphasis has been on integration; in Europe, segregation has been more common.

360. [A, F & L] "School District for the Handicapped," *Overview* (January 1961), 2:36.

A special education school district for the education and training of handicapped children was established in a county in Missouri. Handicapped children from a 500 square-mile area were transported to a central location for a special education program. A description of the legislation, financing, administration and program is given in this article.

361. [A] SCHUCHMAN, LEON. "Current Practices in Administering Home Teaching," *Exceptional Children* (March 1957), 23:246–250 and 266.

A report of a survey designed to determine and describe current practices and facilities for homebound children.

362. [A] SCHWARTZ, JAMES W. (ed.). *The Publicity Process.* Ames, Iowa: Iowa State University Press, 1966, 286 pp.

This book is a collection of articles describing different aspects of effective publicity: methods of effective communication, development of news stories, use of media, and techniques of writing and advertising. These articles have been chosen because of their practical application. Many concepts and ideas are well-illustrated pictorially.

363. [P] SCHWARTZ, LOUIS. "An Integrated Teacher Education Program for Special Education — A New Approach," *Exceptional Children* (February 1967), 33:411–416.

Preparation of the clinician educator, capable of providing diagnosis and remediation of the variety of learning difficulties of exceptional children is discussed. The gap between accumulated knowledge regarding exceptionality and existing teacher education curricula is discussed. The problems of the shortage of teachers is also discussed. The courses in the integrated sequence are described and limitations are noted.

364. [O] SCOTT, WILLIAM G. *Human Relations in Management: A Behavioral Science Approach: Philosophy, Analysis, and Issues.* Homewood, Ill.: Richard D. Irwin, Inc., 1962, 442 pp.

The philosophy and an analysis of human relations are discussed by the author. The works of a number of industrial sociologists are presented.

365. [A, PP, F & L] *Self-Study and Evaluation Guide.* New York, N. Y.: National Accreditation Council for Agencies Serving the Blind and Visually Handicapped, 1968, 348 pp.

Standards developed for agencies over a 3-year period are presented. The following are provided or specified: a manual of procedures for agency self-study, an agency and community profile, agency function and structure, financial accounting and service reporting, personnel administration and volunteer service, physical facilities, public relations and fund raising, library services, orientation and mobility services, rehabilitation centers, sheltered workshops, social services, vocational services, an individual staff member information form, and the evaluation summary and report.

366. [A, F & L, PP] *Self-Study and Evaluation Guide for Sheltered Workshops.* New York: National Accreditation Council for Agencies Serving the Blind and Visually Handicapped, 1968, 213 pp.

This document is designed as an instrument for self study and evaluation of a sheltered workshop for the blind which operates as an independent agency rather than as part of a larger multiservice organization. Forms and a manual of procedures are provided for evaluation of major aspects of administration common to any service organization including function and structure, financial accounting and service reporting, personnel administration and volunteer service, physical facilities, and public relations and fund raising.

367. [P] SELZNICK, HARRIE M. "Direction for Future Action," *Exceptional Children* (May 1965), 31:356–360.

Identifies three possible problems in special education that warrant future action. These include (a) the reconsideration of the classification and grouping of pupils away from medical, diagnostic labels toward more concern for learning needs, (b) the evaluation and examination of programs for preservice preparation of professional personnel and the development of programs of continuing education, along with a need for better teacher training programs and renovation of current conceptualization of professional standards, (c) a re-estimation of our current levels of understanding of children. There are untouched islands of vital and vastly important topics for research in the specializations with the gifted, the mentally retarded, and the culturally disadvantaged. There exists a great need for revisions in the training of specialists, especially considering speech therapy as it now is operated in the schools.

368. [AP] SELZNICK, HARRIE M. "Why and How," *Exceptional Children* (May 1965), 31:477-484.

The author, then president of CEC, presented this paper at the 43rd Annual CEC Convention, Portland, 1965. His remarks suggested some of the unfinished business of special education. Attention was called to the unresponsive manner in which advice of our leadership has been utilized. The long-range concerns for professional standards, continuing education, legislation, class designation, and groups and diagnostic teaching are discussed.

369. [AP] SELZNICK, HARRIE M. "The Education of Exceptional Children: A Positive Factor," *The Teachers College Journal* (1964), 36:42-43.

In every school system there are children with unusual needs. Special skills and services are required to benefit these exceptional children. Special education greets these demands with a sense of equality and consideration of individual differences and needs with the provision of special services. These services are implemented through identification, guidance, counseling, and planning in view of the problems to ensure adjustment and academic success. Special education extends its influence into the regular school and classroom, influencing the philosophy and programming for all children, and it extends its influence to society at large, to the community, and to the parent through its improvement of research, theory, and action in the schools.

370. [A] SHELDON, OLIVER. *The Philosophy of Management.* New York: Pitman Publishing Corp., 1965, 296 pp.

Fundamental concepts in management are presented with a discussion of the author's philosophy of management.

371. [A] SHUCHMAN, ABRAHAM. *Scientific Decision Making in Business: Readings in Operations Research for Nonmathematicians.* New York: Holt, Rinehart & Winston, Inc., 1963, 568 pp.

The tools of operations research are described in this collection of articles, and the development of operations research is traced. Techniques of programing, factor analysis, waiting-line theory, game theory, and the application of operations research are discussed.

372. [A, O] SIMCHES, RAPHAEL F. *A Magna Carta for the Emotionally Disturbed Child. Paper Presented at New York Congress for Mental Health (1st) New York, New York.* 1965, 6 pp.

The author anticipates barriers and problems which might arise when legislation became effective, requiring school districts to provide appropriate education for emotionally disturbed children. Aspects included are problems of definition and diagnosis, community responsibilities in providing cooperative medical and social services, and varying directions of school program organization.

373. [A] SMALTZ, JANET M. (ed.). *Classes for Educable Mentally Handicapped Children — Guides to Special Education in North Dakota. Part II.* Bismarck, N. D.: North Dakota State Department of Public Instruction, 1965, 153 pp.

The first section of this administrative and curriculum guide presents basic information for school administrators and teachers of mentally retarded children. Administrator, parent and teacher cooperation, the retarded child's potential for academic achievement, teaching suggestions, daily schedules, progress reports, and reference lists for parents and teachers are discussed.

374. [AP] SMITH, EUGENE H. "State Level Educational Services to Gifted Pupils," *Exceptional Children* (May 1961), 27:511-513.

The results of a survey of services to gifted pupils in all 50 states, data being secured from questionnaires to the chief state school officers. State level committees on education, state funds for gifted pupils, state educational agency staff members, and proposed expansion in services are discussed.

375. [A] SMITH, J. and CHARLES MARK. "Administrative Problems Connected with Special Programs for the Gifted Children in California Junior High Schools," *Dissertation Abstracts* (1961), 21:2971-2972.

The report of research designed to study the major problems in the administration of programs for gifted children. It was found that schools generally use multiple bases for identification of the gifted, and that financial provisions vary in the schools.

376. [AP] SPARKS, HOWARD L. and LEONARD S. BLACKMAN. "What is Special About Special Education Revisited: The Mentally Retarded," *Exceptional Children* (January 1965) 31:242-247.

Special education has evolved from the democratic idea of equal opportunity for all people. Special class placement versus regular class placement is discussed. Analysis of available evidence points toward the lack of measurable academic achievement in the special class and brings forth questions concerning the adequacy of the special class social environment. Research is needed in the area of teacher preparation for teachers of the educable mentally retarded.

377. [AP] "Special Classes for Handicapped Children," *Research Bulletin,* NEA Research Division (May 1961), 39:43-46.

A study made of urban schools showed more special classes in large districts. The most frequently reported special class was found to be for the mentally retarded. Slow learners have more hope of profiting from education. However, the survey indicated fewer slow learner classes. Speech defects was another area covered in many schools. Physical handicaps seemed to be fairly well covered in large districts although the expense is great. The physically handicapped are generally not retarded and present the teacher with a challenge to make the most of their lives. The emotionally disturbed are the least likely to be provided with special classes.

378. [O] *Special Education for Exceptional Children in Texas.* Texas Education Agency, Division of Special Education, Austin (September 1966), 1-5.
Covers special education for exceptional children in Texas from definition, establishing law, eligibility, through function, special education curriculum, and function of the special education division. Includes organizational chart for special education in Texas.

379. [A] *Special Education Handbook for School Administrators* (Louis Bruno, ed.). Olympia, Washington: The Office of the Superintendent of Public Instruction, 1961.
The philosophy of special education for children with mental, physical, and social deviations; organizational program patterns; roles of the superintendent and school psychologist; methods of financing programs; requirements for special education teachers; and laws pertaining to the education of handicapped children are discussed. In addition, ten programs for specific areas of handicap are presented.

380. [P] *Special Education Teachers Approval Procedures.* (Revised March 1, 1965), Office of Superintendent of Public Instruction, Springfield, Illinois (March 1965), 1-22.
Minimum training requirements for approval of teachers in special education for all areas of exceptionality are discussed. Also programs offered in special education are listed.

381. [P] "Special Professional Personnel in Public Schools," 1966 *NEA Research Bulletin* (December 1967), 45:105-106.
The availability of professional services is still largely a matter of the size of the school system in which the pupil is enrolled. A table depicts the percent of large, medium, and small systems that provide each of five types of specialized professional or in-service personnel on a nationwide basis.

382. [AP] "Special Programs for Gifted Pupils," *Bulletin of the California State Department of Education*, Sacramento (January 1962), 31:167-178.
The characteristics and needs of gifted children, identification of gifted pupils, education planning, guidance of gifted children,

educational administration of programs, specific programs and teachers of the gifted are discussed.

383. [P, R] SPRAGUE, HALL and LLOYD DUNN. "Special Education for the West," *Exceptional Children* (April 1961), 27:415-421.

The report of a survey made by Western Interstate Commission for Higher Education (WICHE) for the purpose of determining how various regions in the West were approaching the problem of the shortage of teachers with special skills needed for instructing exceptional children. Recommendations for special education teacher training were made.

384. [A, P] *The Special Services Program in the Champaign Schools.* Champaign, Ill.: Champaign Community Unit 4 School District, 1967, 102 pp.

An analysis of the administrative structure of the Champaign special services program outlines the relationship of the director of special education to school personnel, community agencies, parents, and children. The relationship between special services personnel and regular school personnel is shown.

385. [A] *Standards for the Education of Exceptional Children.* Department of Public Instruction, Division of Pupil Personnel Services, Pierre, South Dakota (1962), 1-43.

The many aspects of administration of special education at the state level are discussed. The article also entails what the local community's responsibilities should be. It sets up guidelines for standards involved in educating the mentally and physically handicapped.

386. [AP] *Standards for Public School Programs for Severely Handicapped (Trainable) Children.* Kansas State Department of Public Instruction (September 1957), 1.

Standards for many phases of the program are described. Among these phases are the children's eligibility, admissions, trial placement, class size, housing, curriculum, approval and their home training. Also discusses teacher qualification for this program.

387. [O] *Standards for Special Classes for Mentally Retarded Pupils.* State Department of Public Instruction, Division of Special Education, Kansas (1957), 1-9.

The principles of organizing a special class, standards of eligibility for special class placement, housing of the special class, steps in establishing the special class, curriculum, recommended levels for organizing classes, supervision, supplies and equipment, teacher qualifications, training standards, requirements for teachers and reimbursement are discussed.

388. [A, O] *State Plan for Special Education.* Austin, Texas: Texas Education Agency, 1970, 62 pp.

> Information for the initiation, organization, and operation of special education programs in Texas is included in this bulletin. In addition to program descriptions, information is given about local planning, psychological reporting, textbooks, teacher certification, and transportation.

389 [AP, R] "Statistics of Special Education for Exceptional Children," *Special Education for Exceptional Children,* U. S. Department of Health, Education, and Welfare, Office of Education, Biennial Survey of Education, 1952-54., 1-46.

> The data contained in this report pertain to certain types of special instructional programs maintained for exceptional children in public elementary and secondary day schools. Similar data have been collected at five year intervals since 1900. The study attempted to include all programs in all school districts. In all, 4,994 questionnaires were sent out, from which 99.44 percent were returned. The results were analyzed and presented in a comparative format.

390. [AG] STEVENS, GODFREY. *Taxonomy in Special Education for Children with Body Disorders,* Department of Special Education and Rehabilitation, University of Pittsburgh, Pittsburgh, 1962.

> This study points up the "need for an educationally conceived classification scheme for the concepts of special education for exceptional children" and attempts to construct a taxonomy which will be operationally relevant to the central purpose of special education.

391. [A, P] STRAUSS, GEORGE and LEONARD R. SAYLES. *Personnel: The Human Problems of Management.* 2d ed. Englewood Cliffs, N. J.: Prentice-Hall, Inc., 1967, 756 pp.

> The authors discuss the concepts of recruitment, selection, training, management development, and performance appraisal. Methods of rating are given such as forced distribution, forced choice, critical incident technique, and the evaluation interview. The chapters on management training disucss such training techniques as the lecture, guided conference, case method, simulation, and T-group.

392. [P] SUGRUE, TIMOTHY J. "New York City's High School Program for the Deaf, *Volta Review* (April 1967) 69:247-252.

> Describes the programs in New York public school system where teachers are assigned to three academic high schools, a vocational high school for boys, and three coeducational vocational high

schools. These teachers have many functions other than just teaching. For instance, they serve as program directors, consultants, etc. There is also a program under which deaf students are integrated into the programs of schools where there is no teacher of the deaf.

393. [A, AT, O]   TANNENBAUM, ROBERT, IRVIN R. WESCHLER, and FRED MASSARIK. *Leadership and Organization: A Behavioral Science Approach.* New York: McGraw-Hill Book Company, 1961, 456 pp.

The publishers assert this book contains key advances in four major areas: a significant theory of leadership; sensitivity training — an "active" method for leadership development and a way to helping people behave differently; useful concepts and research in the systematic study of organizations; and advances in research design and techniques. The book concludes with independent commentaries written by a social psychologist, a sociologist, and a management theorist and consultant.

394. [AP, R] TENNEY, HENRY C. "The Development of Criteria for the Education of Emotionally Handicapped Children in Special Classes," *Dissertation Abstracts* (1962), 22:2642.

The report of a survey of programs for emotionally handicapped children in public and residential schools. Criteria to be developed were identification and selection of children for the program, placement, and evaluation.

395. [A]   TERRY, GEORGE R. *Office Management and Control.* 3d ed. Homewood, Ill.: Richard D. Irwin, Inc., 1958.

The thesis of this text is that the concept of office management consists of specific fundamental functions which when applied constitute the management process. Specific pertinent sections of the text deal with organizing the work of the office, personnel motivation, and controls for maintaining work of the office.

396. [AG] THAYER, LEE O. *Administrative Communication.* Homewood, Ill.: Richard D. Irwin, Inc., 1961, 344 pp.

The purpose of this book is to offer basic concepts regarding the nature and dynamics of communication in organizations. The author's basic assumption is that the communication process is an administrative tool; hence, it should be studied only in relation to administrative procedures. Two main segments of the book are devoted to the purposes of communication and the methods of administrative communication. In the final parts Thayer discusses current problems and research in this field and brings into sharper focus the personal and organizational aspects of communication. A brief essay on how to write administrative reports and memoranda constitutes an appendix; a bibliography on the literature of communication and organization is provided.

397. [A, O, AP] THOMPSON, JAMES D. *Organizations in Action.* New York: McGraw-Hill Book Company, 1967.

>This book deals with the behavior of complex organizations as entities. Whereas as books on "organizational behavior" focus on the behavior of people in organizational contexts, this book considers individual behavior only to the extent that it helps explain organizations. The book seeks the reasons for existing patterns or organizational design and structure, and methods of coordination, decision, and control. It seeks, also, to account for differences on these topics among organizations.

398. [AP] THOMPSON, MORTON. "The Nassau County Cerebral Palsy Playground: Day Camp Plan for Handicapped Children," *Cerebral Palsy Review* (January-February 1961), 22: 6-7.

>A description of a treatment center and school for cerebral palsied children and adults in Nassau County, New York, which includes in its program comprehensive and unusual recreation facilities. Dr. Thompson describes the playground and the summer day camp grounds in detail.

399. [AP, R] TISDALL, WILLIAM J. "A Follow-up of Trainable Mentally Handicapped Children in Illinois, *"American Association on Mental Deficiency* (July 1960), 65:11-16.

>Data from investigation gave implications for a curriculum development of functional skills, organization of classes with more teachers, more allocation of public school classroom space, support of school authorities and community, postschool accommodations, parent counseling, and parent organizations.

400. [AP] TISDALL, WILLIAM J. and JAMES W. MOSS. "A Total Program for the Severely Mentally Retarded," *Exceptional Children* (March 1962), 28:357-362.

>Pros and cons for the education of trainable mentally retarded children and the results of research studies. Suggestions are made for a total program for the severely retarded child and his family. Kirk, Karnes, and Kirk's model for a program for the severely retarded of all ages is presented.

401. [A, P] *To Meet the Challenge of the Handicapped Child, Report of the Governor's Commission to Study the Educational Needs of Handicapped Children.* Annapolis, Maryland: Maryland Gov. Comm. to Study Educ. Needs of Hand. Child., 1966, 75 pp.

>A special commission appointed in June 1966 studied the educational needs of Maryland's handicapped children. Public hearings were held, and public and private agencies submitted formal statements. Top priority recommendations were made on (1) extension of state financing, (2) administrative reorganization of the state

department of education, (3) scholarships and in-service training for professional personnel, and (4) inter-departmental coordination. In addition to these recommendations, the commission formulated objectives and administrative principles on special education and reported its suggestions concerning definition and classification, coordination and communication.

402. [AP, R] TRAPP, E. PHILIP and PHILIP HIMELSTEIN (ed.). "Incidence Figures of Exceptional Children in the United States," Chapter I in *Readings on the Exceptional Child.* New York: Appleton-Century-Crofts, 1962, 3-6.

The U. S. Office of Education conducted a survey of exceptional children in cities with 2500 population and over and in towns of less than 2500 if the State Department of Education reported that these towns maintained special education programs. The results of the survey are presented in both narrative and tabular forms. Definitions of exceptionalities that were used in reporting enrollment are given in the report.

403. [A] TRAVELSTEAD, CHESTER C. "Problems in the Education of Handicapped Children in Sparsely Settled Areas," *Exceptional Children* (September 1960), 27:52–55.

Discusses the six main problems that face educators of handicapped children in sparsely settled areas and offers possible solutions such as regional cooperation.

404. [O] TRIPPE, MATTHEW J. "Conceptual Problems in Research on Educational Provisions for Disturbed Children, *"Exceptional Children* (April 1963), 29:400–406.

Suggests a broadened concept of the organizational pattern of the school organized to broaden the child's role, to engage them in activities to help them in the many roles of the adult world; it also suggests a broadened conception of the role and function of teachers. It also suggests an increased sensitivity to situational crises in children's lives.

405. [AP] TWITCHELL, THEODORE GRANT. *Programs Initiated by Institutions of Higher Learning for Gifted High School Students of California,* University of Southern California (1964), 436 pp.

The purpose of the study was to investigate programs of advanced placement for gifted high school students of California who attend institutions of higher learning during part of their senior year. Conclusions were that merits of offering part- time college programs for mentally gifted high school students are widely accepted; improvement of all curriculum may be a result of this experimentation. High schools are challenged to develop a more suitable secondary curriculum to meet the students' needs. "Cockiness" and socially immature attitudes may result when students are poorly placed or counseled. There is a need for evaluation of advanced placement.

406. [A, P] *Type B Programs for the Trainable Mentally Handicapped in Michigan.* Lansing, Michigan: Michigan State Department of Public Instruction, 1963, 21 pp.

Administrative practices, including eligibility criteria and evaluation of the trainable mentally handicapped, teaching certification requirements, and the duties of teacher aides, are discussed in this guide.

407. [A] URIS, AUREN. *Developing Your Executive Skills.* New York: McGraw-Hill Book Company, 1955, 270 pp.

The A to Z of executive performance is Ability and Zeal. This book is addressed to both areas: Ability, or skill, experience, training and know-how; and Zeal, of motivation, drive, and applied effort. Writing in a lively style, Uris seeks to attract and assist the executive who wishes to improve his own performance. His long experience as head of human relations programs of the Research Institute of America qualifies him as a knowledgeable mentor for aspiring executives.

408. [A] VUILLEMOT, L. D. *Intermediate School District, Implications for Special Education.* Burnee, Ill.: Lake County Special Education District, 1967, 9 pp.

The compounding problems of a special education program in a school district of less than 15,000 population are outlined by the director of special education in an intermediate school district in Illinois. A variety of adaptive organizational structures is considered.

409. [A, S] VOELKER, PAUL H. "Administration and Supervision of Special Education Programs," Chapter 14 in *Education of Exceptional Children and Youth*, William M. Cruickshank and G. Orville Johnson, Editors. Englewood Cliffs, N.J.: Prentice-Hall, Inc., 1958.

An in-depth discussion of specialized professional skills and knowledge required to administer and supervise special education programs. Recruitment, selection, and training of superior teachers; inservice training; class size; identification services; housing; guidance and counseling services; reporting methods; transportation; and the roles of the state, the county, the local school systems, and state and private residential schools are dealt with in detail.

410. [A, S] VOELKER, PAUL H. and FRANCES A. MULLEN. "Organization, Administration, and Supervision of Special Education," NEA, *Review of Educational Research* (February 1963), 33:5-19.

This article is concerned with research directed at the overall task of providing special education services. In general, problems of organization, administration, and supervision have received little attention from researchers. Several lines of investigation should receive priority consideration: (a) determination of the most effective methods of organizing special education programs, (b) evaluation of instruction, (c) more complete inquiry into the incidence and prevalence of the various areas of exceptionality, and (d) follow-up studies of exceptional youth and adults.

411. [AP] WAGNER, GUY. "What Schools are Doing in Challenging the Rapid Learner," *Education 78,* The Palmer Company (September 1957), 78:59-62.
Gives resumes of six booklets dealing with plans for gifted children. Especially goes into a plan in which rapid learners are separated and chiefly associated with other gifted children. Also touches on stressing independent creative thinking in gifted children, grouping in a regular classroom, special ability groupings and accelerated promotion.

412. [AP] WALESKI, DOROTHY. "The Physically Handicapped in the Regular Classroom," *NEA Journal* (1964), 53: 12-16.
The practice of integrating handicapped children into the regular classroom presents certain difficulties for the teacher and the administrator. However, learning can take place with these children, provided that the teacher has a repertoire of techniques and skills to utilize the functioning aspect of the child's sensory-motor system. The author describes some benefits which result from the placement of handicapped children in the regular classroom, makes estimates of the number of children involved, and offers general recommendations and specific suggestions for the classroom teacher which help the child adjust to his school environment.

413. [A] WEBER, MAX. *The Theory of Social and Economic Organizations.* Edited by Talcott Parsons. Translated by A. M. Henderson and Talcott Parsons. 2d ed. New York: The Free Press, 1957, 436 pp.
A basic sociological analysis of bureaucracy, according to Weber, the most efficient form of administrative organization. The five characteristics of a bureaucracy on which Weber bases his theory are listed and discussed.

414. [A] WESTBY-GIBSON, DOROTHY. *Social Foundations of Education.* New York: The Free Press, 1967.
The text contains sections dealing with social control and support of the schools, organization of the schools, and new directions in curriculum. The school is viewed as a complex social organization.

415. [A] WHEELER, G. J. and D. F. JONES. *Business Data Processing: An Introduction.* Reading, Mass.: Addison-Wesley Publishing Company, Inc. 1966, 152 pp.

This book surveys the field of business data processing, and shows how data processing fits into an organization's overall operations. Terms and techniques used in data processing are explained clearly and comprehensively, and methods and applications of both manual and machine data processing are described. The latter part of the book deals with electronic data processing and explains the concepts of programming, flowcharting, operations research, systems analysis, etc.

416. [AP, R] WHELAN, RICHARD J. "Recent Trends in Educating Emotionally Disturbed Children," *Selected Convention Papers, 42nd Annual CEC Convention*, Chicago (March 1964), 271–276.

A brief historical resume of educational programs for emotionally disturbed children up to the present time. Certain specific experimental research contributions which may have important implications in terms of planning future learning experiences for these children are discussed.

417. [O] WILLENBERG, ERNEST P. "Critical Issues in Special Education: Internal Organization," *Exceptional Children* (March 1967), 33: 1–2.

Forms or types of internal organization to serve exceptional children are discussed. No single pattern is suitable for the needs of all exceptional children. The goal is each child's optimum education and rehabilitation. The concept of flexible internal organization can be scaled from a base requiring minimal modifications. Each successive level above base represents the need for greater modification in the social milieu of the child. Seven levels of varying degrees of modification are presented.

418. [A] WILLENBERG, ERNEST P. "Administration of Special Education: Aspects of a Professional Problem," *Exceptional Children* (1964), 30:194–195.

There is still no single source of comprehensive information providing a rationale, structure, and process for the administration of special education programs. There are simply no textbooks on the subject. Some of the needs for particular attention are a clearly formulated concept of service with the general aims and specific purposes of public education systems. The process of education of the exceptional child must be considered in the fabric of the operational interweavings that constitute the scheme and facilities devised for general education. Other problems in relief are the nature and scope of programs and services, both structural and organizational, and the relationship of instructional services for exceptional children. Among many other focuses are those on instrumentalities for program development, planning, and coordination.

419. [AP] WILLEY, NORMAN R. "An Examination of Public School Speech and Hearing Therapy Facilities," *Exceptional Children* (1961), 28:129-134.

A report of the inadequacies in therapy accommodations used by speech and hearing therapists in Indiana. Cooperation of the administrators and the state department of special education are needed in order to procure adequate facilities and programs.

420. [AP, R] WILLIAMS, CHARLES EDWARD. "Programs for the Educable Pupil in Trenton, New Jersey," *Dissertation Abstracts* (1960), 20:2648-2649.

The report of a study designed to examine an expanding program. Inadequacies were found, but in spite of these, the program was achieving stated objectives. Some recommendations were made.

421. [AP] WILSON, DONALD V. "Should the Disabled be Segregated?" *New Outlook for the Blind*, (November 1964), 58:277-280.

In developing programs for the handicapped, care should be taken to assure that these children have adequate opportunity for interaction with the regular classes where this seems to be feasible and appropriate.

422. [P] WINFORD, BETTY JEAN. *Achievement of Educable Mentally Handicapped Children as Affected by the Level of Teacher Preparation.* Doctor's Thesis, University of Virginia, Charlottesville (1964), 54 pp.

The study is concerned with the differences in effectiveness between teachers in special public school classes for the educable mentally retarded who differed in the degree of their special preparation and the manner of obtaining their preparation. It was found that the educable mentally handicapped children taught by teachers with part-time preparation achieved greater scores in reading than children taught by teachers with full-time preparation. It appears that the depth of teacher education is of greater importance than the manner in which it is acquired. Experience and preparation could be dependent on major variables affecting the achievement level of educable mentally handicapped children. An M. A. in special education was indicated by the study.

423. [AP, R] WISEMAN, JOSEPH A. "An Evaluation of the Special School Services Rendered Youth by Pupil Personnel Officials in Two Maryland County School Systems During a Three-Year Period Beginning in 1955-56 through 1957-58," *Dissertation Abstracts* (1961), 22:1897.

Referral procedures, follow-up activities, and some essential services;

e.g., psychological and psychiatric services for emotionally disturbed children, were lacking in the school systems evaluated.

424. [A] WISLAND, M. W. and T. D. VAUGHN. "Administrative Problems in Special Education," *Exceptional Children* (1964), 31:87-89.

An attempt to identify problems and problem areas which directors and supervisors are currently experiencing in special education to provide empirical evidence for developing better training programs. The factors considered as criteria are size, type of program, and experience of the individual in a current position. The results revealed that very few significant differences exist between the mean ratings of the various groups. A large number of comparisons made in the study could produce a number of statistically mean differences by chance alone. The results did not support the hypothesis that administrative and supervisory problems differ when they are grouped by size, type of program, or experience. However, guidelines can be weaned from the study in developing programs for training future administrators and supervisors in special education.

425. [A, O] WOLF, JAMES M. *The Blind Child with Concomitant Disabilities. American Foundation for the Blind Research Series Number 16.* New York: American Foundation for the Blind, 1967, 120 pp.

Data were collected from 48 chief administrators of schools enrolling 6,696 visually handicapped children to determine enrollment, disabilities, and services. Forty-six percent of the administrators reported that providing services for the multiply disabled blind child will become the major role of the residential school.

426. [AP] WOLFE, WILLIAM G. and L. LEON REID. "Survey of Cerebral Palsy in Texas — Austin, Texas." *The United Cerebral Palsy Association of Texas* (1958).

The background of the research problem, the definitions of terms to be used, a comprehensive review of the literature concerning cerebral palsy, procedures for the study, and the results are presented and discussed.

427. [A] WRIGHT, THEON and HENRY S. EVANS. *Public Relations and the Line Manager.* New York: American Management Association, 1964, 240 pp.

This public relations book is written with the belief that public relations is a management function. The basic functions of a public relations program are outlined and tools of measurement for control are given by the authors. They discuss top management's responsibility for initiating, organizing, and supporting public relations within a company. Although this book is primarily addressed to managers of business enterprises, its practical approach makes it useful for administrators of governmental agencies.

428. [A] YOUNIE, W. J. "A Survey of the Administration of Educational Programs for the Institutionalized Mentally Retarded," *American Journal of Mental Deficiency* (1965), 69:451-461.

    A survey on the educational programs of participating public institutions in the United States and Canada. The administrators' functions, responsibilities, and problems, as well as those of the total instructional staff, are described in terms of selection, salaries, retention, attrition, certification requirements, and inservice educational opportunities. Included in the report are summaries of the screening procedures, curriculum materials, instructional aids, and research activity. Other survey topics include support of the communities and interrelated departments.

429. [A, O] ZERAN, FRANKLIN R. and RICCIO, ANTHONY C. *Organization and Administration of Guidance Services.* Chicago, Ill.: Rand McNally & Co., 1962.

    The authors point out that organization and administration are essential ingredients which go toward distinguishing a program of guidance from incidental guidance, implementation is paramount for an effective program. They emphasize personal assistance to the individual after he has left the school. An important reference for all those concerned with guidance programs.

Selected abstracts on physical environment have been made available for this publication by the Council for Exceptional Children, William C. Geer, Executive Secretary. Project Staff — Bertram Berenson, Alan Abeson, and Deborah Peterson. Grace Warfield, Consultant.

430. EC 003 969
Publ. Date Apr 69
Abeson, Alan
ED pending
13 p.
The Physical Environment: A Brave New World.
Council For Exceptional Children, Washington, D. C.
EDRS not available
The Council For Exceptional Children, 1201 Sixteenth Street, N. W., Washington, D. C. 20036
Paper Presented At The Annual CEC Convention (Denver, Colorado, April 1969) And Published In CEC Selected Convention Papers, 1969.

The failure of classrooms to reflect educational programing and the inadequacy of facilities for exceptional children are cited. Needs in the planning and design of facilities for such children are enumerated as follows: to accommodate change in methods, materials, and equipment; to create expansible, convertible, versatile, and malleable space; to adjust to the child's changing needs as he grows; to involve practitioners in planning so they will utilize the potential of the space designed; and to articulate educational programs upon which to base the environment. Presented as analytical systems for assessing the physical environment-special education relationship are the strictly environmental and strictly educational systems and the system of environmental conceptualizations, which are described, include privacy, scale, consistency, transition, useability, and movement. Solutions demonstrated by slides collected by The Council for Exceptional Children's special project on Physical Environment and Special Education are reviewed, including multipurpose corridors, womb (or quiet) rooms, equipment modifications, storage areas, and architectural character. Physical environment is, in closing, envisioned as a teaching tool which may well advance education for exceptional children. (JD)

431. EC 003 961
Publ. Date 68
Abeson, Alan
ED pending
7 p.
The Design Process in Special Education Facility Planning.
Council For Exceptional Children, Washington, D. C.
EDRS not available
Council For Exceptional Children, NEA, 1201 Sixteenth Street, N.W., Washington, D. C. 20036.
Symposium Held At Annual International CEC Convention (46th, New York City, New York, April 14-20, 1968).

Factors which affect the quality of planning for special education facilities and the effectiveness of the educational program are considered. The problem of presenting the needs to the architect in sufficient detail is described and suggestions are made for bringing educators and architects together. The need for educators to clarify terminology and the need for architects to visit the schools and interview staff members and members of the planning committee are cited. Also discussed is the usefulness of thorough evaluation in determining real needs and desires rather than requiring popularized concepts which may not be used. (RP)

432. EC 002 942
Publ. Date 65
Abeson, Alan; Ackerman, Paul
ED 022 315
14 p.
An Architectural-Educational Investigation of Education and Training Facilities for Exceptional Children (National Education Association, Washington, D. C., September 9-10, 1965).
Council for Exceptional Children, Washington, D. C.
EDRS mf,hc
The Council For Exceptional Children, NEA, 1201 16th Street, N. W., Washington, D. C. 20036

The proceedings of a conference called to institute a dialogue between the architectural and educational professions are summarized. Areas considered include deterrents to efficient dialogue, the need for research, parameters of research (foundational questions; flexibility; furniture, materials, hardware, and teaching equipment; information transmission), 23 suggested educational needs of exceptional children with as many suggested architectural solutions, and building designs for these children following and resulting from the conference. (Author/JD)

433. ED 003 960
    Publ. Date Jan 67
    ED n.a.
    29 p.
    Architectural Considerations for Classrooms for Exceptional Children.
    Texas Education Agency, Austin, Division Of Special Education
    EDRS mf, hc

    Definitions are provided of the following exceptionalities: blind, partially sighted, physically handicapped, minimally brain injured, deaf, educable mentally retarded (primary, junior, and senior high levels), trainable mentally retarded, speech handicapped, and emotionally disturbed. Architectural guidelines specify classroom location, size, acoustical treatment, heat and light, ventilation, electrical outlets, bulletin boards and chalkboards, floors, and drinking fountain, sink, and counter space. Additional specifications are given for certain exceptionalities. (JD)

434. EC 003 877
    Publ. Date May 66
    Bailey, Roger And Others
    ED pending
    187 p.
    Mental Health Facilities for Inpatient Adolescents.
    Architectural Psychology Interdepartment Program, Salt Lake City, Utah
    National Institute of Mental Health, Bethesda, Maryland;
    Utah University, Salt Lake City, Department of Architecture:
    Utah University, Salt Lake City, Department of Psychology
    EDRS not available
    PH-43-65-1068

    Interviews with consultants and visits to institutions are analyzed to determine present practices and trends in treating adolescent mental patients. Information gathered concerns philosophy of treatment and program, the adolescent, and facilities. Three schemes for living areas and architectural character are considered, and suggestions are made and specifications offered for site, admitting and screening, administration and staff living areas, therapy areas, educational program and facilities, and ancillary and utility areas. Findings indicate that plans for facilities are dependent upon the staff-patient ratio and upon regional climactic and social problems, that adolescents require more space than adults; that facilities should be located convenient to the community they serve; and that they should be regarded as a residential school which also provides vocational education. Additional findings concern the ineffective nature of short term help, the need for a continuum of services and facilities within the community, and the use of additional and varied services to lessen the load placed on inpatient facilities. (JD)

435. EC 003 884
Publ. Date Jul 67
Bair, Howard V.; Leland, Henry
ED n.a.
27 p.
The Utilization and Design of Physical Facilities for the Rehabilitation of Mentally Retarded. Final Project Report.
Parsons State Hospital And Training Center, Kansas
Vocational Rehabilitation Administration (DHEW), Washington, D. C.
EDRS mf, hc
VRA-RD-1319-G-64

To. investigate the appropriate design and utilization of physical facilities being constructed as a rehabilitation center, a variety of centers was examined. Conclusions were that flexibility in construction of the physical plant, including nonpermanent walls and fixtures was necessary; program planning should be included in architectural discussions to avoid later modifications; facilities should be designed with the concept of a teaching hospital in mind; equipment and materials for program development, especially technical aids and audiovisual facilities, should be acquired on an experimental basis; design must be based on changing community needs; and the service, research, professional training, and demonstration areas should overlap and flow into and out of each other. Consideration was given to the role of the staff and the kinds of areas they would need, classrooms for training programs, a television studio and control room, advanced planning for installation of audiovisual equipment, varied use of the same space, and facilities for behavior modification training. (Author/RP)

436. EC 003 881
Publ. Date 67
Bayes, Kenneth
ED n.a.
58 p.
The Therapeutic Effect of Environment on Emotionally Disturbed and

Mentally Subnormal Children; A Kaufmann International Design Award Study, 1964-66.
EDRS not available
Kenneth Bayes, 37 Duke Street, London W1, England.

> Environmental influences on emotionally disturbed and mentally handicapped children and the relationship between environment and therapy are investigated. The nature of space and of perception, animal and human behavior, and architectural psychology are described; also described are subjects relating to planning and form: planning for social relationships, transition between areas, avoidance of ambiguity, architectural character and scale, consideration of the size of groups, corridors and circulation, room size and shape, flexibility, child participation, pattern and visual stimuli, furniture, and staff needs. Topics relating to color examined are color perception, the psycho physiological effect of color, color preferences, color schemes, and color and form. Sound, texture, temperature, time, smell, and symbolic significance are other sensory perceptions discussed; research methods and problems and research needs are suggested. A list of persons and institutions visited or consulted about environmental therapy is provided. (RP)

437. EC 003 967
Publ. Date Mar 69
Bednar, Michael J.; Haviland, David S.
ED n.a.
101 p.
The Role of the Physical Environment in the Education of Children with Learning Disabilities. A Position Paper.
Rensselaer Polytechnic Institute, Troy, New York, Center For Architectural Research
Educational Facilities Laboratories, New York, New York
EDRS mf,hc

> Concerned with the role of physical environment in the education of exceptional children, this position paper reviews the general problems and the roles of architects and educators in it. Exceptionality is discussed; learning disabilities are considered as a criterion for educational grouping instead of medical classifications; and the exceptionalities mental retardation, brain injury, social maladjustment, and emotional disturbance are categorized as learning disabilities. A portrait of a brain injured child is provided, and learning disabilities are further classified as perceptual (including sensory hyperactivity, reduced attention span, short memory and poor recall, perserveration, dissociation, and figure-background reversal) motor related (motor hyperactivity and poor motor skills), or psychosocial (poor self concept), distorted body image, and aggrava-

tion by social pressure. Special education programs and methods are described; the role of environment is discussed. The following are then presented: environmental variables, including space, light, color, clutter, sound, texture, climate, and shape; environmental characterizations, including space-time identity, ambiguity, articulation, transition, decisions and alternatives, consistency, scale, and sociopetal-sociofugal, privacy, territoriality, useability, movement, and character; and program factors, including changeability, educational tools, flexibility, the site, and integration and segregation of exceptional children. Directions are proposed for future environmental research in special education. (JD)

438. EC 003 875
Publ. Date 67
Benet, James And Others
ED pending
95 p.
SCSD: The Project and the Schools.
Educational Facilities Laboratories, New York, New York
EDRS not available
Education Facilities Laboratories, 477 Madison Avenue, New York, New York 10022.

A discussion of the School Construction Systems Development project (SCSD), conducted in California and responsible for 11 schools built or under constructions, mentions the consultant role of the staff, the role of local school districts, the development of component parts used in the schools, financial costs, the origins of the project, specifications, and the cooperation of manufacturers in developing the components. Educational requirements flexibility, school organization, environmental requirements, structure, acoustics, fire ratings,· roofing and tolerances, heating, air conditioning, ventilating, lighting, ceilings, performance criteria, partitions, casework and cabinets, and lockers are described, and diagrams are provided; also provided are pictures of the components in use, floor plans, and names, addresses, and construction data on the schools involved. Technical consultants are listed. (RP)

439. EC 003 968
Publ. Date 68
Berenson, Bertram
ED pending
3 p.
The Planned Environment: An Educational Tool.
Council For Exceptional Children, Washington, D. C.
EDRS not available
International Journal Of Educational Science; V2 P123-5 1968

Manipulation of the environment to produce behavior change is discussed in terms of the influence of the physical properties surrounding the learner. The concept of special spaces for special activities focuses on the use of hallways as a resource device. Caution is suggested in the area of flexibility as constancy can be beneficial. Ken Isaac's learning box, in which all six sides contained information, is described and recommended as a classroom resource center audiovisually and kinesthetically producing information which can be ordered and structured to meet individual needs. (RP)

440. EC 003 811
Publ. Date 62
Carter, John Harvey
ED pending
23 p.
Educational Environment for the Orthopedically Handicapped Including the Cerebral Palsied.
California State Department Of Education, Sacramento, Bureau Of Special Education
EDRS not available
John Harvey Carter, 417 20th Street, Sacramento, California 95814.

Prepared as a guide to planners and administrators, the report considers architectural problems in the design of educational facilities for orthopedically handicapped and cerebral palsied children. Factors influencing the learning process and selection of instructional materials are discussed; and daily programs suggesting subject areas, activities, equipment, and schedules are provided for the preprimary, primary, and advanced groups. Further aspects considered include therapy facilities, shop, speech, physical and occupational therapy activities, kitchens, resting room, and classrooms and suggested classroom equipment. Also described are special equipment requirements and sizes, controls for lights and so on, braille identification of facilities, hazards, walks, ramps, toilet rooms, playground facilities and equipment, color, floor materials, storage, and access. Nine references are cited. (JD)

441. EC 303 878
Publ. Date 18 Apr 68
Colvin, Ralph W.
ED pending
8 p.
The Design Process in Special Education Facility Planning Applied to a Day and Residential Facility for the Emotionally Disturbed and Brain Injured.
Child Welfare League Of America, New York, New York
EDRS not available

Paper Presented At The Annual Convention Of The Council For Exceptional Children (New York, New York, April 18, 1968).

The development of a residential treatment center for emotionally disturbed children considers the need for a flexible structure, the number of children that can best be cared for, and the preferable size of educational, recreational, or living groups. The teachers' needs are discussed in terms of small groups and the nearness of offices of supportive staff members. Suggestions are made for consultation with technically knowledgeable people in areas for research and professional training which involve problems of sound and light control, air conditioning, observation areas, and audiovisual equipment. Planning for privacy in bathrooms and bedrooms, classroom size, and nonstimulating decor are discussed. Also discussed is the provision of attractive surroundings as a means of introducing the child to beauty. (RP)

442. EC 000 422
Publ. Date Sep 66
Dale, D.M.C.
ED pending
4 p.
Units for Deaf Children.
London University Institute Of Education, England
EDRS not available
Volta Review; V68 N7 P496–9 Sept 1966
Reprint From The Times Educational Supplement, London.

Integration of deaf and normally hearing children in the schools is considered. An experiment in New Zealand which provides a small room for six to eight deaf students adjacent to a regular class is described; provisions of the program include two teachers, combined classes for most subjects, and special help in communication skills for the deaf. Advantages mentioned are the social benefits to the children and the economic advantages of having the children live at home rather than in a boarding school. A floor plan of the classrooms is provided. (RP)

443. EC 003 656
Publ. Date 68
ED n.a.
261 p.
Designing Instructional Facilities for Teaching the Deaf: The Learning Module; Symposium on Research and Utilization of Educational Media for Teaching the Deaf (4th, Lincoln, Nebraska, February 5–7, 1968.)
Nebraska University, Lincoln, Department of Educational Administration; Midwest Regional Media Center For The Deaf, Lincoln, Nebraska

Office of Education (DHEW), Washington, D. C., Captioned Films For The Deaf Branch
EDRS mf, hc
OEC-3-7-000199-0199(019)

> Eleven conference papers treat designing learning modules, or complete instructional facilities for the deaf. The following aspects are considered: the changing classroom, a multimedia approach to teaching American history, a project design for a special school, and educational implications of architecture for the deaf. Further topics are acoustical design of classrooms for the deaf, the use of amplification in educating deaf children, furnishings in the workshop classroom, and lighting in the learning module. Creating environments for learning, providing through architecture for social needs, and planning the deaf child's complete formal education are also discussed; a report from Captioned Films for the Deaf, conference and discussion summaries, foreword, and introduction are provided. Appended are the program and roster of participants. (JD)

444. EC 003 807
Publ. Date Oct 55
Foote, Franklin M.
ED pending
5 p.
Classrooms for Partially Seeing Children
National Society For The Prevention Of Blindness, New York, New York
EDRS not available
Exceptional Children; V22 N1 P318-20, 41-2 Oct 1955

> Aspects of special classrooms or resource rooms for partially sighted children are described, including type and placement of furniture, special equipment, storage, illumination of the room, and dimensions of the sight conservation room. (JD)

445. EC 003 876
Publ. Date 66
Green, Alan C., Ed. And Others
ED pending
207 p.
Educational Facilities with New Media. Final Report.
National Education Association, Washington, D. C., Department Of Audiovisual Instruction;
Rensselaer Polytechnic Institute, Troy, New York, Center For Architectural Research
Office Of Education (DHEW), Washington, D. C.
EDRS not available

National Education Association, 1201 Sixteenth Street, N. W., Washington, D. C. 20036 (Stock No. 071-02302, $4.50).

An overview of learning media introduces a guide for policy makers on educational facilities and new media. Concerns and directions in contemporary education, the role of media in innovations, status and trends in learning media, implications for planning, and programing, and defining building needs are considered. A guide for the design professions provides information on learning media and facilities, general principles for planning schools, nine categories of facility types: independent study, small group, medium group, large group, flexible group, renovated classrooms, resource facilities, production and support facilities, and new building types; a design criteria is also provided. Technical concerns discussed are lighting, acoustics, climate, furniture, projection systems, and other equipment. An appendix lists resumes of three meetings on facilities and meeting participants. (RP)

446. EC 003 810
Publ. Date (66)
ED pending
6 p.
A Model Setting for a Re-Ed School.
Tennessee Re-Ed Program, Nashville
EDRS not available
Tennessee Re-Ed Program, 3409 Belmont Boulevard, Nashville, Tennessee 37215

The ideal site of Re-Ed schools for disturbed children is described as being both residential and near to a university center for consultation and personnel purposes; present sites are discussed. Cottages to hold eight children are proposed as living units; their components and spaces are listed. Eating arrangements, classrooms, and additional school facilities are also described. (JD)

447. EC 003 808
Publ. Date 60
Nugent, Timothy J.
ED pending
15 p.
Design of Buildings to Permit Their Use by the Physically Handicapped; A National Attack on Architectural Barriers.
National Society For Crippled Children And Adults, Chicago, Illinois
President's Committee On Employment Of The Physically Handicapped, Washington, D. C.
EDRS not available
Reproduced From New Building Research, Fall 1960, Publication No. 910

Building Research Institute, National Academy Of Sciences, National Research Council.

Concerned with the nonambulatory disabled, the semi-ambulatory, the sight and hearing handicapped, and the cerebral palsied and other neurologically impaired, the paper considers the increased numbers of those so handicapped and describes the need for facilities they can use. Basic research and development projects reported include both research reviews and experiments assessing materials, design, and handicapped persons in normal environments. Two programs are surveyed: The University of Illinois rehabilitation-education program and the adaptation and construction of facilities at the University; and the American Standards Association Project to make buildings and facilities accessible and usable to the physically handicapped (ASA Project A-117). An appendix provides a work outline for the ASA Project which lists specifications for several types of facilities. (JD)

448. EC 003 976
Publ. Date Apr 67
ED n.a.
34 p.
Outdoor Recreation Planning for the Handicapped. Bureau of Outdoor Recreation Technical Assistance Bulletin.
Department Of The Interior, Washington, D. C., Bureau Of Outdoor Recreation; National Recreation And Park Association, Washington, D. C.
EDRS mf
Superintendent Of Documents, U. S. Government Printing Office, Washington, D. C. 20402 ($0.40)

The requirement that the handicapped be given special consideration as prerequisite to state participation in the Land and Water Conservation Fund Program is stated, and the following groups of handicapped are specified: the physically, visually, and aurally handicapped, and those persons with special health problems, the mentally retarded, the emotionally disturbed, and the multiply handicapped. Their limitations and what can be done in general and in research to help are discussed; modification of playgrounds, swimming facilities and equipment, camping and fishing and boating; national, state and private agencies in several areas which can help are mentioned and their addresses are given. Case histories are provided of a self guiding nature trail in Aspen, Colorado, camping in San Francisco, California, and adaptation of recreation facilities in New York State (including park planning, access, toilet facilities, swimming pools, picnic areas, play areas, and miscellaneous facilities). Sixty-four references are cited. (JD)

449. EC 003 974
      Publ. Date Spr 64
      Relocatable School Facilities.
      ED pending
      59 p.
      Educational Facilities Laboratories, New York, New York
      EDRS not available
      Educational Facilities Laboratories, 477 Madison Avenue, New York, New
      York 10022

> The support that fluctuating school enrollments and the shortage of
> classrooms lend to the need for relocatable facilities is discussed; the
> development of these facilities is considered. Guides for planning
> relocatable structures include the following: four basic types and
> adequate space, appearance of the units, and the relationship of the
> units to the main buildings; portable facilities and size limitations,
> structural system, limits to moving, and foundation; size limits,
> structure, and foundation of mobile, divisible, and demountable
> facilties. Factors to consider in calculating costs, a checklist of items
> relevant to moving the facilities, and an estimate of demounting
> costs are provided. Case studies of movable classrooms in 21 cities
> give specifications and photographs of the facilities. New develop-
> ments in portable units and a plan for the future are included. (RP)

450. EC 003 657
      Publ. Date May 66
      ED pending
      124 p.
      Salmon, F. Cuthbert; Salmon, Christine F.
      Sheltered Workshops; An Architectural Guide.
      Oklahoma State University, Stillwater, School of Architecture
      Vocational Rehabilitation Administration (DHEW), Washington, D. C.
      EDRS not available

> Based on the observation of 24 sheltered workshops of diverse types
> and sizes, the guide presents information on architectural program-
> ing and planning. The role of the sheltered workshop, community
> needs, site considerations, and the program are described. In
> addition, planning principles, work principles, and the physical plant
> are discussed and graphically illustrated. An appendix provides the
> following; a checklist for planning and construction; an analysis of
> materials and methods of construction; a glossary of commonly used
> terms; American Standard Specifications for making buildings and
> facilities accessible to and usable by the physically handicapped; and
> a list of workshops studied. (JD)

451. EC 003 880
      Publ. Date Oct 64

Salmon, F. Cuthbert; Salmon, Christine F.
ED pending, 82 p.
The Blind, Space Needs for Rehabilitation.
Oklahoma State University, Stillwater
Vocational Rehabilitation Administration (DHEW), Washington, D. C.
EDRS not available

> Based on the observation and analysis of 14 rehabilitation centers for the blind, the report presents to both architect and administrator the following environmental considerations: geographical location; community features, site considerations, site development, program development, planning principles, and environmental experience. Areas of rehabilitation activity explained for the architect include medical services, psychological and social services, mobility and orientation, physical conditioning, communications, occupational therapy, techniques of daily living, vocational evaluation, recreation, residential centers, administration and general activities, and staff-client space estimate. Thirty-five illustrations and 23 references are provided. (JD)

452. EC 003 978
Publ. Date 65
ED pending
765 p.
School Environment Research Publication No. 1; Environmental Abstracts.
Michigan University, Ann Arbor, Architectural Research Laboratory
Educational Facilities Laboratories, Inc., New York, New York
EDRS not available

> Annotated abstracts are presented of selected documents which describe the relationships linking environment with human behavior. Each abstract provides bibliographic information and a summary of the document; some abstracts state the document's conclusions and comments. The bulk of the literature abstracted is from periodicals and is either research or reviews of research. The abstracts are arranged in five categories. The first category, Environment and the Human Senses, includes abstracts on stimulus through the visual, auditory, or olfactory sensory channel, on collateral stimulus through several channels, and on equipment design; the second, Behavior and the Atmospheric Environment, annotates documents on problems related to the atmosphere in general, behavioral problems related to temperature only, and problems related to temperature and humidity. Behavior and the Luminous Environment, the third category, contains problems related to illumination in general and to intensity of illumination, influence of chromatic differentials, and illumination systems and intensity standards; the fourth, Behavior and the Sonic Environment, ranges over the effect

of sound on behavior, physiological and psychological reactions to sonic variations, and communication and task performance in relation to sound; and Behavior and the Social Environment, the final category, consists of characteristics of group composition, the individual in relation to group situations, task performance related to individuals or groups, and learning related to the individual and the group.(JD)

453. EC 002 861
Publ. Date (65)
Vanston, A. Roake and Others
ED 024 189
55 p.
Design of Facilities for the Mentally Retarded; Diagnosis and Evaluation, Education and Training, Living Units. Hospital and Medical Facilities Series.
Public Health Service (DHEW), Washington, D. C., Division of Hospital And Medical Facilities
EDRS mf
PHS-1181-C-1
Superintendent Of Documents, U. S. Government Printing Office, Washington, D. C. 20402 ($0.35).

Elements of architectural planning of new physical facilities for the mentally retarded detailed include programing and writing the project program. Design concepts are considered, and the following are specified: types of physical facilities with sample floor plans; elements of physical facilities, such as staff offices, activity areas, living units, and ancillary areas; basic planning consideration; and construction costs. A chart treats four levels of retardation; tables suggest areas for various facilities and recommend lighting levels. A bibliography cites 23 items. (LE)

annotated list of agencies and organizations concerned with exceptional children *

Alexander Graham Bell Association for the Deaf, Inc.
1537 35th St., NW, Washington, D. C. 20007

The Association works to promote the teaching of speech and lipreading and the use of residual hearing to the deaf. (I, II, V) Membership is open to interested persons for $12 a year. The official journal of the Association is *The Volta Review* (9 issues yearly, $12.50). Numerous books and pamphlets (some free) are published, as well as a newsletter, "Speaking Out." Biennial meetings are held in even numbered years, regional meetings in odd numbered years.

American Academy for Cerebral Palsy
University Hospital School, Iowa City, Iowa 52240

The Academy strives to foster and stimulate professional education, research, and interest in cerebral palsy and related disorders and to correlate all aspects of this endeavor for the welfare of those with the handicap. (III, IV, VI) Publications are the *Journal of Developmental Medicine and Child Neurology.* An annual meeting is held in November or December.

American Academy of Pediatrics
1801 Hinman Avenue, Evanston, Illinois 60201

A national organization of specialty board certified pediatricians in the United States, Canada, and Latin America, the American Academy of Pediatrics fosters and stimulates interest in pediatrics and correlates all aspects of the work for the welfare of children which come within the

*Reprinted by permission of Council for Exceptional Children, Information Center on Exceptional Children.

scope of pediatrics. (I, III, IV, V, VI) Membership is limited to specialty board certified pediatricians and other certified physicians (affiliate members). State chapters have been established in all 50 states and in practically all countries in Latin America. Canadian members belong to proximal state chapters in the U. S. The Academy sponsors an annual national meeting, an annual regional meeting, postgraduate courses, and regional conferences. Publications are the monthly journal, *Pediatrics*, and a bimonthly newsletter.

American Academy of Private Practice in Speech Pathology and Audiology
P. O. Box 53217, State Capital Station, Oklahoma City, Oklahoma 73105
The Academy's purpose is to foster the highest ideals and principles of private practice in speech pathology and audiology within the American Speech and Hearing Association. (VI) Membership is limited to those who hold membership in and certification of clinical competence by the American Speech and Hearing Association, have earned the doctoral degree in speech pathology or audiology, have 5 years of experience in the field, and are actively engaged in private practice. Membership dues are $25 annually. Conventions are held biannually. The periodical publication is *Bulletin of American Academy of Private Practices in Speech Pathology and Audiology.*

American Association for Health, Physical Education, and Recreation
1201 16th St., NW. Washington, D. C. 20036
A national organization to support, encourage, and provide guidance for personnel who are developing and conducting school and community programs in health education, physical education, and recreation, AAHPER includes professional, student, and associate members. (I, III) Periodical publications are the *Journal of Health, Physical Education, and Recreation* (which includes a monthly column, "Programs for the Handicapped"), the *Research Quarterly*, and "Challenge" (bi-monthly newsletter dealing with physical education and recreation for the mentally retarded). Other publications are also issued. AAHPER includes six district associations and state associations. National, district, and state association conventions are held annually in addition to numerous national, district, and local conferences dealing with specific topics. One unit of AAHPER is Programs for the Handicapped which is designed to provide leadership preparation, research, interpretation and development of programs, and distribution of materials for all areas of adapted physical education, corrective therapy, recreation for the ill and handicapped, therapeutic recreation, and health and safety problems of the handicapped.

American Association of Psychiatric Clinics for Children
250 W. 57th St., Rm. 1032, Fish Bldg.
New York, N. Y. 10019
The purposes of this Association are to provide for the coordination of the

activities of psychiatric clinics serving children in the U. S., its territories, and Canada; to help maintain the highest possible standards of clinic practice; to provide opportunities for the exchange of ideas, and for mutual help in the study and solution of clinic problems; to promote the training of clinic personnel; to cooperate with appropriate groups or organizations doing professional placement work in the clinic field; to cooperate with appropriate organizations throughout the world whose purposes may coincide with those of the Association; and to carry on such activities as may advance the field of child psychiatry. (I, III, V) Membership is limited to clinics and other organizations offering psychiatric services to children and meeting specific membership requirements. Annual meetings are conducted in March and November. A Membership Directory is published annually.

American Association of Workers for the Blind, Inc.
1511 K St., NW, Suite 637,
Washington, D. C. 20005

The American Association of Workers for the Blind works to render all possible assistance to the promotion of all phases of work for and in the interest of the blind and to the prevention of blindness throughout the Americas. (I, III, VI) Membership ($15 regular, $5 student) is open to persons interested in the welfare of the blind or in the prevention of blindness. State and local chapters exist throughout the country. Periodical publications are *Blindness* (annually), *The New Outlook for the Blind* (monthly, $6), annual convention proceedings, pertinent papers, and the newsletter "News and Views." In addition, professional handbooks are published. Meetings include biennial conventions, biennial regional conventions, annual state chapter conventions, and other institutes and workshops.

American Association on Mental Deficiency
5201 Connecticut Ave., NW, Washington, D. C. 20015

The organization works to promote human progress and the general welfare of mentally subnormal and deficient persons by furthering the creation and dissemination of knowledge of mental deficiency, by facilitating cooperation among professional persons engaged in work in the field of mental deficiency and allied fields, and by encouraging the highest standards of treatment of the mentally deficient. (III,VI) There are several membership classifications for both experienced professionals and other interested persons. Dues range from $8 to $25 according to membership classification. Periodical publications are the *American Journal of Mental Deficiency and Mental Retardation* (both bimonthly). In addition, books and monographs are published. An annual national convention and 10 annual regional conventions are held.

American Corrective Therapy Association, Inc.
811 St. Margaret's Rd., Chillicothe, Ohio 45601

> The work of the Association is directed toward applying the principles,
> tools, techniques, and psychology of medically oriented physical educa-
> tion to assist the physician in treating handicapped individuals. (I, II, III,
> V, VI) Active membership ($25 annually) is for those with a physical
> education degree and clinical training. Professional and associate member-
> ships are $10 annually. Twelve regional chapters have been established.
> *The American Corrective Therapy Journal* is published six times annually.
> A national conference is held annually in addition to clinical and business
> meetings of regional chapters.

American Foundation for the Blind
15 W. 16th St., New York, N. Y. 10011

> The American Foundation for the Blind is a private, nonprofit agency
> which serves as a clearinghouse on all pertinent information about
> blindness and promotes the development of educational, rehabilitation,
> and social welfare services for the blind and deaf children and adults. (I,
> III, IV, V, VI) Services include publications in print, large type, recorded,
> and braille forms (limited), manufacture and sale of special aids and
> appliances for use by blind people, and recording and manufacture of
> talking books. Additional services are field consultation, research, person-
> nel referral service, legislative consultation and action, public education,
> operation of a special library, fostering of improved programs, service
> information and referral, and processing and distribution of identification
> cards for one-fare travel concession for blind persons. Several periodical
> publications are issued including "AFB Newsletter" (quarterly, free), *New
> Outlook for the Blind* (monthly; $6, ink, braille, recorded), and "Talking
> Book Topics" (six times a year, free to blind persons). Numerous
> professional and public information books and pamphlets are published
> (some free). Institutes and conferences are held.

American Heart Association, Inc.
44 E. 23rd St., New York, N. Y. 10010

> Through programs of research, public and professional education, and
> community services, the American Heart Association, Inc., works to
> reduce premature death and disability caused by cardiovascular diseases.
> (I, III, IV, VI) Membership is open to interested persons. Dues range from
> $2 to $5 annually. Periodical publications are *American Heart* (quarterly),
> "Heart Research Newsletter" (quarterly), *Management Digest* (quarterly),
> *Circulation Research* (monthly), *Cardiovascular Nursing* (quarterly),
> *Stroke — a Journal of Cerebral Circulation*, and "The Heart Bulletin"
> (bimonthly). Affiliated Heart Associations exist throughout the United
> States. Annual scientific sessions, an annual meeting, and various local
> conferences on cardiovascular diseases are held.

The American Legion, National Child Welfare Division
P. O. Box 1055, Indianapolis, Ind. 46206

The Division is a child welfare program with emphasis on services and assistance to children of veterans. Through legislative efforts, dissemination of information on child welfare problems, direct aid to veterans' children, and cooperation with other national organizations, it seeks to improve conditions for all children. (I, II, IV, V) Membership in The American Legion is limited to wartime veterans; dues vary according to local chapters. Five annual regional child welfare conferences are held.

American Nurses' Association, Inc.
10 Columbus Circle, New York, N. Y. 10019

The ANA is a national professional organization which works to foster high standards of nursing practice and promote the welfare and professional and educational advancement of nurses for better nursing care. (I, III, IV, VI) Five divisions are responsible for advancing the standards, knowledge, and skills in specific areas of nursing practice. Membership is open to registered nurses. Dues are $12.50 a year. Publications are the *American Journal of Nursing* (monthly, $5), "ANA in Action" (bimonthly membership publication), division newsletters, and monographs. The Association has 55 state and territorial associations and holds a biennial conference in even numbered years and regional clinical conferences in odd numbered years.

American Occupational Therapy Association, Inc.
251 Park Avenue S., New York, N. Y. 10010

Designed to promote and improve the practice of occupational therapy, the Association accepts members who have a degree in occupational therapy and who have passed the registration examination of the Association. (I, III, VI) Dues are $30 annually. *The American Journal of Occupational Therapy* (bimonthly, $7.50) and other periodicals and publications are issued. Conferences are held annually. Affiliations exist with regional or state occupational therapy associations.

American Optometric Association
7000 Chippewa St., St. Louis, Mo. 63119

As a federation of associations of state, zone, and local optometric societies, the American Optometric Association works to advance, improve and enhance the vision care of the public and to encourage and assist in the improvement of the art and science of optometry, (I, II, III, IV, V, VI) Membership is for optometrists who have graduated from an accredited school of optometry and passed the licensing examination of the board of optometry in the state of practice. Dues vary according to the local society. Publications of the Association are the *Journal of the American Optometric Association* (monthly, $7.50) and "The AOA News" (monthly). An annual congress and various educational conferences are held.

American Orthopsychiatric Association, Inc.
1790 Broadway, New York, N. Y. 10019
>The Association works to unite and provide a common meeting ground for those engaged in the study and treatment of problems of human behavior and to foster research and spread information concerning scientific work in the field of human behavior, including all forms of abnormal behavior. (VI) Membership ($25 for members, $35 for fellows) is limited to those who have worked 3 years in the field, meet the requirements of the professional organization in their discipline, and have obtained the masters degree. Publications include the *American Journal of Orthopsychiatry* (5 issues yearly, $12), the Association newsletter, and individual books. An annual scientific meeting is held.

American Physical Therapy Association
1740 Broadway, New York, N. Y. 10019
>The organization fosters the development and improvement of physical therapy service and education through the coordinated action of physical therapists, allied professional groups, citizens, agencies, and schools to meet the physical therapy needs of people. (I, III, V, VI) Several types of professional and nonprofessional membership are available. Local chapters work with the national organization. Publications include the monthly periodical *Physical Therapy* (monthly, $10), a bimonthly listing of available physical therapy positions, monographs and other professional publications, career literature, and visual aids for rental or purchase. The Association holds an annual conference and periodic symposia.

American Printing House for the Blind
1839 Frankfort Ave., Louisville, Ky. 40206
>Operating under an annual appropriation from the U. S. Congress to promote the education of the blind, the Printing House is a nonprofit publisher of literature for the blind and partially seeing. (I, III) Braille books, braille music, large type textbooks, talking books, recorded educational tapes, and tangible and educational aids for the blind are produced.

American Psychiatric Association
1700 18th St., NW, Washington, D. C. 20009
>Purposes of the Association are to further the study of the nature, treatment, and prevention of mental disorders, to promote mental health and the care of the mentally ill, to advance standards for mental hospitals and facilities, and to make psychiatric knowledge available. (I, III, VI) Membership is open to physicians with some specialized training and experience in psychiatry; dues range from $15 to $55. The Association includes local societies and district branches. Publications include *The American Journal of Psychiatry* (monthly $12), "Psychiatric News"

(monthly newsletter, $3), *Hospital and Community Psychiatry* (monthly, $8), special books and pamphlets, reference works, and research reports. The Association holds an annual meeting and an annual mental hospital institute in addition to divisional meetings and regional research conferences.

American Psychological Association
1200 17th St., NW, Washington, D. C. 20036

The purpose of the American Psychological Association is to advance psychology as a science and as a means of promoting human welfare. Membership is open to professionals who have met specific requirements of education and experience dependent upon class of membership (dues range from $30 to $45). Within the Association are 29 divisions and affiliated state associations. Annual conventions are held in the fall. Journal publications are *American Psychologist* (monthly, $10), *Contemporary Psychology* (monthly, $10), *Journal of Abnormal Psychology* (bimonthly, $10), *Journal of Applied Psychology* (bimonthly, $10), *Journal of Comparative and Physiological Psychology* (bimonthly, $30), *Journal of Consulting and Clinical Psychology* (bimonthly, $10), *Journal of Educational Psychology* (bimonthly, $10), *Journal of Experimental Psychology* (monthly, $40), *Journal of Personality and Social Psychology* (monthly, $30), *Psychological Abstracts* (monthly, $40), *Psychological Bulletin* (monthly, $20), *Psychological Review* (bimonthly, $10), *Developmental Psychology* (bimonthly, $10). Also published are the *Employment Bulletin* (monthly, $8), convention proceedings, and position papers.

American Public Health Association, Inc.
1740 Broadway, New York, N. Y. 10019

The Association works to protect and promote public and personal health and acts as an accrediting agency for schools of public health. (I, III, VI) Membership is open to professionals working in public health and to persons interested in public health (dues range from $15 to $25). Periodical publications are the *American Journal of Public Health and the Nation's Health* (monthly, $15), *Health Laboratories Sciences* (quarterly, $6), and *Medical Care* (bimonthly, $10). Handbooks, guides, monographs, and other publications are also issued. The Association meeting is conducted annually.

American Rehabilitation Counseling Association of the American Personnel and Guidance Association
1607 New Hampshire Ave., NW, Washington, D. C. 20009

The Association which is one of eight divisions of the American Personnel and Guidance Association works to emphasize the social concept that conservation of human resources merits skillful services in the rehabilitation of the handicapped. (III) Membership is for professionals, associates, and students: dues range from $11 to $22. *Rehabilitation Counseling Bulletin* (quarterly, $5) is published by the American Rehabilitation Counseling Association and various books, periodicals, and films are available through the American Personnel and Guidance Association. ARCA has state and local branches and participates in the APGA Annual Convention.

American Schizophrenia Foundation
Box 160, Ann Arbor, Mich. 48107

By promoting research and public and professional education on schizophrenia, the Foundation works for the betterment of schizophrenic patients and their relations with society. (III, IV) Various categories of membership are available to interested persons. The Foundation sponsors forums, conferences, and committee meetings and publishes *Schizophrenia* (quarterly) and "Schizophrenia: Newsletter of the ASF" (quarterly).

The American Speech and Hearing Association
9030 Old Georgetown Rd., Washington, D. C. 20014

The Association is a scientific and professional organization which encourages basic scientific study of the processes of individual human speech and hearing, fosters improvement of therapeutic procedures with such disorders, and stimulates the exchange and dissemination of information. (I, III, V, VI) Members must hold a masters degree or equivalent; dues are $32 a year. Three journals are published: the *Journal of Speech and Hearing Disorders* (quarterly, $15), the *Journal of Speech and Hearing Research* (quarterly, $15), and *ASHA Journal* (monthly, $15). Monographs and reports are published irregularly. Twenty-eight state associations sponsor institutes and workshops and an annual convention is held.

Association for Children with Learning Disabilities
2200 Brownsville Rd., Pittsburgh, Pa. 15210

The Association is designed to advance the education and general welfare of children and youth of normal or potentially normal intelligence who have learning disabilities of a perceptual, conceptual, or coordinative nature or related problems. (I, II, V, VI) Membership, available through the state organization, if established, or through the national organization, is open to parents and professionals. An annual conference is held as well as regional conferences. *Items of Interest* (monthly) and annual conference proceedings are published.

Association for Education of the Visually Handicapped
711 14th St., NW, Washington, D. C. 20005

The Association works to provide periodicals and other communicative media to evaluate problems and provide solutions, to disseminate professional information, and to stimulate an effort toward higher standards in personnel programs and facilities. (I, III, VI) Membership is available to professional workers, parents, and interested adults (dues range from $15 to $25). Publications are the newsletter "Fountainhead" (5 times yearly, $4) and the journal *Outlook.*

The Association of Rehabilitation Centers, Inc.
7979 Old Georgetown Rd., Washington, D. C. 20014

As a federation of rehabilitation centers the Association helps to improve rehabilitation service to handicapped and disabled persons by providing a focal point for unified effective joint action, cooperation with other professional associations, and mutual consultation, together with the study and exchange of ideas among rehabilitation facilities. (I, III, V, VI) Publications include manuals, guides, and workshop proceedings. An annual workshop and several educational seminars are sponsored.

Boy Scouts of America
U. S. Rts. 1 & 130, New Brunswick, N. J. 08903

With its 508 local councils, Boy Scouts of America works to provide scouting programs for all boys, both normal and handicapped. Units for all types of handicapped boys have been established throughout the United States. (I, II, III, IV, VI) Scouting affiliation is open to all boys. The national registration fee is $1; unit dues are determined by the boys themselves. Publications include numerous books, films, and pamphlets (some free). A meeting is held annually.

Child Study Association of America
9 E. 89th St., New York, N. Y. 10028

The Association works to stimulate and further the education of adults in all that pertains to the moral, mental, and physical training and education of children. (I, III, VI) Membership is open to all interested persons and groups; dues are $15. A conference is held annually.

Conference of Executives of American Schools for the Deaf
c/o Dr. Howard M. Quigley, 5034 Wisconsin Ave., NW, Washington, D. C. 20016

The Conference works to further the welfare of the deaf by promoting the management and operation of schools for the deaf along the broadest and most efficient lines and establishing and maintaining minimum standards for teachers through certification procedures and approval of teacher training centers. (I, II) Membership is comprised of executive heads of schools for deaf children in the United States, Canada, and Mexico (dues range from $50 to $100). *American Annals of the Deaf* (5 issues yearly, $6) is published in conjunction with The Convention of American Instructors of the Deaf. The Conference holds an annual meeting and cosponsors the International Conference on Education of the Deaf.

The Convention of American Instructors of the Deaf
c/o Dr. Howard M. Quigley, Executive Secretary, 5034 Wisconsin Ave., NW,
Washington, D. C. 20016
Comprised of persons engaged in educating the deaf, the organization
provides an opportunity for the interchange of views concerning methods
and means of educating the deaf. (III) Publications are *American Annals of
the Deaf* (5 issues yearly, $6), "News Release" (5 issues yearly), and
convention proceedings.

The Council for Exceptional Children
1499 Jefferson Davis Highway, Suite 900, Jefferson Plaza, Arlington, Va. 22202
As a professional organization, CEC works to promote the adequate
education of handicapped and gifted children through cooperation with
educational and other organizations and individuals and through encouraging good professional relationships with various disciplines. (III) Membership, which is organized with chapters at the local level and federations or
branches at the state or provincial level, is open to special educators and
other interested persons. Dues range from $15 to $21 depending upon
state of residence. CEC contains the following divisions for persons
interested in a particular exceptionality or aspect of special education:
Association for the Gifted; Council of Administrators of Special Education; Council for Children with Communication Disorders; Division for
Children with Learning Disabilities; Division on the Physically Handicapped, Hospitalized, and Homebound; Division for the Visually Handicapped; Division on Mental Retardation; and Teacher Education Division.
Publications include *Exceptional Children* (10 issues yearly, $10), *Educa-
tion and Training of the Mentally Retarded* (quarterly, $5), *Teaching
Exceptional Children* (quarterly, $5), books and pamphlets, research
monographs, and annual convention papers. Annual international conventions, regional conferences, and special conferences are conducted.

Council of Organizations Serving the Deaf
4201 Connecticut Ave., NW, Suite 210, Washington, D. C. 20008
The Council, working to promote the best interests of deaf persons, serves
as a central clearing house and contact point for information and
combined action by national organizations serving deaf persons. (I, III, IV)
Membership is comprised of organizations (dues from $35 to $100) and
interested individuals ($5). The Council publishes a periodic newsletter
and the proceedings of the annual forum.

Council on Education of the Deaf
c/o Dr. George T. Pratt, President, Clarke School for the Deaf, Northampton,
Mass. 01060
Comprised of representatives from The Alexander Graham Bell Association for the Deaf, The Conference of Executives of American Schools for
the Deaf, and the Convention of American Instructors of the Deaf, the

Council provides a forum for those organizations concerned primarily with the education of deaf children, so that problems and concerns might be brought under advisement and solutions sought. (I, III) One international congress has been held; future congresses are planned.

Girl Scouts of the United States of America
830 3rd Ave., New York, N. Y. 10002

Working with 400 local Girl Scout Councils, the national organization is designed to inspire girls with the highest ideals of character, conduct, patriotism, and service so that they may become happy and resourceful citizens. (I, II, III, V, VI) Active membership is granted to any girl from age 7 to 17 who has the endorsement of the local council (dues are $1). Publications include *Handicapped Girls* and *Girl Scouting* as well as handbooks, pamphlets, books, and periodicals. The National Council of Girl Scouts meets every 3 years.

Goodwill Industries of America, Inc.
9200 Wisconsin Ave., Washington, D. C. 20014

The corporation is organized to provide rehabilitation services, training, employment, and opportunities for personal growth as an interim step in the rehabilitation process for the handicapped, disabled, and disadvantaged who cannot be readily absorbed in the competitive labor market. (I, III, V, VI) Membership is available to rehabilitation facilities and workshops at the dues rate of up to 1 percent of earned income. Informative pamphlets and manuals (some free) are published. The Delegate Assembly is held annually in June and the annual Conference of Executives is held in February. Autonomous Goodwill Industries number 136; there are 43 branch workshops.

Human Growth, Inc.
307 5th Ave., New York, N. Y. 10016

Begun in 1965 by parents and friends of children with growth problems, Human Growth, Inc., works to help the medical profession understand more about the process of human growth and development and all its deviations, such as dwarfism, gigantism, and failure to thrive. (I, III) Opportunities are provided for families of children with growth disturbances to meet; financially indigent families are assisted in obtaining medical help. Membership is $5; sixteen chapters serve members in certain geographical areas. An annual national meeting is held. "HGI Newsletter" is scheduled to begin as a monthly publication in 1969.

Information Center — Recreation for the Handicapped
Outdoor Laboratory, Little Grassy, Southern Illinois University, Carbondale, Ill.
62901

The Information Center is primarily concerned with the collection and dissemination of information pertaining to recreation for all handicapped persons. (I, II, III, VI) Publications include "ICRH Newsletter" (monthly,) *Recreation for the Handicapped: A Bibliography* (yearly), and monographs. The Training Institute, for Directors and Staff of Day Camps for the Mentally Retarded is held annually under the sponsorship of ICRH.

The International Association of Pupil Personnel Workers
5515 Sheridan Rd., Kenosha, Wisc. 53140

The Association subscribes to the philosophy that education as an experience is not only for the purpose of developing the intellectual capacities of the individual but also the physical, emotional, spiritual, and social being. (I, II, III, IV) Any person working in the field of education which deals with special services to children is eligible to join (dues are $10). A quarterly journal is published and an annual convention is held.

International League of Societies for the Mentally Handicapped
12, rue Forestiere, Brussels-5, Belgium

The purpose of this international organization is to advance the interests of the mentally handicapped without regard to nationality, race, or creed, by bringing about cooperation between organizations representing national endeavor on their behalf. (I, VI) Four types of membership are available to all national organizations working primarily in the interests of the mentally handicapped. Annual dues are adjusted to the size and resources of the member society. Forty-six countries are represented in the League. Publications include working papers and a newsletter. Five International Congresses have been held and the General Assembly meets every 2 years.

International Society for Rehabilitation of the Disabled
219 E. 44th St., New York, N. Y. 10017

As a federation of organizations in 59 countries, the Society works to promote the rehabilitation of the disabled throughout the world. (I, III, IV, V, VI) Regional conferences, seminars, workshops, and a Triennial World Congress are sponsored. Publications are a newsletter, "Prosthetics International," and *International Rehabilitation Review* (quarterly).

Joseph P. Kennedy, Jr. Foundation
719 13th St., NW, Suite 510, Washington, D. C. 20005

The Foundation works to support research into the prevention of mental retardation and to promote programs to give retarded persons a better life. (III, IV, V, VI) Two corporations established by the Foundation are Flame of Hope (a sheltered workshops program) and Special Olympics, Inc. (athletic competition for the retarded). An international awards competition and periodic scientific symposia are sponsored. Leaflets and general informative brochures are published.

Little People of America, Inc.
P. O. Box 126, Owatonna, Minn. 55050

The purpose of the organization is to provide fellowship, interchange of ideas, solutions to the unique problems of little people, and moral support. (IV, V) membership dues schedule is $5 per person, $7.50 per family.

Twelve chapters function on the district level. District and national (monthly) newsletters are published. An annual national convention (July) and annual district meetings are held.

Muscular Dystrophy Association of America, Inc.
1790 Broadway, New York, N. Y. 10019

The objectives of the agency are to foster scientific research into the cause and cure of muscular dystrophy and related neuromuscular diseases; to render services to patients; and to carry on a program of education among physicians, members of the paramedical professions, and the general public. (I, II, III, IV, V, VI) Membership is voluntary with no qualifications or dues required. Publications are *Muscular Dystrophy News* (quarterly) and professional literature. Annual chapter conferences (350 local chapters) and periodic medical and scientific conferences are sponsored.

The National Association for Gifted Children
8080 Springvalley Dr., Cincinnati, Ohio 45236

The Association aids schools, parents, and communities in providing for the gifted. (I, II, III, VI) Membership is open to interested persons; dues are $20 and up. An annual convention is held in addition to local chapter and regional meetings. Publications are the *Gifted Child Quarterly* (quarterly, $10), occasional newsletters, and special feature publications.

The National Association for Mental Health, Inc.
Suite 1300, 10 Columbus Circle, New York, N. Y. 10019

The National Association for Mental Health is a coordinated citizens' voluntary organization working toward the improved care and treatment of the mentally ill and handicapped; for improved methods and services in research, prevention, detection, diagnosis, and treatment of mental illness and handicaps, and for the promotion of mental health. (I, III, IV, VI) Membership in the National Association is through the local chapters and/or state mental health associations. Dues are set by the local or state associations. Publications include monographs, leaflets, and the periodical *Mental Hygiene* (quarterly, $8). Specialty conferences are sometimes held in addition to the annual meeting in November.

National Association for Music Therapy, Inc.
Box 610, Lawrence, Kansas 66055

The Association works for the advancement of research in music therapy by establishing qualifications and standards of training for music therapists and perfecting techniques of music programing which aid medical treatment most effectively. (I, III, IV) Membership is open to professionals, interested persons, and organizations; dues range from $5 to $50. *Journal of Music Therapy* (quarterly, $5), brochures, and handbooks are published. A conference and regional workshops are held annually.

National Association for Retarded Children
420 Lexington Ave., New York, N. Y. 10017
>Working through more than 1,300 state and local units, the Association
>helps to advance the welfare of the mentally retarded of all ages. (I, III,
>IV, V, VI) Membership is through the local unit. An annual convention
>and an annual youth conference are sponsored. "Children Limited" (10
>issues yearly, $2.50) is the periodical publication.

National Association of the Deaf
2025 Eye St., NW, Suite 321, Washington, D. C. 20006
>Comprised of deaf persons, relatives of deaf persons, and individuals
>working in the area of deafness, the Association promotes educational,
>sociological, and economic development of the deaf. (I, II, III, IV, VI)
>Dues are $10. A youth organization, the Junior National Association of
>the Deaf, is active in over 50 schools for the deaf. A biennial convention
>and various programs and seminars are sponsored. Periodical publications
>are *The Deaf American* (monthly, $4) and "NAD Newsletter," in addition
>to numerous pamphlets, books, and films.

National Association of Hearing and Speech Agencies
919 18th St., NW, Washington, D. C. 20006
>The Association works toward solving the problems of hearing, speech and
>language handicapped individuals. Approximately 200 local chapters and
>member agencies assist in the improvement of both the quality and
>quantity of care for the communicatively handicapped. (I, III, V, VI)
>Membership is open to agencies, professionals, and interested persons; dues
>are $10 and up. Annual conventions are held in June. Periodical
>publications are *Hearing and Speech News* (bimonthly, $5) and a
>newsletter, "Washington Sounds" (monthly, $15).

National Association of Sheltered Workshops and Homebound Programs
1522 K St., NW, Washington, D. C. 20005
>The purpose of the organization is to establish and maintain high standards
>of service to handicapped people in agency work programs and to
>demonstrate the significance of these services in the rehabilitation process.
>(I, III, IV, V, VI) Membership is open to agencies and individuals (dues are
>dependent upon the size of the workshop). The *Monthly Information
>Exchange Service* provides information on ongoing programs pertaining to
>workshops. Studies and surveys are also published. The Association has 17
>state chapters and holds an annual conference in addition to short term
>institutes.

National Association of Social Workers
2 Park Ave., New York, N. Y. 10016
>The Association is a professional organization which works to promote the
>quality and effectiveness of social work practice, prevent and control

social problems through a program of legislative and social action, and strengthen research and administration in social work. (III, VI) Members must have a masters degree from a school of social work; dues are $25 a year. Publications are *Social Work* (quarterly, $6), *Abstracts for Social Workers* (quarterly, $4 for members, $10 for nonmembers), newsletters, books, and pamphlets. There are 170 local chapters. Numerous national and regional conferences are sponsored.

National Association of State Directors of Special Education
c/o Dr. Stella A. Edwards, President, Division of Special Education, State Dept. of Education, Frankfort, Ky. 40601

The Association renders services for exceptional children and adults through the establishment of active leadership in educational facilities, planning at state and local levels, discussion forums, and consideration of current problems and issues. (I, III) Membership is open to any person employed as director, supervisor, or consultant in special education by a national or state department of education. Persons employed in provinces of Canada are eligible for associate membership. Membership dues are $15. "State Leadership" is published quarterly. The Association holds an annual meeting.

The National Association of Training Schools and Juvenile Agencies
c/o Windell W. Fewell, Exec. Secretary-Treasurer, 5256 N. Central Ave., Indianapolis, Ind. 46220

The Association works to prevent and control juvenile delinquency and crime by better understanding of the causes and needs of socially maladjusted children. (III, IV, VI) Membership is open to individuals and agencies; dues range from $3 to $25. The Association cosponsors the National Institute on Crime and Delinquency and and holds an annual conference. Conference proceedings are published.

National Catholic Educational Association, Special Education Dept.
4472 Lindell Blvd., St. Louis, Mo. 63108

The NCEA Special Education Department coordinates and promotes all the educational activities of the church which relate in any way to the education, training, and care of handicapped children, youth, and adults. Areas of disabilities organized under the framework of the Department include acoustical, emotional, mental, orthopedic, and visual. (I, III, IV, V, VI) Membership is open to individuals or agencies engaged in some area of Catholic special education. Dues are $10 for individuals and $50 for agencies. Publications include "Special Education Newsletter" (3 issues yearly), *N.C.E.A. Convention Proceedings*, and "Directory of Catholic Special Facilities & Programs in the U. S. for Handicapped Children & Adults." The Special Education Department participates in the annual NCEA Convention and arranges individual conferences.

National Committee for Multi-Handicapped Children
339 14th St., Niagara Falls, N. Y. 14303

The Committee works to inform the general public of the educational, therapeutic, recreational, and social service needs of children who have more than one handicap. Serving as a clearinghouse for information concerning existing programs for the handicapped, the Committee researches the literature in the fields of the blind, deaf, cerebral palsied, and brain injured. (I, III) Membership is open to interested persons; no dues are required.

National Council for the Gifted
700 Prospect Ave., West Orange, N. J. 07052

The Council fosters research in the development of practical programs for the education of the gifted to assure American leadership in the fields of education, science (basic, political, and social), and business. (III)

National Council on Crime and Delinquency
44 E. 23rd St., New York, N. Y. 10010

Working on a community, statewide, and national level, the Council strives to develop effective family and criminal courts to improve probation, parole, and institutional services, and to stimulate community programs for the prevention, treatment, and control of crime and delinquency. (I, III, VI) Membership is open to interested persons; dues are $10. The Council has local affiliates and 18 state citizen action program councils. Two journals, *Crime and Delinquency* (quarterly, $4.50) and *Journal of Research in Crime and Delinquency* (semiannually, $4.50), and a newsletter, "NCCD News" (5 issues yearly), are published. The Council cosponsors the National Institute on Crime and Delinquency.

The National Easter Seal Society for Crippled Children and Adults
2023 West Ogden Ave., Chicago, Ill. 60612

The Society is a voluntary agency providing direct services for crippled children and adults; education of the public, professional workers, and parents; research into the causes and prevention of handicapping conditions and into methods of care, education, and treatment of the patients involved. Members are the affiliated State Societies (II, III, IV, V, VI) Publications are *Rehabilitation Literature* (monthly, $6), "Easter Seal Bulletin" (quarterly, free), *Employment Bulletin* (quarterly, free to professional persons and placement service registrants), and numerous informational fliers. Research institutes, inservice training institutes, special workshops, and annual conventions are held.

National Epilepsy League, Inc.
203 N. Wabash Ave., Rm. 2200, Chicago, Ill. 60601

The League is a voluntary agency which encourages research in epilepsy and provides information about epilepsy, medical resources, and employment to epileptics. The League provides epilepsy medication at low cost and works to increase public knowledge about epilepsy and to widen opportunities for education and employment of epileptics. (I, II) Publications include the newsletter "Horizon," general information pamphlets, and technical publications.

The National Foundation — March of Dimes
800 2nd Ave., New York, N. Y. 10017

The National Foundation exists to lead, direct, and unify the fight against birth defects through support of programs of research, medical care, professional and public education, and community services. (I, II, III, IV, V, VI) Lay and professional volunteers participate in programs through nearly 3,000 local chapters. National, regional, and local meetings and symposia for professional and lay audiences are held. General interest and professional education publications are issued. Films and exhibits are available for loan.

National Health Council, Inc.
1740 Broadway, New York, N. Y. 10019

The principal functions of the Council are to help member agencies work together more effectively, to identify and promote the solution of national health problems of concern to the public, and to further improve governmental and voluntary health services for the public. Membership is limited to national organizations concerned with health. Books and pamphlets concerning health are published. The National Health Forum is held annually.

National Recreation and Park Association
1700 Pennsylvania Ave., NW, Washington, D. C. 20006

As a nonprofit service organization, the Association is dedicated to the wise use of free time, conservation of natural and human resources, and beautification of the total American environment. (I, III, VI) There are several categories of membership including professional and organization membership (dues range from $10 to $50). Several periodical publications, including *Therapeutic Recreation Journal* (quarterly), are issued in addition to books and pamphlets on all phases of parks and recreation. A convention plus eight regional conferences are held annually.

National Rehabilitation Association
1522 K St., NW, Washington, D. C. 20005

The Association works to advance rehabilitation of physically and mentally handicapped persons through public understanding, disseminating information, fostering research, encouraging an interdisciplinary approach to rehabilitation, and developing professional standards and professional training opportunities. (IV) Five professional divisions with membership subject to membership in NRA (dues range from $10 to $20) further meet the needs of members. The *Journal of Rehabilitation* (bimonthly, $5), and the "NRA Newsletter" (bimonthly) are published, as

well as a legislative newsletter. Seventy affiliated state and local chapters
hold chapter conferences in addition to an annual national and eight
regional conferences.

National Society for Low Vision People, Inc.
2346 Clermont, Denver, Colo, 80207
Through programs of training, education, and research, the Society works
to help people with low vision achieve greater independence. (II, III)
Although the Society is not a membership organization, it sponsors various
workshops for parents of low vision children.

National Therapeutic Recreation Society
1700 Pennsylvania Ave., NW, Washington, D. C. 20006
As a branch of the National Recreation and Park Association, the Society
is concerned with the improvement of therapeutic recreation services and
the development of the recreation profession. (I, III, VI) Members include
professionals and agencies; dues range from $12 to $35. The Society
participates in the annual convention of the National Recreation and Park
Association and holds its own district conferences. *Therapeutic Recreation*
(quarterly, $4) is the journal publication.

Pan American Health Organization
Pan American Sanitary Bureau, Regional Office of the World Health Organization, 525 23rd St., NW, Washington, D. C. 20037
The organization is an agency of the United Nations with membership
open to all countries of the region. It acts as a coordinating authority on
international health work, assists governments in strengthening health
services, and furnishes appropriate technical assistance. Other functions are
to establish and maintain epidemiological and statistical services; to
stimulate advance work to eradicate diseases; to promote the improvement
of nutrition, housing sanitation, and other aspects of environmental
hygiene; and to promote maternal and child health and welfare. (III, V)
Several periodicals, including *World Health* and "WHO Bulletin," are
published, as well as pamphlets, papers, and reports.

The President's Committee on Employment of the Handicapped
U. S. Department of Labor, Washington, D. C. 20210
The President's Committee on Employment of the Handicapped is
concerned with promoting full and equal employment of all handicapped
persons and encourages the removal of barriers which stand in the way of
their employment. (I, III) Members, appointed for 3 year terms by the
chairman, are national leaders who have an interest in greater opportunities for the handicapped. Each state has a Governor's Committee on
Employment of the Handicapped, and nearly 1,000 cities have local
committees. All are voluntary. Publications include "Performance"
(monthly) and booklets, pamphlets, brochures, and posters. An annual

meeting is held in May of each year and ongoing promotional campaigns are conducted throughout the year.

President's Committee on Mental Retardation
Washington, D. C. 20201

The Committee works to promote cooperation and coordination among agencies and organizations giving services in mental retardation and allied fields. It promotes awareness of mental retardation needs, surveys mental retardation programs and needs, and advises the President on needed measures. (I, III) The Committee is comprised of the Secretary of Health, Education, and Welfare, the Secretary of Labor, the Director of the Office of Economic Opportunity, and 21 citizens. Special workshops and forums are sponsored. Publications include "PCMR Message" (bimonthly), an annual report to the President, and special reports.

Southern Regional Education Board
130 6th St., NW, Atlanta, Ga. 30313

Comprised of the 15 southern states, the Board is an interstate compact for cooperation in the expansion and improvement of higher education, with a special interest for the broad range of problems in mental health research and training. (I, III) Periodicals include *Mental Health Briefs* (quarterly), *Regional Action* (quarterly), *Regional Spotlight* (monthly), *Summary of State Legislation Affecting Higher Education in the South* (spring and fall). Research monographs and reports are also available The SREB annually supports the following meetings: SREB Board, Commission on Mental Illness and Retardation, Policy Commission for the Institute for Higher Educational Opportunity in the South, Educational Plans and Policies Advisory Committee, and the Legislative Advisory Council. In addition, a variety of special interest and area meetings are held.

United Cerebral Palsy Associations, Inc.
66 E. 34th St., New York, N. Y. 10016

As a voluntary health agency, UCP works to: (a) promote research in cerebral palsy, the treatment, education, and habilitation of persons with cerebral palsy and to promote professional training programs of all types related to the problem of cerebral palsy; (b) further by professional and public education information concerning all aspects of the problem of cerebral palsy; (c) promote better and more adequate techniques and facilities for the diagnosis and treatment of persons with cerebral palsy; (d) cooperate with governmental and private agencies concerned with the welfare of the handicapped; (e) promote the employment of persons with cerebral palsy; (f) solicit, collect, and otherwise raise funds and other property for above purposes and for supporting facilities for the care, treatment, and study of persons cerebral palsy; (g) and to establish and work with local and state affiliates (over 300 currently). (I, II, III, IV, V,

VI) Conferences, workshops, and seminars are conducted. Publications include *The UCP Crusader* (bimonthly free) and professional literature.

U. S. Department of Health, Education, and Welfare

The eight major program units of the Department of Health, Education, and Welfare listed here were selected because each administers several programs for the handicapped. For more detailed information about the specific programs of these and other units within HEW, consult the directory, *Financial Assistance Programs for the Handicapped*, U. S. Department of Health, Education, and Welfare, 1968. Available for $1.00 from the Superintendent of Documents, U. S. Government Printing Office, Washington, D. C. 20402.

U. S. Office of Education, Bureau of Adult, Vocational and Library Programs
7th and D St., SW, Rm. 5050, Washington, D. C. 20202.

As one of five bureaus within the Office of Education, the Bureau of Adult, Vocational and Library Programs administers grants to states for vocational and technical education programs, adult education programs, development and construction of public libraries, and acquisition of library resources. (I, III, IV, VI) Examples of specific programs are the establishment of library services for the physically handicapped and provision of vocational education for the handicapped. Periodic conferences are conducted. Publications include professional literature, curriculum guides, and general information publications.

U. S. Office of Education, Bureau of Education for the Handicapped
7th and D St., SW, Washington, D. C. 20202

As one of the five bureaus within the Office of Education, the Bureau of Education for the Handicapped serves as the principal arm of the Office of Education in administering and carrying out programs and projects relating to the education of handicapped children, including training of professional personnel, research and development, and the provision of special education services. (I, III, IV, V, VI) Bulletins, pamphlets, reports, and surveys are published. The Bureau sponsors conferences of professional personnel on subjects involving the education of handicapped children.

U. S. Public Health Service, Health Services and Mental Health Administration, National Institute of Mental Health
5454 Wisconsin Ave., Chevy Chase, Md. 20015

The agency works for the promotion of mental health, the prevention of mental illnesses, and the treatment and rehabilitation of the mentally ill by conducting or supporting research programs, manpower development and training, demonstrations, and community service. (I, III, IV, V, VI) Special mental health problems such as delinquency and child and family mental health are within the work of the Institute. NIMH produces scientific papers, abstract and index publications, and public information publications. Numerous conferences on topics within the wide subject of mental health are conducted.

U. S. Public Health Service, National Institutes of Health
HEW South Bldg., Rm. 5312, Washington, D. C. 20201

As one of the three major units of the Public Health Service, NIH works to improve the health of citizens by conducting and supporting basic clinical research, training researchers, and educating health professionals to bring research results to practice. (III, IV, V, VI) Research activities are conducted by six disease oriented institutes: National Cancer Institute, National Heart Institute, National Institute of Allergy and Infectious Diseases, National Institute of Arthritis and Metabolic Diseases, National Institute of Dental Research, and National Institute of Neurological Diseases and Blindness, and also through the National Institute of Medical Sciences and the National Institute of Child Health and Human Development. Numerous publications are issued including periodicals, abstract and index publications, technical publications, and public information pamphlets. Meetings and conferences are conducted.

Social and Rehabilitation Service, Assistance Payments Administration
330 Independence Ave., SW, Washington, D. C. 20201

Working as a unit within Social and Rehabilitation Service, the Assistance Payments Administration provides leadership in planning, development, and coordination of SRS programs providing for the administrative and money aspects of public assistance programs. (III, IV) Specific programs provide financial aid to needy handicapped persons. Public information publications are available.

Social and Rehabilitation Service, Children's Bureau
330 C St., SW, Washington, D. C. 20201

The Children's Bureau is a governmental agency established to investigate and report upon all matters pertaining to the welfare of children. It assists in extending and improving maternal and child health and crippled children's and child welfare services through grants to the states and grants for special projects. (I, III, IV, V, VI) The journal *Children* (bimonthly, $1.25) is published in addition to materials on child health and handicapped children.

Social and Rehabilitation Service, Office of Research, Demonstrations, and Training
HEW North Bldg., Rm. 3315, Washington, D. C. 20201

The Office of Research, Demonstrations, and Training is one of several offices within the Office of the Administrator, Social and Rehabilitation Service. The Office is responsible for directing and promoting a research and demonstration program to solve physical, mental, social, cultural, and economic deprivation problems and coordinating and directing all SRS intramural research. (I, III, IV, V, VI) Specific programs provide assistance for vocational rehabilitation of the physically and mentally handicapped. Conferences for state and local specialists in staff development are held. "Research and Demonstrations Brief" is published periodically.

Social and Rehabilitation Service, Rehabilitation Services Administration
330 Independence Ave., SW, Rm. 3139 D, Washington, D. C. 20201

As part of the Social and Rehabilitation Service, this unit provides leadership in the planning, development, and coordination of SRS programs providing rehabilitation and social services to physically, mentally, culturally disabled, and handicapped persons as provided for in the Vocational Rehabilitation Act, as amended, and the Social Security Act, Titles I, II, X, XIV, and XVI. (I, IV, V, VI) Publications available include research reports, bibliographies, *Rehabilitation Record* (bimonthly, $1.75), and a wide range of publications for both professionals and the general public.

Western Institute for the Deaf
215 E. 18th Ave., Vancouver 10, British Columbia, Canada

The Institute is a nonprofit service organization dealing with the problems of the hearing handicapped. (I, II, III, V, VI) Services include job placement, audiological assessment hearing tests, provision of hearing aids to the needy, and education of the general public concerning the many problems of the hearing handicapped. A newsletter, "WID News" is published monthly.

Western Interstate Commission for Higher Education, Special Education and Rehabilitation Program
30th St., University East Campus, Boulder, Colo. 80302

The Special Education and Rehabilitation Program is funded by the United Cerebral Palsy Research and Educational Foundation, Inc., and the Rehabilitation Services Administration. It was established to assist in developing western college and university programs in special education and rehabilitation at the graduate and undergraduate levels and to stimulate coordination of agencies and institutions for the use of all resources available for special education and rehabilitation training. (I, II, III, IV, V, VI) The Program sponsors numerous conferences concerning teacher preparation, patterns of service, and research. Publications include reports and brochures.

list of agencies and organizations by service functions

I. **Provides Consultative Service or Technical Assistance for Individuals or Agencies**

Alexander Graham Bell Association for the Deaf, Inc.
American Academy of Pediatrics
American Association for Health, Physical Education, and Recreation
American Association of Psychiatric Clinics for Children
American Association of Workers for the Blind, Inc.
American Corrective Therapy Association, Inc.
American Foundation for the Blind
American Heart Association, Inc.
The American Legion, National Child Welfare Division
American Nurses' Association, Inc.
American Occupational Therapy Association, Inc.
American Optometric Association
American Physical Therapy Association
American Printing House for the Blind
American Psychiatric Association
American Public Health Association, Inc.
The American Speech and Hearing Association
Association for Children with Learning Disabilities
Association for Education of the Visually Handicapped
The Association of Rehabilitation Centers, Inc.
Boy Scouts of America
Child Study Association of America
Conference of Executives of American Schools for the Deaf
Council of Organizations Serving the Deaf
Council on Education of the Deaf

Girl Scouts of the United States of America
Goodwill Industries of America, Inc.
Human Growth, Inc.
Information Center — Recreation for the Handicapped
The International Association of Pupil Personnel Workers
International League of Societies for the Mentally Handicapped
International Society for Rehabilitation of the Disabled
Muscular Dystrophy Association of America, Inc.
The National Association for Gifted Children
The National Association for Mental Health, Inc.
National Association for Music Therapy, Inc.
National Association for Retarded Children
National Association of the Deaf
National Association of Hearing and Speech Agencies
National Association of Sheltered Workshops and Homebound Programs
National Assocation of State Directors of Special Education
National Catholic Educational Association, Special Education Dept.
National Committee for Multi-Handicapped Children
National Council on Crime and Delinquency
National Epilepsy League, Inc.
The National Foundation — March of Dimes
National Recreation and Park Association
National Therapeutic Recreation Society
The President's Committee on Employment of the Handicapped
President's Committee on Mental Retardation
Southern Regional Education Board'
United Cerebral Palsy Association, Inc.
United States Department of Health, Education, and Welfare
Western Institute for the Deaf
Western Interstate Commission for Higher Education, Special Education and
    Rehabilitation Program

II. Provides Direct Services to Handicapped and/or Gifted Children
American Corrective Therapy Association, Inc.
The American Legion, National Child Welfare Division
American Optometric Association
American for Children with Learning Disabilities
Boy Scouts of America
Conference of Executives of American Schools for the Deaf
Girl Scouts of the United States of America
Information Center — Recreation for the Handicapped
The International Association of Pupil Personnel Workers
Muscular Dystrophy Association of America, Inc.
The National Association for Gifted Children
National Association of the Deaf
The National Easter Seal Society for Crippled Children and Adults
National Epilepsy League, Inc.

The National Foundation — March of Dimes
National Society for Low Vision People, Inc.
United Cerebral Palsy Associations, Inc.
Western Institute for the Deaf
Western Interstate Commission for Higher Education, Special Education and
   Rehabilitation Program

III. Conducts Own Projects, Surveys, Research, and Demonstration

Alexander Graham Bell Association for the Deaf, Inc.
American Academy of Pediatrics
American Academy for Cerebral Palsy
American Association for Health, Physical Education, and Recreation
American Association of Psychiatric Clinics for Children
American Association of Workers for the Blind, Inc.
American Association on Mental Deficiency
American Corrective Therapy Association, Inc.
American Foundation for the Blind
American Heart Association
American Nurses' Association, Inc.
American Occupational Therapy Association, Inc.
American Optometric Association
American Physical Therapy Assocation
American Printing House for the Blind
American Psychiatric Association
American Public Health Association, Inc.
American Rehabilitation Counseling Association
American Schizophrenia Foundation
The American Speech and Hearing Association
Association for Education of the Visually Handicapped
The Association of Rehabilitation Centers, Inc.
Boy Scouts of America
Child Study Association of America
The Convention of American Instructors of the Deaf
The Council for Exceptional Children
Council of Organizations Serving the Deaf
Council on Education of the Deaf
Girl Scouts of the United States of America
Goodwill Industries of America, Inc.
Information Center — Recreation for the Handicapped
The International Association of Pupil Personnel Workers
International Society for Rehabilitation of the Disabled
Joseph P. Kennedy, Jr. Foundation
Muscular Dystrophy Association of America, Inc.
The National Association for Gifted Children
The National Association for Mental Health, Inc.
National Association for Music Therapy, Inc.

National Association for Retarded Children
National Association of the Deaf
National Association of Hearing and Speech Agencies
National Association of Sheltered Workshops and Homebound Programs
National Association of Social Workers
National Association of State Directors of Special Education
National Association of Training Schools and Juvenile Agencies
National Catholic Educational Association, Special Education Dept.
National Committee for Multi-Handicapped Children
National Council for the Gifted
National Council on Crime and Delinquency
National Easter Seal Society for Crippled Children and Adults
The National Foundation — March of Dimes
National Recreation and Park Association
National Society for Low Vision People, Inc.
National Therapeutic Recreation Society
Pan American Health Organization
The President's Committee on Employment of the Handicapped
President's Committee on Mental Retardation
Southern Regional Education Board
United Cerebral Palsy Associations, Inc.
United States Dept. of Health, Education, and Welfare
Western Institute for the Deaf
Western Interstate Commission for Higher Education, Special Education and
  Rehabilitation Program

IV. Subsidizes Research and Demonstration

American Academy for Cerebral Palsy
American Academy of Pediatrics
American Foundation for the Blind
American Heart Association, Inc.
The American Legion, National Child Welfare Division
American Nurses' Association, Inc.
American Optometric Association
American Schizophrenia Foundation
Boy Scouts of America
Council of Organizations Serving the Deaf
The International Association of Pupil Personnel Workers
International Society for Rehabilitation of the Disabled
Joseph P. Kennedy, Jr. Foundation
Little People of America, Inc.
Muscular Dystrophy Association of America, Inc.
The National Association for Mental Health, Inc.
National Association for Music Therapy, Inc.
National Association for Retarded Children
National Association of the Deaf
National Association of Sheltered Workshops and Homebound Programs

The National Association of Training Schools and Juvenile Agencies
National Catholic Educational Association, Special Education Dept.
The National Easter Seal Society for Crippled Children and Adults
The National Foundation — March of Dimes
National Rehabilitation Association
United Cerebral Palsy Association, Inc.
United States Department of Health, Education, and Welfare
Western Interstate Commission for Higher Education, Special Education and
    Rehabilitation Program

V. Subsidizes Scholarships, Fellowships, or Traineeships for Personnel

Alexander Graham Bell Association for the Deaf, Inc.
American Academy of Pediatrics
American Association of Psychiatric Clinics for Children
American Corrective Therapy Association, Inc.
American Foundation for the Blind
The American Legion, National Child Welfare Division
American Optometric Association
American Physical Therapy Association
The American Speech and Hearing Association
Association for Children with Learning Disabilities
The Association of Rehabilitation Centers, Inc.
Girl Scouts of the United States of America
Goodwill Industries of America, Inc.
International Society for Rehabilitation of the Disabled
Joseph P. Kennedy, Jr. Foundation
Little People of America, Inc.
Muscular Dystrophy Association of America, Inc.
National Association for Retarded Children
National Association of Hearing and Speech Agencies
National Association of Sheltered Workshops and Homebound Programs
National Catholic Educational Association, Special Education Dept.
The National Easter Seal Society for Crippled Children and Adults
The National Foundation — March of Dimes
Pan American Health Organization
United Cerebral Palsy Association, Inc.
United States Department of Health, Education, and Welfare
Western Institute for the Deaf
Western Interstate Commission for Higher Education, Special Education and
    Rehabilitation Program

VI. Subsidizes or Conducts Training of Personnel Through Refresher Courses, Institutes, Workshops, or Internships

American Academy of Pediatrics
American Academy of Private Practice in Speech Pathology and Audiology
American Academy for Cerebral Palsy

American Association of Workers for the Blind, Inc.
American Association on Mental Deficiency
American Corrective Therapy Association, Inc.
American Foundation for the Blind
American Heart Association, Inc.
American Nurses' Association, Inc.
American Occupational Therapy Association, Inc.
American Optometric Association
American Orthopsychiatric Association, Inc.
American Physical Therapy Association
American Psychiatric Association
American Public Health Association, Inc.
The American Speech and Hearing Association
Association for Children with Learning Disabilities
Association for Education of the Visually Handicapped
The Association of Rehabilitation Centers, Inc.
Boy Scouts of America
Child Study Association of America
Girl Scouts of the United States of America
Goodwill Industries of America, Inc.
Information Center — Recreation for the Handicapped
International League of Societies for the Mentally Handicapped
International Society for Rehabilitation of the Disabled
Joseph P. Kennedy, Jr. Foundation
Muscular Dystrophy Association of America, Inc.
The National Association for Gifted Children
The National Association for Mental Health, Inc.
National Association for Retarded Children
National Association of the Deaf
National Association of Hearing and Speech Agencies
National Association of Sheltered Workshops and Homebound Programs
National Association of Social Workers
The National Association of Training Schools and Juvenile Agencies
National Catholic Educational Association
National Council on Crime and Delinquency
The National Easter Seal Society for Crippled Children and Adults
The National Foundation — March of Dimes
National Recreation and Park Association
National Therapeutic Recreation Society
United Cerebral Palsy Associations, Inc.
United States Department of Health, Education, and Welfare
Western Institute for the Deaf
Western Interstate Commission for Higher Education, Special Education and
   Rehabilitation Program

key to
annotated index

Section I: Administration

Code
(A)   1. Administration, general
(AP)   2. Administrative Programs
(AG)   3. Administrative Guidelines
(AT)   4. Administrative Theory
(S)   5. Supervision
(O)   6. Organization
(F&L) 7. Finance and Legislation
(R)   8. Research in Administration
(P)   9. Personnel
(PP)   10. Physical Plant

Section II: Areas of Exceptionality

1. Orthopedic and Miscellaneous Physical Handicaps
2. Partially Sighted and Blind
3. Hard-of-Hearing and Deaf
4. Speech Handicapped
5. Mentally Retarded
6. Gifted
7. Emotionally Disturbed and Socially Deviant
8. Homebound and Hospitalized
9. Children with Learning Disabilities

Section I: Adminstration

1. *Administration, general (A).*

   1, 15, 17, 20, 22, 24, 28, 33, 37, 44, 46, 47, 54, 56, 57, 59, 60, 62, 63, 66, 67, 69, 71, 72, 79-81, 83, 85-87, 89, 92, 94, 95, 98, 103, 105, 107, 112, 116, 118, 120-122, 125, 127, 129, 133, 136, 138, 139, 141, 142, 146, 148, 149, 151, 157, 162-164, 167-169, 176-178, 181, 185, 191, 192, 195, 197, 200-202, 204, 207, 208, 210, 213, 214, 217, 221, 222, 224, 228, 230, 231, 232, 234, 235, 237, 239-241, 243, 244, 246-250, 253, 254, 261-263, 267, 270, 271, 273, 276, 279, 281, 283, 284, 290-293, 295, 299, 301, 302, 304, 315, 316, 323, 324, 327, 329, 333, 339, 340, 342, 343-345, 347-350, 352-354, 360-362, 365, 366, 370-373, 375, 379, 384, 385, 388, 391, 393, 395, 397, 401, 403, 406-410, 413-415, 418, 424, 425, 427-429.

2. *Administrative programs (AP).*

   3, 5-7, 11-13, 18, 19, 22, 29, 31, 36, 43, 48, 50, 52, 58, 61, 64, 65, 73, 77, 81, 86, 93, 99, 100, 108, 110, 111, 113, 114, 116, 119, 120, 123, 130, 135, 138, 139, 143, 147, 149, 154-156, 158, 159, 169, 171-175, 185, 187, 189, 190, 193, 194, 207, 213, 216, 218, 220, 225, 229, 231, 233, 236, 240, 242, 257, 265, 266, 268, 269, 272, 275, 277, 281, 282, 286, 287, 291, 296, 300, 302, 308-310, 319, 321, 328, 335-338, 355, 358, 359, 368, 369, 374, 376, 382, 386, 389, 394, 397-400, 402, 405, 411, 412, 416, 419-421, 423, 426.

3. *Administrative guidelines (AG).*

   6, 7, 11-14, 27, 32, 34, 35, 41, 51, 53, 55, 58, 70, 74, 76-78, 86, 90, 96, 101, 104, 109, 110, 115, 123, 124, 126, 134, 160, 170, 171-175, 180, 188-190, 193, 194, 196, 205-207, 215, 225, 227, 228, 231, 233, 236, 240, 245, 251, 260, 264-266, 274, 282, 287, 289, 302, 303, 312, 314, 330, 331, 356, 390, 306.

4. *Administrative theory (AT).*

   8, 24, 34, 68, 91, 96, 128, 152, 165, 166, 179, 198, 219, 226, 278, 284, 306, 393.

5. *Supervision (S).*

   15, 17, 40, 59, 61, 95, 103, 116, 117, 122, 129, 144, 163, 184, 186, 225, 254, 307, 351, 357, 409, 410.

6. *Organization (O).*

   8, 10, 16, 21, 23, 32, 37, 42, 58, 60, 67, 68, 73, 91, 97, 106, 115, 118, 119, 120, 125, 132, 137, 138, 142, 143, 145, 149, 158, 159, 163, 183, 200-203, 205, 209, 213, 223, 231, 233, 238, 240, 253, 255, 256, 266, 272, 287, 295, 302, 305, 307, 313, 317, 318, 320, 324, 326-328, 332, 334, 342, 346, 364, 372, 378, 387, 388, 393, 397, 404, 417, 425, 429.

7. *Finance & Legislation (F & L).*

   2, 9, 12, 30, 49, 69, 80, 82, 98, 102, 107, 111, 149, 150, 153, 161, 162, 169, 199, 228, 239, 259, 272, 322, 332, 339, 349, 360, 365, 366.

8. *Research in Adminstration (R).*

   16, 17, 29, 47, 56, 62, 65, 66, 70, 75, 88, 94, 100, 108, 124, 143, 194, 202, 206, 227, 246, 252, 289, 293, 296, 311, 321, 383, 389, 394, 399, 402, 416, 420, 423.

9. *Personnel (P).*

   4, 25, 26, 33, 38, 39, 44, 45, 50, 64, 74, 75, 77, 84, 85, 88, 95, 103, 105, 106, 133, 134, 140, 156, 182, 185, 192, 202, 211, 212, 232, 236, 240, 258, 272, 279-281, 285, 287 288, 294, 298, 305, 307, 311, 316, 319, 324, 331, 334, 339, 341, 343, 346, 348, 358, 363, 367, 380, 381, 383, 384, 391, 392, 401, 406, 422.

10. *Physical Plant (PP).*

   12, 28, 50, 78, 102, 134, 162, 189, 328, 334, 343, 348, 365, 366, 430-453.

Section II: Areas of Exceptionality

1. *Orthopedic and miscellaneous physical handicaps*

   3, 19, 78, 158, 242, 280, 286, 289, 320, 345, 398, 426, 440, 447, 448.

2. *Partially Sighted and Blind*

   38, 71, 93, 110, 111, 112, 130, 154, 216, 268, 294, 307, 314, 317, 425, 444, 448, 451.

3. *Hard-of-Hearing and Deaf*

42, 52, 66, 93, 112, 229, 324, 328, 331, 357, 392, 442, 443, 448.

4. *Speech Handicapped*

6, 11, 12, 40, 76, 126, 211, 255, 302, 328, 419.

5. *Mentally Retarded*

1, 7, 10, 13, 16, 18, 28, 31, 33, 36, 47, 49, 69, 70, 86, 93, 94, 100, 107, 119, 124, 135, 139, 147, 156, 159, 174, 175, 187, 199, 200, 204, 207, 209, 220, 223, 228, 236, 243, 272, 280, 281, 285, 286, 291, 299, 300, 305, 319, 322, 337, 339, 350, 354, 355, 373, 386, 399, 400, 406, 420, 422, 428, 435, 448, 450, 453.

6. *Gifted*

9, 22, 29, 58, 109, 113, 139, 140, 143, 194, 269, 300, 308, 309, 310, 338, 374, 375, 382, 405, 411.

7. *Emotionally Disturbed*

4, 28, 64, 84, 85, 171, 182, 187, 189, 202, 212, 227, 287, 296, 311, 372, 394, 404, 416, 423, 434, 436, 441, 446, 448.

8. *Homebound and Hospitalized*

48, 77, 155, 255, 361.

9. *Learning Disabilities and MBI*
2, 61, 64, 88, 112, 172, 225, 276, 437, 441.

Date   Due